# Quality of Life Assessment: Key Issues in the 1990s

# Quality of Life Assessment: Key Issues in the 1990s

EDITED BY

**Stuart R. Walker**
Director of the Centre for Medicines Research, Carshalton, and
Honorary Professor, Welsh School of Pharmacy,
University of Wales College, Cardiff, UK

and

**Rachel M. Rosser**
Professor of Psychiatry and Head of Department
University College and Middlesex School of Medicine,
London University, London, UK

**KLUWER ACADEMIC PUBLISHERS**
DORDRECHT / BOSTON / LONDON

**Distributors**

*for the United States and Canada*: Kluwer Academic Publishers, PO Box 358, Accord Station, Hingham, MA 02018-0358, USA
*for all other countries*: Kluwer Academic Publishers Group, Distribution Center, PO Box 322, 3300 AH Dordrecht, The Netherlands


A catalogue record for this book is available from the British Library

ISBN 0-7923-8991-3


**Library of Congress Cataloging-in-Publication Data**

Quality of life assessment : key issues in the 1990s / edited by
   Stuart R. Walker and Rachel M. Rosser.
        p.    cm.
   Includes bibliographical references and index.
   ISBN 0-7923-8991-3
   1. Health status indicators.   2. Quality of life—Evaluation.
   I. Walker, Stuart R., 1944–    II. Rosser, Rachel.
      [DNLM: 1. Quality of Life.   WA 30 Q103]
   RA407.Q3   1992
   615.5′028′7—dc20
   DNLM/DLC
for Library of Congress                                    92-49860
                                                               CIP

Published in the United Kingdom by Kluwer Academic Publishers, PO Box 55, Lancaster, UK.

Kluwer Academic Publishers incorporates the publishing programmes of D. Reidel, Martinus Nijhoff, Dr W. Junk and MTP Press.

Lasertypeset by Martin Lister Publishing Services, Bolton-le-Sands, Carnforth, Lancs.

Printed in Great Britain by Hartnolls Ltd., Bodmin, Cornwall.

# Contents

### III.  Viewpoints and Perspectives

# Preface

It was over five years ago that the Centre for Medicines Research organized a workshop entitled "Quality of Life: Assessment and Application". This workshop brought together a unique group of participants, some of whom had been involved in studies on quality of life for well over a decade, whilst others were meeting the subject for the first time. This blend of experienced researchers and enthusiastic newcomers was a great stimulus to the discussions which followed individual presentations as well as that resulting from the study groups. In the ensuing publication, a balance was sought between a consideration of the complex principles underlying the assessment of quality of life and the application of such assessments to specific clinical conditions which necessitated this approach.

The organization in 1991 of a second workshop entitled "Quality of Life Assessment: Key Issues in the 1990s" resulted in a further consideration of the quality of life philosophy, concepts and key instruments together with an update on assessing quality of life in a number of major disease areas. Of particular importance was an examination of various viewpoints concerned with ethical questions and their implications, and quality of life from industry, regulatory and health care purchasers' perspectives. As a result of this second workshop, the editors of the original book referred to above decided to produce a second edition with a number of updates and additional chapters. It is hoped that, as this topic becomes of increasing importance to the medical profession, the regulatory authorities and the pharmaceutical industry, this volume will be seen to be of value not only to experienced research workers but also to those who might be entering this field for the first time.

I would particularly like to take this opportunity of thanking my co-editor, Professor Rachel Rosser, for her important contribution to this volume and to Sandra Cox for her secretarial support in the editing of these proceedings. Lord Butterfield was kind enough to write the foreword to the original book and I am pleased to be able to include this as well in this second edition.

Professor Stuart R. Walker
September 1992

# Foreword

From the earliest times of the medical profession, it has been clearly understood that physicians may have to strike the balance between the treatments available to deal with the disease involved and the patient's well-being. This is reflected in the two names given to the medical demigod of ancient times – Asclepius in Greece – literally 'continuously gentle' and Aesculapius in Rome – 'pertaining to mistletoe with its semen-like restorative berry juice'[1]. Asclepius was obviously deeply concerned with the patient's point of view, about the quality of his life, Aesculepius with action and treatment.

We still have to face this dichotomy in managing patients today. Perhaps we are fortunate that as a generation the arrival of predictive science at the bedside has, almost within living memory, revolutionized medical treatment. Some shrewd observers link the revolution to the development of insulin therapy in the early 1920s. This created the need for the physician to learn how to vary the insulin dose between patients and, in the same patient with a different lifestyle. He also has to learn how to evaluate the variations clinically, or by blood glucose or glycosylated haemoglobin determinations. Before insulin, doses of drugs were, so to say, in the book, but since then medicines have been developed with an eye to the uniformity of dose that could be used in the formulation.

Currently, predictive science is coming to assessments of the quality of life. This is a psychosocial revolution which may prove as exciting as the pharmacological therapeutic era of sixty years ago. Certainly this may be so for many patients who expect to be told what the doctors have in store for them, and increasingly therefore, for those responsible for developing new medicines.

The editors of this monograph are therefore to be congratulated. They can be confident that they are launching an important publication covering, as it does, so many of the ideas and findings of the pioneers in the development of instruments for assessing quality of life, and of the thinking and philosophy about this side of medicine, which many patients and even some politicians thought was threatened with extinction.

John Butterfield
Cambridge

---

1  See *Greek Myths*, Robert Graves, Cassell & Co. London, 1958, p. 176

# Notes on contributors

**J P Anderson, PhD**, is a medical specialist at the University of California, San Diego. Dr Anderson received his PhD degree from Harvard University and completed post doctoral training at Duke University. In 1974 he joined the San Diego group headed by Jim Bush and has continued to collaborate with Dr Kaplan on the development of a general approach to health outcome measurements. He has been particularly interested in methodological studies relevant to the Quality of Well-being Scale. Some of Dr Anderson's current projects involve patients with HIV disease, arthritis, hearing loss, stroke.

**Professor M Bergner, PhD**, is Professor of Health Policy and Management and a member of the Health Services Research and Development Center at Johns Hopkins University. Her current research includes assessment of the impact of life support for critically ill hospitalized adults on health-related quality of life, development of a health status measure for children, and assessment of the clinical and functional outcomes of cataract surgery.

**M Bullinger, PhD**, is assistant Professor at the Institute for Medical Psychology of the University of Munich. She has an appointment with the Biometrical Centre for Therapeutic Studies, University of Munich. Her interest has been oriented towards conceptual, methodological and practical contributions to the emerging field of quality of life assessment. Of the 85 papers and books she has published, the most recent ones pertain to quality of life assessment, but include also areas such as psychoneuroendocrinology, behavioural medicine and environmental psychology. Dr Bullinger is interested in developing a theoretical model of health related quality of life and in testing and developing quality of life instruments according to psychometric quality criteria. She is member of several working international working groups on instrument development and is interested in cross-cultural issues of quality of life research.

**Professor C Bulpitt, MD, MSc, FRCP, FFPM**, is Professor of Geriatric Medicine at the Royal Postgraduate Medical School, Hammersmith Hospital. His research interests include clinical trials, measurement of health and the epidemiology of various clinical diseases, especially in the elderly. He has written a book entitled 'Randomised Controlled Clinical Trials', published by Martinus Nijhoff in 1983, and has edited a book entitled 'Epidemiology of Hypertension', Volume 6 of the 'Handbook of Hypertension' series published by Elsevier, in 1986.

**Professor L W Chambers, BA(Hons), MSc, PhD**, is the Teaching Health Unit Coordinator in the Hamilton-Wentworth Department of Public Health Services, a teaching health unit affiliated with McMaster University. As a cross appointee, he is the Epidemiology Consultant in the Department and he holds the rank of Professor in the Department of Clinical Epidemiology and Biostatistics, Faculty of Health Sciences, McMaster University, Hamilton, Ontario. In addition, he is the Director of the R Samuel

McLaughlin Centre for Gerontological Health Research in the Faculty of Health Sciences. Dr Chambers' areas of interest are: quantification of quality of health care assessment; development of measures of health-related quality of life; research methodology in health sciences (teaching and experimentation); health care controlled trials. and, continuing education for users of health research information.

**Professor R A Deyo, MD, MPH**, is a member Director of the Northwest Health Services Research and Development Field Program at the Seattle, Washington Veterans Affairs Administration Medical Center. He is also Professor of Medicine and of Health Services at the University of Washington. His current research interests include the measurement of health status in clinical settings; management of common musculoskeletal diseases, and evaluation of common medical practices. He is the author of 85 articles and book chapters in the medical and health services literature. These have covered the use of health status questionnaires in rheumatoid arthritis, the diagnosis and management of low back pain, and the methodology of health status assessment in musculoskeletal diseases.

**P Erickson, MS**, is Chief of the Clearinghouse of Health Indexes, Office of Analysis and Epidemiology, National Center for Health Statistics, US, DHHS. Her current responsibilities include editing the Bibliography on Health Indexes and analysing national data on health-related quality of life for epidemiologic and evaluative purposes. Her publications include "Health Status and Health Policy: Quality of Life in Health Care Evaluation and Resource Allocation" co-authored with Donald Patrick and published by Oxford University Press, 1993. In addition, she serves as consultant to The On-Line Guide to Quality-of-Life Assessment (OLGA).

**A Fletcher, PhD**, is a Senior Lecturer in Epidemiology at the Royal Postgraduate Medical School. Current ongoing research includes the measurement of quality of life in a range of contexts from clinical trials in hypertension, heart failure and diabetes to acute geriatric wards. She is also involved in trials and studies of factors influencing survival in hypertensive patients. Main current interest is in the epidemiology of the elderly with a special emphasis on the prevention of disease.

**T G Ganiats, MD**, is an associate professor, Chief of the Division of Family Medicine and Vice-chair of the Department of Community and Family Medicine at the University of California San Diego (UCSD) School of Medicine. Dr Ganiats received his MD degree from UCSD in 1978. In 1981 he graduated from his family practice residency at UCSD where he was Chief Resident. His practice includes the full range of family practice, from prenatal care through geriatrics. His research interests are in health technology assessment, especially cost/utility analysis. He is an active contributor to the literature in family medicine and medical decision-making. One of his current projects is an evaluation of outcomes in stroke prevention using the Quality of Well-being Scale.

**S M Hunt, MA, PhD, FRIPHH, FRSM**, was formerly Senior Research Fellow at the University of Edinburgh and is now a partner in Galen Research & Consultancy. She divides her interests between measurement issues related to health and socio-epidemio-logical investigations of the relationship between living conditions and ill health. With Steve McKenna, she has recently completed a measure of quality of life, based upon a new conceptual model, for use in depression. She is currently engaged in the development of health measures appropriate to the diversity of European cultures and languages, a measure of the impact of childhood illness on the family and an index of distress/dependency.

**J R Johnson, MD**, is Head of the Oncology Drugs Group at the Unites States Food and Drug Administration. His responsibilities include evaluation of applications for testing and marketing of drugs for the treatment and prevention of cancer. His research interests are developing improvements in the design, conduct and analysis of clinical trials and developing new approaches to assess the patient benefit of anticancer drugs. He is an advocate of including quality of life assessment in cancer clinical trials.

**P W Jones, PhD, FRCP**, is Reader in Medicine and Consultant Physician at St George's Hospital Medical School, London. He is a physician specialising in respiratory disease. His recent research has included development and validation studies for the measurement of health in patients with lung disease. Current research is concerned with cognitive aspects of breathlessness and relationships between disturbed lung function, breathlessness, exercise tolerance, disability and perceived health and well-being.

**Professor C R B Joyce, PhD FBPsS**, is Visiting Professor at the University Psychiatric Policlinic, University of Bern, Switzerland and also at the Royal College of Surgeons in Ireland, and Foreign Associate of the Institute of Cognitive Science, University of Colorado. His five books and over 100 papers are mostly on psychopharmacological topics and the methodology of clinical research.

**Professor R M Kaplan, PhD**, is Professor of Community and Family Medicine and chief of the Division of Health Care Sciences at the University of California, San Diego School of Medicine. A graduate of the University of California, Dr Kaplan has spent most of his career in the San Diego area. In 1973 he joined a research group headed by Jim Bush and has continued to focus his research on health status and quality of life measurement. Dr Kaplan is particularly interested in quantifying outcomes in clinical trials and in health resource allocation problems. His current projects are relevant to chronic obstructive pulmonary disease, cancer, and arthritis. He is the author or editor of 13 books and approximately 180 articles or chapters.

**Professor A. Maynard, BA, BPhil**, is Professor of Economics and Director of the Centre for Health Economics, University of York, England. He was a member of the Health Services Research Committee of the UK Medical Research council 1986-92 and chaired the Evaluation Panel of the 4th Medical and Health Research Programme of the European Commission in 1990-1. His research interests are in the development of mechanisms to ration health resources and the integration of these mechanisms into competitive and other forms of health care reforms.

**Professor J McEwen, MBChB, FRCP(Glasg) FFPHM FFOM**, is Henry Mechan Professor of Public Health and Head of Department of Public Health at the University of Glasgow. While based in the Department of Community Health at the University of Nottingham, with colleagues was responsible for the development of the Nottingham Health Profile. Current work on the field of health status measures includes the use of the Nottingham Health Profile in clinical studies and community surveys and the development of new measures. Other interests include, the evaluation of health education, and health promotion in the workplace, the planning, provision and evaluation of health services and the impact of change in the NHS.

**S P McKenna, PhD**, is a partner in Galen Research & Consultancy who specialise in the measurement of health and quality of life. In this capacity, he and Sonja Hunt have worked with a number of pharmaceutical companies in the design and operation of quality of life trials, with special emphasis on multi-national aspects of measurement and the development of new measures.

**Professor J D Parkes, MD, FRCP**, is Professor of Clinical Neurology at King's College School of Medicine and Dentistry and the Institute of Psychiatry. His clinical responsibilities are those of a Consultant Neurologist specializing in extrapyramidal and sleep disorders. His clinical research has been concerned with different aspects of parkinsonism, physiology and pharmacology of dopamine receptor systems. His current work concerns the relationship between physiological disturbances in parkinsonism and patient disability, as well as the investigation of narcolepsy, sleep apnoea and parasomnias.

**Professor D L Patrick, PhD, MSPH**, is Professor of Health Services and Sociology at the University of Washington in Seattle, USA. He has been working on health and quality of life assessment since 1966 with particular emphasis on resource allocation, the measurement of values associated with health status, and the application of health status measures in older adults and people with disabilities in the United Kingdom and the United States. He is currently conducting studies of the cost-effectiveness of preventive services for older adults, measurement of preferences for states of health considered worse than death, and the development and application of health-related quality of life measures in clinical trials, clinical practice, and health services research.

**M Pekurinen, PhD**, is Project Manager, Health Services Research Limited, Finland. His current research interests are in economic evaluation of health care services, hospital productivity and competition in health care.

**J L Read, MD**, is currently a Principal in Interhealth Limited, an investment partnership in Palo Alto California, USA, with holdings in pharmaceutical and biotechnology companies. He co-founded Affymax NV in 1988, with Dr Alejandro Zaffaroni and served as a Managing Director of this innovative drug discovery company until 1991. Dr Read trained as an internist at the Peter Bent Brigham Hospital in Boston and held appointments in the Departments of Medicine and Surgery at the New England Deaconess Hospital, Harvard School of public Health and Harvard Medical School from 1980-1987. He has authored articles in medical literature on topics of cost-effectiveness analysis, decision analysis, and quality of life measurement. He has also participated in the design of many clinical trials intended to provide data for cost-effectiveness analysis. His interest in the use of expert systems for health promotion lead to the creation of a personal computer software product widely distributed in the United States. Dr Read is now involved in facilitating the commercialization of several early-stage technologies in the biomedical field.

**Professor R M Rosser, MA, MB, BChir, PhD, FRCP, FRCPsych**, is Professor of Psychiatry and Head of Department at University College and Middlesex School of Medicine. From 1985 to 1987 she was President of the Society for Psychosomatic Research. She is currently Treasurer of the International College of Psychosomatic Medicine, Secretary of the Psychiatric Section of the Royal Society of Medicine and a member of the Audit Group of the Royal College of Psychiatrists. Her publications and current research are in the fields of psychosomatic medicine with particular reference to disasters and to cultural differences in clinical presentation, psychotherapy evaluation and health services research.

**S Salek, BSc, PhD, RPH**, is Senior Research Associate, Department of Clinical Pharmacy, and Associate Director of the Medicines Research Unit, University of Wales College of Cardiff. He has developed the United Kingdom version of the Sickness Impact Profile and validated a number of disease areas. His current research interests are in health-related quality of life, in particular, in the dermatology, cardiovascular and respiratory areas. He is the author of over 50 papers and contributed chapters.

**N Sartorius, MD, MA, DPM, PhD, FRCPsych**, specialized in neurology and psychiatry and subsequently obtained a Masters Degree and a Doctorate in psychology (PhD). Dr Sartorius joined the World Health Organization in 1967 and soon assumed charge of the programme of epidemiology in social psychiatry. He was also principal investigator of several major international health studies. In 1977, he was appointed Director of the Division of Mental Health of WHO, a position which he holds today. Dr Sartorius has published some 200 articles in scientific journals, co-authored several books and edited a number of others.

**J Scott, MS**, is Head of the On-Line Guide to Quality-of-Life Assessment (OLGA), an information resource service for the health care profession. OLGA is designed to assist in the selection of quality of life assessments for use in clinical studies. His previous experience has centred on the development of computer systems for analysing and reporting clinical trial and drug information data.

**Professor P Selby, MA, MD, FRCP** has been Professor of Cancer Medicine and Director of the Institute for Cancer Studies at the University of Leeds since June 1988 and a Consultant Physician at St James University Hospital. Before taking up that post he was a Consultant Physician and Senior Lecturer in Medicine at the Royal Marsden Hospital and Institute of Cancer Research in London. He trained as a general physician and medical oncologist in London and Toronto. His research interests are in the clinical features, biology and treatment of cancer. He is establishing the Institute for Cancer Studies at the University of Leeds with funding from the Yorkshire Cancer Research Campaign, the St James's University Hospital Trust and Yorkshire Health.

**Professor H Sintonen, PhD**, is Associate Professor of Health Economics in the Department of Health Policy and Management, University of Kuopio, Finland. He has worked on the measurement and valuation of health and health-related quality of life since the mid '70s, primarily on 15D and EuroQol. At present he is the Convenor of the EuroQol Group. His other research fields are dental economics and economic assessment of health care technologies.

**Professor G Teeling Smith, OBE, BA, FRPharmS, Hon MPharm**, has been the Director of the Office of health Economics since it was first established in 1962. He is also Professor Associate in the Department of Economics at Brunel University, where he teaches an Undergraduate course in health economics and supervises graduate research. His principal interest is in developing the methodology for measuring the outcome of pharmaceutical treatments. He is the author of numerous booklets and papers on all aspects of health economics, and has edited a series of books on the economics of the pharmaceutical industry. He is consultant to a number of organizations on the subject of economic evaluation.

**M J VandenBurg, MB, BS, MRCP**, is currently Chairman of the MCRC Group Limited, a company providing contractual services to the pharmaceutical industry. Prior to forming this company, he was Director of Cardiovascular Research at Oldchurch Hospital, Director of Clinical Research for Merck Sharp & Dohme in the UK and established and ran the London Hospital Hypertension Clinic when he was a lecturer at this hospital. His current research interests are how clinical design may alter the results of studies and the assessment of quality of life. He has over 100 publications in the field of clinical research and has been involved in the development of products in the fields of rheumatology, gastroenterology, ophthalmics, microbiology, neurology and cardiovascular medicine.

**Professor S R Walker, BSc, PhD, CChem, FRSC, CBiol, FIBiol**, is Director of the Centre for Medicines Research and Honorary Professor within the Welsh School of Pharmacy, University of Wales College, Cardiff. He spent ten years at London University which included lectureships in biochemical pharmacology at St Mary's Hospital Medical School and in clinical pharmacology at the Cardiothoracic Institute in London. This was followed by eight years with Glaxo Group Research in the UK where he had international responsibility for several of their clinical research programmes. His current research interests include studies into the process of innovation in drug research and development, an examination of the impact of international medicines regulations and policy issues on drug development, and investigating the role as well as the predictive value of pre-clinical animal toxicology. Professor Walker is a member of several academic, professional and industrial committees and sits on the editorial boards of a number of scientific journals. He is frequently involved in the organization of national and international meetings on key issues that concern the pharmaceutical industry and has co-authored over 120 research papers and edited nine books.

**Professor A Williams, BCom**, is part-time Professor of Economics at the University of York, England. His research field has been the application of cost-benefit and cost-effectiveness techniques to a wide range of public policy issues, but in the last twenty years his attention has been increasingly concentrated on the economics of health and of health care. His applied work has concerned orthopaedics, the care of the elderly, CT scanning, the clinical use of NMR, and the application of the cost-per-QALY approach to a wide range of conditions and treatments. But his main interest is in developing the QALY methodology itself, and in exploring how people value health at different stages in their lives, and which aspects of health are most important to them.

# Section I

# Philosophies, Concepts and Key Instruments Involved in Assessing Quality of Life

# 1 The new era of quality of life assessment

**J. Leighton Read**

Whether or not the appearance of this volume is viewed as a turning point in the evaluation of clinical data, the period from which this work arises represents an important watershed. We are in the midst of a transformation in the way people think about clinical trials: their purpose, what they should be telling us, and the tools we need to make them more useful.

This introduction serves to point out why the deliberate assessment of quality of life in medical research is indeed something new, make a case for why one should be interested in having the effort succeed, and finally address a few issues which might help the reader distinguish the forest of endeavour from a few methodological trees.

## THE NOVELTY OF QUALITY OF LIFE ASSESSMENT

A lay person (anyone not involved in the sponsorship, execution, or interpretation of clinical trials) might imagine that quality of life has always been an important objective of medical research. While the notion was of concern to scientists and physicians as they evaluated their results, until recently, patient quality of life has been addressed only by very indirect inference from more traditional, medical variables.

Since the sweeping technological revolution of the mid-twentieth century, doctors have placed great reliance on highly technical endpoints. The advances which come from such a mechanistic, physiological view of disease have caused a generation of physicians to distrust information which does not come from analytical laboratories. This distrust has been aided and abetted by the highly successful, formalized approaches to experimental design which, to their disadvantage, tend to distance experimental settings from what happens in the real and uncontrolled world of patient care.

In a typical clinical trial, the primary endpoints are based on anatomical, physiological, or chemical variables, although sometimes more global, but still vaguely conceptualized, morbidity measures, such as patient improves/deteriorates, symptoms better/worse, cure affected/or not, can be found. In rapidly life-threatening conditions, the outcome of survival is available. In order to draw conclusions about whether a particular therapy is efficacious, doctors use their knowledge of pathophysiology and the natural history of disease to form expectations, which bridge the difference between the medical endpoints and what will later happen to patients' survival and quality of life.

It would be unfair to ignore some early efforts to include performance or activity measures in clinical studies, dating back to the venerable scales of both Karnofsky and Katz, or the disease-specific metrics promulgated by the New York Heart and the American Rheumatologic Associations. These measures, however, have not gained use outside narrow applications. Moreover, their performance in terms of reliability, sensitivity, and validity has either been poorly studied or shown to be less than satisfactory (for further discussion, see the chapter by Deyo). What sets the new quality of life measures apart from previous efforts is the fact that they are based on explicit conceptual models of health and have been painstakingly evaluated for their reliability and validity.

## MAJOR CHANGES IN HEALTH CARE REQUIRE NEW MEASURES OF OUTCOME

In various ways, each contributor to this volume argues for the need for better measures of what happens in patients' lives following medical intervention. As a prelude, three important interrelated changes in the health care enterprise which have led to the interest in quality of life assessment, will be briefly described: the ascendancy of chronic disease as the primary target of intervention, shifting roles of key health care decision-makers, and a dramatic transition in the ground rules of medical practice.

### Chronic disease

It is no longer newsworthy to state that in the developed countries, chronic conditions such as cardiovascular, pulmonary, rheumatological, and neurological diseases have replaced most of the life-threatening infections which once dominated medical attention (AIDS is now an important exception). This trend is a result of the success in treating many acute conditions, the rise in illnesses related to life-style, and the ageing of the population.

Experience with chronic disease has made it clear to doctors and others that health care does not save lives, but when successful, it can prolong the length of life or can enhance the quality of the remaining survival time. Until now, medical science has been poorly equipped to document the latter. Many promising efforts to improve this situation, however, are outlined in the chapters on important chronic diseases which follow by Selby, Deyo, Shindler *et al.*, Jones, Fletcher and Bulpitt, and VandenBurg.

## New decision-making roles

Along with the importance of chronic diseases, a redistribution of health-care decision-making authority adds to the interest in quality of life measurement. Responsibility seems to be shifting both down from the doctor to the patient and up from the doctor to emerging health-care managers. Consumer movements now have firm roots on both sides of the Atlantic and give patients a new voice in the decisions regarding their care. Traditional paternalistic doctor–patient relationships are becoming more like partnerships.

Patients with chronic conditions are not interested in their laboratory results, except to the extent these variables predict future quality of life or survival. They therefore have good reason to insist that clinical data substantiate the value of alternative therapies in terms of the outcomes about which they care.

Quality of life measures are also of considerable interest to a new breed of health care managers (as described more fully in the chapter by Williams). In most Western countries, regardless of financing system, health-care delivery is evolving from a cottage industry of individual practitioners, to a highly organized enterprise of large-scale proportions. The growing centralization of decision-making has created roles for people (who may or may not be physicians) with a common responsibility to allocate limited budgets to alternative forms of care.

Regulatory and financing authorities are beginning to ask that the net cost impact of new therapies be evaluated before they are approved for marketing or reimbursement under health service systems. They also want to know about the impact on health in terms more directly relevant to the public than the usual physiological endpoints of medical models. Admittedly, the current health status indices and quality of life measures may seem a bit arcane and complicated for universal application, but their great promise is based on the fact that they are built up from questions which directly tap the kind of day-to-day functioning and freedom from symptoms which are the objectives of health care.

## New ground rules

The basic tenets by which physicians regard their actions have undergone dramatic changes in this century. In the pre-antibiotic era, the watchword was *First Do No Harm*, justifiable since medical science had relatively little to offer most patients. The great progress that occurred in the middle of the twentieth century allowed doctors to offer genuine relief to many patients, but they soon found themselves fighting a losing battle to keep up with the pace of scientific advance. By the 1960s, the watchword had changed from *Do No Harm* to *Be Complete*. Thoroughness became the highest professional virtue, along with a firm reliance on technical procedures rather than touch and feel.

The rules have changed again. Those who manage society's investment in health care discovered that doctors not only could, but seemed compelled, to do more than was affordable. Thus, a new rule has been imposed from outside the medical profession – *Give Value for Money*. Techniques for measuring the cost impact of health care interventions are evolving rapidly from well-known accounting procedures. True innovation, however, has been required in the area of quantifying the value of effectiveness of therapy, and that is one of the most important functions of some of the new quality of life measures described here (see the chapter by Kaplan and Anderson, and the chapter by Williams, for more details).

## DISTINGUISHING THE FOREST FROM SOME METHODOLOGICAL TREES

*How do the traditional medical measures fit in with quality of life assessments?*

The distinction between the newer quality of life scores and the usual anatomical, physiological, or chemical variables can be viewed as a distinction between measures of goal attainment and measures which predict goal attainment. The primary goal of health care is to provide incremental survival time and/or incremental quality to that time. These are the valued endpoints, not the blood pressure reading or the biopsy finding. The overview chapter by Patrick and Erickson deals with this topic in some detail, and discussion in those by Kaplan and Anderson, Chambers, McEwen, Bergner, and Joyce should also be noted.

Experiments involving traditional medical variables are the key to understanding disease pathophysiology and the mechanisms by which therapy acts. Insights thus gained can be invaluable in providing clues to better therapeutic approaches and avoidance of toxicity. However, traditional medical measures often do not provide a definitive answer about whether or not a therapy is useful. In the new quality of life measures, we now have the wherewithal to directly measure the extent to which alternative therapies benefit patients, in the relevant terms of day-to-day activity and freedom from symptoms.

An important exception is the case where the time delay from intervention to health outcome is so long that patients cannot practically be kept under observation. One must then rely on an understanding of the relationship between medical predictor variables and ultimate changes in quality of life. For example, it is quite possible to obtain good measures of the decrement in quality of life which accompanies antihypertensive therapy (see the chapter by Fletcher and Bulpitt), but one must study a large population for many years to observe and measure the cardiovascular morbidity which follows from inadequate blood pressure control. The chapter by Patrick and Erickson and the chapter by Kaplan and Anderson further discuss the concept of prognosis in measuring quality of life.

### Are quality of life measures more suited to use in patient care or should they be limited to use in clinical trials?

This question arises out of a concern that perhaps too much is expected of quality of life measures. I am more impressed with the role of quality of life instruments as tools for evaluation studies than in patient care, because I have considerable confidence in most doctors' ability to develop accurate impressions of whether or not their patients are improving, based only on informal face-to-face interaction.

However, it is also true that standardized data collection will bring to light health status information which would not otherwise be documented. Use of such forms is also likely to result in better recording, and therefore recall, of this material. The Chapter by McEwen provides some interesting support for these points. While doctors' impressions may be adequate to guide individual therapy, they are not readily communicated to others in a way that can be collected and analysed for clinical trial purposes. Thus, the more important impetus for developing quality of life measurements is for use in clinical trials, where data must be pooled from many patients.

There is a large class of health-care decisions which are not isolated choices for individuals, but decisions which affect many individuals, for example, shall this drug be allowed for reimbursement or allowed in the formulary? do we invest in a transplantation programme? which antihypertensive is my first choice for otherwise healthy young men? The studies organized to answer these questions are where the new health status indices and functional measures can play an invaluable role. The chapters in this volume provide many specific examples.

### How practical are these scales for use in clinical trials?

This is a relevant question for anyone contemplating the sponsorship or organization of a study using quality of life measures. I would argue, however, that there is a danger of too few, rather than too many resources being expended. The amount of investigator and patient time and effort, as well as the financial investment in data collection with well-studied instruments, should be based on the importance of the answers sought and the likelihood that the study will provide them, not by reference to previous efforts in obtaining patient self-reports or diary data.

### Do quality of life instruments produce hard data or soft data?

This contrast is confusing because the concepts are ill-defined. The question comes up often, however, in conversations with doctors about new measurement approaches, and so it should be addressed, as it is in the chapter by Deyo and the chapter by McEwen, and indirectly, in the comprehensive overview by Patrick and Erickson.

When asked to describe hard data, clinicians use terms such as reliable and reproducible. Unfortunately, clinical researchers do not enjoy a widely accepted, formal theory of measurement on which to draw when they consider the acceptability of different types of data. If asked to sort a list of variables into hard and soft categories, I suspect that the more technological (and perhaps in fee-for-service systems, the more reimbursible) the procedure, the more likely it would be considered to produce hard data. Information which is more cognitive, perceptual, or filtered by human judgement is likely to be considered soft.

Reliability has several well-defined meanings in biostatistics which are certainly relevant to the interpretation of clinical trial endpoints. As Deyo and others point out, some of the quality of life instruments perform better on tests of reliability than many traditional medical tests. There are, however, other important considerations. Chief among these is the validity, or relevance, of the data to the question at hand. Here, I believe that the traditional medical approaches to evaluating data can gain from the more sophisticated theories of measurement used in the social sciences. If the elaborate validation studies described for some of the quality of life measures in this volume seem confusing to doctors, it may be because the usual medical approach to measurement theory is too naïve.

### Which are more useful: disease-specific measures or overall measures of health?

It depends on the purpose of the measurement (as discussed at some length in the chapters by Patrick and Erickson, Kaplan and Anderson and Deyo, who describe the impact of this issue on index sensitivity). Consider one hypothetical quality of life measure which is highly focused on the morbidity associated with rheumatoid arthritis and another which purports to measure overall health. Imagine also that the two instruments contain an identical number of questions, follow the same general measurement strategy and questionnaire design, have demonstrated similar levels of reliability and validity for their respective domains, and require the same degree of respondent and investigator attention.

One might predict the following general findings if these two instruments were used side-by-side in a variety of research studies. First, the arthritis-specific scale would be more likely to show statistically significant differences between effective and ineffective anti-arthritic therapies, that is, the probability of a beta-error would be smaller. At the same time, the arthritis index would offer little or no information on which of the two therapies had the greater toxicity, if that toxicity was manifested in, say, the gastrointestinal or haematological systems. Data from the arthritis index would also be of limited use to a health-service manager who must decide whether to allocate resources to the best available arthritis therapy or, for example, to an expensive new form of anti-cancer therapy.

If, however, one anti-arthritis drug is shown to be more effective than another (or a placebo) on a credible measure of overall health, then one might assume that the net of the therapeutic and toxic effects was favourable. And if therapies for other forms of disease were evaluated with the same measure of overall health, one could potentially draw direct conclusions regarding which of the two competing therapies gives the more health value for the cost. A further advantage of the overall index is more subtle; by summing over many types of health effects, it might detect beneficial effects which are small in individual domains of function but become important in total. Synergistic effects of concomitant therapies or disease might also be better appreciated via more global measures.

### Is the notion of quality of life too personal or individual to be reduced to standardized measures?

One can readily observe that people's perceptions of quality differ for every realm of evaluation imaginable and, furthermore, these differences are generally the result of legitimate individual preferences. There is also a large body of literature to support individual variation in the way various health states are rated.

However, introspection and empirical data also support the argument that, despite the differences, there is a good deal of common ground among people's relative evaluation of health states (see especially the contributions by Bergner and by Kaplan and Anderson). There is a strong consensus for the idea that a day spent with a runny nose is much closer to perfect health than is a day spent confined to bed. Of course, there are exceptions, such as someone who would like a day away from work. To aid the many decisions which must be made for groups of individuals, there is a strong argument for using available information on areas of common ground in valuing health outcomes. This information is available in the form of well thought-out quality of life measures.

**Conclusion**

My comments are meant to provide some clues as to why a number of serious and talented health-care researchers would expend the effort to produce this volume. Hopefully, they have also whetted the reader's appetite for the more substantial discussions which follow.

# 2 Assessing health-related quality of life for clinical decision-making

Donald L. Patrick and Pennifer Erickson

Health-care professionals from many specialties and disciplines are becoming increasingly aware that one of the major goals of medical care and technology is to improve patients' quality of life. Enhancing quality of life is as important as other goals of health and medical care, such as preventing disease, effecting a cure, alleviating symptoms or pain, averting complications, providing humane care, and prolonging life.

Quality of life can be considered in regard both to individual patients and to aggregates of patients. With individual patients, the health-care provider wishes to assess the lives of individual patients and to evaluate the potential and actual impact of treatments on them. Patients, families, and significant others are concerned about the meaning of their particular symptoms and health problems, the outcome of the treatment prescribed for them and the burden it imposes, and the effects that their impaired health and its treatment may have on various aspects of their present and future lives. With groups of patients, the health-care professional is concerned with assessing the current and future status of aggregates of patients by means of standardized criteria and with evaluating the impact of interventions that range from specific pharmacological and non-pharmacological treatments to broad health service and policy initiatives. Trade-offs between quantity and quality of life are important in assessing disease and treatment outcomes both for individual patients and for populations.

Clinical decision-making involves both individual patient care and clinical trials for the purpose of evaluating and deciding among alternatives. Health and quality of life outcomes are used for clinical decision-making in four ways:

(1)   Outcomes are used to monitor and assess patient status, for example, a patient with essential hypertension might be followed using a number

11

of different outcomes ranging from blood pressure to work performance, leisure time activities, and worries about health.

(2)    Health outcomes are used to select treatments, for example, the results
of clinical trials assessing the effects of different anti-hypertensive
agents or anti-inflammatory drugs on quality of life.

(3)    Outcomes are then used to monitor the effects of treatments that have
been selected.

(4)    Health and quality of life outcomes are used to develop a shared view
of the disease and of treatment outcomes with patients. In discussing
the effects of a diagnosis, such as rheumatoid arthritis or hypertension,
the doctor and patient can develop a shared understanding of the disease
impact on the patient by assessing health and quality of life outcomes.

In this paper, we shall discuss different socio-medical approaches to the
definition and assessment of health-related quality of life for clinical decision-making. Particular attention will be paid to the conceptualization of
health and quality of life outcomes and to the methodological and practical
considerations involved in selecting and using standardized measures.

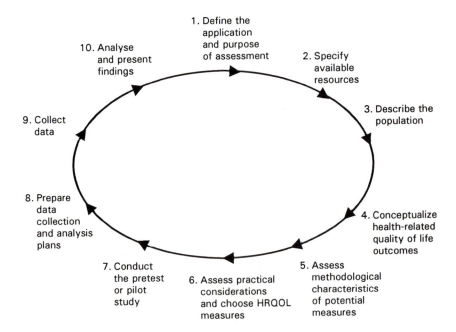

**Figure 2.1** Ten steps in a health-related quality of life assessment

Regardless of the particular application of these measures, the assessment strategy can be viewed as a circular flow comprising the ten steps illustrated in Figure 2.1.

## 1. DEFINE THE APPLICATION AND PURPOSE OF MEASUREMENT

This first step involves describing the decisions to be made and the problem to be addressed. Investigators must specify the objectives of the quality of life assessment and assign priorities to these objectives if there are more than one Kirshner and Guyatt[74] identified at least three major objectives for assessing health status in clinical decision-making: (1) discriminating among persons at a single point in time, similar to psychological measures of traits such as intelligence and personality; (2) predicting some future outcome or the results of a more intrusive or costly criterion measure, commonly referred to as the 'gold standard'; and (3) measuring changes over time, as in the typical design of a cohort study or randomized controlled trial. Methodological and practical considerations are different according to the purpose of assessment, and these considerations may be competing.

For example, a health-related quality of life measure may discriminate adequately between well and ill individuals by using lengthy questionnaire items investigating relatively fixed traits. In contrast, a measure used to evaluate change over time would not benefit substantially from including fixed characteristics. It would be more efficient if it tapped only behaviours or abilities susceptible to change in response to the intervention under study.

Practical considerations also follow from the primary objective of assessment. For example, measures designed to capture change over time may require transition questions, i.e. items written specifically to measure change. For example, respondents can be asked how their quality of life has changed on a seven-point scale ranging from 'much better' to 'much worse'. For discrimination between different groups of persons based on gender, age, or other characteristics, items measuring change may be inappropriate and unacceptable to investigators and respondents.

## 2. SPECIFY AVAILABLE RESOURCES

The major practical consideration involved prior to selecting an assessment strategy and measures of health-related quality of life is the amount of resources to be devoted to the assessment. These resources include time, money, and personnel. The projected burden on respondents, interviewers, data analysts and investigators should be estimated. Identifying resources at this stage not only helps in selection, but also uncovers the interested parties' expectations for the relevance and usefulness of the assessment.

All aspects of assessment – selecting measures, collecting and editing data, analysing data, and presenting findings – are time consuming. Researchers can spend weeks or months developing a comprehensive *and* targeted questionnaire or interview schedule. They must survey the research, specify the problem, and conceptualize the outcomes. Designing an efficient data collection instrument is only the first step to implementation. Preparing even a simple questionnaire can take 10 to 20 versions before it is ready for pretesting.

The entire time-frame for the assessment, analysis, and presentation should be estimated in advance and adjusted for the usual deadlines presented by those sponsoring the research. Developing a timeline, along with a detailed plan outlining all the tasks to be accomplished and the personnel needed for each phase, is recommended. This timeline also helps in budgeting for the assessment. Novice investigators seldom allocate sufficient time, money, and personnel for health-related quality of life assessments. Experienced primary data collectors allow for additional resources to handle unexpected problems in design and implementation. Known resource constraints on time and money provide boundaries for most investigators. Funding agencies also examine budgets in detail for proportion of resources allocated to specific project tasks in relation to project objectives and project design.

## 3. DESCRIBE THE POPULATION

At a minimum, four major characteristics of populations and potential respondents should be considered in selecting measures of health-related quality of life: (i) level of symptoms and disability (well versus ill); (ii) age (younger versus older); (iii) level of cognitive ability (able to provide reasonably accurate information versus disoriented or cognitively impaired); and (iv) ethnic or cultural identity.

Well populations require an assessment strategy and measures different from populations with significant symptoms and disability. Concepts and measures from the more positive end of the health-related quality of life continuum are needed to assess healthy populations[116]. Nearly 70% of the general population reports their health as excellent or very good. Items concerning need for assistance with activities of daily living would, therefore, not be discriminating or responsive measures for such well populations.

Several core domains of health-related quality of life, such as role functioning, physical functioning (ambulation, mobility etc.), and self-care may have little relevance to well populations where dysfunction is rare in work activities, in mobility, and in carrying out the usual activities of daily living. Health status measures based exclusively on these domains may not be broad enough to provide an assessment of well persons on the continuum of health-related quality of life. If the measure does not 'register' for a large percentage of respondents, the content validity of the measure is low for the population under study.

Furthermore, detecting improving health among persons who are already quite well may prove difficult because of the 'ceiling' effect, i.e. if you start out at the top, there is no place to go 'up'. Measures that do not contain items pertaining to minor or common symptoms and signs, health perceptions and psychological well-being generally are not responsive to improvement, since there is nowhere to go at the top of the scale. Inclusion of emotional well-being, positive affect, vitality, and health perceptions aid in discriminating and measuring change in well populations.

As health providers and society, in general, place more emphasis on health promotion and disease prevention, there is increasing need for measures that incorporate the positive benefits that may result from health-promoting environments or behaviours and preventive interventions. These 'positive' measures are especially relevant for assessing changes in relatively well individuals that may result from health-promoting influences and activities. At present, the main approach to assessing the effects of health promotion is to measure subsequent reduction in disease incidence or lengthening of life. Yet, these two outcomes may not be the only outcomes or the most important ones. Even if morbidity and longevity are unaffected, health promotion may enhance health by increasing energy, stamina, feelings of well-being, resilience, autonomy, and productivity. These are outcomes potentially related to behaviour change.

Detecting worsening health among people who are already ill can also be a challenge. Bindman and colleagues[13] studied severely ill patients at two points in time using the Medical Outcomes Study Short Form (MOS-20). Baseline MOS-20 scores for these hospitalized patients were low. While many patients reported worsening health at follow-up, their low baseline scores made it difficult to detect health status decline.

Researchers need more comprehensive generic measures with multiple domains and multiple items to detect subtle changes in both well and severely ill populations. Without such generic measures, they should include disease-specific measures to assess ill respondents. To assess well respondents, they should use specific measures of health perceptions (general and satisfaction with health), resilience, and positive affect. Generic measures provide the basis for population comparisons as well as the assessment of floor and ceiling effects. Specific measures provide the basis for detecting changes at the two ends of health-related quality of life continuum.

Considerable challenges remain to collecting health-related quality of life data on children and older adults. In both age groups, data collection procedures include health examinations and health interviews. Many health examination procedures were developed primarily in the field of medicine. These often include performance-based measures in which respondents are asked to do specific tasks. Their performance on these tasks is evaluated and scored according to stage of development, speed at which the task is performed, or other criteria. Direct measures of older adults' functional status, such as ability to walk, hold objects, open doors, or perform other behaviours, are common in geriatric evaluation. The fifty-foot walk time, Performance Activities of Daily Living[76] and functional vital signs[140] are examples of such direct measures of performance. Health examination data provide the means for obtaining unrecognized and undiagnosed conditions, including non-symptomatic conditions. Recognizing and listing health conditions, however, is less useful in classifying or measuring level of health-related quality of life of children and older adults.

Measures developed primarily from the social sciences include questionnaires, interviewing procedures, and techniques of scale development, including scoring and analysis. Mothers and teachers provide most information about the health status of children, although reliable reports of behaviour have been obtained from children over 12 years of age[49]. Problems exist in obtaining information that is reliable from child to child, given the changes in questionnaire content needed for different age groups. Fink[50] points out the serious limitations to using reported diagnoses, symptoms, impairments, and general measures as reported by parents. The validity of these reports can be questioned along with the difficulties in combining these different reports into a profile of child health status.

The problems are different with older adults. Most well older adults complete self-administered or interviewer-administered health status questionnaires with relative ease, possibly because they have the time and interest to participate in studies. A problem that commonly arises in assessing seniors is asking them to rate their current health in comparison to 'usual' health or asking if reported changes are 'due to health' or 'due to age'. Changes in health status may be attributed by older adults to age and not to health-related conditions. Some measures ask seniors to compare their health to others their own age. Well older adults do not consider their age peers the most appropriate reference group, since a wide spectrum of abilities can be observed at any age, including our 'oldest old' or those 85 years and above.

Cognitive functioning or mental incapacity is of major concern when assessing the health-related quality of life of older or severely impaired adults. With such populations, interviewer-administered questionnaires are recommended to reach a representative sample of the population. If only self-administered questionnaires are used, the resulting sample will include only those capable of completing the instrument on their own or with help from others.

Mental status evaluations are routinely administered at the beginning of interviews with older or disabled adults. Commonly used examples include the Folstein Mini-Mental State[51] and the Short Portable Mental Status

Questionnaire[105]. New cognitive screening tests have also been developed for administration over the telephone[18]. These instruments are short measures of symptoms used to screen for cognitive difficulties. They are not diagnostic tests for dementia or the aetiology of organic diseases such as Alzheimer's disease. Respondents who score below defined cut-off points are generally not interviewed. Instead, a proxy respondent, usually a care-giver, is requested to complete the interview.

The correspondence between respondent and proxy response to health-related quality of life measures varies depending on the domain assessed and the choice of proxy. As might be expected, proxy reports of more observable domains such as physical functioning, activities of daily living, cognition, and social activity are highly correlated with reports from the respondents themselves[46,82,110]. Reports of psychological functioning and satisfaction with health, less observable domains of health-related quality of life, are more moderately correlated.

Proxy respondents tend to consider patients more impaired, i.e. overestimate patient dysfunction, relative to the respondents themselves. Overestimation of disability is particularly characteristic of those proxies with the greatest contact with the respondent. The psychological distress and burden perceived by the proxy respondent can affect their assessments of patients' own psychosocial functioning[110].

Two strategies can be employed to improve proxy reporting. First, respondents can nominate their own proxies; in fact, they tend to select proxies who are able to respond reliably[6,34]. Secondly, investigators can reduce the ambiguity in instructions to proxy respondents, ask proxies to rate their perceived accuracy of the information provided, and use one or more proxies to obtain convergent views of patient status. Perhaps most importantly, investigators should avoid proxy reports of highly subjective domains, since only the person affected can truly communicate their affective feelings and cognitive evaluations of their health and quality of life.

As cultural anthropologists demonstrate repeatedly, a person's conception of what constitutes 'disease' or 'health' can depend on his or her cultural traditions, language, group mores, as well as more individual characteristics such as age, educational level, and income[47,75]. Thus, comparisons between different ethnic groups and across different cultures cannot be made without considering cultural variables. The cross-cultural content of measures, the cultural meaning of different domains, and the translation of measures from one language or culture to another are important considerations in assessing health-related quality of life.

The cross-cultural content of health status measures is relevant to both generic measures and condition or domain-specific ones. Cross-cultural studies of preference weighting using the Sickness Impact Profile[104] and the Nottingham Health Profile[63] suggest a universal ranking or rating of health states. For example, it is better to walk *without* limitations than to walk *with* limitations. The suggestion that health-related quality of life domains can be generalized across different cultures is not surprising. Activities and behaviours related to walking, mobility, sleep, eating, household management, work, and recreation are clearly found in almost every, if not all, cultures. At the most disabling levels of physical activities necessary for human survival, there may be near universal agreement on what is 'bad' and 'good' health.

Although the domains and relative preference for health states may hold for different cultures, the meaning and interpretation of different health states may well vary among these different populations. Symptoms such as bleeding or vomiting, considered undesirable in many Western cultures, may be signs of religious inspiration to others. Persons exhibiting these 'symptoms' under certain conditions may be venerated and held in high esteem. Good and Good[55] provide a 'cultural hermeneutic' model for translating illness realities and decoding a person's symptoms by grounding reports of symptoms in the cultural context of the person rather than using only somatic referents.

In one sense, disease-specific measures are translations of generic health status concepts into the cultural categories, vocabularies, and perspectives of different groups. For example, patients with chronic back pain who attend back pain clinics are a 'subculture'; they communicate with symptoms of back pain, and they evaluate the effectiveness of treatments in somewhat unique terms.

Increasingly, instruments created for use in one language are being translated for use in other cultures and with persons of different ethnic identity. Protocols and techniques for obtaining an accurate and culturally valid second-language translation of health status measures are available[19,54]. For example, many instruments that were originally developed in English are now available in French, German, Spanish, Japanese, and Swedish[2,60,61,121]. Empirical evidence indicates that it is possible to apply instruments developed for use in one culture in a different setting[104].

Investigators still report problems with technically-adequate translations of health status measures[1]. There are many conceptual and linguistic problems to be overcome before a translated version can be used to assess health-related quality of life with confidence. Different dialects and regional, idiomatic language abound within many countries. Hendricson *et al.*[60] conclude that diligent translation may not, by itself, be the key factor. Rather, using a dual-language format and idiomatic language style are crucial factors. Certain aspects of acculturation, particularly familiarity with questionnaire research, may critically affect the validity of the health status data obtained from different cultures[39].

Extreme care must be taken with both generic and disease-specific measures developed in the United States and Europe when applied to populations whose native language is not American or British English, German, or French. The construct validity of the Mexican–Spanish version of the SIP was lower, for example, among patients using this version than among those using the American English version[39]. It is important that people in the community to be investigated translate and format questionnaires. Translations consistent with local dialects and the total 'instrument in translation' should be investigated for reliability and validity before assuming a high correlation with the original language version.

## 4. CONCEPTUALIZE HEALTH-RELATED QUALITY OF LIFE OUTCOMES

Quantity and quality of life can be viewed as distinct but related concepts that are used in evaluating the total present and future state of an individual or a group of people. Quantity of life has been expressed in terms of length of survival, for example, the number of days that a patient survives after undergoing heart transplantation or receiving the newer non-digitalis, positive-inotropic agents, which often improve cardiac function while producing toxic effects. Although it is relatively easy to measure quantity of life objectively in retrospective studies after a patient has died, such quantities as prognosis for survival can only be estimated, and then sometimes without great accuracy. Furthermore, what value is attached to a day of life under the best of circumstances will differ from one person to another[99]. For some, death is preferable to coma, profound pain, or chronic depression[127].

The term, 'quality of life', represents a broad range of dimensions of human experience ranging from those associated with the necessities of life such as food and shelter to those associated with achieving sense of fulfilment and personal happiness. Cultural, psychological, interpersonal, spiritual, financial, political, temporal, and philosophical dimensions may be incorporated into various definitions[26]. These widely valued aspects of human existence may not be thought of as part of personal health status and well-being. A safe environment, adequate housing, a guaranteed income, respect, love, and freedom all contribute to an individual's quality of life[5,84]. The health care system and its providers usually do not assume responsibility for these more global human concerns, even though they may well be adversely affected by disease or treatment and influence disease course and treatment decisions. For example, people with respiratory disease, arthritis, or cardiac disease may experience changes in occupational mobility and income, or require barrier-free housing, or be forced to live in a dry, warm climate. Some patients may also experience stigma, e.g. disapproval from others or social isolation because their friends or family are afraid of 'being with a dying person'. These social, economic and cultural aspects of quality of life are important considerations for patients, families, medical practitioners, and society in general. The focus for clinicians and for clinical trials is primarily on health-related quality of life. Although health status and health services both influence and are influenced by the broader environment, not all aspects of human life are necessarily health or medical concerns.

Because quality of life represents this broad range of human experience, use of this general term in the health field has led to considerable confusion, particularly because of the overlap with the older, more specific concept of health status. To make the meaning more specific and still retain the important aspects of life quality, the term 'health-related quality of life' is both useful and important. *Health-related quality of life is the value assigned to duration of life as modified by the impairments, functional states, perceptions, and social opportunities that are influenced by disease, injury, treatment, or policy*[102].

This definition covers five broad concepts that fall along the continuum shown on the vertical axis in Figure 2.2. This continuum is anchored at the top by an optimal value of 1.0 and at the bottom by a minimal value of 0.0. Specific domains of survival, impairment, functional state, perceptions and opportunities fall along this value continuum and may be negatively or

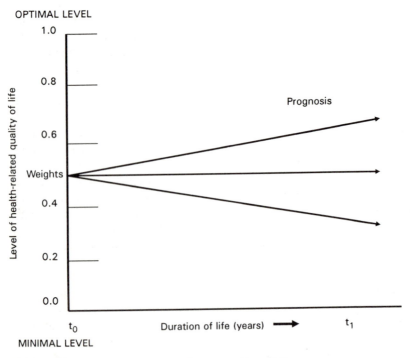

**Figure 2.2** The continuum of health-related quality of life

positively valued to one another. It is the value assigned to a particular state along this continuum that defines quality of life.

It is useful to distinguish health-related quality of life from the social, familial, and personal factors and processes that may influence it. Determinants of health-related quality of life at the individual level include (1) health care, health habits, health knowledge and attitudes, and use of services; (2) social networks and coping skills; and (3) economic, educational, and psychological resources[9]. In addition, elements of the broader social environment such as those noted above may also influence health-related quality of life. Maintaining the separation between these determinants and the concept of health-related quality of life, i.e. the outcome variable, is itself not always straightforward. For example, one might wish to assess well-being and disadvantage because of health among a group of persons with rheumatoid arthritis[80]. This disease affects social functioning, which involves aspects of life well beyond the individual person. Limiting the notion of health-related quality of life only to those elements that are integral to the person is not possible for all applications of health-related quality of life.

Table 2.1 lists the five broad health-related quality of life concepts. These five concepts are defined further by *domains* which are attitudes, behaviours, perceptions, states of being, or other spheres of action and thought in health-related quality of life. For example, the broad concept of functional status is divided into physical, psychological, and social function. Psychological function can be further subdivided into affective and cognitive function. Proposed indicators or measures of the concepts and domains are listed to provide guidance as to how operational definitions are achieved.

Table 2.1 is arranged with the concepts and indicators of death and survival at the bottom and concepts, domains, and indicators of opportunity at the top as though placed on the value continuum from 'least desirable to most desirable'. Individual domains and indicators, however, cannot be easily located hierarchically on the value continuum. Different levels of the concepts cover the entire range of the continuum and interactions of the concepts may map into different levels. For example, minor symptoms may not affect psychological or social well-being and satisfaction with health may be low or negative even though physical, psychological, and social well-being are high or positive. The continuum, however, is useful in considering the contribution of different aspects of health to overall well-being and quality of life.

## Death and duration of survival

Concepts of death and duration of life are obviously necessary for assessing disease and treatment outcomes. From an individual viewpoint, length of life and time of death are of intense interest as well as of considerable importance to family, friends, and care-givers. From the perspective of clinical evalu-

**Table 2.1** Core concepts and domains of health-related quality of life

| Concepts and domains | Definitions/indicators |
| --- | --- |
| *OPPORTUNITY* | |
| Social or cultural disadvantage | Disadvantage because of health; stigma; societal reaction |
| Resilience | Capacity for health; ability to withstand stress; reserve |
| *HEALTH PERCEPTIONS* | |
| General health perceptions | Self-rating of health; health concern/worry |
| Satisfaction with health | Physical, psychological, social function |
| *FUNCTIONAL STATUS* | |
| SOCIAL FUNCTION | |
| Limitations in usual roles | Acute or chronic limitations in usual social roles (major activities) of child, student, worker, independent householder |
| Integration | Participation in the community |
| Contact | Interaction with others |
| Intimacy and sexual function | Perceived feelings of closeness; sexual problems in performance |
| PSYCHOLOGICAL FUNCTION | |
| Affective | Psychological attitudes and behaviours including distress and well-being |
| Cognitive | Alertness; disorientation; problems in reasoning |
| PHYSICAL FUNCTION | |
| Activity restrictions | Acute or chronic reduction in physical activity, mobility, self-care, sleep, communication |
| Fitness | Performance of activity with vigour and without excessive fatigue |
| *IMPAIRMENT* | |
| Symptoms/subjective complaints | Reports of physical and psychological symptoms, sensations, pain, health problems or feelings not directly observable |
| Signs | Physical examination: observable evidence of defect of abnormality |
| Self-reported disease | Patient listing of medical conditions or impairments |
| Physiological measures | Laboratory data, records, and their clinical interpretation |
| Tissue alterations | Pathological evidence |
| Diagnoses | Clinical judgements after 'all the evidence' |
| *DEATH AND DURATION OF LIFE* | Mortality; survival; years of life lost |

ations of disease and treatment outcomes, length of survival has long been a primary endpoint in assessing disease burden and treatment effectiveness.

Advances in biochemical tissue-preserving technology have made exact operational determination of death arbitrary in some cases; irreversible cessation of higher brain activity, for example, has replaced heartbeat and respiration as an indicator of whether one is naturally or artificially alive. Discussing the risk of dying and predicting survival time for individual patients are common tasks for the clinician. Survival is important for patients with conditions that have a poor prognosis. However, it is not the only criterion that patients use when deciding about life-threatening treatments that may improve survival, such as coronary/bypass surgery. For diseases with a more favourable prognosis, such as those for which pharmacological or non-pharmacological treatments are being considered, mortality is a generally insensitive indicator of the impact of therapy. Other aspects of health status and quality of life, such as psychological distress, decreased sexual performance and satisfaction, and the alteration of usual activities must also be considered.

## Impairment

The concept of disease includes most of the classic morbidity category, and it is at the centre of professional appraisal of the presence or absence of abnormalities within the individual, either present at birth or acquired later through pathological processes or injuries. In the medical model of disease, morbidity has included both pathological changes that have not yet been recognized and those that have become evident to the individual or professional. Morbidity concepts thus encompass aspects of both disease and impairment or any loss or abnormality of psychological, physiological, or anatomical structure or function.

Technical distinctions have been made between the various concepts of morbidity and the methods for measuring them. At least six concepts of morbidity can be distinguished, though professionals have different aetiological, anatomical, and physiological criteria for the evaluation of disease. The relative emphasis placed on each type depends on the purpose of assessment and on how the evidence is obtained.

### Symptoms and subjective complaints

Complaints reported by patients or participants in a clinical trial are often not directly observable by an interviewer or clinician. Reports of physical and psychological symptoms, sensations, pain, health problems or other feelings of abnormality are best known to the person who has them, although useful inferences can often be made by objective observers. Problems such as headache, backache, nasal congestion, cough, and tiredness affect millions annually. Four types of complaints are assessed: physical symptoms, health problems, impairments, and pain. Although sensations, feelings, or thoughts are best known to the person who has them, useful inferences can often be made by objective observers, both clinicians and non-professional observers.

Subjective reports of pain are commonly used in clinical decision-making. Approaches to the assessment of pain are numerous[17,72]. Two basic approaches are behavioural assessment and subjective estimates. Behavioural assessment usually involves some measure of activity or morbidity levels and limitations of functioning in vocational, social, and leisure activities[52]. These activity restrictions and limitations in usual social roles are similar to those described in the section of concepts described below as physical well-being. These restrictions and limitations are sensitive behavioural indicators of the effects of painful sensations.

The second basic approach to pain assessment involves numeric estimates of subjective pain states. Subjective judgements can be recorded on numerical or verbal scales[31], but the visual analogue scale approach[113] has gained a wide following. In this approach, the respondent is asked to indicate his or her level of pain by marking a 10-cm line labelled 'no pain' at one end and 'unbearable pain' at the other. The evidence indicates that visual analogue scales produce uniform distributions of responses and consistently and highly correlated with responses to verbal rating scales[17]. The simplicity of the visual analogue scale procedure is also an advantage.

There are also numerous approaches to assessing physical and psychological symptoms. Examples of physical symptom measures are the Symptom-Distress Scale[85] and the Symptom Rating Test[73]. Psychological symptoms are usually measured by a self-response checklist; one of the most comprehensive scales developed for identifying psychological symptoms is the Hopkins Symptom Checklist[38].

*Signs*

Objectively observable evidence or signs obtained through inspection of a respondent adds confirmation to self-reports of symptoms. Some symptoms such as bleeding or health problems such as overweight can be considered signs as well, since examination can confirm self-report. Data obtained through examination by clinicians under standardized conditions are generally considered to be less susceptible to potential non-response bias than data provided by the individuals themselves. The reproducibility of clinical exams, however, may not be any greater than data obtained through self-report. Signs are observed through physical examination, clinical and laboratory tests, and related measurement procedures.

*Self-reported disease*

Clinicians may also hear reports from patients that they have heart disease, cancer, respiratory disease, or some other disease label. These reports may be made both by patients who have been told by a physician that they have a disease and those who have not been told. It is often a good idea to determine whether the patient has been told, since this provides useful information about patient perceptions of disease and illness. Respondents reporting 'diagnoses' unconfirmed by health professionals have evaluated the evidence for themselves, and the basis for these reports is unknown.

### Physiological measures

Clinicians and clinical investigators use a vast number of physiological measures to detect abnormalities, such as blood count, glucose tolerance, and forced expiratory flow. Records from the physiological measuring equipment are observed and interpreted, often by specialists. The records may be single readings or may come from an extensive series of measures, such as prolonged electrocardiographic monitoring to determine the efficacy or toxicity of a drug prescribed to treat cardiac rhythm disturbance.

### Tissue alterations

Alterations in body tissue may be detected by means of pathological evidence obtained either at autopsy or in examination of tissues collected during a surgical procedure or from examination of body fluids. For example, microscopic examination of the heart of a patient with atherosclerotic coronary heart disease can detect pathological processes such as necroses of cardiac muscle. Although this kind of evidence may be important in clinical investigation of disease processes and their complications, such data are not easy to collect because of their intrusiveness. Clinical trials rely on informed consent procedures and patient willingness to participate in collecting and analysing tissue specimens.

### Diagnoses

History, observation, physical examination, symptoms, and physiological measures are used to arrive at both the diagnosis and prognosis of disease conditions for individual patients. Many clinical trials incorporate these diagnostic elements in a systematic protocol that defines diagnostic criteria. Such criteria are essential for disease-specific epidemiological analyses and for locating the clinical course of patients in the natural history of the disease(s) under investigation.

## Functional status

Broadening the assessment of health status to include health-related quality of life indicators is particularly important for assessing the impact of chronic disease and for evaluating rapidly emerging technologies and their effects on the course and outcome of chronic disease such as kidney ailments, chronic respiratory conditions, and cardiovascular diseases. Measures of well-being and quality of life are particularly important for population groups that are dependent on others for essential activities of daily living such as elderly people 85 years and above and people with severely limiting impairments and chronic conditions.

### Physical function

Measures of physical function can be subdivided into two domains: activity restrictions and fitness.

*Activity restrictions* are commonly used by clinicians in obtaining a history from a patient or listening to accounts of the patients' problems. Commonly reported disabilities are restrictions in body movement (e.g. difficulty in walking or bending over), limitations in mobility (e.g. having to stay in bed or not being able to drive a car or use public transportation), or interference with self-care activities (e.g. bathing, dressing, or eating without assistance). Reduced ability to carry out these activities of daily living is also among the most frequently measured concepts of health and well-being in population studies[70]. This is understandable, since the capacity to perform daily routines and tasks determines personal independence, which is a widely-shared value in our society.

Restricted activity days (work-loss, school-loss, bed, or cut-down days) are commonly used measures in evaluating chronic diseases. These are long-term or short-term reductions in a person's capacity to perform the average activities associated with his or her age group. Limitations in role-function, usually long-term, are included below as a domain of social function. Activity restrictions usually refers to a relatively short-term reduction in a person's activities below his or her usual capacity.

*Fitness* is increasingly used as an indicator of health-related quality of life, particularly in evaluating efforts to improve the performance of activity with vigour and without excessive fatigue. Whereas measures of mobility and physical activity assess restrictions or limitations, fitness measures assess energy, endurance, speed, and the more 'positive' nature of physical activity. Individual measures of fitness include such items as the ability to run the length of a football field or the speed with which one can walk 10 yards. What defines physical fitness for groups defined by age, sex, or level of disability differs and fitness measures are difficult to apply across entire populations. Nevertheless, increasingly attempts are made to assess the 'optimal' level of fitness by which to evaluate medical and nutritional interventions.

### Psychological function

Psychological function can sometimes be restricted to affective indicators such as happiness, life satisfaction, morale, or positive affect. Psychological status, on the other hand, can be viewed as pertaining to, or derived from the mind or emotions, including cognitive aspects such as alertness, confusion, or impaired thought and concentration. Both affective and cognitive components of health-related quality of life are important because they are influenced significantly by disease processes and treatment interventions.

*Affective function*, such as psychological distress and well-being, have been usefully distinguished in theory[16,131]. The relationship between positive and negative indicators, however, is not completely understood. Numerous scales have been developed to measure psychological dysfunction and distress, particularly depression and anxiety[7,146]. A number of these scales are used to evaluate psychiatric symptomatology[42] or to produce psychiatric diagnoses according to the American Psychiatric Association Diagnostic and Statistical Manual[114]. Another large body of literature concerns the theory and measurement of positive well-being, and many advances have been made in this field over the last few decades[5,41,57].

*Cognitive function* is also a major component of psychological well-being, although significant mental confusion is uncommon except in persons with severe disease. For example, advanced congestive heart failure may decrease cerebral blood flow and metabolism, thereby producing confusion and difficulty in judgement or reasoning. Clinicians may observe impaired thought and concentration in many patients, particularly elderly ones, because of a wide variety of cerebral processes or therapies. Memory and the ability to carry out intellectual behaviours are of great importance to many people, and loss of cognitive function because of a treatment of disease can provide great psychological distress.

Extensive psychological tests are available to assess intellectual functioning, although these are most often prohibitively costly, beyond the skill of many clinicians, and often inappropriate for study objectives. As mentioned above, mental status items are commonly used to determine reliability of self-report and the need for proxy respondents. Items describing thought and concentration have also been included in general health status measures[11,30]. While impaired alertness, disorientation, and problems in reasoning are significant problems in their own right, such items group with other psychosocial components in aggregated measures[12,32]. The relationship between affective and cognitive measures of psychological well-being is not well understood.

### Social function

Social function has been included in conceptualizations of health since the World Health Organization defined health as 'a state of complete physical, mental and *social well-being* and not merely the absence of disease and infirmity'[145]. Exactly what was meant by 'social well-being' in the WHO declaration is unclear. Social well-being can be viewed as both a component and a determinant of a person's quality of life. Therefore it is difficult to operationalize the content of the social domain without evaluation of the environment external to the individual. In fact, in a reductionist view, social support and health status may be confounded due to biological effects[20]. Social well-being can be viewed as deriving both from individual perception, motivation, attitude and behaviour and from circumstances external to the individual, such as areas of residence, transport and financial resources. Concepts of social well-being, including limitations in usual social roles, social integration, social contact, and intimacy are considered important components of well-being.

*Limitations in usual roles* are assessed in relation to a person's major activity, including holding a job, going to school, parenting, managing a house, or engaging in meaningful activity of some kind. Such limitations are particularly important to people who sustain life-threatening diseases and injuries at any age. Maintaining or restoring functional capacity and preventing deterioration in function are important objectives of treatment. Work activity or 'productivity' is important to most individuals and to society in general. Thus return to work or school and ability to contribute to community life are commonly assessed domains of health-related quality of life.

## Social integration

Durkheim's classic study of suicide[45] has stimulated a great deal of thinking and research concerning the importance of close social ties, and the effects of breakdown of social integration with the emergence of an industrialized, highly technical society. 'Anomie' or the loss of social integration, was considered by Durkheim to be deleterious to psychological well-being. For some people, social participation in the community through membership in social, civic, political, or religious organizations, is highly important to quality of life. Social participation may also confer a high degree of emotional well-being, particularly for people who do not have close family or friendship ties.

Social ties provide the individual with both psychosocial and instrumental support[87]. Psychosocial support derived from social contact provides sympathy, encouragement, and a sense of self-esteem, whereas instrumental support may take the form of practical assistance, financial aid, advice and guidance, which are particularly important for those who require assistance with activities of daily living. Social ties may be particularly important influences on survival, on recovery, on the course of disease, and on other health outcomes[69]. In this sense, social support is a predictor of social well-being, along with other aspects of health-related quality of life.

**Social contact**

Social function as social relationships has been operationalized in diverse ways, with considerable confusion between social networks and the support or benefits derived from one's network. *Quantity* of connections (number of people in the network), *quality* (having people one can trust), *utilization* (actually spending time with people), *meaning* (the importance of social relationships), *availability* (having people, or animals there when needed), and *satisfaction* have all been considered[123]. In addition, there is little consistency in the way in which these concepts have been measured.

Social contact, e.g. frequency of visits with friends/relatives, the number of meetings and community activities attended, or types of social interaction, is another well-recognized component of social well-being[43]. The importance of social contact for different components of health status has not been systematically determined, although mental health outcomes have been implicated most frequently[23].

*Intimacy*

Some of the people in a person's network may provide a feeling of closeness and trust, and such intimacy can be an important determinant of emotional well-being in patients facing a serious illness or death. Social contact and intimacy, of course, are not mutually exclusive; both can be provided by the same person or persons in a social network.

While it is clear that a distinction should be made (1) among subjective perceptions, social behaviours, and external circumstances; (2) between social networks and social support; and (3) between the quantity and quality of social ties, it is by no means clear how to select the most important and most appropriate concepts of social well-being for an operational definition. It is likely that the concepts remain ambiguous because measurement has preceded the development of an adequate definition. The first task, therefore, is to investigate the various concepts of social well-being in association with the increasingly abundant measures of the concepts in order to develop a definition of the concept.

*Health perceptions*

The concepts surveyed so far may be considered specific components of health-related quality of life. There are, however, several general concepts that are important in assessing quality of life, but may or may not include personal health status as perceived by the patient or by others. These concepts describe a combination of the subjective perception of the individual, expressed by opinion or choice, and objective circumstance of both health status and other conditions widely agreed to be a disadvantage to the individual, such as poor nutrition, unemployment, and poverty.

**General health perceptions**

Among the most often used measures of health are general self-ratings such as 'excellent', 'very good', 'good', 'fair', or 'poor'. Self-ratings of health, like more comprehensive and lengthy measures of general health perceptions, include an individual's evaluation of his or her physiological, physical, psychological and social well-being and the effect of health on other aspects of life, such as opportunity and respect[37]. Perceived health may also be an indicator of the value of medical care in reassuring patients and reducing uncertainty as well as an important predictor of mortality[89].

**Satisfaction with health**

The satisfaction derived from activities, relationships, moods, or other states of being is another general component of quality of life that is essential for understanding how people behave, make choices, communicate with professionals, follow treatment regimens, or accept the inevitable. The concept of quality of life incorporates both the individual's objective resources and his or her subjective satisfaction with those resources. Satisfaction is a measure of the extent to which an individual feels that his or her needs or aspirations are fulfilled. The actual feeling that a need is satisfied is only experienced by the person who has the need, though there is wide agreement about the major categories of fundamental life needs. In addition to satisfaction with physical psychological, and social well-being and social role performance, there are spiritual, material, and political needs that should also be considered.

Satisfaction is an elusive concept that raises many methodological and theoretical problems, particularly in relation to related concepts such as happiness and morale. Campbell[28] has stated that 'there is no doubt that happiness and satisfaction have something in common (but) there is also a difference'. Satisfaction, in his view, involves an act of judgement and is not the 'spontaneous lift-of-the-spirits' that characterizes happiness. All three concepts have been distinguished by Stones and Kozma[119]: life satisfaction is 'gratification of an appropriate proportion of the major diseases of life', happiness is 'an activity or state in the sphere of feelings', and morale is 'moral condition as regards discipline and confidence'. While these conceptual differences can be debated at length[53], satisfaction can be viewed as a discrete concept.

**Opportunity**

Opportunity is defined as the potential for an optimal state of health or 'being all that one can be'. Calman[27] suggests that quality of life is the difference between the hopes and expectations of the individual and the individual's present experience. Quality of life therefore involves capacity or potential, an elusive concept to measure whether viewed negatively as disadvantage or positively as resilience.

*Social or cultural disadvantage* involves the major social principle for people with disease, impairment, or disability that all aspects of life should be accessible. These aspects include physical and social access to the environment, to education and training, and to employment. Disadvantage occurs when a person with disease or disability is denied the opportunities generally available in a community for the fundamental elements of living. For example, patients with chronic renal failure that requires dialysis may find it difficult to obtain or keep employment. Persons with congenital heart disease or a history of rheumatic fever may find it difficult to get insurance or to meet the premium requirements. Patients with moderate impairment may also experience difficulty in meeting eligibility requirements for disability income maintenance through the Social Security Disability Insurance Program.

Disadvantage is a social and cultural phenomenon, and being disadvantaged because of health is assessed relative to other people who do not have a particular condition or significant illness. Disadvantage is not only a function of disease or treatment, but also depends on the interplay with environmental factors. For example, vocational disadvantage because of health may depend not only on the impairment and dysfunction experienced by an individual but also on attitudes of employers, demands of the job, availability of employment, and the range of vocational options open to the individual. These factors, in turn, are dependent upon such considerations as age, intelligence, emotional stability, education, and past work experiences.

*Individual resilience* is also a 'capacity for health'. Resilience is defined as a desirable deviation from expected or usual functions, activities, or perceptions that constitute daily life. Resilience is consistent with the concept of physiological reserve[98]. Physiological reserve is the unused capacity of the organism that can be called upon in times of stress, crisis, or increased activity. It decreases with age regardless of an individual's overall health. Capacity for health is most often measured by the ability to cope with or withstand stress or to maintain emotional equilibrium. This approach recognizes that people adjust differently to life situations altered by disease or treatment. While resilience is a difficult domain to assess, coping behaviour and adaptive tasks are important to health maintenance and will be increasingly recognized in health-related quality of life assessments.

## 5. ASSESS CONCEPTUAL AND METHODOLOGICAL CHARACTERISTICS OF POTENTIAL MEASURES

In choosing health-related quality of life measures, trade-offs are most often necessary among competing goals of inquiry. The decision or problem being addressed, the objectives of measurement, and conceptual, methodological, and practical considerations all need to be weighed in making choices. Often less than optimal choices are made, because one or more considerations are neglected. For example, a measure with demonstrated reliability and validity, with comprehensive content, and with a long tradition of application may simply not fit into the practical constraints of resources and investigator willingness to adopt. Major selection criteria involve different types of measures and a wide array of methodological and practical considerations reviewed in the following sections.

### Types of measures

Measures of health-related quality of life can be classified according to (1) the type of scores produced reflecting the level of aggregation across concepts and domains, (2) the range of populations and concepts/domains covered, including the different diseases, health conditions and populations to be assessed and the breadth of concepts and domains included in the measure, and (3) the weighting system used in scoring items and in aggregating within or across different domains.

Single item measures or indicators of health-related quality of life cover one concept or domain, such as a visual analogue pain scale, self-rating of health, or a mortality statistic. With single measures, no explicit weighting scheme is necessary, although mortality measures are weighted implicitly, that is death$=0$ and life$=1$. Composite measures summarize two or more aspects of health status or quality of life in an aggregated index or profile or scores. In contrast to single indicators such as mortality rates or life expectancy, composite measures cover different aspects of function status, positive well-being, pain, and other concepts of health-related quality of life *Health status indexes* are expressed as single aggregated numbers summarizing multiple domains similar to the gross national product (GNP). The term *health profile* refers to those measures in which each domain is assigned a summary score on a metric that can be compared with other domains. Health profiles may also provide an overall or index score that summarizes all component domains. *Health batteries* are collections of different health status and quality of life measures that are scored independently using different metrics and reported as individual scores.

## Single indicators

Single indicators may be used to indicate any one of the five broad concepts or their constituent domains. The mortality rate is the most frequently used single measure of health status. Expressed as crude or adjusted rates, mortality statistics have been used primarily to measure the health of population groups, although patient deaths are important endpoints for many clinical studies involving life extension.

Counts of diseases and disabilities make up the traditional morbidity measures. The most traditional direct measures of morbidity are rates of the incidence or prevalence of specific diseases. Incidence and prevalence rates are valuable epidemiological tools, particularly for single conditions or disease categories. In population surveys, these are obtained through check-lists of acute or chronic conditions and impairments. Conditions are usually coded to the latest version of the International Classification of Diseases with Clinical Modifications (ICD-CM). Incidence of acute conditions has been published annually for the United States since 1957, and no long-range patterns in trends have occurred. In contrast, the prevalence of some chronic conditions has increased for a variety of reasons, not all of which are methodological[143]. Moriyama[88] points out, however, the problems in comparing diseases with one another: 'How (can) one (equate) a case of coryza with a case of primary lung cancer, or a case of congenital anomaly with a case of senile psychosis?' Without some relative weighting of the different diseases in terms of dysfunction, seriousness, occurrence, or prognosis, it is difficult to interpret disease counts as population health status measures.

Disability measures can be used to assess the impact of both acute and chronic illness. Measures of limitation in mobility and limitation in activity assess the long-term impact of chronic illness. Disability days on their own are questionable indicators of population health status change because of variations in health services use and susceptibility to age-related and en-vironmental influences outside the health sector. There are major difficulties in attributing changes over time in these measures to actual changes in disease or practice patterns.

Single indicators of mortality and morbidity will continue to be valuable for population monitoring, particularly since they are the most available data for international comparisons, and they are sensitive to inequities among different population groups. Mortality and morbidity rates, however, are not the most sensitive indicators of population 'health' and 'well-being' since they are indicators of the bottom of the death–health continuum. Composite measures covering more detailed health states and aspects of well-being are necessary to detect health changes and to classify individuals[99].

**Health status indexes**

There are a number of different composite measures of health status and quality of life that are either indexes or profiles, including:

- Arthritis Impact Measurement Scales (AIMS)
- Duke–UNC Health Profile
- Index of Activities of Daily Living (ADL)
- McMaster Health Index Questionnaire (MHIQ)
- Medical Outcomes Study Short Form Health Survey (MOS)
- Nottingham Health Profile (NHP)
- Psychological General Well-Being Index (PGWB)
- Quality of Well-Being Scale (QWB)
- Sickness Impact Profile (SIP)

This list represents only a few of the many measures that have been developed. Selected measures from this list will be used to describe both indexes and profiles.

A number of efforts have been made to combine morbidity and mortality into a single measure. An expanding body of literature is available on health status indexes that provide the methodological basis for collecting combined mortality/morbidity data. Bush and his colleagues have proposed a comprehensive construct of health status including two distinct components: (1) level of well-being and (2) prognosis[25,33,48,65,66,99]. 'Well-being' represents health-related quality of life as comprised of symptom/problem combinations combined with attributes of function status. Levels of well-being are ranked according to subjective preferences that weight time-specific states and function levels. Prognoses are the probabilities of transition among the function levels, as affected by the total environment of the individual.

This conception of health as function and prognosis has been developed extensively over nearly two decades within the framework now defined as a General Health Policy Model[24,68] or Health Decision Model[65]. The policy/decision model incorporates a point-in-time index – the 'Quality of Well-Being Scale' – an additional dynamic or prognostic dimension – 'Well-Life Expectancy' – and a means of incorporating the data into a cost–benefit, cost–utility framework – the 'Policy Space' framework.

Torrance and his colleagues have developed a similar but more extensive health state classification to that proposed by Bush and his colleagues[14,126]. In this multi-attribute classification system, function includes not only physical function, mobility, physical activity, and role function, but also social and emotional function and social activity. Torrance and his colleagues have also developed extensive procedures for cost–utility analysis and have applied these procedures to a number of health programmes[15,130].

Many efforts to develop aggregated measures have focused on the measurement of utilities of different states of illness. The concept of 'Quality Adjusted Life Years' (QALYs), similar to that of 'well-years' has been used by many investigators[139] in cost–effectiveness analyses of health programmes.

## Profiles

Not all developers or consumers of health and quality of life data accept the need for or desirability of summarizing health into a single index number. Like the GNP, a single health index cannot be a clear-cut or wholly comprehensive measure. No single number can take into account all the components of well-being, satisfaction, and opportunity that make up health-related quality of life. For some purposes, specific social indicators of different aspects of health and quality of life are needed to characterize individuals and populations. For example, decision-makers may be interested in evaluating the relative impact of a treatment or intervention on different components of health and quality of life. Using a battery or profile of different health measures or a profile of inter-related components is an alternative strategy to the aggregated index.

Health profiles have been used to characterize health-related quality of life for evaluating the effects of medical interventions. Several health profiles have been developed to cover specific components of health-related quality of life in a systematic and unified manner. The Medical Outcomes Study Short Form Health Survey (SF-36) was developed from measures applied in the Health Insurance Experiment conducted by the RAND Corporation[22]. The Medical Outcomes Study was designed to investigate the outcomes of medical care for different conditions[117]. Physical, social and role functioning scales measure behavioural dysfunction caused by health problems. Subjective measures of well-being include mental health, energy/fatigue, and bodily pain. Overall evaluation of health is captured in the six-question general health perceptions scale. The short-form health survey can be administered to well respondents in 3 minutes, and a mark-sense version of the instrument can be scored using an optical character reader. The different domains can be illustrated according to the effects demonstrated in clinical trials and health-programme evaluations.

The Sickness Impact Profile (SIP) assesses sickness-related dysfunction in 12 areas of activity: sleep and rest; eating; home management; work; recreation and pastimes; body care and movement; ambulation; mobility, emotional behaviour, affective behaviour; social interaction; and communication. This 136-item questionnaire produces a score for each of the 12 categories, a physical dimension score (body care and movement, ambulation, and mobility combined), a psychosocial dimension score (emotional behaviour, affective behaviour, social interaction, and communication combined), and an overall score across all 12 categories. The major strength of this instrument is its broad coverage of dysfunction and its sensitivity to a wide variety of health conditions[101]. A British version of the instrument is available[32,103], including weights for the items obtained from a British population[104].

The Nottingham Health Profile (NHP) is a two-part instrument. Part I contains 38 items that cover 6 domains of experience: pain, physical mobility, sleep, emotional reactions, energy, and social isolation. Scores can be calculated for each of these domains, although no overall scoring system has been developed. The NHP also includes perceived problems in 7 areas of life: paid employment, jobs around the house, personal relationships, social life, sex life, hobbies, and holidays[62]. The NHP has been used widely in evaluating health interventions and in clinical studies.

Composite measures, whether combining mortality with morbidity, or aggregating various concepts of morbidity, have an important place in allocating resources and evaluating health programmes by analysing their contribution to the overall health of the population. At the practical level, both single concept measures and profiles of measures permit analyses of individual components of HRQOL both as independent and dependent variables in causal structures, e.g. the relative impact of a lack of social resources on physical, psychological, or social functioning. Combined indicators are useful for comparing the predicted outputs of different health programmes in resource allocation or policy analysis, and for comparing the results of health interventions on different populations. All three types of measures (single concept indicators, indexes, and profiles) can be used as social indicators for analysing trend in the status of different populations.

## Methodological considerations

Ware[135] has thoroughly reviewed the methodological and practical issues involved in selecting measures of health-related quality of life. Methodological issues involved in the selection of assessment procedures are summarized below. In addition to the important conceptualization issues, these methodological concerns include:

(a) Scaling
        relative frequencies
        relative preferences
(b) Reliability and stability
        interpreting reported coefficients
        suggesting minimum standards
(c) *Validity*
        types and phases of validity measurement

Different concepts of health-related quality of life apply differentially to the clinical decision or problem to be answered. That is, no one single measure will be suitable for all applications. As listed above, methodological issues other than the appropriate concept of health need to be considered in the process of conceptualizing the measure of health-related quality of life for use in answering a specific research question. The relevance of these in terms of selecting a measure of health-related quality of life is discussed below.

## Scaling

Combining measures of components of health-related quality of life into composite measures, either indexes or profiles, implies that the individual indicators must be weighted by some means. Three broad approaches to assigning weights have been used: (1) investigator defined; (2) relative frequencies; and (3) relative preferences.

The first, a procedure in which the investigator assigns higher scores to items of a measure that reflect his view of what is a higher level of well-being or quality of life, is perhaps the simplest and most frequently used method. The investigator assumes social consensus, that is, that these values are widely shared by members of society. However, it has been demonstrated that such consensus does not exist[125]. In addition, the use of investigator-assigned weights to define metric values for measures breaks down when patients rate combinations of attributes. For these reasons most developers of composite measures of health-related quality of life have used either a relative frequencies or a relative preferences scaling method.

The most commonly used frequency methods are factor analytic approaches, with the coefficients being derived for each item of a measure using a statistical technique. Each factor loading is the item weight, and the percentage of variation explained by a particular factor and its items provide weights for the factor itself. As a consequence, items that are infrequently responded to or correlate poorly receive low weights, regardless of how important these items (behaviours or states) may be in social terms[66].

Relative preference methods of assigning weights to health-related quality of life items have been described by a number of different reviewers[94,108,126]. The relative desirability or utility of different states can be obtained using the rules specified by different scaling techniques. A number of techniques have been used to elicit preference judgements, and these have been reviewed in different contexts[14,94,108,126]. Psychometric scaling models encompass a number of indirect and direct methods for eliciting preferences. Indirect methods involve comparisons of alternatives or discrimination between two states or conditions with a scaling model derived from laws of comparative judgement[124].

Direct psychometric scaling models elicit numerical estimates of preference without requiring judges to choose between alternatives. In the method of equal-appearing intervals or category scaling, judges rate the relative desirability of health states or behaviour by assigning each state to a category on a continuous, equal-interval scale with designated anchor points[29,66,96,99,100,125,128]. Magnitude estimation methods require judges to compare states to a selected standard state and to report how much worse or better each one appears[67,96,100,109]. The technique of equivalence requires judges to specify how many people in one health state appear 'equivalent' to a specified number of people in another health state if limited resources required a choice between the two populations[8,96,100].

Utility modelling in health has led to the use of a number of other scaling techniques, most notably the von Neumann–Morgenstern standard gamble where judges are forced to choose between an uncertain or risky alternative with specified probabilities of good and bad outcome and a certain, non-risky alternative with an intermediate outcome[125,128,129,133]. Another technique similar to equivalence methods is time trade-off where judges choose between two health states that have different lengths of time attached[111,125,128,144].

Cumulative evidence from these scaling studies indicates that different scaling techniques lead to different results, although the origin of the difference may not be interpretable. Kaplan et al.[66] found category scaling preferable to magnitude estimation, since magnitude estimates were compressed at the death end of the hypothesized health–death continuum. Comparisons of the standard gamble technique with category scaling and time trade-off have led to the conclusion that the standard gamble technique is difficult to administer[108,125,144]. Unfortunately, few of these methodological studies have been replicated by different investigators, making it difficult to conclude the clear superiority of any one method over another for aggregating health states.

There are other issues involved in applying the relative preference approach, including the stability of the judgements and the zero origin of the well-being continuum[14]. Two additional issues, however, require closer examination. The first concerns factors that significantly influence the preference judgements people make about health and quality of life or the context-independence of direct scaling efforts. The content of the description[111], the mode of presentation[79], the explanation of the scaling task[109], the age of the judge[111], and the medical experience of raters[29,109] have all been found to be significant influences on the utility values obtained. Results are not consistent between studies, however, and the few systematic attempts to investigate the effects of rater characteristics on preference weights have not found significant effects for such important characteristics as age, sex, income, marital status, or cultural group[109]. There is the possibility that the large standard deviations or wide dispersion in scale judgements which have been observed may lead to greater social consensus than actually exists[14,109]. This possibility should be investigated more thoroughly to define more precisely which factors or rater characteristics significantly influence preference judgements.

## Reliability and stability

Reliability is a generic term which refers to the stability and equivalence of repeated measures of the same concept. Reliability coefficients estimate the proportion of the observed variation in a score that can be considered true as opposed to random error[93]. The minimum level reliability differs according to the type of analysis being performed. According to Ware[135] reliability above 0.90 is required for making comparisons between individuals; for group comparisons, on another hand, reliabilities in the 0.50–0.70 range are acceptable. A point-in-time estimate of reliability of a health-related quality of life instrument can be obtained using an internal consistency analysis or the test–retest method of analysis can be used to estimate reliability over time. Internal consistency and test–retest reliability estimates for the same instrument may differ due to changes in health status during the interval.

Before selecting an instrument, not only should the levels of reliability for each instrument be ascertained but also research reports describing how the studies to collect the coefficients were conducted should be studied to detect possible sources of bias. For example, if, with a test–retest reliability analysis, the interval between administrations is too short, the patient may remember previous responses and thus upwardly bias the estimate. On the other hand, if the interval is too long, then the patient's health status may have deteriorated, resulting in a downward bias[135].

While test–retest reliability indicates the extent to which measurements are repeatable over a short time period, usually 2 weeks, measures of stability indicate fluctuations in scores over longer intervals, usually 6 months or more[93]. Since many health status concepts tend to be stable over time, assessment at the beginning of a clinical trial can be used to predict the status of either an individual or a group at the end of a trial. This prediction increases the power of hypothesis testing by reducing the associated error. The consequence of this for clinical trials is that the increased power associated with intertemporal stability can reduce the requisite sample size[106,135].

## Validity

There are many different types of validity, e.g. face concurrent, convergent, predictive or construct validity and many different empirical approaches for measuring validity. Since the focus of this section is on the methodological considerations for selecting an instrument, this paper will not discuss specific methods. Instead, it will briefly review the two phases of measurement validation that have been identified by Ware[135].

The first phase involves assessing bivariate associations by collecting data on other measures of the same component of health-related quality of life. Bivariate validity encompasses concurrent, convergent and predictive validity and usually focuses on what the instrument measures. The second phase is that of multivariate validity assessment encompassing incremental, discriminant and construct validity. This phase provides information that is not available from bivariate analyses. As Ware notes, few health status instruments have reached this stage of analysis.

Another step in the validation process is the determination of meaningful effect size, i.e. the degree to which the null hypothesis is false. A desirable effect size is one that is as small as is reasonable to expect and yet gives results that are medically and socially meaningful. Given a particular effect size, the objective of an experiment is to detect this with high probability. In the design of a study, the investigator is faced with a tradeoff between effect size and sample size. In general, a large sample size is needed to detect a smaller effect size[106]. To date, little is known about various effect sizes in different target populations[135]. However, some empirical evidence on effect size has been calculated using data collected in the Rand Health Insurance Study. For example, Brook *et al.*[21] report that a 5-point difference in general health perceptions is equivalent to the effect of having been diagnosed as having hypertension. Clearly, this is one area of health-related quality of life research that will benefit from additional empirical research.

## 6. ASSESS PRACTICAL CONSIDERATIONS AND CHOOSE HRQOL MEASURES

In addition to the various methodological issues discussed above, there are a number of practical considerations that also need to be considered in selecting health-related quality of life measures for clinical decision-making. These include acceptability to respondents, method of administration, length and cost of administration, method of analysis, and presentation of data. Table 2.2 lists the major topic areas. Each practical consideration has advantages and disadvantages in terms of its use in clinical research. Selecting an instrument or set of instruments for assessing health-related quality of life involves making tradeoffs between these advantages and disadvantages to identify those that best match the context of the study. The following paragraphs present greater detail on some of these points.

**Table 2.2** Practical considerations in HRQOL assessment

---

Standardized or non-standardized assessment strategy
- identification and explanation of real differences among selected clinical populations
- resource requirements – time and effort

Acceptability
- previous experiences in clinical applications
- respondent burden – the 'unhealthy' respondent
- interviewer burden

Method of administration
- direct observation
- face-to-face interview
- telephone interview
- self-administered questionnaire
- proxy respondents

Length and cost of administration
- other components of interview schedule or questionnaire
- completion rates and quality data

Method of analysis and complexity of scoring
- availability of computer scoring
- aggregation or disaggregation into component parts

Presentation of data and usefulness to decision-makers
- degree of certainty on value
- numbers, graphs, and interpretation of data

---

**Standardized or non-standardized?**

In deciding which instrument to use to answer a specific clinical problem, the issue often is one of choosing between developing a new assessment strategy or using an existing, standardized instrument. Developing an instrument for a specific application, i.e. what one might term a non-standardized instrument, is an initially attractive approach because of the apparent uniqueness or complexity of the clinical situation. That is, a problem-specific instrument may seem to maximize the potential for discovering and explaining differences among selected treatment groups. However, to the extent that the instrument is specific to disease, treatment and socio-demographic characteristics of individuals participating in a given clinical trial, it will be difficult to assess whether the findings of the trial are due to the treatments or whether there is some confounding with regard to patient selection. In addition, with a non-standardized instrument results can not be generalized beyond the specific application.

Experience with developing new instruments to assess health-related quality of life has shown that substantial inputs in terms of time, effort, and money are required. Currently available generic health status measures, for example the Medical Outcomes Study SF-36, the Nottingham Health Profile, the Quality of Well-being Scale and the Sickness Impact Profile, have taken more than 5 years to reach the point where each could be widely applied. The reason for the great expenditure of resources has been the need to carefully conceptualize the definition of health-related quality of life, develop an operational definition and take into account the other methodological issues that are summarized in the previous section.

An alternative to developing a completely new instrument is to use a battery of standardized questionnaires. Such an approach can include a generic measure of health-related quality of life as well as measures of specific health concepts such as mood, satisfaction or general health perceptions that are apt to be affected by the chosen treatment. This approach has been taken by Sugarbaker et al.[120] in their study of patients of soft tissue sarcoma. They used the Sickness Impact Profile and complemented this global measure of health status with the Katz ADL, Psychosocial Adjustment to Illness Scale and the Barthel Function Scale. The Nocturnal Oxygen Therapy Trial (NOTT) group[92] also used the Sickness Impact Profile to assess overall health status and included Halsted Impairment Index, Minnesota Multiphasic Personality Inventory (MMPI), and Profile of Mood States (POMS) as other standardized instruments in the total quality of life battery which was fielded in a clinical trial designed to study the efficacy of nocturnal oxygen therapy. In a clinical trial designed to test the relative effectiveness of three antihypertensive agents Croog et al.[35] used the General Well-Being Schedule to obtain data on overall health. Other instruments in the battery included Physical Symptoms Distress Index, Positive Symptoms Index from the Brief Symptom Inventory, and the Wechsler Memory Scale.

Occasionally, no readily available, standardized measure that meets the context of a given clinical study exists. In this case, the short-term alternative is to develop a brief, non-standardized assessment. This can be done by either designing a set of questions de novo or by modifying an existing instrument. Slight modifications may not change the measurement properties of the existing instrument. Major modifications, however, result in a new instrument and thus require reliability and validity testing. Modification may not always be necessary as was shown by Temkin et al.[122]. In this study of patients with head injuries, a modified Sickness Impact Profile gave no better information than did the original, standardized version.

Another advantage of standardized measures is that users manuals are usually available. These manuals which are developed from cumulative experience with each instrument generally include standard instructions for using the instrument, interviewer-training procedures, computer scoring algorithms, and analytic strategies. Standardized administration procedures are important for reducing variation when the same instrument is to be used by many different investigators in different populations, such as in multi-centre clinical trials.

Another important practical consideration in the decision to use standardized or non-standardized instruments is that of identification of differences between treatment groups. An important aspect of clinical research is to be able to generalize from the study populations to the broader populations of interest. Comparability, with regard to health-related quality of life assessment, across different diseases, conditions, populations, or even investigations requires a generic approach to health status assessment. The development of standardized, generic measures of health status and quality of life has permitted comparisons across different patient populations for clinical research and across different interventions in the evaluation of health outcomes for the purpose of resource allocation[68,126]. Generic measures provide a common denominator or common unit of outcome by which to judge the relative severity of health outcomes and the relative effectiveness of health interventions. Many interventions also affect outcomes that are not condition-specific, e.g. prevention programmes to reduce cigarette smoking resulting in heart disease, cancer, and pulmonary disease. Investigators also may not anticipate all the effects of treatment which may be assessed with generic measures.

Disease-specific measures developed on special populations are not intended for general application. The issue of generalizability may still arise, however, in relation to the disease, condition, or population under investigation. Arthritis-specific measures have been applied across a large number of investigations, some involving patients with osteoarthritis and others of patients with rheumatoid arthritis. Measures specific to inflammatory bowel disease were applied in studies of patients with ulcerative colitis and those with Crohn's disease, although there may be concepts and dimensions of health-related quality of life that are more specific to one diagnosis than another. Disease-specific measures need to be 'general' enough for application to these different sub-populations to permit comparisons between different organ-specific diseases.

Proliferation of many specific instruments for the same condition decreases the external validity of study findings. If disease-specific measures are too specific to a given study, they are unlikely to be used in other studies. Investigators working with particular patient populations or highly specific interventions tend to perceive a need for creating new instruments rather than using existing measures. Advances in identifying outcomes across populations and interventions in a single field might well be slowed if measures spawned by single studies subsequently require detailed investigation of measurement characteristics.

Although standardization is a marked advantage, the length and complexity of some measures overshadows this desirable characteristic. Complex questionnaires and scoring algorithms are frequently perceived as requiring resources above and beyond the potential usefulness of the data obtained from their use. The additional time and effort needed to collect and analyse the data discourages the use of some standardized measures in clinical research. To overcome these undesirable properties, short-form generic health status measures are beginning to appear in the literature for self-administration in clinical settings[64,91,117] and in general population surveys[118]. Measures for use in clinical practice must meet the most strenuous criteria of minimum length, maximum validity, reliability, and responsiveness, and low cost.

### Acceptability

The basic notion of acceptability refers to the ease with which an instrument can be used in a particular setting. One set of issues is that associated with how well a given instrument satisfies the research needs and resource constraints of the clinical investigator. Among these concerns are:

(1)    the length of the instrument and how this impacts on other assessments in the study;

(2)    the cost of including a particular instrument in a study in terms of the resources required, e.g. whether interviewers are required, the detail of the data collected with the instrument, and the need for complex computer programs for analysis; and

(3)    the extent of previous experience with the instrument, e.g. whether it has been used in the same type of clinical application. The investigator also needs to be aware of completion rates, prevalence of missing responses or other experiences that will impact on the study outcome.

A second set of issues is that associated with respondent burden which includes both the time and amount of psychological stress required to complete a questionnaire[135]. The length of response time may differ by complexity of the questionnaire and by personal characteristics of the respondent such as age, education, and health status. Longer response times have been observed among the elderly and the dysfunctional[24,135]. Also, persons who are taking medications that affect memory or cognition may have difficulty complying with instructions for either an interviewer- or self-administered questionnaire[115].

The instruments selected for use in a clinical trial also have to be acceptable to the persons responsible for collecting the data. If an interview format, whether face-to-face or telephone, is chosen, the instrument must be acceptable to the interviewer. One questionnaire characteristic that can burden the interviewer is the amount and type of training required. For some instruments, the training is minimal; for others such as the Quality of Well-being Scale and the Sickness Impact Profile, the developers recommend careful instruction and practice for the interviewers who will administer the instruments[10,24]. Another possible burdensome characteristic is the amount of administrative procedures required to successfully complete the interview.

If other, non-interview formats are chosen for collecting the health-related quality of life data, then the staff associated with administering these instruments has to feel that questions make sense. For example, health professionals responsible for rating patient performance have to agree that the appropriate functions are being assessed. Persons who are available to assist the patient with self-administered instruments also need some training as to the purpose and implementation of the instrument. Neither interviewers, raters, nor other persons associated with instrument administration want to be burdened with defending an instrument that has no face validity or one that inquires unnecessarily about embarrassing aspects of the patient's life. One way of examining this burden is to have members of the clinical research team read proposed questionnaires to determine if individual items make sense in the context of the planned study.

## Method of administration

The 6 most commonly used methods for obtaining information on health status and health-related quality of life are listed in Table 2.2. The methods differ in the concepts that can be measured, costs to administer, amount and type of interviewer training and respondent burden[135]. Some instruments have been developed for use according to more than one method of administration[86]. For example, the Sickness Impact Profile can be either interviewer- or self-administered[12]. The developers of the Quality of Well-being Scale, on the other hand, cite lower reliability as the main reason for their recommendation against using the QWB in self-administered form[3].

With direct observation a trained observer, usually an available health professional, rates a patient. Most commonly the rating is done according to a structured checklist such as a list of activities of daily living[71,77,83,112]. Recently a number of performance-based measures, such as the Timed Manual Performance[141], have been developed. With these measures a health professional notes whether or not a patient can perform certain tasks. Direct observation is commonly used in assessment of activity restrictions and self care. This method of collecting information has limited value for measuring perceptual components of health-related quality of life.

An alternative mode of administration is the face-to-face interview. This method may use a structured questionnaire, an open-ended response set or a combination of these two techniques. Like direct observation, an interview administered instrument requires trained personnel to collect the data; the amount of training required depends on the complexity of the instrument. The face-to-face interview has the advantage over direct observation in that it can be used to obtain patient self-reports of health-related quality of life. The telephone interview is a less expensive alternative to the face-to-face interview. A study conducted by the National Center for Health Statistics indicated that the total response rate for a telephone interview for the National Health Interview Survey was 80%. With face-to-face interviews the response rate for this survey was over 96%. One reason for the lower response rate for the telephone survey may be that it is easier to end an interview in the middle than it is if the interviewer is sitting in one's living room. Telephone interviews also may result in biased information, for example, if used in places with less than 100% telephone coverage.

Self-administered, including postal, questionnaires are another method of collecting health-related quality of life information. Self-administered instruments, while a less expensive form of data collection than either the face-to-face or telephone interview, tend to have lower item completion rates. Use of self-administered questionnaires is also inadvisable for patients either who are cognitively impaired or who have problems understanding the questions due to lack of education or to lack of familiarity with either the language, the culture, or both. Self-administered questionnaires are also an important way of collecting information about sensitive topics. For example, people are more willing to admit incontinence on a postal questionnaire than they are in a face-to-face interview[134].

Diaries are useful for collecting detailed information over specified intervals. Information is entered into the diary on a daily basis or at other short intervals determined by the clinical investigator. For example, Verbrugge and Balaban[132] collected daily information on self-rated health, activity level, and health behaviours using a diary format. This method of administration is particularly important to detect daily or short-term fluctuations in health-related quality of life.

Another important practical issue is whether or not an instrument allows for the use of proxy or surrogate responses. Allowing someone other than the patient to supply information about the patient's health-related quality of life may reduce non-response and expense. With some patients, use of proxy respondents may provide more reliable and valid answers than with self response, especially in the case of cognitively impaired persons. In general, instruments comprised of concepts that are perceptual in nature, for example the General Well-being Schedule[44], require self response; those that assess performance, for example, the Quality of Well-being Scale[24] are more likely to allow proxy responses.

**Length and cost of administration**

Length and cost of administration are functions of the context of the study. In the broad scope of any clinical trial which incorporates measures of health-related quality of life, the length and cost of administration will be a function of the total amount of information collected. If there are a number of other components, for example, checklists to identify treatment side effects and adverse reactions and questions about disease history and family medical history, then the overall cost of the trial will be higher than if these components are few and short. More specific to the health-related quality of life aspects of the trial, including more rather than fewer concepts is likely to result in a longer assessment battery and thus to cost more to administer, process and analyse. Also, if the study population is unhealthy, cognitively impaired or illiterate the data collection phase of the study, whether by interview or interviewer-assisted self-administered is bound to take longer. In general, longer assessments, whether measured in terms of number of items or time to administer, translate into higher costs.

Estimating the total costs of conducting a health-related quality of life assessment involves both variable and fixed costs. Included in the fixed costs may be the design of the instrument, amount of interviewer training required, and the overhead involved in the actual data collection. Variable costs will depend on, for example, the sample size, number of interviewers, and number of questionnaires printed. Designing a health-related quality of life assessment with a budget based on political rather than study design considerations prevents the investigator from improving the quality of the study beyond the designated budget, even if the marginal cost of the improvement is minimal[56].

**Method of analysis and complexity of scoring**

When a composite health status or health-related quality of life measure is used, one practical consideration concerns the availability of information about calculating scores after the assessments have been completed by the patient. For all assessments clearly specified algorithms are needed for calculating scores. Some instruments are scored by simply summing the scores to individual items. Others, convert the sum of items to a score ranging from 0 to 100. Yet others require that weights be assigned to individuals in given health states.

For some assessments, these may be simple procedures that can be done efficiently by hand. For others, the logic is sufficiently complex to warrant the use of a computer scoring system to assure accuracy. In this latter situation, a key consideration is whether or not the needed computer programs already exist or if they have to be written. Even if programs exist, it is possible that either the computer language or other machine configuration patterns are incompatible between different computer centres. Even if computer programs are available, scoring manuals should be available so that it is possible for the clinical investigator to clearly understand the scoring process and hence to be able to interpret the data.

The manual should also explain whether or not the measure has an overall score or not, that is, whether or not individual items in a multi-dimensional instrument can be aggregated over all of the items and concepts to form a single indicator of health-related quality of life. Such scores provide a summary of the individual's or the group's health-related quality of life and are useful for assessing global changes due to treatment. On the other hand, summary scores are unable to give much guidance as to which areas are responsible for decrements from optimal function. To identify this information, it is necessary to be able to disaggregate the overall score into its component parts. From this it is possible to calculate the contribution of each concept or domain of health-related quality of life to the overall score.

As indicated by this review of practical considerations selection of different measures of health-related quality of life depends upon the objectives of measurement and environment of the application. Practical considerations will have to be assigned priorities in designing an optimal strategy. That is, it may be more important to use a self-administered questionnaire to obtain perceptual information and accept lower completion rates than to use face-to-face interviews with higher response rates. No single general purpose measure is likely to meet all the needs of investigators and specific populations. Thus it is necessary to make tradeoffs among the practical considerations to select the assessment or battery of assessments that will result in the most responsive health-related quality of life assessment.

## 7. CONDUCT PRETEST OR PILOT STUDY

Once the set of assessments has been selected, taking both methodological and practical considerations into account, the next step is to develop a data collection instrument that integrates the quality of life instruments and the other forms for data collection that are to be used in the study. Drafting the composite questionnaire needs to be completed before a pretest or pilot study can be conducted.

One of the concerns in drafting the data collection instrument is the placement or order of the questions. At one level, the decisions revolve around the order of the various components. For example, in what order will the quality of life, patient characteristics such as age and gender, and clinical information be collected? A narrower level of concerns in drafting the draft instrument revolves around the order in which the quality-of-questions are asked. For example, should physical function items be placed before or after items assessing health perceptions and affective well-being? Danchik and Drury[36] found that response rates to self-rating of health as excellent, good, fair, or poor varied by 20% depending on where in the instrument the question was asked.

Another concern in drafting the instrument is formatting the questions so that they are clear, legible and easy to answer. If the study is to be conducted among older persons and an administered format is to be used, then using a larger type style may enhance the readability of the instrument. Also, the health-related quality of life questions, regardless of the method of administration, need some introductory remarks that clearly state the purpose of the questions. The more detailed the remarks, the better the patient will understand the importance of supplying correct information. Instructions to the respondent as to what he or she is expected to do follow the introductory remarks. These instructions should indicate what responses are appropriate and what to do if questions do not apply.

Before doing a pilot test, some thought needs to be given as to the level of training required for interviewers and other staff who will be responsible for the data collection. If a standardized measure is being used, then one needs to review the interviewer's instruction manual and note any changes that might be needed to conform to the context of the planned study. One change in the instructions might be needed if the original instrument was designed for use in a household interview setting and the clinical trial application will use it in a clinic setting. If a non-standardized measure is being used, then, instructions need to be prepared. The development of standard instructions for administration of the instrument are important for reducing errors in the actual data collection phase.

The extent of the instructions and interviewer training will depend on the experience of the interviewers. If clinicians, other health professionals or clinic receptionists are to collect the data, then, general instructions about how to collect standard data will be needed as well as instrument-specific instructions. If trained survey research interviewers, such as are employed by survey research firms, are used, then the extent of the general instructions will be minimal; the data collection instruction manual will consist mostly of instrument-specific information.

Once the composite data collection instrument and the instructions for administration have been drafted, the instrument should be tested to determine ease of use. The first step in checking the usefulness of both content and format is for the instrument design staff to administer it amongst themselves and other co-workers. This step can identify unclear question wording, awkward response formats, and missing skip patterns. If any one of these goes undetected, the quality of the data obtained will be diminished. After informal testing, pretests or pilot studies are necessary to address methodological and practical considerations in a study group that more nearly resembles that to be used in the clinical trial.

Pretests are generally small investigations involving 5 to 25 administrations of a measure or battery of measures. This helps investigators estimate the length of time the assessment takes to complete, respondent reactions to different measures, completeness of instructions and other instrumentation, format and flow of the questionnaire, and other considerations in health survey research[1]. Investigators should debrief both respondents and interviewers to learn how to improve plans for formatting questionnaires and monitoring and carrying out the assessment. Debriefing involves going over the data collection instrument step by step asking respondents to repeat their understanding of the instructions and the items contained in the questionnaire. Pretests should be conducted using respondents from the population to be assessed and the actual interviewers involved in the study.

Pilot studies are large pretests involving more than 25 respondents and making a complete study including data collection, scoring, and analysis. Pilot studies are often small investigations in their own right and are published separately. Pilot studies are advisable if an investigator wishes to test specific hypotheses prior to the main study; test several different measures or methods of administration; collect data on the reliability, validity, and responsiveness of a measure in a particular application; or 'practice' the assessment on a small number of persons prior to a large-scale investigation. Pilot studies are often methodological in focus, helping the investigators select among different measures or assessment strategies. Such studies can be particularly useful in learning how to analyse and present health-related quality of life data. Often pretests and pilot studies uncover unanticipated problems in conceptualization, methodology, and practical administration of measures, thereby avoiding problems in the main investigation.

## 8. PREPARE DATA COLLECTION AND ANALYSIS PLANS

Experiences from the pretests and pilot studies can be used to guide the development of data collection plans for the full-scale study. One area of concern is scheduling the initiation of the actual data collection. The study should formally begin after all of the adjustments identified during the pretest and pilot study have been completed. For example, if the pilot study indicated that the data collection forms needed to be revised to streamline procedures and improve data quality, then these changes should be finalized before any data collection is started[138]. Also, any modifications to interviewer or other data collection staff instructions should be thoroughly revised and reprinted as part of the data collection plans.

The plans should describe procedures for processing and editing the data as it is being collected. These procedures may include time lines that will indicate when questionnaires are to be submitted for editing, conversion to machine readable formats and basic validity checking. Interim reviews of the data can alert the investigator as to problems that may have emerged during the course of the study. Monitoring the data collection during the course of the study is one way to ensure high quality data. Early identification of problems in the data collection process also provides additional time to develop analytical solutions. For example, in the case of missing data, early identification of the problem gives analysts time to develop solutions, most commonly through the use of one form of imputation or another.

Analysis plans need to be drafted in conjunction with the data collection plans. With this co-ordination, preliminary data can be used to monitor the progress of the study once the data collection phase of the study has started. The analysis plans should allow the investigator to conduct quality control studies while the study is in process. These plans should all be for assessing problems with the data collection and with the treatment arms being used in the clinical study. In addition, the analysis plans should describe how each of the hypotheses in the clinical study are to be tested. Included in the information specified by the plans are the dependent and independent variables, the cutoff points for the health-related quality of life measures that are to be used for the analysis, and the statistical tests to be used to assess statistically significant differences.

For some clinical investigations, external data may be used to validate the study findings. In these situations, the use of the external data needs to be incorporated into the analysis plans. If the external data are not already available, then, they should be obtained at this time. For example, sample surveys conducted by the National Center for Health Statistics may be useful in determining the representativeness of the clinical population with regard to selected physical, social and mental components of health-related quality of life. The most flexible way of making these comparisons is through the acquisition of public use data tapes. Using these files, these external data sources can be analysed according to patient characteristics that are meaningful to the clinical investigator.

Once the plans for the data collection and analysis have been formulated, the next step is the actual collection of the data. Although there may be a tendency by some members of the clinical investigation team to begin collecting data before the plans are finalized, patience is usually rewarded by the higher quality of data that is produced.

## 9. COLLECT DATA

After conducting a pretest and/or a pilot study and developing data collection plans, the next step is to collect the data. Carefully done pretests and pilot studies, as well as thoroughly developed plans, will ensure that as many problems with this phase of clinical research will be eliminated as possible. It is not unusual, however, for events to occur during data collection that have not been expected. 'Surprises' are more likely to occur in multi-centre trials since it is difficult to control all variables in either a pretest or pilot study. In many cases, the most effective way of minimizing the number and impact of the surprises is to carefully choose the principle investigators for the study and to work closely with them throughout the trial. This section identifies several areas where problems might occur and suggests contingency plans for dealing with them.

One area where unforeseen problems may occur is in the use of computers as a means of data collection. Computer-assisted interviewing, whether in person (CAPI) or by telephone (CATI), as well as computer-assisted self-administration (CASA) is being used increasingly[64,90,107,136]. Proponents of this method of data collection point out that computers standardize the administration and the possible responses to a greater extent than do traditional methods of administration. Also, computers can be programmed to screen for invalid responses as the data are being collected, for example, a person who first claims to have had no restricted activity days during the past 2 weeks and then later in the questionnaire indicates that he or she stayed home from work for 2 days during the past week because of a cold. In such cases, the computer can identify the inconsistency and it can be corrected immediately. Editing the data as it is collected has the potential for reducing the amount of missing or unusable data available for analysis. Health-related quality of life instruments that rely on 'skip patterns' for obtaining detailed information on dysfunction also may benefit from computer-assisted administration. Programs can be written to assure that the skip patterns are uniformly followed, regardless of the type of administration.

One potential problem that can arise if using computer-assisted administration during the data collection step stems from respondent unfamiliarity with these procedures. Data collection staff need to be particularly sensitive to patient acceptance of computer-assisted methods in the case of self-administration. If a relatively large number of response forms are returned with missing or unusable data then it may be necessary to revise the instructions to respondents.

Another set of problems that may surface during the actual data collection of the clinical investigation stems from the composition of the study population. It is probably more difficult to accurately predict the study group in the case of multi-centre trials than in single institution studies. In either case, however, if the study group is either older, sicker, less literate or from a different culture than expected, time to collect the data will be longer than predicted. In addition, more missing information might result, depending on the method of administration and the population characteristics. One contingency plan is to switch from self- to an interviewer-administered method of administration; this will be especially suitable if the population is older and/or sicker than expected. If this solution is adopted, however, care must be taken to minimize variation in results by standardizing the interviewing process and training the interviewers. If the problem is one of missing information which is of a sensitive nature, then a different contingency plan is needed. In this case, it would make sense to adopt a self-administered form of the instrument for the sensitive items.

As indicated in step 8, above, the data collection procedures should be monitored at the outset of the trial and at specified intervals throughout the trial. Even if all of the data collection procedures are met in the initial data gathering, changes in staff, clinic location or patient attitude toward the trial may adversely influence data collection as the trial proceeds. Monitoring is an important part of the process whether the staff are regularly employed by the sponsor of the clinical investigation or if the staff are part of a survey research team that have been contracted to conduct the trial.

## 10. ANALYSE AND PRESENT FINDINGS

As preliminary data are being edited and used for reviewing the data collection procedures, analysts can also begin to implement the analysis plans that have been proposed in step 8. In many ways, analyses and presentations of health-related quality of life data are similar to those used with other kinds of health data. For most clinical investigations, analyses will involve calculating means and standard errors both at a point in time and as a change score over time. Graphs used to display these findings should be simple to read without too much data displayed on the same figure.

Health-related quality of life data present special challenges for analysis and presentation of findings in two areas. One is whether to use a summary score or to present component scores, when available, as well as the single number. In some cases, it is desirable to be able to aggregate the various components into a single summary score, for example, to form QALYs for use in cost-utility analyses[68,126,139]. For other purposes, it is desirable to be able to disaggregate the summary score into its component parts to determine which is making the most significant contribution to the overall score.

### Responsiveness and analysis of effects

The ability of a measure to detect changes and the analysis of change scores or effect size are important considerations for all serial applications of health status measures. The inclusion of items sensitive to change is critical to such assessments. Responsiveness of health status measures in clinical research has been assessed using the relative efficiency statistic (a ratio of paired $t$ statistics)[78] correlation of scale changes with other measures[40], receiver operating characteristic curves[40], and a responsiveness statistic (ratio of minimal clinically important difference to variability in stable subjects)[59]. These approaches use similar data in calculating a statistic of responsiveness, although their mathematical relationships have not yet been investigated.

Disease-specific measures with items selected to assess particular concerns or worded to attribute change to the condition of interest, e.g. back pain in the modified SIP, may be particularly sensitive to within-subject changes and thus more responsive than generic measures that contain items unrelated to change. A responsive measure, however, may not demonstrate high test–retest or internal consistency reliability[59]. In this case, a trade-off must be made between responsiveness and reliability.

Analysing and interpreting changes in health status measures are problems for all longitudinal studies. These may be observational case studies, cohort studies, clinical trials, or health services evaluations. Changes in physiological measures such as blood pressure or cholesterol level may be interpreted in terms of prognostic implications and well-established or agreed cut-off points. Changes in generic health measures such as those from the auranofin trial are more difficult to interpret, although even small changes in portions of such measures may be quite useful (for example, changes in physical mobility or self-care are meaningful in disabled populations). Changes in scores on the most general measures, such as health perceptions or global physical and psychosocial dimension scores, can be even more difficult to interpret. The net changes observed may be due to a large number of different transitions or combinations of transitions within the population. Single score or aggregated measures can make it difficult to identify which items or components are responsible for the change. Net changes must also be distinguished from random or systematic changes (learning effects, rumination) that may occur independently of an intervention. Although changes in these scores may reflect sensitive effects, the relative magnitude of the change may be difficult to assess. For example, is a 5-point difference more meaningful than a 3-point difference?

Changes in disease-specific measures may be easier to interpret because they are more specific or more closely associated with changes in clinical measures of disease-activity such as blood pressure or joint inflammation. Clinician or patient assessments of improvement, which are common measures of change or effects, may be more closely associated with changes in disease-specific measures than with those in generic health status measures[81].

Changes observed in studies using the battery approach may not be easy to interpret. Different results in different measures may make interpretation difficult, particularly when multiple comparisons or statistical tests are necessary[58]. In studies using batteries, one measure needs to be chosen as the primary health status outcome to guide interpretation of changes.

Incorporation of quality of life assessment into clinical practice and clinical trials requires brief, well-defined instruments that can be applied and interpreted easily. There is an increasing need for standardization of instruments or the use of standardized, general measures in combination with population-specific or disease-specific measures. The use of these measures for policy analysis and decision-making will be increased by the incorporation of overall scores as well as scores for each component of the quality of life instrument.

Not only technical knowledge but also creativity and conceptual skill are essential in developing appropriate measures of health-related quality of life. As clinicians apply these concepts and measure and assess their usefulness, catholicity of outlook, combined with scientific rigour, will aid them in finding treatments and solutions that enhance well-being and quality of life.

**References**

1. Aday, L.A. *Designing and Conducting Health Surveys: a Comprehensive Guide.* San Francisco, California: Jossey-Bass Publishers, 1989.
2. Alonso, J., Anto, J.M. and Moreno, C. Spanish version of the Nottingham Health Profile: translation and preliminary validity. *Am. J. Public Health* 1990; 80: 704–708.
3. Anderson, J.P., Bush, J.W. and Berry, C.C. Classifying function for health outcome and quality-of-life evaluation. *Med. Care* 1986; 24: 454–469.
4. Anderson, J.P., Kaplan, R.M. and DeBon, M. Comparison of responses to similar questions in health surveys. In Fowler, F.J. (ed.) Conference Proceedings: Health Survey Research Methods. Rockville, Maryland, Agency for Health Care Research, 1989.
5. Andrews, F.M. and Withey, S.B. *Social Indicators of Well-being: Americans' Perceptions of Life Quality.* New York, Plenum Press, 1976.
6. Bassett, S.S., Magaziner, J. and Hebel, J.R. Reliability of proxy response on mental health indices for aged, community dwelling women. *Psychol. Aging* 1990; 2: 1271–1332.
7. Beck, A.T. *Depression: Causes and Treatment.* Philadelphia, Pennsylvania, University of Pennsylvania Press, 1967.
8. Berg, R.L. (ed.) *Health Status Indexes.* Chicago, Hospital Research and Educational Trust, 1973.
9. Bergner, M. Measurement of health status. *Med. Care* 1985; 23: 696–704.
10. Bergner, M. The Sickness Impact Profile. In Wenger, N.K., Mattson, M.E., Furberg, C.D. and Elinson, J. (eds). *Assessment of Quality of Life in Clinical Trials of Cardiovascular Therapies.* New York, LeJacq Publishing Inc, 1984, pp. 152–159.
11. Bergner, M., Bobbitt, R.A., Kressel, S. *et al.* The Sickness Impact Profile:

conceptual formulation and methodological development of a health status index. *Int. J Health Serv.* 1976; 6: 393-415.

12. Bergner, M., Bobbitt, R.A., Carter, W.B. and Gilson, B.S. The Sickness Impact Profile: development and final revision of a health status measure. *Med. Care* 1981; 19: 787-805.

13. Bindman, A.B., Keane, D. and Lurie, N. Measuring health changes among severely ill patients: the floor phenomenon. *Med. Care* 1990; 28: 1142-1152.

14. Boyle, M.H. and Torrance, G.W. Developing multiattribute health indexes. *Med. Care* 1984; 22: 1045-1057.

15. Boyle, M.H., Torrance, G.W., Sinclair, J.C. and Horwood, S.P. Economic evaluation of neonatal intensive care of very-low-birth- weight infants. *N. Engl. J. Med.* 1983; 308: 1330-1337.

16. Bradburn, N.M. *The Structure of Psychological Well-being.* Chicago, Illinois, Aldine Publishing, 1969.

17. Bradley, L.A., Prokop, C.K., Gentry, W.D. *et al.* Assessment of chronic pain. In Prokop, C.K., Bradley, L.A. *et al.* (eds) *Medical Psychology: Contributions to Behavioral Medicine.* New York, Academic Press, 1981, pp. 91-117.

18. Brandt, J., Spencer, M. and Folstein, M. The telephone interview for cognitive status. *Neuropsychiatr. Neuropsychol. Behav. Neurol.* 1988; 1: 111-117.

19. Brislin, R., Lonner, W. and Thorndike, R. *Cross Cultural Research Methods.* New York, Wiley and Sons, 1973, pp. 32-81.

20. Broadhead, W.E., Kaplan, B.H., James, S.A., Wagner, E.H., Schoenbach, V.J., Grimson, R., Heyden, S., Tibblin, G. and Gehlbach, S.H. The epidemiologic evidence for a relationship between social support and health. *Am. J. Epidemiol.* 1983; 117: 521-537.

21. Brook, R.H., Ware, J.E., Rogers, W.H., Keeler, E.B., Davies, E.R., Donald, C.A., Goldberg, G.A., Lohr, K.N., Masthay, P.C. and Newhouse, J.P. Does free care improve adults' health? Results from a randomized controlled trial. *N. Engl. J. Med.* 1983; 309: 1426-1434.

22. Brook, R.H., Ware, J.E., Davies-Avery, A., Stewart, A.L., Donald, C.A., Rogers, W.H., Williams, K.N. and Johnston, S.A. Overview of adult health status measures fielded in Rand's health insurance study. *Med. Care* 1979; 17 (7 Suppl.): iii-x, 1-131.

23. Brownell, A. and Shumaker, S.A. Social support: an introduction to a complex phenomenon. *J. Social Issues* 1984; 40: 1-11.

24. Bush, J.W. General Health Policy Model/Quality of Well-Being (QWB) scale. In Wenger, N.K., Mattson, M.E., Furberg, C.D. and Elinson, J. (eds) *Assessment of Quality of Life in Clinical Trials of Cardiovascular Therapies.* New York, LeJacq Publishing Inc. 1984, pp. 1891-1899.

25. Bush, J.W., Chen, M.M. and Patrick, D.L. Health Status Index in cost-effectiveness: analysis of PKU program. In Berg, R. (eds) *Health Status Indexes.* Chicago, Illinois, Hospital Research and Educational Trust, 1973, pp. 172-208.

26. Calman, K.C. Definitions and dimensions of quality of life. In *The Quality of Life of Cancer Patients.* New York, Raven Press, 1987, pp. 1-9.

27. Calman, K.C. Quality of life in cancer patients—an hypothesis. *J. Med. Ethics* 1984; 10: 124-127.

28. Campbell, A. *The Sense of Well-being in America: Recent Patterns and Trends.* New York, McGraw-Hill, 1981.
29. Carter, W.B., Bobbitt, R.A., Bergner, M. and Gilson, B.S. Validation of an interval scaling: the Sickness Impact Profile. *Health Serv. Res.* 1976; 11: 516–528.
30. Chambers, L.W. The McMaster Health Index Questionnaire (MHIQ): methodologic documentation and report of second generation of investigations. Hamilton, Ontario, Department of Clinical Epidemiology and Biostatistics, 1982.
31. Chapman, C.R. Measurement of pain: problems and issues. In Bonica, J.J. and Albe-Fessard, D. (eds) *Advances in Pain Research and Therapy.* New York, Raven Press, 1976.
32. Charlton, J.R., Patrick, D.L. and Peach, H. Use of multivariate measures of disability in health surveys. *J. Epidemiol. Commun. Health* 1983; 37: 296–304.
33. Chen, M.M. and Bush, J.W. Health status measures, policy and biomedical research. In Mushkin, S.J. and Dunlop, D.W. (eds) *Health: What is it Worth: Measures of Health Benefits.* New York, Pergamon Press, 1979, pp. 15–42.
34. Clipp, E.C. and Elder, G.H. Elderly confidants in geriatric assessment. *Compr. Gerontol.* 1987; 35–40.
35. Croog, S.H., Levine, S., Testa, M.A., Brown, B., Bulpitt, C.J., Jenkins, C.D., Klerman, G.L. and Williams, G.H. The effects of antihypertensive therapy on the quality of life. *N. Engl. J. Med.* 1986; 314: 1657–1664.
36. Danchik, K.M. and Drury, T.F. Evaluating the effects of survey design and administration on the measurement of subjective phenomena: the case of self-assessed health status. *Proceedings of the Social Statistics Section of the American Statistical Association.* Washington, DC, American Statistical Association, 1985.
37. Davies, A.R. and Ware, J.E. *Measuring Health Perceptions in the Health Insurance Experiment.* Santa Monica, California, The Rand Corporation, 1981.
38. Derogatis, L.R., Lipman, R.S. and Covi, L. SCL-9: an outpatient psychiatric rating scale: preliminary report. *Psychopharmacol. Bull.* 1973; 9: 13–28.
39. Deyo, R.A. Pitfalls in measuring the health status of Mexican Americans: comparative validity of the English and Spanish Sickness Impact Profile. *Am. J. Publ. Health* 1984; 74: 569–573.
40. Deyo, R.A. and Centor, R.M. Assessing the responsiveness of functional scales to clinical change: an analogy to diagnostic test performance. *J. Chronic Dis.* 1986; 39: 897–906.
41. Diener, E. Subjective well-being. *Psychol. Bull.* 1984; 95: 542-75.
42. Dohrenwend, B.P., Dohrenwend, B.S., Gould, M.S. *et al. Mental Illness in the United States.* New York, Praeger, 1980, p. 163.
43. Donald, C.A. and Ware, J.E. *The Quantification of Social Contacts and Resources.* Santa Monica, California: The Rand Corporation, 1982.
44. Dupuy, H.J. The Psychological General Well-being (PGWB) Index. In Wenger, N.K., Mattson, M.E., Furberg, C.D. and Elinson, J. (eds) *Assessment of Quality of Life in Clinical Trials of Cardiovascular Therapies.* New York, Le Jacq Publishing Inc, 1984, pp. 1701–1783.
45. Durkheim, E. *Suicide. A Study in Sociology.* Spaulding, J.A., Simpson, G. (transl.) New York, Free Press, 1897/1951.
46. Epstein, A.M., Hall, J.A., Tognetti, J., Son, L.H. and Conant, L. Using proxies

to evaluate quality of life: Can they provide information about patients' health status and satisfaction with medical care? *Med. Care* 1989; 27: S91–98.

47. Fabrega, H. *Disease and Social Behavior: an Interdisciplinary Perspective.* Cambridge, Mass., Massachusetts Institute of Technology Press, 1974.

48. Fanshel, S. and Bush, J.W. A health status index and its application to health-services outcomes. *Operations Res.* 1970; 1021-1066.

49. Fienberg, S.E., Loftus, E.F. and Tanur, J.M. Cognitive aspects of health survey methodology: an overview. *Milbank Mem. Fund Q.* 1985; 63

50. Fink, R. Issues and problems in measuring children's health status in community health research. *Soc. Sci. Med.* 1989; 29: 715–719.

51. Folstein, M.F., Folstein, S.E. and McHugh, P.R. Mini-Mental State—a practical method for grading the cognitive state of patients for the clinician. *J. Psychiatr. Res.* 1975; 12: 1891–1898.

52. Fordyce, W.E. *Behavioral Methods for Chronic Pain and Illness.* St. Louis, Missouri, CV Mosby, 1976.

53. George, L.K. and Bearon, L.B. *Quality of Life in Older Persons.* New York, Human Sciences Press, 1980.

54. Gilson, B.S., Erickson, D., Chavez, C.T., Bobbitt, R.A., Bergner, M. and Carter, W.B. A chicano version of the Sickness Impact Profile (SIP): a health care evaluation instrument crosses the language barrier. *Cult. Med. Psych.* 1980; 4: 1371–1450.

55. Good, B.J. and Good, M.D. The meaning of symptoms: a cultural hermeneutic model for clinical practice. *The Relevance of Social Science for Medicine.* Dordrecht, Holland, D. Reidel Publishing Co, 1980, pp. 1651–1696.

56. Groves, R.M. *Survey Errors and Survey Costs.* New York, John Wiley and Sons, 1989.

57. Gurin, G., Veroff, J. and Feld, S. *Americans View their Mental Health: a Nationwide Interview Survey:* a Report to the Staff Director, Jack E. Ewalt, 1960. New York, Basic Books, 1960.

58. Guyatt, G., Feeny, D. and Patrick, D. Issues in quality-of-life measurement in clinical trials. *Controlled Clinical Trials.* (forthcoming).

59. Guyatt, G., Walter, S. and Norman, G. Measuring change over time: assessing the usefulness of evaluative instruments. *J. Chronic Dis.* 1987; 40: 171–178.

60. Hendricson, W.D, Russell, I.J., Prihoda, T.J., Jacobsen, J.M., and Rogan, A. Development and initial validation of a dual-language English-Spanish format for the Arthritis Impact Measurement Scales. *Arthritis Rheum.* 1989; 1153–1159.

61. Hunt, S.M. Cross-cultural issues in the use of socio-medical indicators. *Health Policy* 1986; 6: 1491–1558.

62. Hunt, S.M., McKenna, S.P., McEwen, J., Backett, E.M., Williams, J. and Papp, E. A quantitative approach to perceived health status: a validation study. *J. Epidemiol. Commun. Health* 1980; 34: 281–286.

63. Hunt, S.M. and Wiklund, I. Cross-cultural variation in the weighting of health statements: a comparison of English and Swedish valuations. *Health Policy* 1987; 8: 227.

64. Jette, A.M., Davies, A.R., Cleary, P.D., Calkins, D.R., Rubenstein, L.V., Fink, A., Kosecoff, J., Young, R.T., Brook, R.H. and Delbanco, T.L. The Functional

Status Questionnaire: reliability and validity when used in primary care. *J. Gen. Intern. Med.* 1986; 1: 143–149.

65. Kaplan, R.M. and Anderson, J.P. A general health policy model: update and applications. *Health Serv. Res.* 1988; 23: 203–235.

66. Kaplan, R.M., Bush, J.W. and Berry, C.C. Health status: types of validity and the Index of Well-being. *Health Serv. Res.* 1976; 11: 478–507.

67. Kaplan, R.M., Bush, J.W. and Berry, C.C. Health Status Index: category rating versus magnitude estimation for measuring levels of well-being. *Med. Care* 1979; 17: 501–525.

68. Kaplan, R.M. and Bush, J.W. Health-related quality of life measurement for evaluation research and policy analysis. *Health Psych.* 1982; 1: 61–80.

69. Kasl, S. Social and psychological factors affecting the course of disease: an epidemiological perspective. In Mechanic, D. (ed.) *Handbook of Health, Health Care and the Health Professions.* Riverside, New Jersey, Free Press, 1983, pp. 683–708.

70. Katz, S. and Akpom, C.A. A measure of primary sociobiological functions. *Int. J. Health Serv.* 1976; 493–507.

71. Katz, S., Ford, A.B., Moskowitz, R.W., Jackson, B.A. and Jaffe, M.W. Studies of illness in the aged. *J. Am. Med. Assoc.* 1963; 185: 914–919.

72. Keefe, F.J., Brown, C., Scott, D.S. *et al.* Behavioral assessment of chronic pain. In Keefe, F.J. and Blumenthal, J.A. (eds) *Assessment Strategies in Behavioral Medicine.* New York, Grune & Stratton, 1982, pp. 321–350.

73. Kellner R, Sheffield B. A self-rating scale of distress. *Psychol. Med.* 1973; 3: 88–100.

74. Kirshner, B. and Guyatt, G. A methodological framework for assessing health indices. *J. Chronic Dis.* 1985; 27–36.

75. Kleinman, A., Eisenberg, L. and Good, B. Culture, illness and care: clinical lessons from anthropologic and cross-cultural research. *Ann. Intern. Med.* 1978; 88: 251–258.

76. Kuriansky, J.B. and Gurland, B. Performance test of activities of daily living. *Int. J. Aging Hum. Dev.* 1976; 7: 343–352.

77. Lawton, M.P. and Brody, E.M. Assessment of older people: self-maintaining and instrumental activities of daily living. *Gerontologist* 1969; 9: 1791–1796.

78. Liang, M.H., Larson, M.G., Cullen, K.E. and Schwartz, J.A. Comparative measurement efficiency and sensitivity of five health status instruments for arthritis research. *Arthr. Rheum.* 1985; 28: 542–547.

79. Llewellyn-Thomas, H., Sutherland, H.J., Tibshirani, A.C., Ciampi, A., Till, J.E. and Boyd, N.F. Describing health states: methodologic issues in obtaining values for health states. *Med. Care* 1984; 22: 543–553.

80. Locker, D. In *Disability and Disadvantage: the Consequences of Chronic Illness.* London, England, Tavistock Publications, 1983.

81. MacKenzie, C.R., Charlson, M.E., DiGiola, D. *et al.* Can the Sickness Impact Profile measure change? An example of scale assessment. *J. Chronic Dis.* 1986; 39: 429.

82. Magaziner, J., Simonsick, E.M., Kashner, T.M. and Hebel, J.R. Patient-proxy response comparability on measures of patient health and functional status. *J. Clin. Epidemiol.* 1988; 41: 1065–1074.

83. Mahoney, F.I. and Barthel, D.W. Functional evaluation: the Barthel Index. *Md State Med. J.* 1965; 14: 61–65.

84. Maslow, A.H. A theory of human motivation. *Psychol. Rev.* 1943; 50: 370–396.

85. McCorkle, R. and Young, K. Development of a symptom distress scale. *Cancer Nurs.* 1978; 373–378.

86. McDowell, I. and Newell, C. *Measuring Health: a Guide to Rating Scales and Questionnaires.* New York, Oxford University Press, 1987.

87. Morgan, M., Patrick, D. and Charlton, J. Social networks and psychosocial support among disabled people. *Soc. Sci. Med.* 1984; 19: 489–498.

88. Moriyama, I.M. Problems in the measurement of health status. In Sheldon, E.B. and Moore, W.E. (eds) *Indicators of Social Change.* New York, Russell Sage Foundation, 1968, pp. 573–600.

89. Mossey, J. and Shapiro, E. Self-rated health: a predictor of mortality among the elderly. *Am. J. Public Health* 1982; 72: 800–809.

90. National Center for Health Statistics. *Concept Design for the NCHS Computer Assisted Personal Interviewing (CAPI).* Gardinier, J.S., Kovar, M.G., Shumate, P., Adams, C. Hyattsville, Maryland, National Center for Health Statistics. 1990.

91. Nelson, E., Wasson, J., Kirk, J., Keller, A., Clark, D., Dietrich, A., Stewart, A. and Zubkoff, M. Assessment of function in routine clinical practice: description of the COOP Chart method and preliminary findings. *J. Chronic Dis.* 1987; 40: (Suppl 1), 55S–69S.

92. Nocturnal Oxygen Therapy Trial Group. Continuous or nocturnal oxygen therapy in hypoxemic chronic obstructive lung disease. *Ann. Intern. Med.* 1980; 93: 391–398.

93. Nunnally, J.C. *Psychometric Theory.* (2nd edn) New York, McGraw-Hill Book Company, 1978.

94. Patrick, D.L. Constructing social metrics for health status indexes. *Int. J. Health Serv.* 1976; 6: 443–453.

95. Patrick, D.L. Health and care of the handicapped in Lambeth: description of objectives and proposed research. London: St. Thomas's Hospital Medical School, Department of Community Medicine, 1979. (Unpublished).

96. Patrick, D.L. Measuring social preference for function levels of health status. PhD Dissertation, Columbia University, 1972.

97. Patrick, D. Standardization of comparative health status measures: using scales developed in America in an English speaking country. In *Health Survey Research Methods: Third Biennial Conference.* Hyattsville, MD, US Department of Health and Human Services, 1981.

98. Patrick, D.L. and Bergner, M. Measurement of health status in the 1990s. *Annu. Rev. Public Health* 1990; 11: 1651–1683.

99. Patrick, D.L., Bush, J.W. and Chen, M.M. Toward an operational definition of health. *J. Health Soc. Behav.* 1973a; 14: 6–23.

100. Patrick, D.L., Bush, J.W. and Chen, M.M. Methods for measuring levels of well-being for a health status index. *Health Serv. Res.* 1973b; 8: 228–245.

101. Patrick, D.L. and Deyo, R.A. Generic and disease-specific measures in assessing health status and quality of life. *Med. Care* 1989; S217–S232.

102. Patrick, D.L. and Erickson, P. What constitutes quality of life? Concepts and dimensions. *Clin. Nutr.* 1988; 7: 53–63.

103. Patrick, D.L. and Peach, H. (eds) *Disablement in the Community*. Oxford, England, Oxford University Press, 1989.

104. Patrick, D., Sittampalam, Y., Somerville, S., Carter, W.B. and Bergner, M. A crosscultural comparison of health status values. *Am. J. Public Health* 1985; 75: 1402–1407.

105. Pfeiffer, E. (ed.) *Multidimensional Functional Assessment: the OARS Methodology. A Manual*. Durham, North Carolina: Duke University, Center for the Study of Aging and Human Development, 1975.

106. Rogers, W.H., Williams, K.N. and Brook, R.H. Conceptualization and measurement of health for adults in the health insurance study: Vol. VII. *Power Analysis of Health Status Measures*. Santa Monica, California, Rand Corporation, 1979.

107. Roizen, M.F., Coalson, D., Hayward, R.S.A. *et al*. Can patients use an automated questionnaire to define their current health status? *Med. Care* 1992; 30: (5 Suppl.): MS74–MS84.

108. Rosser, R.M. A history of the development of health indicators. In Smith, G.T. (ed.) *Measuring the Social Benefits of Medicine*. London, England, Office of Health Economics, 1983, pp. 50–62.

109. Rosser, R.M. and Kind, P. A scale of valuations of state of illness: is there a social consensus? *Int. J. Epidemiol*. 1978; 7: 347–358.

110. Rothman, M.L., Hedrick, S.C., Bulcrot, K.A., Hickam, D.H. and Rubenstein, L.Z. The validity of proxy-generated scores as measures of patient health status. *Med. Care* 1991; 29: 1151–1224.

111. Sackett, D.L. and Torrance, G.W. The utility of different health states as perceived by the general public. *J. Chronic Dis*. 1978; 31: 697–704.

112. Schoening, H.A. Anderegg, L., Bergstrom, D. *et al*. Numerical scoring of self-care status of patients. *Arch. Phys. Med. Rehabil*. 1965; 46: 689–697.

113. Scott, P.J. and Huskinsson, E.C. Graphic representation of pain. *Pain* 1976; 2: 1751–1784.

114. Spitzer, R.L., Endicott, J., Fleiss, J.L. and Cohen, J. The psychiatric status schedule: a technique for evaluating psycholpathology and impairment in role functioning. *Arch. Gen. Psychiat*. 1970; 35: 773–782.

115. Stanton, B. *Quality of Life and Well-being Workshop Report*. Hyattsville, Maryland, National Center for Health Statistics, 1987, pp. 33–37.

116. Stewart, A.L. and Ware, J.E. (eds) *Measuring Functioning and Well-being: the Medical Outcomes Study Approach*. Durham, North Carolina, Duke University Press, 1992.

117. Stewart, A.L., Greenfield, S., Hays, R.D., Wells, K., Rogers, W.H., Berry, S.D., McGlynn, E.A. and Ware, J.E. Jr. Functional status and well-being of patients with chronic conditions: results from the Medical Outcomes Study. *J. Am. Med. Assoc*. 1989; 262: 907–913.

118. Stewart, A.L., Hays, R.D. and Ware, J.E. Jr. The MOS short-form general health survey: reliability and validity in a patient population. *Med. Care* 1988; 26: 724–735.

119. Stones, M.J. and Kozma, A. Issues relating to the usage and conceptualization of mental health constructs employed by gerontologists. *Int. J. Aging Hum. Dev*. 1980; 11: 269–281.

120. Sugarbaker, P.H., Barofsky, I., Rosenberg, S.A. and Gianola, F.J. Quality of

life assessment of patients in extremity sarcoma clinical trials. *Surgery* 1982; 91: 17–23.

121. Sullivan, M. Sickness Impact Profile: Introduktion av en Svensk version for matning av sjukdomskonsekvenser. *Lakartidningen* 1985; 82: 1861–1862.

122. Temkin, N.R., Dikmen, S., Machamen, S. and McLean, A. General vs. disease specific measures: further work on the Sickness Impact Profile for head injury. *Med. Care* 1989; 27: (Suppl), S44-S53.

123. Thoits, P. Conceptual, metholodological and theoretical problems in studying social support as a buffer against life stress. *J. Health Soc. Behav.* 1982; 22: 324–336.

124. Torgerson, W.S. *Theory and Methods of Scaling.* New York, Wiley, 1958.

125. Torrance, G.W. Social preferences for health states: an empirical evaluation of three measurement techniques. *Socio-Econ. Plan. Sci.* 1976; 129–136.

126. Torrance, G.W. The measurement of health state utilities for economic appraisal. *J. Health Economics* 1986; 5: 1–30.

127. Torrance, G.W. Utility approach to measuring health-related quality of life. *J. Chronic Dis.* 1987; 40: 593–600.

128. Torrance, G.W., Sackett, D.L. and Thomas, W.H. Utility maximization model for program evaluation: a demonstration application. In Berg, R.L. (ed.) *Health Status Indexes.* Chicago, Illinois, Hospital Research and Educational Trust, 1973, pp. 1561–1572.

129. Torrance, G.W., Thomas, W.H. and Sackett, D.L. A utility maximization model for evaluation of health care programs. *Health Serv. Res.* 1972; 7: 1181–1233.

130. Torrance, G.W. and Zipursky, A. Cost-effectiveness of antepartum prevention of Rh immunization. *Clin. Perinatal.* 1984; 11: 267–281.

131. Veit, C.T and Ware, J.E. Measuring health and health care outcomes: issues and recommendations. In Kane, R.L. and Kane, R.A. (eds) *Values and Long-term Care.* Lexington, Massachusetts, Lexington Books, 1982, pp. 233–260.

132. Verbrugge, L.M. and Balaban, D.J. Patterns of change in disability and well-being. *Med. Care* 1989; 27: (3 Suppl.), S128-S147.

133. Vertinsky, I. and Wong, E. Eliciting preferences and the construction of indifference maps: A comparative empirical evaluation of two measurement methodologies. *Socio-Econ. Plan. Sci.* 1975; 9: 15–24.

134. Victor, C.R. Survey of the elderly after discharge from hospital in Wales – the long report. St. David's Hospital, Cardiff, Research Team for the Care of the Elderly. 1983.

135. Ware, J.E. Methodological considerations in selection of health status assessment procedures. In Wenger, N.K., Mattson, M.E., Furberg, C.D. and Elinson, J. (eds) *Assessment of Quality of Life in Clinical Trials of Cardiovascular Therapies.* New York, LeJacq Publishing, 1984, pp. 87–111.

136. Ware, J.E. The MOS Short-Form 36: Conceptual Background and Method of Administration. In *MAPI Quality-of-Life Symposium*, 1990.

137. Ware, J.E. Jr. The use of health status and quality of life measures in outcomes and effectiveness research. Rockville, Maryland, Agency for Health Care Policy and Research (forthcoming)

138. Weinberg, E. Data Collection: Planning and Management. In *Handbook of Survey Research*. San Diego, California, Academic Press, 1983, pp. 329–358.

139. Weinstein, M.C. and Stason, W.B. Foundations of cost-effectiveness analysis for health and medical practices. *N. Engl J. Med.* 1977; 296: 716–721.
140. Williams, M.E., Hadler, N.M. and Earp, J.A. Manual ability as a marker of dependency in geriatric women. *J. Chronic Dis.* 1982; 35: 115.
141. Williams, S.J. Chronic respiratory illness and disability: a critical review of the psychosocial literature. *Soc. Sci. Med.* 1989; 28: 791–803.
142. Williams, S.J. and Bury, M.R. 'Breathtaking': the consequences of chronic respiratory disorder. *Int. Disabil. Stud.* 1989; 11: 114-20.
143. Wilson, R.W. and Drury, T.F. Interpreting trends in illness and disability: health statistics and health status. *Annu. Rev. Public Health* 1984; 5: 83–106.
144. Wolfson, A.D., Sinclair, A.J., Bambardier, C. and McGeer, A. Preference measurements for functional status in stroke patients: interrater and intertechnique comparisons. In Kane, R.L. and Kane, R.A. (eds) *Values and Long-term Care.* Lexington, Massachusetts, Lexington Books, 1982, pp. 191–214.
145. World Health Organization. *Constitution of the World Health Organization.* Basic documents. Geneva, Switzerland, World Health Organization. 1948.
146. Zung, W.W.K. A self-rating depression scale. *Arch. Gen. Psychiatr.* 1965; 63–70.

# 3 The Quality of Well-being Scale: rationale for a single quality of life index

Robert M. Kaplan, John P. Anderson and
Theodore G. Ganiats

This chapter provides an overview of the Quality of Well-Being Scale (QWB) and the General Health Policy Model from which it was derived. Our group argues that a single, comprehensive expression of quality of life (a combined index of morbidity and mortality) has many desirable features for policy analysis, evaluation research, and clinical investigation. A recurrent theme in several of our previous publications is that a single index of health status is both feasible and highly desirable[2–5,16,17,19,20,23,31–33,36–47,55,56].

Health status measurement has been characterized by competing traditions; one of the major issues is disease specificity. Some investigators argue that specific measures are required for each disease category; while others, including our group, believe there are many advantages to a general approach. Among those favouring the general approach to health status measurement, some groups have focused on mortality while others have focused on morbidity. Our approach is to integrate morbidity and mortality into common units of health status. In this chapter, we will elaborate each of these issues.

## GENERAL VERSUS DISEASE-SPECIFIC HEALTH MEASURES

Many health-related quality of life measures are designed for use with any population. However, some investigators feel that it is necessary to develop quality of life measures for specific diseases, for example, the RAND Corporation has produced a series of booklets describing the conceptualization and measurement of 'physiologic health' where each booklet describes the problems in conceptualization and measurement of a specific condition, such as anaemia, acne and vision impairment. The rationale underlying the development of these measures is largely clinical. It suggests that medical conditions have very specific outcomes. Thus, for example, diabetic patients are evaluated according to blood glucose, while chronic obstructive lung disease patients are evaluated according to pulmonary function. In addition to general physiological indicators, there are also quality of life measures designed specifically for particular disease groups. For instance, Meenan and colleagues have developed a specific quality of life measure for arthritis patients[50] and this is only one among many approaches to health status assessment for this particular disease[49].

Disease-specific measures can produce follow-up information that will necessarily fall within the error of more general measures. For instance, it may be useful to know that a new treatment for burns generally allows hand burn victims to regain sufficient finger dexterity to open a bag of potato chips, while current treatments do not provide these benefits. Any general measure that attempted to gather this wealth of detail on all conceivable diseases or injuries would soon overwhelm respondents with what might be considered burdensome and trivial questions.

Though useful for many purposes, these disease-specific measures have a weakness from the policy point of view. Their use precludes the possibility of comparing programmes that are directed at different populations or groups suffering from different diseases. Policy analysis requires a more general approach to health status assessment. In addition, many health care interventions affect outcomes that are not system-specific. For example, cigarette smoking may increase the probability of coronary heart disease, peripheral artery disease, cerebrovascular disease, and cancer of the larynx, lung, mouth, oesophagus, bladder, pancreas and stomach, and chronic obstructive pulmonary disease[24]. From this point of view, the impact of smoking upon health is truly overwhelming, but only general health status measures can provide a comprehensive summary of these heterogeneous health effects.

## MORTALITY

Mortality remains the major outcome measure in most epidemiological studies and clinical trials. Typically, mortality is expressed in units of time. In order for mortality data to be meaningful, they must be expressed in the form of a rate, that is the proportion of deaths from a particular cause occurring in some defined time interval (usually per year) and usually, mortality rates are age-adjusted. Case fatality rates express the proportion of persons who died of a particular disease divided by the total number with the disease (including those who die and those who live).

There are many advantages to reporting mortality rates. They are hard data (despite some misclassification bias[53]), and the significance of the outcome is not difficult to comprehend. However, there are also some obvious limitations. Mortality rates consider only the dead and ignore the living.

Many important health care services, including prevention (e.g. childhood inoculations), can be expected to have little or no impact upon mortality. For example, each year there are approximately 1.2 million cataract removal procedures performed in the United States[29]. Although the procedure is essentially non-controversial, cataract removal has little or no impact on mortality and is certainly unrelated to infant mortality. An outcome measure that focused only on mortality would miss the value of this surgery, which may have benefits in as many as 95% of the cases.

## MORBIDITY

The most common approach to health status assessment is to measure morbidity in terms of function or role performance. Morbidity estimates can also include work days missed or bed disability days. Most approaches to health status assessment are essentially morbidity indicators. For example, the Sickness Impact Profile[8] represents the effect of disease or disability upon a variety of categories of behavioural function, while the Medical Outcome Study (MOS) measures include separate items for the effects of disease or health states upon physical function, social function, and mental function[60]. These measures do not integrate morbidity and mortality, although as each birth cohort ages, there is accrual of mortality cases. Death is a health outcome and it is important that this outcome not be excluded from any expression of health status.

To illustrate this, consider evaluating the effect of an integrated support and treatment programme, as opposed to no support or treatment, for randomly assigned groups of very ill, elderly, nursing home residents. Let us suppose that the programme maintained them all at a very low level of function throughout the year, while in the comparison group, the sickest 10% died. Looking just at the living in the follow-up, one finds the comparison group to be healthier, since the sickest had been removed by mortality. By this standard, the programme without supportive treatment might be put forth as the better alternative. However, with a measure that combined morbidity and mortality, the story would be very different, because the mortality effects would drag the overall health of the comparison group to a very low level. The importance of mortality will be discussed in greater depth later in this chapter.

## WELL-YEARS

Our approach is to express the benefits of medical care, behavioural intervention, or preventive programmes in terms of well-years. Others have chosen to describe the same outcome as Quality Adjusted Life Years

(QALYs)[66]. Well-years integrate mortality and morbidity to express health status in terms of equivalents of well-years of life. If a cigarette smoker died of heart disease at age 50 and we would have expected him to live to age 75, it might be concluded that the disease caused him to lose 25 life-years. If 100 cigarette smokers died at age 50 (and also had life expectancies of 75 years), we might conclude that 2500 (100 men by 25 years) life-years had been lost by that group.

Death is not the only outcome of concern in heart disease. Many adults suffer myocardial infarctions leaving them somewhat dysfunctional over a longer period of time. Although they are still alive, the quality of their lives has diminished. Our model permits various degrees of dysfunction to be compared to one another. A disease that reduces the quality of life by one half will take away 0.5 well-years over the course of one year. If it affects two people, it will take away 1.0 well-year (equal to $2 \times 0.5$) over a one-year period. A medical treatment that improves the quality of life by 0.2 for each of five individuals will result in a production of one well-year if the benefit is maintained over a one-year period. Using this system, it is possible to express the benefits of various programmes by showing how many equivalents of well-years they produce. However, not all programmes have equivalent costs. In periods of scarce resources, it is necessary to find the most efficient use of limited funds. The well-year approach provides a framework within which to make policy decisions that require selection between competing alternatives. Preventive services may in this way compete with traditional medical services for the scarce health care dollars and moreover can be competitive in such analyses. Performing such comparisons requires the use of a general health decision model. In the next section, the general model of health status assessment and benefit–cost/utility (BCU) analysis will be presented[3].

## THE GENERAL HEALTH POLICY MODEL AND THE QUALITY OF WELL-BEING SCALE

The General Health Policy Model has been developed over the course of the last 20 years as a method for quantifying health outcomes. The approach depends upon a comprehensive model of the concept 'health' that includes components of functioning, symptoms/problems, preferences, life-expectancy, and prognoses. The Quality of Well-being (QWB) Scale is a method for estimating some components of the general model. The QWB questionnaire categorizes individuals according to functioning and symptoms. Other components of the model are obtained from other data sources.

## COMPONENTS OF THE GENERAL HEALTH POLICY MODEL

The General Health Policy Model includes several components and must be derived from five distinct data sources. The model is based on an underlying conceptualization of the concept 'health' that was first described by Fanshel and Bush[23]. The model was first outlined by J.W. Bush, an experienced clinical physician, who had a strong interest in quantitative studies and mathematical modelling. Bush felt that health and disability had general impacts upon quantifiable outcomes. In conceptualizing health outcomes, several distinct components became apparent. These components include mortality, dysfunction, symptoms/problems, relative importance, prognoses, and costs.

### Mortality

A model of health outcomes necessarily includes a component for mortality. Indeed, many public health statistics focus exclusively on mortality through estimations of crude mortality rates, age-adjusted mortality rates, and infant mortality rates. Death is an important outcome that must be included in any comprehensive conceptualization of health.

### Functioning

In addition to death, behavioural dysfunction is also an important outcome[34]. The General Health Policy Model considers functioning in three areas: mobility, physical activity, and social activity. Descriptions of the measures of these aspects of function are given in several publications (see references 36–37).

### Symptoms/problems

Most public health indicators are relatively insensitive to variations toward the well end of the continuum. Measures of infant mortality, to give an extreme example, ignore all individuals capable of reading this book since they have lived beyond one year following their births (we assume that no infants are reading the manuscript). Disability measures often ignore those in relatively well states. For example, the RAND Health Insurance Study reported that about 80% of the general populations report no dysfunction when they were interviewed. Thus, they would estimate that 80% of the population is well. In our work, symptoms or problems are evaluated in addition to behavioural dysfunction. In these studies, only about 12% of the general population report no symptoms on a particular day[37]. In other words, symptoms or problems are a very common aspect of the human experience. Some might argue that symptoms are unimportant because some are subjective and unobservable. However, symptoms are highly correlated with the demand for medical services, expenditures on health care, and motivations to expend personal resources for altered lifestyles. Thus, we feel that the quantification of symptoms is very important.

**Relative importance**

Given that various components of functioning and mortality can be tabulated, it is important to consider the relative importance of various components. For example, it is possible to develop measures that detect very minor symptoms. Yet, because these symptoms are measurable it does not necessarily mean that they are important. A patient may experience side-effects of a medication but be willing to tolerate them because the side-effects are less important than the probable benefit that would be obtained if the medication is consumed. Not all outcomes are equally important. A treatment in which 20 of 100 patients die is not equivalent to one in which 20 of 100 patients develop nausea, even though statistical tests evaluating the two treatments might come up with the same chi-square value. An important component of the General Health Policy Model attempts to scale the various health outcomes according to their relative importance. This is done by placing all states on a continuum ranging from 0 (for dead) to 1.0 (for optimum functioning). Using this system it is possible to scale the relative importance of states in relation to the life–death continuum. A point halfway on the scale (0.5) is regarded as halfway between optimum function and death. The weighting system has been described in several different publications[31,38,39,43–45].

**Prognosis**

Another dimension of health status is the duration of a condition. A headache that lasts an hour is not equivalent to a headache that lasts one month. A cough that lasts 3 days is not equivalent to a cough that lasts 3 years. In considering the severity of illness, duration of the problem is central. As basic as this concept is, most contemporary models of health outcome measurement completely disregard the duration component. In the General Health Policy Model, the term prognosis refers to the probability of transition among health states over the course of time. In addition to the consideration of duration of problems, the model considers the point at which the problem begins. For example, a person may currently have no symptoms or dysfunction, but may have a high probability of these problems in the future. The prognosis component of the model takes these transitions into consideration.

## DATA SOURCES

Utilization of the General Health Policy Model requires four distinct data sources. These are as follows:

### 1. Life expectancy

Life expectancy data are used to estimate the mortality component of the model. Typically, this information comes from standardized life tables.

### 2. Functional status

A second data source comes from information on the functional states of mobility, physical activity, and social activity. This information is obtained from standardized health status questionnaires. We recommend the QWB 7.0 that obtains the information on six consecutive days using a standardized questionnaire. Symptoms/problems are also obtained using this standardized method. Tables 3.1 and 3.2 summarize the levels of functioning and the symptoms/problems captured by the QWB questionnaire.

### 3. Utilities representing relative importance

A third data source is the utility component that is used to express relative importance of observed states. Standardized utility weights, that have been validated on a general population in San Diego, California, are available. Other investigators have developed similar weights based on specific disease populations, other non-ill populations, and some special interest groups. The generalizability of the weights across different groups has been very high (see 6, 44). These weights are given in Tables 3.1 and 3.2. Other investigators have published weights derived from different utility scaling methods[63]. These weights are applied to observable function in order to evaluate the relative importance of any observed states. Mathematically, the QWB of a population can be expressed as:

$$W = 1/N \sum W_K Y_K$$

where

$W$   is the average symptom/problem-standardized well-life expectancy in equivalents of completely well-years for the population

$N$   is the number of people in the population

$K$   indexes the QWB score

$W_K$   is the QWB score for each combination of CPX, Mobility, Physical Activity, and Social Activity, and

$Y_K$   is the number of people with a given $W_K$ QWB score.

**Table 3.1** Quality of Well-being/General Health Policy Model: elements and calculating formulas (function scales, with step definitions and calculating weights)

| Step No. | Step Definition | Weight |
|---|---|---|
| | *Mobility Scale (MOB)* | |
| 5 | No limitations for health reasons | $-.000$ |
| 4 | Did not drive a car, health related; did not ride in a car as usual for age (younger than 15 yr), health related, *and/or* did not use public transportation, health related; *or* had or would have used more help than usual for age to use public transportation, health related | $-.062$ |
| 2 | In hospital, health related | $-.090$ |
| | *Physical Activity Scale (PAC)* | |
| 4 | No limitations for health reasons | $-.000$ |
| 3 | In wheelchair, moved or controlled movement of wheelchair without help from someone else; *or* had trouble or did not try to lift, stoop, bend over, or use stairs or inclines, health related; *and/or* limped, used a cane, crutches, or walker, health related; *and/or* had any other physical limitation in walking, or did not try to walk as far as or as fast as other the same age are able, health related | $-.060$ |
| 1 | In wheelchair, did not move or control the movement of wheelchair without help from someone else, *or* in bed, chair, or couch for most or all of the day, health related | $-.077$ |
| | *Social Activity Scale (SAC)* | |
| 5 | No limitations for health reasons | $-.000$ |
| 4 | Limited in other (e.g. recreational) role activity, health related | $-.061$ |
| 3 | Limited in major (primary) role activity, health related | $-.061$ |
| 2 | Performed no major role activity, health related, but did perform self-care activities | $-.061$ |
| 1 | Performed no major role activity, health related, *and* did not perform or had more help than usual in performance of one or more self-care activities, health related | $-.106$ |

*Calculating Formulas*

**Formula 1.** Point-in-time well-being score for an individual (W):

$$W = 1 + (CPXwt) + (MOBwt) + (PACwt) + (SACwt)$$

where "wt" is the preference-weighted measure for each factor and CPX is Symptom/Problem complex. For example, the W score for a person with the following description profile may be calculated for one day as:

| | | |
|---|---|---|
| CPX-11 | Cough, wheezing or shortness of breath, with or without fever, chills, or aching all over | $-.257$ |
| MOB-5 | No limitations | $-.000$ |
| PAC-1 | In bed, chair, or couch for most or all of the day, health related | $-.077$ |
| SAC-2 | Performed no major role activity, health related, but did perform self-care | $-.061$ |

$$W = 1 + (-.257) + (-.000) + (-.077) + (-.061) = 0.605$$

**Formula 2.** Well-years (WY) as an output measure:

$$WY = [\text{No. of persons} \times (1.0 + CPXwt + MOBwt + PACwt + SACwt) \times Time]$$

**Table 3.2** Quality of Well-being/General Health Policy Model: symptom/problem complexes (CPX) with calculating weights

| CPX No. | CPX Description | Weights |
|---|---|---|
| 1 | Death (not on respondent's card) | −.727 |
| 2 | Loss of consciousness such as seizure (fits), fainting, or coma (out cold or knocked out) | −.407 |
| 3 | Burn over large areas of face, body, arms or legs | −.387 |
| 4 | Pain, bleeding, itching or discharge (drainage) from sexual organs – does not include normal menstrual (monthly) bleeding | −.349 |
| 5 | Trouble learning, remembering, or thinking clearly | −.340 |
| 6 | Any combination of one or more hands, feet, arms, or legs either missing, deformed (crooked), paralysed (unable to move), or broken – includes wearing artificial limbs or braces | −.333 |
| 7 | Pain, stiffness, weakness, numbness, or other discomfort in chest, stomach (including hernia or rupture), side, neck, back, hips, or any joints or hands, feet, arms, or legs | −.299 |
| 8 | Pain, burning, bleeding, itching, or other difficulty with rectum, bowel movements, or urination (passing water) | −.292 |
| 9 | Sick or upset stomach, vomiting or loose bowel movement, with or without chills, or aching all over | −.290 |
| 10 | General tiredness, weakness, or weight loss | −.259 |
| 11 | Cough, wheezing, or shortness of breath, *with* or *without* fever, chills, or aching all over | −.257 |
| 12 | Spells of feeling, upset, being depressed, or of crying | −.257 |
| 13 | Headache, or dizziness, or ringing in ears, or spells of feeling hot, nervous or shaky | −.244 |
| 14 | Burning or itching rash on large areas of face, body, arms, or legs | −.240 |
| 15 | Trouble talking, such as lisp, stuttering, hoarseness, or being unable to speak | −.237 |
| 16 | Pain or discomfort in one or both eyes (such as burning or itching) or any trouble seeing after correction | −.230 |
| 17 | Overweight for age and height or skin defect of face, body, arms, or legs, such as scars, pimples, warts, bruises or changes in colour | −.188 |
| 18 | Pain in ear, tooth, jaw, throat, lips, tongue; several missing or crooked permanent teeth – includes wearing bridges or false teeth; stuffy, runny nose; or any trouble hearing – includes wearing a hearing aid | −.170 |
| 19 | Taking medication or staying on a prescribed diet for health reasons | −.144 |
| 20 | Wore eyeglasses or contact lenses | −.101 |
| 21 | Breathing smog or unpleasant air | −.101 |
| 22 | No symptoms or problem (not on respondent's card) | −.000 |
| 23 | Standard symptom/problem | −.257 |
| X24 | Trouble sleeping | −.257 |
| X25 | Intoxication | −.257 |
| X26 | Problems with sexual interest or performance | −.257 |
| X27 | Excessive worry or anxiety | −.257 |

Note: X (i.e. X24) indicates a standardized weight and is used because preference studies have not been completed

## 4. Transitions and durations

The final data source considers the transition among states and the duration of stay in the states. This information can come from empirical prospective studies of populations or from judgements obtained from distinguished experts. Consider a person who is limited in ambulation and has pain in both legs. Suppose that this condition described two different individuals – one who was in this condition because of participation in a marathon race and another because of arthritis. The fact that these individuals are in these conditions for different reasons is reflected by different expected transitions to other levels over the course of time. The marathon runner probably is sore from her ordeal, but is expected to be off and running again within a few days. However, the arthritis sufferer will probably continue to convalesce at a low level of function. A General Health Policy Model must consider both current functioning and probability of transition to other function levels over the course of time. When transition is considered and documented in empirical studies, the consideration of a particular diagnosis is no longer needed. We fear diseases because they affect our current functioning, symptoms, or pain either now or at some time in the future. A person at high risk for heart disease may be functioning very well at present, but may have a high probability of transition to a lower level (or death) in the future. Cancer would not be a concern if the disease did not affect current functioning or the probability that functioning would be affected at some future time.

When weights have been properly determined, health status can be expressed precisely as the expected value (product) of the preferences associated with the states of function at a point in time and the probabilities of transition to other states over the remainder of life-expectancy. QWB ($W$) is a static or time-specific measure of function, while the well-life expectancy ($E$) also includes the dynamic or prognostic dimension. The well-life expectancy is the product of QWB and the expected duration of stay in each Function Level over a standard life period and can be expressed as:

$$E = \sum W_K Y_K$$

where
$E$    is the symptom-standardized well-life expectancy in equivalents of completely well-years, and
$Y$    is the expected duration of stay in each function level or case type estimated with an appropriate statistical (preferably stochastic) model.

An example computation of the well-life expectancy is show in Table 3.3. Suppose that a group of individuals was in a well state for 65.2 years, in a state of non-bed disability for 4.5 years, and in a state of bed disability for 1.9 years before their deaths at the average age of 71.6 calendar years. In

**Table 3.3** Illustrative computation of the well-life expectancy

| State | k | $Y_k$ | $W_x$ | $W_xY_k$ |
|-------|---|-------|-------|----------|
| Well | A | 65.2 | 1.00 | 65.2 |
| Non-bed disability | B | 4.5 | 0.59 | 2.7 |
| Bed disability | C | 1.9 | 0.34 | 0.6 |
| Current life expectancy ...................................71.6 life years | | | | |
| Well-life expectancy .......................................68.5 well-years | | | | |

order to make adjustments for the diminished quality of life they suffered in the disability states, the duration of stay in each state is multiplied by the preference associated with the state. Thus, the 4.5 years of non-bed disability become 2.7 equivalents of well-years when we adjust for the preferences associated with inhabiting that state. Overall, the well-life expectancy for this group is 68.5 years. In other words, disability has reduced the adjusted life expectancy by an estimated 3.1 years.

### Estimating the benefit–cost/utility ratio

The concept of a well-life expectancy can be used to evaluate the effectiveness of programmes and health interventions. The output of a programme has been described in a variety of publications as Quality Adjusted Life Years[12], Well-years, Equivalents of Well-years, or Discounted Well-years[16]. Weinstein[67-68] has popularized the concept and calls the same output Quality-Adjusted Life Years (QALYs), and this has been adopted by the Congressional Office of Technology Assessment[54]. It is worth noting that the Quality-Adjusted Life Years terminology was originally introduced by Patrick, Bush and Chen[57], but later abandoned because it has surplus meaning. The term wellness or well-years implies a more direct linkage to health conditions. Whatever the term, the number shows the output of a programme in years of life adjusted by the quality of life which has been lost because of diseases or disability.

By comparing experimental and control groups with a general health status measure, it is possible to estimate the output of a programme in terms of the well-years it produces. This is shown as the area between curves representing the two groups in Figure 3.1. Dividing the cost of the programme by the well-years it yields, gives the Benefit–Cost Utility (BCU) ratio.

There are many attractive elements of general health status measures. We argue that the ultimate purpose of health care and prevention is directed toward two simple objectives: investments in health care are aimed at extending the duration of life, and health care programmes should improve the quality of life while individuals are alive. A comprehensive expression

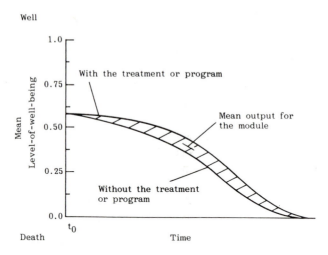

**Figure 3.1** Theoretical comparison of treated and untreated groups. The area between the two curves is the output or benefit of a programme in well-year units. (Reproduced from Ref. 12 with permission)

of health status can determine the effects of a programme using a unit that simultaneously considers risks and benefits. As Mosteller[24] has suggested, specific measures of health outcome often ignore the side-effects of treatment. A treatment for hypertension, for example, may cause gastric irritation, nausea, and bed disability. Health benefits of treatment can be expressed in well-year units, as can health side effects.

## CLINICAL EXAMPLES

This section provides several examples describing how this system might be used to evaluate pharmaceutical products or medical technology. Examples describing the use of the system for the evaluation of health policy alternatives are given elsewhere[3,12].

It is important to emphasize that the QWB scale is the measurement system for a General Health Policy Model. Ultimately, we hope that clinical trials will incorporate these measures so the estimates of treatment effects can be obtained in well-year units. Many of the analyses presented in this section depend upon estimates of QWB scores rather than the actual measurements but are present to emphasize the potential for utilizing quality of life measures for policy studies.

### The tight control of insulin-dependent diabetes mellitus

Several studies have suggested that the degree of hyperglycaemia is associated with the long-term risk of diabetic complications[61]. However, there is no strong experimental evidence confirming that reduction in blood sugar leads to a parallel reduction in diabetic complications. The most frequently cited study purporting to show the benefits of the tight control of diabetes[30] has been aggressively criticized because there were many therapeutic crossovers, data were incomplete, and the difference in blood glucose between experimental and control participants was not large[59]. Other studies have failed to show reversals of microvascular diabetic complications with intensive therapy[7].

The question of tight control of diabetes was considered ambiguous enough for the US National Institutes of Health to begin a prospective clinical trial to evaluate the benefits of tight control versus ordinary care. The trial, known as the Diabetes Control and Complications Trial (DCCT), will include approximately 1400 subjects treated over a 10-year period. We will evaluate a portion of the DCCT subjects using the General Health Policy Model, which may have substantial benefits for estimating treatment benefits. In addition to mortality, diabetes may be associated with poor outcomes in a variety of organ systems. For example, poor control might lead to differential rates of retinopathy, kidney failure, and foot infections. The difficulty is in finding one common expression for these outcomes. Some patients may have foot infections that result in amputations, while others have eye problems that result in blindness. One purpose of our system is to aggregate these outcomes with death to provide a single expression of the impact of poor control. Diabetic coma receives a score of approximately 0.32 on our scale while vision impairment that interferes with driving a car and work, but does not interfere with self-care might receive a score of 0.61. This tells us that two days of diabetic coma add up to less than one day of vision impairment. However, treatment that eliminates diabetic coma (averaged across the duration of the coma) might be considered more valuable than one that reduces vision impairment. The objective is to eliminate any sort of impairment. However, our system does provide for some weighting of the very different outcomes assessed in the study.

The system also includes the capability of expressing side-effects and benefits of treatments in the same unit. For example, suppose that the treatment reduces the probability of retinopathy by 25%. We will assume that 40% of the patients will eventually get serious retinopathy[66]. Suppose further that the retinopathy begins at age 55 and continues until death at age 75. The weight associated with blindness or serious vision impairment might be 0.5. Our system might suggest that the equivalent of chances of developing serious retinopathy (0.4) multiplied by average decrease in well-being over 20 years and then multiplied by the times (0.5) reduction in severity resulting from treatment (0.25) would equal 1.0 well-year. In other words, the improved treatment of diabetes might add up to the equivalent of one healthy year of life expectancy.

Now, we must consider the consequences or side-effects of tight control. For the sake of argument, assume that the intensive treatment begins at age 30. One third of the patients experience nausea and weakness associated with tight control on half of the days. So, let us assume that the duration is 75 – 30 = 45 years, divided by the number of days in which there are symptoms, $0.5 \times 45 = 22.5$ years multiplied by the weight associated with the symptom of sick or upset stomach which is 0.75. The net side effects are 0.33 of all patients $\times$ 22.5 years $\times$ 0.25 average decrease in QWB = 1.87 years. In this example the side-effects might cause a loss of the equivalent of 1.87 years while the benefits produce a benefit of 1.0 years. However, the benefits for other aspects of treatment must also be considered. So, for example, we would also consider the altered probability of kidney disease, heart disease, etc. With these added in, the benefits would most likely outweigh the side-effects.

Ultimately, the net effects of a treatment are expressed in these QALY units. The next question concerns determination of the costs to produce a QALY or well-year unit, from which comparison health care programmes with very different specific objective may be made.

### Auranofin treatment for patients with rheumatoid arthritis

Clinical trials for treatments of rheumatoid arthritis have considered a wide variety of end points. The traditional approach has been to review clinical outcomes such as degree of synovitis. This is typically assessed through tender or swollen joints, grip strength, time to walk 50 feet, or duration of stiffness upon rising in the morning. At an international conference on outcome measurement in arthritis, it was suggested that comprehensive assessments of quality of life outcomes were highly desirable[9]. In a recent clinical trial involving 14 centres, more than 300 patients were randomly assigned to therapy with oral gold (auranofin) or a placebo. A wide variety of traditional and non-traditional measures were used to assess outcome, and among the non-traditional measures was the QWB Scale. The outcome using the QWB is shown graphically in Figure 3.2. There was essentially no change in QWB function for the placebo group while the group receiving auranofin showed a mean improvement of 0.023. This difference was statistically significant beyond the 0.005 level. Auranofin does not reach pharmacologi-cally effective levels in blood until it has been used for about 2 months. It is interesting that QWB scores for the treatment and placebo groups begin to diverge at about 2 months. Considering the many measures used in the trial,

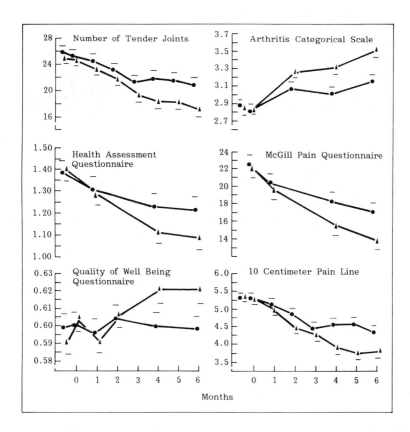

**Figure 3.2** Outcome of patients treated with auranofin (triangles) or placebo (circles) assessed by traditional and non-traditional measures. (Reproduced from Ref. 33 with permission)

the percentage of variance accounted for with the QWB measure was among the very most significant (see Figure 3.2). Outcomes measured using traditional, clinical measures, such as the 50-foot walk and duration of morning stiffness were not statistically significant, although they did favour the auranofin group. In addition, simple self ratings by both patients and physicians failed to detect the significant effect. However, a significant network of associations emerged suggesting that the QWB was associated with other similar measures of general function[10].

It is important to consider the clinical importance of a difference of 0.023. Although this appears to be a small number, the QWB provides a direct translation into clinically meaningful units. A difference of 0.023 translates into 2.3 Quality Adjusted Life Years for each 100 patients who maintain the difference for 1 year. Also, although 0.023 appears to be a small change, the entire continuum from death to optimal health is represented on the 0 to 1.0 scale. The differences observed in the auranofin trial are quite respectable in comparison to those obtained through other medical treatments.

One of the most important aspects of the QWB is its capability of quantifying side-effects as well as benefits. Many of the specific scales used for the auranofin trial were not capable of detecting the general effect of the intervention upon health status. Yet, gold preparations are known to cause significant adverse effects including diarrhoea, headache, rashes, digestive problems and abdominal pain. In fact, 59% of the auranofin treated patients experienced diarrhoea at some point in comparison to 19% of the placebo treated group. The General Health Policy Model allowed these side-effects to be integrated with benefits in order to provide a comprehensive expression of net treatment efficacy[62]. In comparison to control subjects, the costs associated with auranofin treatment were $788 per patient. The investigators estimated the cost/utility of auranofin therapy at just more than $10,000 US dollars per well-year of life. This compared quite favourably to many alternatives in health care.

## Coronary artery bypass grafts or CABG

Despite some controversy[11,28,14], coronary artery bypass graft (CABG) has become a major treatment for symptomatic coronary artery disease. The number of procedures performed in the United States has steadily grown to an estimated 332 000 procedures in 1987 at an estimated cost of $35 000 per operation[64]. The significance of the procedure and expenses associated with it led Weinstein and Stason[67] to conduct a systematic evaluation of the literature on CABG using a cost–utility model with the data provided by clinical reports, systematic longitudinal data banks and clinical trials including the major trials conducted by the European Coronary Surgery Study Group and the Veterans Administrations (VA) Cooperative Study.

The analysis considered the benefit for a 55-year old male population, since 55 years is approximately the median age for receipt of CABG. The analysis considers only those men who would be deemed operable by cardiologists on the basis of clinical characteristics and angiography, and was done separately for men with obstruction (defined as 50% or more) of one, two or three coronary arteries or left main coronary artery disease. In each of these cases, ventricular function was good, with at least a 40% ejection fraction. The analysis for patients with poor ventricular function will not be considered here.

In order to calculate QALYs, Weinstein and Stason needed to integrate morbidity and mortality information. They used data about symptomatic relief from the European study[21,22,13,66] and from the Montreal Heart

Institute[13] and also simulated the benefit results, using a variety of quality judgements for observed levels of functioning and symptomatic angina.

The approach by Weinstein and Stason uses data from different sources. Data from the VA study and the European trial differed in their evaluation of the benefits of surgery for one-vessel and two-vessel disease: the VA data suggest that surgery may be detrimental in these cases, while the European data indicate there will be benefits. Results of these two trials and other data are merged to obtain central assumptions that are operative in the analysis, although the analysis can also consider differing assumptions and the impact these assumptions have upon quality adjusted life expectancy. Under the assumption that the preference for life with angina is 0.7 (on a scale from 0 to 1), Weinstein and Stason estimated the benefits of surgical treatments over medical treatment for the various conditions. They found that the benefits in quality adjusted life years would be 0.5, 1.1, 3.2, and 6.2 years for one vessel, two vessels, three vessels, and left main artery disease respectively.

Next, Weinstein and Stason estimated the cost of the surgery and evaluated cost/utility under the central assumptions. Assuming that the surgery relieves severe angina, the estimates ranged from $30 000/well-year for one vessel disease to $3 800/well-year for left main artery disease. Weinstein and Stason performed these analyses under a variety of assumptions and in doing so, they revealed the impact of considering quality of life. One assumption ignored quality of life and considered only life expectancy. But the cost-effectiveness of bypass surgery for one vessel disease with this assumption cannot be estimated since surgery has no effect upon survival. However, many of the benefits of surgery are directed toward the quality of life rather than survival. If the surgery is performed to relieve mild angina, the cost/utility for one vessel disease exceeds $500 000/well-year (1986 US dollars). A model that did not integrate mortality and morbidity would have missed benefits for some types of surgery.

In summary, the Weinstein and Stason[67] analysis demonstrates that the BCU of CABG differs by characteristic of disease state, but the cost–utility figures compare favourably with those from other widely-advocated medical procedures and screening programmes.


## Adherence to antihypertensive medications

Hypertension is a major public health problem because of its high prevalence and its association with heart disease and stroke. Many people are unaware that they have hypertension, and many of those who are aware are unwilling to take the necessary actions to control the condition.

Weinstein and Stason have calculated the cost–utility for programmes screening severe hypertension (diastolic > 105 mmHg) to be $4850/well-year while the corresponding figure for mild hypertension screening pro-grammes (diastolic 95–104 mmHg) to be $9800/well-year[66].

However, their analysis also considered a variety of factors that influence these cost–utility ratios. One of the most important factors is adherence to the prescribed medical regimen once cases have been detected. The figures given above assume full adherence to the regimen. Yet, substantial evidence reveals that full (100%) adherence is rare[18]. Compliance with antihypertens-ive medications is of particular interest because taking the medication does not relieve symptoms; in fact, medication adherence can increase rather than decrease somatic complaints. More studies have been devoted to compliance among hypertensive patients than to compliance in any other disease category, and some studies suggest that behavioural intervention can be very useful in increasing adherence to prescribed regimens[27].

In their analysis, Weinstein and Stason considered the value of programmes designed to increase adherence to antihypertensive medication. Two separate problems were considered. First, there are drop-outs from treatment, and there is failure to adhere to treatments that have been prescribed. The two cases may differ in their cost. One extreme is the patient who fails to see a physician and purchase medication; here the cost would be very low. The other extreme would be the patient who remains under medical care, purchases medications, but does not take them. In this case, the costs would be high. Weinstein and Stason refer to these as the minimum cost assumption and the maximum cost assumption. Under the minimum cost assumption, patients do not receive the full benefits of medication because of incomplete adherence, but they also do not spend money. Thus according to Weinstein and Stason, the cost-effectiveness under this assumption is very similar to full adherence in which patients receive the benefits of medication but make full expenditures. Under the maximum cost assumption, the effect of incomplete adherence is substantial, particularly for those beginning therapy beyond the age of 50. Earlier, it was noted that the costs to produce a well-year for a national sample (US) were $4850 for those with pretreatment diastolic blood pressure greater than 105 mmHg. With incomplete adherence, these values increase to $6400 under the minimum cost assumption and $10 500 under the maximum cost assumption. For mild hypertensive screening (diastolic blood pressure 95–104 mmHg), the $9880 per well-year under the full adherence assumption rose to $12 500 under the minimum cost assump-tion and $20 400 under the maximum cost assumption.

Since adherence under the maximum cost assumption appears to have a strong affect upon cost-utility, it is interesting to consider the value of behavioural interventions to improve adherence. Several studies have shown the value of behavioural interventions, and it is reasonable to assume that a successful behavioural intervention will improve adherence rates by 50%[27]. Weinstein and Stason considered the cost-utility of interventions that would

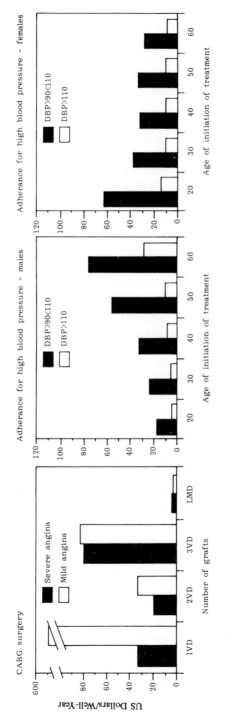

**Figure 3.3** Comparison of cost/utility[a] of CABG: surgery and behavioural interventions for increasing adherence[b] with antihypertensive medications for mean and women( Data for comparisons come from Ref. 72, left panel and Ref. 71 for centre and right panels)

[a] All cost/utility figures adjusted to 1986 dollars

[b] Adherence analyses assume that the programme will increase medication adherence by 50%. These calculations were made under the maximum cost assumption

[c] Severe angina is defined as well-being score of 0.7 on 0–1.0 scale. Mild angina is defined as 0.9 on the same scale.

improve adherence by 50% under the maximum cost assumption. Their analysis of hypothetical programmes that would reduce diastolic blood pressure from 110 mmHg to 90 mmHg suggest a differential expected cost-utility for programmes designed for males and for females. As the figure shows, the intervention would improved the cost-utility for both males and females and at each age of therapy reveals the finding from epidemiological studies that blood pressure is better controlled in women than in men. In summary, the analysis demonstrates that even an expensive programme can improve cost-utility because it produces substantial improvements in outcome relative to its costs.

In the Weinstein and Stason monograph, a variety of other hypothetical conditions were considered. Under the assumption that the programme improves adherence by 50%, a significant benefit of the programme remained under the maximum cost assumption. However, under the minimum cost assumption, the hypothetical adherence intervention would have a significant benefit if it increased adherence by 50% but no significant effect if it increased adherence by only 20%.

Other assumptions in the Weinstein and Stason analysis need to be considered. For example, they make (and discuss) many other assumptions about the relationship between hypertension and outcome, the linear relationship between adherence and outcome, and the effect of adherence programmes. Some data support the reasonableness of each of these assumptions.

Figure 3.3 shows how very different programmes can be compared using the system, and summarizes the two Weinstein and Stason studies discussed above.

## The Acquired Immunodeficiency Syndrome (AIDS)

The Acquired Immune Deficiency Syndrome (AIDS), resulting from infection with the human immunodeficiency virus (HIV) represents one of the most important threats to the world population in the 1990s. The Centers for Disease Control estimates that between one and two million Americans are currently infected with HIV[15]. In April 1990 CDC reported that 50 000 people had died from AIDS and that one million new cases were expected by 1992.

In addition to opportunistic infections and malignancies which define AIDS, HIV infection may cause a broad range of disease. These conditions include persistent lymphadenopathy, thrombocytopenia, immune complex disease, wasting, various constitutional symptoms and HIV neurological diseases. The impact of HIV infection on functioning is equally diverse. For example, HIV infection may result in fatigue, arthritis, blindness, memory loss, or paraplegia. Treatments for HIV infection should be designed to prevent early mortality and to reduce morbidity during periods before death. The diverse impacts of both HIV disease and its treatment require a general approach to assessment.

There have been several previous attempts to evaluate quality of life in HIV infected patients. However, most of these have focused on psychological outcomes. Few studies have attempted to characterize the health status and economic impacts of HIV infection, and we are aware of only three studies that have applied general health-related quality of life scales.

Since September 1987, AZT has been available by prescription to treat patients with advanced HIV infection. This decision was based on the encouraging results of early clinical trials. In the multicentre phase II AZT trial, 19 of 137 placebo recipients died as compared to 1 of 145 AZT recipients. The incidence of opportunistic infections was also significantly reduced among AZT recipients. Thus, in certain groups of patients, AZT may profoundly lower both mortality and morbidity[25]. However, serious side-effects are frequently associated with AZT, including anaemia, neutropenia, nausea, myalgia, insomnia, and severe headache. Nearly one-third (31%) of patients who received AZT required blood transfusions for anaemia[58].

In the San Diego arm of the multicentre AZT trial, Wu et al. obtained outcome data using the QWB and the Karnofsky Performance Status measure[70]. The participants in the study were 31 patients (27 male, 4 female) with a clinical diagnosis of either AIDS or severe AIDS Related Complex (ARC). They were randomly assigned to receive AZT treatment or placebo and were evaluated using the QWB before beginning the trial and at eight follow-up visits over the next 52 weeks. The value of the treatment was estimated using the repeated measures analysis of variance (calculated using a general linear model).

The patients were divided into those with CD4 cell (also know as $T_4$ lymphocytes or T-helper cells) counts less than or greater than $100 \times 10^9$ L. Patients in both groups were comparable at baseline with regard to age, CD4 group, sex, diagnosis (AIDS or ARC), Karnofsky score, and QWB ($t$-test and chi-square, $p > 0.15$). In fact, mean initial CD4 count was significantly higher in the AZT group ($t < 0.3$).

For the QWB measure, the repeated measures ANOVA showed a significant effect of time and an interaction between group and time of testing. This interaction, illustrated in Figure 3.4, is the crucial component in evaluating treatment effectiveness. It suggests that there was a differential rate of change between AZT treated and control groups. As Figure 3.4 demonstrates, QWB scores remained relatively constant over the course of time for the AZT group, while they declined substantially for the placebo group.

These results suggest that the QWB can detect strong treatment effects associated with AZT treatment. One advantage of the QWB system is that it

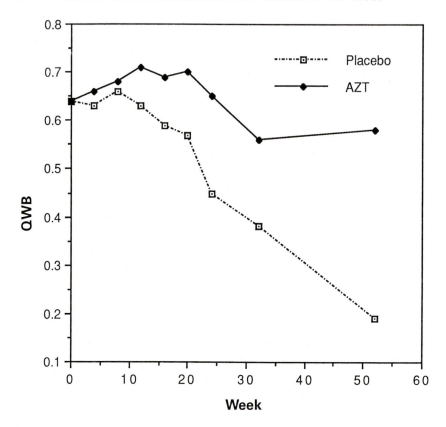

**Figure 3.4** QWB outcomes of AIDS patients treated with AZT or placebo

allows the expression of programme benefits in terms of well-year units and the comparison of treatment alternatives that are very different from one another. In the AZT trial, the placebo-treated group experienced substantial mortality and greater morbidity than the AZT group. Neither measures of mortality alone, nor of morbidity alone, were capable of detecting the potent treatment effect of this medication, as could the QWB. Further, the comprehensive measure takes the side-effects of AZT into account and expresses outcome as the net benefits minus adverse effects.

### The neonatal circumcision controversy

There has been a long standing debate about the medical indications for neonatal circumcision. In 1971, the American Academy of Pediatrics concluded that there were no medically valid reasons for performing circumcisions on newborn males[1]. This position was confirmed by the American College of Obstetrics and Gynecology in 1978[65]. However, an important paper by Wiswell[69] suggested a tenfold increase in urinary tract infections for uncircumcised male infants. As a result of these data, new questions about an old controversy began to arise.

Recently a cost–utility analysis was performed in order to estimate the total health effects and the total costs of neonatal circumcision. The analysis considered the cost of the procedure, the pain associated with the procedure, the probability of urinary tract infections, and the risks of developing cancer of the penis. With the base assumptions, the net discounted lifetime US dollar costs associated with neonatal circumcision were relatively low ($102 US/person). However, the discounted lifetime health costs were also quite low. Under the base assumptions, the expected health loss is about 14 hours of well-life expectancy.

In cases such as the evaluation of neonatal circumcision, it is unlikely that a true randomized trial will ever be conducted. Therefore, the analysis typically considers outcomes under a variety of circumstances. However we are often uncertain about the accuracy of these assumptions. In order to deal with the uncertainty, the assumptions are varied. In the circumcision example, the base analysis assumed that the probability of developing cancer if uncircumcised is 0.0001 while the probability for those who are circumcised is essentially 0.000. In the sensitivity analysis, it was assumed that the probability of developing cancer if uncircumcised is more severe. For example, it may be as high as 1/600 or 0.00167. The development of cancer may also have important cost implications. In the base case it was assumed that the work up and treatment costs would be $25 000. The sensitivity analysis considered a lower estimate of $10 000 and a higher estimate of $100 000. Many variables are considered in the sensitivity analyses. For example, the cost of the procedure is considered to be $150 US dollars in the base case while in the sensitivity analysis a lower cost of $50 was also included. The traditional method for comparing a value to be received in the future (e.g. medical expenses overted) with a value to be given at the present time (in this case the cost of the circumcision) is discounting. With the aim of looking at future gains and comparing them with the amount of money currently at hand, compound discount-rate multipliers are typically included in the analysis. In this analysis discount rates in the base case were 5% while a discount rate of 0% was considered for the sensitivity analysis. The discount rate multipliers were also used with the number of well-years produced. Under the base case assumptions, the costs of routine neonatal circumcision of 1000 newborns are $102 451 and the effects are an average loss of 1.61 well-years. Any programme that damages health as a function of treatment is not advisable. However, under some assumptions, the analysis suggests more benefits. For example, in the case that a patient needs a second circumcision and experiences symptoms for 120 days prior to the second operation, the cost–utility ratio is $18 463/well-year. If the cost of the later circumcision is $5000 US dollars, then the cost–utility ratio becomes $45 673/well-year. The base case assumes that the cost of circumcision is $150 US dollars. Although the cost/utility of the procedure in the base case is questionable, reducing the cost of the procedure to $50 US dollars makes the intervention look more worthwhile at $9054/well-year. The advantage is because money is saved, not because better health is achieved. Overall, the financial and medical advantages of neonatal circumcision cancel each other out. In this case cost/utility analysis helped clarify that the issue is not one of economics or medical outcome. Instead, the debate must be focused on personal preference and social custom[26].

### Policy space for benefit–cost/utility analysis

A two-dimensional health policy space (Figure 3.5), where costs (C) are subtracted from benefits (B) to establish consistency in signs, provides a useful analytic framework for analysing resource allocation and related problems. Net dollar returns (R) per person, where (R = B − C) are plotted on the X-axis, and well-years gained or lost per person (Y) are plotted on the Y-axis. Any alternative action (whether treatment, programme, or policy) can be located in this space according to its dollar return and well-years produced or lost.

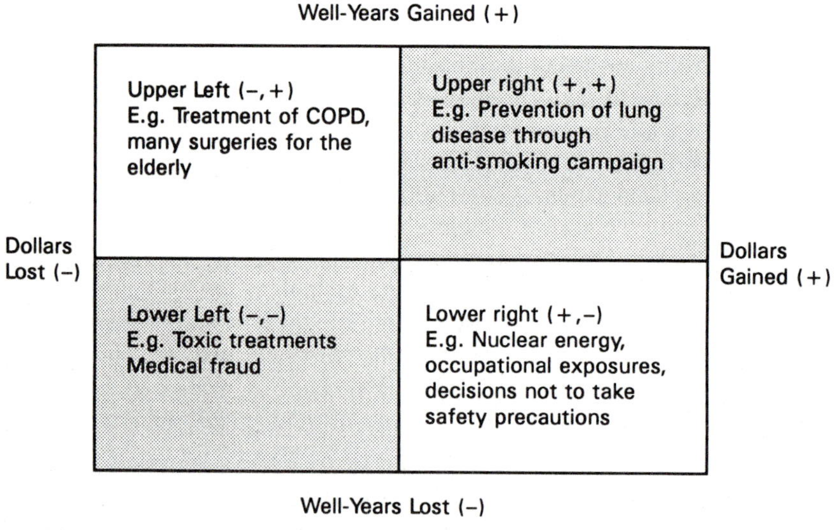

Well-Years Gained ( + )

| | |
|---|---|
| Upper Left (−, +)<br>E.g. Treatment of COPD,<br>many surgeries for the<br>elderly | Upper right ( +, + )<br>E.g. Prevention of lung<br>disease through<br>anti-smoking campaign |
| Lower Left (−,−)<br>E.g. Toxic treatments<br>Medical fraud | Lower right ( +,−)<br>E.g. Nuclear energy,<br>occupational exposures,<br>decisions not to take<br>safety precautions |

Dollars Lost (−)            Dollars Gained ( + )

Well-Years Lost (−)

**Figure 3.5** Two-dimensional policy space. (Adapted from Anderson *et al.*, Ref 3)

Alternatives with net economic benefits ($B > C$) fall in the right half of the plane, while programmes with net costs ($C > B$) fall in the left half. Medical treatment and such things as social policies with positive health effects ($+Y$) fall in the upper half of the plane, while alternatives (policies or practices) with negative health consequences ($-Y$) fall in the lower half.

The left upper quadrant ($-, +$) represents the area for standard BCU analysis, where dollars are being spent to produce well-years, and the negative ratios represent the relative efficiency of the programmes. In the absence of interdependencies and other non-linear constraints, the simple BCU algorithm identifies the optimal set of alternatives within a single budget limit. The left (Figure 3.5) lower quadrant ($-, -$) represents unsatisfactory alternatives where dollars are being spent and well-years are being lost. While unusual, this would include ineffective treatments or practices that incur expense and actually do harm.

The right lower quadrant ($+, -$) represents trade-offs of economic benefits for health as in policies involving nuclear power, pollution control, occupational, environmental and consumer product safety, highway speed limits, the construction of overpasses and aircraft runways. Analytically, society is willing to sacrifice some well-years in return for substantial economic benefits. The General Health Policy Model can contribute to the analysis of such issues generally. All alternatives in the right upper quadrant of policy space ($+, +$) produce not only well-years but also net dollar returns. The ratio of costs to benefits makes sense in the left upper and right lower quadrants of the policy space, but not in the right upper and left lower, where the outcomes are in a general sense additive (dollar returns plus well-years in the right upper quadrant, dollar costs in addition to well-year losses in the left lower)[3].

## SUMMARY

This chapter summarizes some of our current thinking on the potential for a general health policy model. We believe the system can be used as an aid for understanding clinical problems. In our previous work, we have documented the validity[43] and the reliability[5] of the measurement system. In addition, systematic evaluations of the question structure and reliability of administration have been performed[2]. Although some authors[9] suggest that the interview procedure is long and tedious, there is substantial evidence that the extra effort results in greater precision of the instrument[2].

Quality of life is clearly a multi-dimensional construct. However, there is still considerable debate about whether or not multi-dimensional measures are required. Some approaches, such as the SIP, represent the multi-dimensionality by providing quality of life profiles. Other approaches, including our own, attempt to map the multi-dimensional construct of well-being onto a unidimensional scale of preference or desirability. The choice of a unidimensional versus a multidimensional approach depends on the purpose of the study. Multidimensional approaches may provide more clinical diagnostic information about areas in which there are specific problems, for example, the clinician may learn that arthritis patients have difficulty in ambulation but not in sleep. The unidimensional approach is better suited for policy analysis and comparisons of very different alternatives in health care. A related issue is the specificity of the measure. Some investigators prefer measures specific to the symptoms associated with a particular disease. However, we favour the more general approach because it captures both benefits and side-effects (both expected and unexpected) in a single, comprehensive unit. Clearly, the debate will continue on the value of many competing quality of life measures. Future research is required to identify the reliability of preference weights, the value of general versus specific measures, and the desirability of interviewer-administered versus self-administered questionnaires. We also need to learn more about issues of discounting, the comparability of different measures, and the value of economic valuation methods. The inclusion of general quality of life measures in systematic clinical trials will help elucidate many of these issues.

In this paper we offer several suggestions for the use of the QWB in clinical studies. Current research is often divided between measurement studies and policy analysis. The General Health Policy Model includes the measurement system described here. When taken in clinical studies, QWB measurements can be used directly in policy analysis. However, few clinical studies have taken QWB measures directly. We hope to see a wider application of quality of life measurement in future clinical studies.

## References

1. American Academy of Pediatrics, Committee on Fetus and Newborn. *Hospital Care of Newborn Infants*, 5th Edn. American Academy of Pediatrics, Winston, IL., 1971: p. 110.
2. Anderson, J.P., Bush, J.W. and Berry, C.C. Classifying function for health outcome and quality-of-life evaluation. Self versus individual models. *Med. Care* 1986; 24: 454–469.
3. Anderson, J.P., Bush, J.W., Chen, M. and Dolenc, D. Policy space areas and properties of BCU analysis. *J. Am. Med. Assoc.* 1986; 255: 794–795.
4. Anderson, J.P., Kaplan, R.M. and DeBon, M. Comparison of responses to similar questions in health surveys. In Fowler, F. (ed.), *Health Survey Research Methods*. Washington, DC, National Center For Health Statistics, 1989, pp. 13–21.
5. Anderson, J.P., Kaplan, R.M., Berry, C.C., Bush, J.W. and Rumbaut, R.G. Interday reliability of function assessment for a health status measure: The quality of well-being scale. *Med. Care* 1989; 27: 1076–1084.
6. Balaban, D.J., Fagi, P.C., Goldfarb, N.I. and Nettler, S. Weights for scoring the

quality of well-being instrument among rheumatoid arthritics. *Med. Care* 1986; 24: 973–980.

7.  Ballugooie, E. *et. al.* Rapid deterioration of diabetic retinopathy during treatment with continuous subcutaneous insulin infusion. *Diabetes Care* 7: 236–242.

8.  Bergner, M., Bobbitt, R.A., Carter, W.B. and Gilson, B.S. The Sickness Impact Profile; development and final revision of a health status measure. *Med. Care* 1981; 19: 787–805.

9.  Bombardier, C., Tugwell, P., Sinclair, A. *et. al.* Preference for endpoint measures in clinical trials: results of structured workshops. *J. Rheumatol.* 1982; 9: 798–801.

10.  Bombardier, C., Ware, J., Russell, I.J. *et. al.* Auranofin therapy and quality of life for patients with rheumatoid arthritis: Results of a multicenter trial. *Am. J. Med.*, 1986; 81: 565–578.

11.  Braumwald, E. Coronary artery surgery at the crossroad. *N. Engl. J. Med.* 1977; 661–663.

12.  Bush, J.W., Chen, M. and Patrick, D.L. Cost-effectiveness using a health status index: Analysis of the New York State PKU screening program. In Berg, R. (ed.), *Health Status Index*. Chicago, Hospital Research and Educational Trust, 1983, pp. 172–208.

13.  Campeau, L., Lesteiance, J., Hermann, J. *et. al.* Loss of the improvement of angina between one and seven years after aortocoronary bypass surgery. *Circulation* (Suppl. 1), 1979; 60: 1–5.

14.  CASS Principle Investigators and their Associates. Coronary artery surgery study (CASS): A randomized trial of coronary artery bypass survival data. *Circulation* 1983; 68: 939.

15.  Centers for Disease Control Mortality Attributable to HIV infection/AIDS United States, 1981–1990 *Morbidity and Mortality Weekly Report* 40(3), 1991, p. 41.

16.  Chen, M. and Bush, J.W. Maximizing health system output with political and administrative constraints using mathematical programming. *Inquiry* 1976; 13: 215–227.

17.  Chen, M.M., Bush, J.W. and Patrick, D.L. Social indicators for health planning and policy analysis. *Policy Sci.* 1975; 6: 71–89.

18.  DiMatteo, M.R. and DiNicola, D.E. *Achieving Patient Compliance*. Elmsford, NY, Pergamon Press, 1982.

19.  Erickson, P., Kendall, E.A., Anderson, J.P. and Kaplan, R.M. Using composite health status measures to assess the nation's health. *Med. Care* 1989; 27 (Suppl 3): S66–S76.

20.  Erickson, P., Anderson, J.P., Kendall, E.A., Kaplan, R.M. and Ganiats, T.G. Using retrospective data for measuring quality of life: National health interview survey data and the quality of well-being scale. *Quality of Life and Cardiovascular Care* 1988; 4 (4): 179–184.

21.  European Coronary Surgery Study Group. Coronary-artery bypass surgery in stable angina pectoris: Survival at two years. *Lancet* 1979; 1: 889–893.

22.  European coronary Surgery Study Group. Prospective randomized study of coronary artery bypass surgery in stable angina pectoris. *Lancet* 1980; 2: 491–495.

23.  Fanshel, S. and Bush, J.W. A health status index and its applications to health-services outcomes. *Operations Res.* 1970; 18: 1021–1066.

24. Fielding, J.E. Smoking, health effects and control. *N. Engl. J. Med.* 1985; 313: 491–498.

25. Fischl, M.A., Richman, D.D., Grieco, M.H. *et. al.* The efficiency of azidothy-midine (AZT) in the treatment of patients with AIDS and AIDS-related complex: a double-blind, placebo-controlled trial. *N. Engl. J. Med.* 1987; 317: 185–191.

26. Ganiats, T.G., Humphrey, J.D.C., Tares, H.L. and Kaplan, R.M. Routine neonatal circumcision: A cost-utility analysis. *Medical Decision Making*, 1991; 11: 282–293.

27. Haynes, R.B., Sackett, D.L., Gibson, E.S., Taylor, D.W., Hackett, B.C., Roberts, R.S. and Johnson, A.L. Improvement of medication compliance in uncontrolled hypertension. *Lancet* 1976; 1: 1265–1268.

28. Hultgren, H.N., Shettigar, R. and Miller, D.C. Medical versus surgical treatment of unstable angina. *Am. J. Cardiol.* 1982; 50: 663–670.

29. Jaffe, N. *Cataract Surgery and its Complications* (3rd edn). St Louis, C.V. Mosby, 1981.

30. Job, D., Eschwege, B., Guyot-Argenton, C., Aubry, J.P. and Tchobroutsky, G. Effect of multiple daily injections on the course of diabetic retinopathy. *Diabetes* 1976; 25: 463–469.

31. Kaplan, R.M. Human preference measurement for health decisions and the evaluation of long-term care. In Kane, R.L. and Kane, R.A. (eds), *Values and Long-term Care.* Lexington, Mass, Lexington Books, 1982, pp. 157–188.

32. Kaplan, R.M. Quantification of health outcomes for policy studies in behavioral epidemiology. In Kaplan, R.M. and Criqui, M.H. (eds), *Behavioral Epidemiology and Disease Prevention.* New York, Plenum, 1985.

33. Kaplan, R.M. Quality-of-life measurement. In Karoly, P. (ed.) *Measurement Strategies in Health Psychology.* New York, Wiley-Interscience, 1985, pp. 115–146.

34. Kaplan, R.M. Behavior as a central outcome in health care. *Am. Psychologist* 1990; 45: 1211–1220.

35. Kaplan, R.M. Value for money in management of HIV: Health-related quality of life. In Maynard, A. (ed.) *Economic Aspects of HIV Management.* London, Colwood Press, 1991.

36. Kaplan, R.M. and Anderson, J.P. A general health policy model: Update and applications. *Health Serv. Res.* 1988; 23(2): 203.

37. Kaplan, R.M. and Anderson, J.P. The general health policy model: An integrated approach. In Spilker, B. (ed.), *Quality of Life Assessments in Clinical Trials.* New York, Raven Press, 1990, pp. 131–149.

38. Kaplan, R.M. and Bush, J.W. Health-related quality of life measurement for evaluation research and policy analysis. *Health Psychol.* 1982; 1: 61–80.

39. Kaplan, R.M. and Ernst, J.A. Do category scales produce biased preference weights for a health index? *Med. Care* 1983; 21: 193–207.

40. Kaplan, R.M., Anderson, J.P. and Erickson, P. Estimating well-years of life for a new public health indicator. *Proceedings of the 1989 Public Health Conference on Records and Statistics.* HDDS, National Center for Health Statistics. DHHS Publication Number (PHS) 90–1214, 1989, pp. 298–303.

41. Kaplan, R.M., Anderson, J.P., Wu, A.W., Matthews, W.C., Kozin, F. and

Orenstein, D. The quality of well-being scale: Applications in AIDS, cystic fibrosis, and arthritis. *Med. Care* 1989; 27 (Suppl 3): S27–S43.

42. Kaplan, R.M., Atkins, C.J. and Timms, R.M. Validity of a quality of well-being scale as an outcome measure in chronic obstructive pulmonary disease. *J. Chronic Dis.* 1984; 37: 85–95.

43. Kaplan, R.M., Bush, J.W. and Berry, C.C. Health status: Types of validity for an index of well-being. *Health Serv. Res.* 1976; 11: 478–507.

44. Kaplan, R.M., Bush, J.W. and Berry, C.C. The reliability, stability, and generalizability of a health status index. *American Statistical Association, Proceedings of the Social Statistics Section* 1978, pp. 704–709.

45. Kaplan, R.M., Bush, J.W. and Berry, C.C. Health status index: Category rating versus magnitude estimation for measuring levels of well-being. *Med. Care* 1979; 5: 501–523.

46. Kaplan, R.M., Kozin, F. and Anderson, J.P. Measuring quality of life in arthritis patients (including discussion of a general health-decision model). *Quality of Life and Cardiovasc. Care* 1988; 4: 131–139.

47. Kaplan, R.M., Ries, A and Atkins, C.J. Behavioral management of chronic obstructive pulmonary disease. *Ann. Intern. Med.* 1985; 7: 5–10.

48. Klein, R. and Klein, B. Vision disorders in diabetes. In *National Diabetes Data Group – Diabetes in America*, NIH Publication, 1985, pp. 85–1468.

49. Liang, M.H., Katz, and Ginsburg, Chronic rheumatic disease. In Spilker, B. (ed.) *Quality of Life Assessment in Clinical Trials*. New York, Raven Press, 1990, pp. 441–458.

50. Meenan, R.F. AIMS approach to health status measurement; Conceptual background and measurement properties. *J. Rheumatol.* 1982; 9: 785–788.

51. Mosteller, R. Innovation and evaluation. *Science* 1981; 211: 881–886.

52. Mulrow, C.D., Aguilar, C., Endicott, J.E., Tuley, M.R., Velez, R., Charlip, W.S., Rhodes, M.C., Hill, J.A. and DeNino, L.A. Quality-of-life changes and hearing impairment. A randomized trial. *Ann. Intern. Med.* 1990 Aug 1; 113(3): 188–194.

53. National Institutes of Health. *Epidemiology of Respiratory Diseases Task Force Report*. Washington, DC, US Government Printing Office, 1979.

54. Office of Technology Assessment, US Congress. *A Review of Selected Federal Vaccine and Immunication Policies: Bases on Case Studies of Pneumococcal Vaccine*. Washington, DC, US Government Printing Office, 1979.

55. Orenstein, D.M., Nixon, P.A., Ross, E.A. and Kaplan, R.M. The quality of well-being in cystic fibrosis. *Chest* 1989; 95: 344–347.

56. Orenstein, D.M., Pattishall, E.N., Ross, E.A. and Kaplan, R.M. Quality of well-being before and after antibiotic treatment of pulmonary exacerbation in cystic fibrosis. *Chest* 1990; 98: 1081–1084.

57. Patrick, D.L., Bush, J.W. and Chen, M.M. Toward an operational definition of health. *J. Health Social Behav.* 1973; 14: 6–23.

58. Richman, D.D., Fischl, M.A., Grieco, M.H. *et. al.* The toxicity of azidothymidine (AZT) in the treatment of patients with AIDS and AIDS-related complex: a double-blind, placebo-controlled trial. *N. Engl. J. Med.* 1987; 317: 192–197.

59. Schade, D., Santiago, J., Skyler, J. and Rizza, R. Effects of intensive treatment

on long-term complications. In *Intensive Insulin Therapy*. *Princeton Excerpta Medica*, 1983, Chapter 5.

60. Tarlov, A.R., Ware, J.E., Greenfield, S. *et. al.* The Medical Outcome Study: An application of methods for monitoring the results of medical care. *J. Am. Med. Assoc.* 1989; 262: 925–930.

61. Tchobroutsky, G. Relation of diabetic control to development of microvascular complications. *Diabetologia* 1978; 15: 143–152.

62. Thompson, M.S., Read, J.L., Hutchings, H.C., Patterson, M. and Harris, E.D., Jr. The cost-effective of auranofin: results of a randomized clinical trial. *J. Rheumatol.* 1988; 15: 35–42.

63. Torrance, G.W. Utility approach to measuring health-related quality of life. *J. Chronic Dis.* 1987; 40: 593–600.

64. Vital and Health Statistics: National Hospital Discharge Survey, 1987, Series 13, US DHHS, Publication No. (PHS) 89–1760, April 1989.

65. Wallerstein, E. Circumcision – The Unique American Medical Enigma. *Urol. Clin. N. Am.* 1985; 12: 123–132.

66. Weinstein, M.C. and Stason, W.B. *Hypertension: A Policy Perspective*. Cambridge, Mass., Harvard University Press, 1976.

67. Weinstein, M.C. and Stason, W.B. Cost-effectiveness of coronary artery bypass surgery. *Circulation* 1982 (Suppl. 3): 56–66.

68. Weinstein, M.C. and Stason, W.B. Cost-effectiveness of interventions to prevent or treat coronary heart disease. *Am. Rev. Publ. Health* 1985; 6: 41–63.

69. Wiswell, T.E. and Roscelli, J.D. Corroborative evidence for the decrease evidence of urinary tract infections in circumcised male infants. *Pediatrics* 1986; 78: 96–99.

70. Wu, A.W., Matthews, W.C., Brysk, L.T., Atkinson, J.H., Grant, I., Abramson, I., Kennedy, C.J., McCutchan, J.A., Spector, S.A. and Richman, D.D. Quality of life in a placebo-controlled trial of zidovudine in patients with AIDS and AIDS-related complex. *J. Acquired Immune Deficiency Syndromes* 1990; 3(7): 683–690.

# 4 Development, testing, and use of the Sickness Impact Profile *

**Marilyn Bergner**

---

The Sickness Impact Profile (SIP) is a behaviourally based measure of health-related dysfunction. In its final version it consists of 136 items grouped into 12 categories. Three of the categories can be aggregated into a physical dimension; four others into a psychosocial dimension. The remaining five categories cannot be aggregated into a coherent and consistent dimension. A percentage score may be obtained for the entire measure, each of the 12 categories, and the two dimensions. (See Table 4.1 for samples of SIP items grouped by category and dimension.)

The SIP may be self or interviewer administered. In either case, it is meant to be answered by the respondent about himself. The respondent agrees to an item, which is in the form of a first person singular statement, if it applies to him and is related to his health.

## Rationale for development of the Sickness Impact Profile

The SIP was developed in order to provide a measure of health status that would be useful in the assessment of individuals or populations with chronic as well as acute illness. Such a measure was thought to be necessary in order to evaluate clinical interventions and changes in health services delivery, to help in planning services, and to examine cost-effectiveness of new therapies.

A major influence in the development of the SIP was the clinical experience of the physicians who initially expressed the need for a new measure of outcome that addressed the impacts of disease and treatment of the chronically ill. Betty and John Gilson had noted in their respective medical practices, that patients often seem to improve in terms of the activities they undertake, yet their medical condition or pain and symptoms may remain unchanged.

---

* Major portions of this paper have been reported in Refs 3 and 5.

**Table 4.1** Sickness Impact Profile categories and selected items

| Category | Items describing behaviour related to | Selected items |
|---|---|---|
| SR | Sleep and Rest | I sit during much of the day<br>I sleep or nap during the day |
| E | Eating | I am eating no food at all, nutrition is taken through tubes or intravenous fluids<br>I am eating special or different food |
| W | Work | I am not working at all<br>I often act irritable toward my work associates |
| HM | Home Management | I am not doing any of the maintenance or repair work around the house that I usually do<br>I am not doing heavy work around the house |
| RP | Recreation and Pastimes | I am going out for entertainment less<br>I am not doing any of my usual physical recreation or activities |
| A | Ambulation | I walk shorter distances or stop to rest often<br>I do not walk at all |
| M | Mobility | I stay within one room<br>I stay away from home only for brief periods of time |
| BCM | Body Care and Movement | I do not bathe myself at all, but am bathed by someone else<br>I am very clumsy in body movements |
| SI | Social Interaction | I am doing fewer social activities with groups of people<br>I isolate myself as much as I can from the rest of the family |
| AB | Alertness Behaviour | I have difficulty reasoning and solving problems, for example, making plans, making decisions, learning new things<br>I sometimes behave as if I were confused or disorientated in place or time, for example, where I am, who is around, directions, what day it is |
| EB | Emotional Behaviour | I laugh or cry suddenly<br>I act irritable and impatient with myself, for example, talk badly about myself, swear at myself, blame myself for things that happen |
| C | Communication | I am having trouble writing or typing<br>I do not speak clearly when I am under stress |

They reasoned that a systematic knowledge of the behaviour of patients would help assess new or altered treatment, changes in delivery of medical care, and could even be used to plot the impacts of a disease as it progressed.

## Conceptual basis for the Sickness Impact Profile

Performance has several attributes that make it potentially useful as a basis for development of an outcome measure of health care. Performance or behaviour may be reported directly by the individual under consideration; it may also be observed and reported by another respondent about the individual under consideration; it may be affected by medical treatment even though the disease itself may be unaffected; it can be measured whether or not the individual is receiving medical care; and a measure based on performance or behaviour permits the relating of diverse definitions of disease and sickness, by uncovering universal patterns of behavioural dysfunction[13].

Health-related behavioural dysfunction is a concept both familiar and relevant to the individual. As the basis for health status assessment, it assures measurement of significant events from the societal, individual and health care points of view. Health and sickness undoubtedly affect behaviour and role performance. The healthy individual may be thought of as behaving without limitation and, therefore, functioning optimally. The sick individual may be thought of as behaving with limitation and, therefore, exhibiting dysfunction.

### A model of sickness behaviour

A model for measuring sickness-related behaviour should be independent of the conception of health, the health care system or care-seeking behaviour. Such a model should be universally applicable and, in conjunction with the concepts of health, it forms the basis for the development of a useful measure of health outcome. Such a model is presented in Figure 4.1.

In transforming this model into the framework for developing an outcome measure of health, sickness impacts were conceptualized as changes in behaviour associated with carrying out one's daily life activities. These changes in behaviour were considered dysfunctions since they represent deviations from the way an individual usually behaves. Thus, although these changes in behaviour may be functional in accelerating the return to good health, they are dysfunctional in the sense that they represent impaired or ineffective role performance, and it is in this latter sense that the term dysfunction is used here.

The transformation of the model into a set of working definitions is shown in Figure 4.2. Signs and Symptoms are defined as those found in oral reports and/or written records of individuals, patients, doctors, folk healers, nurses, and others. Sickness is defined as an individual's own perception of his health.

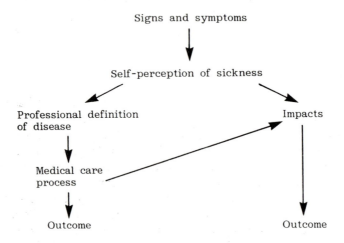

**Figure 4.1** Diagrammatic representation of a model of sickness behaviour

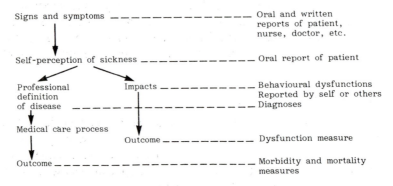

**Figure 4.2** Transformation of a model of sickness behaviour into a set of working definitions

Disease measures are defined as different diagnoses and their severity. Sickness impact is defined as self-reports of dysfunction, clinical reports of dysfunction and tests of dysfunction using other instruments.

These working definitions may be converted into measures with the expectation that they will individually and collectively relate to the dysfunction measure so as to permit a series of validation studies. Such studies are essential to determine both the specificity and sensitivity of the measure and must occur before its generalised use. This assumes, of course, that in addition to assessing the sensitivity of the measure to change, its reliability in terms of reproducibility has also been determined.

## METHODS USED TO DEVELOP THE SICKNESS IMPACT PROFILE

The intent to develop a behaviourally-based measure for assessing the impact of sickness that is comprehensive in scope and applicability, and that is sensitive in detailing the kind and degree of impact, raises the question of what sources to tap to assure a representative catalogue of sickness impacts.

Most function assessment measures are based on statements of dysfunction devised by experts and are principally concerned with the extremely dysfunctional individual. Ideally the measure should be based on all-inclusive, though non-duplicative, list of health-related dysfunctions that cover the range from minimal to maximal dysfunction. Such data could be obtained from self-reports, from reports based on clinical observation or observation by other trained observers, from reports of 'significant others', such as family members, and from existing measures of behavioural dysfunction (see Refs 1, 7, 8, 11, 15, 17-19, 24, 25). This catalogue of sickness-related behaviours could be assembled in an instrument that would measure the impact of sickness on a given individual as perceived by the respondent. Such an empirical approach to extensive sampling of behavioural impacts of sickness appeared to be indicated in the development of the SIP.

### Obtaining the statements

A procedure was devised to obtain statements describing sickness-related changes in behaviour, i.e. sickness-related dysfunction, from patients, health care professionals, individuals caring for patients, and the apparently healthy. Several open-ended request forms were developed. One of each of these forms was directed to health care professionals, to patients, and to significant others accompanying patients for care. Data were collected at several out-patient clinics, a walk-in clinic, a private partnership practice and a prepaid group practice.

Over 1100 completed request forms were collected. Sampling continued until the yield of new and usable statements diminished markedly. As a final step in the empirical search, existing catalogues of behavioural dysfunction related to illness were reviewed and statements were added to the empirically obtained catalogue.

### Processing the raw data

Data obtained in the search were subjected to the following set of criteria to provide a basic catalogue of statements to be used in the prototype SIP. Each statement must (a) describe the behaviour, and (b) specify the nature of the dysfunction. Dysfunction was defined as including modification or impairment in degree or manner of carrying on an activity, cessation of an activity, or initiation of a new activity that interferes with or substitutes for a usual activity.

Statements obtained from the entire sample of subjects, and from the literature, were processed according to these criteria into a set of potential items for inclusion in the prototype instrument. Statements were examined by five staff members. Working independently and then together, they eliminated or re-phrased statements that were ambiguous or were not expressed in sufficiently explicit behavioural terms. During this process, statements considered virtual duplicates were eliminated, and statements that were similar but in which there were significant shades of difference were rewritten to make the differences clear. An item to be used in the SIP had to be unique in terms of at least one of the following criteria: in the behaviour it described, in the nature of the dysfunction described, or in the degree of dysfunction specified.

On completion of this process, the items were sorted independently by each of the five staff members. Items were grouped together if they seemed to refer to a common type of activity. Agreement among staff members on the grouping of items was analysed. The minimum criterion for retaining a pair of items in the same group was agreement by at least three of the five staff members.

In this manner a prototype measure consisting of 312 items grouped into 14 categories was devised.


**Scaling and scoring**

For the instrument to be useful in measuring outcomes, a method of scoring the responses of an individual to the SIP statements was needed. Obviously, the difference between a minor impact of sickness such as walking shorter distances, and a major one, such as not walking at all, had to be recognized in the scoring process in order to convey useful information in a quantitative way. For this reason procedures were developed to scale, or attach weights to, statements and categories. During the development of the instrument a total of 133 judges rated the relative 'severity of dysfunction' of each statement so that scale values could be assigned. The judging group was composed of 108 randomly selected enrollees in a prepaid health plan and 25 health care professionals and pre-professional students. They were asked to rate each statement in terms of severity without regard for who might be experiencing it, what might be causing it, or future implications. Agreement among the judges was very high.

A score for the overall SIP instrument is computed by summing the scale values of all statements checked by a respondent and dividing that sum by the grand total of all statement scale values. This ratio is then multiplied by 100 to convert it to a simple percentage. Similarly, scores can be computed for each SIP category. The higher the score on the SIP, the more dysfunctional the respondent. Thus, a person with a score of 30% is more dysfunctional, or sicker, than a person with a score of 3%.

As part of the developmental process, the interrelations among SIP category scores were examined using cluster and factor analytical techniques. The result of these analyses indicated that two groups of categories consistently clustered together across all field trial samples. Categories A (ambulation), BCM (body care and movement) and M (mobility) constitute a scoring dimension that reflects physical dysfunction. Categories SI (social interaction), C (communication), AB (alterness behaviour) and EB (emotional behaviour) constitute a scoring dimension that reflects psychosocial dysfunction. The remaining SIP categories are scored individually. Percentage scores for the scoring dimensions may be calculated in the same manner as the category overall scores.

## TESTING THE SICKNESS IMPACT PROFILE

Field trials of the SIP were conducted in 1973, 1974 and 1976, and were designed so that the instrument would be tested on subjects that spanned a range of type and severity of illness.

In 1973, a pilot study was aimed at providing preliminary assessments of reliability, validity and ease of administration. Two hundred and forty-six subjects (outpatients, inpatients, home care patients, walk-in clinic patients and other persons) completed SIPs in this field trial. Data were analysed for purposes of item revision, and a statistical analysis was used to revise and shorten the prototype instrument. Items that were relatively independent and accounted for most of the subject variance, items that were insufficiently tested and/or items that were substantively important were retained in a revised SIP for further training.

A 1974 field trial was designed to provide a comprehensive test of the reliability of the SIP, a preliminary assessment of validity, a preliminary test of self-administration and a broad assessment of the revised SIP. The design utilized four subsamples of subjects covering a range of sickness or dysfunction: rehabilitation treatment outpatients and inpatients, speech pathology inpatients, outpatients with chronic health problems and a group of enrollees in a prepaid health plan who had participated in a 20-year long longitudinal study and who were not ill at the time.

The test–retest reliability of the SIP was investigated using different interviewers, different forms, different administration procedures and a variety of subjects who differed in type and severity of dysfunction. Overall the reliability of the SIP in terms of score was high ($r=0.75$–$0.92$) and reliability in terms of items checked was moderate ($r=0.45$–$0.60$). Reliability did not appear to be significantly affected by the variables examined, which suggests that the SIP is potentially useful for measuring dysfunction under a variety of administrative conditions and with a variety of subjects[22,23].

Validity was examined by analysing the relationships between SIP scores and three types of measures: one based on subject self-assessment, one on clinician assessment and one on the subject's score on some other assessment instrument. The SIP scores discriminated among subsamples, and the correlations between each criterion measure and SIP scores provided evidence for the validity of the SIP.

Data from the 1974 field trial were also used in making the second revision of the SIP. The data were analysed to determine the interrelationships among items, the relationships of items to category and overall scores and to the various criterion measures, the clarity of instructions, the reliability and clarity of items and the discriminative capability of items.

A 1976 field trial had three basic aims: determining the final content, format and scoring of the SIP, providing a broad assessment of the discriminant, convergent and clinical validity of the SIP, and comparing the reliability and validity of alternative administrative procedures. A large stratified random sample of members of a prepaid group practice was a major component of the field trial. To assure an adequate frequency of response to SIP items, so that final item analysis would be possible, a sample of subjects who considered themselves sick and were patients of a family medicine clinic were interviewed.

### Reliability

Table 4.2 provides results of reliability testing in all field trails, and shows reliability of the SIP to be compared across all trials. As was expected, reliability in terms of score is high; in terms of item agreement only moderate. This suggests that though subjects change the specific items they respond to within a 24-hour period, the combination of items checked on the two occasions are sufficiently similar in scale value to provide similar overall and category scores.

The 1976 field trial provided an opportunity to compare the reliability of three types of administration of the SIP: an interviewer administration (I), an interviewer-delivered self-administration (ID), and a mail-delivered self-administration (MD). As in the 1974 field trial, high levels of test–retest reliability, evaluated in terms of score correlations, were demonstrated for Is and IDs (no retest on MDs could be obtained) and analyses of variance showed no difference in overall mean scores between administrative types. Internal consistency (Cronbach's alpha) was high for both Is and IDs but substantially lower for MDs.

To further assess the comparability of administration types, the relationship of SIP score to self-assessments of sickness and dysfunction, clinician

Table 4.2 Reliability summary of the SIP across all field trials

| Criterion | 1973 Field trial | 1974 Field trial | 1976 Field trial |
|---|---|---|---|
| Reproducibility | | | |
| overall score | 0.88 | 0.88 | 0.92 |
| item agreement | 0.56 | 0.50 | 0.50 |
| Internal consistency | | | |
| Cronbach's alpha | NA | 0.97 | 0.94 |

NA: not applicable

assessments of dysfunction, and an index of disability derived from the National Health Interview Survey (NHIS) restricted activity days questions, was determined. Although some differences were noted, no single administration type consistently displayed stronger relationships to criterion variables than did any other. Lower correlations were noted for MD overall SIP score and the NHIS index. Separate correlations between category scores and self-assessments of dysfunction for MDs were markedly lower than those of Is and IDs for categories SI (social interaction), E (eating), HM (home management), M (mobility), and BCM (body care and movement).

Thus, it appears that mail-delivered SIPs may not provide data comparable to those obtained by the two other types of administration. These data suggest that self-administered forms may be more valid than interviewer-administered forms when accompanied by a method of administration that assures comprehension of and adherence to SIP instructions and conveys a sense of importance of the task. A trained interviewer who reads instructions and answers questions before the SIP is completed by the subject may be the best assurance of reliable and valid SIP data. If mail-delivered SIPs are to be used, careful follow-up and monitoring is suggested to assure and assess reliability and validity.

## Validity

The validity of the SIP depends on demonstrating the relationship between sickness impacts and behavioural dysfunction. In each field trial an attempt was made to determine the relationship between independent measures of sickness and of dysfunction[3,5].

In the 1974 field trial, preliminary estimates of the validity of the SIP were obtained by examining the relationship between the SIP and self-assessments of dysfunction, between the SIP and other measures of dysfunction, including the Activities of Daily Living Index[17] and between the SIP and selected questions from the NHIS.[27]. In general, the relationships between overall SIP scores and criterion measures were high.

In the 1976 field trial, subject and clinician assessments of health status were obtained and the relationships between SIP scores and these measures were examined. In addition, the relationship between SIP scores and clinical measures of patient progress was determined.

On the basis of previous work[3], we assumed that the strength of the relationship between the SIP and other measures of health status was a function of the similarity of the construct being measured and the similarity of the method of measurement. Therefore, a series of hypotheses concerning these relationships was generated. We hypothesized that SIP score would be more related to those criterion measures reflecting subject perceptions than to other criteria. Specifically, we hypothesized that SIP scores would be most related to subject self-assessments of dysfunction, and that the next highest relationship would be between SIP score and self-assessment of dysfunction and sickness. The construct of sickness and the method used to measure it differed somewhat from those employed in the SIP, but the construct of dysfunction and the method used to measure it closely parallelled the SIP. SIP scores were hypothesized to be less related to the NHIS index than to the self-assessments of dysfunction or sickness, because this index differs from the SIP in two aspects: it refers to a 14-day period rather than the one-day period of the SIP, and it measures restricted activity days in a general fashion. Nonetheless, it reflects the same underlying construct of dysfunction and is a self-perceived report of limitation of activity.

We assumed that the SIP would be less related to measures of sickness obtained from sources other than the subject. Thus, we hypothesized that the SIP would be less related to clinician ratings. Further, we hypothesized that because of the common construct of dysfunction, SIP score would be more related to clinician ratings of dysfunction than to clinician ratings of sickness.

Analysis of the 1976 field trial data confirms these hypotheses. The correlation between SIP score and self-assessment of dysfunction is 0.69; between SIP score and self-assessment of sickness is 0.63; between SIP score and the NHIS index is 0.55; between SIP score and the clinician assessment of dysfunction is 0.50; and between SIP score and clinician assessment of sickness is 0.40. These data across all field trials are summarized in Table 4.3.

The relationships between the SIP and each of the criterion variables were further analysed by the multitrait–multimethod methodology developed by Campbell and Fiske[9]. A discussion of these results may be found in Ref. 4.

## Clinical validity

Another group of criteria against which a health status measure should be validated consists of objective clinical data that are characteristically used to follow the progress of patients with specific diagnostic conditions.

**Table 4.3** Validity summary of the SIP across all field trials

| Criterion | 1973 Field trial | 1974 Field trial | 1976 Field trial |
|---|---|---|---|
| Protocol judgements | 0.85 | NA | NA |
| Self-assessment | | | |
| sickness | NA | 0.54 | 0.63 |
| dysfunction | NA | 0.52 | 0.69 |
| Clinical assessments | | | |
| sickness | NA | 0.30 | 0.40 |
| dysfunction | NA | 0.49 | 0.50 |
| Other instruments | | | |
| NHIS* | NA | 0.61 | 0.55 |
| ADL** | NA | 0.46 | NA |

NA: not applicable.
*National Health Interview Survey Index of activity limitation. Work loss and bed days.
**Activity of Daily Living Index.

The test of this aspect of the SIP involves assessment of the relationship between the SIP and existing clinical measures, and determination of whether the SIP provides additional information not provided by the existing clinical measures. The former is important if clinicians are to be assured that the information obtained from the SIP is consonant with more traditional data obtained on patients; the latter is important in order to assess and specify the types and range of supplemental information that can be provided by the SIP.

Patients who had undergone total hip replacement, hyperthyroid patients and rheumatoid arthritic patients were chosen for study. Although specific tests, time intervals and conditions differed for each group the general format for study of each of these diagnostic groups was as follows: (i) each diagnostic group contained fifteen patients; (ii) patients were measured at least three times during the study period; (iii) follow-up times were specified in advance and procedures developed to assure the timely administration of SIPs and collection of clinical data; and (iv) clinical measures and SIPs were obtained within a 24-hour period.

To assess the relationship between the SIP and the clinical measures, correlations between them were obtained. As can be seen in Table 4.4, these correlations are moderate ($r=0.41$) to high ($r=0.84$). The correlation level appropriately reflects the similarity of the constructs assessed by the SIP overall or dimension score and the clinical measure.

## USING THE SICKNESS IMPACT PROFILE

Since the early publications of the initial development of the SIP, clinical

**Table 4.4** Correlations of SIP scores and clinical measures

| Clinical measures | Correlation with overall SIP score | Correlation with categories that measure | |
| --- | --- | --- | --- |
| | | Physical dysfunction | Psychosocial dysfunction |
| Harris analysis of hip function* | −0.81 | 0.84 | 0.61 |
| Adjusted T4** | 0.41 | 0.21 | 0.35 |
| Activity Index*** | 0.66 | 0.66 | 0.56 |

*An assessment of patients who have undergone hip replacement. A high score on this test indicates better hip function than does a low score.
**A hormonal measure of thyroid function.
***An index developed by Haastaja that combines weighted values for duration of morning stiffness, grip strength, sedimentation rate and joint involvement.

researchers have indicated an interest in using it to assess functional health status or, what the clinical literature often calls, health-related quality of life. During the past 10 years the SIP has been used in a variety of studies that examine the health status of patients with cardiopulmonary disease, joint and bone disease, renal disease and malignant disease. It has also been used by health services' researchers to examine the effects of the organization and delivery of care on health status. More recently, studies have been conducted, often under the auspices of drug and equipment manufacturers, which assess the cost-effectiveness of new therapies and use the SIP as one of the measures of effectiveness.

## Studies of patients

The first large study that used the SIP was a multi-centre randomized controlled trial of the use of 24-hour oxygen, as compared with nocturnal or 12-hour oxygen, for patients with oxygen-dependent chronic obstructive pulmonary disease (COPD). Unfortunately for the patients, and for the several measures of health status used in this study, the single most important outcome was the increased mortality of those on nocturnal oxygen. Fortunately, the study did provide an opportunity to describe the type and level of dysfunction experienced by COPD patients and to examine the relationship between the SIP and several physiological and neuropsychological measures. These data are presented in Figure 4.3 and Table 4.5. As can be seen in Figure 4.3, patients with COPD who are oxygen-dependent are quite dysfunctional. Their overall SIP score is about 25% and they are unlikely to be working, participating in recreational activities or managing their own home. Their sleep and rest is disturbed and they have difficulty in all areas

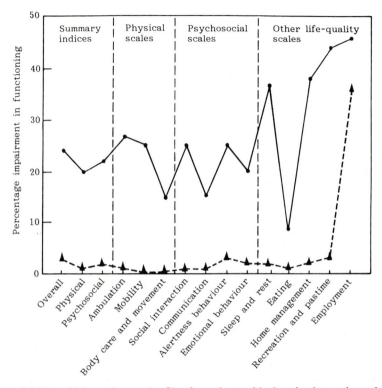

**Figure 4.3** Mean Sickness Impact Profiles for patients with chronic obstructive pulmonary disease (COPD) and control subjects. Patients with COPD are significantly ($p < 0.001$) more impaired on all scales except employment using paired tests ($n = 66$). Solid line indicates patients in the Nocturnal Oxygen Therapy Trial: dotted line, control subjects. (Reproduced with permission from Ref. 20)

**Table 4.5** Pearson's correlations between SIP scores and Nocturnal Oxygen Therapy Trial measures (Reproduced with permission from Ref. 20)

| Measure | r | p |
|---|---|---|
| $PaO_2$ | –0.12 | NS |
| $O_2$ transport | –0.22 | <0.01 |
| Cardiac index | –0.16 | 0.04 |
| COPD severity index | –0.33 | <0.01 |
| Halstead impairment index | 0.34 | <0.01 |
| Average impairment rating (Halstead–Reitan battery) | 0.38 | <0.01 |
| Average impairment rating (Rennich repeatable battery) | 0.45 | <0.01 |
| Global clinical rating | 0.37 | <0.01 |

of activity. Table 4.5 indicates that SIP score is poorly correlated with physiological measures usually used to assess severity of COPD. In this study, these low correlations may result from the restricted range of the physiological measures because of the study criteria for patient inclusion[20]. However, they may reflect the common observation that patients with the same COPD severity exhibit widely different activity levels[2]. The correlations of the SIP with the neuropsychological measures are moderate and may indicate the relatively broad effect of oxygen deprivation.

A randomized clinical trial of early exercise and counselling for myocardial infarction patients used the SIP to determine the impact of the intervention on the usual activities of the patient. The SIP assessments were supplemental to physiological assessments such as treadmill testing for those patients. Physiological outcomes were not found to be affected by early exercise and counselling, neither were physical dimension and overall scores of the SIP, but the psychosocial dimension scores of those who received early exercise and counselling were significantly lower (better) than those who did not[19].

The National Study of End Stage Renal Disease used the SIP as its measure of quality of life for patients treated by four different modalities: transplant, home dialysis, continuous peritoneal dialysis and in-centre dialysis. Hart and Evans[16] report large differentials in SIP scores between these four treatment groups. Some of these differences may be the result of cohort differences, although the authors commented that successful transplant had a statistically significant, independent effect of reducing dysfunction after these differences were statistically controlled.

Performance or behaviour seems an appropriate indicator of treatment effects for those with joint or bone problems. In the early testing of the SIP, it was found to be a sensitive measure of change for patients who underwent hip replacement, and that it accurately reflected the condition of arthritic patients[4].

Follick et al.[14] and Deyo et al.[10] have reported studies of patients with low back pain in which the SIP was used to assess the efficacy of treatment. Follick and his colleagues were able to show that a chronic pain treatment programme was effective in reducing dysfunction in the treatment group as compared with those of the controls. Deyo and his colleagues found no difference in outcome (SIP and other measures) for low back pain patients randomly assigned to 2 days' bed rest or 7 days' bed rest.

The effect of changes in health care delivery have traditionally been difficult to evaluate. Aside from the problems associated with development of a study design from which plausible causal inferences can be made, there is often the added difficulty of choosing measures of efficacy that reflect the potential impacts of the change. Two studies of changes in the organization of care provide examples of the value of the SIP as a measure of impact of organizational change. One was an evaluation of a sophisticated emergency medical service programme that examined the effects of the programme on survival following out-of-hospital cardiac arrest and the functional health status of survivors[2]. In a comparison of age-and-sex matched cardiac arrest survivors, and myocardial infarct survivors, the cardiac arrest survivors reported poorer health status. Further, although cardiac arrest survivors were more dysfunctional than myocardial infarct survivors across all but one SIP category, work, household management and alertness were relatively more impaired in the cardiac arrest victims. The impairment in alertness behaviour is consistent with the oxygen deprivation experienced by these patients. The comparison of levels of dysfunction may help those who must decide whether to implement sophisticated emergency medical services.

A study of the cost and efficacy of sustained home care for patients with COPD used the SIP and other outcome measures to assess the efficacy of the home care programme. The results of the study were unequivocal. None of the measures of efficacy detected any differences between patients randomly assigned to home care and those assigned to regular out-patient care[6]. Of course, it is possible that these measures, even those especially developed for the study, were not sensitive to the benefits of home care, and efforts to develop more sensitive measures may be justified. In the meantime, this study may help inform the discussion about the values of expanded home care services.

The SIP has been used in several drug trials conducted by pharmaceutical companies, although unfortunately the results of these trials have not been published. It is possible to reveal, however, that it is feasible to incorporate the SIP in a drug trial; it can be successfully completed via phone interviews, as well as in-person interviews, and the range and level of responses seem consistent with published data.

## References

1.  Beck, A.T., Ward, C.H., Medelson, M. *et al.* An inventory for measuring depression. *Arch. Gen. Psychiatr.* 1961; 4: 561–571.
2.  Bergner, L., Hallstrom, A.P., Bergner, M. *et al.* Health status of survivors of cardiac arrest and of myocardial infarction controls. *Am. J. Public Health* 1985; 75: 1321–1323.
3.  Bergner, M., Bobbit, R.A., Kressel, S. *et al.* The Sickness Impact Profile: conceptual formulation and methodology for the development of a health status measure. *Int. J. Health Serv.* 1976; 6: 393–415.
4.  Bergner, M., Bobbit, R. A., Carter, W.B. *et al.* The Sickness Impact Profile: development and final revision of a health status measure. *Med. Care* 1981; 19: 787–805.
5.  Bergner, M., Bobbit, R.A., Pollard, W.E. *et al.* The Sickness Impact Profile: validation of a health status measure. *Med. Care* 1976; 14: 57–67.

6.  Bergner, M., Hudson, L., Conrad, D. *et al*. The cost and efficacy of home care from chronic lung patients. *Med. Care* 1988; 26: 566–579.

7.  Brown, M.E., Daily activity inventory and progress recorded for those with atypical movement. *Am. J. Occup. Ther.* 1950; 4: 195–204.

8.  Buchwald, E. *Physical Rehabilitation for Daily Living*. New York, McGraw-Hill, 1952.

9.  Campbell, D.T. and Fiske, D.W. Convergent and discriminant validation by the multitrait–multimethod matrix. *Psychol. Bull.* 1959; 56–81.

10. Deyo, R. A., Diehl, A.K. and Rosenthal, M. How many days of bed rest for acute low back pain? A randomized trial. *N. Engl. J. Med.* 1986; 315: 1064–1070.

11. Dinnerstein, A.J., Lowenthal, M. and Dexter, M. Evaluation of a rating scale of ability in activities in daily living. *Arch. Phys. Med. Rehabil.* 1965; 46: 579–584.

12. Dudley, D.L. *Psychophysiology of Respiration in Health and Disease*. New York, Appleton-Century-Crofts, 1969.

13. Fabrega, H., Jr. The need for an ethnomedical science. *Science* 1975; 189: 969–975.

14. Follick. Personal Communication.

15. Haber, L.D. The epidemiology of disability: the measure of functional capacity limitations. Social Security Survey of the Disabled. Washington DC, US Department of Health, Education, and Welfare, July 1970.

16. Hart, G.L. and Evans, R.W. The functional status of ESRD patients as measured by the Sickness Impact Profile. *J. Chronic Dis.* 1987; 40 (Suppl. 1): 1175–1315.

17. Katz, S., Ford, A.B., Moskowitz, R. W. *et al*. Studies of illness in the aged: the index of A.D.L.: a standardized measure of biological and psychosocial function. *J. Am. Med. Assoc.* 1963; 185: 914–919.

18. Malamud, W. and Sands, S.L. A revision of the psychiatric rating scale. *Am. J. Psychiat.* 1947; 104: 231–237.

19. McReynolds, P. and Ferguson, J.T. *Clinical Manual for the Hospital Adjustment Scale*. Palo Alto, Consulting Psychologists Press, Inc., 1953.

20. McSweeney, J.A., Grant, I., Heaton, R. K. *et al*. Life quality of patients with chronic obstructive pulmonary disease. *Arch. Intern. Med.* 1982; 142: 473–478.

21. Ott, C.R., Sivarajan, E.S., Newton, K. *et al*. A controlled randomized study of early cardiac rehabilitation: the Sickness Impact Profile as an assessment tool. *Heart Lung* 1983; 12: 162–170.

22. Pollard, W.E., Bobbitt, R.A. and Bergner, M. Examination of variable errors of measurement in a survey-based social indicator. *Soc. Indic. Res.* 1978; 5: 279.

23. Pollard, W.E., Bobbitt, R.A., Bergner, M. and Gilson, B.S. The Sickness Impact Profile: reliability of a health status measure. *Med. Care* 1976; 14: 146–155.

24. Skatin, L. and Freed, E.X. A behavioral rating scale for mental patients. *J. Mental Sci.* 1955; 101: 644–653.

25. Shontz, F.C. and Fink, S.L. A method for evaluating psychosocial adjustment of the chronically ill. *Am. J. Phys. Med.* 1961; 40(a): 63–69.

26. Suchman, E.A. Stages of illness and medical care. *J. Health Human Behav.* 1965; 6: 114–128.

27. US Department of Health, Education, and Welfare. Interviewing methods in the health interview survey. Vital and Health Statistics Series 2, No. 48, Washington DC 1972.

# 5 The Nottingham Health Profile

**James McEwen**

The measurement of health is inevitably tied to two inter-linked issues: how health is defined and the purpose for which the measurement is required. Just as it is easier to define disease rather than health so most people who set out seeking to measure health end up measuring departures from health. Accordingly, the ultimate departure from health, death, has long-standing credibility as a useful measure of a nation's health.

The concept of health indicators assumed importance in the 1930s[16] but it was in the 1970s that the explosion of interest began. Health indicators, it is suggested, can be grouped into three main categories[3].

(1) Indicators of health status of individuals in a community, e.g. mortality, morbidity, disability, perceived health.

(2) Indicators of the work, scope and efficiency of health care services, e.g. episodes of illness, bed days, clinic attendances.

(3) Indicators of social or environmental status of the community, e.g. environmental pollution, overcrowding, unemployment.

Reviews of the approaches to health indicators from a theoretical point of view and descriptions of a number of specific indicators are given in other chapters. The development of the Nottingham Health Profile (NHP), which is one measure of perceived health, will be discussed, together with the ways in which it is similar to and different from other indicators. In attempting to describe health, no single approach is likely to be comprehensive or adequate for every situation. Professional descriptions based on physical or biological departures from normal and professional estimates of the effect that such departures have on an individual must be seen against the individual's own view on feeling and function. Magi and Allander[15] proposed a primary classification of: self-assessed need (an individual's assessment of his own situation), and other-assessed need (the assessor and the assessed are not the same person). They suggest that congruence between these two is not usual,

111

because of the unique and introspective character of self-assessed need and because there is likely to be a greater gap in health due to the special position, knowledge and responsibility for service that health professionals have. In the 1970s, one of the major talking points in research was the debate about hard and soft data and how soft data could be made harder. Many student projects were criticized for wanting somehow or other to measure human happiness and to see how it might be improved by various tinkerings with health care. At that time, in the early days of work on the measurement of perceived health, we were not in the era of 'Health for All by the Year 2000' or familiar with the diverse definitions of health promotion. Recognition was given to the fact that people's perception of health contributed to the decision to seek care and was used by individuals to assess their own valuation of the health care they had received.

There have been many attempts to develop a standard measure of self-assessed health for use as a population survey tool and many clinicians have sought to produce a specific instrument to evaluate clinical care in defined diseases. From the population survey perspective, it was hoped that it would be possible to measure the health status of whole populations at a particular point in time, to provide reliable repeated measures over time and to assess the efficacy of health care. Many of the attempts encountered problems of definition, measurement weighting, reliability, validity, sensitivity and speci-ficity. While some instruments have been long, complex and comprehensive, others have been narrow and concentrated on one or more specific aspects of disability. Bearing all this in mind, work started in the Department of Community Health at Nottingham in the mid-1970s to produce a new instrument. Recognizing the culture-specific nature of perceived health it was decided to start afresh, rather than adapt an existing instrument.

Although 15 years seems a long time since work commenced on the NHP, it is generally reckoned that the development and testing of a new instrument takes about ten years. This chapter will describe the development, indicate the current use of the NHP, and review its value and possible future developments.


## THE DEVELOPMENT OF THE NOTTINGHAM HEALTH PROFILE

In 1975, the Department of Community Health, under the leadership of Maurice Backett, began work on an indicator which would describe the typical effects of ill health – physical, social and emotional. The research was supported by the Social Science Research Council with the early work being carried out by Carlos Martini and Ian McDowell and the later research by Sonja Hunt, Stephen McKenna and the present author[8].

Specifically the measure was intended to:

(a) Provide some assessment of a person's need for care which was not based upon purely medical criteria.

(b) Enable the subsequent evaluation of care provided for persons in need.

(c) Make a start on the development of an indicator which could be used for the survey of populations' health status.

Some of the key points in development which distinguish this instrument from some others are described below.

The research team began by interviewing 768 patients with a variety of chronic ailments. These interviews produced 2200 statements describing the effects of ill-health; thus these initial statements were patient-generated, not physicians' views. The statements were grouped according to function. The wording of each statement was scrutinized for redundancy, ambiguity, understandability, clarity, ease of reading, esoteric expressions and reading age. Following this procedure, 138 statements remained. A number of pilot studies were then carried out to refine the list and to test the statements against medical information and in different types of disability. It was shown that the resulting 82 statements covering 12 domains of functioning were of value in distinguishing between different types and levels of disability.

The next stage of research aimed at further refining of the instrument and at the same time sought to expand its use as an instrument, for population survey. Administration of an instrument on a large scale has a number of requirements which may include: being short and simple enough to be self-administered; scoring must be relatively easy; being sensitive to changes in the same individual over time and to differences in the consequences of different pathological states. It was envisaged that the instrument would contribute to: (a) identification of groups in need of care; (b) development of social policy, and allocation of resources; (c) evaluation of health and social services; (d) identification of consumer concerns; and (e) understanding of differential responses to comparable pathologies.

Statements were re-examined, retested and analysed using the following criteria:

- There should be no negative expressions.
- Statements should be easy to understand, unambiguous and easy to answer.
- Statements should be answerable by yes or no.
- Language should conform to standards of a minimum reading age

Items which met these standards were tested on patients and other groups and those which proved satisfactory were retained. The resulting NHP is in two parts. Part I of the NHP comprises 38 items which best reflect problems with health. They fall into six areas: sleep, physical mobility, energy, pain, emotional reactions and social isolation. Within each area statements have been weighed using the Thurstone[17] method of paired comparison. This allows empirical judgements to be based on perceived differences. Subjects, both patients and others, were asked to judge each statement in a section against every other statement in that section in terms of which condition or situation they considered to be worse. Statements were paired at random, with the order of presentation reversed for half the interviews. In all, 1200 interviews were carried out, 200 on each of the sections, and again the statements were weighted by members of the public, not by physicians. The subjects were asked to consider five statements A, B, C, D, E and select which of these two they considered to be the more serious:

| | |
|----|----|
| AB | BD |
| AC | BE |
| AD | CD |
| AE | CE |
| BC | DE |

An example of the weighting obtained by this method is shown in Table 5.1. In this way, the original statements arose from lay perceptions and the final statements were weighted by lay people, thus making the NHP different

**Table 5.1** Examples of weighting for sleep section of NHP

| Statement | Weight |
|---|---|
| I am waking up in the early hours of the morning | 12.6 |
| It takes me a long time to get to sleep | 16.1 |
| I sleep badly at night | 21.7 |
| I take tablets to help me sleep | 22.4 |
| I lie awake for most of the night | 27.2 |

from many professionally determined instruments.

It was decided that all sections should allow scores to range from zero (no problems) to 100 (where all the problems in the section are affirmed).

Part II of the NHP consists of seven statements relating to those areas of life most often affected by health: paid employment, looking after the house, social life, home life, sex life, hobbies and interests, and holidays. Statements in Part II are scored one for an affirmative and zero for a negative.

## TESTING

The NHP has been tested for face, content and criterion validity with groups of elderly people with differing clinical conditions, patients who consult their general practitioners, firemen, mine-rescue workers, pregnant women, patients undergoing minor surgery and fracture victims. Reliability was tested in patients with osteoarthritis and peripheral vascular disease.

### Validation studies

The NHP has been tested for face, content and criterion validity and has been found to be a highly satisfactory measure of subjective health status, in the physical, social and emotional domains; and to be a useful guide to the extent to which health problems are restricting normal physical and social activities.
Testing has taken place with the following groups:

(1) Four groups of elderly people (over 65) comprising 41 people participating in a research programme on physical exercise who could be described as 'fit' on the basis of their exercise heart rate; a sample of 19 patients who had no known illness or disability and who had not contacted a doctor for at least 2 months prior to the study was drawn from the records of a general practitioner; 49 people attending a luncheon club run by the social services and having a variety of health and social problems; and 54 chronically ill patients drawn from general practitioner records.

Results showed that NHP scores effectively differentiated between the well (first two) and ill (last two) groups. The study also indicated that the content of the statements was understandable to and acceptable to elderly persons.

(2) Three hundred and fifty-two persons drawn at random from general practitioners' records and divided into two groups: consulters, i.e. persons who had consulted the general practitioner or obtained repeat prescriptions on three or more occasions in a 6-month period; and non-consulters, i.e. persons who had not consulted the doctor at all in the same 6-month period

Controlling for age, sex and consultation rate, the NHP scores showed significant differences between the scores of the groups on all sections. Scores were also associated with reported absence from work through ill health.

(3) One hundred and fifty-eight firemen representing a fit sample. Profile scores were very low for the group as a whole, but with some individuals achieving very high scores on energy, sleep and emotional reactions.

(4) Ninety-three patients with peripheral vascular disease who were attending an out-patient clinic. Scores reflected the high number of problems

experienced by these patients especially in the areas of pain, sleep disturbance and physical mobility.

(5)    One hundred and forty-one patients attending a fracture clinic and an equal number of control subjects. Profile scores were obtained from patients and controls at a point in time soon after the fracture occurred and again 8 weeks later. Scores were sensitive to changes in perceived health concomitant with the healing of the fracture.

(6)    One hundred and fifty-seven patients attending an out-patient clinic for non-acute complaints such as haemorrhoids, hernias, varicose veins and ulcers. Forty-one of these patients were administered the NHP before and after minor surgery. Results showed the patients, as a whole, to have perceived health status below that of people who consider themselves to be well.

(7)    A random sample of 2173 people drawn from a group general practice in the Nottingham area. Results showed significant differences in scores between members of different social classes, age groups and sexes.

**Reliability**

One of the requirements of a standardized measure is that it should be reliable. Scores should show consistency over time and there should be some numerical estimate of the degree of consistency exhibited by the instrument. There are three well-established methods for estimating reliability:

(1)    The method of internal consistency, where items on an instrument are divided into two equivalent parts (the split half technique) and the correlations between the scores on each part are computed.

(2)    Alternate forms, where two instruments which have been developed in parallel and which measure the same attribute are administered and scores on one form are correlated with the scores on the other.

(3)    The test–retest technique where the same test is administered on two separate occasions to the same group of individuals and the correlation between the two sets of scores is computed.

The first method requires that the items in the instrument should be homogeneous with respect to the attribute being measured and the second method requires that a parallel form of the instrument should exist. Neither of these requirements are fulfilled in the case of the NHP. The third method, test–retest, is thus the preferred one.

Since the NHP yields a high proportion of negative answers when given to a normal population, an investigation of its reliability would need to be carried out on a population which could be expected to give a high proportion of affirmative responses in order to avoid overestimating its reliability. However, to avoid the underestimation of reliability the sample would need to be such that the condition of the respondents would not be expected to change significantly over a short period of time. Two groups of respondents who fulfil these conditions are people suffering osteoarthritis and patients with peripheral vascular disease.

In the first case 58 patients with osteoarthritis were selected for study, specifically those awaiting hip-replacement operations. Each person was sent a NHP and covering letter by mail and a second NHP was sent 4 weeks later. The reliability coefficients obtained are shown in Table 5.2.

**Table 5.2** Correlation coefficients for statements on Part I and II of the NHP with osteoarthritis. (Based on Ref. 8, with permission)

| Part I | | Part II | |
|---|---|---|---|
| *Statement* | *Spearman's r** | *Statement* | *Cramer's C** |
| Energy | 0.77 | Paid employment | 0.86 |
| Pain | 0.79 | Jobs around the home | 0.85 |
| Emotional reactions | 0.80 | Social life | 0.59 |
| Sleep | 0.85 | Family relations | 0.64 |
| Social isolation | 0.78 | Sex life | 0.84 |
| Physical mobility | 0.85 | Hobbies/interests | 0.44 |
| | | Holidays | 0.71 |

* All values are statistically significant ($p < 0.001$)

A second group comprising 93 patients with peripheral vascular disease were given the profile questionnaire to complete and were sent a second one 8 weeks later. The reliability coefficients obtained are shown in Table 5.3. These two studies demonstrate the high level of reliability of the NHP with groups suffering from chronic illness.

It should be noted that certain changes in perceived health may have occurred between the two administrations of the NHP, consequently reducing the correlation coefficient obtained. This is a general problem with testing the reliability of a sensitive indicator, since the greater the sensitivity of the instrument to change, the lower will be the consistency between administrations of the instrument to the same group of people. Within the limitations of time and funding, it is considered that these studies indicate quite a high degree of validity and reliability for NHP for use with a wide range of people and age groups.

**Table 5.3** Correlation coefficients for statements on Part I and II of the NHP for patients with peripheral vascular disease. (Based on Ref. 8 with permission)

| Part I | | Part II | |
| --- | --- | --- | --- |
| Statement | Spearman's r* | Statement | Cramer's C* |
| Energy | 0.77 | Paid employment | 0.55 |
| Pain | 0.88 | Jobs around the house | 0.64 |
| Emotional reactions | 0.75 | Social life | 0.61 |
| Sleep | 0.85 | Family relations | 0.89 |
| Social isolation | 0.77 | Sex life | 0.85 |
| Physical mobility | 0.79 | Hobbies/interests | 0.86 |
| | | Holidays | 0.72 |

* All values are statistically signified ($p : 0.001$)

## Establishing norms

Two large-scale studies have been carried out to develop norms for the NHP. Both were designed to look at the association between sex, age, class and the scores obtained. The first study was of the general population and the second of employees in a large manufacturing organization.

## Norms for general population

The co-operation of a four-doctor group practice near Nottingham was obtained and a random sample of males and females, divided into 5-year age groups, 20–75 years, was drawn. A total of 3200 questionnaires were sent out and 2192 (68%) usable profiles were returned after 10 weeks. The main findings can be summarized as follows for Part I.

- The relation between perceived health and social class occurs only in the age group 20–24. This has important implications at both a theoretical and practical level for explanations of persisting inequalities in health.
- Scores on the NHP convey a clear picture of differences in perceived health problems between social classes for these younger age groups.
- On average, a male in the age range 20–44 and coming from social classes IV and V will score twice as highly as his contemporary from social classes I or II on the energy and emotional reactions section, over three times as high on the sleep section, and four times as high on feelings of social isolation.
- Similar, though less marked findings occurred for females. Some

**Table 5.4** Age, sex and social class norms 20–34 year olds

| | Class I | | Class II | | Class IIInm | | Class IIIm | | Class IV | | Class V | |
|---|---|---|---|---|---|---|---|---|---|---|---|---|
| | Male | Female | Male | Female | Male | Female | Male | Female | Male | Female | Male | Female |
| Energy | 5.90 | 8.84 | 3.73 | 9.75 | 6.91 | 13.19 | 5.18 | 16.54 | 8.96 | 17.45 | 9.14 | 18.32 |
| Pain | 0.42 | 1.83 | 0.97 | 1.03 | 1.88 | 1.39 | 1.94 | 3.21 | 0.97 | 3.24 | 1.58 | 8.68 |
| Emotional | 5.50 | 5.46 | 5.21 | 6.69 | 6.35. | 10.01 | 8.63 | 11.63 | 12.81 | 14.34 | 3.87 | 20.73 |
| Sleep | 5.57 | 5.78 | 3.66 | 5.78 | 6.41 | 7.96 | 8.69 | 11.85 | 11.04 | 14.92 | 2.84 | 24.74 |
| Social | 4.78 | 2.81 | 4.17 | 3.66 | 4.49 | 4.52 | 2.16 | 3.85 | 7.71 | 7.70 | 7.39 | 10.89 |
| Physical mobility | 0.77 | 1.79 | 0.64 | 0.94 | 1.58 | 1.43 | 0.99 | 2.19 | 1.42 | 2.39 | 1.48 | 3.03 |

*Age, sex and social class norms 35–49 year olds*

| | Class I | | Class II | | Class IIInm | | Class IIIm | | Class IV | | Class V | |
|---|---|---|---|---|---|---|---|---|---|---|---|---|
| | Male | Female | Male | Female | Male | Female | Male | Female | Male | Female | Male | Female |
| Energy | 8.17 | 20.80 | 6.31 | 13.58 | 6.31 | 13.44 | 6.58 | 19.05 | 11.37 | 23.39 | 20.39 | 8.62 |
| Pain | 1.49 | 5.67 | 3.93 | 4.47 | 3.77 | 4.13 | 2.22 | 7.45 | 3.40 | 8.27 | 8.45 | 2.4 |
| Emotional | 5.89 | 9.92 | 7.59 | 7.70 | 7.57 | 8.75 | 7.43 | 13.95 | 13.52 | 19.36 | 17.73 | 14.39 |
| Sleep | 5.81 | 9.27 | 8.91 | 9.83 | 6.07 | 12.46 | 8.52 | 15.09 | 10.31 | 19.54 | 22.40 | 19.45 |
| Social | 3.00 | 8.15 | 4.55 | 5.14 | 3.27 | 4.58 | 3.05 | 4.79 | 7.34 | 6.75 | 6.40 | 8.23 |
| Physical mobility | 2.52 | 4.86 | 2.59 | 2.38 | 2.19 | 2.19 | 1.31 | 4.71 | 3.22 | 5.35 | 5.24 | 2.47 |

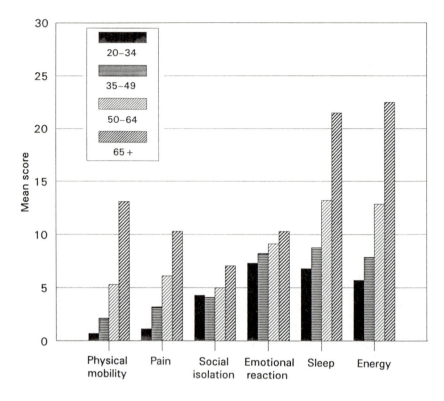

**Figure 5.1** Mean scores on NHP Part I by age for each section (males)

masking of social class effects may have occurred because of the general tendency of females to score more highly than men.
- The lower social classes feel themselves to have a much larger burden of socio-emotional problems than do the others, but this difference becomes less marked after the age of 45

Results from Part II of the NHP support the general themes of those from Part I, though they are not so clear-cut. Men from the lower social classes are significantly more likely to feel the effects of health problems on their daily life.

### Norms for an employed population

It was considered that it would be useful to have separate norms based on industrial and commercial populations and a large company using a variety of industrial and commercial processes and providing diverse types of

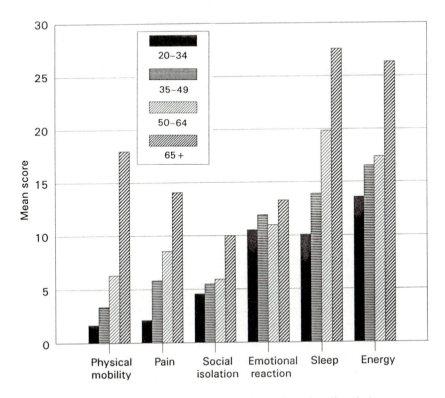

**Figure 5.2** Mean scores on NHP Part I by age for each section (females)

employment agreed to take part. Although some difficulties were evident in the distribution, 1753 usable questionnaires were returned from a total of 3000. It was found that the scores for Part I again showed the characteristic social class gradients, with employees in social classes IV and V having higher scores. Similar traits were found for Part II.

As expected, mean scores for this employed sample population tended to be lower than those for the general population. However, within the healthy workforce there was still an acceptable number of health problems which affected the full range of areas of living.

Full details of the development, administration, analysis and norms, which are now based on a larger data base than the original studies described above, are found in the Nottingham Health Profile Users Manual[8].

Table 5.4 shows the age, sex and social class norms for the age groups 20–34 and 35–49 years old, and Figures 5.1 and 5.2 show the mean scores on NHP Part I for males and females of different age groups

## USE OF NOTTINGHAM HEALTH PROFILE

From the early days of the research project it was noted that the NHP appeared to be of value in both clinical studies and in population surveys. The increased interest during the past few years (by the public, professionals and health service managers) in evaluation has perhaps been responsible for its greater application in studies of clinical care. Population surveys are often more complex, take longer to plan, attract less funding and may rely on established measures to ensure comparability of results The ease of administration of the NHP may encourage its incorporation into either existing or planned studies of a new treatment or form of care.

### Clinical studies

The most frequent use of the NHP has been in intervention studies. Probably the best known and one of the earliest was the national study into the costs and benefits of heart transplantation[1] where the NHP was used to evaluate the quality of life changes. Prior to operation every section of Part I showed levels of perceived distress that were very high with the most affected domains being energy, sleep and physical mobility, accompanied particularly by feelings of social isolation. A significant improvement in perceived health was noted 3 months after transplantation, the effect being most marked for physical mobility. This improvement remained throughout the period of the study and the nature of the change is shown for the energy and physical mobility domains in Figures 5.3 and 5.4. At the same time, patients renewed their normal daily activities particularly in jobs around the home, sex and hobbies as noted in Part II NHP.

A later study on liver transplantation[13] also showed the acceptability and value of the profile in evaluating intervention in serious illness. Although it was not possible to obtain measurement prior to transplantation it was found that generally patients achieved levels of perceived health and feelings similar to that expected (based on age and norms) most particularly for scores on emotional problems, although there were higher scores for physical mobility (Figure 5.5). Transplant patients reported fewer problems in the home life and job of work section in Part II NHP, while the levels of problems encountered in other activities were similar to that expected (Figure 5.6)

The NHP has been used in many studies involving less severe illness. Although in some instances the numbers in such studies are small or the benefits of the intervention are uncertain or likely to result in minimal improvement, most of the published statistics suggest that the NHP has proved useful. For example, in a study[2] into the possible relationships between chronic fatigue syndrome and low red blood cell magnesium and the possible benefits of magnesium treatment, patients claimed improved energy levels,

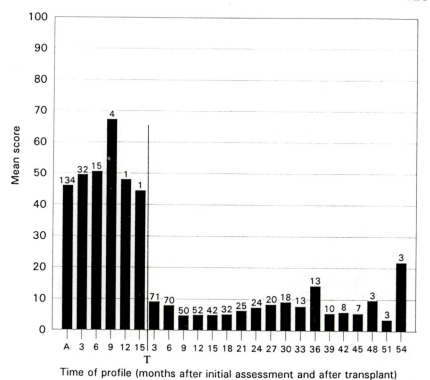

**Figure 5.3** Mean score on Energy section of Part I NHP by 3-month periods from initial assessment (A) and from transplant (T) (number of observations above bars) (Based on Ref. 8 with permission)

better emotional states and less pain. In a large multi-centre study in Belgium into the effects of enalapril on hypertension and quality of life, it was found that there was reduction in blood pressure, and the scores on this NHP were favourably influenced in the patients participating in the study[5].


## Population surveys

Following the initial development work which showed the difference in scores related to socio-economic status, studies in Manchester[12] and London[4] into health and health care in inner city areas showed significant social class differences with NHP scores in Part I being linked to residential area (Table 5.5). Although some findings suggested a positive link between scores and use of health services, this was not a consistent finding and a large study in the South of England which is nearing completion may shed further light on this.

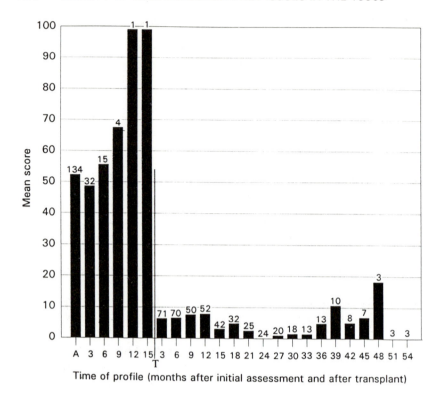

Time of profile (months after initial assessment and after transplant)

**Figure 5.4** Mean score on Physical Mobility section of Part I NHP by 3-month periods from initial assessment (A) and from transplant (T) (number of observations above bars) (Based on Ref. 8 with permission)

**Table 5.5** Mean score on Part I sections of the NHP measured in inner and outer city areas

| Parameter | London | | Manchester | |
|---|---|---|---|---|
| | *Inner* | *Outer* | *Inner* | *Outer* |
| Energy | 15.9 | 11.1 | 17.9 | 14.5 |
| Pain | 8.0 | 4.3 | 6.9 | 6.1 |
| Emotional reactions | 13.7 | 7.1 | 13.2 | 9.2 |
| Sleep | 17.6 | 15.1 | 16.5 | 14.0 |
| Social isolation | 8.6 | 5.1 | 6.7 | 5.1 |
| Physical mobility | 7.8 | 5.5 | 6.6 | 5.9 |

Based on Refs 12 and 4.

**Table 5.6** The perceived health of unemployed and re-employed men: mean scores on the NHP and GHQ

| Health measure | Unemployed (n=114) | Re-employed (n=71) |
|---|---|---|
| Energy | 19.30 | 8.77 |
| Pain | 3.29 | 1.14 |
| Emotional reactions | 33.37 | 7.68 |
| Sleep | 27.57 | 7.63 |
| Social isolation | 15.47 | 3.04 |
| Physical mobility | 2.63 | 0.15 |
| GHQ 12 | 15.67 | 7.84 |
| Depression | 4.13 | 0.72 |
| Anxiety | 8.89 | 4.42 |

In a study by McKenna and Payne[15] the improvement in health of those re-employed after a period of unemployment compared with those remaining unemployed was demonstrated, (Table 5.6).

In two very different studies some of the problems of use of measures such as the NHP are identified. In a study of attendance and non-attendance at a breast screening clinic[6] in a mainly healthy population, while there was a good response to a postal questionnaire, the large number of zero scores suggested that the NHP may not be appropriate for this type of study. In a study of health and housing in a deprived area[7], while there was a highly significant relationship between damp/mouldy housing and certain symptoms of physical and mental health, no relationship between NHP scores and housing conditions was found. It is considered that in an area of multiple deprivation, any effects on NHP scores as a result of housing conditions might be masked by the relatively high scores achieved by the sample as a whole.

## Review

In the 1970s those involved in the development had no thought that in the 1990s the Nottingham Health Profile would be used internationally and accepted as one of the recognised instruments associated with the extensive interest in 'quality of life'. Although terminology has changed from the 1970s when discussion was about socio-medical indicators, the current popularity of the term, quality of life, may be misleading. It is best to regard the NHP as a measure of distress in the physical, mental and social domains and to recognize that it is more correctly (as are most other measures) an indicator of departure from health rather than a measure of health.

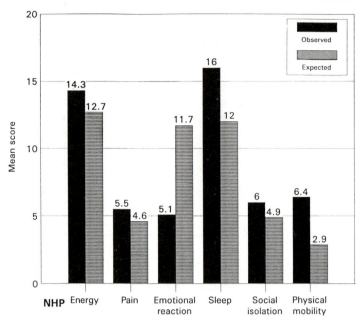

**Figure 5.5** Comparison of mean scores for Part I in liver transplant patients ($n = 58$) and age/sex controlled community population (Based on Ref. 13 with permission)

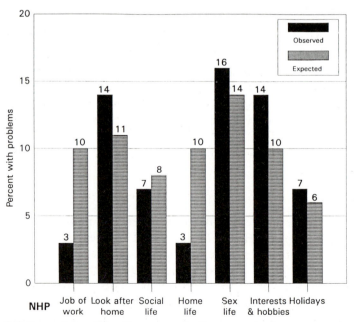

**Figure 5.6** Comparison of Part II responses in liver transplantation patients ($n = 58$) and age/sex controlled community population (Based on Ref. 13 with permission)

There have been a small number of researchers[11] who have been critical of the fundamental concepts or developments of the NHP. Perhaps lack of funding for theoretical research has limited the number of researchers who have been able to undertake critical reviews, or comparisons with other instruments. Studies have examined relationships between the NHP and the general household survey and the General Health Questionnaire. Further studies will be required to confirm the comparative strengths and weaknesses suggested, but it is not surprising that conditions vary as the nature of the instruments are very different. Some of the criticisms were recognised by the authors from the beginning, and the following advantages and limitations still seem to stand.

## ADVANTAGES OF THE NHP

(1) Suitability for use in a wide range of situations from individual clinical interviews to large scale postal surveys.

(2) High reliability and validity.

(3) Easy and cheap to administer.

(4) Takes only a short time to complete and is highly acceptable to respondents.

(5) Easy to score and compute. Particularly suited for experimental analysis using the Statistical Package for the Social Sciences.

(6) Since the NHP does not ask directly if people have *health* problems, it is more likely to pick up people who are ill or at risk but who do not perceive their problems as being related to health.

(7) Scores provide profiles which differ for different medical conditions.

(8) Can be of use to measure general perceived health status and for specific medical conditions.

(9) Age, sex and social class 'norms' available for comparison.

## LIMITATIONS OF THE NHP

(1) The items on Part I represent severe situations. It was found necessary to have such items in preference to less severe statements in order to avoid picking up large quantities of 'false positives', i.e. people who are feeling temporarily 'under the weather'. However, the severity of the items does mean that some individuals who are suffering discomfort may not show up on the NHP.

(2)    'Normal' populations or those with minor ailments may affirm few statements on some sections. This makes it difficult to compare their scores, or to be able to demonstrate changes. In most studies distribution of scores will be highly skewed.

(3)    'Zero scores' cannot be shown to improve on the NHP sections, although in actuality patients may be feeling better than on a previous occasion.

(4)    The NHP does not attempt to cover all possible disabilities; however, the statements have been selected for their applicability to general health status.

(5)    The scores on Part II are a combination of two factors: whether or not the respondent has a health problem and, if so, if it is affecting any of the specified areas. It should not be taken to mean that the individual has that area affected in the *absence* of a health problem. Part II is optional.

(6)    Scoring on Part I involves six scores plus a further seven scores if Part II is used. Analysis can, therefore, become cumbersome if large numbers of other variables need to be taken into account, e.g. in a study where the NHP is only one of the measures.

(7)    The NHP measures health by its absence by focusing on negative aspects of health, i.e. all the statements describe problems.

Perhaps one of the most important problems with any health measure, is its inappropriate use. All measures have limitations, yet there seems to be an assumption that a measure of perceived health does not suffer the same constraints as a clinical, biochemical or physiological measure. In some instances when a general measure is required it may be used alone, in other instances, a combination of measures may be required. In clinical studies as Jonsson[10] has noted it may be 'advisable to use one generic instrument, one disease specific instrument and one study specific instrument'. As with any research the nature and size of the study population and the expected differences in outcome will determine the type of instrument that may be appropriate.

One of the other requirements that has become important in the past few years has been the request for versions in other languages. As would be expected simple word for word translation is quite unsuitable for what is a culture specific instrument. A number of approaches have been tried and there are now several versions (Swedish, Spanish, French and Italian)[9]. Individual researchers have produced versions independently in various ways and indeed in some languages there are several different versions. The authors are concerned about this proliferation of unofficial versions.

## THE FUTURE

The time may now be appropriate for a careful examination of what is required in the next generation of measures. There is a clear need for health status measures which can be used within different countries and for ones suitable for cross-cultural comparisons. Further work needs to be carried out to consider the relationship between general measures and ones related to specific diseases or symptoms. The long-standing debate on the values and limitations of a profile and a single index still continues. The requirement for new measures to cope with the implications of the changes in the health service with the emphasis on needs assessment, evaluation of outcomes, audit and economic comparisons should ensure continuing research and development.

## References

1. Buxton, M., Acheson, R. *et al. Costs and Benefits of the Heart Transplant Programme at Harefield and Papworth Hospitals. DHSS Research Report No 12,* London, HMSO, 1985.
2. Cox, I.M., Campbell, M.J. and Dowson, D. Red blood cell magnesium and chronic fatigue. *Lancet* 1991; 337: 757–760.
3. Culyer, A.J. Health and health indicators. Proceedings of a European Workshop. *Report to the British Social Science Research Council and the European Science Foundation.* University of York, 1981.
4. Curtis, S. *Intra-Urban Variation in Health Care.* Vol. 1 Department of Geography and Earth Science, London, Queen Mary College, London University, 1985.
5. De Lame, P.A., Droussin, A.M., Thonson, M., Ver Haest, L. and Wallace, S. The effects of enalaprolon hypertension and quality of life. A large multi-center study in Belgium. *Acta Cordiogica.* 1989; 44: 289–302.
6. Hunt, S.M., Alexander, F. and Roberts, M. Attenders and non-attenders at a breast screening clinic. *Publ. Health* 1988; 102: 3–10.
7. Hunt, S.M., Martin, C. and Platt, S. Health and housing in a deprived area of Edinburgh. In *Unhealthy Housing: a Diagnosis.* Institute of Environmental Health Officers and Legal Research Institute. University of Warwick, 1986.
8. Hunt, S.M., McEwen, J. and McKenna, S.P. *Measuring Health Status.* London, Croom Helm, 1986.
9. Hunt, S.M., McKenna, S.P. and McEwen, J. *The Nottingham Health Profile. Users Manual.* Revised Edition, 1989.
10. Jonsson, B. Assessment of quality of life in clinical diseases. *Acta Paediatr. Scand.,* 1987; (Suppl.) 337: 164–165.
11. Kind, P. and Carr-Hill, R. The Nottingham Health Profile: a useful tool for epidemiologists? *Social Sci. Med.* 1987; 25(8): 905–910.
12. Leavey, R. *Inequalities in Urban Primary Care Use and Acceptability of the GP Services.* DHSS Research Unit, Department of General Practice, University of Manchester, Manchester, 1982.

13. Lowe, D., O'Grady, J.G., McEwen, J. and Williams, R. Quality of Life following liver transplantation: a preliminary report. *J. R. Coll. Physicians Lond.*, 1990; 24: 43–46.
14. Magi, M. and Allander, E. Towards a theory of perceived and mentally defined need. *Soc. Health Ill.* 1981; 3: 49–71.
15. McKenna, S.P. and Payne, R.L. *Measuring the Perceived Health of U and Re-employed Men.* Memo No 696, Sheffield, MRC/ESRC Social and Applied Psychology Unit, 1984.
16. Stouman, K. and Falk, I. Health indices: a study of objective indices of health in relation to environment and sanitation. *Bull. Health League of Nations*, 1936; 8: 63–69.
17. Thurstone, L.L. *The Measurement of Values.* Chicago, University of Chicago Press, 1959.

# 6 The McMaster Health Index Questionnaire: an update

**Larry W. Chambers**

Many health care interventions are designed to improve the quality of, rather than extend the duration of, the patient's life. Since 1970, when work on the initial version of the McMaster Health Index Questionnaire (MHIQ) began, there has been increasing recognition of the need for direct measures of quality of life/health status to assess the benefit of such interventions as evidenced by a conference and workshops[5,28] devoted to this topic. Quality of life and health status cover a range of diverse components such as the patient's capacity for work, hobbies and psychosocial relationships, as well as the performance of essential acts of daily living in personal hygiene and ambulation. The importance of systematic measurement of these components presents challenges to clinicians and researchers, unlike measurement of inanimate substances and technology used in laboratory measurements. The assessment of quality of life/health status is affected by all the human reactions and variations that can occur when individual persons are the observers and the observed. Guyatt and his colleagues[14] have outlined the several stages in the development and testing of a quality of life/health status measure:
- selecting an initial item pool,
- choosing the best items from that pool,
- deciding on questionnaire format,
- pretesting the instrument,
- demonstrating the responsiveness and validity of the instrument.

They go on to point out that at each stage, the investigator must choose between a rigorous, time-consuming approach to questionnaire construction that will establish clinical relevance, responsiveness and validity of the instrument and a more efficient, less costly strategy that leaves reproducibility, responsiveness and validity untested.

This chapter describes the development of the MHIQ and its application in a number of clinical settings. The general approach to development of the

MHIQ has been of a rigorous and time-consuming nature, hence the ability to report major findings with the instrument some 22 years after it was initially conceived. However, a modified MHIQ or alternative instruments must be developed to address newly identified methodological issues related to such instruments. A later section of this chapter outlines the strengths and limitations of the MHIQ and identifies methodological issues that should be considered by potential users of the MHIQ.

## DEVELOPMENT OF THE QUESTIONNAIRE

### Selection of the initial item pool

Selection of the initial pool of 172 items for the MHIQ was conducted by multidisciplinary teams consisting of experts in internal medicine, family medicine, psychiatry, epidemiology, biostatistics and social science. The World Health Organization[29] definition of health was used as the conceptual basis for defining health status:

> A state of complete physical, mental and social well-being and not merely the absence of disease or infirmity. (WHO, 1958)

The original selection of questionnaire items for inclusion in the MHIQ resulted from a number of different approaches: (a) external consultants, e.g. the St. Thomas Hospital Health Survey in England[3], and the East York Project in Toronto, Ontario[1,2]; (b) brainstorming sessions with faculty and community representatives (physicians and health administrators); and (c) internal consultants from psychiatry, sociology and anthropology, geriatrics, social work and psychiatry.

Items in the St. Thomas Health Survey Questionnaire[3], and the Katz Activities of Daily Living scale[25] were adapted for use as MHIQ items that tapped the physical function area. No single scale was used to develop MHIQ social function items; however, a description of the review process has been reported[9]. MHIQ emotional function items were adapted, and in some instances taken verbatim, from the Social Readjustment Rating Scale[16], the FIRO-B Interpersonal Behaviour scale[24] and instruments presented in Measures of Social Psychological Attitudes[21]. The original draft version of the MHIQ consisted of 172 items.

### Choosing the best items from that pool

The original 172 items, though only a sample of all possible physical, emotional and social function items, took approximately one hour to administer by interview. Also, after numerous occasions of field testing, the wording of some of the original items has been slightly altered.

The best 59 items were identified by assessing their responsiveness to change in function (in before/after interviews of general hospital patients) and their ability to predict family physician global assessments of physical function, emotional function and social function[9]. Linear chi-square trend analyses and multivariate discriminant function analyses were used to identify the best items, using family physician global assessments as the criterion variable. Physicians' assessments are important because the physician is a key decision-maker about what health-system resources should be brought to bear, and indeed whether any response will be made to problems the patient presents.

## Instrument description

The three dimensions of health assessed by the MHIQ are physical, social and emotional function. The 24 physical function items cover physical activities, mobility, self-care activities, communication (sight and hearing), and global physical function. The 25 social function items are concerned with general well-being, work/social role performance/material welfare, family support/participation, friends support/participation, and global social function. The 25 emotional function items are concerned with feelings of self-esteem, attitudes toward personal relationships, thoughts about the future, critical life events, and global emotional function. In total, the MHIQ contains only 59 items, since some of the items address both social and emotional function (see Appendix, p. 449).

All the physical function items are designed to evaluate the patient's functional level on the day the MHIQ is administered. The social function items are explicitly concerned with a specific time period (usually the present). Agree–disagree emotional function items do not refer to a specific time period, but are phrased in the present tense. Other emotional function items refer to the recent past, as specifically defined (e.g. within the last year). None of the items asks the respondent to report changes in physical, social or emotional function.

An attempt was made to phrase all items in the performance mode in order to elicit only information on activities that can actually be observed at the time the MHIQ is completed. The aim of this approach is to avoid the ambiguity of the capacity mode, which may imply either ability or willingness on the part of the respondent. An example of this distinction between the capacity and the performance mode is the difference between the question '*Can* you dress yourself?' (capacity mode) and the question '*Did* you dress yourself?' (performance mode). The extent to which MHIQ items reflect the performance mode is reported in the validity section below.

## Deciding on the questionnaire format

The self-completed version of the MHIQ takes 20 minutes for administration. A recently completed study estimated the degree to which the mode of administration affects the responsiveness of the MHIQ to changes in health status or quality of life[7]. The MHIQ was given to 96 physiotherapy outpatients, who were randomly assigned to one of three methods of administration (self-completion, telephone interview or in-person interview) on four occasions when clinically significant changes in health status had occurred. Social and emotional function scores were not affected by the mode of administration, and as predicted, these scores did not reflect change in the study group. Clinically significant change accounted for up to 30% of variation in physical function, indicating that the mode of administration had little effect and that the physical function component of the MHIQ is responsive to change in any of these three modes.

## Pretesting the instrument

Whenever the MHIQ is used in clinical drug trials, it should be pretested with a group a patients with similar characteristics to those who will be included in the trial. This will assist the investigator in determining the length of time for the MHIQ to be completed, acceptability of the questionnaire to patients and how the MHIQ fits in with other measures also being used in the trial.

## Reliability

Reliability was assessed by asking 30 physiotherapy and 40 psychiatry outpatients to complete the MHIQ at their first visit to their respective clinics and again within one week of the first visit[6]. Patients were not expected to change their functional status in this short period, an observation confirmed by independent assessments by the physiotherapists. Retest reliability coefficients of 0.53, 0.70 and 0.48 (intra-class correlation) for the MHIQ physical, emotional and social function scores, respectively, were observed in the physiotherapy patients. In the psychiatry patients, the coefficients were 0.95 for physical function scores, 0.77 for emotional function scores, and 0.66 for social function scores. In a rehabilitation clinic[11], test–retest physical function scores were reported to be 0.80 (Kappa). An acceptable level of retest reliability of MHIQ physical function change scores was demonstrated for all three methods of administration.

**Validity**

Validity of the MHIQ has been assessed in a wide variety of populations and studies. Validity was assessed by comparison of MHIQ scores with global measures of health status, observed performance, clinical biological indicators and MHIQ scores in different patient groups.

*Global measures*

The MHIQ physical function, emotional function and social function scores have been shown to correlate with global assessments made by health professionals[6,9,11,22].

*Observed performance*

The ability of the MHIQ physical function scores to reflect actual patient performance was examined with 40 patients who first completed the MHIQ and then, immediately after, were observed performing physical functions from areas covered in the Lee Index[19]. A subset of 10 patients was assessed independently by two occupational therapists. A substantial Kappa score of 0.86 was achieved between the two therapists. For the 40 patients, the MHIQ physical function index scores ranged from 0 to 0.76. The MHIQ physical function index correlated with observed patient performance as assessed by the occupational therapists who used the Lee Index to assess patients (see Figure 6.1)[8].

*Clinical/biological indicators*

The 40 rheumatoid arthritis patients who had completed the MHIQ were examined by their rheumatologists, who reported the following clinical/biological indicators: active joint count (the Ritchie Articular Index)[20], duration of morning stiffness and the erythrocyte sedimentation test (ESR)[8]. Table 6.1 gives summary statistics for the three MHIQ indices for different levels on each of the clinical/biological indicators. A gradient is present with the MHIQ physical function index only. The MHIQ scores in Table 6.1 should be useful for estimating sample size requirements for clinical trials.

*Different patient groups*

Figure 6.2 shows the means scores for the three MHIQ indexes obtained in the physiotherapy clinic (96 patients) and in the psychiatry outpatient clinic (40 patients)[6]. The mean MHIQ physical function score in the physiotherapy outpatient clinic was 0.59, whereas the mean physical function score in the psychiatry clinic was 0.89. This difference was statistically significant ($p < 0.01$, unpaired $t$-test), indicating relatively poorer physical function among the physiotherapy patients. Conversely, as predicted, the mean MHIQ emotional scores were 0.66 in the physiotherapy clinic and 0.44 in the

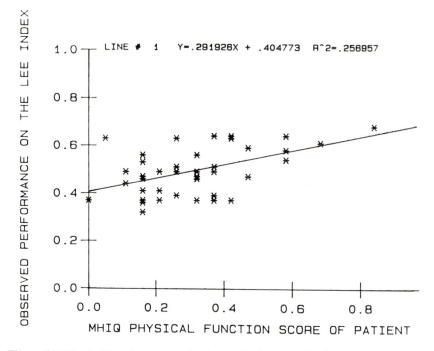

**Figure 6.1** Physical function scores of patients with rheumatoid arthritis versus observed performance on Lee Index

psychiatry clinic, a difference which was statistically significant, and the MHIQ social function scores were also significantly higher in the physiotherapy clinic (0.71).

Further evidence of clinical and biological validity is summarized in Figures 6.3, 6.4 and 6.5. These figures show the MHIQ physical function, emotional function and social function index scores for four different groups of patients; outpatient physiotherapy clinic patients, chronic respiratory disease patients at home, long-term insulin-dependent diabetic patients at home and family practice patients[6].

The family practice patients were hypothesized to have better physical function than the other four groups because these were ambulatory patients presenting with a wide range of complaints. Figure 6.3 shows the distribution of physical function scores with more of the family practice patients having good MHIQ physical function scores than the other three patient groups.

The emotional function of family practice patients was hypothesized to be poorer than the other three patient groups, based on reports from Last and White[18] that approximately 50% of family practice patients present with emotional problems. This trend was found and Figure 6.4 shows the family

**Table 6.1** MHIQ Physical, emotional, social function association with clinical/biological indicators of rheumatoid arthritis (n=40)

| Clinical/ biological indicator | | n | MHIQ Physical Function Index | | | MHIQ Emotional Function Index | | | MHIQ Social Function Index | | |
|---|---|---|---|---|---|---|---|---|---|---|---|
| | | | Median | Mean | SD | Median | Mean | SD | Median | Mean | SD |
| Ritchie Articulator Index* | 0–19 | 11 | 0.37 | 0.42 | 0.21 | 0.54 | 0.56 | 0.15 | 0.61 | 0.65 | 0.14 |
| | 20–29 | 12 | 0.37 | 0.29 | 0.19 | 0.56 | 0.57 | 0.14 | 0.63 | 0.64 | 0.10 |
| | 30–39 | 12 | 0.24 | 0.25 | 0.13 | 0.52 | 0.53 | 0.15 | 0.64 | 0.62 | 0.05 |
| | 40–59 | 5 | 0.17 | 0.23 | 0.13 | 0.48 | 0.48 | 0.10 | 0.63 | 0.62 | 0.05 |
| Age (years) | 15–29 | 1 | 0.74 | 0.74 | 0.00 | 0.46 | 0.46 | 0.00 | 0.64 | 0.64 | 0.00 |
| | 30–49 | 9 | 0.41 | 0.37 | 0.26 | 0.65 | 0.60 | 0.17 | 0.64 | 0.64 | 0.08 |
| | 50–64 | 17 | 0.29 | 0.32 | 0.14 | 0.52 | 0.12 | 0.62 | 0.62 | 0.62 | 0.14 |
| | 65+ | 13 | 0.32 | 0.29 | 0.15 | 0.51 | 0.53 | 0.15 | 0.64 | 0.65 | 0.09 |
| Patient experiences morning stiffness | no | 6 | 0.34 | 0.39 | 0.29 | 0.48 | 0.49 | 0.20 | 0.62 | 0.65 | 0.08 |
| | slight | 8 | 0.29 | 0.34 | 0.22 | 0.48 | 0.50 | 0.16 | 0.64 | 0.62 | 0.10 |
| | moderate | 8 | 0.34 | 0.36 | 0.14 | 0.54 | 0.56 | 0.09 | 0.64 | 0.66 | 0.10 |
| | severe | 10 | 0.24 | 0.25 | 0.12 | 0.51 | 0.50 | 0.09 | 0.56 | 0.56 | 0.08 |
| | very severe | 4 | 0.18 | 0.21 | 0.09 | 0.58 | 0.60 | 0.13 | 0.66 | 0.71 | 0.12 |
| Duration of morning stiffness | 30 min | 9 | 0.42 | 0.41 | 0.23 | 0.49 | 0.52 | 0.18 | 0.67 | 0.67 | 0.09 |
| | >30 min | 31 | 0.28 | 0.31 | 0.17 | 0.53 | 0.55 | 0.13 | 0.62 | 0.62 | 0.11 |
| ESR† (mm/h) | 3–17 | 3 | 0.42 | 0.38 | 0.11 | 0.62 | 0.62 | 0.12 | 0.58 | 0.59 | 0.05 |
| | 18–40 | 12 | 0.29 | 0.35 | 0.24 | 0.61 | 0.55 | 0.20 | 0.64 | 0.65 | 0.08 |
| | 41–70 | 8 | 0.34 | 0.35 | 0.17 | 0.52 | 0.55 | 0.10 | 0.66 | 0.67 | 0.12 |
| | 71–120 | 11 | 0.31 | 0.32 | 0.19 | 0.49 | 0.50 | 0.09 | 0.57 | 0.56 | 0.10 |

* Good articular function = 0, poor = 78.
† ESR = erythrocyte sedimentation rate. (Reproduced from Ref. 8 with permission.)

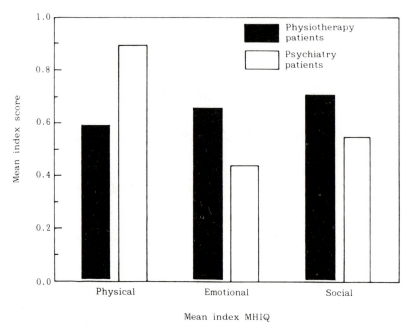

**Figure 6.2** Comparison of mean index score on MHIQ indexes by patient group

practice patients to have poorer MHIQ emotional function scores than the other three groups.

The patients being cared for at home, who included the respiratory disease patients and the long-term diabetic patients, were hypothesized to have poorer social function than the other two groups. Figure 6.5 shows the respiratory disease patients and the long-term diabetic patients had poor MHIQ social function scores compared with the other two patient groups.

### Responsiveness (sensitivity to change in health status)

Figure 6.6 shows the MHIQ physical function index mean and standard error scores for four administration times in the study of physiotherapy outpatients[7]. A one week no-change interval occurred between Time I and II and between Time III and Time IV. Patients entered the clinic at Time I and were discharged from the clinic at Time III. Thus the Time II to Time III interval was expected to show change on the MHIQ. The results confirmed this did occur, with no change, as expected, between Times I and II and Times III and IV. As reported above in the questionnaire format section, the MHIQ scores were responsive to change regardless of the mode of administration

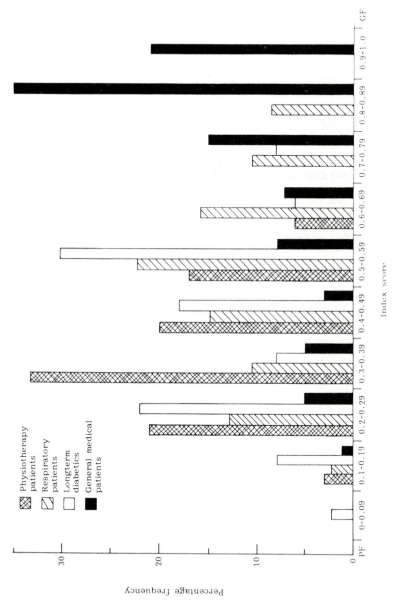

**Figure 6.3** Physical function status of selected populations

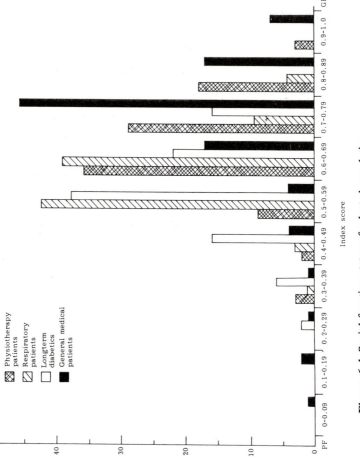

**Figure 6.4** Social function status of selected populations

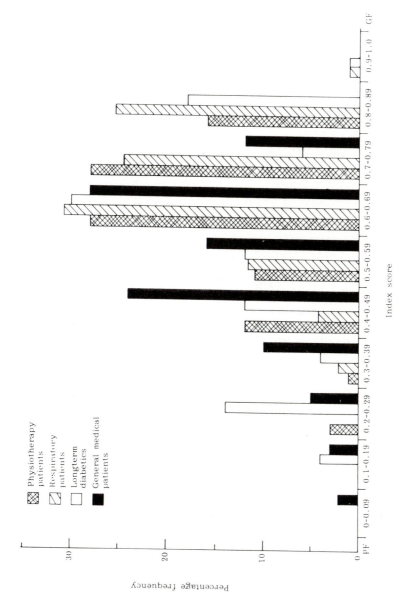

**Figure 6.5** Emotional function status of selected populations

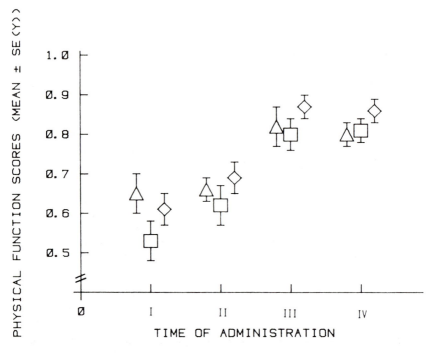

**Figure 6.6** Responsiveness of MHIQ Physical function index scores to change in health status. Physiotherapy outpatients were assessed on four occasions by either self-assessment (triangles); telephone interview (squares); or personal interview (diamonds)

of the MHIQ. Future studies need to be conducted with persons whose social and emotional functioning are known to change in order to determine the responsiveness to change of the MHIQ social and emotional function scores.

## ASSESSMENT OF THE QUESTIONNAIRE

### Applications

The MHIQ has been used in the following patient populations: physiotherapy outpatients[7]; psychiatry outpatients[6]; insulin-dependent diabetic patients receiving home nursing care[6]; chronic respiratory disease patients living at home[6]; family practice patients[22]; patients with rheumatoid arthritis[6]; multiple sclerosis patients living at home[15]; elderly patients under acute care in a hospital[12]; elderly patients discharged from a home care programme by public health nurses[4]; patients at a rehabilitation centre[11]; and patients with acute myocardial infarction[26].

**Strengths and limitations**

In a recent paper, Feinstein and his colleagues[10] outline six main clinical and scientific issues related to the assessment and application of indexes of quality of life/health status (functional disability) such as the MHIQ: the omission of attention to personal collaboration, the role of personal preferences, the measurement of change, the selection and aggregation of components, the strategies used in justifying an index, and the unsatisfactory application of 'established' indexes. Each of these issues now will be briefly outlined and used to describe the strengths and weaknesses of the MHIQ.

*Patient's collaboration*

> When a patient's collaboration is needed to perform a task, the index will be inadequate if it describes only the magnitude of the task while omitting such crucial concomitant factors as the patient's effort or support in the performance. An improved index would appropriately modify the ratings according to these additional factors[10].

As Guyatt *et al.*[14] have shown in a randomized controlled trial, the distance covered in a timed walking test can be substantially increased if a technician walks alongside the patient offering encouragement. The MHIQ adequately taps the magnitude of the task or performance, as outlined above (Instrument description) but it does not include items on the patient's effort or support in performance. Feinstein *et al.*[10] suggest that instruments such as the MHIQ should be supplemented with a single question about the availability of a person who is willing and ready to give support if needed, or, instead of trying to estimate a patient's 'motivation' in working at rehabilitative exercises, nurses or other therapists could be asked to rate the observed effort and cooperation. The MHIQ should also recognize certain non-human sources of support, such as including a question about the use of ramps or elevators for someone who is wheelchair bound, that can also make important distinctions in a patient's ability to function. Inclusion of one or more of these three additions to the MHIQ would address this important issue of patient collaboration and result in an instrument that measures more than just the magnitude of the task alone.

*Patient's preferences*

> If an index refers to multiple disabilities, the focus of the index may become blurred in the combination of ratings for important and unimportant problems. By determining the patient's preferences about the relative importance of the disabilities, and by adjusting the focus of the index accordingly, investigators can aim at clearer targets in planning and evaluating therapeutic interventions[10].

In a recent study of patients with chronic respiratory disease[13], patients were asked to select quality of care/health status items that were important to them and only these were included in a new instrument to measure quality of life for such patients. This study showed that using only items viewed by patients as important can decrease the sample size required in clinical trials, as these items were more sensitive to change when compared to general measures of quality of life/health status such as the MHIQ. Thus, there is now documentary evidence to support the point that unselected items (global measures) create problems of distinguishing changes[10]. In contrast to this new instrument, items in the MHIQ are preselected for the patients and therefore may not include quality of life/health status items that are important to specific patients with specific diseases. The MHIQ is a global measure of physical, emotional and social function. Consequently, it should be supplemented with items that have a specific bearing on the study questions in order to improve the validity of the results in studies that evaluate health care interventions or describe or predict health status/quality of life[17].

### Measurement of changes

Indexes that have been constructed to describe a patient's single state in time may not always be suitable for discriminating changes. The changes may be either poorly discerned if the rating scale has too few categories, or obscured if too many extraneous variables are included in the index. The problem can often be solved by developing indexes that are specifically concerned with transitions and that concentrate on the main attributes of interest[10].

The MHIQ physical function scores have been shown to reflect clinically important change, such as discharge from hospital or an outpatient physiotherapy clinic[7,22]. Also, the single state in time items used to calculate MHIQ physical function scores were found to be correlated with the transition ratings (for example, 'Since – [time of first visit] has the patient's physical function changed? – better, same, worse') of a physiotherapist[7]. This responsiveness is presumably because the MHIQ physical function scores consist of items which cover a range of quality of life/health status categories, and few extraneous items contribute to the MHIQ physical function score.

In a randomized trial evaluating the effects of a drug prescribed to patients with rheumatoid arthritis, the responsiveness of the MHIQ physical, social and emotional function scores to small, clinically significant changes were compared with other instruments including the MACTAR (McMaster Toronto Arthritis) Patient Function Preference Questionnaire[23]. With the MACTAR, it was possible for an interviewer to ask each patient to identify activities related to mobility, self-care, work, and social and leisure activity. Patients were then asked to rank these activities in the order in which they would most prefer to have them improved. At the end of the study (18 weeks) or at the time of dropout, all patients were asked if there had been improvement in the ranked disabilities specified by them at the beginning of the study. The MACTAR outperformed the three MHIQ indexes in reflecting clinically significant changes when compared to physician assessments and patient self-report measures of change. Again, the MHIQ physical function scores outperformed the social function and emotional function scores in reflecting change.

The usefulness of the MHIQ score to detect change, therefore, will depend on the MHIQ's applicability to the study question and analysis of individual item changes to determine which items contributed to the changed MHIQ score. The MHIQ could be supplemented with transition items for the patient to complete in these studies designed to detect change in the quality of life/health status of the patient.

### Hierarchical aggregations

When multiple variables are aggregated, the resulting scale of categories can be arranged as a summation or as a hierarchy. The summations are easier to organize but may be ambiguous because the same summary score can be produced by many different variations in scores of the components. The hierarchical arrangements provide clearer ideas of what is contained in each score but are difficult to construct because the combinations of different components must be ranked for relative importance. The hierarchical decisions can be eased if the 'importance' of individual variables or combinations is determined from patients' preferences, clinical judgements, or documentary correlations[10].

The responses to MHIQ items are dichotomized and weights of one for a good health response and zero for a poor health response are assigned to each item, then added to calculate an MHIQ physical function score, an MHIQ social function score, and a MHIQ emotional function score (see Appendix, p. 449). Function scores are standardized to index values ranging from 0 (extremely poor function) to 1.0 (extremely good function).

The use of other weights for good and poor responses was assessed with a group of chronic obstructive lung disease patients at home[6]. In this study, 12 respirologists based in the Hamilton area identified 94 chronic obstructive lung disease patients in their practices. All patients were experiencing shortness of breath and were over 40 years of age. Trained interviewers administered the MHIQ to these patients in their homes. Some wording of the MHIQ items was altered slightly to refer specifically to chronic respiratory disease and these changes have been reported elsewhere[6]. In addition, health professionals working with chronic respiratory disease patients were approached to assist in developing preference weights for scoring the MHIQ. Each was asked to assign to each item in the MHIQ a score between 1 and 10, according to what they thought was most important for a typical chronic respiratory disease patient's overall social, emotional and physical functioning. Each function area was weighted separately. These scores were averaged and the mean score for each question was used as a weight given to that question in a second analysis, following the analyses using the 0 and 1 arbitrary weights.

The unweighted (zero–one weights) physical and emotional function scores slightly underestimated the function of patients. The results for

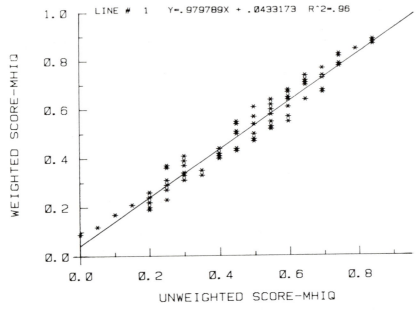

**Figure 6.7** A comparison of weighted versus unweighted MHIQ physical function scores in patients with chronic obstructive lung disease

physical function are shown in Figure 6.7. No systematic differences were found between the weighted and unweighted social function scores. The psychology literature (see from example, Ref. 27) provides evidence that little difference in total explained variance will occur between weighting schemes. However, the ranking of individuals with the MHIQ may differ using different weights and the total explained variance may increase if new health status items are included in addition to MHIQ items.

Early in the development of the MHIQ, a decision was made to report disaggregated physical, social and emotional MHIQ scores and a single MHIQ score was not calculated. Thus, in a clinical trial, an MHIQ profile can be reported showing the separate physical, social and emotional function scores in the experimental and control groups. This profile also leaves it to the investigator or reader of the study results to decide on the relative importance of each of the three components of the MHIQ. As Feinstein *et al.*[10] point out, the relative importance of components could also be decided by the patients themselves. They also suggest that the importance of different components could be determined from their statistical correlation with a selected external variable, such as hours of daily care needed, costs of care, or some other relevant attribute such as the patient's subsequent need for placement in a nursing home. For example, among recently discharged clients from home (public health) nursing care, better MHIQ physical and social function scores were more likely in older persons who received and were given more aid by their social network, but this did not hold for MHIQ emotional function scores[4]. In summary, as documentary evidence accumulates about MHIQ scores, the implications of the method of hierarchical aggregation used in MHIQ scoring will be clarified.

### Documentary justification

Although an index may be reported with an account of its conceptual justification, most indexes have not been accompanied by documentary evidence showing how well they do their job, particularly in comparison with appropriate existing indexes. The absence of such documentation – a striking feature of the published literature – can be remedied by appropriate attention from investigators and editors[10].

As outlined in the Validity section, the MHIQ physical function, emotional function and social function scores correlate with global assessments made by health professionals, and by relatives or friends, with other questionnaires such as the Bradburn Scale of Psychological Well-Being and with biological parameters of severity of disease. The MHIQ was designed to be flexible enough to use in different settings, easily communicable to health professionals, clear in its direction of improvement, and amenable to mathematical index construction. If instruments that the MHIQ was designed to replace did not meet one or more of these prerequisites, they were not compared with the MHIQ. However, future uses of the MHIQ will be better justified if further documentary evidence is accumulated about how it compares with other general measures of quality of life/health status.

### Suitability of established indexes

When investigators choose indexes that have shown good statistical coefficients in tests of 'reliability' and 'validity', the subsequent results may be unsatisfactory because the established indexes are too complex or are not aimed at the specific goal of the study. This problem can be solved by adding 'sensibility' as a criterion for choosing indexes or by creating new indexes as needed[10].

The MHIQ has been widely used because it is simple to use and has proved to be substantially useful as a general measure of quality of life to supplement more specific clinically relevant indicators in clinical trials and health evaluations. As the first part of this chapter demonstrates, the MHIQ has been around long enough to have been applied in a number of settings and this has resulted in the accumulation of evidence regarding its validity and reliability. Future users of the MHIQ must however very carefully assess these data and the usefulness of the MHIQ in addressing the questions they are proposing for their study.

## SUMMARY

On the basis of a review of a number of studies, the accumulated evidence of the validity and reliability of the MHIQ was presented. Application of the Feinstein *et al.*[10] issues related to scientific and clinical problems with indexes of quality of life/health status have shown that the MHIQ:

- does a poor job of tapping patient effort and patient preferences
- is a fair measure of change
- adequately deals with the hierarchical aggregation of the components of quality of life/health status
- has above average documentation that can be used to justify its use
- receives high marks on 'sensibility' as it actually has been used for research studies.

Future use of the MHIQ will depend on the resources available to develop alternative better instruments and the applicability of the MHIQ to the purpose of the study.

## References

1. Allodi, F.A. and Coates, D.B. Social stress, psychiatric symptoms and help seeking patterns. *Can. Psychiat. Assoc. J.* 1973; 15: 153–158.
2. Allodi. Personal Communication.
3. Bennett, A.E., Garrad, J. and Halil, T. Chronic disease and disability in the community: a prevalence study. *Br. Med. J.* 1970; 3: 762–764.
4. Black, M. Health and social support of older adults in the community. *Can. J. Aging* 1985; 4: 213–226.
5. Buchanan, W.W., Tugwell, P. and Bombardier, C. (eds). Proceedings of the Conference on Outcome Measures in Rheumatological Clinical Trials, December 7–8, 1981, Hamilton, Ontario, Canada. *J. Rheumatol.* 1982; 9: 749–806.
6. Chambers, L.W. The McMaster Health Index Questionnaire (MHIQ): Methodologic Documentation and Report of the Second Generation of Investigations. Department of Clinical Epidemiology and Biostatistics. McMaster University, Hamilton, 1982.
7. Chambers, L.W., Haight, M. and Norman, G. *et al.* Measurement of health status: sensitivity to change and the effect of mode of administration on health status measurement. *Med. Care* 1987.
8. Chambers, L.W., MacDonald, L.A., Tugwell, P. *et al.* The McMaster Health Index Questionnaire as a measurement of quality of life for patients with rheumatoid disease. *J. Rheumatol.* 1982; 9: 780–784.
9. Chambers, L.W., Sackett, D.L., Goldsmith, C.H. *et al.* Development and application of an index of social function. *Health Serv. Res.* 1976; 11: 430–441.
10. Feinstein, A.R., Josephy, B.R. and Wells, C.K. Scientific and clinical problems in indexes of functional disability. *Ann. Intern. Med.* 1986; 105: 413–420.

11. Fortin, F. and Kerouac, S. Validation of questionnaires on physical function. *Nurs. Res.* 1977; 26: 128–135.
12. Gibbon, M., Tugwell, P., Chambers L.W. *et al.* Measurement of health status in the evaluation of coordinated home health care. Presented at the 111th Annual Meeting of the American Public Health Association, Dallas, November 1983.
13. Guyatt, G.H., Berman, L.B., Townsend, M. *et al.* A new measure of quality of life for clinical trials in chronic lung disease. *Thorax* 1987.
14. Guyatt, G.H., Bombardier, C. and Tugwell, P.X. Measuring disease-specific quality of life in clinical trials. *Can. Med. Assoc. J.* 1986; 134: 889–895.
15. Harper, A.C., Harper, D.A., Chambers, L.W. *et al.* Physical and psychosocial disability in multiple sclerosis: an epidemiological survey of patients in a regional clinic. *J. Chronic Dis.* 1986; 39: 305–310.
16. Holmes, T.H. and Rahe, R.H. The social readjustment rating scale. *J. Psychosom. Res.* 1967; 11: 213.
17. Kirshner, B. and Guyatt, G. A methodological framework for assessing health indices. *J. Chronic Dis.* 1985; 38: 27–36.
18. Last, J.M. and White, K.L. The content of medical care in primary practice. *Med. Care* 1969; 7: 2: 41–48.
19. Lee, P., Mukundriak, Jassani, W. *et al.* Evaluation of a functional index in rheumatoid arthritis. *Scand. J. Rheumatol.* 1973; 2: 71–77.
20. Ritchie, D.M., Boyle, J.A., McInnes, J.M. *et al.* Clinical studies with an articular index for the assessment of joint tenderness in patients with rheumatoid arthritis. *Q. J. Med. NS* 1968; 37: 393–406.
21. Robinson, J.P. and Shaver, P.R. Measures of Social Psychological Attitudes. Ann Arbor Survey Research Center, Institute for Social Research, University of Michigan, 1973.
22. Sackett, D.L., Chambers, L. W., Macpherson, A.S. *et al.* The development and application of indexes of public health: general methods and a summary of results. *Am. J. Public Health* 1977; 67: 423–428.
23. Tugwell, P., Bombardier, C., Buchanan, W.W. *et al.* Methotrexate in rheumatoid arthritis: impact on quality of life assessed by traditional standard-item and individualized patient preference health status questionnaires. *Arch. Intern. Med.* 1990; 150: 59–82.
24. Schultz, W.C. *The Firo Scales*. Palo Alto, Consulting Psychologists Press, 1967.
25. The Staff of the Benjamin Rose Hospital. Multidisciplinary study of illness in aged persons. I. Methods and preliminary results. *J. Chronic Dis.* 1958; 7: 332–345.
26. Tugwell, P., Sackett, D.L., Goldsmith, C.H. *et al.* Quality of Care in Acute Myocardial Infarction. Final Report, US National Center for Health Services Research Grant No. RO1 HS 03239, October 1983.
27. Wainer, H. Estimating coefficients in linear models: It don't make no never mind. *Psychol. Bull.* 1976; 83: 213–217.
28. Wenger, N.K., Mattson, M.E., Furberg, C.D. *et al.* (eds) *Assessment of Quality of Life in Clinical Trials of Cardiovascular Therapies*. New York, Le Jacq Publishing Company, 1984.
29. World Health Organization. *The First Ten Years of the World Health Organization*. Geneva, World Health Organization, 1958.

# 7 A health index and output measure

Rachel M. Rosser

This is a review of the work done by our group over the past 20 years. During this time some of the problems in designing global indices of health (see Refs 14, 20, 22, 23 and 32) and incorporating the same principles of utility measurement into studies of the output of services and in particular, of hospitals have been investigated[27]. Originally, the aim was to specify minimal data requirements which could be recorded routinely using existing Hospital Activity Analysis Forms, or obtained by minor modifications in the General Household Survey. Recently, more detailed descriptions which are necessary to produce a sensitive measure of change for clinical trials have been studied. This review will consider the following aspects of work: (a) background; (b) model (i.e. algebraic representation of health status); (c) implementation (from model to measure); (d) output measurement (application of model in Health service settings); (e) index of health (application of model to national community data); (f) towards a profile (detailed descriptors for use in clinical trials); (g) recent research (scaling of three-dimensional classification, time-related factors, the effect of diagnosis on the utility of health states and utilities representative of the population); (h) current research; and (i) conclusion (related to policy formation at regional and district levels).

## BACKGROUND

Our work began in the context of the Nuffield Provincial Hospitals Trust Working Party on Medical Care, which produced an important book on the evaluation of screening procedures[17] and also drew on a limited amount of literature on hospital evaluation, dating back to the work of Florence Nightingale[18], and on a more extensive and recent literature on the evaluation of medical care (see for example Refs 1, 4 and 10). Other important early work included practical studies on indices of daily living[12] and theoretical and mathematical papers on the concept of health indicators[5].

Research outside the field of health care was also considered, including fundamental psychometric work on the measurement of perception[34] which had been extended to the measurement of judgement[8]. Psychophysicists had begun to apply their technique to the economic concept of utility[35]. Economic techniques, such as output budgeting (also known as Planned Programme Budgeting Systems) and planning models, such as linear programming, derived from operation research and required measures of output which incorporated utilities. The implications of these developments for health services were being explored[19] but more progress had been made in measuring the output of other public-sector programmes, such as crime prevention[11,33]. This background has been reviewed in detail elsewhere[21]. Our original model had much in common with those developed by groups at York[7], San Diego[9], and Hamilton[37]; all are included in one of our review papers[28], and represented in this volume.

## THE MODEL

We conceived of a unit of the Health Service, such as a hospital, as a system which organizes resources such as staff, beds, and clinics (input) so as to change the state of patients between the point of entry to the system and of exit from the system.

The utility (f) of the state of morbidity (m) of the patient ($i$) at time ($t$) is represented by the term $f_{ijt}m_{it}$ ($j$ is the evaluator term). The treated state is indicated by a prime (m). The output of the system is measured over any given period by the difference between the sum of the utilities assigned to the states of health of the patients on admission and to the state of health on discharge from the system[26]. The formula indicates that utility may be affected, not only by the definition of morbidity state but also by the characteristics of the patient other than attributes of illness, e.g. age, occupation and marital status. It may also reflect characteristics of the judges who provide the valuation (shown by changes in the term $j$), e.g. the value systems of older judges may differ from those of younger ones. In addition, the time at which values are elicited may be important. Consider how attitudes have changed over the past two hundred years to symptoms such as psychosexual difficulties, delusions, depression, or cosmetic defects on the one hand, and coughs, fevers, bacterial infections and diabetes on the other. The terms $i$ and $j$ have been studied, but it is too early to quantify the importance of $t$. This model has been developed in more detail[21,30-32] to accommodate changes attributable to the natural history of disease and changes owing to therapeutic interventions. Using the notation developed above, the total effect of treatment is given by:

$$\sum_{t=0}^{l} [f_{ijt} (m_{it}) - f_{ijt} (m'_{it})] + \sum_{t=l+1}^{k} [D_{ijt} - f_{ijt} (m'_{it})]$$

where, as noted above, f is a function of the characteristics of the patient ($i$) (e.g. his age, sex, etc.), the evaluator ($j$), and the time in the future ($t$) at which the condition will be experienced, and where $l$ is the life-span. The equation represents the difference in the utility assigned to the morbidity experienced by the patient after treatment, compared with that experienced without treatment, during $l$ of the untreated individual, together with the difference between the utility of being dead between the first unit of time after the time at which death would occur without treatment ($k$), compared with the utility of the morbidity experienced by the treated, and therefore surviving, patient between $l + 1$ and $k$. This defines an absolute measure, taking into account spontaneous deterioration and remission. Because of ethical and logistical problems involved in documenting natural history, an absolute measure of outcome is unattainable in practice, and the model was modified to provide a comparative measure. In practice, this limitation complicates the interpretation of data by raising questions about comparability of cohort groups.

A further simplification was the separation of the effect of a service on present morbidity state (EPS), the effect on longer-term morbidity state (ELS) and the effect on mortality (EM). The simplified formula for EPS is:

$$EPS = \sum_{i=1}^{N} f_{ojo} (m_{io}) - f_{ojo} (m'_{il})$$

where $N$ is the total number of patients, $t=0$ is the beginning of an episode of care, and $t=1$ is the end of the episode. This formula permits a comparison between services to similar groups of patients and it was used in our hospital studies.

## IMPLEMENTATION

The model specifies a definition of an episode. Definitions which have been used include admission to discharge (Charing Cross multi-speciality study)[21,24] and admission to first follow-up visit (St. Olave's studies)[20,21,32]. For community care, an episode might be one year of operation of a service. In policy decisions, a year is typically taken as the unit of time. The model also specifies a set of descriptions of states of ill-health and a scale which places values or utilities on each state.

**Table 7.1** Descriptions of states of illness

---

*Disability\**

---

8    Unconscious
7    Not in 8 but confined to bed
6    Not in 7 but confined to chair or wheelchair or able to move around in the home
     only with support from an assistant
5    Not in 6 but unable to undertake any paid employment. Unable to continue any
     education. Old people confined to home except for escorted outings and short
     walks and unable to do shopping. Housewives only able to perform a few simple
     tasks
4    Not in 5 but choice of work or performance at work severely limited. Housewives
     and old people able to do light housework only, but able to go out shopping
3    Not in 4 but severe social disability and/or slight impairment of performance at
     work. Able to do all housework except very heavy tasks
2    Not in 3 but slight social disability
1    No disability

---

*Distress\*\**

---

(a)   *Published set of descriptors*
      Pain and mental suffering
      4  Severe
      3  Moderate
      2  Mild
      1  None
(b)   *Current set of descriptors*
      Pain\*\*\*                  Distress\*\*\*\*
      5  Agonizing pain          5  Extreme distress
      4  Severe pain             4  Severe distress
      3  Moderate pain           3  Moderate distress
      2  Mild pain               2  Mild distress
      1  None                    1  None

|  | Pain\*\*\* | Mental disturbance\*\*\*\* |
|---|---|---|
| State 1 | None | No mental distress |
| State 2 | The patient has occasional mild pain | Mild mental distress |
| State 3 | The patient has moderate pain some of the time | Moderate mental distress |
| State 4 | The patient has severe pain most of the time | Severe mental distress |
| State 5 | The patient has continuous agonizing pain | Distress so severe that sufferer is actively suicidal |

---

\*This describes the extent to which a patient is judged to be unable to pursue the activities of a normal person at the time at which the classification is made. Patients in Class 2 are slightly disabled, but performance in their normal work is not impaired. This degree of disablement affects social activities and personal relations. It includes such conditions as mild cosmetic defects, slight injuries and diseases which may interfere with hobbies but not with essential activities, and some of the less-severe psychiatric states which cause some social disablement.
\*\* This describes the patient's pain, mental suffering in relation to disablement, anxiety and depression.

## Set of descriptions

### Criteria

We used standard descriptions of states rather than scenarios as used by Torrance's group[37]. Therefore, the set of descriptions had to meet the usual minimal criteria for a classification, i.e. the states should be mutually exclusive and jointly exhaustive. Hence it should be possible to assign all members of samples studied to one morbidity class only.

In addition, for routine use, the descriptive system must be shown to be used consistently in studies of inter-observer and test–retest reliability and should be acceptable and quick to use.

### Disability and distress

The descriptive system is shown in Table 7.1. It was derived from studies involving sixty doctors of all specialities who identified the characteristics which they took into account in comparing the severity of patients' states.

The two-dimensional system defines 29 possible combinations of disability and distress. Both dimensions are complex and amenable to further subdivision. Disability subsumes observed mobility and social function; distress subsumes pain and other types of subjective distress, especially endogenous or reactive disturbances of mood and reactions to symptoms such as breathlessness and to disability. Unconsciousness is included under the heading disability. The system was shown to be reliable in use by doctors and multi-disciplinary terms[2,21].

## The scale

### Methods

The principal methods by which scales of value and utility can be obtained are: (i) utility production; (ii) psychometric valuation by interview or questionnaire; and (iii) behavioural analysis.

The classical method of utility production is the Von Neumann–Morgenstern standard gamble, which can be extended to multi-attribute utility measurement. The term psychometric encompasses a large number of techniques and includes methods of magnitude estimation, fractionation, equivalence and category scaling, all of which have been applied to our classification. These all carry the advantage in comparison with behavioural analysis, that the question which is being asked can be specified precisely and the sensitivity of the results to variations in this operation can be tested. However, they have the disadvantage that people may not behave in a way which reflects the attitudes they verbalize. Both the standard gamble and behavioural analysis methods have also been used in our studies.

**Table 7.2** Psychometric scales

| | Version 1 Median scale with interval between first two states set at 1* | | | | Version 2 Geometric mean scale normalized about score for state 1,2 for comparison with median scale** | | | |
|---|---|---|---|---|---|---|---|---|
| Distress | 1 | 2 | 3 | 4 | 1 | 2 | 3 | 4 |
| Disability | | | | | | | | |
| 1 | 0.00 | 1.00 | 2.00 | 6.67 | 0.00 | 1.00 | 2.97 | 13.20 |
| 2 | 2.00 | 2.70 | 5.45 | 13.50 | 2.01 | 3.38 | 6.61 | 24.56 |
| 3 | 4.00 | 5.53 | 8.75 | 17.50 | 4.67 | 6.52 | 10.93 | 40.98 |
| 4 | 7.25 | 8.70 | 11.67 | 26.00 | 8.14 | 11.19 | 16.15 | 55.84 |
| 5 | 10.85 | 13.03 | 20.00 | 60.00 | 13.68 | 16.70 | 27.28 | 100.39 |
| 6 | 25.00 | 31.00 | 64.00 | 200.00 | 35.52 | 47.04 | 107.14 | 274.42 |
| 7 | 64.50 | 87.20 | 200.00 | 497.14 | 108.21 | 155.75 | 343.15 | 732.67 |
| 8 | 405.71 | | | | 609.16 | | | |

\* Score for death on scale of permanent states = 200.00.
\*\* Score for death on scale of permanent states = 262.66.

Version 3
Geometric mean scale
not normalized

| Distress | 1 | 2 | 3 | 4 |
|---|---|---|---|---|
| Disability | | | | |
| 1 | 0.000 | 0.248 | 1.362 | 10.697 |
| 2 | 0.559 | 1.316 | 3.671 | 19.663 |
| 3 | 2.254 | 4.144 | 7.389 | 40.556 |
| 4 | 5.005 | 10.067 | 14.983 | 58.951 |
| 5 | 7.832 | 10.672 | 20.663 | 88.398 |
| 6 | 21.393 | 29.211 | 79.436 | 218.576 |
| 7 | 83.442 | 110.041 | 306.204 | 804.067 |
| 8 | 812.611 | | | |

Version 4
Geometric mean scale with
health set at 1 and
death set at 0

| Distress | 1 | 2 | 3 | 4 |
|---|---|---|---|---|
| Disability | | | | |
| 1 | 1.000 | 0.995 | 0.990 | 0.967 |
| 2 | 0.990 | 0.986 | 0.973 | 0.932 |
| 3 | 0.980 | 0.972 | 0.956 | 0.912 |
| 4 | 0.964 | 0.956 | 0.942 | 0.870 |
| 5 | 0.946 | 0.935 | 0.900 | 0.700 |
| 6 | 0.875 | 0.845 | 0.680 | 0.000 |
| 7 | 0.677 | 0.564 | 0.000 | -1.486 |
| 8 | -1.028 | | | |

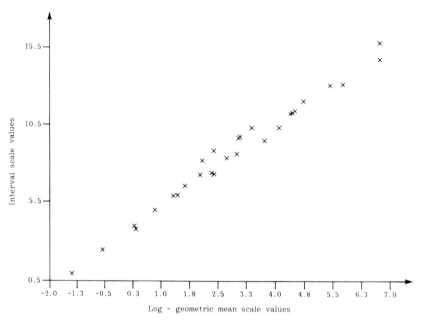

**Figure 7.1** Relationship between log-magnitude estimates and interval values

## Psychometric scales

Table 7.2 shows a psychometric scale obtained by a method of magnitude estimation first used for measuring crime seriousness[11]. Four versions were chosen using both the median and geometric means as measures of central tendency normalized with the interval between the lowest two states set at 1.0, the non-normalized geometric means, and the geometric means transformed onto a scale for permanent states with the state of no disability and no distress set at 1.0 and death set at zero[16,21]. The latter transformation provides comparability with the work of other groups. Features of the scale include a wide range, which is much greater than that achievable by simple ranking of the 29 states. Furthermore, there is a diagonal relationship between scores for states of disability and distress, indicating as expected, some trade-off between the two dimensions. The question arises as to whether true (i.e. cardinal) measurement has been achieved, or whether the judges, who included doctors, nurses, patients and health volunteers, were capable only of simpler mathematical procedures. There is some empirical support for the claim that a cardinal scale has been achieved. If the data are re-analysed on the assumption that judges can make ordinal comparisons between pairs of states but cannot estimate ratios, an interval scale should be achieved. When plotted against the scale derived by magnitude estimation, perceptual data

for physical continua show that the resulting curve should concave–curvili-
near, and a power of logarithmic transformation should result in a linear
relationship. As shown in Figure 7.1, a log-linear relationship is obtained by
transforming our psychometric data. This analysis no only helps to validate
the measurement properties of the scale, but suggests there is scope for briefer
psychometric techniques, supplemented by mathematical transformation, so
that more elaborate descriptions can be placed on cardinal scales[15].

The characteristics of scales derived from judges with different characteristics, designated by $j$ in the equations, have also been examined. Age,
social class, sex, religious belief and other characteristics of the judge were
not correlated with significant differences in scales[25]. However, the experience of illness of the judge, whether as a care-giver or a patient, was
correlated with differences in scale values, and especially with the ratio of
the most severe to the least severe state, as shown in Figure 7.2.

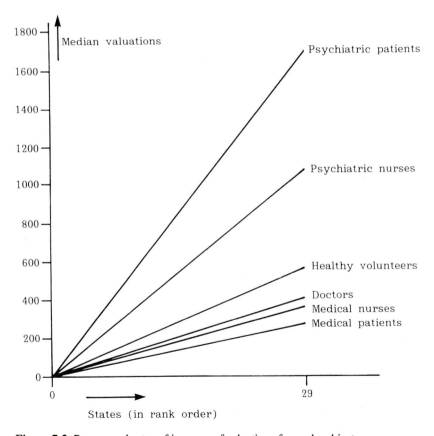

**Figure 7.2** Ranges and rates of increase of valuations for each subject group

*Behavioural scale*

Figure 7.3 shows a comparison between the normalized median psychometric scale, and a scale derived from the analysis of one form of behaviour, the award of compensation in the courts for disability and distress owing to injury or industrial disease[29]. It is notable that the scales are very similar ($r=0.814$, $p<0.001$) except for the most severe states, where the psychometric valuations are higher. This discrepancy appears to be an artefact of the rounding down process which sometimes occurs with very high cost awards in the High Courts. When the total is rounded down, no distinction is made between reductions in the pecuniary and non-pecuniary elements, and it is possible that the discrepancy between the two scales might be less conspicuous if the legal scale were updated to take account of recent very high cost awards.

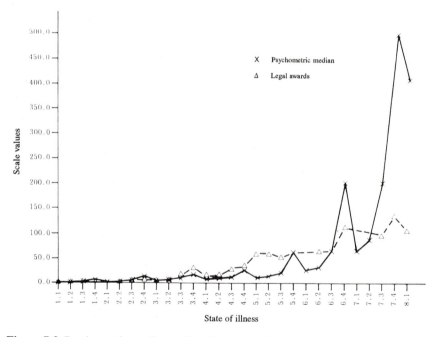

**Figure 7.3** Psychometric median and legal awards scale

## OUTPUT MEASUREMENT

### St. Olave's: first hospital application

This classification was applied to all patients admitted to a 300-bed district general hospital during one month. The quality of data was checked frequently and reliability was maintained. A total 1679 categorizations of patients' states were made by doctors of every speciality and level of seniority. The

**Table 7.3** St. Olave's Study: percentage distribution of patients' distress (1–4) between states in relation to disability (1–8)

| Disability | Admission | | | | Discharge | | | | First follow-up visit | | | |
|---|---|---|---|---|---|---|---|---|---|---|---|---|
| | 1 | 2 | 3 | 4 | 1 | 2 | 3 | 4 | 1 | 2 | 3 | 4 |
| 1 | 19 | 12 | 3 | 1 | 33 | 10 | 1 | 0 | 45 | 7 | 0 | 0 |
| 2 | 10 | 12 | 3 | 1 | 21 | 11 | 1 | 0 | 7 | 11 | 2 | 0 |
| 3 | 1 | 3 | 1 | 1 | 2 | 3 | 1 | 0 | 3 | 4 | 2 | 0 |
| 4 | 3 | 3 | 5 | 1 | 3 | 4 | 1 | 0 | 1 | 2 | 2 | 0 |
| 5 | 1 | 3 | 4 | 2 | 3 | 2 | 2 | 1 | 2 | 8 | 1 | 0 |
| 6 | 1 | 1 | 2 | 0 | 0 | 0 | 1 | 0 | 1 | 1 | 1 | 0 |
| 7 | 1 | 2 | 3 | 1 | 0 | 0 | 0 | 0 | 0 | 0 | 0 | 0 |
| 8 | 0 | 0 | 0 | 0 | 0 | 0 | 0 | 0 | 3 | 3 | 3 | 3 |

return rate was 97% for in-patients and 92% for out-patients. The percentage distribution of patients' states is shown in Table 7.3. There was a clear movement of patients from the more severe categories to the less severe categories between admission and discharge. Of patients in this study, 19% were admitted free of disability and distress, for investigations and treatments directed towards prognosis rather than their present state. The figure of 19% is higher than we have recorded more recently, probably because the reduction is bed numbers and the trend towards day-care for milder cases result in a more ill in-patient population.

Between discharge and one-month follow-up, the movements of patients were not so obvious. Whereas the proportion of patients free of disability and distress increased from 33% to 45%, there was also an increase in the proportion of severely disabled and distressed patients. Whether the value of improvements during convalescence was offset by the deteriorations can only be determined by applying a cardinal scale of valuations of the 29 states.

The difference between the admission and discharge scores of the 475 patients who were admitted and discharged during the study period was calculated by application of the median psychometric scale, normalized around the score for state 1,2. These were expressed as total changes, mean change per patient and percentage contribution to the hospital total. The calculations were repeated after application of sixteen other psychometric or behavioural scales. The teams and specialities were then ranked in terms of their mean effect on present state (EPS) and percentage contribution to the hospital total. The results were found to be relatively insensitive to the choice of scaling technique, statistical treatment of psychometric and behavioural data, or characteristics of the judges who produced the scale. However, the results were highly sensitive to the difference between empirical scales and

**Table 7.4** St. Olave's Study: application of psychometric median scale to specialities

| Parameter | Medicine | Surgery | Psychiatry | Geriatrics | Miscellaneous | Hospital Total |
|---|---|---|---|---|---|---|
| No. Patients | 148 | 199 | 79 | 50 | 79 | 475 |
| Total score at $t_1$ | 3800 | 2436 | 708 | 1829 | 622 | 9395 |
| Total score at $t_2$ | 1824 | 1886 | 462 | 1914 | 298 | 6384 |
| *Effect on Present State (EPS)* | | | | | | |
| Change in total score | 1976 | 550 | 246 | -85 | 324 | 3011 |
| Change (%) | 52 | 23 | 35 | -5 | 52 | 32 |
| Mean score at $t_1$ | 26 | 21 | 9 | 37 | 8 | 20 |
| Mean score at $t_2$ | 12 | 16 | 6 | 38 | 4 | 13 |
| Change in mean score | 14 | 5 | 3 | -1 | 4 | 7 |
| % hospital total at $t_1$ | 40 | 26 | 8 | 19 | 7 | 100 |
| % hospital total at $t_2$ | 29 | 30 | 7 | 30 | 5 | 100 |
| EPS as % of hospital change | 66 | 18 | 8 | -3 | 11 | 100 |

arbitrary scales obtained by ranking the states in order of disability or distress or by diagonal progression across the matrix.

Table 7.4 shows the data by speciality. Internal medicine, the speciality which treated the greatest number of patients, had the highest EPS. The second highest EPS was achieved with a much smaller number of patients under the heading miscellaneous – usually patients admitted briefly as emergencies and not assigned formally to particular consultants. These patients were commonly treated by trainees rather than consultants and the data could therefore be said to prove that doctors' efficacy diminishes with experience! Another and more plausible interpretation of the data would be that these acutely-ill patients were severely distressed when they came into hospital but many had self-remitting conditions or ones which were relatively straightforward to treat. Thus, patient mix would explain the disparity between the results for this group and that of the other three major specialities.

Unexpectedly, surgery came fourth below psychiatry. This result highlighted another problem, namely that surgical patients are commonly admitted from waiting lists, have disability and pain inflicted on them by the surgical procedure, and are discharged to convalesce. Thus, the disparity between medicine and surgery perhaps reflects the choice of definition of episode for the analysis shown in Table 7.4. A better definition of episode for the evaluation of surgery would be the interval between admission to hospital care and first follow-up assessment as an out-patient, as used for Table 7.3. This may not be so appropriate for medicine, because patients who received temporary relief from medical treatment may have begun to deteriorate after discharge. To be unbiased, it is necessary to use both definitions of episode and to examine the sensitivity of any conclusions to the choice of definition.

The geriatric group achieved a negative EPS and thus came last in the order. This was not surprising, since this unit admitted particularly chronic cases who were unlikely to leave hospital in a better condition. For chronic care it is preferable to compare the sum of daily ratings of patient's states[24].

This discussion illustrates some of the methodological and interpretive issues which must be considered before such tabulations could be used in evaluation and in decisions about resource allocation. The tabulations by team (Table 7.5) pose more difficult problems of interpretation. The three medical teams and the three surgical teams treated mainly local patients, predominantly as emergencies, on a one in three daily rota. Each team had some special interests, but these did not have a substantial impact on the patient cohort. Whereas medical team B treated the highest number of patients (80) and achieved the highest mean change in their state, medical team C achieved the greatest proportionate change in its patients, and its low total figures are a result of a low throughput of patients.

How might data like this be used? They might provoke a debate about the

**Table 7.5** St. Olave's Study: application to medial and surgical teams

| Parameter | Medical Team | | | Total medicine | Surgical team | | | Total for surgery | Hospital total |
|---|---|---|---|---|---|---|---|---|---|
| | A | B | C | | X | Y | Z | | |
| No. patients | 62 | 80 | 6 | 148 | 63 | 47 | 9 | 119 | 475 |
| Total score at $t_1$ | 1454 | 2280 | 104 | 3838 | 632 | 1739 | 65 | 2436 | 9394 |
| Total score at $t_2$ | 812 | 984 | 28 | 1824 | 599 | 1228 | 59 | 1886 | 6384 |
| Effect on present state (EPS) (change in total score) | 642 | 1296 | 76 | 2014 | 33 | 511 | 6 | 550 | 3010 |
| Mean score at $t_1$ | 24 | 29 | 17 | 26 | 10 | 37 | 7 | 21 | 20 |
| Mean score at $t_2$ | 13 | 12 | 5 | 12 | 10 | 26 | 7 | 16 | 13 |
| Change in mean score | 11 | 17 | 12 | 14 | 0 | 11 | 0 | 5 | 7 |
| % speciality score at $t_1$ | 38 | 59 | 3 | – | 26 | 71 | 3 | – | – |
| % speciality score at $t_2$ | 45 | 54 | 1 | – | 32 | 65 | 3 | – | – |
| Change (%) | 43 | 57 | 73 | – | 5 | 29 | 10 | – | – |
| EPS as % of change for speciality | 30 | 66 | 4 | – | 6 | 93 | 1 | – | – |
| EPS as % of hospital change | 20 | 43 | 3 | 66 | 1 | 17 | 0 | 18 | 100 |

appropriateness of the selection criteria of the two teams. Medical team A is ranked third on mean score at $t_2$ and change in mean score. This finding would stimulate other enquires. For example, we might wish to compare mean lengths of stay for the three team. It could be that consultant A discharged his patients relatively early and that they convalesced successfully at home, whereas consultant C kept them in for an unnecessarily long period to recover fully in hospital. Or perhaps consultant A admitted the wrong patients; they were less ill than those of consultant B, and might not be sufficiently ill to really need hospital treatment. On the other hand, they may have been more ill than those under consultant C, and might be too ill to benefit from admission. The distribution of the results must be examined, since average figures might have been distorted by one or two patients who seriously deteriorated.

A study of the change in individual patients supported the view that team A admitted several seriously-ill patients and also a number of minimally-ill patients, whereas team B admitted more moderately-ill patients. Team A's diagnostic mix might now be further examined, and eventually questions might be asked about the standards of care provided by the team.

The data on surgical teams in Table 7.5 raise yet another question. The team which was ranked lowest for mean change treated the highest number of patients. This raises the question of whether this team was inappropriately motivated by existing methods of evaluating performance. The data most widely available on the teams' activities at present are numbers of patients treated (patient throughput). The best way to perform well by this criterion is to admit large numbers of mildly-ill patients and discharge them quickly. In this instance, this suspicion proved correct! This team was indeed particularly sensitive to existing performance indicators and may have been focusing on numbers of patients treated at the expense of more clinically-relevant criteria. Had figures on their EPS been available, perhaps they would have responded differently.

**Charing Cross: second hospital application**

This study covered fewer specialities, only fifty beds, and excluded out-patients. It lasted for 3 months, because this was the duration of rotational house officers' stay.

All the in-patients under the care of two nephrologists, three respirologists and two psychiatrists were classified by house officers and registrars as in the first study and the quality-control procedure was identical, including frequent checks of inter-observer and test–retest reliability. A total of 476 categorizations were made by doctors and the return rate was nearly 100%. In a parallel study of the same patient population, data were provided by nurses[2]. In this instance it proved feasible to collect data daily on all the

**Table 7.6** Charing Cross Study: percentage distribution of patients' distress by state

| Disability | Admission | | | | | Discharge | | | | |
|---|---|---|---|---|---|---|---|---|---|---|
| | 1 | 2 | 3 | 4 | Total | 1 | 2 | 3 | 4 | Total |
| 1 | 3 | 1 | 1 | 0 | 5 | 11 | 3 | 1 | 0 | 15 |
| 2 | 5 | 11 | 1 | 0 | 17 | 14 | 16 | 3 | 0 | 33 |
| 3 | 1 | 12 | 10 | 0 | 23 | 5 | 16 | 7 | 0 | 28 |
| 4 | 0 | 7 | 6 | 0 | 13 | 2 | 5 | 1 | 0 | 8 |
| 5 | 1 | 5 | 8 | 1 | 15 | 5 | 5 | 5 | 0 | 15 |
| 6 | 1 | 5 | 8 | 1 | 15 | 0 | 1 | 0 | 0 | 1 |
| 7 | 1 | 3 | 1 | 1 | 6 | 0 | 0 | 0 | 0 | 0 |
| 8 | 6 | | | | 6 | 0 | | | | |
| Total | 18 | 44 | 35 | 3 | 100 | 37 | 46 | 17 | 0 | 100 |

patients in medical and surgical wards. The return rate was 100% and the results of inter-observer and test–retest reliability checks were all statistically significant.

During the study, 138 complete episodes of in-patient care were documented, the remaining 216 episodes being incomplete because the patients were in hospital at the start or end of the study. The percentage distribution of patient states is shown in Table 7.6, which shows that all states were represented and few patients were admitted free of disability and distress.

In this study, teams were operating under even more similar conditions than in the St. Olave's study and additional data were collected to investigate some of the issues discussed above. The disparities in the apparent productivity of teams treating similar patients under similar conditions provokes a debate about more subtle issues.

As shown in Table 7.7, ranking in terms of EPS was different from that in terms of patient throughput. The large differences in the ranking of the two psychiatry teams and of the three respirology teams are striking, since they were practising under similar conditions.

If the figures had been collected in a management appraisal the consultants might now be asked to comment. Some important differences would emerge. Consultant 1 was an NHS consultant psychiatrist and consultant 2 had a university appointment. The question of research activities yielding outputs other than effects on patients' state therefore arises. (This issue also arose with consultants C and X in the first study.) Furthermore, consultant 1 perhaps treated more formal psychiatric illness and emphasized physical methods of treatment. Consultant 2 was more interested in personality disorders and placed more emphasis on psychotherapy. A study of the diagnostic returns would not have revealed this because patient of consultant 2

**Table 7.7** Charing Cross Study: team performance on various indicators (ranks shown in parentheses)

| Team | Psychiatry | | Nephrology | | Respirology | | |
|---|---|---|---|---|---|---|---|
| | 1 | 2 | 3 | 4 | 5 | 6 | 7 |
| No. Patients | 6 (7) | 8 (6) | 13 (4) | 34 (1) | 25 (3) | 34 (1) | 10 (5) |
| Mean length of stay | 47 (7) | 15 (6) | 8 (1) | 10 (4) | 15 (5) | 9 (2) | 14 (4) |
| Deaths | 0 (1) | 0 (1) | 4 (6) | 3 (4) | 3 (4) | 7 (7) | 1 (3) |
| Deaths predicted at admission | 0 | 0 | 0 | 0 | 0 | 0 | 0 |
| Prognosis at 1 year: | | | | | | | |
| better | 2 | 2 | 5 | 18 | 5 | 16 | 6 |
| same | 1 | 3 | 8 | 13 | 14 | 11 | 4 |
| worse | 3 | 3 | 0 | 3 | 6 | 7 | 0 |
| Prognosis ranked by % same or better | 7 | 6 | 1 | 3 | 5 | 4 | 1 |
| Prognosis ranked by 1% better | 4 | 6 | 3 | 2 | 7 | 5 | 1 |
| Ranking by EPS | 51 (2) | 3 (7) | 21 (4) | 32 (3) | 20 (5) | 102 (1) | 11 (6) |
| Mean admission score | 58 | 10 | 28 | 36 | 27 | 108 | 16 |
| Change from $t_1$ to $t_2$ (%) | 89 | 29 | 72 | 88 | 74 | 94 | 68 |

tended to be admitted in crisis and to receive similar diagnostic labels to those of consultant 1. It is only the subsidiary diagnoses which revealed the differences in patient mix and approach. Furthermore, many of the patients of consultant 2 were transferred from elsewhere in the hospital. Their more acute distress may have been ameliorated before transfer. They were transferred from medical or surgical wards when no further treatment could be offered there, and they had residual intractable physical disabilities. The scope for further improvement in a psychiatric unit might be limited.

If these explanations were correct, we would predict that consultant 2 would be willing to admit patients who were less severely disabled and distressed, would focus more on change in prognosis than on change in present state, as measured by EPS, and would probably tolerate a longer mean length of stay. The data confirmed the supposition about disability and distress (the mean score on admission for patients under consultant 1 was 58 compared with 10 for consultant 2) but the data for mean length of stay are not as predicted (mean length of stay under consultant 1 was 47 days and for consultant 2, 15 days).

Data on the effect of prognosis are also shown in Table 7.7. Patients were categorized at admission and at discharge as likely to be better, likely to be the same or likely to be worse in one year's time. (This categorization proved to be highly reliable.) The ranking of the teams by their effect on prognosis differs from the ranking of EPS, and the ordering of consultants 1 and 2 is now reversed.

Data on people's valuations of future, as contrasted with present, health are not yet available to enable us to say which system of ranking is the more appropriate, but these data demonstrate that the inclusion of prognosis in the output measurement could be important.

Consultants 5, 6, and 7 are all academic respirologists. Sub-specialization might account for some of the discrepancies in the results, but they remain perplexing. Further analysis of the data showed the average utilities of the states of patients on admission under these three consultants were 27, 108 and 16 respectively (to nearest whole figures). Thus the ranking of the three teams by percentage change parallels their ranking by severity of states of their patients on admission. The debate would now focus on whether this had arisen by change, by conscious policy, or as a corollary of selection criteria used by the three consultants. If it did not occur by chance, the appropriateness of the disparities in admission policy could be discussed. The data on prognosis show that consultant 6, whose patients seemed to improve most during treatment as shown by EPS, achieved relatively less improvement in terms of prognosis. Furthermore, a higher proportion of the patients under consultant 6 died. If prognosis were to be incorporated into the measure, it would become legitimate to incorporate the valuation of death which has already been elicited in scaling experiments[13], and thus to rank teams 5, 6, and 7 in terms of a composite measure of the relative effects on present state, future state and mortality.

Teams 3 and 4, who are nephrologists, differed less than the others. This perhaps reflects the policy of this unit, where sharing of patients by consultants was the policy and sub-specialization did not occur.

### General conclusion

One conclusion from both these hospital studies is that the measure of EPS seems to be yielding information and insights which cannot be obtained from routinely-available data and which are relevant to clinical practice and Health Service management and policy. The method is now being incorporated into a computerized management and evaluation package for use in primary care (T.S.R. Benson and J. Read, unpublished).

## INDEX OF HEALTH

### General Household Survey

The legal awards' scale was applied to the General Household Survey (GHS), which provides nationwide data on disability approximating to our states, but no information about states of distress[32]. A comparison between years was not possible because of changes in the format of the GHS; stability of format is clearly important if health indicators are to be used to make informed decisions. Analysis showed that the GHS scale contributed much less to community data than to hospital and clinical team data, since only a modest adjustment in life-expectancy data occurred by weighting for quality. This, in line with observations from other research teams[3], suggests that indicators may be most useful for measuring the output of programmes and services and for health-policy planners about treatment alternatives.

However, one of the limitations of the GHS analysis was the dominance of mortality over morbidity data and the lack of a meaningful scale value for death using this particular method of utility estimation. This was not a problem in the OPCS analysis described below.

### Office of Population Census Statistics (OPCS)

A second exercise used Office of Population Census Statistics data for 1976, and applied psychometric weightings for death[13] and for states of disability. An estimate was made of the probability of a person in each age group being in any particular state at the time of the Census. The psychometric scale of values was applied to these probabilities. The adjustment of the raw data attributable to the application of the scale rose steeply for groups over 45 years old. The value assigned to death accounted for only 2.6% of the total adjustment of people aged between 5 and 14, but as much as 74% for people aged between 65 and 74.

## TOWARDS A PROFILE FOR USE IN CLINICAL TRIALS

The global index developed is being applied in a variety of clinical trials and some results are already available.

In a controlled trial of the outcome of home visits by a respiratory health worker to patients with chronic obstructive airways disease, mortality improved, but not morbidity as measured by index and by respiratory function tests[6]. This result is not surprising, in view of the chronic and irreversible nature of the condition, and is comparable with the findings in studies applying the Sickness Impact Profile (SIP) to a sample of patients with this condition (see Bergner, p. 95). However, because the global index incorporates a score for death, unlike the SIP, it was possible to assign a utility to the change in mortality.

Preliminary results are also available from a study of the neuropsychological and psychiatric sequelae of coronary bypass surgery compared with other operations (P. Joseph, S. Newman, and P. Smith *et al.*, unpublished). The global index distinguished between the outcome of patients with and without post-operative psychiatric morbidity. When the data were disaggregated it emerged that for a given level of disability, patients who were found to be probable psychiatric cases were rated as having higher levels of distress.

The original model provides a framework for a more detailed and potentially more sensitive measure of health status. The term $f_{ijj}m_{it}$ indicates that the utility assigned to state m may depend on characteristics of the patient *i* other then those included in the definition of state m (in our example, disability and distress). These might fall anywhere on the spectrum between unequivocal illness characteristics, e.g. symptoms, to unambiguously personal characteristics, e.g. the sex of the ill person. The identification and quantification of these characteristics is the next step in the derivation of a more refined instrument, intended as a cross-diagnostic outcome measure in clinical trials. This has been approached in a pilot study in which other characteristics of people who they would wish to consider in assessing the severity of their state of ill-health were elicited from 70 subjects who acted as judges in the psychometric scaling of disability and distress. Another 64 descriptors were elicited, of which 33 were suggested by more of compound descriptors to ensure that all their elements have been identified, re-scaling, and then the derivation of a statistically taxonomy of all the descriptors.

Some of the descriptors which were assigned low scale values in this study may nevertheless have important effects on the utilities assigned to health states. For example, we studies the effect of defining the age of the ill person on the valuation by healthy volunteers of six combinations of disability and distress. The majority of subjects assigned maximal values to states in young adults, lower values to states in infants and the elderly and the lowest values to states in the very old. However, a minority of subjects assigned the highest values to states in infants and the very old. It appeared that rates took into account many factors, including the probable suffering of the individual described, the expected state of an average individual of a particular age, the maximum possible duration of the state based on life expectancy, and the assumed prognosis of people of different ages in the particular state. These time-related factors need further analysis.

These results raise issues of concern for future research. In particular, there is a question about the discrepancy between the rankings by frequency of suggestion and by psychometric scaling, together with the omission of descriptors such as machine-dependence, which were rated as very important when suggested by the interviewer. This indicates that the usual method of eliciting descriptors by soliciting suggestions from patient, professional and community samples, may not be the best way of identifying the most important aspects of health states. Furthermore, certain quite specific descriptors, e.g. breathlessness, received higher ratings than such general descriptors as institutionalization and ability to sleep, which feature in other instruments. The issues of descriptors for indicators and profiles is important and clearly remains unresolved at this stage.

## RECENT RESEARCH

### Scaling of three-dimensional classification

Disability and distress measures were rescaled with distress disaggregated into ten levels along two dimensions. Standard gamble was applied to separate levels and combined states of one year's duration.

### Time-related factors

Our group has examined the effect on utility of duration of illness (one day, one week or one year). We found that time was not perceived in a linear way and varied according to the severity of the illness state being considered.

We have also looked at the time in the future when the state is experienced. Illness states starting at five different times in the future ranging from the present to 50 years were examined. We found that the value of future health is not discounted over shorter periods (10 years); discount rates were not uniform and varied according to the severity of the illness state.

**Table 7.8** Descriptor features

| Descriptors ranked by frequency | Equivalents in other instruments | | | | |
| --- | --- | --- | --- | --- | --- |
| | SIP | MHIQ | QWB | NHP | HSCS |
| *Suggested more than once:* | | | | | |
| Attitudes to illness | – | – | – | – | – |
| Self-perception | EBB | E | – | SI* | – |
| Age of ill person | – | – | In Scale | – | – |
| prognosis | – | – | – | – | – |
| Social circumstances | SHEW | S | SAC | – | SEF |
| Family/dependents | – | S | – | Part II | – |
| Diagnosis | – | – | – | – | – |
| State of consciousness | – | – | CPX | – | – |
| Cognitive state | AB | E | CPX | – | HP |
| Occupation | W | S | SAC | Part II | RF |
| Sex (male or female) | – | – | – | – | – |
| Duration of illness | – | – | – | – | – |
| Dependency on people | EB/BCM/A | P | SAC | PM | PF |
| Dependency on drugs | – | – | CPX | – | – |
| Pain threshold | – | – | – | SI* | – |
| Pain tolerance | – | – | – | SI* | – |
| Paralysis | A/M/BCM | – | PAC/CPX | – | PF |
| Caring relatives | – | S | – | – | – |
| Treated in community | – | – | MOB | – | – |
| Premorbid function of ill person | – | – | – | – | – |
| Marital status | – | SE/ | – | – | – |
| Communication/speech | C/SI | P/S | CPX | SI* | SEF/HP |
| Previous illness | – | – | – | – | – |
| Terminal illness | – | – | – | – | – |
| Insight/belief | – | – | – | – | – |
| Part of body/organ | A | – | CPX | – | – |
| Mutilation/amputation/disfigurement | – | – | CPX | – | HP |
| Adequacy of treatment | – | – | – | – | – |
| Importance of hobbies to individual | – | S | – | – | – |
| Impairment/deafness/blindness | C | P | CPX | – | HP |
| Religion of individual | – | – | – | – | – |
| Ability to eat | E* | P | CPX | – | RF |
| Underlying conditions | – | – | – | – | – |
| Expectations of individual | EBB | E | – | – | – |
| Ability to sleep | SR | – | – | S* | – |
| Sexual function | SI | – | – | Part II | – |
| Loneliness/isolation | SI | S | – | SI* | SEF |
| Access to outside entertainment | RP | S | MOB | Part II | – |
| Access to social services | – | S | – | – | – |
| Nationality | – | – | – | – | – |
| Premorbid level of happiness of individual | – | – | – | – | – |
| Anti-social traits | SI | – | – | – | – |
| Social acceptability of illness | – | – | – | – | – |
| Breathlessness | – | – | CPX | – | – |
| Symptoms | – | – | – | – | – |
| Social class | – | S | – | – | – |
| Family history of longevity | – | – | – | – | – |

**Table 7.8** *(cont)*

| Descriptors ranked by frequency | Equivalents in other instruments | | | | |
|---|---|---|---|---|---|
| | *SIP* | *MHIQ* | *QWB* | *NHP* | *HSCS* |
| Control of bowels | BCM | – | – | – | – |
| Flexibility of lifestyle | – | E | – | – | – |
| Specific social disabilities | SHEW | S | SAC | – | – |
| Fatigue | SR | – | CPX | E?? | – |
| Premorbid lifestyle of individual | – | – | – | – | – |
| Ability to travel | M | P | MOB | – | PF |
| Contribution to society | RP | S | – | – | – |
| Attitude towards death | – | – | – | – | – |
| Presymptomatic disease | – | – | – | – | – |
| Capacity to form relationships | SI | S/E | – | Part II | – |
| Wounds | – | – | CPX | – | – |
| Size of ill person | – | – | – | – | – |
| Relationship with Health Service staff | – | – | – | – | – |
| Criminal record | – | – | – | – | – |
| Previous pattern of illness | – | – | – | – | – |
| Compliance with treatment | – | – | – | – | – |
| Dependence on drugs which affect perception | – | – | – | – | – |
| Appearance of illness | – | – | CPX | – | – |
| Genito-urinary symptoms | BCM | – | CPX | – | – |
| Nausea | EBB | – | CPX | – | – |
| Depersonalization/derealization | – | – | – | – | – |
| Diagnostic uncertainty and awareness | – | – | – | – | – |
| Suggested by interviewer but rated as important by > 50% of subjects: | | | | | |
| Dependence on a machine | – | – | – | – | – |
| Institutionalized | – | – | MOB | – | – |
| Original index: | | | | | |
| Disability | | | | | |
|   mobility | M/A | P | MOB/PAC | PM | PF |
|   role function | HM/W | S/P | SAC | Part II | RF |
|   consciousness | – | – | CPX | – | – |
| Distress | | | | | |
|   pain | EBB | – | CPX | P | HP |
|   anxiety | EBB | – | – | ER | SEF |
|   depression | EBB | E | CPX | ER | SEF |
|   reaction to distressing symptoms | SI | – | – | – | – |

*Key*: BCM, body care and movement; EBB, emotional behaviour; E, emotional function; SI, social interaction; W, work; SR, sleep and rest; CPX, symptom/problem complex; MOB, M, mobility; PAC, physical activity; SAC, social activity; C, communication; AB, alertness behaviour; RP, recreation and pastimes; A, ambulation; E*, eating; HM, home management; S, social function; P, physical function; S*, sleep; SI*, social isolation; PM, physical mobility; E??, energy; ER, emotional reaction; PF, physical function; RF, role function; HP, health problem; SEF, social-emotional function.

**Table 7.9** Ranking and scaling of 41 descriptors

| Descriptors in psychometric rank order | Psychometric weights (whole sample) | Psychometric ranks[*] | | | |
|---|---|---|---|---|---|
| | | I | II | III | IV |
| 1   Loss of consciousness | 346 | 1 | 6 | 1 | 2 |
| 2   Distress – subjective suffering including pain/anxiety/reaction to illness | 281 | 2 | 2 | 2 | 5 |
| 3   Diagnosis | 269 | 6 | 8 | 6 | 1 |
| 4   Disability – loss of mobility and social and work-role functions | 229 | 8 | 1 | 4 | 8 |
| 5   Dependence on a machine | 227 | 3 | 4 | 3 | 10 |
| 6   Prognosis | 202 | 4 | 14 | 9 | 3 |
| 7   Breathlessness – difficulty with breathing | 185 | 7 | 5 | 8 | 9 |
| 8   Symptoms | 181 | 5 | 18 | 7 | 7 |
| 9   Mutilation/amputation/disfigurement | 167 | 10 | 3 | 5 | 17 |
| 10  Adequacy of treatment | 153 | 9 | 15 | 15.5 | 6 |
| 11  Dependence on others | 140 | 14 | 21 | 24 | 4 |
| 12  Ability to communicate | 122 | 12 | 12 | 13 | 12 |
| 13  Cognitive state – ability to think clearly | 117 | 13 | 9 | 14 | 14 |
| 14  Duration of illness | 111 | 16 | 16.5 | 12 | 13 |
| 15  Pain tolerance – how much pain the ill person can bear | 111 | 11 | 7 | 17 | 24 |
| 16  Dependence on drugs | 99 | 19 | 16.5 | 11 | 16 |
| 17  Part of body affected | 95 | 17 | 10.5 | 19 | 19 |
| 18  Pain threshold – sensitivity to pain | 92 | 15 | 13 | 23 | 21 |
| 19  Isolation/loneliness | 88 | 21 | 20 | 10 | 18 |
| 20  Deafness/blindness | 85 | 24 | 10.5 | 15.5 | 25 |
| 21  Ability to eat | 78 | 25 | 26 | 22 | 11 |
| 22  Capacity for suffering | 73 | 22 | 19 | 20 | 23 |
| 23  Institutionalized in a home or hospital | 69 | 26 | 22 | 18 | 20 |
| 24  Self-perception | 62 | 18 | 24.5 | 25 | 30 |
| 25  Attitudes towards illness | 62 | 20 | 23 | 27 | 29 |
| 26  Ability to sleep | 61 | 23 | 27 | 21 | 22 |
| 27  Control of bowels | 57 | 29 | 24.5 | 26 | 15 |
| 28  Age of ill person | 33 | 27 | 30 | 29 | 28 |
| 29  Family dependants | 29 | 28 | 29 | 31 | 31.5 |
| 30  Social acceptability of illness | 26 | 30 | 28 | 32 | 36 |
| 31  Social circumstances | 26 | 31 | 33 | 30 | 27 |
| 32  Sexual function | 25 | 35 | 34 | 28 | 26 |
| 33  Flexibility of lifestyle | 20 | 32 | 31 | 33.5 | 35 |
| 34  Occupation | 18 | 33.5 | 32 | 33.5 | 31.5 |
| 35  Marital status | 13 | 37 | 36 | 36 | 33 |
| 36  Family history of longevity | 11 | 33.5 | 37 | 35 | 38 |
| 37  Importance of hobbies | 10 | 38 | 35 | 38 | 39 |
| 38  Social class | 9 | 37 | 36 | 36 | 33 |
| 39  Sex of ill person | 7 | 40 | 38 | 37 | 37 |
| 40  Religion | 4 | 41 | 40 | 40 | 41 |
| 41  Nationality of ill person | 4 | 39 | 41 | 41 | 40 |

[*]Key to groups, $w$ = Kendall's coefficient of concordance:
I.   Nurses (high technology specialities), $w = 0.6$
II.  Patients
        surgical, $w = 0.5$
        medical, $w = 0.5$
        psychiatric, $w = 0.5$
III. Healthy volunteers, $w = 0.6$
IV.  Doctors, $w = 0.7$.

## The effect of diagnosis on the utility of health states

Our study revealed a considerable discrepancy between the utilities assigned to the same health state in different diagnostic groups. Mental conditions were consistently perceived as being worse than physical conditions and the reasons for this are being identified. This was the first exercise in disaggregating our compound descriptors.

### Representative utilities

A self-administered questionnaire was used to elicit the utilities assigned to disability, distress and discomfort of a random sample (size of sampling frame = 1000) of the population of Bloomsbury, the Inner London Health District within which University College is located. This sample was used to provide further descriptors and to place values on these. In this study we combined the approach to descriptors used by Bergner's group in the early stages of SIP design and the methods used by Torrance's group in Hamilton to elicit scales of utility.

## CURRENT RESEARCH

Our group has been developing and applying a new instrument, the Index of Health-related Quality of Life (IHQL) which measures physical, psychological and social adjustment. The results of this work are reported in Chapter 8, the Index of Health-Related Quality of Life (IHQL): A New Tool for Audit and Cost-per QALY Analysis.

## CONCLUSION

The global index has provided the basis for Quality Adjusted Life Years (QALY) estimates, as described by Williams (p. 427) and in this form it can be used to make decisions about Health Service policies. It is now being applied at District and Regional level in policy formation. However, in its original format, the index was not designed to provide a sensitive outcome measure for clinical trials, rather the opposite, for it can place in perspective the magnitude of the results of a particular trial. It may, for example, indicate that the impact of statistically, and even clinically, significant research findings in one condition and speciality is trivial when compared with the impact of established or new treatments in other conditions. This perspective can be useful in determining which discoveries should be chosen for further development.

However, there is a need for more sensitive measures of health status for clinical trials. At present, we recommend the SIP to investigators enquiring about such instruments, but no single instrument is likely to address all research needs and there is scope for more work in this field. We hope that the particular contribution of our group will be the development of an instrument which combines the advantages of a global index with the advantages of a health profile, and is potentially of use both in clinical research and for informing clinical audit and policy decisions.

## References

1. Ashley, J.S.A., Howlett, A. and Morris, J.W. Case fatality of hyperplasia of the prostrate in two teaching and three regional-board hospitals. *Lancet* 1971; ii: 1308–1311.
2. Benson, T.J.R. Classification of disability and distress by ward nurses. A reliability study. *Int. J. Epidemiol.* 1978; 7: 359–361.
3. Bush, J.W., Chen, M.M. and Zaremba, J. Estimating health program outcomes using a Markov Equilibrium Analysis of disease development. *Am. J. Public Health* 1971; 61: 2362–2375.
4. Butterfield, W.J.H. *Priorities in Medicine.* Rock Carling Fellowship. Oxford, Oxford University Press, 1968.
5. Chiang, C.L. *An Index of Health: Mathematical Models.* Public Health Service Publication No 1000. Series 2, No. 5, Washington, U.S. Government Printing Office, 1965.
6. Cockcroft, A., Bagnall, P., Heslop, A. *et al.* Respiratory health worker visiting patients with chronic respiratory disability. *Br. Med. J.* 1987 (In press).
7. Culyer, A.J., Lavers, R.J. and Williams, A. *Social Indicators: Health Social Trends,* 31–42. London, Her Majesty's Stationery Office, 1971.
8. Ekman, G. Measurement of moral judgement: a comparison of scaling methods. *Percept. Mot. Skills* 1962; 15: 3–9.
9. Fanshel, S. and Bush, J.W. A health status index and its application to health service outcomes. *Operation Res.* 1970; 18: 1021–1066.
10. Feldstein, M.S. *Econometric Analysis for Health Service Efficiency.* Amsterdam, North-Holland Publishing Company, 1967.
11. Gibbs, R.J. Performance Measures in Public Services. Ph.D. Thesis, University of Warwick, 1974.
12. Katz, S., Ford, A.B., Moskowitz, R.W. *et al.* Studies of illness in the aged. The index of ADL: a standardized measure of biological and psychological function. *J. Am. Med. Assoc.* 1963; 185: 914–919.
13. Kind, P. and Rosser, R.M. Death and dying: scaling of death for health status indices. In Barber, B., Grémy, F., Überla, K. *et al.* (eds) *Lecture Notes on Medical Informatics,* Vol. 5., Berlin, Springer-Verlag, 1979, pp. 28–36.
14. Kind, P. and Rosser, R.M. Health indicators: sensitivity and robustness. In Tilquin, C. (ed.) *Systems in Health Care,* Oxford, Pergamon Press, 1981, pp. 579–586.
15. Kind, P. and Rosser, R.M. The quantification of health. *Eur. J. Social Psychol.* 1988; 18: 63–77

16. Kind, P., Rosser, R.M. and Williams, A. Valuation of quality of life: some psychometric evidence. In Jones-Lee, M.W. (ed.) *The Value of Life and Safety.* Amsterdam, North-Holland Publishing Co. 1982, pp. 159–170.
17. McKeown, T., Butterfield, W.J.H. and Cochrane, A. *Screening in Medical Care, Reviewing the Evidence*, a collection of essays. Oxford, Oxford University Press, 1968.
18. Nightingale, F. *Notes on Hospitals* (3rd edn) London, Longman, Roberts and Green, 1863.
19. Packer, A.H. Applying cost-effectiveness concepts to the community health system. *Operations Res.* 1968; 227–253.
20. Rosser, R.M. Recent studies using a global approach to measuring illness. *Med. Care* 1976; 14, No. 5, (Suppl.) 138–147.
21. Rosser, R.M. A Set of Descriptions and a Psychometric Scale of Severity of Illness: An Indicator for use in Evaluating the Outcome of Hospital Care. Ph.D. Thesis, University of London, 1980.
22. Rosser, R.M. Issues of measurement in the design of health indicators: a review. In Culyer, A.J. (ed.) *Health Indicators.* Amsterdam, North-Holland Biomedical Press, 1983, pp. 34–81.
23. Rosser, R.M. A history of the development of health indicators. In Teeling Smith, G. (ed.) *Measuring the Social Benefits of Medicine.* London, Office of Health Economics, 1983, pp. 60–62.
24. Rosser, R.M. and Benson, T.J.R. New tools for evaluation: their applications to computers. In Andersen, J. (ed.) *Lecture Notes on Medical Informatics*, Vol. 1. Berlin, Springer-Verlag, 1978, pp. 701–710.
25. Rosser, R.M. and Kind, P. A scale of valuations of states of illness - Is there a social consensus? *In. J. Epidemiol.* 1978; 7: 347–358.
26. Rosser, R.M. and Watts, V.C. *The Output of a Health Care System*, Presented at the Annual Conference of the Operational Research Society of American, Dallas. 1971.
27. Rosser, R.M. and Watts, V.C. The measurement of hospital output. *In. J. Epidemiol.* 1972; 1: 361–368.
28. Rosser, R.M. and Watts, V.C. Health and welfare systems. In Ross, M.W. (ed.) *OR 72.* Amsterdam, North-Holland Publishing Company, 1972, pp. 655–669.
29. Rosser, R.M. and Watts, V.C. Disability: a clinical classification. *N. Law J.* 1975; 125: 323–328.
30. Rosser, R.M. and Watts, V.C. *Operational Objectives for Health Services.* Proceedings of the Conference of the European Federation of Operational Research Societies (Euro II), Stockholm, 1976, pp. 421–433.
31. Rosser, R.M. and Watts, V.C. *Measurement of the Effectiveness of Health Services.* Proceedings of the International Congress on Computing in Medicine (Med. Comp. '77) Berlin. Outline Conferences, 1977, pp. 559–572.
32. Rosser, R.M. and Watts, V.C. The measurement of illness. *J. Operational Res.* 1978; 29: 529–540.
33. Sellin, T. and Wolfgang, M. *The Measurement of Delinquency.* New York, John Wiley and Sons, 1964.
34. Stevens, S.S. On the theory of scales of measurement. *Science.* 1946; 103: 677–680.

35. Stevens, S.S. Measurement, psychophysics and utility. In Churchman, C. W. and Ratoosh, P. (eds) *Measurement, Definitions and Theories,* New York, John Wiley, 1959, pp. 18–63.
36. Torrance, G.W. Measurement of health state utilities for economic appraisal. A review. *J. Health Econ.* 1986; 5: 1–30.
37. Torrance, G.W., Thomas, W.H. and Sackett, D.L. A utility maximization model for evaluation of health care programs. *Health Serv. Res.* 1972; 7: 118–133.

# 8 The Index of Health-related Quality of Life (IHQL): a new tool for audit and cost-per-QALY analysis

Rachel Rosser, Richard Allison, Carole Butler, Michaela Cottee, Rosalind Rabin and Caroline Selai

Measurement of health-related quality of life is complex[1] and it raises many difficult philosophical questions[4]. Its role in informing NHS policy planners has become one of fundamental importance[11] yet the choice of instruments is very limited[3].

The Index of Health-related Quality of Life (IHQL) is a new instrument which measures social, psychological and physical adjustment and combines these at five different levels of aggregation on a scale of values or utility. The process of aggregating the scales into a single figure simplifies the interpretation of complex data sets from clinical trials, especially in situations where improvements in some dimensions are offset to some degree by deterioration in others. Detail is preserved because of the multi-level procedure used to derive a final single figure. The instrument combines the advantages of conventional rating scales and profiles with those of a health index[2].

The first stage in the development of the IHQL was the derivation of a three-dimensional classification system from the original two-dimensional Rosser index based on the dimensions of disability and distress[5,6]. Distress was separated into physical and emotional components, to give the three dimensions of disability, (physical) discomfort and (emotional) distress. Valuations for the 175 composite health states which can be described using the three-dimensional classification system (excluding unconsciousness) were obtained using standard gamble for states of one year's duration and are presented in Table 8.1.

**Table 8.1** Three-dimensional classification system: composite state valuations (0–1 scale of values)

|    |    | E1 | E2 | E3 | E4 | E5 |
|----|----|------|------|------|------|------|
| P1 | D1 | 1.000 | 0.970 | 0.894 | 0.791 | 0.643 |
|    | D2 | 0.990 | 0.960 | 0.884 | 0.781 | 0.632 |
|    | D3 | 0.971 | 0.940 | 0.864 | 0.762 | 0.614 |
|    | D4 | 0.946 | 0.917 | 0.840 | 0.738 | 0.590 |
|    | D5 | 0.917 | 0.887 | 0.811 | 0.710 | 0.561 |
|    | D6 | 0.885 | 0.855 | 0.780 | 0.678 | 0.530 |
|    | D7 | 0.838 | 0.804 | 0.729 | 0.628 | 0.481 |
| P2 | D1 | 0.944 | 0.915 | 0.838 | 0.736 | 0.588 |
|    | D2 | 0.934 | 0.904 | 0.828 | 0.726 | 0.578 |
|    | D3 | 0.915 | 0.885 | 0.810 | 0.708 | 0.559 |
|    | D4 | 0.891 | 0.861 | 0.785 | 0.684 | 0.537 |
|    | D5 | 0.861 | 0.831 | 0.756 | 0.654 | 0.508 |
|    | D6 | 0.829 | 0.799 | 0.724 | 0.623 | 0.477 |
|    | D7 | 0.779 | 0.750 | 0.675 | 0.574 | 0.427 |
| P3 | D1 | 0.867 | 0.837 | 0.761 | 0.660 | 0.513 |
|    | D2 | 0.857 | 0.827 | 0.751 | 0.650 | 0.503 |
|    | D3 | 0.837 | 0.808 | 0.732 | 0.631 | 0.485 |
|    | D4 | 0.814 | 0.784 | 0.709 | 0.608 | 0.461 |
|    | D5 | 0.785 | 0.755 | 0.680 | 0.579 | 0.433 |
|    | D6 | 0.753 | 0.723 | 0.648 | 0.548 | 0.402 |
|    | D7 | 0.702 | 0.674 | 0.598 | 0.498 | 0.353 |
| P4 | D1 | 0.714 | 0.685 | 0.610 | 0.510 | 0.365 |
|    | D2 | 0.703 | 0.675 | 0.599 | 0.499 | 0.354 |
|    | D3 | 0.685 | 0.656 | 0.581 | 0.481 | 0.337 |
|    | D4 | 0.661 | 0.632 | 0.557 | 0.458 | 0.313 |
|    | D5 | 0.632 | 0.604 | 0.528 | 0.429 | 0.285 |
|    | D6 | 0.601 | 0.572 | 0.497 | 0.399 | 0.254 |
|    | D7 | 0.551 | 0.522 | 0.449 | 0.350 | 0.207 |
| P5 | D1 | 0.468 | 0.439 | 0.365 | 0.267 | 0.125 |
|    | D2 | 0.457 | 0.428 | 0.355 | 0.257 | 0.114 |
|    | D3 | 0.439 | 0.410 | 0.337 | 0.239 | 0.097 |
|    | D4 | 0.416 | 0.387 | 0.314 | 0.216 | 0.074 |
|    | D5 | 0.387 | 0.358 | 0.285 | 0.188 | 0.047 |
|    | D6 | 0.356 | 0.327 | 0.255 | 0.159 | 0.017 |
|    | D7 | 0.308 | 0.279 | 0.207 | 0.111 | −0.030 |

In developing the IHQL, the three dimensions of disability, discomfort and distress have been sub-divided into seven attributes (dependency, dysfunction, pain/discomfort, symptoms, dysphoria, disharmony and fulfilment), which in turn have been further sub-divided into 44 scales. The 107 descriptors have 225 descriptor levels between them. These steps were essential for the development of an instrument which combines the properties of both a profile and a global index.

### Derivation of descriptors

There are more than 100 descriptors. These were derived by questionnaire surveys of random samples of the population of Bloomsbury, in the course of psychometric interviews with convenience samples of people with widely different experience of illness, both professional and personal, and from a review of the literature. Only items which were virtually identical in meaning were eliminated.

### Scaling

The IHQL has a hierarchical and multi-dimensional structure. The multi-stage scaling method which is used to derive values at each of the five levels is described by Rosser *et al.*[7]. This approach is based on multi-attribute utility theory and has been described by Torrance *et al.*[10] for application at two levels of complexity, but the use of the approach to produce values at more than two levels is unique.

Valuations are obtained from subjects using category rating scales. In the first stage, subjects judge the relative desirability/undesirability of the most detailed descriptors. The end-points of the scales used in this first stage are defined by the descriptive items at the next level of aggregation. This technique is repeated in a step-wise fashion until stage five, the dimensions of disability, discomfort and distress are scaled in relation to their effect on health-related quality of life (HQL).

Finally, in order to index quality (HQL) with quantity (life-years), the worst defined condition of morbidity is scaled in relation to 'being dead'. 'No impairment in health-related quality of life' is assigned a utility of 1 and 'being dead' given a utility of 0. Values for health states are computed as the sum of their valued component parts and represented on the standard 0–1 scale (with negative values possible for the most extreme states of morbidity).

### Reliability

Reliability concerns the extent to which individual differences in scores are due to 'true' differences in the characteristics under consideration.

Reliability studies are ongoing but preliminary results have demonstrated good inter-rater reliability with Kendall's coefficient of concordance, $W = 0.89$, $p < 0.001$, 10 df.

### Validity

The validity of a measure defines the meaning of a score. Validity is not absolute; it is relative to the domain about which statements are made. The lack of a criterion – a single measure that corresponds even roughly to what is meant by 'well-being' or 'health-status' – is the first and foremost reason for developing an index.

#### Convergent validity

A self-administered version of the IHQL was completed along with the General Health Questionnaire (GHQ) and the Symptom Check List-90 (SCL-90) by 94 subjects taking part in a psychotherapy trial after extreme trauma. IHQL values for degrees to which the person's quality of life was impaired by the condition of their health correlated significantly with both of these measures. For the symptom distress scale of the SCL-90, Pearson's product moment correlation $r = 0.77$, $p < 0.001$ and with GHQ total, $r = 0.65$, $p < 0.001$.

### Testing

Full testing of the scaling (test–retest reliability and stability) is ongoing. Three different versions of the IHQL are being developed: self-rated, observer-rated, relative-rated. Detailed reliability and validity studies for the three different versions of the IHQL are in progress using different patient groups.

### Freedom to modify

In our experience people do modify instruments. An example measuring quality of life in cancer patients is provided by Selby[9]. The IHQL can be used in conjunction with the Brief Psychiatric Rating Scale (BPRS) (for psychiatric populations) and other instruments. We would strongly discourage subtraction of items at this stage although we would expect to produce shorter editions in the future. If researchers wish to use diagnosis specific instruments and place them on a utility scale they are encouraged to do so.

## Applications

The instrument is being used to assess a variety of psychiatric services including post-disaster interventions and changes in quality of life of patients on a pychosomatic ward. We have found the IHQL to be of value in clinical trials combined with conventional clinical rating scales. We sound a note of caution when users make their choice of the most appropriate use of summary statistics for cost–utility analysis and informing policy[4,8]. This procedure is no substitute for careful debate of the detailed data and of the principles underlying decisions which implement the results.

## Acknowledgements

The Department of Health for its continued support, John Murphy, and to Steven Dewar, Gary Jackson and James Thompson for access to clinical audit data.

## References

1. Joyce, C.R.B. Quality of life: the state of the art in clinical assessment. In Walker, S.R. and Rosser, R.M. (eds) *Quality of Life: Assessment and Application.* Lancaster, MTP Press, 1988, pp.160–180.
2. Rosser, R.M. A health index and output measure. In Walker, S.R. and Rosser, R.M. (eds) *Quality of Life: Assessment and Application.* Lancaster, MTP Press, 1988, pp. 133–160.
3. Rosser, R.M. Quality of life: consensus, controversy and concern. In Walker, S.R. and Rosser, R.M. (eds) *Quality of Life: Assessment and Application.* Lancaster, MTP Press, 1988, pp. 247–304.
4. Rosser, R.M. From health indicators to quality adjusted life years: technical and ethical issues. In Hopkins, A. and Costain, D. (eds) *Measuring the Outcomes of Medical Care.* RCP Publications, 1990, pp.1–17.
5. Rosser, R.M. and Watts, V.C. The measurement of hospital output. *Int. J. Epidemiol.* 1972; 1,4: 361–8.
6. Rosser, R.M. and Watts, V.C. The measurement of illness. *Journal of the Operational Research Society* 1978; 29,6: 529–540.
7. Rosser, R.M., Cottee, M., Rabin, R. and Selai, C. *The Index of Health Related Quality of Life.* London, RCP Publications (in press).
8. Selai, C.E. and Rosser, R.M. Good quality quality? Some methodological issues. *J. R. Soc. Med.* (in press).
9. Selby, P.J. Measuring the quality of life of patients with cancer. In Walker, S.R. and Rosser, R.M. (eds) *Quality of Life: Assessment and Application.* Lancaster,

MTP Press, 1988.

10. Torrance, G.W., Boyle, M.H. and Horwood, S.P. Application of multi-attribute utility theory to measure social preferences for health states. *Operations Research* 1982; 30: 1043–1069.

11. Williams, A. The importance of quality of life in policy decisions. In Walker, S.R. and Rosser, R.M. (eds) *Quality of Life: Assessment and Application.* Lancaster, MTP Press, 1988.

# 9 A fifteen-dimensional measure of health-related quality of life (15D) and its applications

**Harri Sintonen and Markku Pekurinen**

The rise of medical technology assessment and QALY ideology have intensified the need and demand for a generic (disease-independent), sensitive, valid, reliable and easy-to-use measure of health-related quality of life (HRQOL). However, none of the measures and approaches suggested and developed over the years can claim to have established a position as **the** measure, either as a way of classifying and describing states of HRQOL or for valuing them. In addition, most of them have problems in meeting more than one of the above criteria.

In this chapter we introduce a generic fifteen-dimensional measure of health-related quality of life (15D). First, the measure itself, the accompanying valuation method and their properties in terms of the above criteria are described. Then, some interim results and experiences from applications of the measure are presented. Finally, other application areas and future directions of work are discussed.

## THE 15D MEASURE

When first published, the measure included 12 dimensions: moving, mental functioning, seeing, hearing, eating, communicating, sleeping, breathing, eliminating, working, social participation and perceived health. The choice of dimensions is discussed elsewhere[5,6]. Each dimension was divided into between four and five discrete levels or descriptive statements, by which more or less of the attribute were identified. For example, the descriptions for each level of the moving dimension are given in Table 9.1. A state of

**Table 9.1** The descriptions for levels of the moving dimension and their 'social' values (average of 80 hospital patients)

| | |
|---|---|
| I am able to move (walk) normally, i.e. without difficulties indoors, outdoors and on stairs | 1.000 |
| I am able to move (walk) without difficulties indoors, but outdoors and/or on stairs with difficulties | 0.689 |
| I am able to move (walk) without help indoors (with or without appliances), but outdoors and/or on stairs only with help from others | 0.502 |
| I am able to move (walk) only with help from others indoors also | 0.301 |
| I am completely bed-ridden and unable to move about; if helped, I may sit on a chair | 0.090 |

health-related quality of life was defined as a combination or profile of the levels, one from each dimension.

In this way about 80 million mutually exclusive states of HRQOL were defined. Such a number of states represented a considerable improvement in sensitivity compared with most previous measures. Recently, three dimensions measuring depression, distress and pain were added and the levels of some dimensions were reformulated. Theoretically the measure now defines ten billion states.

Ticking, on a self-administered 15D questionnaire, the level of each dimension that best describes the respondents' present status, is all that is required from patients using the measure. Usually, that takes only 5–10 minutes. This easy approach makes it possible to measure frequently the status of the same patients and to obtain a high degree of compliance. This is a great advantage, since rapid status changes are readily detected.

## THE VALUATION METHOD

The novelty of this measure, which allows a great number of states to be defined (i.e. high sensitivity) was the valuation method used, namely a two-stage method, based on the multi-attribute utility theory. The theoretical model behind the approach has been presented in detail earlier[5,6]. The value of a state for an individual is assumed to be a function of (a) the value placed on the level of each dimension and (b) the relative importance or weight attached to each dimension. If an additive aggregation rule is assumed, the value of state $H$ for individual $i$ is thus:

$$V_{iH} = \sum_j I_{ij} [W_{ij} (x_j)]$$

where $I_{ij}$ = a positive constant for the $j$th dimension, representing the relative importance individual $i$ attaches to it ($j = 1, 2, ...,m$), and $W_{ij}(x_j) = $ a numerical function on the $j$th dimension, representing the value individual $i$ places on various levels of the dimension.

The individual is thus faced with a two-stage valuation task. First, (s)he is asked to choose the most important dimension of HRQOL in her/his opinion and give it a value of 100 on an adjacent 0–100 ratio scale. Then all other dimensions are given a value on the scale in relation to this most important dimension. These values are divided by 100 to bring them to a 0–1 scale and then transformed to satisfy $\Sigma I_{ij} = 1$. 'Social' importance weights ($I_j$) are formed by averaging these individual weights over the sample (or groups).

Second, the subject is asked to give a value to the various levels of each dimension on an adjacent 0–100 ratio scale. The value of 100 is given to the best/most desirable level on each dimension and the other levels are valued on the scale in relation to the best level. These values are divided by 100 to attain individual level values and 'social' level values [$W_j(x_j)$] are calculated by averaging them over the sample.

A computer algorithm is used to combine the social importance weights and level values to the levels ticked by the respondents on the 15D questionnaire and to calculate the 15D score for them. The best score is 1 and worst 0.

## RELIABILITY AND VALIDITY OF VALUATIONS

When eliciting the importance weights and level values in various population groups (e.g. hospital patient groups, health-care planners and administrators, health professionals), a self-administered questionnaire has been used. On average, it takes about an hour to complete the valuation task and it does not impose an unreasonable burden upon respondents. For example, in a sample of 80 hospital patients the transformed 'social' importance weights ($I_j$) turned out as shown in Table 9.2.

**Table 9.2** Transformed 'social' importance weights for the 15 dimensions (80 hospital patients)

| | | | | | |
|---|---|---|---|---|---|
| 1. | Breathing | 0.0805 | 9. | Eating | 0.0662 |
| 2. | Mental functioning | 0.0787 | 10. | Eliminating | 0.0652 |
| 3. | Communicating | 0.0736 | 11. | Sleeping | 0.0636 |
| 4. | Seeing | 0.0735 | 12. | Distress | 0.0605 |
| 5. | Moving | 0.0727 | 13. | Pain | 0.0552 |
| 6. | Working | 0.0722 | 14. | Social participation | 0.0545 |
| 7. | Perceived health | 0.0687 | 15. | Depression | 0.0473 |
| 8. | Hearing | 0.0676 | | | |

The reliability of the 'social' importance weights is quite good: the Spearman correlations between the mean weights elicited from various groups have varied between 0.695 and 0.958, and the corresponding rank correlations between 0.630 and 0.916.

The reliability of the 'social' level values within the dimensions is very good: for all dimensions, the intergroup Spearman correlations have been about 0.99. An example of the 'social' level values for the level descriptions of one dimension (moving) are included in Table 9.1*.

Generally, a subject's age, sex, education and duration of illness were not found to be significantly correlated with the individual importance weights. The relatively high correlations between the mean importance weights in different patient groups suggest also that the type of illness may not have a major effect on valuations.

To test the validity of values produced by the two-stage method for different states, three versions of direct valuation were applied in addition to the two-stage method in a small-scale pilot experiment. In it the first version of the EuroQol© measure was used. It consisted of six dimensions, each divided into two or three levels[2]. Out of 216 possible states, seven states covering the range from good (best level on each dimension) to poor health (worst level on each dimension), were chosen for direct valuation.

The versions of direct valuation were a vertical visual analogue scale (VAS) (VERT1), a horizontal VAS (HORIZ), and a vertical ratio scale with adjacent statements indicating the relative desirability that certain numbers on the 0–100 scale represent in comparison with the value of 100 (the most desirable state) (VERT2). Using a self-administered questionnaire all respondents (doctors, head nurses and health-care students) did the two-stage method ($n=35$) and in addition, either VERT1 ($n=24$), VERT2 ($n=11$) or HORIZ ($n=20$) on the basis of a random assignment (VERT2 was used in one group only).

The mean values of the seven health states on a 0–1 scale obtained by various valuation methods are illustrated in Figure 9.1.

The three direct valuation methods produced quite similar mean values, whereas those by the two-stage method were consistently higher. The relation between the two-stage values and the values produced by the other methods can be described very closely by the following regression equations:

TWO-STAGE  $= 0.1804 + 0.0088$ (VERT1), $R^2 = 0.991$
TWO-STAGE  $= 0.1962 + 0.0086$ (VERT2), $R^2 = 0.978$
TWO-STAGE  $= 0.1963 + 0.0088$ (HORIZ), $R^2 = 0.972$

There may be several factors, especially contextual ones, that explain this

---

* The 15D questionnaire (in English) for ticking the levels by the respondents is available from the authors upon request.

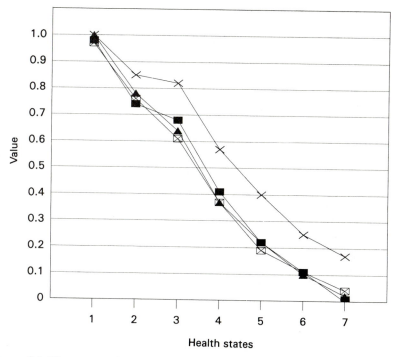

**Figure 9.1** The mean values of seven health states obtained by various valuation approaches on a 0–1 scale. Squares = VERT1; triangles = VERT2; squares = HORIZ; crosses = two-stage

difference. Their potential effect is still to be tested. Should the consistent difference persist after all and should the scientific community agree that the results of direct valuation are the gold standard, against which the validity of values produced by other methods are to be ascertained, the two-stage method still produces valid values: the values obtained by it can obviously be converted to 'direct values' with a simple linear transformation (yet to be established when dealing with 15 dimensions). Thus the situation resembles measuring temperature in Fahrenheit and in Celsius. However, if there is a great number of states to be valued, it is impossible in practice to use direct methods. In such a situation the two-stage method could be applied and the results converted to 'direct values'.

## APPLICATIONS OF THE 15D MEASURE

### Comparison of personal doctor service models

The fifteen-dimensional measure was used to compare three experimental

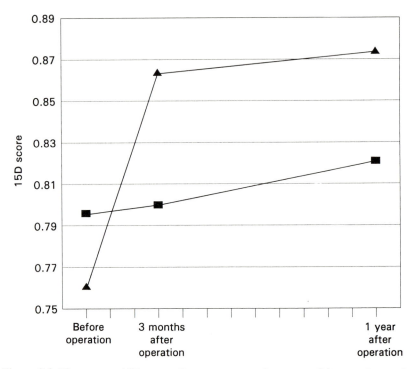

**Figure 9.2** The average 15D score of coronary artery bypass candidates at three points of time (triangles = operated patients, squares = unoperated)

models of organizing personal doctor service with the traditional public health centre service in a number of health centres[3]. A sample of 1815 patients coming to the health centres completed a 15D questionnaire. About half a year later 1700 of them were requested to complete the questionnaire again. The response rate was 72%. On both occasions they also assessed their status overall on a 0–100 ratio scale.

Both the average 15D score and the overall assessment changed clearly in the same direction as the health status change perceived by the patients during the half-year period. Similarly, for those who felt their status had remained the same, both measures reflected virtually no average change.

A regression model explained 11.6% of the variance of the change in 15D score ($F = 13.2$, df 6,601). In addition to the constant term, the coefficients of age and initial 15D score differed significantly from 0, whereas those of the experimental models, represented by dummies, did not. This implies that in none of the experimental models did the changes in HRQOL deviate significantly from those in the traditional model. Due to the simple study design, the internal validity of the results may leave something to be desired. Yet this illustrates one way in which the measure can be used – the study

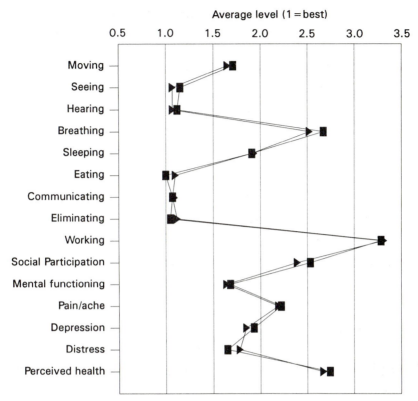

**Figure 9.3** 15D profile: patients waiting for the bypass operation (squares = first measurement; triangles = 3 months after)

design, among other things, determines how reliable and valid the results are.

## Coronary artery bypass patients

Some very preliminary results are available showing the development of HRQOL using the 15D measure, from a project where a sample of candidates for coronary artery bypass surgery ($n$=93) was followed-up[1]. The first measurement took place while the patients were on the waiting list. In those eventually undergoing surgery ($n$=41), the follow-up measurements took place 3 months and 1 year after the operation. In the unoperated group ($n$=52) the measurements took place at similar times.

Figure 9.2 shows how the average 15D score developed over a period of 1 year among the operated and unoperated patients. While on the waiting list, the average 15D score of the eventually operated patients was slightly,

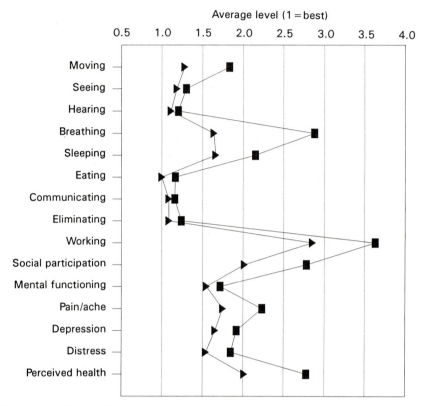

**Figure 9.4** 15D profile: operated patients (squares = before operation; triangles = 3 months after)

but not significantly lower than that of the unoperated. Three months after operation the difference was highly significant to the advantage of those operated and their average score was also significantly higher than before operation. However, 1 year after operation the average score of these patients was not significantly higher than at 3 months and the difference between the operated and unoperated patients had slightly reduced.

Figures 9.3 and 9.4 show the average 15D profiles of the groups in the first and second measurement. Figure 9.4 indicates that in the unoperated group the changes in all dimensions were marginal. In the operated group a marked improvement took place, especially in breathing, working, social participation, perceived health and moving, but also in pain, sleeping and in mental condition.

This project illustrates yet another way of using the measure. The final results complemented with clinical measurements will be available in due course.

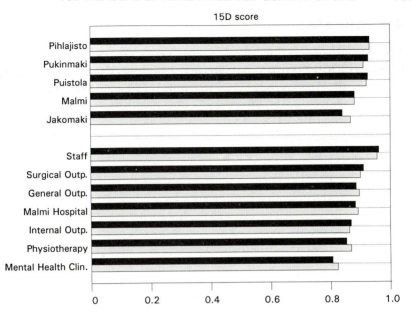

**Figure 9.5** Average 15D scores of patients visiting various health centres and hospital outpatient clinics in Helsinki (black = unstandardized; grey = standardized for age and sex)

### Comparison of patient materials

The fifteen-dimensional measure can also be used as a descriptive tool to compare in a condensed and uniform way whether, for example, patients visiting in various ambulatory settings differ in terms of HRQOL and in what respect. Such a comparison was carried out recently in one health care area of the city of Helsinki. The 15D questionnaire was given to consecutive adult patients upon arrival at five public health centres (Pihlajisto, Pukinmaki, Puistola, Malmi and Jakomaki) and at the outpatient clinics of Malmi Hospital (altogether 1600 questionnaires). The response rate (valid responses) was about 60%.

Figure 9.5 illustrates the average 15D score of patients (with and without a standardization for age and sex) in various settings. Many of the differences in average 15D scores between the settings were significant. This observation may be useful for resource planning purposes. Interesting differences in the 15D profiles between the settings were also found, showing the dimensions from which the differences in the average scores originated.

### Other applications

The 15D questionnaire is currently being used to compare the effectiveness of two drug-based breast cancer treatment regimens. Tentative results from a double-blind, randomized clinical trial with 35 patients in each group and a follow-up period of 3.5 years, suggest that one of the regimens has so far produced about 15% more progression-free, quality-adjusted months than the other regimen. 15D measurements take place every two months. The project is ongoing and treatment remains double-blind.

In a long-term outcome follow-up of cerebral trauma patients ($n=45$), the 15D measure was used together with the Karnofsky scale and the Glasgow Outcome Scale (GOS). In a measurement at an average of 6 years after trauma the correlations of the 15D score with the Karnofsky score and the GOS were 0.669 and 0.561 respectively[4].

There are still a number of projects where the 15D measure is being used in the assessment of effectiveness or cost-effectiveness, but from which no results are yet available. These include different rehabilitation schemes for stroke and asthma patients, early rehabilitation for workers, artificial joint operations, some new technical appliances for disabled people living at home, treatment alternatives for brain tumours, sleep apnea, asthma, renal failure/insufficiency, low back pain and depression. The 15D measure is also being used in an experiment to measure hospital output.

## CONCLUSIONS AND FUTURE DIRECTIONS OF WORK

The approach suggested here for measuring and valuing individuals' HRQOL seems feasible, practicable, easy to use and it produces reliable results. Yet the 15D measure as it stands now cannot be described as 'ready' and 'fully validated' (whatever the last phrase may imply). Further research and work are needed and are in progress to test it in real life situations.

It is likely that some refinements in the measure will take place in the future. So far we have used self-administered questionnaires to elicit valuations. The intention is also to use interview techniques to check whether the manner of organizing and administering the valuation task affects the results. Also, further comparisons of the two-stage valuation method with direct methods will be carried out. Further comparisons of valuations by patients/ordinary people with different characteristics (age, illness etc.), health authorities and various groups of health professionals are on the agenda. 'Final' valuations for the measure will be elicited from a representative sample of the general public. Comparisons between the results produced by the 15D measure and other similar types of measures are under way.

So far we have used an additive aggregation rule for calculating the index score. Other possible aggregation rules will also be explored.

## References

1. Brommels, M. Assessing coronary artery bypass surgery: survival, physical ability and quality of life. In ISTACH. Abstracts of the Sixth Annual Meeting, Houston, Texas, USA, (May 20–23) 1990, p. 8.
2. EuroQol Group. EuroQol® – a new facility for the measurement of health-related quality of life. *Health Policy* 1990; 16:199–208.
3. Pekurinen, M., Vohlonen, I. and Sintonen, H. Redefining incentives in primary medical care: The Finnish demonstration project. In Lopez-Casasnovas, G. (ed.) *Incentives in Health Systems*. Heidelberg, Springer Verlag, 1991, pp. 224–238.
4. Rönty, H. Cerebral trauma. A clinical, computed tomography, quantitative EEG, blood circulation isotope and neuropsychological follow-up study. *Acta Universitatis Ouluensis*, Series D, Medica 182, Oulu, University of Oulu Printing Center, 1988.
5. Sintonen, H. An approach to economic evaluation of actions for health. A theoretic-methodological study in health economics with special reference to Finnish health policy. Official Statistics of Finland, Special Social Studies XXXII: 74, Helsinki, Government Printing Centre, 1981.
6. Sintonen, H. An approach to measuring and valuing health states. *Soc. Sci. Med.* 1981; 15C: 55–65.

# 10 The EuroQol© quality of life project

**Rachel Rosser and Harri Sintonen**

For several years meetings have been held between a selected number of multi-disciplinary groups in various European countries. Cross-cultural, inter-disciplinary and cross-language issues have provided unique challenges and forced some compromises in the interests of producing an operational instrument.

The particular characteristics of the original instrument were:

1.   Six dimensions encompassing two or three levels of severity which produce 216 possible composite states.

2.   Category scaling of a sub-sample of these composite states on an international basis. One member (Allison[1]) has also shown consistency with multi-attribute scaling compared with scaling of composite states, opening up the potential for scaling a more complex range of descriptors. The details of the instrument were published in *Health Policy*[3].

After publishing the above article the EuroQol Group continued to experiment with various aspects of the instrument. New postal surveys with different versions of the EuroQol questionnaire have been conducted and their results partly reported. On the basis of experiences thus gained the descriptive classification system was recently changed and fixed for at least 2 years. The classification now reads as follows:

**EuroQol Descriptive Classification**

*Mobility*
1.      I have no problems in walking about
2.      I have some problems in walking about
3.      I am confined to bed
*Self-care*
1.      I have no problems with self-care
2.      I have some problems washing or dressing myself
3.      I am unable to wash or dress myself

*Usual Activities*
1.      I have no problems with performing my usual activities
        (e.g. work, study, housework, family and leisure activities)
2.      I have some problems with performing my usual activities
3.      I am unable to perform my usual activities

*Pain/Discomfort*
1.      I have no pain or discomfort
2.      I have moderate pain or discomfort
3.      I have extreme pain or discomfort

*Anxiety/Depression*
1.      I am not anxious or depressed
2.      I am moderately anxious or depressed
3.      I am extremely anxious or depressed

---

The change in classification has also implied considerable changes in the content of the health states (boxes) included in the standard valuation task. Therefore, new valuations have to and will be elicited. Comparisons of the thermometer-based valuation method with other valuation methods and the EuroQol instrument as a whole with other instruments are priority areas in the future work.

The EuroQol has attracted both users and critics (Carr-Hill)[2]. Time and more research will tell whether it is useful and relevant to decision-making and comparative evaluation of services on an international basis. Research at present focuses on the measurement properties of the instrument. An unresolved issue is the low return rate from random samples of the population attempting the scaling exercise. It seems possible solutions may include a household interview survey and a more user-friendly scaling system.

## Appendix
## Membership of the EuroQol[©] Group

Health Economics Research Group
Brunel University
Uxbridge, Middlesex
 England, UK
        Martin Buxton*
        Moira O'Hanlon
        Julia Rushby

Academy of Finland
        Markku Pekurinen*
        National Public Health Institute
        Elimäenkatu 25 A
        SF-00510 Helsinki, Finland

Swedish Institute for Health Economics
PO Box 1207
S-22105 Lund, Sweden
        Stefan Bjork*
        Björn Lindgren
        Ulf Persson
        Richard Brooks

National Institute of Public Health
Geitmyrsveien 75
0462 Oslo 4, Norway
        Erik Nord*

Harri Sintonen
University of Helsinki
Mannerheimintie 172
SF-00300 Helsinki, Finland

Erasmus University Rotterdam
PO Box 1738
3000 DR Rotterdam
The Netherlands
Gouke Bonsel*
Marie-Louise Essink-Bot
Ben van Hout
Institute for Medical Technology
   Assessment
Department of Public Health and
   Social Medicine
Jan van Busschbach
Frank de Charro
Department of Economics
Faculty of Law

Department of Academic Psychiatry
Middlesex Hospital
Mortimer Street
London W1N 8AA, England, UK
Jacqui Allen
Michaela Cottee*
Rosalind Rabin*
Rachel Rosser
Caroline Selai

Centre for Health Economics
University of York
York YO1 5DD, England, UK
Claire Gudex
Paul Kind*
Alan Williams
Paul Dolan

*EuroQol® liaison officers for each research group.

### References

1. Allison, R. and Rosser, R. (in preparation).
2. Carr-Hill, R.A. A second opinion: health related quality of life measurement – Euro style. *Health Policy* 1992;20:321–328.
3. The EuroQol Group. EuroQol® – a new facility for the measurement of health-related quality of life. *Health Policy*, 1990;16:199–208.

# 11 A WHO method for the assessment of health-related quality of life (WHOQOL)

**Norman Sartorius**

Prevention of most diseases depends on human behaviour. Political bodies can adopt legislation restricting the risk of becoming ill; communities or administrators can prescribe behaviour which could prevent the appearance or spread of diseases. In the vast majority of instances however the success of such measures will depend on the degree to which the measures proposed interfere with the quality of life of individuals or social groups which have to undertake some action.

An individual can be expected to agree to behave in a 'healthy' way and to comply with medical prescriptions as long as the requirements to avoid diseases do not clash with activities which the individual sees as essential to maintaining or improving the quality of his/her life. This does not mean that people will only do things which are, say, painless: it is the nature of their goals and the congruence of their activities with their value system which will determine what they will do. Sometimes people's value systems will lead them to undertake activities which are harmful to their health and highly, unpleasant: they will however persist in doing them if these activities enhance their feeling of worth or in other ways improve the quality of their life.

The success of medical treatment depends on the patient's acceptance of the treatment; this, in turn, is affected by the changes in quality of life which the patient expects might happen during treatment or in the future, after it is completed. If the treatment is easy to take, without side-effects, short-lasting and very effective, acceptance is probable and concern with quality of life issues may not be determinant for the success of the intervention. Unfortunately, however, for most of the serious diseases – and for most of the unpleasant situations in life – there are no such solutions. Treatments are often painful, long-lasting, causing secondary difficulties, expensive and do not always result in cure. Patients' acceptance of therapy and their compliance with the measures recommended by the physician in such situations will depend on the balance between expectations of gain from treatment and danger from not having it. These expectations are not expressed in medical terms but translated by the patients into assessments of their overall condition, their functional capacity and a forecast of how they might feel in the situations which will result from their decisions on treatment.

It is also likely that quality of life and its changes play an important role in the pathogenesis of disease, both mental and somatic. A systematic exploration of relationships between stress, quality of life, immunological states of the organism and the occurrence or continuation of diseases has not yet been performed, although interesting but isolated findings and intriguing hypotheses would seem to indicate that this would be a promising avenue of search for a better understanding of disease and health. This search may well prove that these relationships are so complex and intricate that much more work is needed. Even so, it would be worthwhile to undertake it on a broad scale and at different service levels, because it might make health workers and researchers more aware of the human dimensions of health care and also help to make the practice of medicine less mechanistic and more focused on the needs of the population.

## QUALITY OF LIFE AND HEALTH CARE

In the light of the above considerations it is surprising that so little attention has been paid to the research and action concerning quality of life in relation to health care. This neglect may have several causes. First, there is no unanimity about the meaning of the words 'quality of life'. Some people believe that quality of life of an individual is synonymous with his or her capacity to perform in social and personal roles appropriate to others of the same age, sex, intelligence and social class. Others consider that quality of life is an individual's perception of his well-being (or lack of it). Still others feel that there are some objective indicators of quality of life, for example availability of food, of shelter, of employment, of human rights. Words such as 'positive health', 'well-being', 'satisfaction' and 'happiness' have also been used as if they were synonymous with quality of life. The result of this epistemological and semantic confusion has been a misuse of the term, a lack of concerted effort by health decision-makers and by scientists, and a reluctance of research funding agencies to support relevant research.

Second, it may be that the technological achievements earlier in this century created the illusion that it is only a matter of a very short time before all diseases would be amenable to effective and definitive treatment. If this were so, measuring quality of life would be a superfluous task since perfect treatments would be applied to remove the disease as soon as it was discovered. Gradually, however, it became clear that this is not so; that most diseases will not be amenable to treatment for many years to come; that even if excellent treatment methods became available economic imperatives would prevent their universal application; and that the universe of disease is not finite and that it is highly probable that new diseases for which no treatments will be available, will be appearing to the despair of governments and patients alike. This, in more recent years, lead to the awareness that we will have to know whether our interventions are helpful to the patient and his family even if no perfect cure can be achieved. Similarly, we will have to use the results of such measurements for determining priorities and for identifying disease groups which are most damaging to societies and individuals in terms of reducing their quality of life.

Third, the limits of medicine are not at all clearly defined. For some the task of medicine is to treat specific diseases, reduce pain and postpone death. All other matters are outside the field of action for medicine. For others the task of medicine is to teach people how to live and behave so as to avoid illness and, in case that illness has struck, to help them overcome it. If the first conception of medicine is accepted, the doctor does not really need to worry about changes in the quality of life of his patients since it is his duty to remove illness and not to worry about the meaning of illness for the patient nor about its consequences. If the second conception is held, the doctor's duty is to seek partnership with people who suffer from a disease and have to cope with it, so as to be able to help them. In setting goals for action in this partnership, quality of life plays a major role and the medical partner must worry about it just as much as the patient.

## ASSESSMENT OF QUALITY OF LIFE

Quality of life can be defined as the individuals' perception of their position in life, in relation to their goals and the value system which they have accepted and incorporated into their decision making. This definition places primary importance on the perception of individuals and makes the measurement of quality of life primarily dependent on the individuals' willingness and capacity to communicate their feelings. This represents a disadvantage when quality of life has to be measured in children and in individuals with severe communication difficulties, e.g. those with asphasia or severe mental retardation. The advantage however is that the measurement becomes less dependent on having (objective) norms of capability and performance for the population to which the individuals belong.

The instruments proposed by various authors for the measurement of quality of life express their understanding and definition of quality of life. They vary in their structure, length, sophistication and manner of application.

Some concentrate on performance, others on the state of the organism or on the environment in which the individual lives; some are very close to scales for the measurement of mood and to checklists of activities of daily life. Some are exclusive and deal only with items relevant to the care of a particular type of patient. None of them seems to have given sufficient attention to the objective state *and* the subjective feelings of the individual whose quality of life is to be measured.

The difference in the focus of assessment is not the only difference between the methods currently used in various settings. The difference in the choice of the 'agency' which is to determine what quality of life people have, can also lead to difficulties in comparing data. There have been, explicitly or implicitly, at least three positions taken by designers of instruments and practitioners: first, that the individuals whose quality of life is measured should be the arbiters of their quality of life; second, that it is the immediate family or those living with the individual who are best able to make a statement; and third, that some appointed agent – for example the treating physician or the governmental agency having access to objective data – is to be asked about the quality of life of individuals or social groups whose quality of life is to be assessed.

Instruments also vary in their choice of points of reference for the measurement of quality of life. While some investigators take the individuals' previous state (best ever, average over life, before disease, etc.) as the yard-stick, others take the average value seen in others (suffering from the same disease, having the same education, same social class etc.) as the point of reference. Others still, take the platonic view and compare the individual's state with the imagined position that the person should have (ideal self, doctor's impression of how well the individual could have been had there not been the disease, etc.)

## THE WHO INSTRUMENT FOR QOL ASSESSMENT

The instrument which is being developed in WHO's study (WHOQOL) will be recording the objective state and functioning of individuals in personal and social roles, as well as their perception of that position and of their functional capacity. For the former ratings – dealing with domains such as social relationships, work, physical capacity and impairments – the WHOQOL will use assessments by doctors and others knowledgeable about the culture and about the areas to be assessed. For the latter, the perception of the individuals' condition in life, ratings will be based on the subjective judgement of the persons unless their disease prevents them from clearly communicating their feelings, in which case proxy assessments by people close to the subjects will be used.

The instruments will be constructed in a manner which will allow the assessment of quality of life in different situations. At present it is envisaged that it should be applicable in the measurement of quality of life in at least four groups of individuals: people suffering from a disease (such as AIDS or cancer); people who look after sick individuals professionally or for other reasons (e.g. nurses, family members); people who live in particularly stressful situations (e.g. in refugee camps); and individuals who are unable to communicate their feelings (e.g. those in states of profound dementia). The instrument will have a modular structure with a core module which will be applicable to all the groups and special modules which will be produced for use with different groups and subgroups (e.g. for cancer in a particular location).

The fact that WHOQOL will be designed for widespread and regular use in different cultural settings and that its results should be suitable for cross-cultural comparisons, imposes certain requirements on its construction. First, the instrument will have to be developed in close collaboration with people who will develop it for use in their culture; second, in order to be attractive and competitive the instrument will have to satisfy the usual requirements for similar instruments – be short, simple, valid, usable on several occasions, sensitive to change, producing data which can be aggregated across groups; third, the instrument will use terms or criteria which are compatible with those used in other WHO instruments (e.g. those for the measurement of disability); and fourth, the process of developing the instrument will aim to result not only in producing good data but also in strengthening the team or centre that have developed the method.

The procedure which will be used in developing the instrument will involve several steps. The first which has already taken place was the definition by WHO – in collaboration with experts from different countries – of several domains of functioning (somatic, e.g. sleep; psychological, e.g. memory; independence, e.g. in looking after activities of daily living and social relationships). The description of the environment in which the person lives and of social services at his or her disposal will also be included in the instrument. A limited number of 'facets' for each domain (e.g. sleep in the area of somatic functioning) has also been defined. The schedule will make provisions for recording the situation concerning a facet and for recording the subjective perception of that situation by the subject. It is likely that the instrument will be prepared in a form suitable for self-administration and in another designed for use by an interviewer.

For each of the facets, investigators in different cultural settings will devise questions which would be used in obtaining the necessary information. These will be brought together, edited and applied in rather large samples of individuals in different cultures. The results of these tests should allow the finalization of the list of domains and facets and the drafting of their precise definitions; at the same time, they should result in sets of items meaningful and applicable in the countries participating in the first group of studies. If later investigators in other cultural settings wish to use the instrument it will be necessary to carry out some further work to adapt the instrument using specific instructions which will accompany it. In this sense the WHOQOL will be an example and a description of a method rather than a rigid questionnaire. Items used in the instrument will be culture-specific. The ratings made on the basis of answers, however, will allow cross-cultural comparisons. Previous work (e.g. on depression) demonstrated that this way of proceeding is useful and productive[4].

Experience which WHO has gathered in other cross-cultural studies will also be used in this study. Difficulties of translation, for example, and the production of equivalent versions of an instrument may be overcome by creating small groups of bilingual experts with whom the principal investigator works on all matters concerning the study and in particular on issues concerning the translation and equivalence of the texts, and in training interviewers. The bilingual group can be used in the 'committee' work on translations[1] and its members can become leaders of focus groups of monolingual subjects brought together to examine the semantic space occupied by a concept or a group of concepts. The members of the bilingual groups can also conduct interviews with representative informants familiar with the cultural norms, supervise the performance of interviews and do other work[5].

The WHOQOL will be developed in a collaborative fashion in some six to eight centres located in different parts of the world. The principles which will govern this collaboration have been described elsewhere[3]. The centres will be selected so as to differ in terms of levels of industrialization, service organization and descriptors of culture relevant for work on quality of life (e.g. the perception of time[2], the perception of self, culture-specific perceptions of death). WHO will also give preference to institutions which will be able to function as part of a network of centres for further research and training on quality of life and its assessment.

The timetable which WHO has proposed[6,7] depends to a large degree on the availability of resources: currently it is expected that the development of the instrument and its field testing will start in the course of 1992. The field work should be completed early in 1993. The evaluation of findings may take several months, so that the final version of the instrument with the accompanying training materials, reports of field tests, and so forth, should be released in 1994.

### References

1. Sartorius, N. Cross-cultural psychiatry. In Kisker, K.P., Meyer, J.E., Müller, C. and Strömgren, E. (eds) *Psychiatrie der Gegenwart BD I/1*, 2nd edn. Berlin,

Heidelberg, New York, Springer-Verlag, 1979, pp. 711–37.
2. Sartorius, N. Cross-cultural comparisons of data about the quality of life: a sample of issues. In Aaronson, N.K. and Beckmann, J. (eds) *The Quality of Life of Cancer Patients*. New York, Raven Press, 1987, pp. 19–24.
3. Sartorius, N. Cross-cultural and international collaboration in mental health research and action: Experience from the mental health programme of the World Health Organization. In Jansson, R. and Perris, C. (eds) *Acta Scand. Psychiatr.* 1988; 78, Suppl. 344: 71–74.
4. World Health Organization. Depressive disorders in different cultures: WHO Schedule for Standardized Assessment of Depressive Disorders. Geneva, WHO, 1983, 150 p.
5. World Health Organization. WHO/ADAMHA Joint project on diagnosis and classification of mental disorders, alcohol- and drug-related problems: Report of a meeting of investigators conducting the studies on cross-cultural applicability research. (document MNH/MND/91.19, 1991, unpublished).
6. World Health Organization. Report of a WHO meeting on the assessment of quality of life in health care held in Geneva in February 1991. (document MNH/PSF/91.4, 1991 unpublished).
7. World Health Organization. Report of a meeting on quality of life held in Geneva in February 1992 (unpublished document).

# 12 Indices versus profiles – advantages and disadvantages

Monika Bullinger

In assessing quality of life, the question arises which measurement strategy is most appropriate in a given clinical trials situation. Choices may pertain to the inclusion of generic versus disease-specific instruments, to patient self-ratings versus expert ratings or to the administration interviews versus questionnaires[1,10]. Of special importance for the type of data gathered is the decision between the use of indices versus profiles for the assessment of quality of life. This decision requires a reflection on the conceptual, methodological and practical issues involved in making such a choice.

Conceptually, the present paper provides a clarification of the underlying problem, the current terminology and the existing definitions. Methodologically, quality criteria for instruments, examples available tools and implications for statistical analyses are reviewed. Finally, practical issues related to indication for the use of indices or profiles, an evaluation of pros and cons as well as guidelines for choice are given.

## CONCEPTUAL ISSUES

### Problem

In spite of the existing scepticism regarding the determination of what is meant by the term quality of life, a consensus emerges throughout the literature. This consensus indicates that the term denotes a multi-dimensional construct, i.e. a not directly observable phenomenon, which can be operationalized and measured via specification of essential underlying components. These components include physical, psychological and social aspects of well-being and/or function as perceived by patients and/or observers[5,25].

In the health sciences, the term 'health-related quality of life' (HRQOL) has been coined by Patrick and Erickson[19].

For the assessment of HRQOL the problem arises to what extent the multi-dimensionality of the construct should be reflected. The question is: should one try to assess in a detailed fashion many different components of quality of life or would an assessment combining such information within a single number suffice? Basically, this question refers to the necessity of differentiation versus abstraction in measuring quality of life.

**Terminology**

Quality of life is usually assessed with instruments such as interviews or ratings in the form of questionnaires[23]. This latter tool consists of various items (e.g. statements, questions, adjectives or nouns) with different response categories (i.e. answer possibilities ranging from yes or no to more differentiated endorsements). While each of these items may be analysed (single items), most often items are combined to form a scale (e.g. for the assessment of anxiety) or – in more comprehensive instruments – to form different subscales within one questionnaire (e.g. assessing anxiety, physical health, social interactions and so forth). These more comprehensive instruments are called profiles. A review of the literature shows that the term 'profile', in fact, is reserved for instruments focusing on the assessment of different components of a construct within one measurement approach.

In contrast, the term 'index' is used to denote a single number which may be derived from various sources (see Figure 12.1). It can originate from a single item (i.e. from a question like 'how is your quality of life today?'), from a scale (of which it is the sumscore) or from a profile (of which it can be a specific subscale score).

Methodologically, the use of the term 'index' for such information is not correct. While all numerical information about quality of life is an 'indicator', the terms 'profile' and 'index' need a more thorough explanation.

**Definitions**

Subsequently the term 'profile' will be used for an instrument that provides scores for more than two components of quality of life. These scores are derived from subscales having been developed for assessment of these components within one instrument. Profiles thus yield more than two (i.e. multiple) indicators for quality of life components. Profiles and batteries are comparable in arriving at information on multiple components of quality of life. Their difference lies in batteries assembling this information from different sources. Batteries are composed of scales or subscales from different

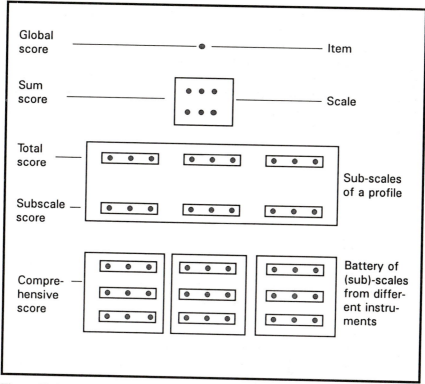

**Figure 12.1** Overview

instruments, while profiles are *a priori* developed as one comprehensive instrument.

An 'index' does not primarily refer to an instrument but to a specific type of numerical information, which is derived from a combination of indicators for a construct. Nevertheless, the term index is often equated with an instrument which gives the above described information. While there is a longstanding tradition in theoretical and empirical work on health status indices[3] the confusion about the term 'index' in HRQOL shows that the quality of life area seems not to have profited from this. For definitive purposes, an index is characterized by providing a single score for HRQOL assessment. This score can be derived from an aggregation of either several single items, subscales of a profile or several scales assembled in a battery (see Figure 12.1). Thus an index can, but must not, be derived from an instrument constructed for this purpose. The aggregation can be refined by weighing procedures for the constituents and can be performed by any mathematical operation (usually summation). In contrast to the health index literature, the theory and practice of weighing and aggregating models has not yet received much attention in quality of life research (exceptions are the QWB and the NHP, see 'Examples' to follow).

The difference between an index and a single (i.e. global) item or scale (e.g. subscale) score is that an index requires aggregation across several distinct constituents. Ideally an index should also have ratio-scale on at least an interval-scale level. Furthermore, each index value should represent distinct diagnostic categories.

## METHODOLOGICAL ISSUES

### Quality criteria

Questionnaires yielding information of the profile or index type should meet quality criteria in order to be candidates for quality of life assessment. Important among these are data on reliability, validity and responsiveness resulting from psychometric testing[9,25,26]. Reliability includes the coherence of items forming a scale (internal consistency), their interchangability (split half) and the scale's reproducibility over time (test–retest). Validity pertains statistically to the questionnaire's potential to reflect the underlying theoretical model (construct validity) or to meet specific criteria (criterion validity) in terms of, for example, differentiating between patient subgroups (discriminant validity), correlating with similar questionnaires (convergent validity) or correctly forecasting outcomes (predictive validity). Responsiveness or sensitivity denotes the questionnaire's potential to reflect over time the effects of specific interventions (e.g. treatments). The responsiveness can be assessed against a criterion or be derived from the pattern of variance in responses over time[11].

While these psychometric criteria require rigorous statistical analyses according to psychological test theory, feasibility criteria do not, but pertain to the application potential of questionnaires. These depend on the length of the instrument and related time requirements for responses, to the clarity of instructions and to the formulation of the questions as well as answer categories in order to ensure acceptability among respondents[1].

A final set of quality criteria relates to the evaluation of an instrument in a research context and includes the conceptual foundation of the instrument, the number and kind of patient groups it was administered to and the international proliferation in terms of frequency of use as well as the availability of psychometrically tested versions in different languages[5].

**Examples**

Recently, a rich source of information on instruments for the assessment of health and of health-related quality of life has become available[16,21,25]. In these publications descriptions of various indices and profiles can be found, pertaining however, mostly to generic instruments. Information on disease specific instruments is available mostly within oncology, while other medical disciplines only recently have engaged in the development of such tools.

Within the generic instruments (see Figure 12.2), examples for indices include the Quality of Life Index (QLI)[22], in which five dimensions of quality of life 'activity', 'daily living', 'health', 'support' and 'outlook' are scored by the physician using values between 0 and 2 and are added to yield an index between 0 and 10. The Quality of Well-being Scale (QWB)[13] involves an intensive interview with the patient and subsequently yields a weighted index to assess the patient's quality of life.

Examples of profiles include the Nottingham Health Profile (NHP)[12], which yields scores for six dimensions relevant to health status (e.g. pain, mobility). The Profiles of Mood States (POMS)[17] assesses short-term psychological state in six mood dimensions (e.g. depression, vigour).

While both NHP and POMS do not provide a total score, other instruments do and therefore yield index- as well as profile-type information. Examples for such scales are the Sickness Impact Profile (SIP)[4] and the Psychological General Well-Being Index (PGWB)[8]. The SIP measures 12 dimensions and

|  | Index | Profile | Both |
|---|---|---|---|
| QLI Spitzer<br>Quality of Life Index | x |  |  |
| QWB Bush<br>Quality of Well-being Scale | x |  |  |
| NHP Hunt<br>Nottingham Health Profile |  | x |  |
| POMS McNair<br>Profile of Mood States |  | x |  |
| SIP Bergner<br>Sickness Impact Profile |  |  | x |
| PGWB Du Puy<br>Psychological General Well-being Index |  |  | x |

**Figure 12.2** Examples

also yields an overall score as does the PGWB with its six dimensions (anxiety, depression, well-being, vitality, self-control, health). Many more examples can be found for the generic health measures, some also in oncological quality of life scales, such as the Karnofsky Index as an indicator of functional status or the EORTC quality of life questionnaire yielding a battery approach to a set of scores for cancer-related quality of life dimensions[2]. While the latter scale is available and psychometrically tested in different languages, most questionnaires are not. It is essential to carry out a state-of-the-art translation and psychometric testing before using the scale in a national context in order to ensure its applicability[6].

## Statistical analyses

Statistical analysis of quality of life data often poses problems to clinicians and biometricians because of its perceived complex nature and its assumed 'subjectivity'. A special deterrent seems to be the amount of information to be processed[5]. Profiles and batteries are thought to yield a multitude of data, while indices are considered a more parsimonious approach. As a consequence, the latter tend to be preferred in clinical trials, while the former are more valued in epidemiological research. An exception is the study by Croog and colleagues[7] in which a battery approach was used for quality of life assessment in comparing three antihypertensive treatments. Here subscale results were presented for each treatment and analysed for significant differences. The treatment with advantages in the majority of quality of life domains was rated superior.

The problem with profiles and batteries is how to deal with multiple testing, resulting from comparisons across scales, between respondents and over time[20]. This problem can and should be minimized by *a priori* statements of hypotheses and required comparisons, so that inferential testing can be carried out for the main research questions. In addition, statistical tools for correcting the significance level in multiple comparisons are available such as Bonferoni adjustment in analyses of variance and corresponding non-parametrical approaches. Recently, the use of global statistics has been recommended as a way of circumventing a multitude of single comparisons[24]. Such approaches have traditionally been followed in clinical and experimental psychology (e.g. MANOVA techniques), but have been regarded with scepticism by the biometrical community.

Indices on the other hand condense information to a point where the sensitivity of a scale may be jeopardized. They do, however, have the advantage of circumventing the multiple testing problem, of yielding clinically directly interpretable information and of being a time-conserving strategy for analyses. Statistically the main advantage of indices is the possibility of incorporating them into survival analyses. They can be used to calculate quality adjusted survival time (and related endpoints, such as time to progression) and can also contribute to analysing transition probabilities between states[18].

## PRACTICAL ISSUES

### Indication

Of practical importance, yet related to conceptual and methodological issues, is the question when to include indices or profiles in a study. The use depends on the objectives of quality of life assessment in terms of scientific focus, research questions, study design and desired type of outcome data (see Figure 12.3). Thus, although psychometric criteria, feasibility and spread are characteristics of an instrument, its application potential is not. There is no ideal quality of life instrument *per se*, but only for a specific research context[10]. With regard to the scientific focus, a distinction should be made between

- clinical descriptions (e.g. analysis of quality of life in a group of treated epileptics in order to identify interventions potentials),
- therapeutic decisions (e.g. in a randomized clinical trial comparing two antihypertensive treatments in order to determine the best medication as regards quality of life),
- health care allocation (e.g. determining the quality of life 'gain' in

---

The use of profiles vs. indices depends on the objectives of HRQOL assessment in terms of

- Scientific focus:         clinical description
                            therapeutic decisions
                            health care allocation

- Research questions:       discrimination, prediction,
                            evaluation

- Study design:             cross-sectional,
                            longitudinal

- Outcome data:             detailed vs. aggregated

---

**Figure 12.3** Indication

ESRD patients treated with kidney transplantation vs. dialysis in order to find out which treatment is superior on health economic grounds.

While indices may be of special value in the latter case, they may prove too crude for the first problem. Profiles, on the other hand could be profitable for the first two cases, but questionable in the last one.

A second objective is the research question as such. Discriminative questions (differences between groups of persons) and predictive ones (forecasting an outcome) lend themselves more to the use of indices, while evaluative questions may require the detection of subtle differences in various aspects of quality of life[15]. In terms of study design indices seem more appropriate for cross sectional studies and profiles more for longitudinal research. The reason for this is the potential lack of sensitivity of indices.

Finally the desired type of outcome data is of special importance. An interest in a detailed and multi-faceted description of quality of life would call for a profile, while single numerical information would call for indices.

## Pros and cons

Before contrasting indices and profiles, the lack of distinction between them in different aspects should be taken into account. Both indices and profiles may or may not be theoretically explicit, developed carefully, standardized in administration, weighted, psychometrically well-tested, generic or disease-specific, providing reference data on patient groups, and applicable as patient or observer rating.

There are, however, dimensions, along which indices and profiles can be distinguished (see Figure 12.4). These include the application (time requirements), the parsimoniousness of information (condensed vs. detailed), the statistical analysability of data (easy vs. difficult), the interpretability of results (straight vs. controversial), the specific strengths for research (dis-

| INDICES | PROFILES |
| --- | --- |
| – economical | – time-intensive |
| – condensed | – detailed |
| – easy to analyse | – difficult to analyse |
| – straightforward | – controversial |
| – discriminative strengths | – evaluative strenths |
| – insensitive to change | – sensitive to change |
| – criterion validity | – construct validity |

**Figure 12.4** Pros and cons

criminative vs. evaluative), the potential to detect changes over time (sensitive vs. insensitive) and the type of underlying validation (criterion vs. construct).

In addition, each form of quality of life assessment has its specific pitfalls. For indices of functional disability, Feinstein and colleagues[9] identified six areas of problems. These include influences on the results by patients' increased effort and by the usually unassessed inter-individual differences in relative importance of items. Also, the justification for use of a specific index in comparison with alternatives may be weak, and the index can be unsatisfactory for study purposes in spite of good psychometric test results. Finally, an index as a single timepoint measure may not be sensitive to change and the aggregation may not be sophisticated enough (e.g. summation instead of hierarchical weighting). Detailed analyses for profiles may show similar pitfalls. Depending on the specific comparison between an index and a profile however, the characteristics of each instrument may prove any list of pros and cons inadequate. Thus, a choice between indices and profiles should not be made in general, but with regard to a specific problem.

**Guidelines for choice**

Most important in the process of making a choice between indices and profiles is firstly a specification of the study objectives. As described in the 'indication' section, the scientific focus, research questions, study design and desired type of outcome data should be recalled.

Subsequently, a characterization of the study across these objectives helps to classify it within a broader research context. One example would be a longitudinal evaluative study to decide between treatment alternatives in terms of quality of life to be combined with clinical data in a survival analysis. Another example would be a discriminative cross-sectional description of different patient groups with a specific treatment to determine maximum quality of life indication for this treatment.

The third step involves writing and prioritizing a list of ideal properties of an instrument that corresponds to the study objectives and type of intended research. This can be done by using the 'quality criteria' format described above.

The fourth phase consists of screening the literature for published instruments and to rate them according to the study objectives and quality criteria. This can be done with the help of a matrix format for criteria with a special rating system (e.g. between excellent and poor). From this matrix two or more instruments may emerge as ideal or at least acceptable candidates for choice.

In a further step, these instruments should be examined empirically by administering them in a pilot phase of the research. It is important that this pilot phase has clear and pre-defined goals with regard to the kind of information needed for making final choice (e.g. is instrument A or B sensitive?).

Finally, reapplying the list introduced in step three, a choice may be made on empirical grounds. If this poses problems and feasibility allows, a profile may be preferred to an index if it yields a defined index score. Likewise if allowed and making sense, an index could be broken down to its constituents, thus yielding a rich information source for exploratory analyses.


## CONCLUSION

The question of whether indices or profiles should be used in health-related quality of life research cannot be answered *a priori*. Although both types can be judged according to their psychometric quality, feasibility and spread in research, the decision for or against implementation of one or the other depends on the specific nature of the planned research. Advantages and disadvantages can be listed for both types, the value of such a generalized list however has to be examined in a concrete situation in which specific indices or profiles are contrasted.

In general, although the question of single vs. multi-outcome measures in quality of life research is receiving increased attention[14], several activities are needed to tackle pending problems. As apparent from the discussion of the conceptual issues, there is a lack of precision in defining indices and profiles in the quality of life field. A taxonomy on 'indices' and 'profiles' could help to clarify these issues.

Furthermore, in view of the methodological issues, an identification of instruments fulfilling quality criteria could be useful. However, as relates to practical issues, such a list of recommendations remains theoretical, unless examined in actual studies. Thus the implementation of indices and profiles for specific study objectives (also comparatively within one investigation) is needed. With such an empirical basis, the body of knowledge of advantages and disadvantages will increase and form a solid foundation for decisions about instruments. This step should be accompanied by further development and refinement of statistical models for data analysis – especially also with regard to loss-to-follow-up-problems and to the combination of clinical with quality of life in information.

Deciding between indices and profiles basically refers to the choice between single- versus multi-outcome measures. However, such choice might not be necessary if instruments are used that provide both types of information. Quality of life research might profit from such instruments given that they have been developed according to a defined conceptual basis, to rigorous quality standards and to easy applicability. Their value, for example in clinical trials, lies in providing both detailed information on quality of life components affected differentially by the treatment arms and a single measure of the overall effect. This single measure would be optimal if derived from well thought-out weighting operations and if usable as an unequivocal scale with defined segments. Depending on the study objective, either the profile part or the index part of the instrument could be chosen for hypothesis testing.

In conclusion, research into specific methodological problems of quality of life assessment as concerns the use of indices or profiles merits the effort. Not only are these problems interesting because they are also tied to conceptual and practical considerations, but they have consequences for how the quality of life assessment can be optimized. Such optimization in turn may positively affect the conduct of studies, the transparency of results and the discussion about implications of quality of life research for patients, physicians and the health care system.

## References

1. Aaronson, N.C. Quality of life assessment in clinical trials: methodologic issues. *Contr. Clin. Trials* 1989; 10: 1955–2085.
2. Aaronson, N.K., Bullinger, M. and Ahmedzai, S. A modular approach to quality of life in cancer clinical trials. *Rec. Res. Cancer Res.* 1988; 111: 231–249.
3. Berg, R.L. *Health Status Indices*. Hospital Research and Educational Trust, Chicago, 1973.
4. Bergner, M., Bobbit, R.A., Carter, W.B. and Gilson, B.S. The sickness impact profile. Development and final revision of a health status measure. *Med. Care* 1981; 19: 787–805.
5. Bullinger, M. and Hasford, J. Testing and evaluating quality of life measures for German clinical trials. *Contr. Clin. Trials* 1991; 12: 915–1055.
6. Bullinger, M., Heinisch, M., Ludwig, M. and Geier, S. Skalen zur Ferfassung des Wohlbefindens. Psychometrische überprüfung des Profile of Mood States (POMS).*Z. Diff. Diag. Psychol.* 1990; 11: 53–61.
7. Croog, S.H., Levine, S., Testa, M.A. *et. al.* The effects of antihypertensive therapy on the quality of life. *N. Engl. J. Med.* 1986; 314: 1657–1664.
8. DuPuy, H.J. The Psychological General Well-Being (PGWB) index. In Wenger, N.K., Mattson, M.E., Furberg, C.D. and Ellinson, J. (eds). *Assessment of Quality of Life in Clinical Trials of Cardiovascular Therapies*. New York, LeJacq Publishers, 1984, pp. 170–183.
9. Feinstein, A.R. *et. al.* Scientific and clinical problems in indices of functional disability. *Ann. Intern. Med.* 1986; 105: 413–420.
10. Guyatt, G.H. and Jaeschke, R. Measurement in clinical trials-choosing the appropriate approach. In Spilker, B. (ed.) *Quality of Life Assessment in Clinical Trials*. New York, Raven Press, 1990, pp. 37–46.
11. Guyatt, G., Walter, S. and Norman, G. Measuring change over time – assessing the usefulness of evaluative instruments. *J. Chronic Dis.* 1987; 40: 171–178.
12. Hunt, S. The Nottingham Health Profile. In Wenger, N.K., Mattson, M.E., Furberg, C.D. and Ellinson, J. (eds) *Assessment of Quality of Life in Clinical Trials of Cardiovascular Therapies*. New York, LeJacq Publishers, 1984.

13. Kaplan, R.M., Bush, J.W. and Berry, C.C. Health status: types of validity and the index of well-being. *Health Serv. Res.* 1976; 11: 478–507.
14. Kaplan, R. and Stewart, L. Pros and cons of single vs. multi outcome quality of life assessments. In Shumaker, S.A. and Furber, C. (eds). *Research on Quality of Life and Cardiovascular Disease. Am. J. Prevent. Med.* (in press).
15. Kirshner, B. and Guyatt, G. A methodological framework for assessing health indices. *J. Chronic Dis.* 1985; 38: 27–36.
16. McDowell, I. and Newell, C. *Measuring Health: A Guide to Rating Scales and Questionnaires.* New York, Oxford University Press, 1987.
17. McNair, D., Lorr, M. and Droppelman, L.F. *Manual for the Profile of Mood States.* California, Educational and Industrial Testing Service, San Diego, 1971.
18. Olschewski, M. and Schumacher, M. Statistical analysis of quality of life data in cancer clinical trials. *Stat. Med.* 1990; 9: 749–763.
19. Patrick, D.L. and Erickson, P. Assessing health-related quality of life for clinical decision making. In Walker, S.R. and Rosser, R.M. (eds). *Quality of Life: Assessment and Application.* Lancaster, MTP Press, 1988, pp. 183–197.
20. Pocock, S.J., Geller, N.L. and Tsiatis, A.A. The analysis of multiple endpoints in clinical trials. *Biometrics* 1987; 43: 487–498.
21. Spilker, H. *Quality of Life Assessment in Clinical Trials.* New York, Raven Press, 1990.
22. Spitzer, W.Q., Dobson, A.J., Hall, J., Chesterman, E., Levi, J., Shepherd, R., Battista, R.N. and Catchlove, B.R. Measuring the quality of life of cancer patients. A concise QL-Index for use by physicians. *J. Chronic Dis.* 1981; 34: 585–597.
23. Streiner, D.L. and Normann, G. *Health Measurement Scales – a Practical Guide to their Development and Use.* Oxford, Oxford University Press, 1989.
24. Tandon, P. Applications of global statistics in analysing quality of life data. *Stat. Med.* 1990; 9: 819–827.
25. Walker, S.R. and Rosser, R.M. *Quality of Life Assessment and Application.* Lancaster, MTP Press, 1988.
26. Ware, J.E. Standards for validating health measures; Definition and content. *J. Chronic Dis.* 1987; 40: 503–512.

# 13 The On-Line Guide to Quality-of-Life Assessment (OLGA): resource for selecting quality of life assessments

**Pennifer Erickson and Jeffrey Scott**

The approach taken to assess quality of life depends on both the purpose of measurement and the characteristics of the population being assessed. Measurement strategies differ if the aim is to monitor the population's level of health, investigate determinants of health, allocate resources or evaluate the impact of different treatment interventions. For either monitoring or epidemiological investigation, a measure that combines both mortality and morbidity, such as quality-adjusted life years, may be the most suitable measure. For resource allocation, measures that include trade-offs between different levels of health-related quality of life are needed. Clinical trials that follow persons over relatively short periods and require detailed information about changes in functioning attributable to the intervention being studied are more likely to require batteries or profiles of health-related quality of life assessments.

Patient characteristics, especially age, level of disability and cognitive function are also important in selecting a measure of health-related quality of life. For example, a different measure will be used to study effectiveness of an oral gold preparation in persons with moderate arthritis than to study the effectiveness of an ACE inhibitor in persons with mild hypertension. Arthritis patients are likely to be older and to have more limitations in mobility, whereas persons with hypertension are likely to be younger and limited in their ability to work.

As these examples suggest, no single assessment or combination of assessments is valid for all studies. Rather, the selection of assessments depends on the context in which they are to be used. Selecting an assessment or set of assessments then becomes a matter of clearly specifying the purpose and features of the quality of life study, identifying one or more assessments suitable for use in this context, and selecting those that meet practical considerations and resource constraints.

To date there have been a number of guidelines for selecting assessments according to their methodological and practical features[1,2,4,7,10,21]. In addition, a number of books have been published recently that summarize many of the existing assessments[8,9,12,15]. Both the guidelines and compendia address the context-specific nature of quality of life assessment. As yet, no one has proposed a method for selecting an optimal quality of life assessment that is based on matching assessments with the context of the study.

This chapter describes The On-Line Guide to Quality-of-Life Assessment (OLGA), a system that has been developed to readily identify assessments for specific applications[6]. The following section presents the background for the system by describing essential considerations in selecting quality of life assessments. Key features, as well as problems and limitations with these approaches, are discussed. That is followed by a general description of OLGA.

Two features of OLGA allow for selection of assessments based on the context of the study: a comprehensive database of assessments and their applications; and decision-theoretic algorithms – 'OLGArithms' – for selecting from among the available assessments those that best satisfy the criteria that define the context of the study. The OLGArithms compare expected quality of life impacts in terms of treatment benefits and side effects, characteristics of the study population, and practical considerations, with features of available assessments, to find the best match. Although the issues are similar, whether assessing quality of life for resource allocation, evaluation, population monitoring, the main focus here is on pharmaceutical studies, and on clinical trials in particular.

## SELECTING AN ASSESSMENT

Selecting an assessment starts with the investigator thoroughly specifying the details of the study, to set the context for the quality of life assessment. The *optimal* assessment matches the study context and is thus able to detect change in quality of life as a result of treatment. Table 13.1 describes the major study characteristics that need to be defined in order to select assessments that will detect quality of life changes.

The type and purpose of the study are important in determining whether an index, profile, or battery is the most appropriate measure to use. Characteristics of the study population are used along with treatment benefits and side-effects to determine operational definitions of the concepts and

**Table 13.1** Important study characteristics for specifying the context for quality of life assessment

---

Conceptual considerations
    Identify the type and purpose of study:
       –   Randomized clinical trial, an evaluation study, or other
       –   Treatment arms
       –   Random sample, convenience sample, or other
    Identify the study population:
       –   Age and sex of the target group
       –   Relevant co-morbidities to include and exclude
       –   Stage(s) of disease to be studied
    Treatment benefits and side-effects:
       List all positive and negative effects of treatment. For example,
       signs and symptoms, depression and other affective functions, role
       performance and other types of social well-being
    Method of administration:
       Match possible methods of administration with sensitive concepts and
       persons with disabilities. For example, self administration for sensitive
       concepts and domains of health-related quality of life, and interviewer-
       administered for people with disabilities
Resource considerations
    Total budget
       –   Staff with sufficient skill to collect, process and analyse data
       –   Cost to obtain respondents
       –   Respondent and interviewer burden
    Time frame
       Maximum interval between start of study until presentation of findings

---

domains of health-related quality of life to be measured. Patrick and Erickson[18] defines a broad range of concepts and domains and gives selected examples of operational definitions of each. Available resources help to determine the scope of the quality of life study. After specifying information according to each of the major categories shown in Table 13.1, the investigator evaluates existing assessments for use in the context of this study.

Quality of life assessments are also context-specific. That is, each assessment has been developed for a particular purpose and for use with specific populations. The concepts and domains of health-related quality of life included in each assessment are relevant for the purpose and population. Some are generic measures that can be applied across diseases, conditions, populations and concepts, such as the Quality of Well-being Scale, the Short-Form 36 and the Sickness Impact Profile[4,13,20]. Others are specific measures that have been developed for application to an individual disease or condition, population, or concept or domain of health-related quality of life, such as the Arthritis Impact Measurement Scales, the Index of ADL and the CES-Depression Scale[14,16,19].

Assessments also differ with regard to the type of scores produced, whether indicators, indexes, profiles or batteries. The taxonomy developed by Guyatt et al.[11] is useful for understanding advantages and disadvantages of various types of quality of life assessments and for evaluating each in the context of a given study.

The evaluation of each assessment in terms of the proposed study context involves reviewing literature on the conceptual rationale for its development as well as empirical studies on its application. Assessments can be excluded from further consideration if they fail to satisfy the criteria used for specifying the context of the quality of life study. Examples of this evaluation process, items to be evaluated, and the action taken are given in Table 13.2. For each assessment the investigator needs to know the rationale for development and link this with the purpose of the current quality of life study. Information on an assessment's conceptual framework as well as its measurement properties can be obtained from basic documentation of the assessment.

Although empirical studies may provide information about reliability and validity, as well as information about practical considerations, their main contribution is to provide evidence about how an assessment performs in a given population. Published articles on clinical quality of life studies usually present average scores at baseline as well as at various intervals over the course of the study. These data can be used to determine an assessment's

**Table 13.2** Example of evaluation logic for identifying quality of life assessments for use in a given study

Match concepts of study and assessments according to:
- *Purpose*, e.g. eliminate screening instruments if the goal is to assess outcomes
- *Defined population*, e.g. eliminate measures of activities of daily living if the target population is middle aged, mildly hypertensive persons
- *Concepts and domains of health-related quality of life*, e.g. eliminate measures of cognitive function if the population is alert and the treatment is not expected to impair cognition
- *Methods of administration*, e.g. give higher priority to measures of sensitive topics that are self-administered

Review measurement properties and resources for:
- *Reliability*, e.g. give higher priority to assessments that have test–retest and internal consistency coefficients greater than 0.50 and demonstrated in the same type of population as is to be used in the given study
- *Validity*, e.g. give higher priority to assessments with larger coefficients for construct validity, especially if obtained in the same type of population as is to be used in the given study
- *Time to administer*, e.g. eliminate assessments that require over an hour to administer if only 10 minutes is available
- *Languages*, e.g. give higher priority to assessments for which translations are available

ability to detect changes due to treatment. These data can also be used to determine whether or not an assessment has been used only in the context for which it was developed, or if its use generalizes to broader contexts.

In addition, some empirical studies may include a discussion of the method of administration and respondent acceptability. From this information the investigator can get an indication as to whether or not the claims of the developers are justified when their assessment is applied by other investigators.

After evaluating the assessments and associated empirical literature, the investigator will often be left with a small set of assessments, each of which fits the study context in at least some of the categories of interest. If one assessment meets all of the criteria that define the study's context, then the decision as to which assessment to select for use in the given study is obvious. Complete agreement is rare, however. In the case of incomplete agreement, the investigator must decide which assessment, or possibly battery of assessments, to use. If the only problem is one of too few resources, and if more resources can be brought to bear, then, again, the choice is obvious. Most decisions are neither so obvious nor so simple. In most cases the investigator has to compromise on the amount of detail to satisfy the study context within the resource constraint.

In working out the compromise, the goal is to identify an assessment, or set of assessments, that correctly identifies changes in quality of life over the course of the study. The investigator is most likely to select an optimal assessment if compromise from the ideal is made in practical, rather than in conceptual, considerations. For example, if an assessment includes concepts needed to assess treatment benefits and side-effects but exceeds the resource constraint, then one compromise may be to use a self-administered rather than an interviewer-administered version of the questionnaire. This will reduce the overall cost of data collection. Another compromise, given that an assessment includes the relevant concepts and domains, is to use a short form rather than a longer version. This will not only reduce the overall costs but will also reduce response time and respondent burden.

These two examples illustrate how it is possible to choose among assessments to satisfy resource constraints by restricting all compromises to practical considerations. In some studies, however, the resource constraint· may also require compromises associated with treatment benefits and side-effects. This problem is most likely encountered when treatment benefits and side-effects encompass many different concepts and domains of health-related quality of life, and there are relatively few resources allocated to the quality of life component of the study.

For example, preliminary studies may suggest that physical activity, social contact, affective well-being, health perceptions and physical and mental symptoms are the relevant concepts and domains of quality of life to assess for a given treatment. Study planners may provide resources for 10 minutes of data collection. If the target population is reasonably healthy, e.g. having mild to moderate hypertension, then it may be possible to collect data on all concepts and domains in 10 minutes or less, especially if a self-administered questionnaire can be used. If the population is relatively unhealthy, it is less likely that data on all of the concepts and domains can be collected in 10 minutes, regardless of method of administration.

Since the purpose of study and target population are relatively fixed, most of the choices lie in an interaction between treatment benefits and side-effects on the one hand and alternative formats for collecting the information within the given resource constraint on the other. Therefore, the investigator must reach a compromise, by trading off not only various practical considerations but also some concepts and domains of health-related quality of life. To detect change in quality of life over the course of the study, however, as much detail about concepts and domains as possible should be retained in the quality of life assessment.

The compromise involves re-evaluating the study context to set priorities among treatment benefits and side-effects. Then, the most efficient method of collecting the information, starting with the highest priorities, is sought. Efficiency of method may mean using a short form rather than a longer version, using a self-administered rather than an interviewer-administered questionnaire, or using a self-administered questionnaire rather than a rating form filled out by a health professional. Following an iterative process between conceptual and practical considerations leads to the optimal assessment, or set of assessments, being selected.

If the study context is not clearly specified, or if the investigator gives priority to practical rather than conceptual considerations, then a less than optimal assessment will be selected. Failure to detect a change in quality of life may occur when the level of function in the study population is different from that measured in the selected assessment. For example, the Sickness Impact Profile (SIP) was developed to assess impact of sickness. Applications of the SIP indicate that in a study to detect change in quality of life among persons with mild to moderate hypertension, the SIP will indicate very little dysfunction at baseline[17]. Thus the opportunity for detecting improvement due to treatment will be small; this is referred to as the ceiling effect. Baseline scores at the lowest end of an assessment's capacity indicate that the measure will be unable to detect changes for the worse, i.e. the floor effect. An optimal quality of life assessment within a given context will avoid ceiling and floor effects.

Less than optimal selections, i.e. assessments that fail to detect change in quality of life, may occur because the investigator starts with a subset of assessments. In theory, selecting a quality of life assessment starts with *all* available assessments being evaluated against the study context; this evaluation includes both the conceptual frameworks and the empirical evidence.

In practice, however, clinical investigators start with a selected subset of assessments. This subset may represent familiar assessments, e.g. those that have been previously used by the investigator, or may have been identified through a literature search of studies that have been done.

Even if the selected subset of assessments is evaluated carefully, starting with less than all the possibly useful assessments can limit the results of a quality of life study. One problem is that the subset may be biased. Bias may occur, for example, if the assessments in the subset are identified by use in a previous study, as for treatment of mild hypertension, and the current study is to be conducted among persons with asthma. Another source of bias is that if the subset is based on a literature search, then the investigator is restricted to what *has been* done, rather than what *can be* done. In either case, the investigator may be led to a less than optimal assessment, or set of assessments.

Evaluation of the subset may also lead the investigator to the incorrect conclusion that there is no currently available assessment that contains the concepts and domains needed for the intended study. In this case a new assessment may be commissioned. Even if this relatively costly and time consuming process is taken, a new assessment creates its own set of problems. For example, results of the study can not be compared with similar studies in which different assessments have been used. Lack of comparability with similar studies weakens claims that can be made based on the study results.

Failure to detect change in quality of life may also result from lack of attention to measurement properties, especially reliability, validity and responsiveness. Some information may be readily available, perhaps even supplied by the developers of the assessment. For any given assessment, however, readily available data are usually limited to a few populations and studies. Although more data on reliability and validity may be published, this is frequently difficult to locate using traditional literature retrieval systems, such as the US National Library of Medicine's Medline.

Although reviewing all assessments and their measurement properties, and evaluating them in terms of practical considerations, leads to the best match with the study context, this approach is rarely, if ever, used in practice. One reason is that there is a lack of assembled information about the development of quality of life assessments and their empirical applications. Another is the lack of resources with which to locate and summarize all of the information needed within a given time frame. And a third reason is lack of experience in setting priorities and making the compromises needed to select an optimal assessment.

The On-Line Guide to Quality-of-Life Assessment (OLGA) has been developed to overcome these limitations. This system is a resource which has been designed specifically to provide investigators with complete quality of life information in a single location and in an easy-to-use form. The next section describes how OLGA can help investigators select the optimal quality of life assessment.

## THE ON-LINE GUIDE TO QUALITY-OF-LIFE ASSESSMENT (OLGA)

OLGA has been developed to help in the selection of a quality of life assessment, and to do this in a fraction of the time needed for the traditional literature search, review and evaluation. To meet this objective, OLGA consists not only of information needed to match the study context with available assessments but also of decision-theoretic algorithms – 'OLGA-rithms' – to identify compromises, or trade-offs, among assessments. This combination of complete information and OLGArithms for matching the study context with available assessments leads to the selection an optimal assessment strategy, and one which fits within the resource constraints of a given study.

In addition to facilitating the design of quality of life studies, using OLGA helps improve the science of quality of life assessment in the following ways:

(1)   OLGA helps investigators select an assessment that detects true changes in quality of life, that is, one that maximizes the detection of true positive and true negatives.

(2)   Use of OLGA increases the likelihood of replication through the emphasis on the use of existing assessments.

(3)   OLGA makes it possible to formulate hypotheses about the relationships between treatments and their quality of life impacts. Quality of life assessment becomes, therefore, an integral part of a treatment evaluation, rather than an *ad hoc* addition to a clinical study. Hypotheses formed in this way can be rigorously tested and, since there is a theoretical basis for the hypothesized relationships, predictions can be made.

Each assessment in the OLGA database is thoroughly reviewed and comprehensively categorized according to its conceptual and practical considerations. This information is summarized in standardized, easy-to-read formats designed to assist the investigator in choosing between quality of life assessments. The database also contains references to empirical studies in which the assessments have been used. This includes research using clinical trial designs as well as cost–effectiveness or cost–utility analysis and evaluation studies. Each study is identified by the quality of life assessments used as well as other key features for retrieval. Reference to the empirical studies is presented in standard bibliographical format, with the quality of life assessments in each study clearly identified. Abstracts that describe the quality of life aspects are available for recent studies.

OLGArithms assist the investigator in evaluating and re-evaluating the study and assessment contexts and various measurement options, to select an optimal quality of life assessment or set of assessments. For example, for a set of assessments that meet the study's conceptual considerations, OLGA-rithms assist the investigator in making compromises in practical consider-ations: to identify those assessments that meet the resource constraints. Or, if the study's context and resources require making compromises between treatment benefits and side-effects, OLGArithms assist the investigator in evaluating various trade-offs: to select the optimal assessment or set of assessments. In performing these evaluations, OLGA uses information contained in both the assessment summaries and the references to empirical studies that have used the assessments.

OLGA is updated three times each year. Updates include new material to the database and improvements in the OLGArithms. Material for the updates is identified by a comprehensive search of on-line bibliographical retrieval systems as well as personal review of over 60 professional journals that repeatedly publish articles dealing with quality of life assessment. The database includes references to English and non-English language writings: published and unpublished articles, and monographs.

OLGA is designed for use in standard IBM-compatible personal com-puters. The computer programs are especially easy to use, employing checking/correcting features for user input. Output formats are designed to present information needed for selecting a quality of life assessment in one easily accessible location, and to allow for matching the study context with that of each assessment.

This section has described the rationale for the development of OLGA and has described essential features of the system for selecting a quality of life assessment that is optimal for a given study. The next section discusses the advantages of using this system compared to the existing strategies for selecting an assessment.

## ADVANTAGES OF USING OLGA

Using OLGA and its comprehensive database overcomes one of the major problems in quality of life assessment: selecting sub-optimal assessments, i.e. those that fail to detect change in quality of life due to treatment. Quality of life assessments are more thoroughly reviewed and indexed in OLGA than in other, traditional reference materials. For example, although the US. National Library of Medicine's *Medline* database may indicate that there are many articles that discuss quality of life, assessments are not referenced systematically by name. Thus there is no way to search for assessments such as the Sickness Impact Profile, the Arthritis Impact Measurement Scales, etc., in a comprehensive, systematic fashion.

Assessment names in the title of an article or in the author-supplied abstract, may lead to confusion, since some assessments are referenced by several different names. For example, the General Well-being Schedule developed by Dupuy has been variously referred to as Dupuy's Well-being Scale, and the Psychological General Well-being Schedule.

As another example, in studies that use quality-adjusted life years (QALY), the underlying quality of life assessment may not be named. Instead, the abstract may note only that a QALY has been used to assess quality of life. In this way, use of traditional reference searching can result in many quality of life assessments being overlooked.

OLGA is also more comprehensive than traditional searching systems because it includes newly-developed assessments. New assessments will be overlooked if the investigator is looking to 'what has been done' in traditional reference and searching systems. OLGA, however, shows not only what has been done but also what can be done. For example, the Dementia Behaviour Disturbance Scale[3] may be the ideal assessment to study the impact of a new treatment for Alzheimer's disease. However, unless this assessment has been used with Alzheimer's patients, it would most likely be overlooked in a literature search. This type of omission will be particularly common in areas where quality of life has not as yet been assessed.

Another way OLGA's unique features improve on the currently available methods for selecting a quality of life assessment is by providing complete information on not only available assessments but also on empirical studies in which these assessments are used. If an investigator does not have the resources to fully identify which assessment can be used in a given context, then the review stops before all possible assessments are identified and evaluated. This tends to result in only the easily accessible assessments being considered for use. Traditional search procedures are generally less thorough than the information contained in OLGA. Lack of thoroughness can result in biased selection, resulting in an assessment that fails to detect change in quality of life.

Also, OLGA uses standard terminology, so that it is easy to compare across assessments and from assessments to the empirical research. In contrast, when using traditional searching and review procedures, the investigator faces problems of non-standard terminology and jargon that are used from one journal article to another, and even from one compendium to another. Sorting through the jargon to fully understand its meaning requires many years of experience in working in the field of quality of life assessment.

Although OLGA has been primarily developed for selecting a quality of life assessment for use in a given study, the OLGArithms and database are sufficiently flexible to satisfy other needs, as noted in Table 13.3.

**Table 13.3** Main uses of OLGA

| |
|---|
| Design quality of life assessment strategies for various clinical studies |
| Evaluate the quality of life assessment strategy used in another study |
| Gain a deeper understanding of the strengths and weaknesses embodied in various approaches to assessing quality of life |
| Identify quality of life consultants |

For example, OLGA can be used to validate the assessment strategy used by another investigator. The conceptual considerations of the other investigator's study are supplied to the OLGArithms which then identify optimal assessments for use in this context. Comparing OLGA's selection with that actually used serves as a validity check on the other investigator's approach to quality of life assessment.

With its comprehensive database, OLGA can assist the user in identifying consultants relevant for various studies. For example, each assessment summary lists the name and address of the assessment's principal developer. The empirical references indicate who is actively working on quality of life in specific diseases and health conditions. Also, for persons new to the field of quality of life assessment, OLGA can serve as a tutor. Repeated use of the OLGArithms, and studying the results, will inform the user of the key concepts and developments in assessing quality of life. Lastly, OLGA's developers are committed to providing high-quality technical support.

Overall, OLGA is a multifaceted resource that has been developed to assist investigators select optimal assessments for use in quality of life studies. The goal is to supply high-quality information in an easy-to-use format, thereby improving the science of quality of life.

## References

1. Aaronson, N.K. Methodological issues in psychosocial oncology with special reference to clinical trials. In Ventafridda, V., vanDam, F.S.A.M., Yancik, R. *et al.* (eds) *Assessment of Quality of Life and Cancer Treatment.* Amsterdam, The Netherlands: Excerpta Medica, 1986, pp. 29–42.
2. Barofsky, I., Cohen, S.J. and Sugarbaker, P.H. Selecting a quality of life assessment: standardized tests, clinical assessments, or custom-designed instruments. In Wenger, N.K., Mattson, M.E., Furberg, C.D. *et al.* (eds) *Assessment of Quality of Life in Clinical Trials of Cardiovascular Therapies.* New York, Le Jacq Publishing, 1984, pp. 239–249.
3. Baumgarten, M., Becker, R. and Gauthier, S. Validity and reliability of the dementia behavior disturbance scale. *J. Am. Geriatr. Soc.* 1990; 38(3): 221–226.

4. Bergner, M., Bobbitt, R.A., Carter, W.B. *et al.* The Sickness Impact Profile: development and final revision of a health status measure. *Med. Care* 1981; 19(8): 787–805.

5. Bergner, M. and Rothman, M.L. Health status measures: an overview and guide for selection. *Annu. Rev. Public Health* 1987; 8: 191–210.

6. Erickson, P. The On-Line Guide to Quality-of-Life Assessment. *CMR News* 1990; 8(3): 5.

7. Erickson, P. and Patrick, D.L. Guidelines for selecting quality of life assessment: methodological and practical considerations. *J. Drug Ther. Res.* 1988; 13(5): 159–163.

8. Fallowfield, L. *The Quality of Life: The Missing Measurement in Health Care.* London, Souvenir Press Ltd., 1990

9. Frank-Stromborg, M. (ed.) *Instruments for Clinical Nursing Research.* Norwalk, Connecticut, Appleton and Lange, 1988.

10. Guyatt, G.H. and Jaeschke, R. Measurements in clinical trials: choosing the appropriate approach. In Spilker, B. (ed.) *Quality of Life Assessments in Clinical Trials.* New York, Raven Press, 1990, pp. 37–46.

11. Guyatt, G.H., Veldhuyzen Van Zanten S.J.O., Feeny, D.H. *et al.* Measuring quality of life in clinical trials: a taxonomy and review. *Can. Med. Assoc. J.* 1989; 140(12): 1441–1448.

12. Kane, R.A. and Kane, R.L. *Assessing the Elderly: A Practical Guide to Measurement.* Lexington, Massachusetts, Lexington Books, 1981.

13. Kaplan, R.M. and Anderson, J.P. A general health policy model: update and applications. *HSR: Health Serv. Res.* 1988, 23(2): 203–235.

14. Katz, S., Ford, A.B., Moskowitz, R.W. *et al.* Studies of illness in the aged: the index of ADL: a standardized measure of biological and psychosocial function. *J. Am. Med. Assoc.* 1963; 185(12): 914–919.

15. McDowell, I. and Newell, C. *Measuring Health: A Guide to Rating Scales and Questionnaires.* New York, Oxford University Press, 1987.

16. Meenan, R.F., Gertman, P.M. and Mason, J.H. Measuring health status in arthritis: the Arthritis Impact Measurement Scale. *Arthritis Rheumatism* 1980; 23(2): 146–152.

17. Patrick, D.L. and Deyo, R.A. Generic and disease-specific measures in assessing health status and quality of life. *Med. Care* 1989; 27(3 Suppl.): S217–S232.

18. Patrick, D.L. and Erickson, P. What constitutes quality of life? Concepts and dimensions. *Quality of Life and Cardiovascular Care* 1988; 4(3): 103–127.

19. Radloff, L.S. The CES-D Scale: A self-report depression scale for research in the general population. *Appl. Psychol. Meas.* 1977; 1(3): 385–401.

20. Stewart, A.L., Hayes, R.D. and Ware, J.E. The MOS short-form general health survey: reliability and validity in a patient population. *Med. Care* 1988; 26(7): 724–732.

21. Ware, J.E. Methodological considerations in the selection of health status assessment procedures. In Wenger, N.K., Mattson, M.E., Furberg, C.D. *et al.* (eds) *Assessment of Quality of Life in Clinical Trials of Cardiovascular Therapies.* New York, Le Jacq Publishing, 1984, pp. 87–117.

# Section II

# Assessing Quality of Life in Major Disease Areas

# 14 Measuring the quality of life of patients with cancer*

Peter Selby

The traditional goal of cure for localized cancer by surgery or radiotherapy is now supplemented by an intention to cure many patients who have widespread disease with drugs. However, the majority of patients with common cancers will not be cured by local or systemic therapy. For these patients the purpose of medical care is to prolong their lives and to maintain the quality of those lives. The quality of life may be impaired by the disease, but treatments may also have deleterious effects so that overall benefit from a treatment is often uncertain.

This review is concerned with the issue of measurement of quality of life. Quality of life may not be reflected by the length of survival or by clinical and laboratory measurements of the activity of the illness. For instance, if the success of a treatment is indicated by a reduction in the volume of a tumour, but this is only achieved at the cost of adverse reactions, then it may not be associated with an increase in well-being. On the other hand, partially successful therapy may produce remarkable relief of symptoms. To achieve a successful balance we need to be able to measure the net benefit, that is improvement in quality of life.

Interest in direct methods for measuring quality of life in cancer is a relatively recent development. Bardelli and Saracci[4] reviewed all the clinical studies published in six major cancer journals between 1956 and 1976 and found that less than 5% reported attempts to measure any aspect of quality of life. Since 1976 there has been a substantial increase in studies on this subject, reflecting a recognition of the limitations and potential hazards of

---

* Based in part on assessing quality of life in cancer patients. *British Journal of Cancer* 1989;60:437–440 and Measurement of the quality of life – the particular problems of cancer patients. *Proceedings of a Royal College of Physicians* meeting, 1992, with permission.

modern treatment. A great deal of the work in the last decade has focused on methodology, but the techniques and concepts have been largely borrowed from psychometry in psychology, sociology and educational psychology[50]. The methods of psychometry are not familiar to oncologists and are somewhat obscured by a plethora of sometimes ill-defined terms. An outline of some of the important principles which are essential to the proper choice and development of measurement methods for quality of life will be given here and the available methods and some of their applications are discussed. Reviews of this field are given by Fayers and Jones[23], Holland[30], Selby and Robertson[62] de Haes and van Knippenberg[18], Ventafridda et al.[72] and Clark and Fallowfield[15], McDowell and Newell[45] and Selby[63].

In 1989 the United Kingdom Medical Research Council Working Party carried out a review of methods available for evaluating quality of life. This considered the function, format, administration, scoring, structure and clinical usage of a wide range of questionnaires. Their psychometric properties and the extent to which they were evaluated were assessed and some interim recommendations for measurement of quality of life in cancer patients were made. In this report we will summarize the conduct and conclusions of that Working Party which have been published Maguire and Selby[42].

## DEFINITION

There appears to be no agreed definition of the term quality of life[5,14,18]. The concept clearly involves physical and psychosocial well-being; to be comprehensive, religious, cultural and political facets of life might be specified. A fully satisfactory quality of life might be regarded by some as a return to the situation before an illness began, whereas others would require the attainment of an ideal quality[13,58]. Most authors recognize that a satisfactory quality of life is an individual judgement and that there are differences between individuals.

Two pragmatic solutions to the problems of definition may be proposed. Firstly, the World Health Organization's traditional definition of health as 'physical, mental and social well-being and not merely the absence of disease or infirmity' (see Ahmed and Kolker[3]), is a useful statement of those areas which must be considered in the measurement of quality of life. They represent the minimum requirement and the use of this definition does not preclude consideration of, for instance, the spiritual aspects of life where this seems appropriate. This definition includes our view that quality of life has multiple dimensions and that the hypothesis that there is a useful, integral and single dimension expressed by a single number should be viewed cautiously. Secondly, in cancer medicine we are concerned with the effect of the disease and its treatment upon the patient. Our goal is to return them, as far as possible, to normal. The upper limit of measurement should be normality for that patient, not an ideal of perfect quality of life.

## SPECIAL DIFFICULTIES MEASURING QL IN CANCER PATIENTS

### Difficulties related to disease

*Physical dimension*

The symptoms associated with local or advanced cancer are many and varied. For many common cancers the long-term prognosis is still extremely poor. Although the severity of symptoms and the threat to patient's lives may not be greater for many cancers than for other common life threatening conditions such as ischaemic heart disease, they do present special difficulties in the measurement of quality of life. The difficulties arise from the multiplicity of cancer presentations and disabilities. Each cancer site is associated with a spectrum of presentations and stages and the measurement of quality of life needs to encompass all of these. This presents a problem in the generation of generic instruments which has yet to be adequately addressed.

In addition to the problems presented by the multiplicity of cancer presentations, their severity can generate restrictions on the measurement of quality of life. The ill patients with advanced and/or recurrent cancer require extensive and intensive care and it is important that the measurement of quality of life in this context should not be onerous for the patient. The need to restrict questionnaires in length confounds the difficulties presented by the multiplicity of features that must be measured. The reduction of questionnaires to the minimum possible is necessary.

*Psychology*

Cancer patients suffer depression, anxiety and experience anger frequently as a reaction to their illness. They are, of course, not alone in experiencing emotional disorder as a result of the presence of physical illness but, again, there are particular aspects of their illness which makes the measurement of quality of life in this context especially difficult. Emotional well-being is an independent factor determining quality of life for cancer patients which requires measurement[10].

Why is the screening of cancer patients for psychiatric morbidity by using psychometric questionnaires more difficult than for other diseases? One answer is technical and relates to the construction of such instruments. Many methods draw upon the somatic symptoms of psychiatric illnesses to identify the diagnosis and quantify severity. A good example is the weight loss commonly associated with depression. These somatic symptoms are frequently manifestations of the physical disorders associated with cancer, particularly when it is advanced. The value of many psychometric questionnaires is therefore limited in cancer patients and those which, like the Hospital Anxiety and Depression Scale[80] seek to avoid the use of somatic symptoms are especially valuable.

Despite these difficulties, a substantial body of information exists about the psychological disabilities and psychiatric disorders of cancer patients and the application of measurement methods has been in general terms successful. The availability of useful questionnaires which are relatively independent of somatic symptoms and which have been validated in the context of cancer patients by comparison to more extensive questionnaires provides the researcher and the cancer physician with valuable tools.

### Social

The social problems for the cancer patients are particular and severe compared to the other major life threatening illnesses. Cancer is our major medical metaphor for evil[65]. It inherited this mantle from infectious diseases such as tuberculosis in the early part of this century and holds its position without challenge. In two areas this is most clear. First, the illness is used as a metaphor for much that is evil within our society. A certain political system may be described as being 'a cancer within our country'. The 'cancerous' role of individual military dictators within their countries has been often quoted. Second, discussions of cancer often make use of metaphors drawn from the battlefield. There are charities described as 'The War on Cancer', patients do 'do battle' with their illness, we are all members of 'campaigns'. Cancers are 'invasive' etc., etc. The social implications of being afflicted by a metaphor for evil are inadequately explored but some manifestations are clear. Cancer patients can become socially isolated at home and in the workplace. Fear of infection is used as an excuse for isolating the cancer patient. Jobs have been lost and families have been broken by this process which is entirely without substance in any clinical or biological form.

Susan Sontag[65] has examined the metaphor of cancer in some detail. A failing incidence of common cancers, which is predicted by epidemiological observations, may not reverse the process of metaphor. Only a reduction in case fatalities can do this, as with tuberculosis, and there is not immediate prospect for a major reduction in case fatalities for common cancers in this century.

Financial disability generated by illness is easy to ignore in the context of busy clinical practice. The cancer patient is not unusual or special in this respect but his or her well-being may be considerably impaired by frequent hospital visits and loss of career prospects even if the disease is effectively controlled.

## Difficulties related to the treatment

The treatment of most cancers is highly unsatisfactory. Areas of success include complete surgical resection of primary cancer which is still the main curative treatment modality (e.g. 30% cure rate in lower gastrointestinal cancers), curative radical radiotherapy for cancer of the cervix or cancers of the head and neck and curative combination chemotherapy for a small number of relatively uncommon cancers. Apart from its general inadequacy, the hall-mark of cancer treatment is that it is associated with deleterious effects upon the patient. In many cases these are not qualitatively different from those experienced by other patients undergoing, for instance, major surgical procedures. However, in some cases it is possible to characterize the deleterious effects of cancer therapy and their impact is more severe than that experienced by patients with other life threatening disorders.

### Surgery

The degree of damage associated with cancer surgery can vary from straightforward laparotomy with full bowel reconstruction through to major excisions like fore or hind quarter amputations. Few other diseases can be associated with range of permanent resection sometimes unavoidable for the cancer patient. In general there have been striking improvements in the aftermath of surgical procedures for cancer in the last 10 years. Notably the move from radical to conservative surgery for breast cancer, the availability of reconstructive techniques in the head and neck, the availability of microvascular techniques for rebuilding soft tissues in all parts of the body and the use of prosthetic techniques to replace resected bone have greatly reduced the mutilation suffered by patients undergoing cancer operations. However, amputations, mastectomy, laryngeal and pharyngeal resections are still sometimes unavoidable.

### Radiotherapy

The morbidity of radiotherapy may be either acute in association with inflamed epithelial surfaces, generalize malaise or nausea and vomiting or chronic when fibrosis, or even malignant change can occur. Carefully delivered therapy can usually avoid the most severe of these reactions although a fine balance between toxicity and efficacy is usual.

### Chemotherapy

Toxicity associated with chemotherapy is well described. Common toxicities include alopecia, nausea and vomiting and milia suppression and less frequent toxicities include cardiac renal neurological damage. Patients place nausea and vomiting at the top of their list of acutely identified toxicities but also give a high priority to hospitalization and financial burdens associated with recurrent treatments of the kind commonly employed.

As noted above, in cancer medicine and surgery discussions about treatment are complicated balancing acts between efficacy and toxicity. When the treatment is potentially curative in a high proportion of cases a high level of toxicity may be acceptable. When their treatment is palliative it should not be given unless there is a net improvement in the patients well-being such that the benefits outweigh the toxicity. In deciding the level of acceptable toxicity for any given probability of remission, both the patient's and the physician's views should be influential. In good practice the decision is reached by a process of discussion. Not all patients will manage to resolve a choice about treatment options. Many will ultimately turn to their physician for guidance and at that point it would be necessary for him to offer clear advice. Research into the balance of risks against benefits has generally indicated that there are differences between cancer patients, cancer doctors and the general population. In a study by Slevin and colleagues[64] the level of efficacy which was perceived to be sufficient to justify a given level of toxicity was evaluated in patients, in the general population and members of the medical and allied professions. Broadly, people were prepared to undergo moderately toxic treatment for quite a small probability of achieving a remission of their disease. For patients moderate toxicity was acceptable in one study for only 1% chance of improvement of their disease even if this improvement was not curative. Doctors (including professional oncologists) are, in general, less prepared to undergo toxic treatment unless the probability of improvement of their tumour is higher than that expected by the general population and by cancer patients. The interpretation of these observations is quite complex and it may not be a simple indication that toxic treatment should be given even if there is a tiny chance of effect. It probably should be used to indicate that the decision making process must be explored carefully with the patient who should be warned against the dangers of 'grasping at straws'.

In oncology the issues of 'balance' between toxicity and efficacy are particularly striking. In this case the effect of the illness can be severe in terms of symptoms and in terms of reduction of life expectancy. The toxicities employed may also be moderate or severe and there may be a risk of treatment related deaths. In medical specialities the balance between toxicity and efficacy must be sought but the immediacy of threat to the patient and the degree of toxicity contemplated may be less than for cancer patients. Measurement of quality of life should be an aid in decision taking in this area particularly if it is possible to develop instruments which measure quality of life with reasonable reliability and validity that take on board the complexity of the treatment and disease related damage that cancer patients may experience.

## PSYCHOLOGICAL MEASUREMENT METHODS

Valuable information about the quality of cancer patients' lives may be gained from descriptive studies which do not use specific measurement methods. For instance, a study describing the proportion of patients who suffer specific symptoms, lose their jobs, or lose their sexual drive because of a particular disease or treatment will be useful to allow plans for care and comparisons between treatments to be made. However, when precise quantification is needed for mathematical analysis, a psychological measurement method must be used. The design of such methods for cancer patients presents some special problems.

### Method of quantification of response

Several standard methods exist in psychometry for converting the subjective response of the interviewer or interviewee into a number. The commonest methods are linear analogue scoring or category rating.

At first sight, the choice of a method of quantification and the way it is presented may seem simple. However, it is clear from the literature of experimental psychology that the presentation of questions may dramatically influence results obtained. An example drawn from the measurement of physical stimuli serves to illustrate this point. Oborne and Clarke[51] investigated the influence of the addition of descriptive phrases along a linear analogue scale relating to comfort during a helicopter ride! Their experiment and results are described in Figure 14.1, which shows the large effect of altering the format of the question. The conclusion from their studies is that a plain line with simple descriptive phrases at either end is the most satisfactory form of presentation. This conclusion is supported by results obtained for pain measurement[59].

Relatively few studies have sought to compare linear analogue scales with other rating methods. Remington et al.[55] compared linear analogue scales with a categorical rating method for psychiatric symptoms, using items drawn from the Present State Examination[78]. Their conclusion was that reliability for the two different approaches was similar and concurred with an earlier observation made for validity for linear analogue scales[43]. There is a need for a study to compare these methods for their suitability to collect data in cancer patients. For the present it seems reasonable to conclude that the choice of method of quantification lies with the investigators and should be tailored to suit individual studies and purposes.

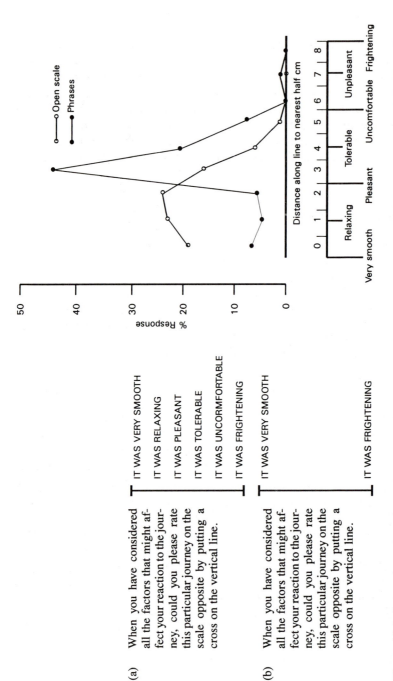

**Figure 14.1** Comparison of comfort ratings when an open scale or phrases are used. (From BEA helicopter survey, 1970)(Reproduced from Ref. 51 with permission)

## Scope of enquiry

The choice of an appropriate scope of enquiry for cancer patients is determined by the purpose of the investigation. If the questions are focused upon a single area they may fail to assess the impact of disease on the patient's whole life. On the other hand, an enquiry which seeks to be comprehensive may not adequately assess an important symptom and will be lengthy and time-consuming. Lengthy interviews may be particularly inappropriate when frequent assessments are needed to follow a patient's clinical course. Problems of compliance may be expected to accumulate during lengthy studies[6].

If only one measurement instrument is used to assess quality of life then the inclusion of several areas of enquiry is suggested by our definition:

- physical well-being, e.g. symptoms of disease or treatment such as pain, fatigue or nausea, physical activity and activity for work, recreation and self-care;
- psychological well-being, e.g. presence of emotional distress or a formal psychiatric illness such as depression;
- social well-being, in particular the support of family and friends and sexual relationships.

These suggestions are broadly similar to those of Aaronson[1], who also includes an enquiry about satisfaction with medical care as an important area requiring attention. It seems likely that the interaction with health care teams will have a major influence on a patient's perception of his quality of life during a period of life-threatening illness. However, cancer patients may not readily admit to dissatisfaction[61].

Some symptoms or problems may be particularly important for different disease sites or treatments, for example, dysphagia for oesophageal cancer or cystitis with oxazaphosphorine chemotherapy. However, it is not possible to include questions about all of these in all instruments without excess length and irrelevance for many patients. This may be overcome by the use of interchangeable groups of items (modules), within a questionnaire, which are chosen for particular studies. This approach was explored in our studies at the Ontario Cancer Institute (see below and Refs 60 and 75), where a group of items of general relevance was used in all studies and alternative, additional groups developed for breast cancer, lung cancer and ovarian cancer studies.

When all of these areas are considered, the resulting questionnaire frequently includes 20–40 items. Although such questionnaires are useful, they may still be too lengthy for frequent administration in clinical trials. Many investigators have sought to reduce such methods to about five questions by factor analysis or related methods[42,58]. Studies to evaluate the utility and sensitivity of shortened scales will be discussed below.

### Interviewer or self-report?

Self-assessment has the advantage of avoiding bias introduced by the interviewer, but it requires careful explanation to the patient. Professional interviewers produce high-quality data, with fewer errors and greater reliability[61] and with careful training, interviewers can uncover important information that patients may not volunteer. The choice of an interviewer or self-assessment depends on the resources available and the measurement method. Simple linear analogue scales or Likert scales are reliable for self-assessment when they are introduced in a clear and standardized way.

### Time focus

A patient may be asked to report on quality of life during time periods ranging from 24 hours to an infinite period. Few data are available to help in the choice of time focus. Reliability is similar for linear analogue scales with a 1-day or 7-day time focus, but care is needed when major events, such as a chemotherapy schedule, occur in the time period, since confusion and apparent reduction in reliability may then occur[61]. At present, a focus on 1 week is useful and suitable for studies with repeated tests every few weeks[1].

### Summation of scores

Each item in a questionnaire will evaluate one small aspect of a patient's life, but it may be desirable to add the scores into a sum. A simple addition is inappropriate for most purposes because it ignores the relative importance (weight) of each question. A more valid summation may require the deduction of weights for each question and these values may be used to produce a weighted sum.

The idea of a weighted sum is often expressed mathematically. If $y$ represents a value for a weighted sum of several items $x_1$, $x_2$, $X_3$, ... $x_n$, then:

$$y = w_1 x_1 \text{ i} + w_2 x_2 ... w_n x_n + e$$

or

$$y = {}^n w_i x_1$$

where $w_1$ is the weight for item $x_i$ and $e$ is the error of measurement. This representation of the concept of a weighted sum may be useful for many experimental purposes. However, it is severely limited. It is not possible to demonstrate that a linear relationship between an overall score and the independent items is the case, while the underlying assumption that all of the independent items are drawn from the same domain may not be appropriate.

It seems improbable that any single number can describe all the aspects of cancer patients' lives that are relevant to the overall concept of quality of life. Certainly, efforts to aggregate scores for different aspects of physical functioning into a single number have proved too technically difficult[67]. It was not possible to create a single cumulative scale that aggregated activity and mobility together with work or leisure roles. This argues strongly that an attempt to produce a single sum which covered all of these domains might be misleading. However, individual items which are linked to a single underlying theme such as physical activity may probably be safely summed[1].

## Normal ranges and calibration

The development of normal ranges is only necessary for some purposes. When a measurement method is to be used to compare two groups of patients, for instance in a comparative trial of a clinical cancer treatment, then normal ranges are unnecessary. However, when the purpose is to assess the degree of abnormality, for instance to assign a need for psychiatric or social referral, then a normal range must be established and must allow for the age distribution and underlying physical illness of the patients. Blohnik[11] demonstrated that some psychological differences between cancer patients and controls may disappear when age corrections are applied. Calibration of the linear analogue scales or of category rating methods has not been successfully achieved in many areas. In psychiatry, scores for many methods have been calibrated by comparison with diagnosable psychiatric syndromes. Particular scores may be associated with a high probability of needing psychiatric care[25]. However, for overall quality of life in cancer, no such ready calibration exists and investigators have fallen back on estimating scores between patients from clinically distinct groups of patients (e.g. remission versus relapse) to indicate the meaning of different scores[6,61].

## EVALUATION OF MEASUREMENT METHODS

The previous section has illustrated the options that present themselves to an investigator seeking to design or choose a suitable measurement method for evaluating quality of life, suitable for a particular purpose. The important properties of any measurement method used in oncology can be considered as follows:

### (1) Acceptability

This general term can be used to cover a description of the speed of completion of the questionnaire and the proportion of patients who find it difficult, impossible or unacceptable for any reason.

*(2) Reliability*

The reliability of a method is an indication of the extent to which it is reproducible and therefore of the amount of random error associated with its use.

*(3) Validity*

The validity of a measurement is the extent to which it appropriately measures that which it is intended to measure. Commonly in science this can be assessed by comparison of a measurement to a 'gold standard'. Unfortunately for most quality of life and other psychological measurements no such gold standard exists and indirect approaches to the validation of a measurement method are taken. Face or content validity is said to be present when a team of experts or users regard the items included within a measurement as appropriate and the presentation of the test as reasonable. Clearly this is open to many possible sources of bias. Concurrent validity involves a comparison between many different measurements each of which purports to measure a particular item or domain. In practice this commonly means comparison of a new measurement method to established measurement methods. The concept of construct validity is rather more ill-defined. At its simplest level it involves confirming that inter-item correlations within a test conform to a predictable pattern. Examples of construct validation are considered in the next section. The term 'predictive' validity is used in various ways by different authors; in its simplest form it may mean the degree of correlation of the method with external criteria, such as clinical status. The term 'discriminant' validity describes the ability of a method to assign different scores to distinct groups – to discriminate between groups – a similar concept to predictive validity.

## EXISTING METHODS FOR MEASUREMENT AND THEIR APPLICATION

There is a large range of quantitative questionnaires available for measuring some aspects of the quality of life of patients. A comprehensive review of all psychological measurement methods that may be applied in cancer patients is beyond the scope of this chapter, but some examples are given below. The much smaller number of methods which have been developed specifically for quality of life measurement in cancer patients will be reviewed in some detail.

### General methods that may be used in oncology

Methods which have been developed for application in psychiatry and other areas outside oncology may be very useful in cancer patients. In Table 14.1,

**Table 14.1** General methods that may be used in oncology

| Domain | Instrument | Nature |
|---|---|---|
| Physical domain | Activities of Daily Living Index[38,39] | Scales for the ability to perform bathing, dressing, toileting continence, mobility, and feeding developed for assessing the aged |
| | Barthel Index[41] | 10 Scales for basic physical and bodily functions |
| Psychological and social domain | Psychosocial Adjustment to Illness Scale[49] | Four-point scales for 45 items grouped under health care orientation vocational and domestic environments, sexual relationships, family relationships, social environment and psychological distress |
| | General Health Questionnaire[74] | 28 items covering depression, anxiety, confidence including somatic symptoms and measured on a 4 point scale |
| | Present State Examination[74] | 140 items covering psychiatric symptoms scored on a 3-point scale: given by trained non-medical interviewers may be shortened |
| | Symptom Check List-90[21] | 90 items covering 9 areas of symptoms (anxiety, depression and so on) on a 5-point scale |
| | Hospital Anxiety and Depression Scale[77] | 14 items describing non-somatic symptoms of anxiety and depression assessed on 4-point scales |
| Methods of broad scope | Sickness Impact Profile[9] | Impact of health on behaviour and function in 12 areas, e.g. social interactions, work mobility and emotional behaviour |
| | Personal Health Survey[66] | 200 items divided into 12 areas of physical and psychological functioning |
| | Index of Well-being | Scores for function levels in physical activity, mobility and social activity |

examples are given of methods that may be used for assessing either physical or psychosocial well-being and function as well as some methods which have a broad scope.

### Psychiatric aspects

Quantified measurement methods have been used in psychiatry for several decades and these have been very usefully applied in cancer medicine[29]. For instance, the incidence of depressive illness has been studied in detail in breast cancer patients[41,44] and lymphoma patients[21]. Most of these methods have been developed for use in psychiatric patients and have to be very carefully evaluated before their reliability or validity can be accepted in cancer patients. This is illustrated by considering the methods designed to detect clinical depression, which may depend upon the collection of positive scores for depressed mood as well as scores for somatic symptoms associated with depression such as weight loss or sleeplessness. Such somatic symptoms may be present in a non-depressed cancer patient.

### Physical aspects

The application of descriptive methods and simple measurement instruments has yielded valuable information about physical aspects of cancer patients' lives. This allows some comparisons between treatments, although the groups of patients studied are often not strictly comparable (i.e. not randomized groups). The symptomatic problems associated with major surgery and chemotherapy are well documented[47,53,73,76] and in this area comparisons suggest that for prostatic cancer, radiotherapy has less deleterious after-effects than radical surgery[38]; for rectal cancer, sphincter-saving surgery produces better quality of life than abdominoperineal resection[76] and for breast cancer, combination chemotherapy produces a more negative impact on quality of life than single-agent chemotherapy[53].

### Terminal care

The quality of life during terminal phases of cancer has been extensively discussed[68]. Specific measurements are less commonly made[48] methods for judging pain control being most frequent[12].

## Quality of life measurement instruments for cancer patients

A relatively small number of questionnaires have been developed specifically to measure quality of life in cancer patients. Performance status scores have been used for four decades[34]. Other early workers in the field used essentially descriptive methods. Further interest in the technical aspects of the work was stimulated by an influential paper from Priestman and Baum in 1976[54], and since then, a great deal of methodological work has been done. Although development of methods is still incomplete, the existing methods illustrate the techniques involved and represent the choices available for studies in this field.

The Medical Research Council's Working Party considered a series of questionnaires which hold promise for use in cancer patients. These have been described[42] and included:

(a) Global measures
    (i) Gough's Visual Analogue Scale[28]
    (ii) Rosser and Kind's Distress/Disability Matrix[56]
    (iii) Quality of Life Adjusted Years (QALYs)[77]

(b) Performance indices
    (i) Karnofsky *et al.*[34]
    (ii) ECOG, Eastern Co-operative Oncology Group[81]
    (iii) Katz Activities of Daily Living[36]
    (iv) World Health Organization scales[79]

(c) Scales measuring several dimensions
    (i) Iszack and Medalie Index[32]
    (ii) Priestman and Baum Linear Self-assessment System[54]
    (iii) Functional Living Index for Cancer[57]
    (iv) Ontario Cancer Institute Quality of Life Questionnaire[10,60]
    (v) Padilla QL Questionnaire[52]
    (vi) QL Index[66]
    (vii) EORTC QL Questionnaire[1]
    (viii) Rotterdam Symptom Checklist[18,19]

(d) Psychological dimension
    (i) Hospital Anxiety and Depression Scale[80]
    (ii) General Health Questionnaire[26]

The comments of that Working Party were:

(a) Global measures
    (i) Gough's Scale. Patients are required to rate a 10 cm line in terms of 'How would you rate your feeling of well-being today?' The authors would argue that it performs as well as more complex scales (The Spitzer QL index (objective and subjective versions), Baum and Priestman LASA system). This conclusion is erroneous since it is based on an over-reliance on correlation coefficients and a failure to examine areas of significant disagreement between different measures. No data are given about how well this scale measures changes over time. Nor does this global rating of well-being give information about the relative contributions of the component dimensions. It was not considered a serious contender despite its simplicity.

(ii)    Rosser and Kind's Disability/Distress Matrix. This method requires patients with physical or psychiatric illness and health care professionals to evaluate 29 combinations of disability ($0$ = no disability to $8$ = unconscious) and distress (no distress to severe distress). It involves a lengthy interview of between $1\frac{1}{2}$ and 4 hours, which is acknowledged to be 'potentially distressing and traumatic'. Scores are presented as group medians and there is no interest in the scores of individual patients since this measure seeks to determine a consensus view of the relative importance of differing states of disability and distress. While data about such views could inform decisions about priorities within health care they do not enable quality of life to be measured within clinical trials.

(iii)   Quality of Life Adjusted Years index (QALYs). This measure is designed to take account of the quality as well as the duration of survival in assessing the outcome of health care procedures and services. Unfortunately, the judgements on which it rests are drawn from small samples of respondents who were chosen arbitrarily. There is no evidence that these judgements bear much relationship to real judgements made by patients with cancer when facing decisions about the utility of different treatments set against the possible adverse effects on their lives. Thus, it is not known what the trade-offs would need to be in terms of change in quality of life before a patient or clinician elected to undergo or reject a given treatment.

While the QALY index is important conceptually and could be used to compare different treatments within a trial, work is needed to determine the judgements of real patients in real predicaments.

(b)  Indices of physical performance

(i)    Karnofsky index. The Karnofsky index is a valid if crude predictor of survival. It emphasizes physical performance and dependency. Scores are weighted heavily on the physical dimensions of quality of life. Consequently, Karnofsky scores can give a misleading picture of the social and psychological dimensions. It has limited reliability in routine clinical application[31]. While its accuracy in measuring performance can be improved by training the assessors this would still fail to measure quality of life adequately, particularly variation in psychological status (Table 14.2).

(ii)   ECOG. This provides a 5-point scale of performance in contrast to the 10-point Karnofsky scale. It is simple to use and has a

**Table 14.2** The Karnofsky performance index

| Description | Scale (%) |
|---|---|
| Normal, no complaints | 100 |
| Able to carry on normal activities; minor signs or symptoms of disease | 90 |
| Normal activity with effort | 80 |
| Cares for self. Unable to carry on normal activity or to do active work | 70 |
| Requires occasional assistance but able to care for most of his needs | 60 |
| Requires considerable assistance and frequent medical acre | 50 |
| Disabled; requires special care and assistance | 40 |
| Severely disabled; hospitalization indicated although death not imminent | 30 |
| Very sick. Hospitalization necessary. Active supportive treatment necessary | 20 |
| Moribund | 10 |
| Dead | 0 |

**Table 14.3** WHO performance status; a five-grade scale is recommended

| Grade | Performance status |
|---|---|
| 0 | Able to carry out all normal activity without restriction |
| 1 | Restricted in physically strenuous activity but ambulatory and able to carry out light work |
| 2 | Ambulatory and capable of all self-care but unable to carry out any work; up and about more than 50% of waking hours |
| 3 | Capable of only limited self-care; confined to bed or chair more than 50% of waking hours |
| 4 | Completely disabled; cannot carry on any self-care; totally confined to bed or chair |

        precise but narrow function. It is less easy to use and interpret than the comparable WHO scale.

(iii)    WHO scale. This measures physical performance on a 5-point scale. It is easy to use and interpret but has a limited function[79], Table 14.3.

(c)    Scales measuring several dimensions

    (i)    Iszack and Medalie ability index. This provides a series of simple rating scales to measure physical, social and psychological variables. These are tailored to specific cancers and treatments and are not generalizable across different cancers or different treatments. They seem of most use in helping clinicians assess rehabilitation needs and monitoring outcome in relation to specific cancers.

(ii)   Baum and Priestman LASA system. Their set of linear analogue scales originally covered ten aspects: well-being, mood, activity, pain, nausea, appetite, housework, social activity, anxiety and help from treatment. It has been used in patients with cancer of the breast and appears of most value in picking up strong treatment effects over time. They expanded the scale to 25 items and included more relating to psychological aspects. It has not been compared with other QL methods or with gold standard interviews. Consequently, its validity and reliability have still to be determined but it seems to detect change over time and to distinguish between different treatments.

(iii)  Functional living index for cancer (Figure 14.2). The FLIC includes 22 items covering physical symptoms, mood, physical activity, work and social interaction. Items are presented in a linear analogue format. Each line is divided into seven and covers 'now' or the 'past two weeks'. The items derive from a pool suggested by a panel of patients and health professionals involved in cancer care. The index consists of a number of sub-scales which are derived from factor analysis and have been replicated. It is easy to use, administer and score. It has been validated in a cross-sectional study of patients with different stages of cancer and on different treatments.

The word cancer is used in several items and has distressed patients. Validity has been tested only by comparing different groups and by correlation with other self-rating instruments. Performance in detecting changes over time has yet to be assessed. Nor has it been assessed or calibrated against 'gold standard' interviews. Consequently, scores on the component sub-scales are difficult to interpret. There are so few items on each dimension that its ability to measure significant changes over time may be poor. For example, few physical symptoms are included.

These factors prevented the working party from recommending its use in clinical trials despite the attractiveness of simplicity and ease of use.

(iv)   Ontario Cancer Institute/Royal Marsden Scale. Linear analogue self-assessment (Ontario Cancer Institute and Royal Marsden

**MANITOBA CANCER TREATMENT & RESEARCH FOUNDATION
FUNCTIONAL LIVING INDEX: CANCER (FLIC)**

Date

1  Most people experience some feelings of depression at times. Rate how
often you feel these feelings

| | | | | | |
1      2      3      4      5      6      7
Never                                    Continually

2.  How well are you coping with your everyday stress?

| | | | | | |
1      2      3      4      5      6      7
Not well                                 Very Well

3.  How much time do you spend thinking about your illness?

| | | | | | | |
1      2      3      4      5      6      7
Constantly                               Never

4.  Rate your ability to maintain your usual recreation or leisure activities

| | | | | | |
1      2      3      4      5      6      7
Able                                     Unable

5.  Has nausea affected your daily functioning?

| | | | | | |
1      2      3      4      5      6      7
Not at All                               A Great Deal

6.  How well do you feel today?

| | | | | | |
1      2      3      4      5      6      7
Extremely                                Extremely
Poor                                     Well

7.  Do you feel well enough to make a meal or do minor household repairs
today?

| | | | | | |
1      2      3      4      5      6      7
Very                                     Not
Able                                     Able

8.  Rate the degree to which your cancer has imposed a hardship on those
closest to you in the past 2 weeks

| | | | | | |
1      2      3      4      5      6      7
No                                       Tremendous
Hardship                                 Hardship

PLEASE INDICATE — YOUR RATING

**Figure 14.2** Sample of the Manitoba Cancer Treatment and Research Foundation
Functional Living Index: Cancer questionnaire

Hospital). In a study beginning in 1981, patient's self-report on simple linear analogue scales was used to collect data[61]. The intention was to design a measurement method which could be used for comparative purposes in clinical trials, in a range of disease sites, being modified for each site. For this reason, the items in the questionnaire were divided into two groups. Firstly, a group of 18 items which assessed general aspects of health (global enquiry) were derived from an established method for assessing the effect of health upon behaviour and function, the Sickness Impact Profile (SIP)[9]. These included work, homework, recreation, mobility, concentration, eating, sleep, social life, family relationships, self-care, physical activity, anxiety, depression, anger, speech and writing. The second group of 13 items was disease-specific, and in the initial studies were developed for breast cancer, comprising pain, breathing, sore mouth, nausea, vomiting, hair loss, attractiveness, appearance, burning on passing urine, constipation, diarrhoea, fatigue, and satisfaction with information received. The disease-related items were produced by a panel of physicians and nurses and from an open questionnaire to patients attending a Medical Breast Cancer Clinic. This approach was also used in subsequent studies of lung cancer and ovarian cancer patients.

The reliability of this measurement method was assessed by test–retest comparisons and by Cronbach's alpha statistic[17]. Correlation coefficients for test and retest were generally $> 0.7$, an acceptable level for a research instrument. Comparisons to the SIP Karnofsky indices and to a physician's scoring on linear analogue scales were used to assess concurrent validity. Correlations were generally high. A factor analysis showed apparent relationships between items which would be expected in this disease (Table 14.4). The measurement was shown to discriminate between clinically distinct groups of patients with breast cancer (hormone treatment versus cytotoxic treatment; localized versus advanced disease), to detect changes occurring during treatment, and to discriminate between patients receiving differing doses of drugs. Although preliminary attempts at the deduction of weights for the different items within the questionnaire were made in these studies, the issues of weighting, normal ranges and calibration have not been resolved. As with the FLIC scale, this approach to the measurement of quality of life in cancer patients must be considered to be still under development[10].

(v)    Padilla QL scale. This is a short 14 item scale containing three sub-scales. It covers the 'present time' and takes less than 5

**Table 14.4** Correlations between items: factor analysis

| Factor 1 | | Factor 2 | | Factor 3 | | Factor 4 | | Factor 5 | |
|---|---|---|---|---|---|---|---|---|---|
| Housework | (0.89) | Pain | (0.60) | Depression | (0.80) | Nausea | (0.86) | Attractiveness | (0.64) |
| Recreation | (0.85) | Physical activity | (0.57) | Anger | (0.77) | Vomiting | (0.85) | Family relations | (0.63) |
| Social life | (0.71) | Bowel habit | (0.54) | Anxiety | (0.68) | Eating | (0.38) | Hair loss | (0.35) |
| Mobility | (0.49) | Breathing | (0.42) | Appearance | (0.40) | | | | |
| Fatigue | (0.46) | | | Concentration | (0.40) | | | | |
| Writing | (0.44) | | | Family relations | (0.38) | | | | |
| Physical activity | (0.42) | | | | | | | | |
| Concentration | (0.40) | | | | | | | | |

Figure in parentheses are rotated factor loading. All loadings > 0.3 are shown. (Reproduced from Ref. 60 with permission).

minutes to administer. It is easy to score. Unfortunately, data on reliability and validity are lacking and there are too few items to reflect changes on key dimensions. It appears inferior to the FLIC and OCI Scales.

Linear analogue scales in general can be used to map out differences between different illnesses but are most valid in monitoring the impact of treatment regimes over time. They can tap all dimensions, are simple to administer and score. However the time periods covered are often unstated or vague. It is difficult to interpret the clinical significance of the scores. Parametric methods of statistical analyses are suspect. There is no evidence that they are superior to categorical rating methods.

(vi)  Spitzer QL index. This index measures five areas including physical activity, daily living, perception of own health, support from family and friends and outlook on life. The scores are summed to produce an overall score of quality of life. It has the attraction of being simple, easy and quicker to administer. It is available in clinician- and patient-rated versions. It was carefully developed by reference to patients with cancer, patients suffering from other chronic diseases, their relatives, people who were free of disease, doctors, nurses and social workers. Unfortunately, the reduction to five aspects of quality of life reflects an over-reliance on correlations between the different items that go up to make each dimension. Consequently it does not do justice to the different aspects of quality of life. Nor is there evidence that this index has yet been used successfully within clinical trials to reflect change over time. Recent studies have found a poor correlation between the clinician and patient rated versions. They have suggested that the overall score is unduly affected by clinicians' judgements about the extent of the cancer and associated physical disability.

(vii)  EORTC questionnaire. This questionnaire was designed for heterogeneous groups of cancer patients. It seeks to measure key dimensions, including symptoms of disease, side-effects of treatment, physical functioning, psychological distress, social interaction, sexuality, body image and satisfaction with medical care. It is a self-administered scale and the format varies according to the dimensions being addressed. Items on physical activity comprise 'yes or no' responses whereas questions on symptoms use a categorical form asking for answers ranging from 'not at all' to 'very much'. The checklist of symptoms assessed varies according to the type of cancer being studied. It is designed for administration by a nurse within clinics and takes up to 10 minutes to complete. It is easy to score and produces both an overall score and scores on each sub-scale. Unfortunately norms do not yet exist but work is under way to establish norms and check reliability and validity.

While the scale was carefully developed on the basis of existing measures, its reliability and validity have yet to be properly assessed. It has to be checked against 'gold standard' interviews to see how well it performs. The sub-scales and factor structure have yet to be replicated. Thus, although it is promising it is still being developed and is probably not ready for inclusion in large scale clinical trials. Initial feedback suggests that the acceptance rate is variable (ranging between 33 and 90%) but it appears to reflect changes over time as well as differences between different diseases and treatments. A major validation study is under way to address the questions of how well it performs within major clinical trials.

(viii) The Rotterdam Symptom Checklist. This was carefully derived from a pool of items based on existing questionnaires, together with checklists from interviews with cancer patients.

It compromises 38 items and each item is rated on a four-point scale (0 = not at all, 3 = very much). It is well laid out and asks respondents to indicate how much they have experienced particular symptoms over the last week. It is readily administered by nurses and takes 5–10 minutes to complete. All items appear understandable and acceptable. It is easy to score and produces distinct sub-scale scores.

It provides two main sub-scales measuring physical and psychological dimensions. It is considered to be a good, clear and simple questionnaire which has been validated against independent interviews and found to have high sensitivity and specificity in measuring the psychological dimensions. It has been used successfully within busy clinics and seems as effective in advanced cancer patients with early disease. It seems to measure physical and social dimensions equally well but this requires confirmation.

(d) Psychological dimension
(i) Hospital Anxiety and Depression Scale. This 14-item scale has the advantage that it was developed for patients with physical disease and excluded items like tiredness that could be both due to mood disturbance and physical illness. Of the 14 items seven are concerned with anxiety and seven with depression. It is completed by patients and is easy and quick to administer. It has

proved capable of measuring change over time within different groups of cancer patients. Recent studies have suggested that a cut-off point of 10/11 distinguishes between patients who are coping well with their cancer and those who have developed morbid anxiety or depression.

It therefore seems a useful tool for measuring the psychological dimensions of quality of life cancer patients.

(ii)    General Health Questionnaire. This 28-item version includes four sub-scales which measure anxiety, depression, social functioning and physical symptoms. Preliminary evidence suggests that it works less well with cancer patients than those who are free of illness in detecting change over time and determining probable cases of anxiety. It has lower sensitivity and specificity than the more easily administered hospital anxiety and depression scale and Rotterdam Symptom Checklist.

## Conclusions of MRC Working Party

(1)    The current 'best-bet' for tapping key dimensions of quality of life is the Rotterdam Symptom Checklist. Work is ongoing to check further its performance in patients with different stages of cancer and on different treatments.

(2)    When additional items are needed to assess illness or treatment related variables which are not covered by the RSCL these can be added in categorical form.

(3)    The hospital anxiety and depression scale appears particularly useful in assessing levels of anxiety and depression in cancer patients.

(4)    Linear analogue systems (see Refs 54 and 60) are useful in highlighting major differences between treatment regimes in respect of adverse effects and disease response but clinical interpretation of scores is difficult.

(5)    A multi-dimensional scale which is specific to patients with cancer, meets all the assessment criteria and provides scores which have relevance to clinical judgement remains to be developed. This could be done in three phases:

(i)    In-depth interviews with a representative sample of cancer patients to determine which aspects of quality of life most concern them and change for the better or worse over time.

(ii)    The construction of a categorical self-rating questionnaire which measures the most salient aspects of quality of life in a way which reflects both clinically relevant changes and changes which concern the patient.

(iii) Validation of this questionnaire cross-sectionally and over time against independent in-depth assessments by trained interviewers.


## TWIST ANALYSIS

Different treatments may have different impacts upon quality of life from their impacts upon survival; a marginal survival benefit may result from a very toxic treatment. It is tempting to consider amalgamation of the endpoints to allow a single comparative analysis. Such a combined morbidity–mortality health index would be useful to measure the overall health of a population and to compare programmes. The mathematical basis upon which such integration could be done has been investigated[70,71]. However, the approach has many limitations. It requires a single number description of quality of life which, as we have discussed above, is conceptually and technically elusive. Even if such a number were available, the weight that should be given to quality of life when compared to quantity is a value judgement, which is difficult to deduce for populations and then it is doubtful if it is relevant to an individual. Gelber *et al.*[24] have introduced the concept of TWiST (Time Without Symptoms and Toxicity) into the area of amalgamation of quality and quantity of life. They subtracted time with any disease, or treatment-related morbidity, from the overall survival time, and the resulting TWiST times can be used to compare groups of patients on different treatment. Although interesting and attractive, this does not solve all the measurement problems. No different weights are given to different degrees of morbidity from disease or treatment and the patients' evaluation of their time-quality is not considered.


## FACTORS DETERMINING QL

A number of workers have sought to define the principal factors which determine the quality of life of cancer patients by the technique of factor analysis[27]. The items included in our questionnaire in Toronto and the Royal Marsden Hospital are listed in Table 14.4. Factor analysis was used to deduce common factors to which individual items were correlated and the results of this analysis are shown in the factor structure (Table 14.4) for the data from Canada. It can be seen that factors identified are activities of everyday living, emotional well-being and gastrointestinal or alimentary well-being are clearly defined and these were confirmed in a subsequent study[10]. Factors relating to appearance/attractiveness and to separate symptoms and a number of items are less well defined in these analyses. The extensive work required to explore such an analysis fully is beyond the scope of this paper and has been submitted for publication[10]. Our results are broadly in agreement with studies carried out using the Rotterdam Symptom Checklist[19]. In that questionnaire it was apparent that psychological distress and physical distress were separate factors together with alimentary problems in two of their three factor analyses. In the third study alimentary problems were difficult to analyse because of a skewed distribution of answers. Schipper et al.[58] identified physical well-being, emotional well-being and nausea as distinct factors as we have and in keeping with the Rotterdam Symptom Checklist. In addition, Schipper's Questionnaire, the Functional Living Index with Cancer Scale, tapped aspects of family hardship and disruption which emerged as a separate factor and had not been adequately identified in other questionnaires including our own.

We do not believe that further factor analyses are likely to greatly define or refine our knowledge of the things that determine quality of life in cancer patients. There will be differences between patient populations. Studies of this area have to be carried out in large patient numbers if the factor analysis is to achieve any sort of stability. There will always be particular items that are separate and are of importance to small numbers of patients within any group. These are unlikely to emerge in an overall statistical analysis but cannot be ignored in detailed consideration of quality of life in the individual patient's case.


## POSSIBLE APPROACHES TO MEASURING QL

The approach to measuring quality of life in a particular study or practice must depend on the purposes of that measurement and the resources available:


### Multiple generic questionnaires

There now exist a substantial number of questionnaires which are capable of assessing general aspects of dysfunction of behavioural changes in relation to disease (e.g. Sickness Impact Profile or the Nottingham Health Profile) or else detailed questionnaires which will quantify psychiatric morbidity (e.g. The Present State Examination). These can and should be used in cancer patients in detailed studies of disability, distress and emotional disorder. They can have no place in the routine performance of cancer medicine or a large scale cancer clinical trials because of their length and complexity.

## Cancer-specific questionnaires

The MRC Working Party considered a range of cancer specific questionnaires and concluded that the Rotterdam Symptom Checklist was probably the present 'best buy'. Since that time further work on the validation of the EORTC questionnaire has been completed which has the advantage of offering a range of options related to the specific cancer site and further work on the validation of the new analogue scale systems has been completed and in some cases reported. These systems are valuable in a research setting when the particular focus of the research is quality of life measurement. However, although they are perceived as being quite brief by workers in the quality of life field they are perceived as being lengthy and onerous by many cancer physicians and surgeons and many cancer patients. Compliance is often poor and there is an unwillingness on the part of busy cancer doctors to incorporate them routinely into clinical practice. This is a substantial restriction and it may be appropriate to consider a trade off between the carefully evaluated questionnaires developed by the research groups and even briefer approaches which can be used in routine practice.

## Reductionism and pragmatism

If the measurement of quality of life in cancer patients is to come of age and be integrated into routine practice in clinical research and clinical service, we will need instruments with a very small number of individual questions, perhaps between two and ten. This number of questions might be integrated into the evaluation of the cancer patient in all situations. The junior doctor in out-patients or when 'clerking' a patient into the ward or, the nurse on the ward could reasonably be expected, or even required, to accumulate information about a small number of facets of a patients life that might be reasonably uniform and valuable as endpoints in clinical trials or in the evaluation of the quality of a service.

The ultimate exercise in reductionism would be to the single question. However, there are a number of reasons for proposing that a single question about quality of life would be inadequate. Factor analysis demonstrates the independence of at least two major factors, activities of every day living and emotional well-being[10]. A single question about quality of life cannot encompass both of these or describe either adequately.

It is not yet clear what the gains or the losses of a reduced and pragmatic approach to evaluating quality of life might be. Obvious gains in terms of brevity, patient and health care worker compliance and ease of data handling are apparent. How much information is lost when only a small number of questions are used?

We have addressed this question in a study in which quality of life was assessed by using linear analogue scales to ask questions about each of the factors derived from our quality of life study in Toronto. In addition, patients completed an overall score for quality of life called the Uniscale. As a further part of this study they completed the whole questionnaire with 28 items. We have used multiple regression analysis to assess the relationship between the five individual items and the overall quality of life score in the Uniscale. This is clearly a highly stylised system which can allow questions to be asked about the contribution to quality of life scores from each of the five main factors in cancer patient populations.

The analysis was performed using data for 296 patients and the final model selected had an adjusted coefficient of regression of 0.704, that is to say, the final model apparently explained 70.4% of the variation in the Uniscale measurements. In a range of alternative analyses and models the questions based on the five factors are capable of explaining 58–70% of the variation in the overall QL score. The importance of Activities of Everyday Living and Emotional Well-being was clearly demonstrated.

These studies in this system suggest that a small number of questions carefully directed at the factors which determine quality of life in cancer patients can explain between 50 and 70% of the variation in quality of life. This proportion was not greatly improved when multiple regression was carried out using the 28 items in the original questionnaire. This suggests that a small number of questions is capable of explaining a great deal of the variance in quality of life and that the larger number of questions, although perhaps important in a descriptive way, do not contribute a great deal more information. There will be a proportion of the variation in the quality of peoples lives which will never be tapped by questionnaires of this kind because it will relate very much to that patients individual interests and priorities.

Questions tapping the major factors that determine quality of life in cancer patients which appear to be the Activities of Everyday Living, Emotional Well-being and perhaps Appearance/Attractiveness are sufficient for some purposes. In individual studies or individual clinical practices it may well be important to add items that describe individual areas of great of importance. For instance, in an assessment of an oesophageal cancer it will be appropriate to ask a question about difficulty in swallowing regardless about what other information may be collected. If appropriate descriptive items are included and a question about emotional well-being and a question about activities of everyday living is asked and recorded in a simple quantitative way for most practical purposes no other effort to measure quality of life may be required in routine clinical work. They may be extended for specific purposes by a range of existing questionnaires.

It must be emphasized that this is a rather personal view of the subject. After extensive research in this area it may be that the measurement of quality of life has been explored in cancer patients and defined with sufficient precision to allow us to choose carefully and pragmatically the sort of information that must be collected in the management of the cancer patient. If this is kept to a minimum it may be possible to integrate it into clinical practice and clinical trials routinely, even if a small amount of information is lost.

## CONCLUSIONS

In this review, both the structure of measurement methods and the available methods have been considered. It can be concluded that no single measurement method for quality of life in cancer patients has yet been developed satisfactorily. It is also doubted whether any single method will be suitable for all purposes. The appropriate approach to this question is to choose measurement methods for specific purposes. The length of the questionnaire and the number of questionnaires that may be used will depend upon the clinical context and brief questionnaires may be satisfactory for some purposes. There remains a need for developmental work on measurement methods to increase and improve the range available to investigators. This field now has to move forward into widespread application in clinical trials and practice. In these, the value of the different methods will become apparent. Quality of life is an important endpoint in most cancer care and should not be restricted to studies of psychosocial aspects of patient care.

## ACKNOWLEDGEMENTS

In this paper I have quoted extensively from the conclusions of the Medical Research Council's Working Party of Quality of Life Measurement in Cancer Patients and I am grateful to my co-author of that report (Dr Peter Maguire) and to the Chairman of the Cancer Therapy Committee of MRC for their permission to do so. I am also grateful to the editors and publishers of the *British Journal of Cancer* for their permission to quote extensively from that paper (Maguire and Selby, Assessing quality of life in cancer patients, *British Journal of Cancer* 1989;60:437–440. The section on Special Difficulties Measuring Quality of Life in Cancer Patients draws heavily on my paper by that title in press with the Royal College of Physicians and I am grateful to Dr Anthony Hopkins for his permission to do so.

## References

1. Aaronson, N.K. Methodological issues in psychosocial oncology with special reference to clinical trials. In Ventafridda, V,. Van Dam, F.S.A.M., Yancik, R. *et al.* (eds) *Assessment of Quality of Life and Cancer Treatment*. Amsterdam, Elsevier Science Publishers, 1986, pp. 19–29.
2. Aaronson, N.K., Bakker, W., Stewart, A.L. *et al.* A multidimensional approach to the quality of life in lung cancer clinical trials. In Aaronson, N.K. (ed.) *Quality of Life in Cancer*, EORTC Monograph Series. New York, Raven Press, 1986, pp. 171–192.
3. Ahmed, P.I. and Kolker, A. The role of indigenous medicine in WHO's definition of health. In Adhmed, P.I. and Coelho, C.O. (eds) *Towards a New Definition of Health*. New York, Plenum Press, 1979, p. 113.
4. Bardelli, D. and Saracci, R. Measuring the quality of life in cancer clinical trials. Methods and impact of controlled therapeutic trials in cancer. *IUCC Technical Report Series*, 1978, No 36, pp. 75–97.
5. Barofsky, I. Function states: quality of life. In Holland, J.C.B. (ed.) Proceedings of Conference on Research Methodology in Psychosocial Oncology. *Cancer* 1984; 53 (Suppl): 2299–2302.
6. Baum, M., Priestman, T., West, R.R. *et al.* A comparison of subjective responses in a trial comparing endocrine with cytotoxic treatment in advanced carcinoma of the breast. In Mourisden and Palshof (eds) *Breast Cancer – Experimental and Clinical Methods*. London, Pergamon Press, 1980, pp. 223–228.
7. Bell, D.R., Tannock, I.F. and Boyd, N.F. Quality of life measurement in breast cancer patients. *Br. J. Cancer* 1985; 51: 577–580.
8. Bergner, M., Babbitt, R.A., Carter, W.B. *et al.* The Sickness Impact Profile: development and final revision of a health status measure. *Med. Care* 1981; 19: 787–805.
9. Bergner, M. Development testing and use of the Sickness Impact Profile. In Walker, S.R. and Rosser, R.M. (eds) *Quality of Life: Assessment and Application*. MTP Press, Lancaster, 1988, p. 79.
10. Bliss, J.M., Selby, P, Robertson, B. and Powles, T.J. A method for assessing the quality of life of cancer patients: replication of the factor structure. *Br. J. Cancer*, 1992. In press
11. Blohnik, 1980, quoted by Fox, B.H., 1984 (See Ref. 25).
12. Bond, A. and Lader, M. The use of analogue scales ID rating subjective feelings. *Br. J. Med. Psychol.* 1974; 47: 211–218.
13. Calman, K.C. Quality of life in cancer patients – a hypothesis. *J. Med. Ethics* 1984; 10: 124–127.
14. Campbell, A., Converse, P.E. and Rodgers, W.L. *The Quality of American Life*. New York, Sage, 1976, p. 4.
15. Clark, A. and Fallowfield, L.J. Quality of life measurements in patients with malignant disease: a review. *J. R. Soc. Med.* 1986; 79: 165–169.
17. Cronbach, L.J. Coefficient alpha and the internal structure of tests. *Psychometrika* 1951; 16: 297–334.
18. de Haes, J.C.J.M. and van Knippenberg, F.C.E. The quality of life of cancer patients: a review of the literature. *Social Sci. Med.* 1985; 20: 809–817.

19. de Haes, J.C.J.M., van Knippenberg, F.C.E. and Neijt, J.P. Measuring psychological and physical distress in cancer patients: structure and application of the Rotterdam Symptom Checklist. *Br. J. Cancer* 1990; 62: 1034–1038.

20. Derogatis, L.R., Akeloff, M.D. and Melisaratos, N. Psychological coping mechanisms and survival time in breast cancer. *J. Am. Med. Assoc.* 1979; 242: 1504–1509.

21. Devlen, J.L. The psychological and social consequences of Hodgkin's disease and its treatment. In Selby, P. and McElwain T.J. (eds) *Hodgkin's Disease.* Oxford, Blackwell Scientific Publications, 1986.

23. Fayers, P.M. and Jones, D.R. Measuring and analysing quality of life in cancer clinical trials. *Sial Med.* 1983; 2: 429–446.

24. Gelbert, R.D. and Goldhirsh, A. A new endpoint for the assessment of adjuvant therapy in postmenopausal women with operable breast cancer. *J. Clin. Oncol.* 1986; 4: 1772–1779.

25. Goldberg, D.P. *Detection of Psychiatric Illness by Questionnaire.* Oxford, Oxford University Press, 1972.

26. Goldberg, D. and Hillier V.F. A scaled version of the General Health Questionnaire. *Psychol. Med.* 1979; 31: 139.

27. Gorsuch, R. L. *Factor Analysis.* Philadelphia, Saunders, 1974.

28. Gough, I.R., Furnival, C.M., Schilder, L. and Grove, N. Assessment of the quality of life of patients with advanced cancer. *Eur J. Cancer Clin. Oncol.* 1983; 19: 1161.

29. Greer, S. Cancer: psychiatric aspects. In Granville-Grossmark, K. (ed). *Recent Advances in Clinical Psychiatry.* Volume 5. London, Churchill Livingstone, 1985, pp. 87–104.

30. Holland, J.C.B. (ed). Proceedings of Conference on Research Methodology in Psychosocial Oncology. *Cancer* 1984; 53; (Suppl): 2217–2384.

31. Hutchinson, T.A., Boyd, N.F. and Feinstein, A.R. Scientific problems in clinical scales as demonstrated in the Karnofsky index of performance status. *J. Chronic Dis.* 1979; 32: 661–666.

32. Iszack, F. and Medalie, J.H. Comprehensive follow up of carcinoma patients. *J. Chronic Dis.* 1971; 24: 179.

33. Kaplan, R.M., Bush, J.W. and Berry, C.C. Health status: types of validity for an index of well-being. *Health Serv. Res.* 1976; 11: 478–507.

34. Karnofsky, D.A., Abelmann, W.H., Craver, L.F. and Burchenal, J.H. The use of nitrogen mustards in the palliative treatment of carcinoma. *Cancer* 1948; 1: 634.

35. Karnofsky, D.A. and Burchenal, J.H. The clinical evaluation of chemotherapeutic agents against cancer. In McLeod, C.M. (ed.) *Evaluation of Chemotherapeutic Agents.* New York, Columbia University Press, 1949.

36. Katz, S. and Akpom, C.A. A measure of primary sociobiological functions. *Int. J. Health Serv.* 1976; 6: 493–499.

37. Katz, S., Ford, A.B., Moskowitz R. W *et al.* Studies of illness in the aged. *J. Am. Med. Assoc.* 1963; 185: 914–919.

38. Leibel, S.A., Pino, Y., Torres, J.L. *et al.* Improved quality of life following radical therapy for early stage carcinoma of the prostate. *Urol. Clinic N. Am.* 1980; 7: 593–604.

39. Mahoney, F.I. and Barthel, D.W. Functional evaluation: the Barthel Index. *Md State Med. J.* 1965; 14: 61–65.

40. Maguire, G.P., Tait, A., Brook, M. *et al.* Psychiatric morbidity and physical toxicity associated with adjuvant chemotherapy after mastectomy. *Br. Med. J.* 1980; 281: 1179–1180.

41. Maguire, G.P. *et al.* Psychiatric problems in the first year after mastectomy. *Br. Med. J.* 1978; 1: 963–965.

42. Maguire, P. and Selby, P. Assessing the quality of life in cancer patients. *Br. J. Cancer* 1989; 60: 437.

43. Matell, M.S. and Jacoby, J. Is there an optional number of alternatives for Likert scale items? *Educ. Psychol. Meas.* 1971; 31: 657–674.

44. McArdle, C.S., Calman, K.C., Cooper, A.F. *et al.* The social, emotional and financial implications of adjuvant chemotherapy in breast cancer. *Br. J. Surg.* 1981; 68: 261–266.

45. McDowell, I. and Newell, C. *Measuring Health. A Guide to Rating Scales and Questionnaires.* Oxford, Oxford University Press 1987, p. 204.

46. Medical Research Council, quoted by Fayers, P.M. and Jones D.R. 1983 (see. Ref 24).

47. Meyerowitz, B.E., Watkins, I.K. and Sparks, F.C. Quality of life of breast cancer patients receiving adjuvant chemotherapy. *Am. J. Nurs.* 1983; 2: 232–235.

48. Morris, J.N., Suisson, S., Sherwood, S. *et al.* Last days: a study of the quality of life of terminally ill cancer patients. *J. Chronic Dis.* 1986; 39: 47–62.

49. Morrow, G.R., Chiarello, R.J. and Derogatis, L.R. A new scale for assessing patients' psychological adjustment to medical illness. *Psychol. Med.* 1978; 8: 605–610.

50. Nunnally, J.C. *Psychometric Theory.* 2nd edn. New York, McGraw–Hill, 1978.

51. Oborne, D.J. and Clarke, M.J. Questionnaire surveys of passenger comfort. *Appl. Ergonom.* 1975; 6: 97–103.

52. Padilla, G., Presant, C.A., Grant, M. *et al.* Assessment of quality of life in cancer patients. *Proc. Am. Assoc. Cancer Res.* 1981; 22: 397.

53. Palmer, B.V., Walsh, G.A., McKinnae, J.A. *et al.* Adjuvant chemotherapy for breast cancer, side effects and quality of life. *Br. Med. J.* 1980; 281: 1594–1597.

54. Priestman, T.J. and Baum, M. Evaluation of quality of life in patients receiving treatment for advanced breast cancer. *Lancet* 1976; 1: 899–901.

55. Remington, M., Tyrer, P.J., Newsom-Smith, J. *et al.* Comparative reliability of categorical and analogue rating scales in the assessment of psychiatric symptomatology. *Psychol. Med.* 1979; 9: 765–770.

56. Rosser R.M. and Kind, P. A scale of valuations of states of illness; is there a social consensus? *Int. J. Epidemiol.* 1978; 7: 347.

57. Schipper, H., Clinch, J., McMurray, A. *et al.* Measuring the quality of life of cancer patients. The functional living index – cancer: development and validation. *J. Clin. Oncol.* 1984; 2: 472–483.

58. Schipper, H. and Levitt, M. Quality of life in cancer trials: What is it? Why measure it? In Ventrafridda, V., van Dam, F.S.A.M., Yancik, R. *et al.*. (eds) *Assessment of Quality of Life and Cancer Treatment.* Amsterdam, Elsevier Science Publishers, 1986, pp. 19–29.

59. Scott, J. and Huskinsson, E.C. Graphic representation of pain. *Pain* 1976; 2: 175–184.
60. Selby, P.J., Chapman, J.A., Etazadi Amoli, J. *et al.* The development of a method for assessing the quality of life of cancer patients. *Br. J. Cancer* 1984; 50: 13.
61. Selby, P.J. Measurement of the quality of life after cancer treatment. *Br. J. Hosp. Med.* 1985; 33: 267–271.
62. Selby, P. and Robertson, B. Measurement of quality of life in patients with cancer. *Cancer Surveys* 1987; 6: 521.
63. Selby, P. Measurement of the quality of life – the particular problems of cancer patients. Proceedings of a Royal College of Physicians meeting, 1991.
64. Slevin, M., Stubbs, L., Plant, H. *et al.* Attitudes to chemotherapy: comparing views of patients with cancer with those of doctors, nurses and general public. *Br. Med. J.* 1990; 300: 1458–60.
65. Sontag, S. *Illness as a Metaphor.* Penguin Books, 1988, London.
66. Spitzer, W.O., Dobson, A.J., Hall, J. *et al.* Measuring the quality of life of cancer patients. *J. Chronic Dis.* 1981; 34: 595–597.
67. Stewart, A.L., Ware, J.E. and Brook, R.H. Advances in the measurement of functional status: construction of aggregate indices. *Med. Care* 198 1; 19: 473–488.
68. Stoll, B. *Coping with Cancer Stress.* Dordrecht, Martinus Nijhoff, 1986.
69. Thorne, F.C. The personal health survey. *J. Clin. Psycho.* 1978; 34: 262–268.
70. Torrance, G.W. Health status index models: identified view. *Management Sci.* 1976; 22: 990–1001.
71. Torrance, G.W. Towards a utility theory foundation for health status index models. *Health Serv. Res.* 1976; 11: 349–369.
72. Ventafridda, V., van Dam, F.S.A.M., Yancik R. *et al.* (eds) *Assessment of Quality of Life and Cancer Treatment.* Amsterdam, Elsevier Science Publishers, 1986.
73. Vera, M.I. Quality of life following pelvic exenteration. *Gynaecol. Oncol.* 1981; 12: 355–366.
74. Walker, S.R. and Rosser, R.M. (eds) *Quality of Life Assessment and Application.* MTP Press, Lancaster, 1988.
75. Warde, P., Sturgeon, J.F., Fine, S. *et al.* Quality of life assessment in patients with carcinoma of the ovary. *Proceedings ASCO* 1984; 3: 68.
76. Williams, N.S. and Johnston, D. The quality of life after rectal excision for low rectal cancer. *Br. J. Surg.* 1983; 70: 460–462.
77. Williams AH. Economics of coronary artery by-pass grafts. *Br. Med. J.* 1985; 291: 326.
78. Wing, J.K., Nixon, J., Mann, A. *et al.* Reliability of the PSE used in a population study. *Psychol. Med.* 1977; 7: 505–516.
79. World Health Organization. *WHO Handbook for Reporting Results of Cancer Treatment.* Geneva, WHO, Geneva Offset Publication No. 48, 1979.
80. Zigmond, A. and Snaith, P. The Hospital Anxiety and Depression Questionnaire. *Acta Scand. Psychiat.* 1983; 67: 361–368.
81. Zubrod C.G., Schneiderman, M., Frei, E. *et al.* Appraisal for methods for the study of chemotherapy in man. *J. Chronic Dis.* 1960; 11: 7.

# 15 Measuring the quality of life of patients with rheumatoid arthritis

### Richard A. Deyo

Rheumatoid arthritis is a prototypical chronic disease, as its impacts are largely functional and rarely fatal. Because cure or death are rare outcomes, rheumatologists have entirely sought alternative measures of therapeutic response, and have recently devised several arthritis-specific measures of health status. The purpose of this chapter is to review the pressures for improving health status assessment in arthritis, to examine whether newer instruments offer an advantage over older ones, and to review the performance of several recently devised scales. Finally, the particular problem of measuring changes over time, as in the typical design of a therapeutic trial, will be considered.

There is a tendency for clinicians to equate quality of life with health status, although the latter may not consider important aspects of quality of life such as self-esteem, personal control, and supportive relationships. None the less, this review will adhere to convention, and consider primary instruments which are labelled health status or functional status measures.

## WHY MEASURE QUALITY OF LIFE IN ARTHRITIS?

Hard measures are clearly preferred over soft data in studying therapeutic efficacy. Thus, there has been a traditional preference for laboratory data or at least observable physical findings in assessing patient outcome. In contrast, patient self-reports of symptoms or behaviour have been regarded as subjective, unreliable, and soft. Most trials have therefore emphasized the outcomes noted at the top of Table 15.1, and given less attention to those measuring disability or dysfunction.

However, the distinctions between hard and soft data easily blur. For example, interobserver reliability in rating joint tenderness, grip strength,

**Table 15.1** Potential outcomes to be assessed in therapeutic trials for rheumatoid arthritis – examples of each of the 8 D's

| Disease activity | Disability and Dysfunction |
|---|---|
| painful/tender/swollen joints | physical function |
| grip strength | self care |
| sedimentation rate (ESR) | mobility |
| morning stiffness | physical ability |
| walking time | social function |
| radiographic erosions | work |
| isotope uptake | household |
| Distress | emotional function |
| pain | Disharmony (family function) |
| Death (infrequent) | Dissatisfaction |
| Disadvantages/drug effects | |

Reproduced with permission from Tugwell, P. and Bombardier, C. *J. Rheumatol.* 1982; 9: 758–762.

and joint circumference can be surprisingly poor[5]. In other settings, agreement between examiners is often much better for items of patient history than for physical examination findings[44]. While hardness is often equated with objectivity (physician judgement versus patient observation), preservability (an X-ray or histological specimen), or dimensionality (quantitative laboratory data), Feinstein argues that the crucial attribute of hardness is reliability or reproducibility[14]. By this standard, the newer questionnaire techniques for assessing health status may be at least as hard as more traditional measures.

Besides pitfalls in measurement, many traditional outcomes (especially those derived from the laboratory) have no inherent value to either patients or society[15]. Table 15.2 illustrates the judgement of one author[15] about the relevance and reliability of several outcome measures which are used in clinical trials. Patients wish to be free of pain and to perform their accustomed activities. The erythrocyte sedimentation rate (ESR), titre of rheumatoid factor, or activity on a joint can have no intrinsic importance either to patients or society. The joint count, grip strength, or walking time come closer to the patient's concerns, but still may reflect little about his symptoms, functional ability, or psychological adjustment; the former are useful primarily to the degree that they correlate with the latter. The newer health status measures, however, seek to quantify symptoms, function and psychological status directly, rather than to infer them. To the extent that they are successful, they better reflect patient and societal concerns.

If there were a precise correlation between laboratory measures or physical findings and patient function, it would be unnecessary to measure the latter. Unfortunately, however, dissociations between various outcome measures are common and well described. Some rheumatoid patients, for example,

**Table 15.2** Relevance and reliability of various outcome measures for arthritis trials[*]

| Type | Measures | Estimated patient relevance | Estimated variability (same laboratory or observer) |
|------|----------|:---:|:---:|
| Laboratory | Sedimentation rate (ESR) | 0 | 20% |
| | Latex fixation titre | 0 | 2 tubes |
| | Haemoglobin | + | 5% |
| Surrogate measures of outcome | Grip strength | + | 20% |
| | Walking time | + | 20% |
| | Patient global assessment | + + | 1 grade |
| True outcome measures | Disability | + + + + | 7% |
| | Physical discomfort | + + + + | 15% |
| | Financial impact | + + + + | 10% |

[*] Adapted from Ref. 15.

develop fixed serological abnormalities (e.g. elevated ESR) which persist even when joint inflammation subsides. McCarty has described the discrepancies that occurred between ESR (little change) and onset on new radiographic bone erosions (sharply reduced) in a trial of cyclophosphamide for rheumatoid arthritis[31]. Table 15.3 illustrates the dissociation between laboratory and clinical outcomes in a trial of plasmapheresis for rheumatoid arthritis. While several laboratory measures were significantly improved after apheresis, patient performance and symptoms changed little. Furthermore, the functional and symptomatic changes that did occur were no greater than those following sham apheresis. Thus, if we are concerned about symptoms and function, we must measure them directly, and not assume that proxy measurements are sufficient.

## WHAT'S WRONG WITH OLDER FUNCTIONAL SCALES?

Functional status assessment is not new, although it is becoming more sophisticated. It is reasonable, then, to ask if the new generation of functional and health status measures truly offer any advantage over scales which were devised in the 1940s and 1950s for assessing arthritis-related dysfunction, and also if the lengthy, newer scales offer any advantage over a single item asking patients to rate their function.

One of the earliest functional scales for arthritis was that devised by the American Rheumatism Association (ARA)[41]. This scale simply identified four functional classes:

(I)  Complete functional capacity with ability to carry on all usual duties without handicaps

**Table 15.3** Laboratory versus clinical outcomes in a trial of plasmapheresis (true therapy versus sham therapy) for rheumatoid arthritis

| Laboratory measures | | Clinical measures | |
|---|---|---|---|
| Test | Significance of advantage for true plasmapheresis | Test | Significance of advantage for true plasmapheresis |
| ESR* | $p = 0.001$ | Subjective improvement | NS** |
| IgM | $p = 0.045$ | Number of active joints | NS |
| Complement ($C_3$) | $p = 0.005$ | Grip strength | NS |
| Rheumatoid factor | $p = 0.01$ | Walking time | NS |

\* ESR = erythrocyte sedimentation rate
\** NS = not significant

(II) Functional capacity adequate to conduct normal activities despite handicap of discomfort or limited mobility of one or more joints

(III) Functional capacity adequate to perform only little or none of the duties of usual occupation or self-care

(IV) Largely or wholly indicated, with patient bedridden or confined to wheelchair, permitting little or no self-care.

One drawback of this scale is that it clarifies patients into only four categories, thus registering only gross changes in function. In many clinical settings over half the patients with rheumatoid arthritis are in functional class II[34,43], so that the scale does not provide a smooth distribution of scores. Furthermore, the scale is ambiguous, not defining such terms as normal activities or usual duties.

We have examined the construct validity of the ARA scale by testing its correlation with other measures of disease severity in rheumatoid arthritis, and comparing it with other functional scales (Table 15.4)[12]. We expected only moderate correlations since none on the biological measures is truly an indicator of function. None the less, we may presume that a functional scale showing better correlations is more valid than one showing weaker correlations. Table 15.4 shows that the ARA scale had weaker associations with several validating measures than a newer (and longer) functional scale, the Sickness Impact Profile (SIP). Furthermore, when patients were rated unchanged at follow-up by both the patient and a clinician, there was virtually no correlation between initial and follow-up ARA ratings. While the initial clinician and the follow-up evaluator were rarely the same in this study, the results illustrated the limited reliability and validity of the ARA scale.

Could patients simply be asked to rate their functioning on a single unidimensional scale (e.g. from 'not at all affected' to 'extremely affected')?

**Table 15.4** Validity and reliability of traditional scales and the Sickness Impact Profile (SIP): correlations* between functional scales and biological variables, and between repeated administrations

| Comparison variable | Self-rating 7-point scale | ARA classification | SIP, physical dimension |
|---|---|---|---|
| Grip strength | −0.19 | −0.28 | −0.33 |
| ESR | 0.24 | 0.33 | 0.44 |
| X-ray stage | −0.03 | 0.27 | 0.31 |
| Test–retest correlation | 0.65 | 0.0 | 0.95 |

*Partial correlations for grip strength and ESR, after controlling for age and sex. Spearman rank correlations for X-ray stage and test–retest correlations. For each scale, higher scores indicate worse function. (Adapted from Ref. 12.)

In the study described above we also asked patients to rate their functioning on a seven-point scale with these extremes, and compared the reliability and validity of the responses with those of the ARA scale and the SIP[12]. As Table 15.4 shows, these unidimensional self-ratings appeared to be less valid than either the ARA or the SIP, and less reliable than the SIP. In a clinical trial of auranofin for rheumatoid arthritis[3], two newer health status questionnaires (the Stanford Health Assessment Questionnaire (HAQ)[16] and Bush's Quality of Well Being (QWB) scale[19,36]) both showed differences between treatment groups more strongly than global visual analogue scales. Thus, the newer health status scales appear to offer substantial advantages in performance over a single self-rating item, physician ratings on a more traditional scale, or ratings on a single visual analogue scale.

A large number of scales of Activities of Daily Living (ADL) were devised in the 1950s and 1960s for use in rehabilitation medicine[13,21,30,35,40]. Some were used in studies of hip fracture and arthritis patients[21,40], and it should be determined whether the newer scales offer an advantage over these established ADL scales. Though direct comparisons are virtually non-existent, examination of the ADL scales reveals important differences from the newer generation of health status indexes[8]. In many ways, the ADL scales were the predecessors of the newer scales, but they were aimed at the severely dysfunctional inpatients found on rehabilitation wards. Thus, their items on personal hygiene, continence, and feeding are rarely applicable to ambulatory arthritis patients. Attention to less severe dysfunction (e.g. fine hand activities) is very limited, probably reducing their sensitivity to the functional changes observed in an ambulatory population. Finally, most of the ADL scales have very limited coverage of psychosocial functioning, so that the newer health status scales are typically more comprehensive.

Thus, the ADL scales may not be well suited to assessing ambulatory arthritis patients. Studies with the SIP and other health status instruments clearly demonstrate that it is possible to improve over the simpler, traditional unidimensional scales. While there are few comparative studies, the careful development, testing and validation of several new arthritis-specific questionnaires suggest that most are likely to be superior to the older scales. These newer instruments are described in more detail in the next section.

## SELECTED HEALTH STATUS MEASURES WHICH HAVE BEEN USED IN ARTHRITIS RESEARCH

A complete review of functional scales for arthritis patients is not feasible in the space of a brief overview. This discussion focuses, therefore, on the newer instruments which have been most widely applied and carefully evaluated, or are most representative of the newer questionnaires.

The instruments discussed here in greatest detail include the HAQ developed at Stanford University[16], the Arthritis Impact Measurement Scales (AIMS) developed at Boston University[33], the SIP from the University of Washington (Seattle)[2], and the instrument devised by Jette for a Pilot Geriatric Arthritis Program[18]. Other instruments such as those of Lee *et al.*[24] and Convery *et al.*[7] have also been validated, but have been less extensively used in the United States.

These instruments are compared on the following criteria:

- *Applicability*: How have the instruments most often been used? Are they appropriate for outpatient rheumatology trials?
- *Practicality*: What is the time required for administration? Can the instruments be self-administered? Could telephone interviews be used?
- *Comprehensiveness*: Types of function or other impacts considered.
- *Reliability*: Test–retest and inter-rater reliability are both considered, as well as internal consistency measures.
- *Validity*: No 'gold standard' is available, so correlations with biological indicators of disease severity or other markers of health status are considered (construct validation).
- *Responsiveness*: Does the instrument detect changes over time, and can it detect subtle, but clinically important change?

It can be argued that the last characteristic, responsiveness, is crucial in clinical trials, and has received insufficient attention. The next section deals with this particular problem more extensively.

All of the instruments discussed here have been used in outpatient studies of arthritis patients; in fact, these instruments were designed primarily with outpatients in mind. Table 15.5 lists some examples of clinical studies which have employed each of the scales. Since all appear to be appropriate for outpatient therapeutic trials, the criterion of applicability is met by all.

The HAQ is the shortest of these scales, and requires the least time for administration and scoring[16]. It drew health status questions from multiple sources, including the instruments of Convery[7], Katz[20] and Mahoney[30], and has been successfully used in a trial of educational intervention for rheumatoid arthritis[26], in studies of health care costs and utilization[28], a survey of the natural history of rheumatoid arthritis[39], and a large drug trial[3]. As shown in Table 15.6, test–retest reliability is good. Validity was assessed by having patients perform the activities included on the questionnaire in their own homes, with a trained observer recording their performance, and was shown to be substantial. Furthermore, this scale, and all the others described here, have been correlated with one another. The global health status scores showed intercorrelations which ranged in every case between 0.73 and 0.87 (Ref. 25). Like all the arthritis-specific scales discussed here, the HAQ includes a scale of pain symptoms as well as functional ability, and, in its complete

**Table 15.5** Descriptions of four health status instrument which have been tested in rheumatoid arthritis patients

| Health status instrument | Number of items | Subscales | Time for administration | Successfully tested in self-administered format | Examples of application |
|---|---|---|---|---|---|
| HAQ | 23 health status items | Dressing and grooming, arising, eating, walking, hygiene, reach, grip, activity, sex, pain | 5–10 min: scoring: 1 min | Yes | Trial of education interventions, study of health costs, drug trial |
| AIMS | 45 health status items | Dexterity, physical activity, mobility household activities, ADL, depression and anxiety, pain | 15–20 min | Yes | Drug trials |
| SIP | 136 items | Ambulation, mobility, home management, self-care, social interaction, communication, emotional behaviour, alertness eating, work, sleep and rest, recreation | 20–30 min: scoring: 5 min | Yes | Trial of continuing education, studies of back pain |
| Jette-FSI | 54 items | Gross mobility, hand activities personal care, home chores interpersonal activities | 10–30 min | ? | Evaluation of multidisciplinary care for older patients with arthritis |

form, includes questions on treatment side-effects and costs of care, as well as health status.

Of the scales considered here, the AIMS[33] has probably had the greatest use in clinical therapeutic trials. Its items were drawn in part from Bush's Index of Well Being[19,36] and the Rand Health Insurance Experiment batteries[4]. The questionnaire is intermediate in length, with 45 health status items (Table 15.5). As shown in Table 15.6, it is a reliable measure that has shown moderate relationships with several biological markers of disease severity. In this situation, since the validation variables are not actual measures of health status, high-validity correlations are not expected, only correlations of moderate strength, and in the expected directions. The AIMS has been shown to correlate closely with the HAQ, at least in the physical function scales[17], and the overall AIMS score correlates well with all the scales described here (0.84–0.87)[25]. The AIMS investigators have also examined the value of assessing pain in a health status questionnaire. They found that pain scores explained medication use better than did physical disability or psychological status. Furthermore, regression models showed that the pain scales made a substantial contribution to explaining both physician and patient overall health assessments, above and beyond the contributions of physical and psychological function[22]. These data provide

**Table 15.6** Validity and reliability of four health status instruments which have been tested in rheumatoid arthritis

| | | Physical activity subscales | | |
| | HAQ | AIMS | Overall SIP | Jette–FSI |
| --- | --- | --- | --- | --- |
| *Validity* | | | | |
| Grip Strength | ** | 0.45 | 0.35 | 0.20[*] |
| Morning stiffness | ** | – | 0.23 | 0.08[*] |
| Professional assessment of | | | | |
|   disease activity | ** | 0.35 | 0.40[†] | 0.20[*] |
| ARA functional class | ** | 0.50 | 0.30 | – |
| Patient self-rating of function, | | | | |
|   health, or joint condition | ** | 0.45 | 0.52 | 0.39[*] |
| *Reliability* | | | | |
| Internal consistency | – | 0.80[††] | 0.93[††] | 0.80[‡] |
| Test–retest | 0.85 | ≥0.80 | 0.87[§] | 0.70[§] |
| Interobserver | – | – | – | 0.70[†] |

** Validation performed by direct observation of behaviour in questionnaire, not against these biological measures.

* Based on an early, lengthier version than described in text.

‡ Spearman–Brown formula.

§ Statistic accounting for chance agreement (weighted kappa or intraclass correlation coefficient).

†† Cronbach's alpha.

† From patients with conditions other than rheumatoid arthritis.

a persuasive case for including pain scales as part of health status assessments among arthritis patients.

The SIP[2] is the only instrument considered here which is not arthritis-specific. The SIP was designed to measure health status in a comprehensive manner for general populations or for persons with a wide variety of medical conditions and has most often been used for studying patients with chronic diseases (arthritis, chronic obstructive lung disease and coronary heart disease). The entire questionnaire is behaviourally based, and does not consider symptoms (including pain) *per se*. It does, however, include behavioural items which reflect underlying pain (e.g. 'I often moan and groan in pain and discomfort'; 'I keep rubbing or holding areas of my body that hurt or are uncomfortable'). The SIP is by far the longest of the instruments considered, though the time required for administration is still reasonable (20–30 minutes), and when used in a self-administrated format, this is a relatively minor problem. The SIP has been used successfully in studies assessing the impact of continuing physician education on outcome for patients with rheumatoid arthritis[42], in methodological development of other arthritis-related scales[27], and in studies of the musculoskeletal conditions such as low back pain[10,11]. As shown in Table 15.6, the construct validity of the SIP, demonstrated through correlations with biological measures or other judgements, is comparable to that for the disease-specific questionnaires, and reliability is consistently high in many settings. The high level of internal consistency for the SIP is not surprising, since internal consistency coefficients tend to rise with increasing numbers of items.

Jette's Functional Status Instrument (FSI) was developed for evaluating a pilot arthritis programme in geriatric patients[18]. It asks patients to make three judgements concerning each of 18 activities of daily living: the degree of dependence in that activity (need for someone to assist); level of pain associated with the activity; and how difficult (how hard or easy) the activity is to perform. Thus, 54 separate judgements are required, using a five-point Likert scale for each. The time required is close to that for the SIP. Experience with the FSI outside of its original programme evaluation use has been limited, and while validity and reliability have been established, the data in Table 15.6 suggests that they may be slightly less than those of the other scales considered.

Other scales for measuring arthritis-related dysfunction have been developed, but are not described in detail here. Convery and his colleagues, for example, developed a functional scale[7] for use with arthritis patients which adapted items from the Barthel Index[30]. A four-point rating was made for each of 19 ADL items. Validity was assessed by comparisons with physician judgements and the ARA functional classification. Unfortunately, more extensive validation was not undertaken, conventional reliability statistics were not reported, and the scale has not been widely used elsewhere.

A scale developed by Lee and associates[24] used 17 ADL items, each rated on a three-point scale. Strong validity correlations were shown with walking time, grip strength and the Ritchie Articular Index, but again, conventional reliability statistics were not reported, and the scale has not been widely used in therapeutic studies. Neither of these scales considers psychosocial function, and the Convery scale does not consider pain.

Aside from these disease-specific scales, one other general health status index, the QWB Scale[19,36] has been well studied in patients with rheumatoid arthritis and was used successfully in a recent trial evaluating the effectiveness of auranofin[33]. Like the SIP, it is applicable to a wide variety of diseases, but has performed well in this disease-specific application. The overall scale appears to be responsive to clinical changes[3,25] and the item weights have been scaled specifically for rheumatoid arthritis patients (with results very similar to scaling in a general population)[6]. The list of scales presented here is not exhaustive; a number of other health status or functional status scales have been used to study arthritis, but have not been widely adopted.

## MEASURING CHANGES IN FUNCTION: THE APPLICATION OF SCALES TO CLINICAL TRIALS

The design of a questionnaire in clinical medicine or the social sciences may vary substantially according to the purpose of the scale. Kirshner and Guyatt have pointed out that quality of life scales may be used for three purposes: discriminating between subjects, predicting either prognosis or the results of some other test, and evaluating change over time[23]. When physiological or laboratory tests are considered, the requirements for development and successful application are similar for all three purposes. However, for quality of life measures, the requirements of a scale may vary with its intended use, and the requirements for one purpose may actually interfere with other purposes[23].

The development of many instruments for survey or social science applications has focused on scale performance at a single time, usually for discriminating two groups. For example, intelligence tests distinguish between children's learning abilities, and health status measures might be used to compare the burden of illness in different communities. In this setting, items are selected to tap all important components of the domain, and to be universally applicable to respondents. Large intersubject variation is desired, and cross-sectional construct validity (relation between the scale and external measures at a single time) is most important.

In contrast, when used for therapeutic trials, the purpose of a health status scale is not to discriminate between subjects at a single time, but to detect individual changes which occur over time. Item selection should then be focused only on components of the domain which are amenable to change.

Intrasubject variability becomes the most important aspect of reliability, with the goal of insignificant variation between changes in an index and changes in some external measure over time, now becomes crucial. The critical issue is responsiveness of the scale, so that small but clinically relevant changes with therapy can be detected. This may require deleting unresponsive items from a questionnaire.

Arthritis investigators have been attentive to the issue of responsiveness, and this characteristic has been examined in several ways. Perhaps the simplest method is to administer scales before and after an intervention which is known to cause substantial clinical change. Responsiveness is then judged by the magnitude of a paired $t$-statistic for the before–after comparison. The scale with the largest value would be judged most responsive. A second method is to correlate functional score changes which occur over time with changes in biological or other variables. A third method is to consider scales to be 'diagnostic tests' for clinical changes over time. By this criterion, the best scale would be that which best discriminates subjects who improve from those who do not improve. Each of these methods has been used in arthritis-related applications, and representative findings are considered below.

**Method 1**

Liang and colleagues compared the HAQ, AIMS, SIP and FSI with regard to their ability to detect improvement after joint replacement[25]. Subjects with rheumatoid arthritis or osteoarthritis who underwent total hip or knee replacement comprised the study population. The different subscales and content in the instruments meant only three dimensions of health status were considered: mobility, social function and pain. In addition, global scores for each complete instrument were assessed. Scores for each scale were linearly transformed to a common range of possible values (0–100) for comparison. The efficiency of each scale in detecting change was tested by examining paired $t$-statistics, based on within-patient changes. The relative efficiency (RE) of scales was judged by comparing each to an arbitrary standard (in this case the FSI) by squaring the ratio of the appropriate $t$-statistics. For example,

$$\text{RE (AIMS versus FSI)} = (t\text{AIMS}/t\text{FSI})^2$$

An RE greater than or less than 1.0 means that the instrument is more (or less) efficient for measuring change than the FSI. Table 15.7 shows a comparison of four scales using this method.

It can be seen that the AIMS, FSI and SIP are similar in detecting mobility improvement, with a slight advantage to the SIP, but the HAQ was considerably less efficient. The FSI and SIP were similar in detecting changes in social function, while the AIMS was less efficient. With regard to pain, the

**Table 15.7** Comparison of scale responsiveness following joint replacement in arthritis patients. Values represent Relative Efficiency in detecting change compared to Jette's Functional Status Instrument (FSI). Values greater than 1.0 or less than 1.0 represent greater or lesser efficiency. (See text for calculation of Relative Efficiency.)

| | Instrument | | | |
| --- | --- | --- | --- | --- |
| Dimension | FSI | AIMS | HAQ | SIP |
| Mobility | 1.00 | 0.85 | 0.48 | 1.11 |
| Social | 1.00 | 0.18 | 0.62 | 0.74 |
| Pain | 1.00 | 0.79 | 0.57 | – |
| Global | 1.00 | 4.12 | 1.15 | 3.51 |

FSI appeared best, while the SIP had no specific pain scale. When considering global change, the AIMS and SIP were more than three times as efficient as either the FSI or the HAQ. Though not shown in Table 15.7, Bush's QWB Scale was also examined in this study. Its overall score was the most responsive of the scales tested, though its mobility and social subscales were relatively less responsive. Thus, in a setting of surgical intervention for lower extremity arthritis, certain scales appeared to be more efficient than others, but the instruments varied in relative efficiency for detecting change on specific dimensions.

This method of assessing responses can be quite useful, and would certainly help to identify unresponsive items or subscales for deletion in a particular clinical trial. However, this method assumes that an overall improvement is occurring in the patients studied, and does not indicate how well each scale may distinguish between those who improve and those who do not. Changes in scale scores may therefore be sensitive, but not very specific for clinical change (i.e. score changes may be relatively common even among clinically stable patients).

## Method 2

Meenan has tested the responsiveness of the AIMS in a clinical trial of auranofin and injectable gold for rheumatoid arthritis[32]. Changes in the AIMS physical dimension correlated significantly with changes in other measures, such as joint tenderness, joint swelling and grip strength. Furthermore, the AIMS scores after treatment were significantly different among the three treatment groups (placebo, oral gold and injectable gold). A discriminant analysis was performed when the data were complete, to determine which outcome variables best distinguished among treatment groups. The AIMS data correctly assigned subjects to the true drug category at a rate virtually identical to the clinical data (swelling, tenderness, grip and patient overall assessment), namely 43% compared with 42%. When the two types of data were combined, the percentage correctly classified was even greater.

## Method 3

Assessing scale responsiveness can be considered in some ways analogous to assessing a diagnostic test[9]. In this case, the condition to be diagnosed is whether or not a clinically important change has occurred. Health status scales will show random variability over time, and can never provide perfect measurements. Thus, score changes over time may either be true-positives reflecting real patient change, or false-positives reflecting other score variability. One could therefore describe the responsiveness of a health status scale in terms of its sensitivity and specificity for detecting change as established by external criteria. As this argument suggests, the issue in most therapeutic trials is not merely sensitive to change, but ability to discriminate between those who improve and those who do not. Like most diagnostic tests, it may be that the sensitivity and specificity of functional scales are to some extent inversely related. Thus, the use of receiver operating characteristic (ROC) curves[38] to characterize scale responsiveness has been proposed[9].

An ROC curve can synthesize information about scale sensitivity and specificity for detecting improvement by some external criterion. The true-positive rate (sensitivity) is plotted against the false-positive rate (1 – specificity) for each of several possible cut-off points for score change. Thus, sensitivity and specificity can be calculated for a one-point score change, two points, five points, and so forth. A score change of one point, for example, might be highly sensitive to change (most patients who improve show this much change) but also be fairly non-specific (many unimproved patients might have a change of this magnitude). A score change of five points might be somewhat less sensitive, but more specific (clinically stable patients would be unlikely to have this great a score change). The area under an ROC curve in this setting is proportional to the ability of a scale to discriminate subjects who improve from those who do not.

Though we have not used this method to examine scale performance among rheumatoid arthritis patients, we have studied patients with back pain using the SIP, its physical and psychosocial dimensions, and a brief 24-item scale adapted from the SIP by British investigators (the Roland Scale)[37]. The items chosen for the Roland Scale were those thought by experts to be most relevant to back pain, and they were reworded to include the phrase 'because of my back'. We tested each scale's ability to detect changes over a three-week treatment period[9]. Two external criteria were used to define improvement: the patient's own judgement of whether or not he had resumed full activities,

**Table 15.8** Responsiveness of functional scales for detecting improvement of low-back pain in a 3-week interval. Tabled values represent areas under the receiver operating characteristic (ROC) curve for each scale in detecting change by the criteria shown[*] (Adapted from Ref. 9 with permission)

|  | Using return to full activities as the criterion for improvement | Using consensus patient and clinician judgement as the criterion for improvement |
|---|---|---|
| Roland Scale | 0.72 | 0.67 |
| Sickness Impact Profile (SIP) | 0.70 | 0.61 |
| SIP physical dimension | 0.68 | 0.59 |
| SIP psychosocial dimension | 0.60 | 0.52 |

[*] The ROC are represents each scale's ability to discriminate improved from unimproved patients. An area of 1.0 would represent perfect discrimination and 0.5 no discrimination.

and a clinician–patient consensus that there was any degree of improvement on a six-point scale of change.

Table 15.8 shows the area under the ROC curves for each scale studied. It is apparent that the brief Roland Scale was as responsive (or slightly more so) than the lengthier SIP or its two major subscales. These results were concordant with an analysis similar to that of Method 2 noted above, but ranked the scales differently than an analysis using Method 1 (Ref. 9).

Though not conclusive, our data suggested that in some cases a shorter scale might be more responsive than a longer one. This may have occurred because items unrelated to back pain (and unresponsive to intervention) were removed from the parent questionnaire. It appears that the ROC method may be useful in assessing scale responsiveness, and may provide results that differ from simple before–after score comparisons. This may occur because it considers not only the ability of scores to change, but their ability to discriminate improvers from non-improvers.

Thus, the responsiveness of a scale is a crucial attribute in its application to clinical trials; cross-sectional reliability and validity are necessary, but not sufficient. For evaluation over time, unresponsive items should be deleted from a scale, to improve responsiveness and statistical power for detecting treatment effects. So far, relatively little attention has been given to responsiveness, although arthritis investigators may be ahead of those in most other clinical areas. Work to date suggests that different instruments excel in different dimensions. Generally, the AIMS and the SIP appear to be the most responsive of the scales examined here for studying arthritis (at least in the lower extremity), but it appears likely that even these can be improved. Different methods by which responsiveness might be assessed have also been discussed. A number of investigators have begun to study methods for improving scale responsiveness, including the use of key functional behaviours which could be patient-specific[29]. However, this work remains preliminary, and such scales have not been used in clinical trials.


## OTHER ASPECTS OF QUALITY OF LIFE

This chapter has focused on health status measures which have been used in arthritis research. However, there are dimensions of quality of life, which are not assessed by any of these scales. For example, Burkhardt examined correlates of quality of life for patients in an arthritis clinic, using a wide variety of instruments[6]. She used a composite of several scales including a Life Satisfaction Index to operationalize quality of life, and found that perceived support from a social network, self-esteem, sense of internal control over health, and negative attitude toward the illness were all important correlates of quality of life. Each of these constructs required a separate measurement scale. Her data suggested that pain and health status (using an adaptation of the AIMS) influenced quality of life primarily by affecting the attitude toward the illness, self-esteem, and sense of internal control over health (the mediating variables). Thus, comprehensive assessment of quality of life may require more than health status measurement alone, but there is relatively little experience with these other dimensions.


## CONCLUSIONS

Arthritis investigators have developed a major interest in health status assessment during the past 5 years. Drawing on the earlier development of ADL scales and general health status scales, they have devised several arthritis-specific measures of health status. Pain appears to be an important dimension of such scales. The reliability, validity and comprehensiveness of these newer instruments is quite good, easily exceeding those of earlier and simpler arthritis functional measures. The responsiveness of these scales to clinical changes over time has been demonstrated in varying degrees, suggesting some important differences among them. However, this aspect of their performance has not yet been fully assessed, and methods for testing responsiveness are still evolving. There presently exist both arthritis-specific and general health status measures which appear to be useful for studying patients with arthritis, and which can be confidently used in clinical trials today. However, we can expect this field to continue evolving, with refinements and adaptations of current scales promising even better performance in the future.

## References

1. Balaban, D., Sagi, P.C., Goldfarb, N.I. *et al.* Weights for scoring the quality of well-being instruments among rheumatoid arthritics: a comparison to general population weights. *Med. Care* 1986; 24: 973–980.
2. Bergner, M. Bobbit, R.A., Carter, W.B. *et al.* The Sickness Impact Profile: development and final testing of a health status measure. *Med Care* 1981; 19: 787–805.
3. Bombardier, C., Ware, J. Russell, I.J. *et al.* Auranofin therapy and quality of life in patients with rheumatoid arthritis: results of a multicenter trial. *Am. J. Med.* 1986; 81: 565–578.
4. Brook, R.H., Ware, J.W., Davies-Avery, A. *et al.* Overview of adult health status measures fielded in Rand's Health Insurance Study. *Med. Care* 1979; 17 (7 Suppl.): iii–x, 1–131.
5. Buchanan, W.W. Assessment of joint tenderness, grip strength, digital joint circumference and morning stiffness in rheumatoid arthritis. *J. Rheumatol.* 1982; 9: 763–766.
6. Burckhardt, C.S. The impact of arthritis on quality of life. *Nurs. Res.* 1985; 34: 11–16.
7. Convery, F.R., Minteer, M.A., Amiel, D. and Connett, K.L. Polyarticular disability: a functional assessment. *Arch. Phys. Med. Rehabil.* 1977; 58: 494–499.
8. Deyo, R.A. Measuring functional outcomes in therapeutic trials for chronic disease. *Control. Clin. Trials* 1984; 5: 223–240.
9. Deyo, R.A. and Centor, R.M. Assessing the responsiveness of functional scales to clinical change: an analogy to diagnostic test performance. *J. Chronic Dis.* 1986; 39: 897–906.
10. Deyo, R.A. and Diehl, A.K. Measuring physical and psychosocial function in patients with low-back pain, *Spine* 1983; 8: 635–642.
11. Deyo, R.A., Diehl, A.K. and Rosenthal, M. How many days of bed rest for acute low back pain? A randomized clinical trial. *N. Engl. J. Med.* 1986; 315: 1064–1070.
12. Deyo, R.A. Inui, T.S., Leininger, J.D. *et al.* Measuring functional outcomes in chronic disease: a comparison of traditional scales and a self-administered health status questionnaire in patients with rheumatoid arthritis. *Med. Care* 1983; 21: 180–192.
13. Donaldson, S.W., Wagner, C.C. and Greshaw, G.E. A unified ADL evaluation form. *Arch. Phys. Med. Rehabil.* 1973; 54: 175–179.
14. Feinstein, A.R. Clinical biostatistic, XLI. Hard science, soft data, and the challenges of choosing clinical variables in research. *Clin. Pharmacol. Ther.* 1977; 22: 485–498.
15. Fries, J.F. Toward an understanding of patient outcome measurement. *Arthritis Rheum.* 1983; 26: 697–704.
16. Fries, J.F., Spitz, P., Kraines, R.G. *et al.* Measurement of patient outcome in arthritis. *Arthritis Rheum.* 1980; 23: 137–145.
17. Fries, J.F., Spitz, P.W. and Young, D.Y. The dimensions of health outcomes: the Health Assessment Questionnaire, disability and pain scales. *J. Rheumatol.* 1982; 9: 789–793.

18. Jette, A.M. Functional Status Index: reliability of a chronic disease evaluation instrument. *Arch. Phys. Med. Rehabil.* 1980; 61: 395–401.

19. Kaplan, R.M., Bush, J.W. and Berry, C.C. Health status index: category ratings versus magnitude estimation for measuring levels of well-being. *Med. Care* 1979; 17: 501–523.

20. Chat, S., Ford, A.B., Moskowitz, R.W. *et al.* Studies of illness in the aged: the index of ADL: a standardized measure of biological and psychosocial function. *J. Am. Med. Assoc.* 1963; 185: 914–919.

21. Katz, S. Vignos, P.J., Moskowitz, R.W. *et al.* Comprehensive outpatient care in rheumatoid arthritis. A controlled study. *J. Am. Med. Assoc.* 1968; 206: 1249–1254.

22. Kazis, L.E., Meenan, R.F. and Anderson, J.J. Pain in the rheumatic diseases: investigation of a key health status component. *Arthritis Rheum.* 1983; 26: 1017–1022.

23. Kirshner, B. and Guyatt, G.A methodological framework for assessing health indices. *J. Chronic Dis.* 1985; 38: 27–36.

24. Lee, P., Jasani, M.K., Dick, W.C. *et al.* Evaluation of a functional index in rheumatoid arthritis. *Scand. J. Rheumatol.* 1973; 2: 71–77.

25. Liang, M.H., Larson, M.G., Cullen, K.E. *et al.* Comparative measurement efficiency and sensitivity of five health status instruments for arthritis research. *Arthritis Rheum.* 1985; 28: 542–547.

26. Lorig, K. Lubeck, D., Kraines, R.G. *et al.* Outcomes of self-help education for patients with arthritis. *Arthritis Rheum.* 1985; 28: 680–684.

27. Lorish, C.D. and Maisiak, R. The face scale: a brief, nonverbal method of assessing patient mood. *Arthritis Rheum.* 1986; 29: 906–909.

28. Lubeck, D.P., Spitz, P.W., Fries, J.F. *et al.* A multicenter study of annual health service utilization and costs in rheumatoid arthritis. *Arthritis Rheum.* 1986; 29: 488–493.

29. Mackenzie, C.R., Charlson, M.E., DiGroia, D. *et al.* A patient-specific measure of change in maximal function. *Arch. Intern. Med.* 1986; 146: 1325–1329.

30. Mahoney, F.I. and Barthel, D.W. Functional evaluation: the Barthel Index. *Md. Med. J.* 1965; 14: 61–65.

31. McCarty, D.J. Clinical assessment of arthritis. In McCarty, D.J. (ed.) *Arthritis and Allied Conditions*, 9th edition, Philadelphia, Lea and Febiger, 1979, pp. 131–147.

32. Meenan, R.F., Anderson, J.J., Kazis, L.E. *et al.* Outcome assessment in clinical trials: evidence for the sensitivity of a health status measure. *Arthritis Rheum.* 1984; 27: 1344–1352.

33. Meenan, R.F., Gertman, P.M. and Mason, J.H. Measuring health status in arthritis: the Arthritis Impact Measurement Scales. *Arthritis Rheum.* 1980; 23: 146–152.

34. Meenan, R.F., Yelin, E.H., Nevitt, M. *et al.* The impact of chronic disease: a sociomedical profile of rheumatoid arthritis. *Arthritis Rheum.* 1981; 24: 544.

35. Moskowitz, E. and McCann, C.B. Classification of disability in the chronically ill and aging. *J. Chronic Dis.* 1957; 5: 342–346.

36. Patrick, D.L., Bush, J.W. and Chen, M.M. Toward an operational definition of health. *J. Health Soc. Behav.* 1973; 14: (3) 6–23.

37. Roland, M. and Morris, R. A study of the natural history of back pain. Part I: Development of a reliable and sensitive measure of disability in low-back pain. *Spine* 1983; 8: 141-144.

38. Sackett, D.L., Haynes, R.B. and Tugwell, P. *Clinical Epidemiology: A Basic Science for Clinical Medicine.* Boston, Little, Brown and Co., 1985, pp. 100-108.

39. Sherrer, Y.S., Block, D.A., Mitchell, D.M. *et al.* The development of disability in rheumatoid arthritis. *Arthritis Rheum.* 1986; 29: 494-500.

40. Staff of the Benjamin Rose Hospital: multidisciplinary study of illness in the aged person. *J. Chronic Dis.* 1958; 7: 332-344.

41. Steinbrocker, O., Traeger, C.H. and Batterman, R. C. Therapeutic criteria in rheumatoid arthritis. *J. Am. Med. Assoc.* 1949; 140: 659-662.

42. Stross, J.K., Schumacher, H.R., Weisman, M.H. *et al.* Continuing medical education: changing behaviour and improving outcomes. *Arthritis Rheum.* 1985; 28: 1163-1167.

43. The Cooperating Clinics of the American Rheumatism Association: a seven day variability study of 499 patients with peripheral rheumatoid arthritis. *Arthritis Rheum.* 1965; 8: 302-334.

44. Wood, R.W., Diehr, P., Wolcott, B.W. *et al.* Reproducibility of clinical data and decisions in the management of upper respiratory illnesses. *Med. Care* 1979; 17: 767-779.

# 16 Measuring the quality of life of patients with Parkinson's disease

J.S. Shindler, R. Brown, P. Welburn and J.D. Parkes

Parkinson's disease affects about one in a hundred of the UK population over the age of 60, with a total of 60–80,000 recognized cases. The extent of false-negative diagnosis is not known, but at least one-third of parkinsonian patients are said to receive an incorrect initial diagnosis[14]. Similarly, in one-third of the patients, there has been a more than three-year delay in making the diagnosis after the initial symptoms. This suggests that diagnosis other than Parkinson's disease have been considered[17]. In addition, recent surveys have indicated that perhaps a third of all established cases in the community may be unrecognized. A four-fold difference in disease prevalence has been reported from different countries, but accurate statistics for the worldwide incidence of Parkinson's disease are not available.

Parkinson's disease is mainly a disorder of late life, with a mean age of onset of 59, but there are many younger-onset cases of both idiopathic Parkinson's disease and parkinsonian syndromes. Sex incidence is approximately equal.

In retrospective surveys, tremor is said to be the initial symptom by 70% of patients with Parkinson's disease[10]. Initial symptoms are ascribed mainly to hypokinesia and rigidity in one-fifth of the patients, including stiffness, gait disturbance, loss of arm swing, handwriting difficulty, loss of dexterity and speech difficulty. Some patients with hardly noticeable motor symptoms show general fatigue or depression, or, very rarely, apparent dementia. Unusually, painful foot cramp is the first symptom.

Two broad patterns of disease can be identified, one mainly tremulous and with a fairly good prognosis, the second mainly bradykinetic and with a worse outlook. In the pre-levodopa era, the course from onset to death averaged 11 years. Treatment has restored life expectancy towards normal, but despite treatment, disability is slowly progressive in two-thirds of all patients,

289

although in the others, disease severity does not greatly increase during patients' lifetime.

## DISABILITY IN PARKINSON'S DISEASE

What are the major effects of Parkinson's disease on quality of life? The condition is readily recognized by the onlooker, on account of the basic clinical features of tremor, rigidity, akinesia, postural instability and postural deformity. Most rating scales of disease severity rely heavily on these features. However, in the influential report by Hoehn and Yahr[10] on the natural history of parkinsonism, the authors indicated there was a marked discrepancy between observable signs, such as rigidity and tremor, and the degree of functional incapacity.

A recent study by Gotham *et al.*[9] found patients' self-report of depression and functional disability and clinical rating of disease severity was correlated, but the two ratings shared only 27% of common variance, indicating the knowledge and overall clinical state is a poor predictor of the degree of functional disability as perceived by the patient.

Quality of life, however, cannot be equated simply with disease severity or degree of disability. Psychosocial factors may be far more important than akinesia and tremor in determining life quality. Most patients view Parkinson's disease in terms of a progressive and very disabling illness causing embarrassment, loneliness and depression, with increasing dependence on others, as well as one producing slowness and falls. Side-effects of many antiparkinsonian drugs, particularly in the late stage of illness, are frequent and severe, and their use may lead to an overall deterioration, not improvement, in life quality.

Major problems in life for the parkinsonian patient include difficulties in communication, as well as the more obvious problems with movement. The illness is accompanied by depression in approximately 30% of subjects, and subtle cognitive and sensory abnormalities add to the patient's burden. The evaluation of these and other selected features in parkinsonism, and the effect on quality of life, is considered below.

## VARIATION IN PARKINSON'S DISEASE

A characteristic feature of parkinsonism is sudden extreme change in disease severity. These variations take two main forms, those natural to the disease and those occurring as a result of treatment. Both types of response variation are very difficult to quantify.

Exercise, fatigue, sleep, emotion, anxiety, infection, dehydration, concurrent illness, drugs and alcohol all cause circadian variation in the symptoms of parkinsonism, while unpredictable as well as predictable response swings occur with levodopa treatment. Clinically, three stages of response variation to levodopa can be identified with disease progression, each stage lasting from perhaps three to seven years, depending on the rapidity of progression of parkinsonism.

(1)   Initial phase of good stable response to levodopa. Here overall disability is usually mild to moderate, and despite 6–8 hourly drug dosage, even occasionally alternate day drug dosage, the level of disability is fairly stable.

(2)   Intermediate response phase. Initially levodopa produces improvement for 4–6 hours, but this period progressively shortens, with levodopa dose-related response fluctuations.

(3)   Marked variability or poor response phase. This indicates the end stage of illness, when response variations become increasingly obvious. The expected drug response may not occur, and dyskinesias and psychiatric side-effects of levodopa and dopamine agonists become more frequent, severe and disabling.

The assessment of these complicated fluctuations in the course of Parkinson's disease largely depends on the continued presence of a trained observer[20]. Some patients can be taught to recognize and record the different types of disease and drug-related fluctuations, and keep accurate On–Off charts themselves, but both day and night recordings may be essential to gain an accurate picture of the problems of end-stage parkinsonism.


## COMMUNICATION

A recent survey of 203 parkinsonian subjects showed that communication difficulties were one of the major problems of disease. On a self-rating Activity of Daily Living (ADL) questionnaire, 50% of patients considered themselves unable to write a letter, and 33% thought their speech was sometimes unintelligible[9]. Oxtoby[19] asked 261 patients if they had difficulty with various activities when they were feeling 'at their worst'. Perhaps because of the difference in wording, this study indicated an even greater level of disability, 83% of patients with writing disability. A smaller survey of 57 patients in Northampton found that 70% of subjects had unintelligible speech[28].

Speech abnormality, paucity of facial movement, and drooling of saliva, are embarrassing and ostracizing symptoms. Speech is generally lower in volume, higher in pitch, and faster than normal, with a disorder of prosody or metred speech rather than errors in articulation[25]. Videofluoroscopy studies confirm this disorder is due to abnormal oropharyngeal mobility, and show that swallowing is also impaired, tracheal aspiration being far more common than is realized[22].

As with most other aspects of parkinsonism, the evaluation of speech and communication difficulties, and the effects of antiparkinsonian drugs or speech therapy on these, has proved extremely difficult. Fatigue, natural variation (see below) and drug-induced dyskinesias, which may increase rather than relieve dysphonia[5,16] all make evaluation difficult. Relatives, but not medical attendants, may comprehend the patient.

Paradoxical kinesia may result in comprehensible speech in stressful clinic surroundings, but not under normal home circumstances. Additional speech disorders in the elderly, related to stroke, laryngeal problems and deafness, may compound incomprehensibility. In addition, rigid facies deny the patient non-verbal communication. Written communication is impaired as handwriting becomes difficult, and although many resort to slow writing in capital script, illegibility is still very common. Handwriting and speech improve with levodopa[18] but, using currently-available evaluation methods, it has been difficult to show that speech therapy is definitely beneficial in the long term. Other studies[23,25-6] have indicated that speech improvement, at least in the short term, is possible using individual and group techniques. It has likewise proved difficult to evaluate the various electronic feedback devices available to improve voice intensity[24], as well as determine if other aids, including pointer boards, typewriters and electronic 'communicators' are of real value to the majority of parkinsonian patients.

## MOBILITY

In the study of Gotham et al.[9] 15% of parkinsonian patients could not walk indoors without assistance, and 40% had problems with outdoor mobility. The Northampton study reported that 47% had difficulty in walking unaided, 44% had problems with bathing and personal hygiene[28], whilst only 9.6% reported by Oxtoby[19] walked normally; 63% had difficulty in turning over in bed, and 67% had difficulty with fine movements such as doing up buttons and zips[19].

The Parkinson's Disease Society survey[19] provided detailed information about loss of outdoor mobility. The preferred mode of travel was by private car, but only 18% of respondents were able to drive themselves. The public bus and train were rarely used. In particular, great difficulty was documented in the use of bus services. Most patients felt that their lack of independent mobility was a major problem.

Evaluation of walking is difficult because of the inherent variability of parkinsonism. Simple assessments of mobility can be made by walking patients along a marked floor and recording the time to walk a set distance, measuring stride length (distance between two ipsilateral heel strikes) and total number of steps in a specific distance. More sophisticated testing can be performed with video recording and polarized light goniometry (see Knuttsen)[13]. However, none of these measures one fundamental disability; fear of falling, with loss of postural stability. The recognition of this fear, rather than the measurement of stride length, may be all-important in quality of life determination in parkinsonism.

Everyday tasks become difficult as manual dexterity and find hand control fail. These tasks include cutting food, dressing and grooming, pill-taking and simple housework. The assessment of the individual's home needs is very important, and once tried, many simple aids are accepted[2]. These aids include easy-grip cutlery and non-slip mats and trays, as well as kitchen, toilet and bath modification. Hand function may be improved by drug treatment, but there is no evidence that physiotherapy is beneficial. The occupational therapist may be able to help the patient achieve a new level of function, and group therapy has been recommended to improve fine motor skills with games and group activity[6].

## RECREATIONS AND SOCIAL LIFE

An aspect of living that is largely neglected in the evaluation of parkinsonian disability is recreational and social life. Seventy-five per cent of patients in a pilot study in the King's College Hospital Parkinson's Disease Clinic had forgone some or all of their hobbies. A survey in Glasgow[15] assessed hobbies and disease severity. Sedentary activities such as reading and watching television were little altered, whereas outdoor activities were markedly affected, including outdoor gardening, lunching out, and going to church and clubs. Few new activities were commenced after the onset of illness. Many patients are widowed, an event that affects social functioning in itself.

A survey by Singer[27] attempted to define the 'social cost' of parkinson's disease. As with the Glasgow study, sedentary, solitary activities were not affected, and indeed were more common in the patient sample. More striking, however, was the amount of time spent idle during the day; 41% of patients spent four or more hours each day idle, compared with only 8% in the general population of the same age. The patients were also much more likely to be isolated from close social contacts, and the discrepancy from normal levels was particularly marked in the younger patients. The Oxtoby survey[19] asked patients to name their most serious non-medical problems. The two most common were lack of company (21%) and problems in using transport (19%). In other words, 40% felt loneliness or lack of mobility outside the home to be the areas where help was most needed in their lives. In evaluating the findings from her study, Singer concluded that the impact of Parkinson's disease on the individual's life was a type of premature social ageing, which was particularly marked in the younger patients.

## DEPRESSION IN PARKINSON'S DISEASE

From the studies above, a picture emerges of social isolation, resulting in part at least from problems with mobility, together with a decrease in purposeful activity and an increased dependence on others, both in and out of the home. Such a pattern can have serious consequences for the patient's sense of emotional well-being. Although figures vary, studies in Parkinson's disease suggest a high frequency of depression, possibly 30% of all subjects. Despite many detailed studies, it is still not apparent whether such depression is specifically related to the pathology of parkinsonism or merely the consequence of progressive chronic illness.

Several studies, employing disease control groups, have found a higher prevalence of depression in the Parkinson's disease groups than in the other disease states, although in no case was the comparison group ideal. Robbins[21] used patients with severe chronic physical handicaps, including hemiplegia, amputation, spinal cord disease and cerebrovascular disease. In this study, as in the others, the patients with Parkinson's disease were found to be more depressed than the other groups. However, the controls used by Robbins did not serve as an ideal comparison with parkinson's disease, as many had illnesses of relatively rapid onset which, while chronic, were not associated with progressive deterioration. Many patients consider static disability to be less distressing than the realization that further decline is inevitable. Recently, Gotham et al.[9] compared the level of depression in Parkinson's disease with that in a group of patients with rheumatoid arthritis, with equivalent levels of functional disability. No difference was found in the levels of depression in the two groups.

Attempts to relate the severity of depression to the degree of disability have not been very successful, and most studies show no significant correlation. However, Gotham et al. found a correlation of 0.43 between scores on their ADL and the Beck Depression Inventory, although even that association represented only 18% of common variants. This suggests that either the ADL scale was not tapping the relevant aspects of functional disability or, more likely, that factors other than functional disability were important in determining which patients would become depressed. This may depend on age and rate of progression of illness more than level of functional disability; if deterioration is rapid, then the ability of the patient to adapt may be compromised. Any cross-sectional study will, therefore, fail to capture the picture of change in disability.

Brown and MacCarthy[3] reassessed 210 patients studied by Gotham et al.[9] after 12 months, using the Beck Depression Inventory and ADL scales. Taking a conservative cut-off score of 17 on the Beck Depression Inventory, patients were divided into four groups according to their depression status by the two assessments: (1) 16% were depressed by both assessments; (2)

63% were not depressed on either assessment; (3) 11% were depressed on the initial but not the second assessment; and (4) 11% were depressed on the second but not the initial assessment.

In terms of their ADL scores, patients in group (1) were the most severely disabled by both assessments, while those in group (2) were the least disabled. Patients in group (4) (i.e. those that had become depressed) started with the same ADL score on the initial assessment as that of group (2), but had experienced a much greater degree of functional deterioration over the 12-month period. Finally, group (3) patients (i.e. those that had become non-depressed) were of intermediate levels of disability on the initial assessment. While their ADL scores increased over the follow-up period, the degree of change was slight, and parallelled the changes in the patients in group (2).

These findings suggest that depression in Parkinson's disease may be of at least two types. First, there are patients who are severely disabled and who may have a chronic or recurring depression. Secondly, there are those patients in the early stages of the illness who are only mildly disabled, but who suffer a marked deterioration in functional ability over a short period of time.

A major factor which influences adjustment to Parkinson's disease is age. Perhaps surprisingly, across a range of chronic physical illnesses, psychological adjustment is sometimes worse in younger than in older age groups[3,4]. In the study of Brown and MacCarthy[3], the group who became depressed were on average five years younger than the other groups. Older people may be better able to cope with the prospect of increasing disability than younger patients. Alternatively, the social cost of the disease may be less in older people. Age itself has a social cost in terms of retirement, decreased income, shrinking social networks and declining health. The impact of Parkinson's disease on old people may be very different from that on young subjects.

Age is not the only variable which may modify an individual's psychological reaction to the stresses caused by disease and disability. In acute illness, a wide range of psychosocial factors has been shown to influence the impact of the illness on the individual and even the speed and thoroughness of recovery, including: casual and moral explanations which the patient may have for the onset and consequences of his illness; beliefs about personal ability; controllability of the illness; future expectations; and quality and quantity of social support available; and the personal resources available to assist the patient to cope. The influences of these different factors have been demonstrated in many illnesses, including serious accident, spinal injury, cancer and recovery from surgery.

## ANTIPARKINSONIAN DRUGS

There is no doubt that quality of life has been dramatically improved in Parkinson's disease since the introduction of levodopa and dopamine agonists.

However, psychosocial factors undoubtedly influence the degree to which patients can adjust to chronic progressive disability, and medical treatment should not ignore such factors in favour of the alternative, easier and cheaper drug-based approach. Drug treatment in Parkinson's disease should be aimed not at the symptoms themselves, but at the broader target of improved quality of life. However, to date, the primary evaluation of antiparkinsonian drugs has considered their effects on various aspects of functional disability rather than on overall quality of life. Unfortunately, levodopa and dopamine agonists have a narrow therapeutic index between wanted and unwanted effects and, at least in the late stages of disease, it may be necessary to accept certain side-effects as the price of improved mobility. Side effects include postural hypotension, serious nausea and sickness, disability and often painful involuntary movements and, in up to a third of all patients treated with antiparkinsonian drugs at some stage of illness, severe psychiatric problems. Despite between one and two decades of use, there are many unsolved controversies about the overall effect of specific antiparkinsonian drugs on life quality. Ill-defined areas include the questions as to whether to start levodopa in the early or late stages of the disease, in low or high dose, and how one can weigh early benefit versus the likelihood of subsequent disabling side-effects; another question is the exact role of dopamine agonists such as bromocriptine, pergolide and lisuride in Parkinson's disease (since most patients report that bromocriptine given alone, and irrespective of dosage, is just not 'as good' as levodopa); and the role, if any, of the monoamine oxidase type B (MOAB) inhibitor deprenyl in delaying progression of disease (deprenyl will prevent $N$-methyl-4-phenyl-tetrahydropyridine (MPTP) toxicity resulting in parkinsonism in primates). Some recent attempts to evaluate the continuous lisuride pump in parkinsonism (analogous to the insulin pump in diabetes) have foundered on the emphasis on major sustained motor improvement, sometimes at the expense of severe drug-related psychiatric problems, rather than on the achievement of a more modest motor response, but limitation of psychiatric problems.

## QUALITY OF LIFE

It is apparent from the above discussion that standard methods for the evaluation of parkinsonism will not necessarily reflect quality of life. The available scales vary from the simple to the complex, and although of great value in assessing overall disease progression, the effect of antiparkinsonian drugs, and in the detailed evaluation of specific aspects of parkinsonism, such scales mainly reflect the doctor rather than the patient viewpoint. Many of the more simple scales are widely used, if not fully validated. For example, the simple five-point assessment of Hoehn and Yahr[10] is in widespread use[12] despite some inaccuracies. More complicated scales have been developed

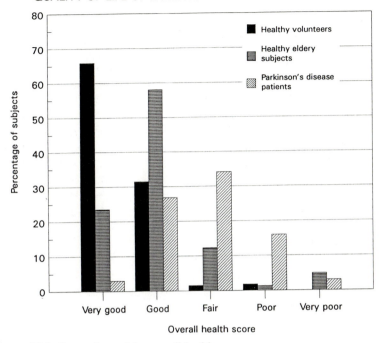

**Figure 16.1** Comparison of the overall health scores

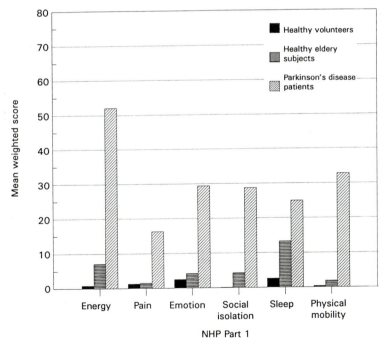

**Figure 16.2** Comparison of the NHP Part 1 scores

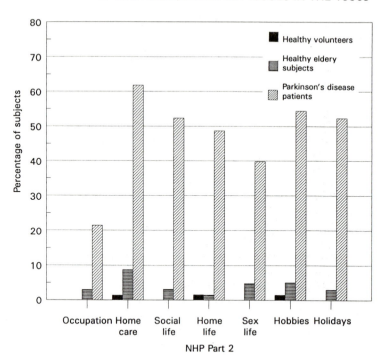

**Figure 16.3** Comparison of the NHP Part 2 scores

(see for example Godwin-Austin *et al.*[8] and Marsen *et al.*[16]). Characteristically these scales combine scores for general history, functional disability, examination and results of various tests, and also record the overall opinion of the patient and his carers. The Barthel ADL index is well validated, but is limited in use since it does not consider communication scales. Evidence suggests that it is also necessary to assess psychological and social factors. Standardized interviews will probably provide the most useful results, because of the flexibility they allow in individual clinical problems. However, important information can be obtained using reliable questionnaires and scales. Figures 16.1 and 16.2 show results from a study using the Nottingham Health Profile[9]. This scale measures a wide range of psychological and social factors, and may prove useful for the routine assessment of individual cases[11].

Finally, cognitive changes, both subtle and profound, are common in Parkinson's disease. Studies of cognitive function and vigilance have used scoring systems of great complexity with subtle neuropsychological tests for verbal and non-verbal memory, motor speed, visuo-motor speed, language function and vigilance. Such assessments are very time-consuming, and not universally applicable. However, the potential impact of cognitive loss on the patient's life cannot be ignored. With all these scales, the success of individual clinical assessment can be judged empirically by response, but if any assessment scale is to be developed it must satisfy tests of validity.

## References

1. Andrews, K. Rehabilitation of conditions associated in old age. *Int. Rehabil. Med.* 1985; 7: 125–129.
2. Beattie, A. and Caird, F.I. The occupational therapist and the patient with Parkinson's disease. *Br. Med. J.* 1980; 280: 1354–1355.
3. Brown, R.G. and MacCarthy, B. Social, psychological and physical factors in Parkinson's disease. Paper presented at the British Psychological Society London Conference. December 1985.
4. Cassileth, B.R., Lusk, E.J., Strouse, T.B. *et al.* Psychosocial status in chronic illness – a comparative analysis of six diagnostic groups. *N. Engl. J. Med.* 1984; 311: 506–511.
5. Critchley, E.M.R. Peak dose dysphonia in parkinsonism. *Lancet* 1976; i: 544.
6. Davis, J.C. Team management of Parkinson's disease. *Am. J. Occup. Ther.* 1977; 31: 300–308.
7. Gibbard, F.B., Page, N.G., Spencer, K.M. *et al.* Controlled time of physiotherapy and occupational therapy for Parkinson's disease. *Br. Med. J.* 1981; 282: 1196.
8. Godwin-Austin, R.B., Tomlinson, E.B., Frears, C. C. *et al.* Effects on l-dopa in Parkinson's disease. *Lancet.* 1969; 2: 165–168.
9. Gotham, A.M., Brown, R.G. and Marsden, C.D. Depression in Parkinson's disease: a quantitative and qualitative analysis. *J. Neurol. Neurosurg. Psychiat.* 1986; 49: 381–389.
10. Hoehn, M.M. and Yahr, M.D. Parkinsonism: onset, progression and mortality. *Neurology* 1967; 17: 427–442.
11. Hunt, S.M., McEwen, J. and McKenna, S.P. Measuring health status: a new tool for clinicians and epidemiologists. *R. J. Coll. Gen. Pract.* 1985; 35: 155–158.
12. Kennard, C., Munro, A.J. and Park, D.M. The reliability of clinical assessment of Parkinson's disease. *J. Neurol. Neurosurg. Psychiat.* 1984; 47: 322–323.
13. Knuttson, N. An analysis of parkinsonian gait. *Brain* 1972; 95: 475–486.
14. Lees, A.J. Early diagnosis of Parkinson's disease. *Br. J. Hosp. Med.* 1981; 26: 511–518.
15. Manson, L. and Caird, F.I. Survey of the hobbies and transport of patients in Parkinson's disease. *Occ. Ther.* 1985; 7: 199-200.
16. Marsden, C.D. and Parkes, J.D. 'On–off' effects in patients with Parkinson's disease on chronic levodopa. *Lancet* 1976; 1: 292–296.
17. Marttila, R.J. Epidemiological, clinical and virus-serological studies of Parkinson's disease. Reports from the Department of Neurology, University of Turku, No. 6, Turku, 1974.
18. Mawdsley, C. and Gamsu, C.V. Periodicity of speech in Parkinson's disease. *Nature* 1971; 231: 315–316.
19. Oxtoby, M. *Parkinson's Disease Patients and their Social Needs.* Parkinson's Disease Society publication, 1982.

20. Quinn, N., Marsden, C.D. and Parkes, J.D. Complicated response fluctuations in Parkinson's disease: response to intravenous infusion of levodopa. *Lancet* 1982; 2: 412–415.

21. Robins, A.H. Depression in patients with parkinsonism. *Br. J. Psychiat.* 1976; 128: 141–145.

22. Robbins, J.A., Logemann, J.A. and Kirshner, H.S. Swallowing and speech production in Parkinson's disease. *Ann. Neurol.* 1986; 285–287.

23. Robertson, S.J. and Thomson, F. Speech therapy in Parkinson's disease: a study of the efficacy and long term effects of intensive treatment. *Br. J. Dis. Commun.* 1900; 19: 213–224.

24. Rubow, R. and Swift, E. A microcomputer-based wearable biofeedback device to improve transfer of treatment in parkinsonian dysarthria. *J. Speech Hear. Disord.* 1985; 50: 178–185.

25. Scott, S., Caird, F.I. and Williams, I. Speech therapy for Parkinson's disease. *J. Neurol. Neurosurg. Psychiat.* 1983; 46: 140–144.

26. Scott, S. and Caird, F.I. The response of the apparent receptive speech disorder of Parkinson's disease to speech therapy. *J. Neurol. Neurosurg. Psychiat.* 1984; 47: 302–304.

27. Singer, E. The social costs of Parkinson's disease. *J. Chronic Dis.* 1973; 26: 243–254.

28. Sutcliffe, R.L., Prior, R., Mawby, B. and McQuillan, W.J. Parkinson's disease in the district of the Northampton Health Authority (UK): a study of prevalence and disability. *Acta Neurol. Scand.* 1985; 72: 363–379.

# 17 Measurement of health-related quality of life in asthma and chronic obstructive airways disease

**Paul W. Jones**

This review will concentrate on the measurement of health-related 'quality of life' in diseases of the airways – asthma and chronic obstructive airways disease. These are numerically by far the largest group of non-malignant lung diseases, 4% of the population have asthma. Aspects of questionnaire design that are pertinent to airways disease will be covered, particularly where these may be important to users of the questionnaires. However the review will concentrate chiefly on the validation and application of existing questionnaires to diseases of the airways.

## THE CLINICAL PROBLEM

### Patho-physiology of the diseases

Asthma and chronic obstructive airways disease (COAD) share many clinical characteristics and in patients aged over 40 it may be difficult to distinguish between them. The symptoms are essentially the same – breathlessness, wheeze, cough and sputum production. In many respects the disturbances of lung structure and function are also similar – fixed and variable components to airways obstruction and excess production of mucus. In addition, in COAD, loss of alveoli results in emphysema, with resulting pulmonary hypertension and heart failure. While these processes do not occur in asthma, their chief effect is to cause breathlessness – a symptom common to both diseases. In the context of health measurement, there are two broad differences between

301

asthma and COAD that may be important. The first is that COAD is unusual below the age of 40 years unlike asthma which may occur at any age. The second generalization is that asthmatic patients, particularly the younger age group, exhibit greater variability in their airways obstruction compared to COAD patients, however with increasing age, the fixed component of airways obstruction tends to increase in both diseases.

## The natural history of the diseases

COAD and asthma are chronic diseases. Asthma may last six or more decades, while patients with COAD live with progressively increasing impairment for at least 20 years from diagnosis. Cure is not yet possible in asthma and there is little evidence that the natural history of asthma in adults may be modified by therapy. The mortality of asthma is significant. There are around 2000 deaths per year in the UK, some of which may be preventable, although there are few reliable predictive factors. COAD is not curable. In these patients, age is the best predictor of death, closely followed by forced expiratory volume in one second ($FEV_1$). The cessation of smoking before age 55 years is the most effective therapy, although there is a now some evidence that steroid prophylaxis may reduce the rate of progression[31]. Overall, however, the picture for both diseases is one in which doctors currently appear to have little impact on mortality or natural history.

## Therapeutic aims in airways disease

In large measure, current therapy is directed towards reducing symptom severity, frequency of exacerbations and demands on health care. There is evidence that comprehensive treatment programmes may reduce the number of acute exacerbations, visits to primary care physicians and hospital admissions[6,26], but by their nature these studies have concentrated largely on benefits to patients with recurrent acute exacerbations of asthma. The vast majority of patients do not die and, for much of the time, most of them are not having acute exacerbations. They just live with the daily disturbances produced by their condition.

There are two basic forms of therapy – short acting drugs that give rapid improvement in symptoms for a few hours and prophylactic drugs that have no immediate effect but reduce inflammatory processes in the lungs. The latter may reduce the number and severity of acute exacerbations, but for most patients for most of the time, their purpose is to produce symptomatic improvement.

## MECHANISMS LINKING LUNG DISEASE TO HEALTH

The links between lung disease and impaired health are complex. The pathways shown in Figure 17.1 are drawn on the basis of current knowledge. They should not be taken to be the definitive description of mechanisms causing impaired health in lung disease, but they illustrate some important principles. First, the dominant symptom is breathlessness. This is not to deny the importance of cough and sputum production, but breathlessness leads to exercise limitation and is probably the key to a large part of the morbidity associated with these diseases since it produces physical disability. The perception of breathlessness is still poorly understood. In disease-free subjects there are large inter-individual variations in the estimation of breathlessness that are still unexplained[1,40]. Very little is known about the factors that determine the perception of breathlessness in disease. Recently, we have shown that normal subjects can discriminate between the level of their breathlessness and the amount of distress their breathlessness caused them, but wide inter-individual variations were again found[40]. It is not known what limits physical activity – the actual magnitude of breathlessness or the patient's affective response to it.

It will be noted that some of the pathways in illustrated Figure 17.1 form loops, thereby allowing the development of feedback. This feedback may permit the development of self-reinforcing changes that then become independent of the original stimulus and may persist even after removal of the original trigger. An example of this is disuse-induced muscle wasting in the legs resulting from reduced physical activity brought about by breathlessness. Full and immediate cure of the underlying lung disease would not immediately reverse the patient's disability.

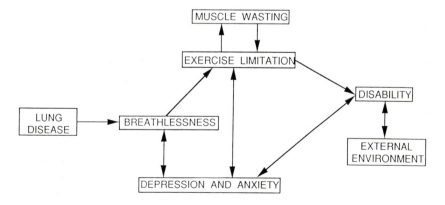

**Figure 17.1** Pathways linking disease in the lungs to impairment, disability and handicap in diseases of the airways

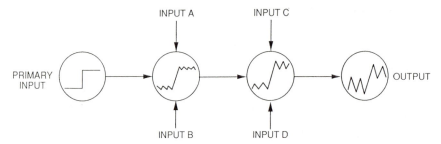

**Figure 17.2** Schematic view of a simple pathway with two intervening steps between input and output. The primary signal is a simple step change. At each step the other inputs (Inputs A–D) feed in to modulate the primary signal so that the output signal contains an element that is recognisably related to the input, but has 'noise' due to the other inputs superimposed upon it

Clinicians operate within in a model, similar to that in Figure 17.1, in which the basic assumption is that improvement in disease process in the lungs will result in beneficial results flowing along the same pathways. Furthermore there is a tendency to believe that there will be a simple quantitative relationship between improvement in lung disease and improved patient well-being. This is probably optimistic in view of the complexity of the pathways involved. This may be illustrated by a simple model, illustrated in Figure 17.2, in which the effect of therapy on a basic disease process is seen as a square wave input into a simple system with a few steps intervening between input and the final output. At each step the signal may amplified or attenuated. In addition, other signals (Inputs A–D) feed in to modulate the primary signal. When the system is assessed simply in terms of its input–output characteristics, these other signals could be considered to be just part of the noise that occurs within any system. This narrow view may be misleading and fail to take into account the important modulating role of these other inputs. This becomes clear if we label the input signal as improved airway calibre, the output signal as perceived well-being and one of the other inputs as the nature of the patients' paid employment. It will be noted that these other input signals may be unrelated to the underlying disease and beyond the limits of therapeutic intervention by the clinician. Continuing with this simple model, it will be seen that the overall effect of therapy on health and well-being will depend on four factors: first, the operating characteristics of the pathway from lung disease to ill health (which may be non-linear and difficult to predict); second, the size of the improved lung function; third, the effect of random variation and noise; fourth, the effect of important modulating inputs.

The theoretical discussion presented above is supported by experimental data demonstrating a generally poor correlation between impaired lung function and physical disability and health. While a rather better correlation has been found between measures of physical impairment (e.g. exercise tolerance) and health. I have reviewed this in detail elsewhere[16]. While correlations may be found between measures of airways obstruction and health, the correlations are too poor to allow accurate prediction of one from the other. Under these circumstances, the outcome of interest (i.e. health) should be measured directly rather than be estimated through a surrogate variable (e.g. $FEV_1$).

## MEASURING IMPAIRED HEALTH IN DISEASES OF THE AIRWAYS

### General requirements

The general requirements of a measure of health in airways disease are no different from any other condition – it should measure health with good accuracy and repeatability. For practical purposes there are two other important properties that have to be assessed. One is the capacity to differentiate between different levels of health in different patients – often termed reliability. The other is the ability to detect changes in the state of health within an individual patient. Theoretically, reliability and sensitivity to change should be closely related properties since a reliable questionnaire should also be sensitive. In practice this may not be the case. Assessments of a questionnaire's reliability tend not to provide a clear indication of the precision with which it discriminates between different levels of health. A questionnaire may have quite coarse scaling intervals and still be reliable if tested on a population with a sufficiently wide range of health states.

Another important property of a health questionnaire is that it should be standardized to allow comparative measurements of health between patients and study populations. The established general health indices are all standardized, but this attribute has been sacrificed in some disease-specific questionnaires to enhance their sensitivity to change. For example, one way in which sensitivity may be increased is through the use change or transition scores in which each patient's response to therapy is measured relative to his or her baseline state. This approach is exemplified in a sensitive measure of breathlessness – the Transition Dyspnea Index[24]. An alternative approach is 'individualization' which allows the subject to tailor parts of the questionnaire to meet his or her specific requirements. This approach, which does not constrain the patient's scoring of disturbance of 'quality of life' to conditions set by the questionnaire's originator, has been used in the Chronic Respiratory Questionnaire[8]. Both of these questionnaires have been used to estimate changes in disability or health following therapy for airways disease, but both suffer from the disadvantage that they are not sufficiently standardized to allow direct comparisons of the size of the therapeutic benefit between different studies. In respiratory medicine it is established practice to use standardized questionnaires such as those produced by the Medical Research Council or American Thoracic Society for the collection of data on respiratory symptoms. I believe that the application of 'quality of life' measures will be limited until measures are available that are both sensitive and standardized. Lung function measurements are internationally standardized, measurements of health in lung disease should be standardized in the same way. Progress has been made in the standardization of respiratory symptom questionnaires in different European languages[5] and we have observed that the level of distress associated with respiratory symptoms appears to be largely independent of language or culture[33]. Standardization is clearly possible, the challenge is to couple this with sensitivity.

### Testing the validity of health measures for use in airways disease

All good health measures have undergone validity testing during their development. While these processes will not be discussed further here, it should be understood that although statistical tests are used at each stage of a questionnaire's development, they do no more than guide the developers in making decisions concerning content and structure. It is not always appreciated how many decisions have to be made during a questionnaire's development and despite the sophistication of the statistical tools used to aid these processes, the questionnaire inevitably reflects the developers' prejudices. It is important that the user of any questionnaire takes steps to establish its validity as a measure of health in the particular disease that they wish to study. The first step is simply to examine its content. When inspecting the Sickness Impact Profile for its applicability to airways disease, one would note that it contains no items that specifically address wheeze, cough or sputum production. These items may be inappropriate in a questionnaire designed to assess the impact of all types of disease on daily life, but their absence should alert one to the possibility that the questionnaire may have low sensitivity in this particular application.

The next step is to test whether the questionnaire actually measures impaired health in the population of interest. This process usually involves tests of convergent validity – comparisons between the questionnaire and other relevant measures of disease activity or health. This presents a problem, since there is usually no single reference measure with which to compare the instrument. Disturbance to health in airways disease is multi-dimensional. Whilst limitation of physical activity may be the single most important determinant of impaired 'quality of life' in diseases of the airways, it is not the only one. For example there is a high degree of psychological morbidity particularly in COAD[4,19,28,35,37], but also in asthma[41]. A multi-dimensional approach to this aspect of validation is required. We have used a panel of reference measures of disease activity, disability and distress that appear to be appropriate to the diseases under study. These include: standard measures of lung spirometry; arterial oxygen saturation; walking distance and ergometer tests of physical exercise tolerance; an established measure of disability – the MRC Dyspnoea Scale; the MRC Respiratory Questionnaire as a measure of respiratory symptoms and the Hospital Anxiety and Depression Scale[42] to measure mood state. The latter was used because it was developed specifically for use in patients with organic disease. One of the questions in the depression limb has quite a high somatic activity component, but we have found little evidence that this item caused any major confounding effect between psychological and physical causes of low physical activity. A further refinement of this validation process is an analysis of the specificity of the questionnaire and its component parts since it is also necessary to demonstrate the absence of an association between one component of the questionnaire and a reference measure concerned with a different aspect of the disease. For example, it has been reported that mood state may have a non-specific effect on responses to questionnaires concerned with specific respiratory symptoms.

The result of all these analyses is a large body of statistical tests in which both positive and negative associations are examined. A single test is rarely of over-riding importance, evidence for the validity and reliability of the questionnaire being built up from many pieces of information. This multivariate approach is not suitable for testing another aspect of the questionnaire's function, however. Many questionnaires produce an aggregate score or index that attempts to sum different aspects of impaired health into a single dimension. The multi-dimensional approach to assessing convergent validity, just described, cannot test the success of these aggregation processes. To address this problem in the context of the validation of a new disease-specific measure – the St George's Respiratory Questionnaire[20], we have drawn upon a slightly circular argument used in a major paper that compared three important general health measures[34]. These three measures were each developed from a different theoretical base with a different structure and scoring system. When applied to a large study population, significant correlations were found between them. On the basis of this finding, the authors argued that each of these measures provided a valid estimate of general health. We have applied a similar argument during the validation of a new measure for airways disease. We used the SIP, one of the three general health measures in the study just described, as a standard against which to compare the new questionnaire. This analysis was not a simple direct comparison of the scores from the two questionnaires since its purpose was to compare the response of the two questionnaires to different aspects of disturbed health and well-being in airways disease. For each of the reference measures of disease activity listed above, we compared the correlation and slope of the regression between the reference measure and the scores for each of the two questionnaires. We argued that if the new questionnaire was correctly constructed, it would show the same pattern of associations with the different areas of disease activity as those found with the Sickness Impact Profile, but with greater sensitivity. Furthermore, we argued that the relative sensitivity of the two questionnaires should be the same across all the different areas of health that were examined. The results of this analysis will be discussed below.

The reader will have noted that considerable emphasis is placed in this review on methods of testing the convergent validity of a questionnaire. The reason for this is that patient populations differ and it cannot be assumed that a questionnaire, no matter how carefully developed, will provide valid, precise and sensitive measurements of health in all populations to which it may be applied. Responsibility for testing the suitability of a particular questionnaire's application lies with the user. Such testing may appear to be complex and multi-faceted, but it is essential. Assays of proven specificity and sensitivity are used elsewhere in medicine, the same standards should apply to measurements of health.

## MEASURES OF GENERAL HEALTH IN DISEASES OF THE AIRWAYS

The use of a general health measure is attractive. These are widely available and have been subject to careful development. I will confine my discussion to two that have been used in asthma and COAD – the Quality of Well-being Scale (QWB) and the Sickness Impact Profile (SIP).

### Quality of Well-being Scale

The validation of this comprehensive measure in airways disease was carried out as part of a study designed to improve compliance to exercise among COPD patients[22]. These patients had severe airways obstruction, their $FEV_1$ was only 36% of the predicted value for their age, height and sex. This study showed significant correlations between the QWB score and spirometric measurements of airways function and exercise tolerance although the shared variance ($r^2 \times 100$) was quite modest (<30%) in each case. There was also a significant correlation between change in exercise tolerance and change in QWB score over a 3-month period, with 16% shared variance. There was no correlation between change in QWB and change in the spirometric measures over the 3-month period. The authors note that when they compared the change in $FEV_1$ with change in QWB score over 18 months, the correlation was significant. They present no details of the size of the relative changes in $FEV_1$ over this period and do not indicate the statistical model used for this analysis. The text does not make it clear whether the analysis was performed using results from all assessments made over the 18 month period or whether it was a straight two time-point comparison. Despite these slight concerns regarding the sensitivity of the QWB, the results from this study clearly show that the QWB has validity as a measure of health in airways obstruction. It should be noted, however, that this study was performed in patients with severe disease, a point that will be discussed at greater length with reference to the SIP. This measure has not been used in any other currently published trials in airways disease, apart from an uncontrolled study of the effect of antibiotic therapy in cystic fibrosis[30].

**Sickness Impact Profile**

This measure was used in two major National Institutes of Health studies in COAD: the intermittent positive pressure bronchodilator (IPPB) study[14] and the long term oxygen therapy study ( the NOTT study)[29]. It is worth noting that the SIP was applied to these studies before its validity for use in such patients was established, although data from the NOTT study was used to establish some validity for its use in that trial[23]. Since that time the SIP has been used in a number of studies[3,19,36,39] and has been shown to discriminate

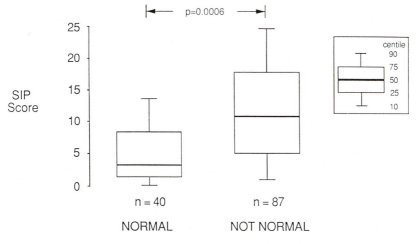

**Figure 17.3** Box plot of total SIP score in 40 patients whose breathing returned to normal between attacks of breathlessness and wheeze and 87 patients whose breathing never returned to normal. The data are from Reference 19, with permission

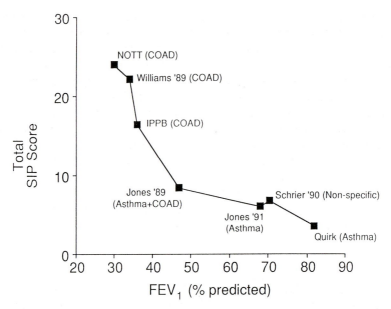

**Figure 17.4** Summary data from seven studies in airways disease relating airways obstruction (FEV$_1$) to Total SIP score. The references are all cited in the text, with exception of Quirk and Jones which are unpublished observations. The total number of patients included in these studies is more than 2000

between different levels of health in patients with airways disease. An example from Ref. 19 is shown in Figure 17.3 which illustrates that the SIP distinguished between patients whose breathing returned to normal between attacks of breathlessness and wheeze and those whose breathing was never normal. Figure 17.4 displays summary data from a number of studies relating FEV$_1$ to SIP score. The physical and psycho-social scores from the SIP show a similar pattern to the total SIP score. It is clear that the SIP score becomes progressively higher with worsening disease, however this relationship is non-linear. Below an FEV$_1$ of 50% predicted, the SIP score appears to rise more rapidly for a given reduction in FEV$_1$ than above this level. With mild disease, large changes in airway function do not appear to be accompanied by commensurately large changes in SIP score. This implies that the SIP may be insensitive to changes in the health of patients with mild to moderate disease. This group includes the great majority of asthmatics.

The SIP has been used in few published controlled clinical trials in airways disease. The IPPB study[14] was not a fair test of its performance because the therapy itself appeared to have no benefit. In the NOTT study[29], there were two groups of patients. One received oxygen for about 12 hours a day while the others received it for 20. At the end of 1 year of therapy, the mortality in the 12 hour group was twice that in the 20 hour group. The SIP scores improved significantly in both, but there was no difference in the improvement in SIP score between the two. There are three possible reasons for this. First, mechanisms responsible for the reduction in mortality may have been unrelated to any factor that altered the impact of the disease on daily life. Second, the SIP may have been too insensitive to detect differences in respiratory-related health. Third, there was a placebo or 'study effect' on the patients' measured well-being that was of sufficient size to mask any differences between treatments. None of these hypotheses can be adequately tested retrospectively. A recent randomized controlled trial of the effect of asthma prophylaxis on the health of asthmatic patients found a rather similar pattern of results to those from the NOTT study. There were highly significant improvements in SIP score but the changes were virtually identical in both treatment and placebo limbs[17]. Using other criteria, however, the patients in this trial who received the active drug – nedocromil sodium – had a significantly greater reduction in the severity of their asthma compared to the placebo group[2]. The implications of these findings will be considered below.

In summary, the SIP is clearly a valid measure of impaired health in patients with diseases of the airways. It appears to be relatively less sensitive for mild to moderate disease compared to severe disease and it is unlikely to have sufficient sensitivity to be of value as a measure of outcome in clinical trials in all but the most severely ill.

## General health measures in airways disease – conclusions

Discussions of the sensitivity of a measure also have to take into account the signal to noise ratio in the measurements. Problems of sensitivity are often associated with a small number of relevant items, however the non-relevant items in the questionnaire may not be simply passive components. In our own studies using the SIP, we found that patients with moderate to severe airways disease did not respond to nearly one third of SIP items. In mild disease, almost 100 items appeared to be largely irrelevant for most patients. This is important, because it is a common experience that patients are content to complete health questionnaires that are relevant to them, but they become bored, irritated or confused when asked to complete a questionnaire with a large number of irrelevant items. Such items may also degrade the accuracy of the the questionnaire if they are misinterpreted or responded to inappropriately by patients suffering from a mild intercurrent illnesses. This may occur with any questionnaire, but matters less when many items can be responded to appropriately. With a low number of appropriate responses, even a few inappropriate responses could have a major effect on the signal to noise ratio of the final score.

Despite the disadvantages of using general health questionnaires in airways disease, I believe that they still have a place such studies. There is now a good body of data describing the relationship between SIP scores and other measures of health and disease in a wide variety of patients with airways disease. Profiles for the SIP category scores from populations of differing severity of airways obstruction have also been published[19,23,36]. Currently, no other standardized questionnaire has been so widely used in airways disease, so the SIP may still act as a standard reference measure of general health in any study of airways disease in which health and well-being are important variables. This picture may change if standardized disease-specific measures become available.

## DISEASE-SPECIFIC MEASURES

Disease-specific measures were developed to provide questionnaires that had greater sensitivity for airways disease than the general health measures. Currently there are three comprehensive disease-specific measures for these diseases and whilst there are differences in the philosophies underlying their development, there is also a common theme since they were each designed to provide a true reflection of the overall impairment of health of the patient population for which they were designed.

To achieve a high level of sensitivity and precision, the items in a disease-specific measure usually address a range of related aspects of the disease for which it was designed. In contrast, a general health measure can afford only limited coverage of the impact of a particular type of clinical condition. Its measurement intervals for any given disease tend to be coarse. Precision in estimates of health have tended to attract less attention than other aspects of questionnaire development and validation, yet it is precision that determines the repeatability and sensitivity of the instrument. This requirement may lead to a major design difference between a general and a disease-specific measure. The former endeavours to avoid redundancy and duplication of items, whereas the latter tends to encourage it. In a general health measure, the presence of multiple items addressing the same aspect of the disease may imbalance the questionnaire in terms of its generalizability. In contrast, the developers of a disease-specific measure may deliberately incorporate a number of related questions to aid precision of measurement in the same way as duplicate or triplicate measures are used in other forms of assay. The first application of this principle to airways disease was in the Dyspnea Index described by Mahler[24]. This instrument, although not a comprehensive measure of health has been used to demonstrate changes in disability with bronchodilators[25] and inspiratory muscle training[11].

## The Chronic Respiratory Questionnaire

This was developed by Guyatt to provide a comprehensive measure of health suitable for detecting changes following therapy in patients with COAD[8]. The questionnaire has four dimensions: dyspnoea, fatigue, emotional function and the patient's feeling of control over the disease (mastery) and was designed to be completed by trained interviewers. It was developed after asking 100 patients with chronic airflow limitation how their quality of life was affected by their illness[7]. It has been shown to be stable with a good level of repeatability when tested six times at 2-week intervals[8]. This questionnaire was designed to measure change, so data concerned with its validation have concentrated on this. It has demonstrated responsiveness to changes in health following a respiratory rehabilitation programme[8] and has been used in a double-blind randomized placebo-controlled study of bronchodilators[10]. In a subsequent analysis of the latter study, the authors demonstrated that changes in spirometry and walking test score correlated with change in Chronic Respiratory Questionnaire score rather better than they did with changes in two measures of disability – the Oxygen Cost Diagram and the MRC Dyspnoea Scale[9]. For example, the shared variance with changes in walking distance was 27% in the case of the Chronic Respiratory Questionnaire, but only 10% with the MRC scale.

The disadvantage with this questionnaire is that the breathlessness comparisons which make it sensitive are not valid between subjects so it is not possible to use the questionnaire to define a population or to make comparisons between patients. It has been stated that a 'significant' change in health will have occurred if, within in each component of the questionnaire, there had been an average improvement per question of half a point (on a seven point scale)[27]. Clinical experience with this questionnaire has lead the authors to state that a change in score of 4 or more in dyspnoea score represents a clinically important difference in physical function[9]. This conclusion does not appear to be the result of any formal sensitivity testing.

This questionnaire was the first comprehensive measure of health specifically developed for use in a disease of the lungs. Although it has certain limitations due to its non-standardized design, it has been shown to achieve its design aim of being able to detect changes in health due to therapy in chronic obstructive airways disease. Perhaps its greatest contribution will have been to introduce many chest physicians to the concept of health measurement.

## The St George's Respiratory Questionnaire

This self-completed questionnaire was designed to meet the need for a sensitive measure of health for use in airways disease that was completely standardized thus allowing comparative measurements between patients and

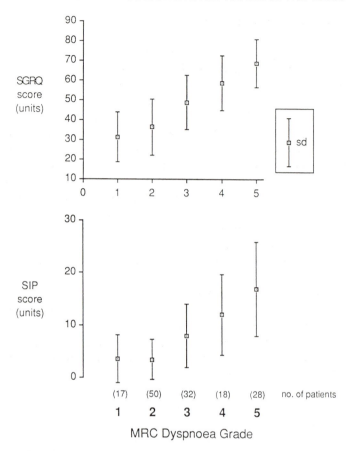

**Figure 17.5** Relationship between disability measured using the MRC Dyspnoea Scale and scores for the Sickness Impact Profile and St George's Respiratory Questionnaire. The data are from reference 19, with permission

between therapies[20,21]. It has three component scores: symptoms which quantify the distress due to respiratory symptoms themselves; activity – a measure of the disturbance to physical activity; impacts – a measure of the overall disturbance of daily life and well-being. A total score is also calculated. The weights for each item in the questionnaire were obtained in a wide range of patients. Age, sex, disease severity and duration appeared to have little effect on the weights[32]. The weights were also obtained from patients in six different countries[33]. There were no differences between weights collected in five of the countries (England, USA, Finland, Italy and Thailand) and interestingly the weights obtained in Thailand and the USA were almost identical. Holland was the only exception where patients tended to indicate a greater level of distress than elsewhere.

The questionnaire has been subject to comprehensive tests of its convergent validity. It showed a pattern of correlation with different measures of disease activity that were very similar to that obtained with the SIP. It was also consistently about two and a half times more sensitive than the SIP across a range of areas of disease activity[20]. The increase in sensitivity was especially apparent in mild disease. This is illustrated in Figure 17.5 which demonstrates that the St George's Questionnaire unlike the SIP, did show a graded difference in scores over all levels of respiratory disability as assessed using the MRC Dyspnoea Scale. The questionnaire has demonstrated sensitivity to changes in a number of aspects of the health of patients with airways disease over a period of a year and has been shown to aggregate these changes together. An attempt has also been made to establish a threshold score for a clinically significant difference in health measured with this questionnaire[20]. It has been used in a 1-year study of the effect of prophylaxis with nedocromil sodium in asthma. The preliminary results from this trial have shown that it can respond to improvements in health following therapy and differentiate quantitatively between the effects of active drug and placebo[17]. A number of other studies using this instrument are under way.

In summary, this questionnaire was designed to provide a standardized measure of health suitable for short or long term studies in patients with a wide range of severity of airways disease, whether asthma or COAD. It is more sensitive than the SIP, but it appears to have an overall balance quite similar to this general health measure. It has demonstrated an ability to detect and quantify health benefits of drug therapy in asthma.

### The Living with Asthma Questionnaire

This questionnaire was designed to provide a quality of life scale which could be used by researchers to evaluate the effectiveness of treatment management programmes for adult asthmatics[13]. It was designed for self-administration. The final 68-item set was identified after a rigorous and large scale programme of evaluation and refinement of items initially identified during focus group sessions. The questionnaire covers 11 domains of life experience. Principal factor analysis demonstrated that while the quality of life of asthmatics covered a number of domains, there was a high degree of cross-correlation between responses in different domains. This suggested that the majority of the domains were uni-dimensional. The scoring system produces a single summary score. The test–retest repeatability for this measure was high. There is little data concerning the validation of this measure against other indices of disease activity and impaired health. The proportion of the variance ($r^2 \times 100$) shared with peak expiratory flow measurements was reported to be 19% and the shared variance with the SIP reported to be 44%[12]. Full details of these validation studies have not been published. Trials are under way using this questionnaire. A preliminary result suggests that the Living with Asthma Questionnaire could detect differences in the health of patients with asthma treated with the long acting bronchodilator salmeterol compared to placebo[15], however no quantification of this difference has yet been published.

### Comparisons between the three disease-specific measures

A comparison of the papers concerned with the development of these three questionnaires illustrates clearly different approaches to the same problem. The development of the Living with Asthma Questionnaire concentrated on the collection of a psychometrically correct questionnaire item set. The St George's Respiratory Questionnaire highlighted the need for standardization and the demonstration of convergent validity, while the Chronic Respiratory Questionnaire placed greatest emphasis on the development of a measure that was sensitive to change. The St George's Questionnaire is thought to be suitable for both asthma and COAD, whilst the other two instruments were specifically designed for use with one or other disease. It is not clear whether separate instruments for these two conditions are needed, or even warranted, since in several respects the two diseases are very similar and often difficult to separate. In addition, development studies for one of the questionnaires could find little influence of age or disease severity on the distress that patients associated with disturbances to their health produced by airways disease[32]. Each appears to have fulfilled the design aims of its originators. It is not possible to make definitive judgements as to which is the 'better' instrument for a particular purpose.

## 'QUALITY OF LIFE' STUDIES IN ASTHMA AND COAD

There are an increasing number of studies using quality of life measures in diseases of the airways. One or two early patterns are emerging. First, there appears to be a disadvantage in using a non-standardized questionnaire since it is not possible to directly compare different patient groups. A second more general problem is the well known 'study effect' on the health of patients recruited to any clinical trial. Quality of life questionnaires allow measurement of the actual size of this effect for the first time. In the NOTT study, significant improvements in SIP scores were recorded in all patients in the study[29]. In the study using nedocromil sodium in mild to moderate asthma ($FEV_1$ 68% predicted), highly significant improvements in the health of patients receiving both placebo and active therapy were recorded using both the SIP and the St George's Respiratory Questionnaire[18], but only the latter detected the health gain due to the active drug[17]. In this study the SIP score fell by nearly 20% from a low baseline score of 6.3. This observation attests to effect on the health of recruiting patients to a clinical trial. In another recent study using the Chronic Respiratory Questionnaire in patients with COAD receiving an inhaled steroid, large and inconsistent placebo effects were recorded in addition to an effect on breathlessness attributable to therapy[38]. These measured improvements in health are probably not directly due to the influence of placebo on the responses to the questionnaires but reflect a true improvement. In the nedocromil sodium study, for example, significant improvements in other measures of disease activity occurred in the group receiving placebo[2]. There are probably a number of reasons for this including greater use by the patients of their routine (i.e. non-study) medication and earlier intervention by clinicians during acute relapses.

The improvements in the health of placebo treated patients may require particular consideration in the design of studies in airways disease. The specific requirements for therapeutic trials on 'quality of life' in airways disease will only emerge with greater experience of the use of these questionnaires in this application. It is already abundantly clear, however, that all studies utilizing these instruments must be strictly randomized, placebo controlled and double blind.


## CONCLUSIONS

There are a range of physiological measurements available for assessing the severity of airways obstruction but these do not appear to provide reliable estimates of impaired health in disease. Over the last few years established measures of general health have been applied to asthma and COAD and new measures developed. An ideal questionnaire would incorporate the specific strengths of each type of measure – standardization and provision of reliable estimates of the overall disturbance of health, as exemplified by the general health measures, coupled with precision and sensitivity to change as demonstrated by the disease-specific measures. The user of any questionnaire will always need to establish that their chosen measure is suitable for the population and study that they are considering. Future developments in health measurement in airways disease will depend on the knowledge gained from the application of these measures to formal clinical trials.


## References

1. Adams, L., Chronos, N., Lane, R. and Guz, A. The measurement of breathlessness induced in normal individuals: individual differences. *Clin. Sci.* 1986; 70: 131–140.

2.  Benbow, A.G. Asthma symptoms and pulmonary function: a one year, placebo controlled study of nedocromil sodium. *Eur. Respir. J.* 1991; 4 (Suppl. 14): 332s.

3.  Bergner, M., Hudson, C.D., Conrad, D.A., Patmont, C.M., McDonald, G.J., Perrin, E.B. and Gilson, B.S. The cost and efficiency of home care for chronic lung patients. *Med. Care* 1988; 26: 566–579.

4.  Borak, J., Sliwinski, P., Piasecki, Z. and Zielinski, J. Psychological status of COPD patients on long term oxygen therapy. *Eur. Respir. J.* 1991; 4: 26–30.

5.  Burney, P.G.J., Laitinen, L.A., Perdrizet, S., Huckauf, H., Tattersfield, A.E., Chinn, S., Poisson, N. and Heeren, A., Britton, J.R. and Jones, T. Validity and repeatability of the IUATLD 1984 bronchial symptoms questionnaire: an international comparison. *Eur. Respir. J.* 1989; 2: 940–945.

6.  Charlton, I., Charlton, G., Broomfield, J. and Mullee, M. Audit of the effect of a nurse run asthma clinic on work load and patient morbidity in a general practice. *Br. J. Gen. Pract.* 1991; 41: 227–232.

7.  Guyatt, G.H., Townsend, M., Berman, L.B. and Pugsley, S.O. Quality of life in patients with chronic airflow limitation. *Br. J. Dis. Chest* 1987; 81: 45–54.

8.  Guyatt, G.H., Berman, L.B., Townsend, M., Pugsley, S.O. and Chambers, L.W. A measure of quality of life for clinical trials in chronic lung disease. *Thorax* 1987; 42: 773–778.

9.  Guyatt, G.H., Townsend, M., Keller, J., Singer, J. and Nogradi, S. Measuring functional status in chronic lung disease: conclusions from a randomized control trial. *Respir. Med.* 1989; 83: 293–297.

10. Guyatt, G.H., Townsend, M., Pugsley, S.O., Keller, J.A., Short, D., Taylor, D.W. and Newhouse, M.T. Bronchodilators in chronic air-flow limitation. *Am. Rev. Respir. Dis.* 1987; 135: 1069–1074.

11. Harver, A., Mahler, D.A. and Daubenspeck, J.A. Targeted inspiratory muscle training improves respiratory muscle function and reduces dyspnea in patients with chronic obstructive pulmonary disease. *Ann. Intern. Med.* 1989; 111: 117–124.

12. Hyland, M.E. The Living with Asthma Questionnaire. *Respir. Med.* 1991; 85 (Suppl. B): 13–16.

13. Hyland, M.E., Finnis, S. and Irvine, S.H. A scale for assessing quality of life in adult asthma sufferers. *J. Psychosom. Res.* 1991; 35: 99–110.

14. Intermittent Positive Pressure Trial Group. Intermittent positive pressure breathing therapy of chronic obstructive pulmonary disease. *Ann. Intern. Med.* 1983; 99: 612–620.

15. Jones, K.P., Coward, G.A., Hyland, M.E. Salmeterol hydroxynaphtoate in the treatment of mild asthma in primary care. *Eur. Respir. J.* 1991; 4 (Suppl. 14): 332s.

16. Jones, P.W. Quality of life measurement in diseases of the airways. *Thorax* 1991; 46: 676–682.

17. Jones, P.W. Symptoms and 'quality of life' in asthma – a one year placebo controlled trial with nedocromil sodium. *Thorax* 1991; 46: 759p.

18. Jones, P.W. Quality of life in asthma following therapy with nedocromil sodium – a one year placebo controlled trial. *Eur. Respir. J.* 1991; 4 (Suppl. 14): 333s.

19. Jones, P.W., Baveystock, C.M. and Littlejohns, P. Relationships between general health measured with the Sickness Impact Profile and respiratory symptoms,

physiological measures and mood in patients with chronic airflow limitation. *Am. Rev. Respir. Dis.* 1989; 140: 1538–1543.

20. Jones, P.W., Quirk, F.H. and Baveystock, C.M. The St George's Respiratory Questionnaire. *Respir. Med.* 1991; 85 (Suppl. B): 25–31.

21. Jones, P., Quirk, F., Baveystock, C. and Littlejohns, P. A self-complete measure for chronic airflow limitation – the St George's Respiratory Questionnaire. *Am. Rev. Respir. Dis.* 1991 (In press).

22. Kaplan, R.M., Atkins, C.J. and Timms, R. Validity of a well-being scale as an outcome measure in chronic obstructive pulmonary disease. *J. Chronic Dis.* 1984; 37: 85–95.

23. McSweeny, J., Grant, I., Heaton, R.K., Adams, K.M. and Timms, R.M. Life quality of patients with chronic obstructive pulmonary disease. *Arch. Intern. Med.* 1982; 142: 473–478.

24. Mahler, D.A., Weinberg, D.H. and Wells, C.K., Feinstein, A.R. Measurement of dyspnoea. Contents, interobserver correlates of two new clinical indexes. *Chest* 1984; 85: 751–758.

25. Mahler, D.A., Matthay, R.A., Snyder, P.E., Wells, C.K. and Loke, J. Sustained-release theophylline reduces dyspnea in nonreversible obstructive airways disease. *Am. Rev. Respir. Dis.* 1985; 131: 22–25.

26. Mayo, P.H., Richman, J. and Harris, W.H. Results of a program to reduce hospital admissions for adult asthma. *Ann. Intern. Med.* 1990; 112: 864–871.

27. Morgan, M.D.L. Experience of using the CRQ (Chronic Respiratory Questionnaire). *Respir. Med.* 1991; 85 (Suppl. B): 23–24.

28. Morgan, A.D., Peck, D.F., Buchanan, D.R. and McHardy, G.J.R. Psychological factors contributing to disproportionate disability in chronic bronchitis. *J. Psychosom. Res.* 1983; 27: 259–263.

29. Nocturnal oxygen therapy trial (NOTT) group. Continuous or nocturnal oxygen therapy in hypoxemic chronic obstructive lung disease. *Ann. Intern. Med.* 1980; 93: 391–398.

30. Orenstein, D.M., Pattishall, E.N., Nixon, P.A., Ross, E.A. and Kaplan, R.M. Quality of well-being before and after antibiotic treatment of pulmonary exacerbations in patients with cystic fibrosis. *Chest* 1990; 98: 1081–1084.

31. Postma, D.S., Peters, I., Steenhuis, E.J. and Sluiter, H.J. Moderately severe chronic obstructive airways obstruction. Can corticosteroids slow down obstruction? *Eur. Respir. J.* 1988; 1: 22–26.

32. Quirk, F.H. and Jones, P.W. Patients' perception of distress due to symptoms and effects of asthma on daily living and an investigation of possible influential factors. *Clin. Sci.* 1990; 79: 17–21.

33. Quirk, F.H., Baveystock, C.M., Wilson, R.C. and Jones, P.W. Influence of demographic and disease related factors on the degree of distress associated with symptoms and restrictions on daily living due to asthma in six countries. *Eur. Respir. J.* 1991; 4: 167–171.

34. Read, J.L., Quinn, R.J. and Hoefer, M.A. Measuring overall health: an evaluation of three important approaches. *J. Chronic Dis.* 1987; 40 (Suppl.): 7s–21s.

35. Rosser, R., Denford, J., Heslop, A., Kinston, W., Macklin, D., Minty K, Moynihan, C., Muir, B., Rein, L. and Guz, A. Breathlessness and psychological

morbidity in chronic bronchitis and emphysema: a study of psychotherapeutic management. *Psychol. Med.* 1983; 13: 93–110.

36. Schrier, A.C., Dekker, F.W., Kaptein, A.A. and Dijkman, J.H. Quality of life in elderly patients with chronic non-specific lung disease seen in family practice. *Chest* 1990; 98: 894–899.

37. Swinburn, C.R., Wakefield, J.M., Newman, S.P. and Jones, P.W. Evidence of prednisolone induced mood change ('steroid euphoria') in patients with chronic obstructive airways disease. *Br. J. Clin. Pharmac.* 1988; 26: 709–713.

38. Weir, D.C. and Burge, P.S. The short term effect of 1500 mcg and 3000 mcg per day of inhaled beclomethasone diproprionate (BDP) in patients with chronic airflow obstruction (CAO). *Eur. Respir. J.* 1991; 4 (Suppl. 14): 251s.

39. Williams, S.J. and Bury, M.R. Impairment, disability and handicap in chronic respiratory illness. *Soc. Sci. Med.* 1989; 29: 609–616.

40. Wilson, R.C. and Jones, P.W. Differentiation between the intensity of breathlessness and the distress it evokes in normal subjects during exercise. *Clin. Sci.* 1991; 80: 65–70.

41. Yellowlees, P.M. and Ruffin, R.E. Psychological defenses and coping styles in patients following a life-threatening attack of asthma. *Chest* 1989; 95: 1298–1303.

42. Zigmund, A.S. and Snaith, R.P. The hospital anxiety and depression scale. *Acta Psychiatr. Scand.* 1983; 67: 361–370.

# 18 Measuring quality of life in hypertension

**Astrid Fletcher and Christopher Bulpitt**

The treatment of hypertension is long-term and is directed towards the reduction of mortality and morbidity, especially from stroke and heart disease (CHD). Although treatment undoubtedly reduces strokes, and to a lesser extent CHD events[4], there are a variety of unresolved issues. These include what levels of blood pressure should be treated, whether indications for treatment should also include prognostic factors such as age, gender, and the presence of other cardiovascular risk factors, which treatment to use (including non-pharmacological approaches), adverse effects and the monetary costs of treatment. Adverse effects include factors which may affect morbidity, such as elevated blood lipids, uric acid, glucose intolerance, and more diffuse side-effects which impair well-being, and may cause patients to discontinue treatment. In the trial of the European Working Party on High Blood Pressure in the Elderly (EWPHE) it was calculated that in every 1000 patients treated for one year, active treatment (a potassium sparing diuretic combination, plus methyldopa in one third) was associated with an excess over placebo of four cases of gout, 23 of an abnormal serum creatinine, nine of diabetes, 124 with a dry mouth and 71 complaining of diarrhoea[13]. In this trial there were relatively few withdrawals due to side-effects. In contrast over the 5 years of the Medical Research Council trial, 16% of patients on active treatment had withdrawn owing to side-effects: impotence, lethargy, nausea, dizziness and headache were the major reasons[20].

Active treatment was discontinued in 9% of patients for definite side-effects over the 5 years of the Hypertension Detection and Follow-up Program (HDFP)[7] and in a further 23% for possible side-effects. Eight percent of all male patients discontinued treatment because of sexual problems. Lethargy and gastrointestinal symptoms were the commonest reasons for discontinuation (4–6%) in all patients.

Psychological well-being may also be affected both by drug treatment and by labelling the patient with a diagnosis of hypertension[29]. Studies have suggested impairment of memory and learning ability in both treated and untreated hypertensives[14,18,27,28].

Earlier case-reports indicated an association between depression and beta-blocker therapy in hypertensive patients, ranging from 0.1 to 6%[26]. More recently, an excess use of tricyclic antidepressants was found in patients on β-adrenoceptor blocking drugs compared to other forms of anti-hypertensive therapy in a large random sample of Medicaid recipients[1].

Although all these studies suggest impairment in quality of life due to side-effects of treatment, a more precise evaluation and quantification of the effects of therapy is required. In the next section we will discuss some of the issues involved in the measurement of quality of life in trials of anti-hypertensive therapies.

## WHAT ASPECTS OF QUALITY OF LIFE SHOULD BE MEASURED?

Some authors advocate the investigation of a whole constellation of variables which have been shown to be important in determining quality of life[21,24]. This would include determination of:

*Demographic* variables such as work, educational income, status, *social* membership and participation in social and family groups, work satisfaction, and the ability to feel a worthwhile member of a group[17]. The pursuit of leisure time interests is also relevant in Western society. Social support has been shown to be an influential factor in the maintenance of health[3].

*Psychological*: emotional level, psychiatric morbidity, intellectual performance, ability to perform tasks, loss of libido.

*Physical* performance of the individual at work, aspects of self-care such as bathing and dressing, mobility and confinement.

*Spiritual*, namely the ability of the individual to transcend everyday life by aesthetic or religious experiences.

It may be argued that, ideally, long-term and comprehensive evaluation of the effect of antihypertensive treatment on quality of life should include all the above components. There are, however, serious restrictions to this approach in terms of the feasibility, design and costs of such a study: a large battery of tests and questionnaires would be needed requiring a variety of specialist training staff. Also, patients may be reluctant to undergo several hours of tests and many measures, for example social support, are unlikely to be sensitive to the short term effects of drug treatment. When a quality of life evaluation is included in trials primarily designed to assess the efficacy of drugs in lowering blood pressure, only those variables that are likely to be fairly immediately responsive to the effect of a drug should be included. It is unlikely that any major demographic changes would occur over a short period, even if the treatment did, in fact, improve the patient's physical and mental well-being sufficiently for a change in work or housing life-style to be considered.

Having selected the areas to be covered, the measurements of these must be appropriate to the condition and its treatment, for example general profiles such as the Sickness Impact Profile (SIP[2]) and the Nottingham Health Profile (NHP[16]) describe limitations in life-style due to ill health, such as loss of self care and mobility. These would not be appropriate for the majority of hypertensive patients who are free of symptoms prior to diagnosis and may experience only the possible psychological effects of labelling[19] and the adverse effects of drug treatment. However in a long term study, a proportion of hypertensive patients will suffer stroke or develop heart disease with consequent loss of dependence, and in this situation, these questionnaires (SIP, NHP) would be appropriate. In this chapter we will consider only the measurement of QOL in short-term trials ($<1$ year) of antihypertensive treatments.

The measures involved in the assessment of QOL, like any measure, need to be valid, repeatable, and capable of change (responsive) in order to detect any differences in QOL occurring as a result of treatment or when comparing treatments. The questions should be acceptable to the patient.

The questionnaire should include symptomatic (physical) well-being, psychological well-being and perception of the effects of antihypertensive treatment on life-style, measure of positive well-being, such as vitality and performance and satisfaction at work. Objective tests of cognitive function may also be included.

## STANDARDIZATION OF METHODS

The patients should provide the information in response to a self-administered questionnaire or directly to an interviewer who asks an exactly defined question. A third party should not be consulted and therefore the patients must give their response in a quiet area without the possibility of interruption. This is best provided in a separate room, the patients giving their answers before seeing any medical staff. In this situation they will not be able to consult their family, nor will they be influenced by such factors as knowledge of their current blood pressure, or need for an increase in tablets.

Whether it is better for a questionnaire to be administered by an interviewer or self-completed depends on the complexity and difficulty of the interview, the health status and literacy of the subject, the skills of the interviewer and costs and other practical considerations. Self-administered questionnaires are most commonly used in large multi-centre trials where training, stan-dardising, and deploying interviewing staff may not be feasible. A researcher or medical practitioner may not be the best interviewer, since they are likely to inject considerable bias, albeit unconsciously, into the interview process.

In a single-blind European trial of antihypertensive therapies, the questionnaires were designed to be completed by the patients, but in fact 50% were administered by the patient's physician. Although the responses and psychological well-being were similar in the self-assessed and doctor-assessed groups at the start of the trial, the results at the end of the trial showed a considerable discrepancy. Using the data from the self-administered questionnaires, both drug groups showed an improvement after 3 months' treatment, but the fall in the symptom complaint rate was significantly greater in patients treated with an angiotensin converting enzyme (ACE) inhibitor than a centrally acting drug[9]. The physician-assessed group showed a different pattern of results; patients on the centrally acting drug showed deterioration in most areas, while those on the ACE inhibitor showed considerable improvement. These data suggest bias owing to the physicians' expectations of the effects of a drug and highlight the unreliability of assessment of quality of life in single-blind or open trials. The nature of the reporting of effects of treatment, and the desire of the patient to please the physician, seen as a giver-of-care, has frequently been discussed.

## MULTI-NATIONAL TRIALS

The result of trials of therapy should be generalizable to the patient population. Concern is often expressed that quality of life methods may not be valid in different countries. Several quality of life instruments have been used in different Western countries, and in general, shown similar patterns of scores. In the SIP each statement has a weighted value based on perception of its relative severity by ratings from health service professionals, and a sample of general practice patients in the United States. The SIP, with a few modifications to colloquial English, was used in a longitudinal study of disability in an inner city area in London[25]. There was very little difference between the new weights derived for the English population and the original American version. Methods used in antihypertensive trials in Europe showed a similar response in the reporting of symptoms[9]. Westernized countries, however, probably share a cultural uniformity of life-style, values and health beliefs.

In international trials of quality of life, it is particularly important to standardize methods at training sessions. Questionnaires should be translated and back-translated by a different person who has not seen the original to ensure that the translation is accurate. The language must also be acceptable to the person in the street. Sometimes it is not possible to find an equivalent meaning. For example, in our experience, the Dutch do not have vivid dreams, only nightmares, and the Germans never feel shaky!

## RESULTS FROM TRIALS OF ANTIHYPERTENSIVE TREATMENT USING QUALITY OF LIFE MEASURES

### 1. Quality of life measures in comparative trials of ACE inhibitors

In 1986 Croog and colleagues published the results of the first major trial using quality of life methods in hypertension and conducted in the United States (US)[6]. This was a randomized double-blind trial of 6 months duration in 626 men with mild to moderate hypertension randomized to captopril, methyldopa, or propranolol. Hydrochlorothiazide was added as needed to control the blood pressure. The trial employed interviewers and used a large number of measures of QOL. After 6 months treatment a significant benefit for captopril compared to methyldopa was shown in a measure of overall well-being, in physical symptoms, in self rated work performance, in a measure of cognitive function, and in an overall measure of Life Satisfaction. There were fewer differences between captopril and propranolol with significant differences being found in favour of captopril in general well-being, sexual dysfunction and physical symptoms. Propranolol patients did better than methyldopa in work performance.

Certain reservations were expressed about the trial, primarily in the choice of comparator drugs, and in the exclusion of women. It should be pointed out however that at the time this trial was set up, propranolol and methyldopa were among the most commonly prescribed antihypertensive agents in the US, and that both these drugs had been used in the large placebo controlled trials which had established the benefits of stroke reduction by anti-hypertensive treatment.

Since then several trials have examined whether these benefits for ACE inhibitors are also found when compared to newer drugs[5,11,12,15,23,30]. In all the studies atenolol was one of the comparator drugs and in two trials the third treatment group was a calcium channel blocker, either verapamil or nifedipine.

Similar dimensions of quality of life were assessed in all trials and included those aspects which potentially might be affected by antihypertensive treatment. These included psychological well-being, work performance, sexual and sleep dysfunction and symptomatic complaints. Objective tests of cognitive function were included in some trials. The questionnaires used to measure quality of life included standard instruments with reasonable reassurance about the reliability of the instruments used and their ability to show changes.

### Global measures

The trials found no differences between ACE inhibitors, atenolol, and the calcium channel blockers, (verapamil or nifedipine) in global measures of psychological and general well-being and life satisfaction. The adverse effect of propranolol suggested in the 1986 Croog study was confirmed in the trial by Steiner and colleagues. Both atenolol and enalapril were associated with positive changes on the life satisfaction scale compared to negative changes on propranolol. In a further trial nifedipine was associated with a significantly higher level of side-effects and withdrawal rate, despite a possible reduction in fatigue[11]. The Psychological Well-Being Index was used in four of the trials. In the original Croog study significant differences of 3.8 units were observed between captopril and methyldopa, and of 2.5 units between captopril and propranolol. In general the differences observed between ACE inhibitors and atenolol were of a smaller order than those seen between ACE inhibitors and either propranolol or methyldopa. In the trial comparing cilazapril with atenolol and nifedipine, the largest of the recent trials and of the same duration as the 1986 Croog study, the average result showed only a very small difference between the ACE inhibitor and atenolol (0.7 units), and nifedipine (0.5 units). The 95% confidence intervals excluded an effect between cilazapril and atenolol, and between cilazapril and nifedipine of the size seen for captopril and for methyldopa but not the difference of 2.5 between captopril and propranolol.

### Mood

Measures of overall well-being may conceal specific effects on mood. In Steiner et al.'s study both captopril and enalapril were significantly different from atenolol and propranolol in the depressed mood subscale although the adverse effect for atenolol was less than for propranolol. None of the other trials reviewed found significant differences in measures of depression. The percentage increase in score on measures of depressed mood ranged from 3% in favour of cilazapril compared to atenolol[11] to an increase of 19% by atenolol compared with captopril[12], with 95% confidence limits from the two largest trials from –22% to +22%[11,23]. Differences between ACE inhibitors and beta blockers may also reflect improvements in mood as a result of ACE inhibition. In the early days of ACE therapy there were suggestions of an anti-depressant[32] or indeed potentially euphoric effect of ACE inhibitors. Steiner et al. found similar improvements in vitality and positive well-being with ACE inhibitors and atenolol but not propranolol. Little change was observed with ACE inhibitors compared either to atenolol or to nifedipine in measures of vigour[11,23]. Overall these results do not support an association of ACE inhibitors with mood elevation but the instruments used may not have been sensitive to more subtle effects.

## COGNITIVE FUNCTION

### Psychomotor speed and concentration

Trail Making B is a test of the time taken to join letters and numbers in sequence, and was used in several of the trials[5,6,11]. Significant differences were found between captopril and methyldopa (8 seconds in favour of captopril) but not between propranolol and captopril (2 seconds). In the study of black hypertensives there were differences in favour of atenolol compared to captopril for men (12 seconds) and in favour of captopril compared to atenolol for women (4 seconds)[5]. The sample size was smaller and these differences were not significant. Very small differences were observed between cilazapril, atenolol and nifedipine with atenolol and nifedipine treated patients being 2–3 seconds faster than cilazapril patients[11]. The 95% confidence intervals for the differences ranged from –7 to +3 excluding the size of difference between captopril and methyldopa observed in the Croog et al. trial[6]. This suggests that the differences previously observed reflected adverse effects of methyldopa rather than improvements with captopril.

Other workers have found differences between ACE inhibitors and beta blockers in other measures of psychomotor speed and alertness. Herrick and colleagues reported that, in the Digit Symbol Substitution Test and Paced Auditory Serial Addition Task, hypertensive patients treated with enalapril showed significantly greater improvement compared to baseline than atenolol treated patients[15].

*Verbal and visual memory*

In three trials verbal memory was assessed using Digit Span tests (repetition of digits both forwards and backwards). No differences were found between ACE inhibitors, propranolol, atenolol or verapamil[5,15,30]. Steiner et al.'s trial also and showed no comparative effects on a range of other test of verbal memory, and both Croog et al.[6] and Herrick et al.[15] reported no differences between ACE inhibitors, beta blockers and methyldopa in tests of visual memory.

No differences in a scale of self reports of problems with memory or concentration were found between ACE inhibitors and atenolol in two large trials[11,23]. A benefit for both captopril and propranolol in comparison with methyldopa in self reported work performance was found[6]. Propranolol patients showed little change.

In conclusion, when ACE inhibitors and atenolol are compared neither drug appears to offer any important benefits over the other. The question of whether atenolol produces more subtle effects on mood and cognition, both benefits and disadvantages, still remains. Nor can we completely exclude the possibility of similarly subtle effect with ACE inhibitors.

## 2. Quality of life measures in comparative trials of calcium channel blockers

Two trials discussed above included a calcium channel blocker. In the Croog *et al.*[5] study no differences were observed between verapamil and either atenolol or captopril in black hypertensives. However the results were presented separately for men and women and the sample sizes were rather small. The results of the trial comparing nifedipine with atenolol and cilazapril showed mixed effects[11]. Symptomatic complaints were more frequent in the nifedipine group throughout the trial and also accounted for a significantly higher discontinuation rate on this treatment (17% discontinued compared to 8% and 5% on atenolol and cilazapril respectively). On the other hand, nifedipine patients reported significantly fewer problems in the fatigue score than patients on either cilazapril or atenolol.

Testa and colleagues reported the results of a 24 week comparison of atenolol with nifedipine gastrointestinal therapeutic system (GITS)[31]. Only men were included and nifedipine was used in a novel preparation. Their results, showing a significant benefits for nifedipine compared to atenolol across a range of quality of life dimensions, were based only on the patients who completed the trial although a large proportion of patients on nifedipine (40%) and atenolol (32%) withdrew. Analysis of all randomized subjects indicated very little difference in quality of life between the two drugs. Withdrawal due to adverse effects was more common on nifedipine (16%) compared to atenolol (4%), $p < 0.001$.

There have been a few other trials in which calcium channel blockers have been evaluated against other therapies.

We have reported the results of a randomized double blind trial of verapamil compared with propranolol in the UK[10]. Patients were either new hypertensives identified through screening, or treated hypertensives who had failed to respond to previous therapy and who satisfied the blood pressure entry criteria after a 3 week wash-out period. The BP entry criteria were a diastolic pressure on two consecutive occasions within 3 weeks of 95–115 mmHg. After a 3 week single blind placebo run in, patients were randomized to double blind treatment with either verapamil (240–480 mg daily) ($n = 47$) or propranolol (160–320 mg daily) ($n = 47$) for 4 months. Quality of life questionnaires were completed by the patients under standardized conditions in the clinic, at the end of the placebo run in and after 6 and 16 weeks on double blind treatment. The questionnaires consisted of the following QOL measurement. Symptomatic side-effects of treatment were evaluated from a checklist of 23 symptoms and side-effects. A complaint rate was derived from this checklist. An activity and well-being index (Health Status Index) was derived from responses to questions on work, sickness absence, and interference with life-style caused by treatment. Psychiatric morbidity was assessed by the Symptom Rating Test, both overall and for five subscales: anxiety, depression, somatic, cognitive and hostility. The quality of life results showed an overall trend of improvement with verapamil and deterioration with propranolol. Little change was observed in the verapamil patients in the reporting of symptoms and side-effects compared to an increase in propranolol ($p < 0.05$). The Health Status Index increased on verapamil and fell on propranolol ($p < 0.05$), a rise indicates an improvement. Psychiatric morbidity tended to improve in patients on verapamil while patients taking propranolol showed deteriorations in all the psychological scores except hostility. However only the somatic scale was significantly different between the drugs. Patients on propranolol reported significantly more weak limbs, blocked nose and a slower walking pace compared to verapamil, while the prevalence of constipation increased significantly on verapamil compared to propranolol. Nine patients on verapamil and 13 on propranolol withdrew before the end of the double blind period, principally for side-effects (five on verapamil and eight on propranolol).

We evaluated QOL in a 6-month double-blind trial in six European countries of patients on a diuretic and randomized to additional pinacidil ($n=110$) (25–100 mg daily) or nifedipine slow release ($n=107$) (2080 mg daily)[8]. Blood pressure entry criteria were a sustained diastolic pressure over 95 mmHg and previously uncontrolled on a diuretic plus one additional antihypertensive agent. The measurements of QOL were essentially the same as in the trial described above, but with additional questions on expected side-effects such as hirsutism, and heartburn. Eighteen patients on pinacidil and 12 on nifedipine withdrew due to side-effects such as oedema (both drugs) and flushing (nifedipine).

The average number of symptomatic complaints fell on both drugs with significant decreases in the reporting of headaches, sleepiness and blurred vision on nifedipine. Complaints of heartburn increased significantly on nifedipine and of body hair on pinacidil. The drugs differed in their effect on psychiatric morbidity, as measured by the Symptom Rating Test. At the end of the trial patients on pinacidil showed a significant improvement in the total and cognitive scores compared to nifedipine ($p < 0.05$). The Health Status Index improved on both drugs.

The trials described above have shown different results on the effects of calcium channel blockers on QOL. A part of this difference may be attributed to the different pharmacological properties of the drugs used. Nifedipine and nitrendipine, calcium channel blockers of the dihydropyridine class, are potent vasodilators while verapamil has greater chronotropic and inotropic depressant action. The results of a randomized controlled trial that directly compared verapamil slow release with nifedipine retard have recently been published[22]. The statistically significant increase in symptoms on nifedipine was due mainly to swollen ankles and flushing. Measures of psychiatric morbidity tended to improve on verapamil and deteriorate on nifedipine. Only the change in cognitive function was significant between the drugs, being worse on nifedipine ($p = 0.05$).

The two drugs therefore differed in their effects on measures of quality of life. The improvements in symptomatic complaints and psychological well-being on verapamil may have been due to inclusion in a trial, although we cannot exclude the possibility of a drug effect. Conversely the increase in symptoms and self assessed cognitive impairment on nifedipine were considered to be side-effects of the drug.

## CONCLUSIONS

In this chapter we have reviewed some of the methodological considerations in measuring quality of life in comparative trials of antihypertensive treatments, and described some results from such trials. It is important to be aware that we cannot make a direct interpretation of the absolute effects on quality of life of the antihypertensive agents without a comparison with a placebo group. Our interpretation is based on the relative effects of drugs in a trial. This is less satisfactory than a comparison with placebo, and there is a strong argument for incorporating a placebo comparison, at least at lower levels of blood pressure.

We conclude that formal assessment of quality of life in trials of antihypertensive treatments has provided the treating physician with a more comprehensive picture of the adverse effects and benefits of drug treatment. The well-being of patients on long term antihypertensive treatment is too important to be left to anecdotal reports.

## References

1. Avorn, J., Everitt, D.E. and Weiss, S. Increased anti-depressant use in patients prescribed beta-blockers. *J. Am. Med. Assoc.* 1986; 255: 357.
2. Bergner, M., Bobbitt, R.A. and Carter, W.B. *et al.* The Sickness Impact Profile: development and final revision of a health status measure. *Med. Care* 1981; 19: 787–805.
3. Cassel, J. The contribution of the social environment to host resistance. *Am. J. Epidemiol.* 1976; 104: 107.
4. Collins, R., Peto, R. and MacMahon, S. *et al.* Blood pressure, stroke and coronary heart disease. Part 2, short term reductions in blood pressure: overview of randomised drug trials in their epidemiological context. *Lancet* 1990; 335: 827–38.
5. Croog, S.H., Kong, W., Levine, S., Weir, M.R., Baume, R.M. and Saunders, E. Hypertensive black men and women. Quality of life and effects of antihypertensive medications. *Arch Intern Med.* 1990; 150: 1733–41.
6. Croog, S.H., Levine, S., Testa, M.A., Brown, B., Bulpitt, C.J., Jenkins, C.D., Klerman, G.L. and Williams, G.H. The effects of antihypertensive therapy on the quality of life. *N. Engl. J. Med.* 1986; 314: 1657–64.
7. Curb, J.D., Borhani, N.O., Blaszkanski, R.P., Simbaldi, F. and Williams, W. Long-term surveillance for adverse effects of antihypertensive drugs. *J. Am. Med. Assoc.* 1985; 253: 3263.

8. Fletcher, A.E., Battersby, C. and Bulpitt, C.J. on behalf of the European Pinacidil Study Group. Quality of life on hypertensive treatment: results from a randomised double blind trial of pinacidil and nifedipine. *J. Hypertens.* 1989; 7: 3645.

9. Fletcher, A.E., Hunt, B.M. and Bulpitt, C.J. Evaluation of quality of life in clinical trials of cardiovascular disease. *J. Chronic Dis.* 1989; 40: 557–66.

10. Fletcher, A.E., Chester P.C., Hawkins, C.M.A., Latham, A.N., Pike, L.A. and Bulpitt, C.J. The effects of verapamil and propranolol on quality of life in hypertension. *J. Human Hypertens. 1989; 3: 125–30.*

11. Fletcher, A.E., Bulpitt, C.J., Chase, D., Collins, W., Furberg, C.D., Goggin, T.K., Hewett, A.J. and Neiss, A.M. Quality of life on three antihypertensive treatments: cilazapril, atenolol, nifedipine. Second International Symposium on ACE Inhibition, London, 17–21 February 1991.

12. Fletcher, A.E., Bulpitt, C.J., Hawkins, C.M., Havinga, T.K., ten Berge, B.S., May, J.F., Schuurman, F.H., van der Veur, E. and Wesseling, H. Quality of life on normotensives on the Wechsler adult intelligence scale: initial findings. *J. Gerontol.* 1986; 41: 169.

13. Fletcher, A., Amery, A., Birkenhager, W., Bulpitt, C., Clement, D., De Leeuw, P., Deruyterre, M.L., De Schaepdryver, A., Dollery, C., Fagard, R., Forette, F., Forte, J., Henry, J.F., Koistinen, A., Leonetti, G., Lund-Johansen, P., Nissinen, A., O'Brien, E., O'Malley, K., Pelemana, W., Petrie, J., Staessen, J., Terzoli, J., Thijs, L., Tuomilheto, J., Webster, J. and Williams, B. Risks and benefits in the trial of the European Working Party on High Blood Pressure in the Elderly. *J. Hypertens.* 1991; 9: 225–30.

14. Franchesci, M., Tancredit, A., Smirne, S., Mercinelli, A. and Canmal, N. Cognitive process in hypertension. *Hypertension* 1986; 21: 641.

15. Herrick, A.L., Waller, P.C., Bern, K.E., Pringle, S.D., Callender, J.S., Robertson, M.R., Findlay, J.G., Murray, G.D., Reid, J.L., Lorrimer, A.R., Weir, R.J., Carmichael, H.J., Robertson, J.I.S., Ball, S.G. and McInnes, G.T. Comparison of enalapril and atenolol in mild to moderate hypertension. *Am. J. Med.* 1989; 86: 421–6.

16. Hunt, S.M., McEwen, J. and McKenna, S.P. *Measuring Health Status.* Croom Helm, London, 1986.

17. Levine, S. and Croog, S.H. The primary care physician and the patients' quality of life. *Qual. Life Cardiovasc. Care*, 1984; 1: 129.

18. Lichter, I., Richardson, P.J. and Wyke, M.A. Differential effects of atenolol and enalapril on tests of memory during treatment for essential hypertension. *Br. J. Clin. Pharmacol.*, 1986; 21: 641.

19. McDonald, L.A., Sackett, D.L., Haynes, R.B. and Taylor, W. Hypertension: the effects of labelling on behaviour. *Qual. Life Cardiovasc. Care* 1985; 1: 129–39.

20. Medical Research Council Working Party on Mild to Moderate Hypertension. Adverse reactions to bendrofluazide and propranolol for the treatment of mild hypertension. *Lancet*, 1981; 2: 539.

21. Najman, J.M. and Levine, S. Evaluating the impact of medical care and technologies on the quality of life: a review and critique. *Soc. Sci. Med.*, 1981; 15: 107.

22. Palmer, A., Fletcher, A., Hamilton, G., Muriss, S. and Bulpitt, C. A comparison of verapamil and nifedipine on quality of life. *Br. J. Clin. Pharmacol.*, 1990; 30: 365–70.

23. Palmer, A.J., Fletcher, A.E., Rudge, P., Andrews, C., Callaghan, T.S. and Bulpitt, C.J. Quality of life in hypertensives treated with atenolol or captopril: a double blind cross over trial. Second International Symposium on ACE Inhibition, London, 17–21 February 1991.

24. Patrick, D.L., Bush, J.W. and Chen, M.M. Towards an operational definition of health. *J. Health Soc. Behav.*, 1973; 14: 6.

25. Patrick, D.L., Sittampalam, Y., Somerville, S., Carter, W.B. and Bergner, M. A cross-cultural comparison of health status values. *Am. J. Publ. Health*, 1985; 75: 1402.

26. Paykel, E.S., Fleminger, R. and Watson, J.P. Psychiatric side effects of anti-hypertensive drugs other than reserpine. *J. Clin. Psychopharmacol.*, 1982; 2: 14.

27. Schultz, N.R., Dineen, J.T., Elias, M.R., Pentz, C.A. and Wood, W.G. WAIS performance for different age groups of hypertensive and control subjects during administration of a diuretic. *J. Gerontol.* 1979; 34: 246.

28. Schultz N.R., Elias, M.F., Robbins, M.A., Streeter, D.H.P. and Blakeman, N. A longitudinal comparison of hypertensives and normotensives on the Wechsler adult intelligence scale: initial findings. *J. Gerontol.*, 1986; 41: 169.

29. Solomon S., Hotchkiss, E., Saravay, S.M., Bayer, C., Ramsey, P. and Blumm, R.S. Impairment of memory function by antihypertensive medication. *Arch. Gen. Psychiat.* 1983; 40: 1109.

30. Steiner, S.S., Friedhoff, A.J., Wilson, B.L., Wecker, J.R. and Santo, J.P. Antihypertensive therapy and quality of life: a comparison of atenolol, captopril, enalapril and propranolol. *J. Hum. Hypertens.* 1990; 4: 217–25.

31. Testa, M.A., Hollenberg, N.K., Anderson, R.B. and Williams, G.H. Assessment of quality of life by patient and spouse during antihypertensive therapy with atenolol and nifedipine gastrointestinal therapeutic system. *Am. J. Hypertens.* 1991; 4: 363–73.

32. Zubenko, G.S. and Nixon, R.A. Mood-elevating effect of captopril in depressed patients. *Am. J. Psychiat.* 1984; 141: 110–11.

# 19 Measuring the quality of life of patients with angina

M.J. VandenBurg

Medical treatment of chronic conditions is directed at both the alleviation of symptoms and, if possible, the prolongation of life. As cure is often not possible, the goals of therapy are also to limit the complications of the disease process both medical and symptomatic so that life may be comfortable, functional and satisfying[13]. This is an important concept, since prolongation of life may lead to an inadequate quality of life, in which case lengthened life may not be an acceptable endpoint of therapy for the patient or for their closest relatives, friends and supporters. This is one of the reasons why there is a growing interest in the definition, measurement and documentation of life's qualities.

There are, however, specific reasons for a growth in this area of research. These are related to the growing wish of patients to receive, and physicians to prescribe, therapies for chronic conditions, in attempts to make patients totally symptom-free and to lengthen life, due in part to patients' expectations of modern all-curing medicine. However, even when such therapy is effective, there are often residual limitations on the patient, both physical and psychological. Therapy itself may cause problems or adverse effects which may adversely affect the patient's lifestyle and psychosocial well-being, and patients often state that their treatment has improved or worsened their well-being without corresponding and appropriate alteration in objective measures and clinical parameters of their disease. It is necessary that such limitations and effects should be measured and documented so that they may be taken into account when assessing therapeutic strategies scientifically and so that physicians and patients can make clinical judgements in an informed way. Similarly, the effects of therapies, and particularly drugs, on social and behavioural status must be assessed. It is this concept of total well-being incorporating both physical and psychological factors which has been termed the quality of life. In this chapter how these generalizations relate to the assessment of angina will be discussed.

## ANGINA

Angina, a pain related to an imbalance of oxygen supply to, and the oxygen requirement of, the heart, impacts on patients' physical and psychosocial capacities, enjoyment and well-being. Patients are often unable to continue enjoying their hobbies or pastimes, and sexual activity may all be limited, as may other social and recreational activities. They are often unable to take part in productive employment, which may not only lead to boredom and feelings of inadequacy, but to problems of financial hardship. Psychological factors, such as emotional excitement, may lead to angina, and the reverse is certainly true; namely knowing that you have angina produces psychosocial problems resulting from being labelled with the condition, worrying about having coronary artery disease (CAD) and anxiety about future coronary events. The experience of a single anginal attack may be quite terrifying, with the patient experiencing thoughts of impending death. The relief of anginal chest pain may reverse or relieve all these anxieties.

## AIMS OF TREATMENT – IMPLICATIONS ON WELL-BEING

### Prophylaxis of coronary artery disease (CAD)

The prophylaxis of CAD will, in the future, increase in prominence as a major therapeutic goal, but, in altering patients' lifestyle by prescribing low-fat diets and abolition of smoking, one may adversely affect overall well-being and enjoyment. Similarly, the identification and treatment of high blood pressure, if indeed its reversal is beneficial to CAD, may bring morbidity by both labelling of patients as hypertensive and by exposing patients to possible adverse effects of antihypertensive medication[10].

### Prophylaxis of attacks

Once a patient is diagnosed as having CAD, prevention of anginal pains may be attempted by recommending alterations in lifestyle, both by curtailing individual activities or recommending that the speed or amount of these is reduced. Indeed, patients often make these alterations on their own. Sublingual glyceryl trinitrate (GTN) may be used prophylactically, but whether this has beneficial effects on well-being is yet to be determined. Other drug therapies such as beta-blockers and calcium antagonists may similarly be given on a long-term basis. These drugs may prevent pain or allow an increase in activities, but all have other adverse effects which may be detrimental to total wellness. Future studies have to elicit this balance.

**Pain relief during an attack**

Sublingual GTN either tablet or spray abates the acute attack. Sprays may act more quickly and cause less headaches, and a recent study found that they were more effective than tablets[11].

**Surgical treatment for angina**

Coronary artery bypass surgery (CABG) has been used extensively to relieve anginal pains. Several studies have attempted to measure quality of life after operation.

*Coronary Artery Surgery Study (CASS)*

This study[2] reported results obtained from comparing surgically- and medically-treated patients and claims to show advantages in quality of life in surgically-treated patients. This attempt was the first of its kind, but the variables measured were as much clinical as related to well-being. The claim is based on better relief of chest pain, a diminished need for drug therapy, significantly longer treadmill exercise times and less limitation of normal daily activities (measured on a scale of (1) none, (2) intermittent, (3) mild, (4) moderate, (5) severe, (6) uncertain). Employment status ((1) unemployed, (2) not employed) and recreational status ((1) strenuous, (2) moderate, (3) mild, (4) sedentary) were no different between groups. The study therefore assumes that, because clinical parameters are better in surgically-treated patients, quality of life is also improved; the study is therefore making assumptions that may or may not be true.

*Columbian Presbyterian Coronary Artery Bypass Study*

Kornfield *et al.*[6] have reported an open, non-controlled, sequential study of patients undergoing CABG at Columbia University. They used a modified psychiatric evaluation form to assess effect, behaviour and social role, supplemented by the CAT 16 Personality Factor Questionnaire and a standard Roseman Friedman interview to measure Type A personality. In addition, 3.5 years after surgery another questionnaire was used, asking for changes on a balanced five-point scale ranging from much better to much worse in terms of: pleasure (65% much better), nervousness (30%), mood (40%), job satisfaction (41%), family relationships (48%) and sexual satisfaction (21%). As one would expect, there was little change in personality type, and as with the CASS study there was no alteration in employment status with less angina and increased exercise capacity. However, although the parameters measured had perhaps more to do with well-being than in the CASS study, it was entirely open and the possibility that the benefits were owing to an operation *per se*, or from receiving greater care and/or comfort from being in a study, cannot be excluded.

### Other studies post-CABG

Wortman and Yeaton[14] reported an analysis of data obtained from published literature, including 14 controlled trials, using only the data on those patients who were angina-free to estimate the quality of life. They reported a 25–50% greater chance of a patient being angina-free if they received surgery.

Russell[7] reviewed the ability of patients to return to work after CABG as a measure of quality of life and concluded that as there appeared to be no benefit in this, other measures to assess quality of life in patients after CABG should be used. Similarly, Smith has written two reviews[8,9] on quality of life after bypass surgery and contends that there is little correlation between return to work and physical well-being, and that there is very little, if any, data on the patients' own perception of their health and lifestyle.

## WHY IS THERE A NEED FOR MEASURING QUALITY OF LIFE IN ANGINA

At present, measurement of efficacy of anginal medication has been restricted to simple clinical measures such as the number of attacks of angina and GTN consumption, or more complex laboratory measures such as exercise testing or radionuclide studies. Both have severe limitations.

The simple clinical measures are totally inadequate as a true measure of disease because patients alter their lifestyle either consciously or subconsciously to prevent the occurrence of pain. They may experience the same number of attacks of pain, but may be doing more exercise or less exercise. In the first case they are improving, in the second worsening their lifestyle. Also, patients relate the intensity of a single attack of pain as the most important parameter of their angina and this is often not recognized[12].

The treadmill time test in an exercise laboratory is an attempt to reproduce the daily exertional pattern in a controlled way, but is a totally artificial environment that does not take into account the realities of life and is therefore a poor measure of possible lifestyle activities. Objective measures of ischaemia, such as ST-segment depression on exercise testing, as well as being inaccurate because of false-positives and negatives, lack correlation with the patient's assessment of his angina (VandenBurg, unpublished observations) and fail to take into account that psychological factors make a contribution to the patient's perception of, and severity of, his angina. Not only is this perception of pain altered by emotion and psychological status, the overall problems associated by patients with angina may be secondary to changes in activities or psychological factors[1].

Problems in assessment and documentation of angina suggest measurement of the amount of disability and the psychological profile of patients with angina should be useful. Clinical and laboratory measures do not indicate what happens to patients during the normal circumstances of their life, nor how treatment totally affects their health and quality of life. Assessment of quality of life should, therefore, play a part in future studies in angina.

## SELF-ADMINISTERED QUESTIONNAIRES IN PATIENTS WITH ANGINA

Self-assessment by patients allows documentation of all the effects of treatment and disease on physical, social and psychosocial parameters and is a useful way to measure total health[4]. As reviewed in the previous section, studies to date have investigated isolated problems concurrent and associated with angina, but no study has evaluated total disability, both physical and psychological, consequent on angina.

There is no global measure of dysfunction by which to evaluate the patient with angina. Various visual analogue scales have been tried. In answering the question 'How bad has your heart pain been?', 53% of patients stated that they used the severity of an individual attack to determine their response, 26% the number of attacks, 9% the duration of an attack and 6% a combination[12]. In contrast, when answering the question 'How much trouble to you has your heart disease been?', 39% chose frequency, 28% severity, 17% duration and 13% a combination to measure their response. Despite this difference, both sets of answers correlated best with the patient's perception of the intensity of pain associated with an individual attack, rather than other more useful clinical parameters[12].

There is no self-administered questionnaire specifically developed for patients with angina. There are studies currently underway using the Sickness Impact Profile (SIP)[3] and the Nottingham Health Profile (NHP) to assess various formulations of GTN. Pilot studies have recently evaluated both questionnaires in patients with angina. Patients with angina and known to have ischaemic heart disease (positive stress test, previous myocardial infarction or stenosis on coronary angiography) completed one or both of the questionnaires. In all cases, patient and doctor rated overall health on a 1–5 balanced scale (very good, good, fair, poor, very poor) at the same time.

### Cross-sectional use of the Nottingham Health Profile (NHP) in patients with angina

Responses of 100 patients with angina to part 1 and part 2 of the NHP are shown in Table 19.1. They indicate that all activities, particularly interests and housework, are affected, although no activity was affected by health for

**Table 19.1** Frequency of affirmative responses (*n*) to the NHP

PART 1 STATEMENT

| *Energy* | | *Social isolation* | |
|---|---|---|---|
| I'm tired all the time | 27 | I feel lonely | 5 |
| Everything is an effort | 23 | I'm finding it hard to make contact with people | 7 |
| I soon run out of energy | 52 | I feel there is nobody I'm close to | 7 |
| | | I feel I'm a burden to people | 8 |
| | | I'm finding it hard to get on with people | 6 |

| *Pain* | | *Sleep* | |
|---|---|---|---|
| I have pain at night | 30 | I take tablets to help me sleep | 14 |
| I have unbearable pain | 15 | I'm waking in the early hours of the morning | 46 |
| I find it painful to change position | 13 | I lie awake most of the night | 23 |
| I'm in pain when I walk | 40 | It takes me a long time to get to sleep | 32 |
| I'm in pain when I' standing | 15 | I sleep badly at night | 34 |
| I'm in constant pain | 5 | | |
| I'm in pain when going up and down stairs | 32 | | |
| I'm in pain when sitting | 17 | | |

| *Emotions* | | *Physical mobility* | |
|---|---|---|---|
| Things are getting me down | 32 | I can only walk around indoors | 12 |
| I've forgotten what it's like to enjoy myself | 23 | I find it hard to bend | 27 |
| I'm feeling on edge | 36 | I am unable to walk at all | 2 |
| The days seem to drag | 13 | I find steps and stairs difficult | 32 |
| I lose my temper easily | 41 | I find it hard to reach for things | 19 |
| I feel as if I'm losing control | 6 | I find it hard to dress | 5 |
| Worry is keeping me awake | 13 | I find it hard to stand for long | 30 |
| I feel that life is not worth living | 4 | I need help to walk about outside | 7 |
| I wake up feeling depressed | 12 | | |

| Part 2 | Job | Housework | Social life | Home life | Sex life | Interests | Holidays |
|---|---|---|---|---|---|---|---|
| *n* | 29 | 35 | 28 | 27 | 28 | 38 | 22 |

more than 38% of the population. Responses to part 1 indicate that energy, pain and sleep were frequently affected, social isolation problems being rare. Age did not affect the results and in general neither did the patient's sex, other than sleep and physical mobility, which were more affected in females. Patients' assessment of their own health was consistently and significantly worse than their doctors' rating and correlated better with the NHP responses. Patient-related health correlated well with NHP part 1 and part 2 scores, frequently with pain and physical mobility, least with social isolation. Stress

**Table 19.2** Functional impairment in angina patients and in healthy volunteers as measured by the Sickness Impact Profile*

| Category or dimension | No. of items in each category and dimension | Mean (SD) scores for angina patients (n = 50) | | Mean (SD) scores for healthy volunteers (n = 50) | |
|---|---|---|---|---|---|
| Overall SIP score | 136 | 8.2 | (7.4) | 0.57 | (1.65) |
| Physical dimension | 45 | 5.0 | (6.4) | 0.37 | (1.70) |
| body care and movement | 23 | 3.3 | (6.4) | 0.28 | (1.42) |
| mobility | 10 | 4.8 | (8.8) | 0.20 | (1.42) |
| ambulation | 12 | 9.6 | (10.1) | 0.70 | (3.60) |
| Psychosocial dimension | 48 | 7.6 | (9.5) | 0.50 | (2.10) |
| emotional behaviour | 9 | 8.4 | (11.9) | 0.92 | (3.85) |
| social interaction | 20 | 9.5 | (11.6) | 0.19 | (0.99) |
| alertness behaviour | 10 | 7.7 | (15.6) | 0.96 | (6.79) |
| communication | 9 | 3.0 | (7.7) | 0.19 | (1.30) |
| Independent categories | | | | | |
| sleep and rest | 7 | 13.2 | (14.9) | 0.25 | (1.73) |
| home management | 10 | 10.3 | (15.2) | 1.05 | (6.35) |
| work | 9 | 27.1 | (32.6) | 0.65 | (2.60) |
| recreation and pastime | 8 | 14.0 | (16.0) | 1.00 | (3.61) |
| eating | 9 | 3.6 | (5.1) | 0.00 | (0.00) |

*Possible range of scores is 100% impairment.

**Table 19.3** Correlation* for four categories of the SIP and NHP

| | NHP | | | |
|---|---|---|---|---|
| SIP | Sleep (SL) | Emotional reactions (EM) | Physical mobility (PM) | Social isolation (SO) |
| Sleep and rest (SR) | 0.707† | – | – | – |
| Emotional behaviour (EB) | – | 0.658† | – | – |
| Physical** dimension (PD) | – | – | 0.633† | – |
| Social interaction (SI) | – | – | – | 0.550† |

* Spearman's rank order correlation.
** Physical dimension = ambulation (A) + mobility (M) = body care and movement (BCM).
† $p < 0.01$.

test results bore no relationship to patient-rated health. it was concluded that NHP identified problems which patients may not normally volunteer and qualifies many aspects of quality of life. Its use in therapeutic studies of angina may give a clearer understanding of the effect that angina is having on patient's life and how this is affected by therapy.

### The Sickness Impact Profile (SIP)

Fifty patients with angina completed the SIP. Table 19.2 shows the structure of the SIP and the mean weighted scores for the overall questionnaire and each dimensions as well as each category independently, compared with the responses of healthy volunteers. The scores of the patients with angina were higher in each case and this supports the hypothesis that a patient's quality of life is severely affected by his symptoms as a result of their impact on daily routines. Work and recreation were most affected; the psychosocial dimension was also considerably affected; communication, body care and movement and eating were least affected.

Stress test results showed no relationship to SIP scores. The SIP and its subscores were found to correlate well with patient-rated overall health but not with doctor-rated health. There was no correlation between doctor-rated health and patient-rated health, patients considering themselves sicker.

### Comparison of NHP and SIP

Fifty patients have completed both NHP and SIP. Although the two questionnaires are structured differently, they both measure similar disabilities resultant on the impact of the patient's sickness. It is possible to select four categories from the SIP and NHP part 1 which appear to measure the same dysfunctional capacities. Table 19.3 shows these categories; there was a significant correlation between them.

### CONCLUSIONS

In the assessment of patients with angina it is necessary to be able to assess the effect of the disease on patients' lifestyle as this is far more useful in assessing benefits of therapy than objective psychosocial measures and doctors' opinion, both bearing little relationship to the patient's assessment of overall health. Previous studies have used poor measures of quality of life in assessing patients with angina. We have now shown that both the SIP and NHP can be useful and provide relevant information about the quality of life of patients with angina. Our data indicate that there is substantial functional impairment, psychosocial as well as physical, associated with this disease. The questionnaires correlate well with each other, as well as with patients' overall assessment of their own health, but poorly with both doctors' opinion and the stress test results. It is thus possible for therapies to improve patients without demonstrably altering either. In future studies of patients with angina, we should ask the patient if there are benefits of therapy, not the doctor or the treadmill.

## Acknowledgements

I should like to thank all the staff of Romford Cardiovascular Research, Medical and Clinical Research Consultants Limited and the Centre for Medicines Research, especially Sister Wan Thai Wiseman, Jane Stephens and Sam Salek and Astrid Fletcher for helping me with my work; Valerie Parkinson for turning unreadable scribble into a publishable manuscript, and to Professor Chris Bulpitt and Professor Stuart Walker for encouraging an interest in quality of life as well and especially in the development of angiotensin converting enzyme inhibitors and new nitroglycerine formulations, for making a knowledge of it mandatory for me.

## References

1. Bruce, R.A. and Hossack, K.F. Rationale of physical training in patients with angina pectoris. *Adv. Cardiol.* 1982; 31: 186–190.
2. CASS Principle Investigators and their Associates. Coronary Artery Surgery Study (CASS): a randomised trial of coronary artery bypass surgery. Quality of life in patients randomly assigned to treatment groups. *Circulation* 1983; 68: 951–960.
3. Fletcher, A.E. and Bulpitt, C.J. Assessment of quality of life in cardiovascular therapy. *Br. J. Clin. Pharmac.* 1986; 21: 173S–181S.
4. Grasser, C. and Craft, B.J. The patient's approach to wellness. *Nurs. Clin. North Am.* 1984; 19: 207–218.
5. Hounslow, N.J., Wiseman, W.T., Stephens, J.D. *et al.* Pilot study to assess the use of Visual Analogue Scales in the assessment of angina. *Clin. Sci.* 1987; 72(Suppl. 16): 10P.
6. Kornfeld, D.S., Heller, S.S., Frank, K.A. *et al.* Psychological and behavioural responses after coronary artery bypass surgery. *Circulation* 1982; 66 (Suppl. 111): 24–28.
7. Russell, R.O. Return to work after coronary bypass surgery and quality of life. *Qual. Life Cardiovasc. Care* 1984; December: 66–77.
8. Smith, H.C. Quality of life after coronary bypass surgery. *Qual. Life Cardiovasc. Care* 1985; 11–21.
9. Smith, H.C., Frye, R.L. and Piehler, J.M. Does coronary bypass surgery have a favourable influence on the quality of life? *Cardiovasc. Clin.* 1983; 13: 253–264.
10. VandenBurg, M.J., Evans, S.J.W., Kelly, B.J. *et al.* Factors affecting the

reporting of symptoms by hypertensive patients. *Br. J. Clin. Pharmac.* 1984; 18: 189S–194S.

11. VandenBurg, M.J., Griffins, G.K. and Wight, L.J. Information recall in patients receiving nitroglycerine. *Clin. Sci.* 1987; 72 (Suppl. 16): 76–77P.

12. VandenBurg, M.J., Hounslow, N.J., Tamrazians, S. *et al.* Difficulties of a Visual Analogue Scale in the assessment of angina. *Br. J. Clin. Pharmac.* 1987; 123: 109P–110P.

13. Wenger, N.K., Matson, M.E., Furgerg, C.D. and Elinson, J. Overview: assessment of quality of life in clinical trials of cardiovascular therapies. In Wenger, N.K., Matson, M.E., Furgerg, C.D. *et al.* (eds) *Assessment of Quality of Life in Clinical Trials of Cardiovascular Therapies.* New York, Le Jacq Publishing Inc., 1984, pp. 1–22.

14. Wortman, P.M. and Yeaton, W.H. Cumulating quality of life results in controlled trials of coronary artery bypass surgery. *Controlled Clin. Trials* 1985; 6: 289–305.

# 20 Measuring quality of life in psychiatry

**Sonja M. Hunt and Stephen P. McKenna**

Interest in quality of life measures for outcome assessment in psychiatry has been much slower to develop than in other disciplines such as cardiology, oncology and rheumatology. At first sight this is curious since it might be expected that psychiatrists would be more aware of the importance of social and psychological concomitants of illness and treatment. Unlike most medical specialties the accounts given by psychiatric patients and/or their relatives tend to form a major part of the material used in making a diagnosis and assessing improvement. However, even within psychiatry there is a strong tendency for the focus to be on the aetiology of the condition and those aspects of the patient's function and feeling which are believed to be of *clinical* significance.

Two explanations can be put forward for this apparent lack of interest in quality of life in psychiatry. First, psychiatry may be seen as less in need of such studies *because* of the greater concern of psychiatrists for the impact of symptoms on patient's lives. Secondly, no scales exist which are specific to psychiatric conditions, except for those which are symptom oriented, such as the Hamilton Psychiatric Rating Scale for Depression[15]. The General Health Questionnaire[13], designed to be completed by the patient, is also available, but this is concerned almost entirely with changes in mood.

## THE NEED FOR QUALITY OF LIFE MEASURES IN PSYCHIATRY

Currently, particularly in Britain, the commonest form of treatment for all kinds of mental disorders is medication. While there is a great deal of information available on the biochemistry of these pharmaceutical preparations, their impact on symptoms and their side-effects, very little is known about how they affect those wider aspects of a patient's well-being which can be summarized under the term 'Quality of Life'.

The debate within psychiatry between biological theorists and those who prefer to focus on the psychological consequences of adverse living experiences is highly pertinent here. The further one moves from the purely biochemical, the more problematic becomes the distinction between clinical diagnosis and assessment and lay perceptions of ill health. Szasz[12,29,33] and others have drawn attention to the way in which attributions of psychiatric illness are strongly influenced by a comparison process between the norms and values of the psychiatrist and those of the patient.

Eisenberg[8] has suggested that exclusively biological and exclusively psychological models have the same relation to each other as do wave and particle theory in physics and that whatever the biological basis of the mind, psychiatry will always need to take into account the socio-cultural and psychological context in which the illness is embedded.

Therefore, it can be argued that the evaluation of treatment is particularly problematic in psychiatry because outcomes are often related to the approximation of the patient's mood and behaviour to some socio-cultural 'norm'.

Undoubtedly the main aim of both psychotherapy and pharmacological therapy is the alleviation of symptoms. However, a recent review of conceptual and methodological issues in the comparison of drug and psychotherapy, did not quote a single study of quality of life or, indeed, make any reference to the perceptions and preferences of the patient. All outcomes were therapist defined[9,10].

It has long been known that the utilization of health services is more closely linked to how people feel than to their actual medical condition. Research in medical sociology has shown that whether or not people seek medical attention is less dependent on the 'objective' presence of symptoms than on the person's perception that something is amiss, or on the judgement of some significant other[24,35]. Indeed, the majority of people with symptoms of mental illness who are identified in community surveys have not been in touch with health services[14].

Compliance with treatment regimens is also largely dependent upon the impact of the treatment on the patient's feelings of well-being[4]. Several investigations have shown that a high proportion of prescribed drugs are not taken, but are given away, disposed of or left on a shelf[3,28]. The extent and nature of people's anxieties about taking drugs – especially psychoactive ones – is an under-researched area.

The issue of who is the best judge of the efficacy of treatment has also come under scrutiny with the publication of several studies which have shown that, when it comes to the outcome of medical treatment, there is often disagreement between doctor and patient[18,26,34]. The doctor may be satisfied that the patient has improved, but the patient may feel worse than before. Conversely, the patient may feel herself to be cured, whilst the physician remains unconvinced that this is the case.

Since quality of life is assumed to encompass psycho-social elements which are not normally accessible to the doctor, it is possible to argue that the patient is the best judge of quality of life and that it is the patient's self-report which should carry most weight. However, within psychiatry, this position is complicated by the feeling that psychiatric patients could be 'untrustworthy' respondents, or (by virtue of mental impairment) are unable to make reliable and valid judgements.

A study by May and Tuma[23] appears to have been influential in this area. They found very low correlations between self-assessment, by schizophrenics, using the Minnesota Multiphasic Personality Inventory to measure psychotic symptoms and the evaluations of nurses and therapists. The assumption was made that the professional assessment was more accurate, with little value being attached to the views of the patients. Subsequently, there seems to have been a tendency on the part of clinicians and researchers to give little weight to self-reports of severely ill or overtly psychotic patients.

Since that early study there has been little research within psychiatry which has attempted to compare clinician- and patient-rated severity of symptoms. A study by Prusoff et al.[27], compared severity of depression as rated by the clinician using the Hamilton Psychiatric Rating Scale for depression with that of the patient on a 110 item self-report inventory. This exercise showed that there was moderate agreement on the presence of symptoms, but a correlation of only 0.36 between clinician and patient ratings of the severity of those symptoms. Ten months later, when most of the patients had improved, this concordance had risen to 0.81. Some of the variance in the discrepancy between patient and physician judgements can be accounted for by differences in the measuring instruments and the research conditions. However, the authors suggest that patients lack a basis for judging severity, unlike the clinician who is familiar with such cases. The clinician also uses cues of expression, voice and dress and more specific criteria. However, studies of utilization of services, mentioned earlier, indicate that it is the severity of the symptoms, as judged by the patient, which determine whether treatment is sought and the degree of compliance with treatment regimens.

Currently, acceptability of treatment in clinical trials tends to be gauged by the occurrence of adverse symptoms, withdrawal from trials and compliance with treatment. Assessing acceptability in this way can be misleading. For example, a patient who feels that her condition has improved sufficiently may well drop out of a trial and, since it is customary to carry forward the assessments of those who withdraw from a trial, this improvement will not be reflected in the final analysis of the results.

Such observations imply that the patient's perception of his or her own condition has an important role to play in the evaluation of health care and in trials of new treatments.

## THE AIMS AND DEFINITION OF QUALITY OF LIFE MEASUREMENT

The aim of quality of life measurement is to quantify the impact of both clinical condition and treatment on the wider aspects of the patient's life by going beyond physician dominated indicators of the patient's progress. There is no doubt that psychoactive drugs can be efficacious in terms of alleviating the presenting problem, but it is also known that they can adversely affect cognition, function, emotional tone and energy levels. This has implications for the competence and enjoyment with which the patient performs the tasks of daily life.

Before quality of life can be assessed, two issues need to be considered;

(a)    the purpose of measurement, and

(b)    the definition of quality of life.

(a) The purpose of measurement is relatively easy to describe.
It may be for:

- the gathering of baseline data,
- defining the current need for care in a population or in special groups (such as the frail elderly),
- monitoring changes over time,
- assessing the effects of medical, social or other interventions,
- evaluating the relative impact of alternative treatments,
- or comparing groups in order to set priorities for the allocation of resources.

(b) The definition of quality of life raises many difficulties. Clinical judgements tend to be based upon a return to optimal functioning, such as ability to go to work, mental clarity, the abatement of symptoms, or to biochemical or physiological norms. However, patients are idiosyncratic in their criteria and may be more concerned with their ability to enjoy themselves or to fulfil their household duties, or may be disturbed by feelings of lack of energy and loss of interest.

The different concerns of doctor and patient can be illustrated by considering the difference between achieving a diagnosis and the perception of illness. Diagnosis is a process engaged in by the psychiatrist, the main aim of which is to decide what is wrong with the patient, in order that the appropriate treatment can be prescribed. The diagnosis involves biomedical language which reflects the responsibilities and interests of the medical profession and is largely incomprehensible to the lay person. In psychiatry, the term disease is no longer considered appropriate by many practitioners, but the concept of physician defined disorder within a medical nosology remains.

In contrast, illness may be defined as the experience of some distress or discomfort based upon the perception of the person that some change has occurred in customary function and/or feeling. The perception of illness is a subjective process with idiosyncratic elements and is usually relative to a background of 'noise' – that is, slight malfunctions or feelings of unease to which the individual has become accustomed. A person may feel ill, but not fall into any particular diagnostic category. Conversely, they may be diagnosed as suffering from some medical condition without feeling ill. This might be the case with some psychoses.

The disease/illness distinction is complicated further by what sociologists refer to as 'sickness behaviour'. This is defined as socially acceptable ways of indicating illness, including the means by which distress is communicated to others. These may involve a variety of behaviours, such as seeking medical attention, absence from work or staying in bed. Neither illness nor a diagnostic label necessarily imply sickness. That is to say, a person may be found to be suffering from a medical disorder without behaving in such a way as to indicate sickness. On the other hand, a person may display sickness behaviour without being either ill or diseased. In such cases he or she may be called a 'malingerer'.

The terms 'well-being' and 'quality of life' are probably best regarded as hypothetical constructs, which may be defined and operationalized for specific purposes.

The confusion which attends definitions of 'quality of life' is important from the point of view of measurement, since it accounts for the diversity of content in so-called 'quality of life' measures, many of which have been developed without a firm rationale or conceptual model, making it difficult to interpret the results they produce.

A distinction is sometimes made between components of quality of life which can be categorized as follows:

*Experiential.* These are the subjective values and expectations of the individual; feelings of malaise, distress and discomfort.

*Functional.* This refers to the ability to carry out the tasks of everyday life, including social and occupational obligations, intellectual functioning and personal relationships.

*Symptomatic.* These are the consequences of disease, illness, disability and the adverse effects of treatment.

These three components are not separate and static but interact in a dynamic fashion. By keeping them separate, certain aspects of quality of life may become amenable to measurement by standard means. However, the essence of the concept will remain elusive.

Currently only the presence or absence of the negative aspects of quality of life is measured and quality of life is often assumed to have improved because some previous distress or discomfort has lessened or gone away.

The most common method of measuring quality of life is by questionnaire and there are several standard measures available which explore these different components. It is, at this point, important to make a distinction between three types of questionnaire;

(a)    those which are completed by an observer, for example, the Montgomery–Asberg Depression Rating Scale[25],

(b)    those which are completed by the patient, but which are oriented towards the concerns of the clinician, for example, the Beck Depression Scale[1],

(c)    those which are self-administered and focus upon matters of concern to the patient, for example, The General Well-Being Index[5,6].

Of these only the third type can be said to approximate to quality of life.

Measurement of quality of life requires the development of questionnaires which incorporate the subjective elements of everyday experience and functioning and their quantification in an accurate, valid and reliable manner. It is this systematic evaluation by the use of well tested and standard methods, used to aggregate data from many patients, which distinguishes quality of life assessment from clinical judgement.

### Quality of life and quality of care

It is essential to make a distinction between quality of life and quality of care. The latter is usually based upon 'expert' criteria and standards which scarcely involve the patient at all. Standards of care relate to how and when a given amount of resources should be used to maximize the ratio of health benefits to health risks for a majority of patients. Guidelines are based upon clinical opinion and empirical studies of the outcome and the process of diagnosis and treatment. There is a tendency to divorce quality of care from the fate and feelings of the patient[20]. Moreover, it has been observed, for instance, that many mental health quality assurance monitoring systems in the USA lack any empirical basis for the selection of clinical factors to be monitored[11].

### Studies of quality of life in psychotic patients

Very few studies have used self-report to measure quality of life in psychotic patients. However, recent studies have shown that chronically ill patients can be relied upon to give valid reports of their experiences and circumstances.

One of the very few drug trials to include measurement of some element of quality of life – social disability – was set up by the Medical Research

Council Drug Trials Committee in 1972. The aim of this investigation was to assess the relative efficacy of two compounds in patients returning to the community after an acute schizophrenic episode, for which they had been hospitalized. In addition to measures of symptoms, adverse effects, relapses and return to hospital, patients were given the Social Performance Schedule[32] which assesses leisure activities, domestic relationships, household tasks, child care, dependence and overt behavioural disturbance.

Although both drugs gave rise to similar outcomes in relation to the clinical measures and adverse effects, one drug proved superior to the other in terms of social functioning. These findings were explained in terms of the need to consider the interaction of the drug with the mode of social interaction of schizophrenic patients[30] and demonstrate the value of including measures of social function.

Other so-called quality of life studies have focused on living conditions. For example, Lehman et al.[19] looked at satisfaction with living situation, family relationships, social relations, leisure activities, work, finances, safety and health, in groups of mentally disturbed patients living in 'board and care' homes in the United States. The findings showed that patients expressed most dissatisfaction with unemployment, money and personal safety and a higher percentage were dissatisfied with leisure facilities than was the case in the general population. Importantly, the study showed that the information collected was reliable as reflected by high internal consistencies in the data.

A comparison of patients on a ward of a District General Hospital with patients in a group home used similar measures to those of Lehman et al., plus the Patient's Attitude Schedule[36]. This study found that well-being and satisfaction were greater in the group home than the ward, with more comfort, social contacts and a better financial situation[31].

Quality of life studies of chronically ill patients are particularly important since there is little possibility of cure. Therefore, the task of treatment must be to enhance care and management, for the benefit both of the patient and for carers. At the very least the treatment should not have an adverse effect on quality of life.

## Quality of life in depressed patients

The general symptoms of depression are well known and include loss of interest, lack of motivation, inability to concentrate, inability to make decisions, sleep disturbance, feelings of hopelessness, lack of affect and the presence of suicidal thoughts. These symptoms are distressing enough, but their effects spread into all areas of the patient's life. Thus work performance will be disrupted, raising issues of financial and occupational insecurity. Marital disharmony may arise leading to quarrelling, possible breakup of the marriage and disruption of children's lives. Relationships with friends and acquaintances may be marred and social activities become attenuated. Sexual interest may disappear, with further repercussions for marriage or intimate relationships. There is also likely to be less interest in hobbies and leisure pursuits.

Medication may well alleviate all or some of these symptoms and, thereby, reverse some of the disruption of those components which make up the person's quality of life. However, medication in itself may have adverse effects. It is known that anti-depressants may cause some or all of the following problems; nausea, dizziness, anxiety, tremor, headache, blurred vision and insomnia. Their action within the central nervous system can interfere with attention, skilled performance, sensori-motor co-ordination, short-term memory and other forms of information processing. These adverse effects will also have implications for work performance, marital relations, social and sexual behaviour and for the appreciation of life.

A search of the literature failed to reveal any studies of quality of life in depressed patients, but a recent investigation by McKenna and Hunt[21], used the General Well-Being Index (GWBI) in a study of patients being treated for depression. The GWBI was developed and tested in the USA[7] and has been adapted for use in Britain by Hunt and McKenna[16]. The questionnaire contains 22 items covering feelings of anxiety, self-control, positive well-being, depression, vitality and general health. There are five response categories for each item, which range from very positive to very negative. The scale thus has the advantage of allowing for movement in both directions along a continuum from very good to very poor well-being.

Patients were assessed on three occasions, prior to treatment and after 3 and 6 weeks of treatment. Presence of symptoms and their severity was assessed by psychiatrists using the Montgomery–Asberg Depression Rating Scale[25]. Patients were given the GWBI to complete immediately after their clinical assessments. The results showed that poor well-being was significantly related to withdrawal from the study by the patient, although severity of depression was not. There were wide variations in well-being scores at any given level of depression as assessed by the psychiatrist. This finding suggests that some people are able to cope with depressive symptoms better than others. Although there was a significant correlation between depression and well-being scores, unemployed men, in particular, were less likely to show an improvement in well-being with treatment, even though their symptoms were alleviated. This indicates that other factors, in addition to the depressive symptoms, determine the patient's response to treatment. Findings such as these go some way to improving our understanding of the factors affecting compliance, variability in reactions to depressive symptoms and the role of social and economic conditions on the life of patients.

Recently, a new measure of quality of life suitable for patients suffering from depression has been developed by the authors. This measure is based upon a needs fulfilment concept of quality of life which goes beyond the somewhat functional orientation of most measures[17,22].

### Measuring the quality of life by proxy

A further issue which deserves more attention is the assessment of quality of life in patients judged to be unreliable informants. These would include the demented elderly, the mentally handicapped, brain damaged patients and people with severe psychotic symptoms.

In such cases it may be possible to use proxy measures, in which relevant others (for example, spouses or carers) are asked to report on the mood and/or behaviour of the patient. Great care is needed in the development and testing of such proxy measures if they are to prove valid, reliable and responsive to changes in the patient.

The well-being of carers is of relevance to the health services and to the patients themselves. Great reliance is placed upon the care and support that they provide and it is known that their own health and emotional state can play a considerable part in the prognosis of the patients in their care[2]. A treatment which improves the quality of life of a patient may have an indirect benefit on the carer's well-being, which in turn may lead to the provision of better care.

Studies of quality of life in psychiatry should consider assessments of the patient, their carer(s) and the people with whom they live.

### Quality of life measurement in the clinical situation

As we have seen, the criteria used by practitioners to assess improvement are not necessarily those of the patients and discrepancies are bound to arise.

The fact that the psychiatric disorder is alleviated, but quality of life remains unchanged or worsens, may be a consequence of the patient's social and/or economic circumstances, or it may mean that the adverse effects of the medication are affecting the patient's functioning. This can only be resolved through further enquiry and psychiatrists may need to make decisions about where their responsibility ends.

The symptoms of psychiatric illness are such that quality of life is bound to be severely impaired. However, for some groups, especially elderly people who are socially isolated, pre-existing quality of life can be so poor as to give rise to psychiatric symptoms. In such cases treating the symptoms is likely to be of limited benefit and attention should be directed to social circumstances. Here, quality of life measures have a particular value in helping to clarify aetiological and contributory factors.

## CONCLUSIONS

Clinical trials of psychoactive drugs which include quality of life assessments will become increasingly common. The value of such studies lies in the facilitation of decisions about the best treatment, for which patients, under what conditions. They will also serve to increase our understanding of the repercussions of psychiatric illness and its treatment, from the patient's perspective.

Both objective and subjective indicators measure different but complementary aspects of the patient's life. Objective measures may appear more appealing because they are familiar, tangible, reflect accepted norms and directly address behaviour that can be manipulated. Their disadvantages are that they tell us little about how the patient feels and exclude the patient from involvement in the planning of her treatment. Identification of discrepancies between the judgement of the clinician and the views of the patient may form a basis for negotiations for improvements in care.

Quality of life measures are by no means a substitute for clinical judgement, but rather an adjunct to such judgement, widening the lens through which patients are viewed and facilitating their input to the treatment process.

Considering that one fifth of all disability is caused by psychiatric illness, it is unfortunate that so few quality of life studies of patients have been undertaken. In relation to drug treatment, tranquillizers and anti-depressants are used by a large number of people, yet, as far as can be ascertained, there has been no empirical study of the subjective effects of these drugs. Indeed, an understanding of the effects of such preparations on quality of life might well have led sooner to greater attention being paid to the consequences of their widespread prescription.

## References

1.  Beck, A.T., Ward, C.H., Mendelson, M., Mock, J. and Erbaugh, J. An inventory for measuring depression. *Arch. Gen. Psychiat.* 1961; 4: 561–571.
2.  Carnwath, T. and Johnson, D. Psychiatric morbidity among spouses of patients with stroke. *Br. Med. J.* 1987; 294: 409–411.
3.  Cartwright, A. *Health Surveys*. King Edward's Hospital Fund. London, 1983.
4.  Coronary Drug Project Research Group. Influence of adherence to treatment and response of cholesterol on mortality in the coronary drug project. *N. Engl. J. Med.* 1983; 303: 1038–1041.
5.  Dupuy, H. Developmental rationale, substantive, derivative and conceptual relevance of the General Well-Being Schedule. (Unpublished manuscript), 1973.
6.  Dupuy, H. The psychological section of the current health and nutrition examination survey. In *Proceedings of the Public Health Conference on Records and Statistics*. June 12–15th. DHEW Publication No. 74-1214. Washington DC, US Government Printing Office, 1974.

7. Dupuy, H. The Psychological General Well-Being Index. In Wenger, N.K. *et al.* (eds) *Assessment of Quality of Life in Clinical Trials of Cardiovascular Therapies.* New York, Le Jacq, 1984, pp. 170–183.

8. Eisenberg, L. Mindlessness and brainlessness in psychiatry. *Br. J. Psychiat.* 1986; 148: 497–508.

9. Elkin, I., Pilkonis, P.A., Doherty, J.P. and Sotsky, S.M. Conceptual and methodological issues in comparative studies of psycho- and pharmacological therapy. I: Active ingredients and mechanisms of change. *Am. J. Psychiat.* 1988; 145: 909–917.

10. Elkin, I., Pilkonis, P.A., Doherty, J.P. and Sotsky, S.M. Conceptual and methodological issues in comparative studies of psycho- and pharmacological therapy: II: Nature and timing and treatment effects. *Am. J. Psychiat.* 1988; 145: 1070–1076.

11. Fauman, M. Quality assurance monitoring in psychiatry. *Am. J. Psychiat.* 1989; 146: 1121–1130.

12. Goffman, E. *Asylums: Essays on the Social Situation of Mental Patients and other Inmates.* Garden City, Anchor Books, 1971.

13. Goldberg, D. *The Detection of Psychiatric Illness by Questionnaire.* London, Oxford University Press, 1971.

14. Goldberg, D. and Huxley, P. *Mental Illness in the Community: the Pathway to Community Care.* London, Tavistock, 1980.

15. Hamilton, M. Standardised assessment and recording of depressive symptoms. *Psychiat. Neurol. Neurochir.* 1969; 72: 201–205.

16. Hunt, S.M. and McKenna, S.P. Adaptation of the General Well-Being Index for use in Britain. (Under editorial consideration), 1992.

17. Hunt, S.M. and McKenna, S.P. The LQD: A new measure of quality of life for use with depressed patients. (Under editorial consideration), 1992.

18. Jachuck, S.J., Brierley, H., Jachuck, S. and Willcox, P. The effect of hypertensive drugs on the quality of life. *J. R. Coll. Gen. Practit.* 1982; 32: 103–105.

19. Lehman, A., Ward, N. and Linn, L. Chronic mental patients: the quality of life issue. *Am. J. Psychiat.* 1982; 139: 1271–1275.

20. McAuliffe, W.E. On the statistical validity of standards used in profile monitoring of health care. *Am. J. Public Health* 1978; 68: 645–651.

21. McKenna, S.P. and Hunt, S.M. Quality of life in depressed patients. (Under editorial consideration), 1992.

22. McKenna, S.P. and Hunt, S.M. Reliability and validity of the LQD; a new measure of quality of life in depression. (Under editorial consideration), 1992.

23. May, P. and Tuma, A. Choice of criteria for the assessment of treatment outcome. *J. Psychiat. Res.* 1964; 2: 199–209.

24. Mechanic, D. The concept of illness behaviour. *J. Chronic Dis.* 1962; 17: 189–194.

25. Montgomery, S.A. and Asberg, M. A new depression scale designed to be sensitive to change. *Br. J. Psychiat.* 1978; 134: 382–389.

26. Orth-Gomer, K., Britton, M. and Rehnqvist, N. Quality of care in an out-patient department: the patient's view. *Soc. Sci. Med.* 1979; 13A: 347–351.

27. Prusoff, B., Klerman, G. and Paykel, E. Concordance between clinical assess-

ments and patients' self-report in depression. *Arch. Gen. Psychiat.* 1972; 26: 546–552.

28. Rashid, A. Do patients cash prescriptions? *Br. Med. J.* 1982; 284: 24–26.
29. Scheff, T. *Becoming Mentally Ill.* Chicago, Aldine, 1961.
30. Shepherd, M. and Watt, D. Impact of long-term neuroleptics on the community: advantages and disadvantages. In Boissier, J.R. *et al.* (eds) *Neuropsychopharmacology.* New York, Elsevier, 1975.
31. Simpson, C. Hyde, C and Faragher, E. The chronic mentally ill in community facilities: a study of quality of life. *Br. J. Psychiat.* 1989; 154: 77–82.
32. Stevens, B. Dependence of schizophrenic patients on elderly relations. *Psychol. Med.* 1972; 2: 17–32.
33. Szasz, T. *The Manufacture of Madness.* London, Routledge and Kegan Paul, 1971.
34. Thomas, M. R. and Lyttle, D. Patient expectations about the success of treatment and reported relief from low back pain. *J. Psychosom. Res.* 1980; 24: 297–301.
35. White, K. L., Williams, T.F. and Greenberg, B.G. The ecology of medical care. *N. Engl. J. Med.* 1981; 265: 885–892.
36. Wykes, T. A hostel ward for 'new' long stay patients: an evaluation study of a 'ward in a house'. In Wing, J.K. (ed.) *Long-Term Community Care: Experiences in a London Borough.* Psychological Medicine Monograph Suppl. 2, 1982, pp. 55–97.

# 21 Measuring the quality of life of patients with skin disease

M.S. SALEK

The effect of a skin disease on a patient's quality of life is often of more importance than the discomfort of having a rash or the presence of skin lesions. Clinical decisions on therapy often take this into account, and assessment of the effectiveness of new management techniques ought ideally to include formal measurement of quality of life and should represent the final common pathway in the treatment of skin diseases. Nevertheless, the concept of health-related quality of life in skin disease like other chronic conditions continues to generate interest and controversy both in respect of its relevance as a therapeutic outcome measure and the methodology used for its measurement. Many different methods are used to measure the clinical severity of skin disease[14], such as the Psoriasis Area and Severity Index (PASI)[10], but these do not tell us to what extent the disease influences the patient's functional behaviour, either physical and psychosocial. Thus, methods of health-related quality of life assessment are needed in dermatology for three reasons: (1) it provides an additional measure of disease status relevant to the patient for clinical decision-making, selection of treatment and monitoring; (2) it gives an ability to assess the effectiveness of both existing and novel management techniques; and (3) it provides an important comparator with systemic diseases when arguing for more resources for dermatology.

## PSYCHOSOCIAL DISABILITY IN SKIN DISEASE

Although the cause of most skin diseases remain unknown[3], they lead to psychosocial disturbances particularly of self image[23]. In most patients the symptoms of skin disease are controlled with emollients and topical steroids. However, the psychosocial aspects of skin disease may continue to seriously damage a patient's self-esteem and ability to cope with the disease[11], especially when it remains through teenage years and adult life. Despite the importance of the problem, the psychosocial impact and quality of life impairment of such a disabling chronic condition has rarely been addressed.

## APPLICATION OF GENERAL QUALITY OF LIFE INSTRUMENTS IN DERMATOLOGY

These combine physical functioning, social and emotional factors into one instrument providing a comprehensive measurement of health. This new generation of instruments evolved during the 1970s, reflecting a global approach to assessing well-being.

Methods of assessing the impact of skin disease on the patient's quality of life have been described previously[7,16]. but these questionnaire techniques have been disease-specific and are therefore not designed for providing a comprehensive picture of a patient's functional behaviour. To overcome this limitation of disease-specific instruments, we need to be able to use a general quality of life measure which has been validated in both dermatological and non-dermatological disease areas in order to make comparisons of the disability experienced by patients with different skin disease or other chronic conditions such as cardiovascular problems. An instrument which may be of value in this context is the United Kingdom Sickness Impact Profile (UKSIP). The UKSIP is a comprehensive general quality of life measure which has been used and validated in a number of chronic diseases[2,8,13,20,22] to assess the impact of the disease and drug treatment on a patient's quality of life. The UKSIP (United Kingdom version of the American Sickness Impact Profile)[1] is briefly described below.

### United Kingdom Sickness Impact Profile (UKSIP)

This reflects a subject's perception of performance of daily activity and specific conditions of sickness-related dysfunctions, both physical and psychosocial, giving a comprehensive list of health problems. It is useful in the clinical situation in assessing a wide range of functional outcomes and is unique in producing a single rating score as well as category scores. Furthermore, since scores are generated for each of 12 different categories of functional behaviour, changes in certain types of function may be examined separately from other types of function.

The UKSIP consists of 136 health-related dysfunctions grouped into 12 different areas of daily activity which require tick-box answers (sample questions and format – Figure 21.1). Three of these areas (body care and movement, mobility, ambulation) concern a physical dimension (45 items), while four others (emotional behaviour, social interaction, alertness behav-

**PLEASE TICK ONLY THOSE STATEMENTS THAT YOU ARE SURE DESCRIBE YOU TODAY AND ARE RELATED TO YOUR HEALTH**

**A**

*These statements describe your sleep and rest today*

1.  I spend much of the day lying down in order to rest ....................... ☐

2.  I sit for much of the day .................................................. ☐

3.  I am sleeping or dozing most of the time – day and night ............... ☐

4.  I lie down more often during the day in order to rest.................... ☐

5.  I sit around half asleep.................................................. ☐

6.  I sleep less at night, for example, I wake up easily, I don't fall asleep ..... ☐
    for a long time, I keep waking up

7. ' I sleep or doze more during the day .................................... ☐

**Figure 21.1** Sample questions and format of the United Kingdom Sickness Impact Profile

iour, communication) concern a psychosocial dimension (48 items). The remaining five areas form the so-called independent categories. These are sleep and rest (seven items), home management (ten items), work (nine items), recreation and pastime (eight items), and eating (nine items). For the purpose of completing the UKSIP, the patients are asked to consider the effects of the disease and/or treatment on them that day. In addition to the 136 questions, patients are asked to give an 'overall health' rating on a five-point scale choosing from a range of 'very good' to 'very poor'. The UKSIP can be either interviewer-administered or self-administered. The self-administered method may be more valid and reliable than the interviewer-administered[1]. However, a trained interviewer who reads the instructions and answers any queries before the UKSIP is completed by the patient may be the best assurance of reliable and valid UKSIP data[1]. The UKSIP scores are calculated by summing the scale values (weightings based on estimates of the relative severity of each dysfunction) of items ticked divided by the sum of the scale values for all items multiplied by 100. Thus, the UKSIP score could be aggregated to provide a single overall quality of life score (index) as well as providing numerical values for each category and dimension (profile).

## APPLICATION OF DISEASE-SPECIFIC QUALITY OF LIFE INSTRUMENTS IN DERMATOLOGY

Recognition of the importance of functional as well as biomedical outcomes in the 1940s led to the development of simple disease-specific quality of life questionnaires in most therapeutic areas. Most of these indices suffer from ambiguity and lack of comprehensiveness. Also, reliability and validity have not been demonstrated in most instances and their sensitivity to clinically important changes (e.g. following treatment) are limited[6,12]. However, the measurement of quality of life in dermatology has only started to generate interest in the last decade with the development of a few dermatologically specific measures such as the Psoriasis Disability Index[7], Eczema Disability Index and Acne Disability Index[16]. These indices have been used in the clinical situation and validated against general quality of life measures. A selection of the most widely used disease-specific quality of life measures in dermatology are briefly described below.

### Psoriasis Disability Index (PDI)

This is a short questionnaire which consists of 15 questions answered on a 1 to 7 linear analogue scale representing grades from 'not at all' to 'very much'. The 15 questions are grouped under five headings; daily activity (five items), work or school (three items), personal relationships (two items), leisure (four items) and treatment (one item). When completing the PDI, patients are asked to consider the effect of the disease and/or treatment on them over the previous month only. The PDI score is calculated by summing the scores for each question.

### Eczema Disability Index (EDI)

Like PDI this is a short compact questionnaire which consists of 15 questions answered on a 1 to 7 linear analogue scale representing grades from 'not at all' to 'very much'. The grouping of questions and scoring is similar to PDI.

### Acne Disability Index (ADI)

This is an acne-specific questionnaire which is self-scored on a linear analogue scale. The ADI consists of 48 statements in eight categories; psychological (14 items), Physical (four items), recreation (three items), employment (three items), self-awareness (three times), social reaction (14 items) skin care (three items) and financial (four items). This is the revised version of the ADI questionnaire described previously[16]. When completing the ADI, patients are asked to consider the effect of the disease on them over the past 4 weeks only. ADI scores are calculated by summing the scale values of attempted items divided by the total possible scale values for all items multiplied by 100.

## PRACTICALITY OF QUALITY OF LIFE MEASUREMENT IN SKIN DISEASE

In general, patients with skin disease are suitable candidates for using the self-administered method of quality of life assessment. These patients are usually very co-operative and seem to enjoy the exercise. The completion time required for both general (15–20 minutes) and disease-specific (10–15 minutes) measures is within the acceptable range for self-administered questionnaires.

A question often asked is how patients receive the questionnaire? Do they consider it an inconvenience, especially with a long questionnaire such as the UKSIP? Do they consider it a problem in that the physician is avoiding talking to them and instead giving them a piece or pieces of paper to work on? The answers based on the author's experience with self-administered questionnaires is that it is important that patients are given adequate information at the onset of filling out the questionnaire. Of equal importance is the setting in which the patient fills out the questionnaire. He or she should be situated in a quiet room with reasonable privacy.

It should be emphasised to them that it is very important that they comply with the introductory comments and instructions. They must complete the questionnaire accurately because it is concerned with their reaction and perception of disease, its treatment and their overall sense of well-being. Furthermore, in the author's experience, patients with skin disease usually do not object to completing questionnaires, even when asked to complete several on the same occasion. Similarly, they do not appear to object to personal questions being posed such as questions about sexual function, as long as they have been prepared properly and reassured about the confidentiality of the questionnaire. Moreover, patients with skin disease, in general, are very positive about the fact that the physician and others involved care about them as patients and not just about their disease. Also they appreciate that interest is being shown in what they think about their condition and its effect upon all aspects of daily living.

## MEASUREMENT OF QUALITY OF LIFE IN PATIENTS WITH SKIN DISEASE

The simple clinical assessment of patients with skin disease using traditional outcome measures is inadequate in describing a complete picture of the disease because patients' lifestyle is greatly affected. Thus, measurement of quality of life (the extent of disability and the psychosocial profile) of patients with skin disease should be useful in the clinic to aid routine management and in clinical research to assess the values of new management techniques. To further illustrate the importance of measuring quality of life of patients with skin disease some recent studies using the self-administered methods (both general and disease-specific) described earlier are presented below.

### Psoriasis

A prospective cross-sectional study of 32 patients (15 male, 17 female) with psoriasis was carried out[8] to validate the use of the UKSIP, a general health-related quality of life measure in psoriasis and to compare its sensitivity with the PDI, a psoriasis-specific measure. The patients were aged betwen 14 and 73 years (median 35 years) of which 23 (72%) were in-patients admitted because of their psoriasis. Nine patients were attending a dermatology out-patient clinic. The nature of the study was described to each patient; no patient declined to take part. The UKSIP and the PDI questionnaires were explained to each patient by the author in a standard scripted fashion and then completed by each patient with him present. A measure of the extent and severity of the patient's psoriasis was recorded by the examining physician using the 'Psoriasis Area and Severity Index' (PASI) method[10]. In the PASI scoring system, four main body areas are assessed: the head, trunk, upper extremities and lower extremities, corresponding to 10%, 20%, 30% and 40% of the body area, respectively. The area of psoriatic involvement of these four main areas is given a numerical value from 0 to 6 corresponding to 0–100% involvement. In each area erythema, infiltration and desquamation are assessed on a 0–4 scale. The PASI score (0–72) is then calculated to give an overall score for clinical degree of psoriasis.

The clinical severity of psoriasis in the patients studied ranged from PASI scores of 2–24, median 5.5. The scores for the PDI ranged from 7 to 88, median 38, with the following distribution: PDI < 31 (10 patients) PDI = 31–50 (11 patients) and PDI > 50 (11 patients). The PDI scores correlated with the PASI scores ($rs = 0.40$, $p < 0.05$). In contrast, overall UKSIP scores did not correlate with PASI; this may be accounted for by the differences in the type of questions asked in the two questionnaires. There was good correlation between the PDI and the overall UKSIP score ($p < 0.01$) and strong correlations between the PDI and all UKSIP subsections, except with body care, alertness, communication and eating (Figure 21.2). The scores for the UKSIP are given in Table 21.1, along with scores from a healthy group of volunteers with similar age and sex distribution for simple comparative purposes. The overall UKSIP mean score for the patients with psoriasis was 9.9 (SD = ±8.7, $n = 32$). As expected psoriasis had only a moderate impact on the patients' ability to move around or take care of themselves, but the psychosocial effects of the disease were profound. There was also a major impact on the patients' ability to sleep, manage their homes, and on their recreational activities. Work was an area particularly affected, reflecting substantial numbers of patients who are unemployed due to their psoriasis (32%).

When the results for the 15 male and 17 female patients were compared, there were no significant differences in PASI, PDI, overall UKSIP scores or in the UKSIP subsections. These findings were further confirmed by the lack of correlation with gender in all areas examined as demonstrated by Spearman rank correlation coefficients. Similarly, age did not correlate with PASI, PDI or the UKSIP, except for the subsections of home management, ambulation and employment ($rs > 0.33$). The overall UKSIP score and most UKSIP subsections correlated well ($p < 0.01$) with the patients' global-rated health assessment (i.e. very good, good, fair, poor, very poor). The patients' global rating of overall health correlated most closely with psychosocial behaviour ($rs > 0.46$). The PASI score did not correlate with patients' global rating of overall health. However, those with only a moderate area of psoriasis involvement did have a better perception of their overall health.

This study has demonstrated that the UKSIP may be effectively used in patients with skin disease such as psoriasis. It has also demonstrated that the

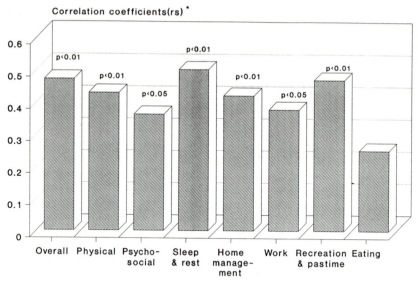

**Figure 21.2** Correlation between Psoriasis Disability Index and UK Sickness Impact Profile

PDI, a much shorter and more compact disease-orientated measure, is effective in measuring the same disability. As the two questionnaire methods are conceptually quite different, one arising from interviews with patients with a specific disease, while the other is designed as a general measure of health status applicable to chronic and acute illness, the close correlation between their final scores indicates that they are both successful in measuring the same 'core' of the patients' problems. These techniques may also provide a useful measure for monitoring drug therapy in situations such as psoriasis where functional results rather than laboratory parameters or survival are of primary interest. Thus instruments such as the UKSIP and PDI, if used together, could be complementary in identifying the breadth and extent of patient's physical and psychosocial functional limitations. These findings have also shown that chronological age and sex do not have any bearing on psoriatic patients' perception of their health status. However, age may affect the degree of a patient's dependency in daily living with respect to various support services. Unemployment is certainly an important issue among patients with psoriasis and thus return to work constitutes one of the major aims of treatment.

**Table 21.1** Quality of life scores in patients with psoriasis and healthy volunteers as measured by the UK Sickness Impact Profile (UKSIP)*

| Category or dimension | Number of items | Mean (SD) scores psoriasis patient (n=32) | Mean (SD) scores healthy adults (n=50) |
|---|---|---|---|
| Overall UKSIP | 136 | 9.9  (8.7) | 0.57 (1.7) |
| Physical dimension | 45 | 3.6  (7.0) | 0.37  (1.7) |
| Body care and movement | 23 | 3.4  (5.6) | 0.28  (1.4) |
| Mobility | 10 | 4.0  (8.9) | 0.20  (1.4) |
| Ambulation | 12 | 3.9 (11.3) | 0.70  (3.6) |
| Psychosocial dimension | 48 | 12.6 (12.4) | 0.50  (2.1) |
| Emotional behaviour | 9 | 18.9 (19.2) | 0.92  (3.8) |
| Social interaction | 20 | 15.9 (16.3) | 0.19  (0.9) |
| Alertness behaviour | 10 | 8.4 (19.0) | 0.96  (6.8) |
| Communication | 9 | 4.3  (8.8) | 0.19  (1.3) |
| Independent categories | | | |
| Sleep and rest | 7 | 15.2 (12.9) | 0.25  (1.7) |
| Home management | 10 | 12.0 (16.6) | 1.05  (6.4) |
| Work | 9 | 27.1 (31.0) | 0.65  (2.6) |
| Recreation and pastime | 8 | 20.6 (20.9) | 1.00  (3.6) |
| Eating | 9 | 2.9  (5.3) | 0.00  (0.0) |

* Improvement with a decreasing score.

## Acne

Acne is a chronic skin disorder commonly affecting the face. The visibility of the disease seems to have a great concern not only to those who are affected by acne, but also those who are in direct contact with the patients such as family members and friends. Acne is usually maximal during adolescence, a period of uncertainty in life, when the individual is making the psychosocial and physical transition from childhood to adulthood. Thus, this important phase of social development is adversely affected by acne and therefore its impact on quality of life (both physical and psychosocial) requires a very careful consideration in the management of patients with acne. Several studies of the psychosocial consequences of acne have been reported in the literature but these findings are of conflicting nature[4,15,18,19,24].

A study of 100 patients (60 male, 40 female) with mild to severe acne, recruited sequentially, was carried out to examine the validity of three self-administered quality of life measures; one being a general (UKSIP) and the other two acne-specific measures, namely the Acne Disability Index (ADI) and Cardiff Acne Disability Index (CADI); in determining the impact of acne on patients' quality of life, physical as well as psychosocial. The patients

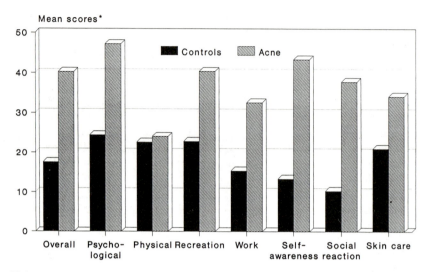

* Higher score represents more impairment
* Possible range of scores is 0 to 100%

**Figure 21.3** Measurements of quality of life in patients with acne as measured by ADI

were aged from 15 to 51 years (median age 22 years). All patients were attending the dermatology outpatient clinic. In addition to the quality of life questionnaires, severity of the patients' acne was recorded using the Cunliffe Grading Method[5], the Acne Clinical Severity Index (ACSI). ACSI is a standard photographic grading method derived from face, back and chest[17]. The severity of the photographs of face, back and chest ranges from 0 to 8 with total possible severity score of 24.

The clinical severity of acne in the patients studied ranged from ACSI scores of 0–11, median 3.5. The scores for the overall ADI ranged from 15–79, median 40, with the psychological activity showing the most impairment and physical activity the least. Scores for ADI categories compared with controls are shown in Figure 21.3. The scores for the overall CADI (a short version of ADI) ranged from 7 to 93 (mean=42, SD = ±19). The CADI scores correlated with ACSI scores ($p < 0.05$). In contrast ADI and UKSIP scores did not correlate with ACSI, this may be accounted for by the fact that these two questionnaires are comprehensive, measuring the extent of both physical and psychosocial impairment, and therefore have very little relationship to ACSI which is a objective measure of the severity and involvement of acne. Table 21.2 shows the structure of the UKSIP and the mean weighted scores for the overall questionnaire and each dimension as well as each category independently, compared with the responses of healthy volunteers. The quality of life scores of patients with acne were higher in all aspects of

**Table 21.2** Quality of life scores in patients with acne and healthy volunteers as measured by the UK Sickness Impact Profile (UKSIP)*

| Category or dimension | Number of items | Mean (SD) scores Acne patients (n=100) | Mean(SD) scores healthy volunteers (n=50) |
|---|---|---|---|
| Overall UKSIP | 136 | 5.6  (4.7) | 0.57  (1.7) |
| Physical dimension | 45 | 1.0  (2.5) | 0.37  (1.7) |
| Bodycare and movement | 23 | 0.6  (2.3) | 0.28  (1.4) |
| Mobility | 10 | 1.3  (2.9) | 0.20  (1.4) |
| Ambulation | 12 | 2.1  (4.9) | 0.70  (3.6) |
| Psychosocial dimension | 48 | 9.9  (8.7) | 0.50  (2.1) |
| Emotional behaviour | 9 | 18.2 (16.9) | 0.92  (3.8) |
| Social interaction | 20 | 11.0 (11.1) | 0.19  (0.9) |
| Alertness behaviour | 10 | 9.2 (13.7) | 0.96  (6.8) |
| Communication | 9 | 0.5  (2.1) | 0.19  (1.3) |
| Independent categories | | | |
| Sleep and rest | 7 | 5.7  (9.7) | 0.25  (1.7) |
| Home Management | 10 | 4.7  (9.6) | 1.05  (6.4) |
| Work | 9 | 7.3 (16.2) | 0.65  (2.6) |
| Recreation and pastime | 8 | 13.7 (14.2) | 1.00  (3.6) |
| Eating | 9 | 0.6  (2.1) | 0.00  (0.0) |

* Improvement with a decreasing score.

daily activity (higher scores represent more impairment). Like psoriasis, patients with acne were also severely affected in the psychosocial aspect of their quality of life with its emotional behaviours component showing the highest impairment. Among other areas of daily activity, recreation and pastime were affected the most by patients' acne. Unlike patients with psoriasis, work was not so much of a problem area in patients with acne.

The findings from this study have demonstrated that the UKSIP provides a sensitive method of identifying different aspects of disability caused by acne. The moderate correlation exhibited between the UKSIP and CADI validates CADI as a simple practical measurement technique with which to monitor acne patients' quality of life. Furthermore, the degree of clinical severity of acne does not necessarily reflect the extent of quality of life impairment experienced by patients. In summary, these methods of quality of life measurement provide a new dimension of assessing the impact of acne on a patient's health-related quality of life.

**Atopic dermatitis (eczema)**

Thirty three patients with severe disabling atopic dermatitis were recruited in a recent multicentre clinical trial in the UK to measure the impact that cyclosporin treatment has on the quality of life of patients with eczema [23]. Each patient was randomized to a two period crossover clinical trial of cyclosporin or placebo in a double blind fashion. Patients were prescribed 5 mg/kg/day of cyclosporin or placebo. Health-related quality of life was assessed at 0, 8 and 16 weeks using the UKSIP, EDI and a global 5-point rating scale of overall health (very good to very poor). In addition, the area and severity of eczema was assessed at each 2 weekly visit to determine the effectiveness of treatment.

The results (Figures 21.4 and 5) using the UKSIP and EDI indicated a major improvement in the quality of life and disability of patients receiving cyclosporin in all areas of daily living, in particular for psychosocial, work, sleep and recreational activities parameters ($p < 0.01$). The findings also indicated that although relapse (measured by severity and area) occurred early after 2–4 weeks, benefit expressed in terms of quality of life was prolonged for up to 8 weeks and possibly longer (i.e., a carry over effect could be seen). These findings clearly indicate that cyclosporin has a major beneficial impact on quality of life of patients with severe atopic dermatitis.

Measurement of health-related quality of life in the above dermatological conditions demonstrates the potential usefulness/applicability of the instruments used (i.e., UKSIP, PDI, ADI, CADI, EDI) and the importance of quality of life data in the clinical decision-making process for patients with skin disease.

## DISCUSSION

Measurement of quality of life in dermatology is useful in different contexts and may affect clinical decisions, patient–physician relationship and decisions about allocation of resources compared with other systemic diseases. Clearly, an improved patient–physician relationship and shared decision-making in choice of treatment regimens is of great benefit to both physician and patient. In this context, a self-administered quality of life questionnaire is likely to be more comprehensive than a personal interview in identifying patient problems because it depersonalizes the questions posed. One of the interesting points that has emerged from studies presented above, examining different skin diseases, is that physicians should listen to the patients and note their comments regarding the effect that the skin disease and its treatment is having on their quality of life. Patient complaints cannot be considered as minor issues because these concerns may impair quality of life and lead to poor compliance with drug therapy.

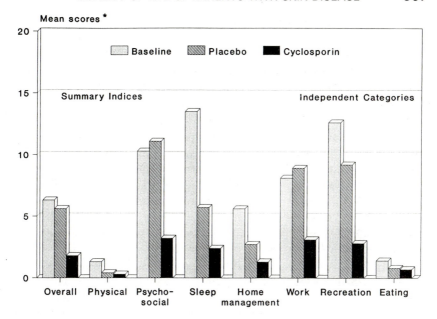

* Improvement with a decreasing score

**Figure 21.4** Measurement of quality of life in patients with eczema as measured by UKSIP

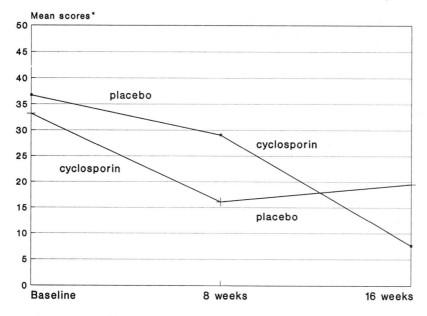

* Improvement with a decreasing score

**Figure 21.5** Measurement of quality of life in patients with eczema as measured by EDI

Assessment of health-related quality of life was proved to be a valuable contribution in making clinical judgements. This was particularly demonstrated when measuring the eczema patients' perception of their quality of life in the double-blind, crossover study with the United Kingdom Sickness Impact Profile (UKSIP) because the instrument relates well to all aspects of daily activity, both physical and psychosocial.

It is now possible to compare quantitatively for the first time the disability experienced by patients suffering from skin disease with that experienced by patients suffering from other systemic diseases. For example, data is available concerning cardiovascular disease[21]. The mean UKSIP score for patients with hypertension was 7.0 (SD = $\pm$7.7, $n$=52), with angina the mean was 8.2 (SD = $\pm$7.4, $n$=50) while with cardiac failure the mean was 10.4 (SD = $\pm$8.1, $n$=53). In the psoriasis study, presented above, the UKSIP mean score was 9.9 (SD = $\pm$8.7, $n$=32). The interviewer delivering the UKSIP to the patients and being available throughout the completion period was the same in each study, thereby removing one possible source of bias. Although the psoriasis patients were not directly matched for age with the patients in the other study, the comparison indicates that a group of hospital-treated patients with psoriasis suffer less disability than patients with cardiac failure but may suffer at least a level of disability equivalent to that of patients with angina or hypertension.

However, the major debate of disease-specific versus general or generic measures continues to be an issue in the field of health-related quality of life. One way of resolving the dilemma of whether to choose a general or specific measure is, as presented here, to apply an approach that combines a general measure such as the UKSIP with a disease-specific questionnaire such as PDI, ADI and EDI. Thus, adapting this approach the two instruments, if used together, could be complementary. This also ensures comprehensiveness and scope, as well as identifying the breadth and extent of a patient's physical and psychosocial functional limitation without losing specific clinical information and the ability to detect treatment induced changes. Furthermore, in clinical situations where a simple rapid overall measure of quality of life is required, either in individuals or in groups of patients with skin disease, it is appropriate to use a disease-specific measure. However, in research studies or in situations where it is necessary to compare quality of life in skin diseases with non-dermatological diseases, it is appropriate to use a general quality of life measure such as the UKSIP, which provides a more comprehensive picture of the impact of disease on a patient's life style. It is hoped that the data provided here should encourage acceptance by physicians and awareness of the need for such measures in dermatology, both in clinical practice and research.

# References

1. Bergner, M., Bobitt, R.A., Carter, W.B. and Gilson, B.S. The Sickness Impact Profile: development and final revision of a health status measure. *Med. Care* 1981; 19: 787–805.

2. Berry, H., Bloom, B., Shayegan-Salek, M.S., Luscombe, D.K. and Walker, S.R. Quality of life – Does it matter? *Br. J. Rheumatol.* 1987; 26 (Suppl. 2): 205.

3. Clark, R.A.F. Cell-mediated and IgE-mediated immune responses in atopic dermatitis. *Arch. Dermatol.* 1989; 125: 413–416.

4. Cunliffe, W.J. Acne and unemployment. *Br. J. Dermatol.* 1986; 115: 386.

5. Cunliffe, W.J. The grading of acne. In Cunliffee, W.J. *A Pocket Guide to Acne.* London, Science Press, 1988, pp. 25–33.

6. Deyo, R.A. Measuring functional outcomes in therapeutic trials for chronic disease. *Contr. Clin. Trials* 1984; 5: 223–240.

7. Finlay, A.Y. and Kelly, S.E. Psoriasis – an index of disability. *Clin. Exp. Dermatol.* 1987; 12: 8–11.

8. Finlay, A., Khan, G.K., Luscombe, D.K. and Salek, M.S. Validation of UK Sickness Impact Profile and Psoriasis Disability Index in Psoriasia. *Br. J. Dermatol.* 1990; 123: 751–756.

9. Finlay, A., Salek, M.S., Khan, G.K., Luscombe, D.K., Allen, R., Berth-Jones, J., Camp, R., Gardner, T., Graham-Brown, R., Marks, R., Motley R, Ross, J. and Sowden, J. Quality of life improvement in cyclosporin treated atopic dermatitis patients – a double-blind crossover study. *Br. J. Dermatol.* 1991; 125 (Suppl. 38): 16.

10. Fredriksson, T. and Pettersson, U. Severe psoriasis – oral therapy with a new retinoid. *Dermatologica* 1978; 157: 238–244.

11. Logan, R.A. Self help groups for patients with chronic skin diseases. *Br. J. Dermatol.* 1988; 118: 505–508.

12. McDowell, I. and Newell, C. *Measuring Health: A Guide to Rating Scales and Questionnaires.* New York, Oxford University Press, 1987.

13. Malone, M., Salek, M.S., Luscombe, D.K. and Harris, A.L. Assessment of health-related quality of life in patients with cancer: using the UK Sickness Impact Profile. *Pharm. J.* 1991; 247 (6657): R50.

14. Marks, R., Barton, S.P., Shuttleworth, D. and Finlay, A.Y. Assessment of disease progress in psoriasis. *Arch. Dermatol.* 1989; 125: 235–240.

15. Medansky, R.S., Handler, R.M. and Medansky, D.L. Self-evaluation of acne and emotion: a pilot study. *Psychosomatics* 1981; 22: 379–383.

16. Motley, R.J. and Finlay, A.Y. How much disability is caused by acne? *Clin. Exp. Dermatol.* 1989; 14: 194–198.

17. Motley, R.J. and Finlay, A.Y. Practical use of diability index in the routine management of acne. *Br. J. Dermatol.* 1990; 123 (Suppl. 37): 12.

18. Rosenberg, M. *Society and the Adolescent Self-image.* Princeton, NJ, Princeton University Press, 1965.

19. Rubinow, D.R., Peck, G.L., Squillace, K.M. and Gantt, G.G. Reduced anxiety and depression in cystic acne patients after suceessful treatment with oral isotretinion. *J. Am. Acad. Dermatol.* 1987; 17: 25–32.

20. Salek, M.S., Peacock, I., Nee, B. and Luscombe, D.K. Is health-related quality

of life assessment important in monitoring patients with diabetes? *Proceedings 19th European Symposium on Clinical Pharmacy, Optimising Clinical Pharmacy Practice*, Amsterdam Medical Press, The Hague 1991; 65–68.

21. Salek, M.S., Luscombe, D.K., Walker, S.R., Grob, P.R., VandenBurg, M.J. and Lewis, M.J. Cardiovascular disease and quality of life. *Br. J. Clin. Pharmacol.* 1988; 26: 628.

22. Salek, M.S., Luscombe, D.K., Walker, S.R., Pughs, S. and VandenBurg, M.J. Quality of life assessment in patients with angina using the UK Sickness Impact Profile. *Br. J. Clin. Pharmacol.* 1988; 25: 99–100.

23. Shuster, S., Fisher, G.H., Harris, E. and Binnell, D. The effect of skin disease on self image. *Br. J. Dermatol.* 1978; 99 (Suppl. 16): 18–19.

24. Van der Meeren, H.L.M., Van der Schaar, W.W. and Van den Hurk, C.M.A.M. The psychological impact of severe acne. *Cutis* 1985; 36: 84–86.

# Section III

# Viewpoints and Perspectives

# 22 Ethical questions and their implication for QOL studies

**C.R.B. Joyce**

In 1983, Culyer[3] pointed out that 'Values impinge in two... ways upon the health indicator's research programme. The first... is that the socio-economic environment... affects not only the way in which policy concerns emerge and are dealt with but also affects researchers themselves: often affecting subconsciously the way in which research questions are put, whether or not particular questions get put at all, and always requiring a sceptical attitude on the part of the researcher as to whether he or she may not be infiltrating values into an apparently "objective" or "scientific" research task'.

'The second arises whenever *action* is based upon health status information, necessarily entailing as it does, either the explicit or implicit weighting of alternative outcomes in terms of "better" or "worse" or, in cost–benefit analysis, the explicit or implicit weighting of benefits (in terms of health improvements or prevention of deterioration) against the costs of attaining them.... . The sorts of issue arising in the first type of value question', he continues, 'are extremely difficult to set out in an orderly fashion'. As an economist concerned with research upon health status, Culyer is chiefly preoccupied with group-based, social and financial rather than personal and psychological consequences. Were this not so, he would certainly have conceded that the kinds of issue arising in connection with the need to *act* and with the form that the action itself will take are also 'extremely difficult to set out in an orderly fashion'. He regrets that, by 1983 at least, extraordinarily little research had been carried out upon these problems. The fact that, 8 years later, the observation is still largely true is the reason for the present short review.

## MORAL SCIENCE AND MEDICAL ETHICS

A moral science, in a European rather than American sense, is a body of knowledge about the subject, including methods. The *Concise* (3rd and 8th editions, 1934 and 1990) and *Shorter Oxford* dictionaries have ethics as the 'science of morals, (a) treatise on this, moral principles, rules of conduct, (the) whole field of moral science;' or 'the science of morals in human conduct; moral principles; rules of conduct; a set of these' and cite 'medical ethics', in parentheses, as a specific example. The American Merriam-Webster dictionary (1974), on the other hand, defines ethics sternly as 'a discipline dealing with good and evil and with moral duty'; or as 'moral principles or practice'.

What do philosophers themselves mean by ethics? Although they may agree with each other as little as lexicographers, most philosophers, at least those of the school that derives from Aristotle, probably hold that moral science, or ethics, is 'the practical science which aims at procuring man's unqualified good...its distinctive object is not the perfection of the works produced and fashioned by man but the good and perfection of the agent himself...' [9]. This definition seems particularly relevant to medicine, where perfection of the work is usually unattainable. Gillon[5], specifically defining medical ethics, refers to the subject as 'the analytic activity in which the concepts, assumptions, beliefs, attitudes, emotions, reasons and arguments underlying medico-moral decision making are examined critically'. He continues: 'at one level the purpose... is simply to make such decision making more thoughtful and intellectually rigorous'. At this level we can surely all agree to conduct our ethical debates.

Medical ethics, as a defined subject area, is considered by the Oxford dictionaries to have appeared for the first time in 1884, although its practice, not labelled as such until then, was an implicit and important part of the practice of Aesculapius and Hippocrates. Health-related quality of life[10] studies (or health status studies, as they are perhaps more accurately called), especially those properly planned and executed, began to appear about 80 years later (i.e. in the 1960s).

Explicit concern about the ethics of decision-making in relation to quality of life, however, is first detectable only within the last decade or so. Indeed, as recently as 4 years ago the distinguished chairman of a National Ethical Review Committee strongly advised that the protocol of a study to develop new methodologies for studying quality of life be reviewed, although no therapeutic interventions were involved, if only because the editor of a journal asked to publish the completed study might otherwise refuse to do so. In fact, every investigation involves an intervention of some kind. The mere adminsitration of a questionnaire is an intervention, and may have positive or negative consequences. The Coronary Artery Surgery Study, among others, has shown (incidentally to its main purpose) that participation in a clinical trial is of itself beneficial to the patient[2].

## POLICY DECISIONS

'Policy-making' conveniently describes compromise among different judgements in order to get something done. In the medical context, vital policies determine the allocation of increasingly scarce resources among competing consumers, and many other issues that require the formulation of a specific policy quickly suggest themselves.

Doctors, administrators and nurses are more and more frequently demanding the expression of clear policies about such matters as resuscitation (or 'do-not-resuscitate') orders and congenital malformations, and curricula that include teaching and discussion of these issues. There is concern about the 'quality of dying' as well as the quality of living. The contribution of the nursing profession to a debate that is increasing in intensity is notable. Nearly a quarter of about 150 papers on the relationship between quality of life and ethics published in the medical literature in the last 7 years have appeared within the last 12 months. Just over one-third of the total have appeared in nursing or related journals. Other members of the community, economists, civil servants and politicians, are concerned about the allocation of resources between patients suffering from conditions that vary greatly in prevalence, incidence and prognosis, and in the social and individual burdens that these impose upon groups that differ widely as to age and disadvantage. Taxpayers and payers of insurance premiums, as well as politicians, insurers and health administrators are worried about cost containment. Such problems require ethical discussion.

A cynic might comment that the multiplication of policies, guidelines and curricula is due to increasing need for self-protection in an ever more aggressive and litigious society. An alternative view is that there is an increasing desire to recover some of the certainty in action that has been progressively lost in the contemporary triumph of relative thinking over older, more absolute ways. And because this is a deeply divided and separated time, the discussion must be both wider and deeper than policy-making in the sense of either medical or administrative management. The isolated individual is no longer immune, nor is his undiscussed standpoint sufficient.

The chief problems with which ethics is concerned are[12]:

(1)  definition of an ultimate standard of right conduct;

(2)  identification of the source from which knowledge of standards is derived;

(3)  definition of the sanctions that apply to such conduct; and

(4)    understanding the motives that prompt the application of sanctions.

Gillon advances four general principles that apply in particular to philosophical medical ethics: respect for autonomy; beneficence; non-maleficence; and justice. These are as relevant to quality of life as to the rest of medicine. As an example, the principle of autonomy is invoked by a conflict between a patient's assessment of quality of life and the doctor's assessment of that patient's physical and other needs. The principle of justice is invoked to ensure that resources are fairly allocated; and so on. It may not be too much to claim that medical ethics illuminates the great discourse, rather than the other way about, for it is concerned with wide ranging questions 'about the scope of our moral obligations to human beings at different stages of their lives[6].'

There is generally little disagreement about the identification of situations that pose ethical problems, but disagreement arises when their solutions are sought. Does the pursuit of happiness, the search for perfection or the execution of duty offer a better guide to right conduct? Is knowledge of the standards of right conduct best derived empirically, by experience and learning from others, by rational thought, or by intuition? Or is it 'given' in some other way, by *Diktat* or revelation? Is the *summum bonum*, the greatest good, a sufficient justification in itself for the application of its own sanctions, or do moral sanctions have a religious, political, legal or other social base? Easy or pure answers are seldom easy to find, especially insofar as medical research is concerned, and even more especially in regard to quality of life.

The critical examination and analysis of the factors underlying 'medico-moral decision-making' do not therefore lead to tablets of stone engraved with the answers to every problem, in part because so-called standards arrived in a relative way, but more because each problem is unique to the individuals concerned. There are no absolutes, not even 'Thou shalt not kill', if a decision to save the baby may lose the mother, and vice versa.

Reference to 'policies' about therapeutic decisions has reminded some critics of National Socialist attitudes to medicine. Irrelevant emotions are aroused because 'value' is confused with 'quality' of life[1]. Each life has a quality, good or bad, as every life has a value; but no estimate of the quality of a life, however arrived at, ought ever to influence judgement of its value. The distinction is crucial.

## ETHICAL DECISIONS IN QUALITY OF LIFE RESEARCH

### Clinical research

Information about the benefits of a new treatment becomes available when the drug enters clinical research, but information about risks has to await its appearance on the market, with the well-known and largely unsolved methodological difficulties that evaluation then presents. In clinical research, as in medical practice, the first law is that the interest of the individual patient is paramount. An experiment that may damage an individual without possibility of benefit (especially to his or her quality of life) is not justified, even if it is known that it will provide information of great value to an untold number of others, *unless* the individual concerned, having been as fully informed as possible of the risks and the lack of benefits, agrees to take part. Known material risks must be disclosed to the patient, who is not, however, thereby fully informed. (Consent can never be given on the basis of full information, however common the belief that this is so; for if full information about the risks and benefits of the intended intervention were available, there would be no need for an experiment and it would therefore be unethical to perform it.) Nevertheless, when the patient is consulted in this – inevitably restricted – way, individual autonomy is respected and the research can accommodate the individual good that would otherwise not be one of its aims.

Levine[8] has described criteria for determining the need for quality of life assessments with any new form of therapy, based upon the concept of material risk, that conflict somewhat with this point of view. He considers that research will be needed when 'there are good reasons to predict that (the) results will yield information that will be of practical utility to doctors and patients making choices about whether to use the new therapy and when the importance of such information justifies the costs and risks of developing it'. Such 'good reasons', Levine suggests, will also include 'a finding that the new therapy has an effect that is likely to impair quality of life... for example, protracted nausea, exercise intolerance or the dumping syndrome.' Although he refers to this aid to decision-making as a guideline, he admits that 'terms such as "practical utility", "importance" and "justifies" do not have precise, inelastic meanings. Deciding what is important or justified in particular cases cannot be accomplished according to an ethical algorithm'. However, where the criteria can be satisfied, it will be unethical *not* to carry out quality of life studies with new drugs (or, we may add, with old drugs too).

Even if the intervention can be expected to have as beneficial an effect upon the patient (including his quality of life) as the best alternative treatment, the individual's own reaction to such predictions must dominate. A life-saving (or, less inaccurately described, a life-prolonging) treatment is by no means always an acceptable one. How can the patient's perspective on such matters be incorporated?

Some of the interesting but rather artificial methods (such as the 'time trade-off' and the 'standard gamble') currently used by those approaching the topic from the standpoint of health economics, to estimate the exchange that subjects are prepared to make of length of life for life quality, themselves appear to pose ethical problems. Should patients actually suffering from severe, possibly terminal, diseases be asked to estimate these 'trade-offs' between time, or cash, and quality of life even – perhaps especially – on their own behalf? It seems unlikely that healthy subjects normally reason about these matters in such terms either. Even if they did, the information provided would scarcely be relevant to the sick; the healthy are not in distress and their choices are thus hypothetical. Although such criticisms call in question the methodology and value of estimating Quality Adjusted Life-Years (QALYs), research is still worth pursuing, for only if better methods are found can the realism and hence usefulness of the information be improved.

As already pointed out, even non-intervention is an event: total inaction or avoidance of contact by medical staff is correctly perceived by the patient as a powerful communication. So, just as an ethical, traditional clinical trial ensures that medication found to benefit each individual will continue to be provided during an appropriate period of follow-up, the quality of life of patients who have been studied in this way should similarly be followed up. This is not only to observe the long-term effects of the active and control interventions on the quality of life itself, but because the very procedures of assessing quality of life often provide important support, or other benefits. Patients taking part in trials of this nature not infrequently testify that 'no one ever asked me that kind of question before'; or 'no one ever took so much interest in what I thought'. If the investigator charged with collecting the information is skilful and empathetic, his or, more probably, her behaviour may be therapeutic for the patient. Hence, it may diminish the scientific value of the information collected. If so, individual interests, as always, must be given precedence, unless the patient voluntarily consents to subordinate them.

### Industrial research

As the assessment of quality of life is increasingly incorporated into research by the pharmaceutical industry, it becomes more and more necessary for such members of a drug company as financial directors, product managers and field representatives, not to speak of shareholders, to examine their decisions in an ethical light. A single person will rarely be able to make an ethical decision about a quality of life problem unaided, although such an individual may often make one that is unethical. Almost always, at least two persons will be involved: the medical director with an investigator; the clinical researcher designing the trial with the statistician; the finance director or chairman of the board with the majority shareholder; the editor with one of his or her authors; and, most obviously and importantly, not only the doctor with the patient, but also the patient with one or more members of the immediate family. It will almost always be useful, and frequently essential, to involve a third person (with a neutral standpoint) in the decision.

They will not always be seen as coming under this heading, but ethical questions in research and development, product management and marketing will often arise in connection with 'me-too' drugs, or even more tellingly, 'me-agains'[7]. It may seem paradoxical to suggest that a study making use of quality of life assessments as outcome measures may be an ethically satisfactory way of justifying the continuation of research with such substances. This is because a new compound that is otherwise indistinguishable from a 'me-too' drug may improve the quality of life of at least some patients whose quality of life was not improved by the congener. There is no doubt of the validity of the 'horses-for-courses' argument (that there are drugs that suit some patients and not others, like doctors). A study of their effect upon quality of life may also be the only way to differentiate members of a group of life-saving but very toxic drugs.

It is unethical for those who market a drug to claim that it improves quality of life without defining what they mean by the term, and still more so to fail to substantiate the claims that they make. This behaviour (it may almost be called a habit), has been so prevalent at times in regard to quality of life, and the anxiety not to miss the economic bandwagon it was expected to represent so great, that the very concept has at times appeared likely to fall into disrepute. Fortunately, the danger seems to have lessened recently (or perhaps for various reasons the volume of ethically unsatisfactory medical advertising has been reduced).

Product managers not uncommonly 'position' the same drug differently in different markets. If a claim for enhanced quality of life is made in one market it should be made in all others; if such a claim has failed in one market, it should not be made elsewhere unless there is clear justification (such as demonstrated cultural differences). Other instances of ethically doubtful behaviour may be no less important.

There is always a strong drive in industrial (as well as academic) research to get 'positive' results. One of the most reliable ways to show interesting differences between treatments is to choose controls that are not the best competitors but those likely to perform least well. One of the earliest of the still rather small number of published so-called quality of life (i.e. health status) clinical trials committed this sophistry, and it is not uncommon for marketing departments to plead for controls of this kind to be used, a practice indeed not unknown in traditional trials. Related unacceptable practices with a long history (and no doubt, alas, a long future as well) include decisions not to carry out a study if the effects on quality of life are expected to be negative, and failure to publish the results if they turn out, unexpectedly, to be so.

What if the effect of a compound that has been studied in a satisfactory way also satisfies clinical criteria for improvement (for example: reduction of blood pressure, control of blood sugar) but causes patients to report an unacceptable deterioration in their quality of life for other reasons? It would seem that if the condition from which they are suffering is life-threatening, clinical criteria should predominate. But this is not necessarily so; a medical decision not to change a clinically successful treatment may unjustifiably interfere with the patient's autonomy. It is a matter for the patient and the physician to decide together, but if such cases occur often enough, the producer will have to consider whether or not to keep the drug on the market. An even more difficult decision would have to be taken if a drug were found that prolonged, but did not necessarily improve the quality of, the life of patients suffering a chronic disease, the treatment of which involved heavy social as well as individual costs. Both these not necessarily hypothetical situations obviously involve social policy, but the contribution of the industrial decision maker to their ethical solution cannot be ignored. A decision to develop a new drug showing evidence of greater efficacy than existing compounds but involving higher costs to the patient, thus reducing resources available for purposes that are perhaps as important, or more so, should also give rise to ethical discussions at the social as well as the individual level.

### Publishing decisions

And then there are the editors of the medical as well as the popular press. The responsibility of the journal editor is not exhausted on being satisfied that the authors have carefully carried out the plan that they originally submitted to ethical review. Feinstein, writing about the consequences of the publicity given to epidemiological research upon the alleged carcinogenicity of diethylstilboestrol, has pointed out that 'even if it does indeed cause clear cell cancer of the female genital tract, the risk is so small that no such cancers were found in two properly assembled cohorts containing about 2500 exposed women. In the meantime, because of the publicity, several million women (and men) exposed *in utero* before the 1960s have been leading lives of cancerophobic terror, dreading the imminent development of genital tract malignancy. Has this adverse effect on the quality of so many lives been suitably evaluated?[4].' The example is not isolated; as short a period as one week elapsed between the publication in a Sunday newspaper of a serious but uncommon adverse effect of a life-saving drug and the death of a patient who ceased to take it upon reading an uncritical and ill-advised report. The change in the quality of life of this lady thus brought about was dramatic indeed, though only indirectly medical (the reporter was the newspaper's lay medical correspondent). One can only speculate about the incidence of similar events. A general obsession with the avoidance of medical risk has perhaps been fed to surfeit by members of the profession and their associates who too often seem to prefer to publish bad news. It is true that unwanted reactions can sometimes damage the quality of life of individual patients, or even shorten the lives of some; but there is an ethical obligation to try to weigh against these the beneficial effects upon the lives of a usually far greater number. The obligation to demonstrate, and fully document in both clinical research and practice, effects of both kinds is even stronger.

## CONCLUSION

The ethical issues raised by research involving the assessment of quality of life are not fundamentally different from those in other areas of medicine. As so often, the general task has been stated in lapidary fashion by Bertrand Russell: 'Without civic morality, communities perish; without personal morality, their survival has no value'[11]. The greatest need does not therefore appear to be for specialized research, but for the far more difficult, self-imposed, task of deciding at every step of practice or research if an ethical issue arises. Unless this reaction becomes habitual, the answer will be given by default. The best odds that a default answer will prove correct are no better than one in two, and these are totally insufficient where matters of life and death are concerned. They will certainly not satisfy those who become aware of them.

### Acknowledgement

I am very grateful to Dr Hannah McGee for thought-provoking suggestions on a draft.

### References

1. Cohen, C.B. "Quality of Life" and the analogy with the Nazis. *J. Med. Philos.* 1983; 8: 113–135.
2. Coronary Artery Surgery Study Principal Investigators and their Associates. Coronary Artery Surgery Study (CASS) A randomized trial of coronary artery bypass surgery. Quality of life in patients randomly assigned to treatment groups. *Circulation* 1983; 68: 951–960.
3. Culyer, A.J. (ed.). *Health Indicators.* Oxford: Martin Robertson, 1983, pp. 18–20.
4. Feinstein. A. Scientific news and epidemiologic editorials: a reply to the critics. *Epidemiology* 1990; 1: 170–180.
5. Gillon, R. *Philosophical Medical Ethics.* Chichester: John Wiley, 1986, p. 2.
6. Gillon, R. *Philosophical Medical Ethics.* Chichester: John Wiley, 1986, p. 183.
7. Joyce, C.R.B. "Me-toos", "me-agains" and the risk of drugs. *Br. Med. J.* 1980; 2: 286–287.
8. Levine, R.J. An ethical perspective. In Spilker, B. (ed.) *Quality of Life Assessments in Clinical Trials.* New York: Raven Press, 1990.

9. Maritain, J. *An Introduction to Philosophy*. London: Sheed and Ward, 1930.
10. Patrick, D.L. and Erickson, P. What constitutes quality of life? Concepts and dimensions. *Qual. Life Cardiovasc. Care* 1988; 103–127.
11. Russell, B. Unpublished lectures on Ethics, University of Cambridge, 1947–8.
12. Wolf, A. Ethics. *Encyclopaedia Britannica* 8: 757 *et seq.*, 1946.

# 23 Industry perspectives on quality of life

**Stuart R. Walker**

Since the 1950s the double-blind controlled clinical trial has become the standard by which the efficacy of a new medicine is determined. However, while traditional endpoints are still crucial in measuring the benefits of new and existing therapy, the question is now 'do we need innovative outcomes to more fully appreciate the benefits of medicines from the standpoint of the patient, the physician and the pharmaceutical company?'.

The historical background to the development of socio-economic measurements of health outcome and the effectiveness of drug therapy (Figure 23.1) indicates that, since the 1950s, the controlled clinical trial has answered the question 'does the treatment work?'. The introduction of cost–benefit analyses in the 1950s and 1960s provided the framework for measuring the overall economic benefits of medical care and setting them against the corresponding costs by answering the question 'does the treatment pay off?'. During the 1960s and 1970s the economic emphasis swung away from cost–benefit analysis to the concept of cost–effectiveness analysis which questioned 'which is the most effective treatment using given resources?'. However, since the 1980s the principles of cost–utility analysis have introduced the concept of utility as a measurement of value to complement the financial aspects and answer the question 'how does the treatment impact on length and quality of life?'.

It is useful in any discussion of quality of life to define what we mean by certain terms, for to be involved in valid quality of life studies requires a clear definition of the terminology which is broadly accepted and understood by those involved in this research. 'Health status' is a measure of an individual's function in terms of physical, social and mental well being, while 'quality of life' is more related to how a person feels and functions in his or her everyday life. 'Quality of life' has been defined as a concept encompassing a broad range of physical and psychological characteristics and limitations which describe an individual's ability to function and derive satisfaction from so doing. However, with regard to measuring the benefits of medicines

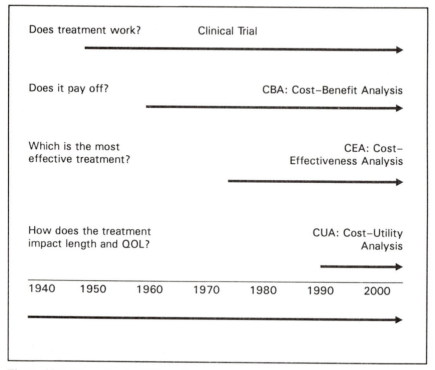

**Figure 23.1** Measuring health benefits

'health-related quality of life' is probably the key term and this is defined as the level of well being and satisfaction associated with an individual's life and how this is affected by disease, accidents and treatment.

## THE NEED

It was Ware et al.[5] in 1981 who indicated there were a number of reasons for studying health status which could well apply to quality of life, namely, measuring the effectiveness of medical intervention, improving clinical decisions, assessing the quality of care, estimating the needs of the population and understanding the causes and consequences in differences in health. The need to move from solely traditional endpoints to innovative outcomes is underlined by the fact that today's goal is perhaps not so much seeking the cure for a disease, but rather an improvement in function, the resolution of symptoms and the opportunity to limit the progression of the disease and to improve a patient's quality of life.

In a recent article Buxton and Drummond[1] identified three main reasons

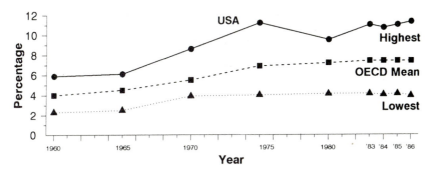

**Figure 23.2** Total health care expenditure, percentage of gross domestic product – OECD countries, 1960–86 (23 countries, excluding Turkey). Based on data in ref. 3

why quality of life data are so important in assessing the impact of medical intervention. They stated first, that while it is still possible to identify new interventions that extend life such as medicines for AIDS, most modern drugs are concerned with improving the quality not quantity of life. Therefore, measures are required to assess the impact of intervention for chronic conditions such as rheumatoid arthritis, cardiovascular disease, and so forth. Secondly, most medical interventions are not entirely beneficial. They have associated risks of side-effects which need to be considered alongside their therapeutic characteristics. Thirdly, some interventions have serious associated risks that could reduce life expectancy but offer, in return, improvements in the quality of life, e.g. open heart surgery. Alternatively, some interventions may extend life yet have serious unpleasant adverse effects, e.g. cancer chemotherapy. In such situations one not only wants to measure quality of life but also assess how individuals trade-off length of life for improvements in quality. The measurements of utilities – the relative evaluation of alternative outcomes – permits this assessment and the 'quality adjusted life-year' or QALY is now the most familiar of such measures.

Currently the trends in health care expenditure in major countries such as the USA, UK, Sweden, Japan and Germany underline the increasing importance, as well as the increased cost, of meeting the health care needs of patients in these countries (Figure 23.2). In addition, a number of current government initiatives have provided a further stimulus to those involved in the evaluation of new medicines to make sure that we have the most appropriate means of determining their benefits. Some of these initiatives include global budgets for hospitals, cash limits on health authorities, clinical budgeting experiments, positive and negative lists of medicines, monitoring of physicians' prescribing costs and the limiting of reimbursement for medicines.

Quality of life measurements, therefore, offer direct assessment of those features of medical interventions which are typically measured indirectly as

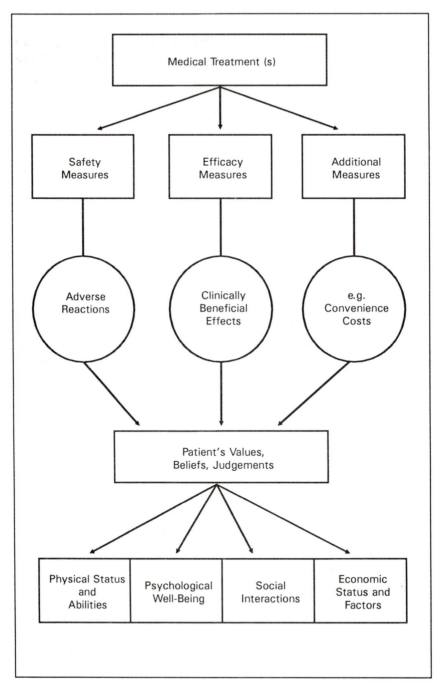

**Figure 23.3** Reproduced from Ref 4, with permission

well as giving the overall impact on the patient of a combination of effects which could be both adverse and beneficial. This latter point is illustrated in Figure 23.3

Currently there is a need for further studies on:

1.  The role of quality of life assessment incorporated within medical practice as this ultimately can affect both perception and actual measures of therapeutic efficacy.

2.  The importance and nature by which the type of disease in certain cultural settings affects assessment of quality of life using standard instruments.

3.  How the measurement of quality of life can be practicably translated into information which can be broadly and consistently useful for understanding the benefits of pharmaceuticals.

## THE BENEFITS

The potential benefits of measuring health-related quality of life should concern a number of groups, namely, patients, physicians, pharmaceutical companies, regulatory authorities and health authorities. The opportunity for patients to express and assess the impact of their disease and subsequent treatment on life-style is often of more importance to them than the impact of treatment on clinical parameters. The immediate benefits on their quality of life, again, is often of more interest than the long term gain which may include extension of life. For physicians the ability to have alternative methods of measuring outcome may, subsequently, influence their prescribing patterns. For pharmaceutical companies these innovative measures are of value in comparing different therapies, assessing the outcome of treatment and are of value in the drug development process as well as providing data which may allow the repositioning of medicines and a re-assessment of the balance between benefits and risks. The regulatory authorities are becoming increasingly interested in health-related quality of life measures. Buxton and Drummond[1] stated that 'licensing authorities sometimes have to make difficult decisions relating to the trade-off between risks and benefits of new medicines'. These decisions are taken on a case-by-case basis and depend critically on the likely use of the medicine and the existence of acceptable clinical alternatives. Clearly such decisions cannot always be determined totally by objective criteria. Some information from patients or members of the general public, who may be potential patients and who make the trade-offs between benefits and risks, could be of value and ultimately influential in making the appropriate regulatory decision. For health authorities who may be involved in determining which medicines are reimbursed and which are admitted to a formulary, health-related quality of life may be of increasing importance.


## THE OPPORTUNITIES

There is undoubtedly a need in the evaluation of new medicines for the determination of hard clinical endpoints, as well as an agreement as to what change will represent a clinically significant difference. The degree of the difference that is considered clinically significant, is a judgement often made by the researchers based on their knowledge of prognosis with and without treatment. However, in the absence of quality of life data it is often not clear whether the difference in a clinical measure, such as forced expiratory volume in one second ($FEV_1$), as measured in chronic obstructive lung disease, is really significant to the patients concerned and, if so, whether it is relevant as a prognostic indicator or as a determinant of current quality of life. The situation is further confounded if the treatment itself has side-effects that affect the patient's health status. There is, therefore, a heavy onus on those involved in developing and advocating the use of quality of life measures to ensure that these measures have been subjected to the rigorous assessment of validity and reliability[1].

There is undoubtedly a number of disease areas where the inclusion of health-related quality of life data would be of utmost value in determining outcome. Leighton Read[2] has suggested that, in any area where quality of life is being considered, an important step is to develop a medical model of the disease to be investigated which should, subsequently, be compared with the socio-economic model. This chapter provides a medical model for respiratory diseases and demonstrates how this could be considered in terms of socio-economic issues (Figure 23.4 and 23.5).

A major opportunity provided by 'health-related quality of life' assessment might well allow the repositioning of a new or established medicine in terms of the benefit/risk ratio. The following figures demonstrate that with information on clinical benefits and a knowledge of risks from a particular treatment, it should be possible, ideally, to place any medicine within one of the four quadrants (Figure 23.6). In general terms a medicine with major clinical benefits but low risk would indicate a breakthrough drug while a medicine with minor clinical benefits but high risks would indicate a disaster. Low benefits and low risks might be a poor situation for any medicine while, in special circumstances, high risks might be tolerated for major clinical benefits in certain life threatening diseases.

However the following figure (Figure 23.7) indicates that the position of any medicine in Figure 23.6 could well be altered by measuring and then combining the clinical benefits with quality of life measurements and

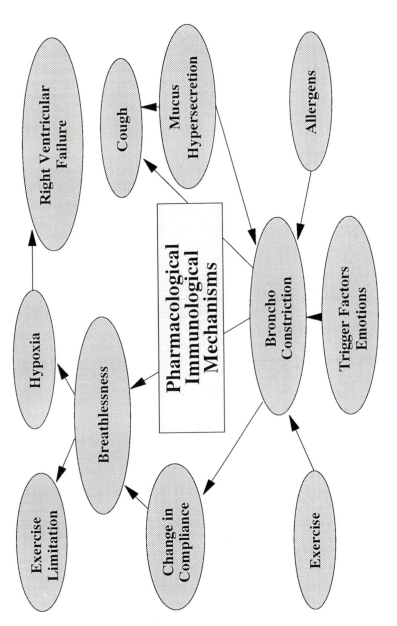

**Figure 23.4** Respiratory disease – a medical model

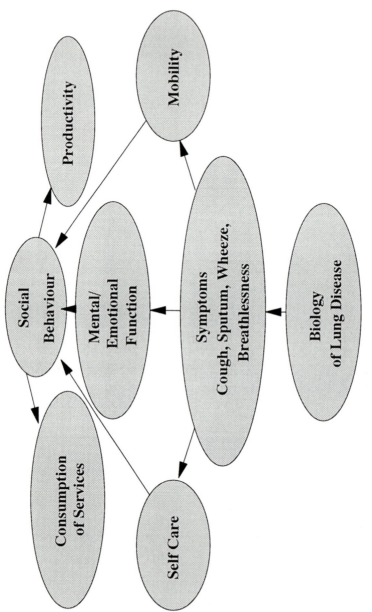

**Figure 23.5** Respiratory disease – a socio-economic model

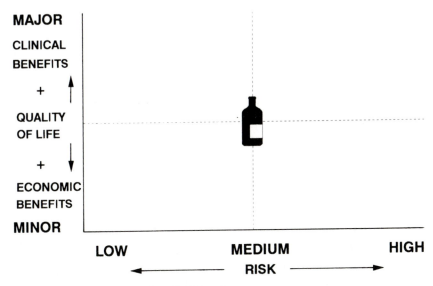

**Figure 23.6** Medicines – the benefit/risk ratio

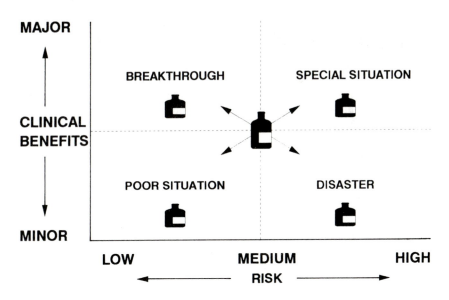

**Figure 23.7** Medicines – the benefit/risk ratio

economic outcomes. The measurement of such additional benefits could move a medicine from the lower part of the graph to the higher quadrants.

## THE PRINCIPLES

In considering health-related quality of life studies the plan for a pharmaceutical company should be as follows:

1. Define what one means by 'health-related quality of life';

2. Develop a conceptual framework initially producing a medical model of the disease and, subsequently, a socio-economic model;

3. Review the generic and specific instruments available rather than developing a new instrument unless one is prepared to go through the various issues and procedures required for validating a new instrument;

4. Having selected the appropriate instrument, assess its potential value in the disease area to be examined, and

5. Complete a pilot study to identify the applicability and suitability of using such an instrument in the study proposed before a full scale evaluation is carried out.

Spilker[4] has indicated in a recent book entitled 'Quality of Life Assessments and Clinical Trials' that the quality of life field is a rapidly changing and developing medical area. The standards developed over the next few years will probably have a major influence on this area for a very long period. Whilst it may be considered premature to define the golden rules of this field, there is no doubt that serious consideration should be given to the move from solely traditional endpoints to innovative outcomes in estimating the benefits of medicines.

## References

1. Buxton, M.J. and Drummond, M.R. Quality of life measurement in the development of medicines. *J. Pharmaceut.* 1990; 3 Mar: 260–2.
2. Read, J.L. From medical to socioeconomic evaluation of drug therapy. In van Eimeren, W. and Horisberger, B. (eds) *Socioeconomic Evaluation of Drug Therapy.* Springer-Verlag, Berlin, Heidelberg, New York, Tokyo, 1988, pp. 72–81.
3. Schieber, G.J. and Poullier, J.P. Health spending and utilization trends. *Health Aff.* 1988; 7(4):105–112.
4. Spilker, B. *Quality of Life Assessment in Clinical Trials.* New York, Raven, 1990
5. Ware, J.E., Brook, R.H., Davies-Avery, A. and Lohv, K.N. Choosing measures of health studies for individuals and general population. *Am. J. Publ. Health* 1981; 71: 620–625.

# 24 A regulatory view

## J.R. Johnson

Improvement in quality of life (QOL) is an important objective of treatment for many illnesses. Thus the United States Food and Drug Administration (FDA) is interested in assessing the effect of new drugs on QOL. There has been more internal FDA discussion and more collaboration with industry and academia on QOL assessment in cancer than other diseases. Cancer will be used in this chapter as a model for describing the FDA perspective on QOL assessment in clinical trials.

The two objectives of cancer treatment are prolongation of life and improvement in QOL. All other efficacy endpoints, such as objective tumour response (tumour shrinkage), response duration and time to tumour progression are only possible surrogates for prolongation of survival or improved QOL. Often the cancer drug regimens are known not to improve survival and the only objective of therapy is palliation or improvement in the QOL. Cancer drugs usually have severe side-effects. Yet most cancer drug studies do not include any direct assessment of QOL other than recording the side-effects of the drugs.

Quality of life assessment is important not only when palliation is the sole objective, but also in comparing curative regimens where there is more than one alternative.

Improvement in QOL in cancer patients is a sufficient basis for FDA approval of cancer drug marketing applications. The FDA view on assessment of QOL in cancer drug clinical trials has previously been described[3]. Quality of life assessment can be divided into four categories. These are QOL surrogates, relief of cancer specific symptoms, decreased adverse effects of treatment and QOL instruments.

## QUALITY OF LIFE SURROGATES

In some circumstances the FDA has accepted surrogates for QOL without any direct measurement of QOL. For example, complete responses of long duration in acute leukaemia are assumed to result in improved QOL and have been the basis for drug marketing approval even in the absence of other

393

evidence of improved QOL and even in the absence of an improvement in survival. Another example is that increased disease free survival due to adjuvant drug therapy of breast cancer is assumed to result in improved QOL and has been the basis for marketing approval even in the absence of other evidence of improved QOL and in the absence of an improvement in survival. An important factor here is that 80% of breast cancer patients are symptomatic at the time of recurrence. Also the mental impact on patients of knowing that they may be cured is an important factor.

Gelber and co-workers have described a method called TWIST (time without symptoms or treatment) for assessing QOL in breast cancer studies when the adjuvant drug therapy is toxic. The objective is to determine the amount of 'good' time the adjuvant therapy adds to no treatment. The median time without either toxic therapy or disease symptoms in the treated patients should exceed the median time without disease symptoms in the untreated control patients[1]. This method is appropriate for cytotoxic drugs with strong side-effects, but is less appropriate for drugs with modest side-effects such as tamoxifen. TWIST is an 'all or nothing' method and does not allow for differences in side-effects of treatment regimens.

A modification of TWIST called Q-TWIST credits some value to time on treatment and time with symptoms by using utility coefficients for time on treatment and time with symptoms. The utility coefficients may be estimated based on clinical experience, but are preferably calculated using QOL data[2]. For example, one might determine that the time on adjuvant treatment with a particular drug has a utility coefficient of 50%. Thus 12 months of adjuvant treatment with this drug would be credited as 6 months of 'good' time. This modification of TWIST is applicable regardless of the severity of drug side-effects.


## RELIEF OF CANCER SPECIFIC SYMPTOMS

Quality of life can be evaluated on the basis of relief of disease specific symptoms. For example, $\alpha$-interferon was approved for treatment of hairy cell leukaemia based on a decrease in transfusion dependence and in the incidence of acute infections. Sandostatin, a somatostatin analogue, was approved on the basis of relief of the watery diarrhoea hypokalaemic acidosis syndrome seen in patients with VIPomas without any antitumour effect being demonstrated. Other possibilities would include relief of an obstructed hollow viscus (e.g. oesophagus or bronchus), gain in weight (lean body mass) in cachectic patients or relief of pain.

## DECREASED ADVERSE EFFECTS OF TREATMENT

Quality of life assessment in cancer drug studies may involve comparing the side-effects of drug analogues or regimens containing different drugs. New drugs may also be tested to determine if they prevent the side-effects of cancer drugs, e.g. antiemetic. Other examples are drugs to prevent renal toxicity of cisplatin, cardiotoxicity of doxorubicin and haematological toxicity of myelo-suppressive drugs. A decrease in toxicity is meaningful only if the drug is an effective anticancer drug in the first place and if the anticancer effect is not unduly diminished along with the toxicity.

## QUALITY OF LIFE INSTRUMENTS

### A Hypothetical Instrument

Table 24.1 Hypothetical QOL Instrument Spectrum

| Disease specific | Disease specific symptoms |
|---|---|
| | General symptoms |
| | Specific physical function (ambulate, walk, stairs) |
| | General physical function (work, sports) |
| | General well-being |
| | Social function |
| Abstract | Global evaluation |

Table 24.1 shows the spectrum of a hypothetical QOL instrument. As we progress down this spectrum from disease specific symptoms to global evaluation, physicians become progressively less confident in the QOL assessment. Depending on the disease being assessed we lose most physicians when we progress beyond assessment of physical function, if not sooner. Yet symptoms are a measure of the disease, not the patient's life. If we want to measure the effect of the disease on the patient's life, we must measure the more abstract components at the bottom of the table.

### Uses

Quality of life instruments can be used in clinical trials as discriminants, prognostic factors or outcome measures. A discriminant may distinguish between patients who are very sick and those who are not. It could be used for selection of patients for a clinical trial. A prognostic factor predicts

**Table 24.2** QOL Instrument Uses

| | |
|---|---|
| Discriminant | Patient selection |
| Prognostic factor | Pre-randomization stratification |
| Outcome parameter | Outcome in randomized trial |

outcome and could be used for pre-randomization stratification of patients. An outcome measure could be used in a randomized clinical trial to compare outcomes of the treatment arms (Table 24.2). An outcome measure must be responsive to change and be sufficiently sensitive to detect a clinically meaningful difference between treatments. A QOL instrument useful for any one of these purposes (discriminant, prognostic factor or outcome measure) is not necessarily useful for the others. The QOL instrument must be validated for the specific purpose for which it is used.

### Validation

Quality of life instruments used in cancer clinical trials must be validated for cancer and probably for each specific kind of cancer. Perhaps a basic QOL instrument can be developed for cancer with a separate module (component) that can be changed for each kind of cancer.

Most interest in cancer clinical trials involves use of QOL assessment as an outcome measure. It is necessary that the QOL instrument be validated as an outcome measure in cancer. One sometimes hears that a particular QOL instrument has been validated in cancer. Often most of the validation has been in other diseases and the validation in cancer has been as a discriminant or a prognostic factor. The FDA knows of no QOL instrument that has been adequately validated to measure the difference in outcome between treatment arms of a randomized cancer clinical trial.

The question arises how a QOL instrument can be validated for use in cancer. Because there is no gold standard for measurement of QOL, we must depend on showing construct validity (comparison to other QOL instruments) and concurrent validity (comparison to other efficacy parameters). We can do this only by incorporating the best instruments into randomized cancer clinical trials and using them repeatedly until we gain confidence in them. This is starting to happen in the United States. The National Institutes of Health held a Workshop on QOL evaluation in cancer clinical trials in July 1990 and is beginning to encourage more measurement of QOL in cancer clinical trials.

Quality of life advocates believe QOL instruments measure something that is both important and different from other efficacy parameters. If this is correct, we must have sufficient confidence in the QOL instrument to accept the result even when it is different from other efficacy parameters.

**Table 24.3** Karnofsky Performance Status Scale

| | |
|---|---|
| 100 | Normal. No complaints. No evidence of disease |
| 90 | Normal Activity. Minor signs or symptoms of disease |
| 80 | Normal activity with effort. Some signs or symptoms of disease |
| 70 | Cares for self. Unable to carry on normal activity or do active work |
| 60 | Requires occasional assistance, but able to care for most of needs |
| 50 | Requires considerable assistance and frequent medical care |
| 40 | Disabled. Requires special care and assistance |
| 30 | Severely disabled. Hospitalization indicated,but death not imminent |
| 20 | Hospitalization necessary. Very sick. Active supportive treatment necessary |
| 10 | Moribund. Fatal processes progressing rapidly |
| 0 | Dead |

### Define QOL Instrument in Clinically Meaningful Terms

Quality of life instruments should be defined in clinically meaningful terms. For example, the Karnofsky Performance Status scale is a measure of physical function that assesses ability to perform work and self-care activities (Table 24.3). The scale runs from 0 to 100 in 10 point increments with 0 being dead and 100 being normal. Note that each interval is defined in clinically meaningful terms. Thus if a patient's score improves from 50 to 80, the clinician can assess whether this is a clinically meaningful change. Contrast this with a 100 point LASA scale (Table 24.4). The intervals along the scale are not defined in clinically meaningful terms except at each end. The clinician does not know in clinical terms what benefit an improvement of 50 to 80 on this LASA scale represents. One needs to know that the change is not only statistically significant but also clinically significant.

**Table 24.4** LASA Scale

$$
\begin{array}{c}
100 \quad \text{Good} \\
\vert \\
0 \quad \text{Lousy}
\end{array}
$$

### TIMING OF QOL ASSESSMENT

Another QOL issue is the timing of QOL assessments in cancer clinical trials. Should assessment of QOL be during maximum toxicity of therapy or after maximum recovery from toxicity or both? Certainly there must be equal assessment of QOL in all treatment arms of the trial. Usually change from baseline is used rather than the absolute QOL score. This should be measured at fixed intervals after the treatment. Alternately a survival curve type analysis can be done, defining a specific change from baseline as an event. The most impressive result is an improvement over baseline rather than only a difference in the rate of decline. With cancer clinical trials a rather high QOL score (e.g. physical performance status) is often a requirement for study entry. In this situation there is not much room for improvement.

In cancer clinical trials one must consider the effect of 'time bias' on QOL assessment. If patients are dying at a faster rate on one treatment arm, a time may be reached when there is worse QOL on the treatment arm with the best survival.

Where QOL assessments continue over long periods of time, changing patient expectations and adjustments to illness occur. These may affect the results of QOL assessment.

## MISCELLANEOUS QOL ASSESSMENT ISSUES

Some additional issues regarding QOL assessment are:

(1)    Is QOL best assessed by the patient, the family or the health professional? These assessments sometimes differ considerably. Most workers in this field believe QOL is best assessed by the patient. The health professional is best at assessing the severity of the illness.

(2)    Should both the patient and the health professional assessing QOL be blinded as to objective tumour response? Obviously if the patient is told the tumour is dramatically responding, this may impact on the QOL assessment.

(3)    Should the components of the QOL instrument be totalled for one score?

(4)    If each component of the QOL instrument is separately analysed, how are the multiple comparisons addressed statistically?

(5)    How is the result interpreted if only a minority of the QOL components are affected at a statistically significant level?

(6)    Are linear analogue scales linear? Is a numerical change at one end of the scale equivalent to the same change at the other end of the scale?

## CANCER DRUG MARKETING APPLICATIONS

Very few studies in cancer drug marketing applications have attempted to measure QOL using QOL instruments. The QOL portion of the studies have not been well conducted, with a substantial number of eligible patients not participating and much missing data. No cancer drug has been approved by the FDA based on improved QOL as measured by QOL instruments. The FDA does not believe that any QOL instrument has been adequately validated as an outcome parameter in randomized cancer clinical trials. Drug companies and the academic community are strongly encouraged to include QOL evaluation in cancer clinical trials, so that the QOL assessment methods can be validated.

## A REGULATORY VIEW

A drug regulatory agency can use QOL assessment as the principal basis for marketing approval, supportive of other efficacy parameters as a basis for marketing approval or comparison of treatments for labelling or promotional purposes. The FDA has approved cancer drug marketing applications on the basis of improved QOL, but not on the basis of QOL assessment using QOL instruments. In discussions with my colleagues in other drug groups at the FDA they indicate that QOL data is not submitted in applications for drug marketing. They occasionally see QOL data in post marketing studies comparing treatments as a basis for supporting labelling claims or promotional activities. It is for this use that QOL assessment has the most support at the FDA. This is on condition that the QOL evaluation is based on disease specific symptoms or drug side-effects. None of the colleagues that I discussed this with at the FDA accepts QOL evaluation based on the more abstract domains of QOL instruments, such as general well being or social function. Because this kind of QOL assessment is not presently submitted by drug companies in marketing applications, the FDA staff has not had reason to study this issue in depth. They are willing to look at any data that QOL proponents wish to present.

## FINANCIAL CONSIDERATIONS IN DRUG REGULATION

Government regulatory agencies might also consider financial costs in making regulatory decisions. Some methods that could be used are cost effectiveness, cost utility, or cost benefit. Cost benefit is not as attractive to health professionals because it requires placing a dollar value on human life. The FDA does **not** consider financial cost at all in making decisions on applications to market drugs.

## CONCLUDING REMARKS

There is an obvious need for good methods to assess QOL in cancer patients.

After all, the purpose of most drug treatment of cancer is palliation and improved QOL. The FDA strongly urges incorporation of QOL assessment into cancer drug clinical trials so that the QOL instruments can be validated for comparison of outcomes in randomized trials in cancer patients.

For diseases other than cancer the FDA encourages better QOL assessment, emphasizing comparison of drugs for side-effects and relief of disease specific symptoms. A QOL instrument should be validated in the disease where it will be used and defined in clinically meaningful terms.

## References

1. Gelber, R.D. and Goldhirsch, A. A new endpoint for the assessment of adjuvant therapy in postmenopausal women with operable breast cancer. *J. Clin. Oncol.* 1986; 4: 1772–1779.
2. Gelber, R.D., Simes, R.J., Castiglione, M. *et al.* Evaluating prognoses and treatment effects using a quality of life oriented endpoint (Q-TWIST) rather than conventional endpoints (disease free survival and overall survival) alone. *Am. Soc. Clin. Oncol. Proc.* (March) 1990: 302.
3. Shoemaker, D., Burke, G., Dorr, A. *et al.* A regulatory perspective. In Spilker, B. (ed.) *Quality of Life Assessments in Clinical Trials*. New York, Raven Press, 1990, pp. 193–201.

# 25 The cost effectiveness of pharmaceuticals

**George Teeling Smith**

---

Worldwide, in the 1990s, the central issue for health care is going to be 'cost effectiveness'. This is very different from the emphasis on mere 'cost containment' in the 1980s. During the past decade there was a fashionable view that health care costs were somehow 'out of control'. The costs of health services were thought to be rising too fast, and this opinion was supported by evidence of 'waste' in medical care. Gradually, however, as we enter the last decade of this century a new attitude to medicine is emerging. Governments and social security organizations are coming to realise that the public place an extremely high priority on 'better health'. As more and more people experience for themselves the problems of ageing relatives, they can see the urgent need to spend more money improving people's health and the quality of life, especially amongst older people. It is the shortage of health care rather than its cost which is now seen to be the problem.

The British Government, perhaps ahead of those in other countries, has recognised this change in attitude. But they have very properly adopted the position that if substantially more money is to be made available for the Health Service, it must be seen to be spent effectively. Wasteful expenditure cannot be tolerated. Hence the emphasis of 'cost effectiveness' in the recent reorganization of Britain's National Health Service. It seems certain that this British initiative will be followed by all other countries within the next few years. Extra money will be made available for medical care as soon as it can be demonstrated that it is 'cost effective'. Hence the opening statement in this paper. In many ways, the pharmaceutical profession and the pharmaceutical industry are in a better position than any other section of the health services to respond to this challenge. This paper reviews some of the evidence which is already available to show that medicines can be extremely 'cost effective', and it goes on to discuss the new work which is being done to demonstrate more clearly the way in which medicines also improve the quality of life.

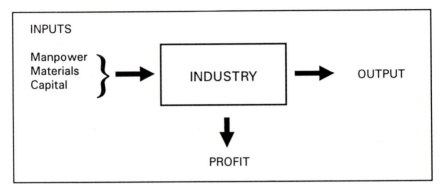

**Figure 25.1** The basic economic model

Starting with some very elementary economic theory, Figure 25.1 shows the way in which, in industrial economics, classical 'inputs' of capital, manpower and materials are converted into 'outputs'. The efficiency with which this is done is generally measured by the profit earned. (Incidentally, profit is much more important as a measure of efficiency than it is simply in providing an income for investors). Figure 25.2 indicates that health service economics follows the same basic model, but 'output' is now replaced by 'outcome' and profit is no longer the usual measure of efficiency. In health economics, both outcomes and efficiency are generally harder to measure than in classical industrial economics, but the principles are the same.

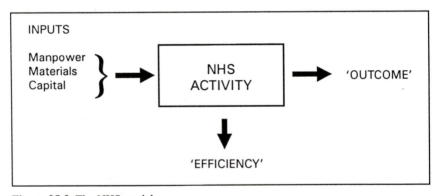

**Figure 25.2** The NHS model

The outcome of health care can take three forms. First, the improved survival and well-being of the patient; this will be discussed later. Second, savings for other parts of the health service; third, savings for the economy through reduced sickness absence and the avoidance of premature death. These last savings are important for the economy of the nation as a whole, but unfortunately, are rarely taken into account by health service managers

**Table 25.1** Savings from nine groups of diseases

|  | Bed days (1957) | Bed days (1982) | Hospital savings (£million) |
|---|---|---|---|
| Asthma | 394 331 | 297 281 | 7 |
| Epilepsy | 500 053 | 247 352 | 19 |
| Glaucoma | 148 969 | 89 096 | 4 |
| Hypertension | 1 204 277 | 185 510 | 77 |
| Bronchitis | 1 262 028 | 471 459 | 60 |
| Skin disease | 1 122 385 | 966 204 | 9 |
| Tuberculosis | 6 886 552 | 106 323 | 509 |
| Other infections | 2 766 190 | 533 947 | 167 |
| Mental ilness | 52 487 000 | 27 324 630 | 847 |
| Total saving |  |  | 1 699 |
| Manufacturers' cost of *all* pharmaceuticals |  |  | 1 225 |
| 'Cost–benefit pay-off' |  |  | 474 |

Source Teeling Smith and Wells, 1985

or those who have to provide the funds for medical care. Thus, the next part of this paper concentrates on financial savings for the health service itself.

Table 25.1 shows that the reduction in numbers of hospital beds in England and Wales between 1957 and 1982 for nine groups of disease amounted to about 25 million bed days. This represented a saving of £1699 million in 1982[12]. Of course not all of this reduction was due to better medicines, and there was a small offsetting item for extra bed days caused by adverse effects of pharmaceuticals. In addition, there were extra costs maintaining some, for example, psychiatric patients in the community. Nevertheless, it is interesting to compare this figure of 'savings' with the total cost of *all* medicines prescribed in the same year of £1225 million. In very approximate terms, it can be said that there was a 'saving' to the Health Service of £474 million.

Another example is the specific case of the reduction in the number of strokes as a result of the control of hypertension. It is estimated that in general practice in England and Wales the number of strokes per 1000 patients fell from 2.4 in 1954/55 to 1.75 in 1981/82. The actual cost of strokes to the Health Service in 1984 was £550 million. If there had not been the reduction in the number of cases between the 1950s and the 1980s, the cost would have been £754 million. Thus there was a saving of £204 million. This can be compared to the cost of all hypotensive medicines of £185 million. Once again, there is a net saving to the Health Service from the use of pharmaceuticals[10].

The use of hormone replacement therapy (HRT) to reduce osteoporosis and the risk of fracture of the hip, particularly in elderly women, is another example. In 1985 the cost to Britain's National Health Service was £128 million. It is estimated that half of these fractures could be avoided if the 25% of post-menopausal women most at risk were given HRT for ten years. The cost of this would be £31.25 million. The saving from reduction in fractures – admittedly at a later date – would be £64 million, at 1985 prices. Taking account of inflation, it is likely that the real savings in later years would be much greater so even discounted back to 1985 values it would still show a true saving[3].

Asthma is a case where prophylaxis shows a substantial saving. The result of an American double-blind trial of disodium cromoglycate (Cromolyn) showed that in the treated group there was a large reduction in the use made by patients of the hospital emergency room from 2.75 users per year to 0.15. In the control group there was no such reduction[8]. A British study is currently costing this sort of saving over an 18-month period (Elegant: private communication).

In an example from Japan, vaccination was shown to reduce the cost of hepatitis B. Taking the estimated cost of the disease before immunization as 100, the Japanese Institute of Statistics estimated that the cost after immunization was reduced to 14, while the cost of vaccination itself represented 6.7.

The last illustration of reduced costs due to pharmaceuticals comes from the hospital sector. This concerned the use of glycerol trinitrate patches applied to the veins to reduce the failure of intravenous infusions through clotting. This in turn reduced the need to set up a new infusion at a new site. Figure 25.3 shows the reduction in risk of failure for the active patch against a placebo over a period of time. Figure 25.4 estimates the cost, based on observations and the actual work done setting up the new infusion. This figure shows that it would be cheaper – taking account of the cost of the patch – to use it rather than not to do so, provided the infusion was to last for more than 48 hours[5].

The next three cases illustrate another important point. A more expensive medicine may work out cheaper than a less expensive one, when total health service costs are taken into account. Table 25.2 compares the cost of using the newer anticancer agent carboplatin against the older generic cisplatin. Carboplatin is more than ten times as expensive, but because it can be given on an out-patient basis, the total cost is less than that of cisplatin, whose adverse effects require hospital admission[13].

Table 25.3 shows a similar picture for antibiotics used as prophylactics to prevent post-operative infection. The third generation cephalosporin is the most expensive, but because it shows the greatest reduction in risk of a delay in hospital discharge caused by infection, it works out to be the cheapest overall[6].

A last example in this set compares sublingual buprenorphine against

**Table 25.2** Comparative cost (£) for carboplatin and cisplatin

| Item | Carboplatin | Cisplatin |
|---|---|---|
| Carboplatin 450 mg ro cisplatin 100 mg | 205.71 | 17.90 |
| Dexamethasone i.v. mg + 2 mg tablets×4 for 4 days | 2.34 | |
| Metoclopramide 150 mg i.v. | | 3.30 |
| Domperidone tablets 20 mg×4 for 4 days | 3.47 | |
| 0.9% i.v. saline | 0.55 | 3.60 |
| Hospital bed | 8.00 | 324.00 |
| Registrar's time (1 h) | 8.70 | |
| **Total** | **228.77** | **347.90** |

Source: Tighe and Goodman, 1988

**Table 25.3** Savings ($) from antibiotic prophylaxis in surgery per 100 patients

| | Extra hospital cost | Cost antibiotic | Net extra cost |
|---|---|---|---|
| No antibiotic | 707 600 | — | 707 600 |
| 1st generation cephalosporin | 246 100 | 5 000 | 251 100 |
| 3rd generation cephalosporin | — | 11 800 | 11 800 |

Source Mandell-Brown *et al.*, 1984

**Table 25.4** Comparative costs for analgesia (£)

| | Injectable papaveretum | Sublingual buprenorphine |
|---|---|---|
| Medicament | 0.11 | 0.240 |
| Consumables | 0.114 | 0.001 |
| | 0.225 | 0.241 |
| **Notional staff costs** | | |
| Pharmacy | 0.090 | 0.082 |
| Ward | 0.573 | 0.394 |
| Total | 0.663 | 0.476 |

Source Wittrick, 1987

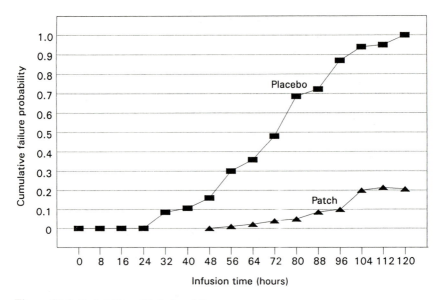

**Figure 25.3** Probability of infusion failure

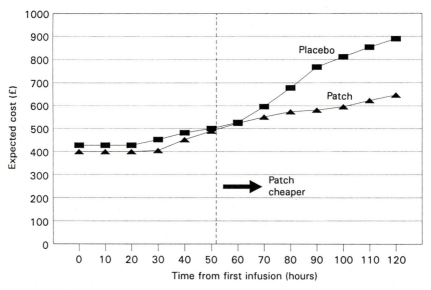

**Figure 25.4** Expected cost per infused patient

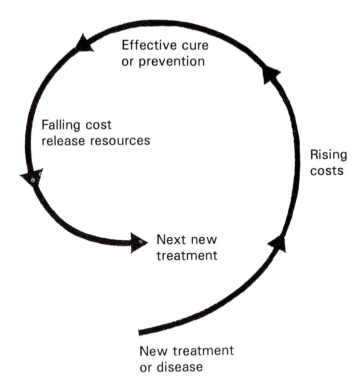

**Figure 25.5** The health–cost spiral

injectable papaveretum, both opiates used for pain control (Table 25.4). Because the latter needs to be injected, and to be subjected to controlled drug restrictions, it is more expensive to use than buprenorphine, even though the latter is more than twice as expensive[14].

All of these examples illustrate the basic principle that it is *total* health service costs which must be taken into account, rather than the cost of the medicine alone.

However, the 'savings' resulting from using a more cost-effective therapy do not normally result in a reduction in total expenditure on the health service. Figure 25.5 illustrates the reason for this. It can be described as 'the spiral of health care costs'.

When a new disease emerges – like AIDS – or when a new palliative treatment for an existing disease is developed, the cost of the disease rises steeply. Previously, when the disease or the treatment was unknown, it had cost nothing. Only when an effective curative treatment or a new preventative measure emerges do costs start to fall. Eventually, as in the case of smallpox, the costs may be eliminated altogether. However, these 'savings' do not result

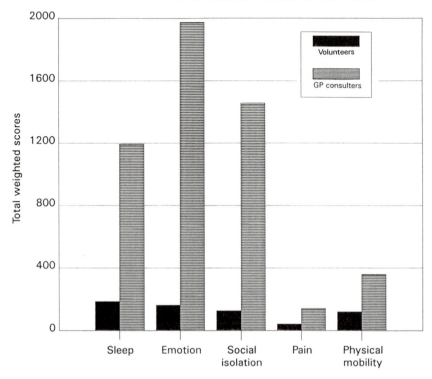

**Figure 25.6** Nottingham Health Profile scores for GP consulters and controls

in an overall reduction in health care costs. Those resources which are released by the 'savings' will immediately be used to provide the new treatment, either for a newly emerging disease or for the treatment of one for which no treatment was previously possible. Thus, historically, savings from the prevention and the rapid and inexpensive treatment of infectious diseases were quickly absorbed to provide the newly emerging treatments for the chronic diseases. This does not mean that advances in medicine are of no economic importance. Indeed just the reverse is true. By making savings on 'older' diseases, resources are more readily available to improve the quality of life and survival of patients suffering from 'newer' diseases.

All this means is that much of health economics in the past few years has been concerned not only with the cost of illness but also with the degree of well-being of the population. The purpose of medical care is to improve health and to reduce disease, not to save money.

Patients quality of life can be measured by two broad methods. The first is a Health Profile and the second is a Health Index. Figure 25.6 shows the use of the Nottingham Health Profile to compare patients attending their doctor with a group of healthy volunteers[9]. The height of the column for

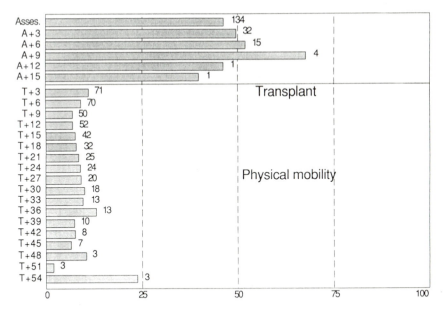

**Figure 25.7** Profile: before and after heart transplant

each parameter measures the extent of disability and distress which the person is suffering. These measures are obtained by asking the individuals simple questions about their life – can they, for example, easily walk upstairs? No attempt is made to combine the different measures, so a true 'profile' of the person's well-being is produced.

Figure 25.7 shows the effect on one parameter (physical mobility) for patients as a result of a heart transplant. The reduction in disability and distress at the point of transplant is dramatic[1]. In general, the use of pharmaceutical treatments produces smaller changes, and economic studies are now in progress to try to improve on the Nottingham Health Profile, in order to more accurately measure smaller changes in patients' well-being.

A 'Health Index' is an even more ambitious approach, attempting to measure patients' well-being on a single numerical scale. Each of a range of defined states of health is given a specific value, and the individual patient's condition is then matched as accurately as possible with one of these defined states. The numerical values for the different states can be obtained in a number of ways, all of which try to obtain a consensus of people's 'valuation' of each defined state of health. Table 26.3 shows the values obtained using one of these methods by Professor Rachel Rosser. She defined 29 different states of health in a matrix formed by four degrees of 'distress' and eight degrees of 'disability'. They are scored on a scale of one for perfect health to zero for death. Three of the resultant 32 squares have no values because they represent states where the patient is unconscious and can therefore suffer no distress[7].

There are two comments on Rosser's values. First, many states of health score very high values (greater than 0.9 on the scale of zero to one). This is surprising as it means that on this scale a patient suffering quite severe distress and disability is still rated '90% fit'. Other methods of valuing the same states produce lower values, which seem more realistic. Second, two states score values less than zero. That is, according to this scale these patients would be better off dead. This has interesting ethical implications, if the scoring is valid.

Although Rosser's values cannot be regarded as a 'gold standard' for measuring quality of life, they have been used to develop the concept of the 'quality adjusted life year' (QALY). This is based on the belief that a person's quality of life should affect the value (or 'utility' in economic jargon) of that particular year of his or her life. Hence, if a person is only 50% 'well' over a 10-year period, he or she would score only five QALYs for those 10 years.

Table 25.5 shows the 'cost' of purchasing an extra QALY for a patient as a result of a variety of medical interventions. There is an enormous range from £170 for a quality adjusted year by advising patients to stop smoking up to £14 000 for hospital haemodialysis for end stage renal failure[11]. Clearly, preventive medicine comes well out of the Table, with antihypertensive therapy to reduce strokes costing only £600 per QALY. At present, it would be wrong to use the numbers in this sort of table as a specific guide to health

**Table 25.5** 'League table' of costs and QALYs for selected health care interventions (1983–1984 price)

| Intervention | Present value of extra cost per QALY gained (£) |
|---|---|
| GP advice stop smoking | 170 |
| Antihypertensive therapy to prevent stroke (ages 45–64) | 600 |
| Pacemaker implantation for heart bloke | 700 |
| Hip replacement | 750 |
| CABG for severe angina with LMD | 1 040 |
| GP control of total serum cholesterol | 1 700 |
| CABG for severe angina with 2VD | 2 280 |
| Kidney transplantation (cadaver) | 3 000 |
| Breast cancer screening | 3 500 |
| Heart transplantation | 5 000 |
| CABG for mild angina with 2VD | 12 600 |
| Hospital haemodialysis | 14 000 |

CABG = coronary artery bypass graft; LMD = left main disease; 2VD = two-vessel disease.
Source: Teeling Smith, 1989

care policy, but the concept of providing more cost effective treatments in place of very expensive alternatives will increasingly start to be taken into account.

Thirty years ago the principle of controlled double blind clinical trials to assess the safety and efficacy of new medicines was only just starting to be universally accepted. A distinguished pharmaceutical physician, for example, at that time published a paper in *The Lancet* entitled 'The Feet of Clay of the Double Blind Trial'[2]. Economic analysis is in the same situation today, 30 years later. There is little doubt, however, that it is going to be more and more important in the future to demonstrate that any new therapy is cost effective before it is generally introduced. As this paper has suggested, this will often be easier to do for pharmaceuticals than for more complicated and perhaps less effective alternatives. Pharmacists and others have a major role to play in the future in helping to demonstrate the cost effectiveness of the preparations which they manufacture and dispense. They must do this taking into account the total economic consequences for the health service, and also the comparative benefits which their medicines can bring to patients by improving their quality and length of life. Any tendency towards a 'cheap medicine' policy must become a thing of the past.

## References

1. Buxton, M., Acheson, R., Caine, N. *et al. Costs and Benefits of the Heart Transplant Programmes at Harefield and Papworth Hospitals.* London, HMSO, 1985.
2. Cromie, B.W. The feet of clay of the double blind trial. *Lancet* 1963; 2: 994–997.
3. Griffin, J.R. *Osteoporosis.* London, Office of Health Economics, 1990.
4. Institute of Statistical Research. *Technological Assessment of Drug Therapy: Analysis of Cost–Benefit Study and Research on Pharmaceuticals.* Tokyo, 1988
5. Khawaja, H.T., O'Brien, B., Buxton, M. and Weaver, P. C. Cost minimisation study of transdermal glyceryl trinitrate in reducing failures of peripheral intravenous infusion. *Br. Med. J.* 1989; 299: 97.
6. Mandell-Brown, M., Johnson, J.T. and Wagner, R.L. Cost effectiveness of prophylactic antibiotics and head and neck surgery. *Otolaryngol. Head Neck Surg,* 1984; 91: 520–523.
7. Rosser, R.M. The history of the development of health indicators. In Teeling Smith, G., (ed.) *Measuring the Social Benefits of Medicine.* London, Office of Health Economics, 1984.
8. Ross, R.N., Morris, M., Sakowitz, S.R. and Berman, B.A. Cost effectiveness of including Cromolyn sodium in the treatment program for asthma: a retrospective record based study. *Clin. Ther.* 1988; 10: 188–203.
9. Stevens, J. PhD Thesis. In *CMR News,* Centre for Medicines Research, Carshalton, Surrey, 1984; 2: 3.
10. Teeling Smith, G. Economics of cardiovascular disease. In Sleight, P. (ed.) *Postgraduate Cardiovascular Seminars, I.* London, Mediq Ltd, 1988.

11. Teeling Smith, G. *Measurement and Management in the NHS*. London, Office of Health Economics, 1989.
12. Teeling Smith, G. and Wells, N.E.J. The economic contribution of the industry in England and Wales. *Pharm. J.* 1985; 235: 178–179.
13. Tighe, M. and Goodman, S. Carboplatin versus cisplatin. *Lancet* 1988; 2: 1371–1373.
14. Wittrick, A. Measuring the cost of drugs. *Health Serv. J.* 1987; 97: 678.

# 26 Requirements for health care purchasers

**Alan Maynard**

## INTRODUCTION

In many health care systems there is an increasing recognition that markets, which are networks of buyers and sellers, may be made to work more efficiently if the roles of purchaser and provider are more clearly separated. Such a separation permits a clear definition of the roles of the contractors for health care services and facilitates greater openness and accountability in decision making.

An essential ingredient into the processes by which purchasers and providers make contracts for the supply and finance of health care services is the measurement of health outcomes, in particular the identification, quantification and valuation of the impacts of competing interventions, be they diagnostic or therapeutic, on the quality of life of patients.

## THE ROLE OF THE PURCHASER

What is the role of health care purchasers and what information do they require to perform their tasks efficiently? The British Government has implemented reforms which from April 1991 separated the purchaser/provider roles. The purchaser is required to identify the health care needs of the local population and to buy cost effective services to meet those needs.

The first of these tasks is made complex because there are two purchasing authorities which overlap. The District Health Authority (DHA) purchaser holds the budget to buy care for, on average, a population of about 250 000. However some groups of general practitioners (GPs) in primary care can elect to become budget holders for pharmaceuticals, diagnostics and cold (non-emergency) elective care. To the extent that they do so, the residual budget of the DHA purchaser is reduced. This fragmentation of the purchasing task means that DHA purchasers and GP budget holder purchasers have to integrate their measurement of health needs and agree the methods for

413

assessing the cost effectiveness of competing therapies. For the first time in the history of the NHS there are sharp incentives for District Health Authorities to take account of the preferences of primary care providers. This change in the power structure will have profound effects on health care delivery.

But what are health needs? Need may be a demand or supply concept[28] but for the purposes of NHS resource allocation, need will be defined as a two-part decision process:

(1)    a technical judgement by medical and other experts about the extent to which competing therapies enhance the length and quality of life. This judgement will determine how much patients will benefit from health care in terms of producing additional well-years or quality adjusted life-years (QALYs).

(2)    a social judgement as to whether it is worthwhile to treat patients. This judgement is a reflection of how much society is prepared to pay for an additional QALY.

### Information needs and information availability

The purchaser requires information about the cost effectiveness of competing health treatments in order that she can target her resources on those activities which increase the patients' health the most, at least cost. Unfortunately this information is not widely available in all health care systems.

Indeed scientific knowledge about the cost effectiveness of treatments offered by doctors is so poor that Black[2] has asserted that only 10% of interventions are grounded in good evidence. Fuchs[11] has argued that 10% of health care expenditures harm patient health, 10% of expenditure has no effect on health and 80% of expenditure improves patient health. The problem, argues Fuchs, is that no one knows which therapies lie in the 10 and 80% categories! An additional problem is how Fuchs reached his 10 and 80% groupings?

There are many causes of this ignorance. For a long time in the post-war period there was an assumption that increased health care expenditure increased patient health. This cosy assumption was challenged by McKeown[18], who argued that the prior cause of improved health in the past was nutrition and public health, not health care, and by Cochrane[4] who argued that ignorance was prevalent and that the methodology advocated by Brad-ford-Hill in the 1930s, randomized control trials, needed adopting urgently.

Much 'evaluative' activity continues to be focused on process rather than outcome and this can be explained by the ease of measuring what is done to patients (process) as opposed to whether the processes of care improve patient health. Measuring outcomes, in terms of enhancements in the length and quality of life, is complex because of the inherent complexity of the concepts as well as the absence of routine data about these aspects of care.

The purchaser of health care in Britain's National Health Service (NHS) and increasingly in other health care systems (e.g. the USA where the determination of the 'appropriateness' of treatment requires measurement of cost effectiveness) needs information about the outcomes and costs of alternative treatments. Cost data are poor, with more market orientated health care systems having price data (e.g. DRG prices) which bear little relation to the opportunity cost (the value of what is foregone) of the treatment. Mortality data are segmented and also are inadequate measures of outcome as they do not indicate the quality of survival, an aspect of outcome which is of crucial importance in resource allocation decisions.

The purchaser/provider reforms have created a demand for such data. What was once esoteric and marginal, the results of economic evaluation of treatment options, is now at the 'centre of the stage'[6]. Purchasers have to identify efficient practices and use this information to ration in the UK NHS and to reformulate reimbursement rules in the USA and other health care systems where cost containment pressures are intense. Regardless of the structure of health care systems, the results of outcome measurement and cost evaluation are central ingredients into the processes of determining who will live and who will be denied treatments from which they could benefit.

## OUTCOME MEASUREMENT

### Some history of outcome measurement

The recognition of the central role of outcome measurement in the design and evaluation of health care systems is not a new discovery. Indeed it is a classic example of the rediscovery of the wheel!

The Babylonians recognized not only the need to define outcomes but the necessity to link success (and failure) to a reward system.

> 'If a surgeon has made a deep incision in the body of a man with a lancet of bronze and saves the man's life, or has opened an abscess in the eye of a man and has saved his eye, he shall take 10 shekels of silver.

> If the surgeon has made a deep incision in the body of a man with his lancet of bronze and so destroys the man's eye, they shall cut off his forehand'. Babylon, 1792 BC

Clearly the Babylonian measures of outcome and the reward mechanism they proposed were crude but the lessons are obvious for all those seeking to implement medical audit in the UK and the rest of the world.

More recently, there was a focus on the duration of survival as an indicator of 'success' advocated and used by policy makers. Francis Clifton, the physician to the Prince of Wales argued that:

> 'In order, therefore to procure this valuable collection, I humbly propose, first of all, that three or four persons should be employed in the hospitals (and that without any ways interfering with the gentlemen now concerned), to set down the cases of the patients there from day to day, candidly and judiciously without any regard to private opinions or public systems, and at the year's end publish these facts just as they are, leaving every one to make the best use he can for himself.'   Francis Clifton (1732).

Clifton was quoted with approval by the editor of the *Lancet* in 1841 who advocated the introduction of survival measurement as a performance indicator for the health care system:

> All public institutions must be compelled to keep case-books and registers, on an uniform plan. Annual abstracts of the results must be published. The annual medical report of cases must embrace hospitals, lying-in hospitals, dispensaries, lunatic asylums, and prisons.   *Lancet* (1841) pp. 650–651.

This advocacy was associated with legislative action. The 1844 Lunacy Act required the managers of all psychiatric hospitals to evaluate the success of their institutions by reporting annually patient outcomes in relation to three criteria: were the patients dead, relieved or unrelieved? As can be seen from the records of all public psychiatric hospitals these data were collected throughout the remainder of the nineteenth century.

It was these measures, dead, relieved and unrelieved, that were advocated by Florence Nightingale and used also in some English acute hospitals in the nineteenth and twentieth centuries. Nightingale, in advocating the use of these measures, remarked that:

> 'I am fain to sum up with an urgent appeal for adopting this or some uniform system of publishing the statistical records of hospitals. There is a growing conviction that in all hospitals, even in those which are best conducted, there is a great and unnecessary waste of life. In attempting to arrive at the truth, I have applied everywhere for information, but in scarcely an instance have I been able to obtain hospital records fit for any purpose of comparison. If they could be obtained, they would enable us to decide many other questions besides the ones alluded to. They would show subscribers how their money was being spent, what amount of good was really being done with it, or whether the money was doing mischief rather than good.'   Florence Nightingale (1863)

Whilst the routine collection of Nightingale–Lunacy Act data does not appear to have survived far into the twentieth century, and certainly not beyond the creation of the NHS in 1948, the National Health Service has required Districts to collect both activity, process and mortality data: Hospital Activity Analysis (HAA) data set. Despite the collection of mortality outcome data for 20 years to 1985, and since then the Korner mortality data (for those Districts who have managed to complete returns!), these data have not been used to evaluate performance.

These data are crude. Kind[14] used the 1985 Hospital In-patient Enquiry (HIPE) data (a one in ten sample of HAA) to illustrate the variations in inpatient mortality between English NHS hospitals (Table 26.1). This use of these data concentrated attention on the causes of these variations: were they caused by inaccurate data collection? Were they due to variations in case severity or socio-economic class? Obviously the data and the ways in which they can be used to investigate variations in health outcomes are limited but this work focused attention on the need to link mortality data sets to appraise long term survival, and the need to address the measurement issues in quality of life.

**Table 26.1** Death rates in English health authorities

| Health Authority | No of cases | Actual no of deaths | Crude mortality rate | Expected no. of deaths | Standardized mortality rate |
|---|---|---|---|---|---|
| **Northern RHA** | | | | | |
| Hartlepool | 1403 | 76 | 5.4 | 72.1 | 1.055 |
| North Tees | 1752 | 112 | 6.4 | 85.0 | 1.317 |
| Darlington | 1515 | 67 | 4.4 | 73.8 | 0.908 |
| **Yorkshire** | | | | | |
| Hull | 3936 | 221 | 5.6 | 210.7 | 1.049 |
| Grimsby | 1930 | 124 | 6.4 | 87.7 | 1.414 |
| Harrogate | 1676 | 84 | 5.0 | 112.4 | 0.748 |
| **North West Thames** | | | | | |
| North West Hertfordshire | 1838 | 108 | 5.9 | 71.5 | 1.510 |
| Harrow | 2202 | 75 | 3.4 | 129.9 | 0.577 |
| **North East Thames** | | | | | |
| Bloomsbury | 5353 | 133 | 2.5 | 206.6 | 0.644 |
| **South Western** | | | | | |
| Somerset | 3121 | 230 | 7.4 | 169.7 | 1.355 |
| **Mersey** | | | | | |
| Wirral | 3758 | 238 | 6.3 | 264.3 | 0.900 |

Source: Kind, 1988.

**Measuring health outcomes**

In principle outcome measurement is simple. It is necessary to collect information about:

(1)    the duration of survival (life expectancy after treatment),

(2)    the quality of survival (describing the quality of life (QOL)),

(3)    the values attached to different health states (valuing alternative combinations of descriptors),

(4)    low benefits accruing to different people are to be added together.

When evaluating competing treatments for a given presentation the first task is to identify the relative difference, if any, in the duration of survival after treatment. Routine data, such as those used by Kind, are an incomplete measure of survival as they do not follow the patient out of the hospital to measure survival in the community. To do this record linkage is necessary. Whilst this is feasible it is difficult and expensive, as can be seen from the experience of the Oxford Record Linkage work (see for example Refs 1 and 13 and the Medical Outcomes Study (MOS) in the USA[26]).

The quality of survival has several aspects: physical (including energy), social and psychological. Relevant physical attributes might include activities of everyday living such as ability to get out of bed independently, wash, dress, feed, clean the house, go to the shops and participate in work.

Social well-being might include attributes such as social isolation and integration (or its absence) in family and neighbourhood networks. Psychological well-being might include characteristics such as 'being happy, some or part of the time'.

These illustrative descriptors are used in varying ways in the many measures of the impacts of health care on the quality of life (QOL) and patient well-being. There are hundreds of such measures[10,23,24]. A useful distinction can be made between disease-specific QOL measures and generic measures. The former relate to disease categories, for instance cancer or mental health, and are useful for measuring changes in well-being within that disease category only. The latter can be used across diseases so that the well-being changes produced by investments in dissimilar therapeutic areas can be identified, measured and valued.

The generic measures are particularly useful for providing for purchasers measures of the effects of competing therapies on the patients' quality of life. Measures such as this include the Sickness Impact Profile (SIP), the McMaster Health Index, the Nottingham Health Profile (NHP), and the Quality of Well-Being measure. Some might add to this list the instrument used in the Medical Outcomes Study and the Rosser index.

There is no agreement about a 'gold standard' amongst these measures and the usual advice is to use a portfolio of specific and generic instruments in any prospective trial. Furthermore the measures are evolving, in that descriptors have not reached a 'steady state' and valuation methods remain an area of dispute. The alternative valuation methods (e.g. time trade off standard gamble and linear analogue) have yet to be compared and contrasted with a given set of descriptors in many therapeutic areas. As a consequence the QOL instruments have to be accepted as experimental and crude but their careful use is unavoidable if purchasers' decisions are to be better informed.

Not only are the descriptors and valuation methods a matter for argument amongst practitioners, but there is also little agreement about how benefits accruing to different people are to be added together. Often this issue is not confronted explicitly and benefits accruing to different age groups and social classes are implicitly assumed to be of equal value. But is an additional year of good quality life for a 35 year old of equal value as an additional good quality year of life for a 70 year old? Is an additional year of life for a poor man of equal value to an additional year of life for a rich woman?

These are empirical questions: social values about these aspects of outcome measurement need to be identified, measured and valued. The results should then be used to adjust estimates of additional years of life, QOLs and quality adjusted life-years.

**Prioritizing health care treatments**

One approach to prioritizing competing health treatments using a generic quality of life measure is that using the Rosser matrix. Rosser descriptors generate an eight by four matrix of disability and distress states described in Table 26.2.

Using a small sample of respondents Rosser generated a matrix with median values ranging from 1 (no disability and distress) to dead 0. As can be seen from Table 26.3, some health states were viewed as worse than dead[22].

Williams and subsequent researchers have used this matrix to generate 'guestimates' of the cost–QALY[29] characteristics of competing therapies. A 'league table' produced by this work, adjusted to 1990 prices, is set out in Table 26.4.

The implications of these data, given that they are the best guestimates available and there are no diminishing returns, are that treatments at the top of the table are good value for money, and those at its foot should not be funded in a health care system anxious to use resources efficiently, i.e. produce improved health at least cost. Purchasers would, thus, target their expenditure away from kidney dialysis, erythropoietin treatment and some neurosurgical interventions.

**Table 26.2** The Rosser descriptors

| | *Disability* | |
|---|---|---|
| I | No disability | A. No Distress |
| II | Slight social disability | B. Mild |
| III | Severe social disability and/or slight impairment of performance at work. Able to do all housework except very heavy tasks | C. Moderate<br>D. Severe |
| IV | Choice of work or performance at work severely limited. Housewives and old people able to do light housework only but able to go out shopping | |
| V | Unable to undertake any paid employment. Unable to continue any education. Old people confined to home except for escorted outings and short walks and unable to do shopping. Housewives able only to perform few simple tasks | |
| VI | Confined to chair or to wheelchair or able to move around in the house only with support from an assistant | |
| VII | Confined to bed | |
| VIII | Unconscious | |

Source: Rosser, Kind and Williams, 1982.

**Table 26.3** Rosser valuation matrix

| Disability rating | Distress rating | | | |
|---|---|---|---|---|
| | A | B | C | D |
| I | 1.000 | 0.995 | 0.990 | 0.967 |
| II | 0.990 | 0.986 | 0.973 | 0.932 |
| III | 0.980 | 0.972 | 0.956 | 0.912 |
| IV | 0.964 | 0.956 | 0.942 | 0.870 |
| V | 0.946 | 0.935 | 0.900 | 0.700 |
| VI | 0.875 | 0.845 | 0.680 | 0.000 |
| VII | 0.677 | 0.564 | 0.000 | -1.486 |
| VIII | -1.028 | | Not Applicable | |

Source: Rosser, Kind and Williams, 1982.

**Table 26.4** The cost per quality adjusted life-year (QALY) of competing therapies: some tentative estimates

| | Cost/QALY £ Aug 1990 |
|---|---|
| Cholesterol testing and diet therapy only (all adults, aged 40–69) (source A) | 220 |
| Neurosurgical intervention for head injury (B) | 240 |
| GP advice to stop smoking (C) | 270 |
| Neurosurgical intervention for subarachnoid haemorrhage (D) | 490 |
| Anti-hypertensive therapy to prevent stroke (ages 45–64) (C) | 940 |
| Pacemaker implantation (D) | 1100 |
| Hip replacement (D) | 1180 |
| Valve replacement for aortic stenosis (D) | 1410 |
| Cholesterol testing and treatment (A) | 1480 |
| CABG (LMVD, severe angina) (D) | 2090 |
| Kidney transplant (D) | 4710 |
| Breast cancer screening (E) | 5780 |
| Heart transplantation (D) | 7840 |
| Cholesterol testing and treatment (incrementally) of all adults 25–39 years (A) | 14150 |
| Home haemodialysis (D) | 17260 |
| CABG (1 vessel disease, moderate angina) (D) | 18830 |
| Hospital haemodialysis | 21970 |
| Erythropoietin treatment for anaemia in dialysis patients (assuming a 10% reduction in mortality) | 54380 |
| Neurosurgical intervention for malignant intracranial tumours (B) | 107780 |
| Erythropoietin treatment for anaemia in dialysis patients (assuming no increase in survival) (F) | 126290 |

Sources: Updated cost data applied to results in Department of Health (1990), Pickard *et al.* (1990), Teeling Smith (1990), Williams (1985), Department of Health and Social Security (1986) and Leese *et al.* (1990).
CABG = coronary artery bypass graft; LMVD = left main vessel disease; CAPD = continuous ambulatory peritoneal dialysis

## Whither outcome measurement?

The techniques used to produce cost QALY estimates are crude. An outline of some of their defects would include the following:

(1)   There is no agreement about the appropriate set of descriptors. Both the Rosser group and the Williams group at York have abandoned the original Rosser descriptors and the valuations matrix (Tables 26.2 and 26.3 above). The Williams group has now adopted a different set of descriptors to produce, with other European groups, the EuroQoL measure[30].

(2) There is no agreement about valuation methods. Is the time trade off method superior to the standard gamble approach and do these methods give results similar to those derived by magnitude estimation?

(3) There is uncertainty about the replicability and robustness of the QOL measures.

(4) The cost–QALY estimates are often presented as point estimates with no sensitivity analysis and emphasis on average values rather than incremental (marginal) estimates.

(5) The issue of how to weight benefits accruing to different groups or classes of people is generally ignored.

(6) There is greater scope for the use of sensitivity analysis and for the identification of incremental cost–QALY data.

(7) The merits of keeping measures simple in terms of design, analysis and reporting are great.

These defects may be sufficient to induce some to discard these measures as of little practical use. However the issues of identifying appropriate (efficient) technologies to contain costs and of prioritizing competing treatments, all of which cannot be afforded, remain. These choices are made every day on the basis of guesses, shroud waving and political chicanery.

An explicit framework in which costs and outcomes are estimated and the estimates are publicly available for all to challenge with better data is to be preferred on political and efficiency grounds to implicit mechanisms which determine difficult health care choices. In a publicly financed system of health care, choices should be made explicitly with the best data available. Such a framework creates incentives for researchers and clinicians to produce better data and make better choices.

Replacing implicit rationing with explicit rationing inevitably provokes criticism even if it does have the virtue of producing, via *glasnost*, greater accountability. A decision to favour some treatments and discriminate against others creates sharp responses from the losers. In the USA the State Managers of Medicaid programmes, which provide health care for some of the poor, have responded to cost inflation by restricting access to the programmes' benefits by making some groups ineligible for benefits.

In Oregon the response to this behaviour has been to step back and explicitly prioritize treatments on the basis of the best scientific evidence (which is poor in quality and quantity), local preferences (revealed from polls and local meetings) and political choices. The results are controversial and have changed over time as can be seen (Table 26.5). They are derived from literature review, professional advice, the values of the local population and the choices of the members of the Health Services Commission[12]. Some have

**Table 26.5** Oregon priorities: some examples

---

**(a) February 1990 list**

| | |
|---|---|
| 1 | Pneumococcal pneumonia |
| 2 | Tuberculosis |
| 3 | Peritonitis |
| 23 | Low birth weight (1250 g and over) |
| 73 | Low birth weight (1000–1249 g) |
| 358 | Low birth weight (500–749 g) |
| 695 | Liver cirrhosis |
| 707 | Terminal HIV, with 10% chance of 5 year survival |
| 713 | Low birth weight (less than 500 g, under 23 weeks gestation) |

**(b) May 1991 list**

| | |
|---|---|
| 1 | Pneumococcal pneumonia |
| 2 | Tuberculosis |
| 3 | Peritonitis |
| 22 | Low birth weight (500 g and over) |
| 73 | Drug reactions and intoxications specific to the newborn |
| 587 | Oesophagitis |
| 600 | Breast reconstruction after treatment for a neoplasm |
| 708 | Low birth weight (below 500 g) |

---

Source: Health Services Commission, 1991.

criticized these processes as prioritizing in a 'data free environment', others have been less pessimistic[17,25]. The Oregonian legislature chose to fund up to line 587 and, if Federal approval is forthcoming, this process will be implemented with evaluation in mid-1992. If adopted by the legislature they will target Oregon Medicaid expenditure away from groups such as low birth weight neonates and those with AIDS and facilitate the expansion of provision of prioritized and valued health care treatments for the poor.

The investment made by the numbers of the Oregon Health Services Commission was significant and it has produced a crude prioritization which will be revised biannually in the light of new knowledge and can be used as a guide for the production of similar lists for purchasers in other countries. The processes by which Commission members used telephone poll results and their own consensuses, to reorder the listing derived from the views of experts about the cost effectiveness of alternative treatments, again offer purchasers a guide as to how they might integrate social values and scientific guestimates of outcomes.

## CONCLUSIONS

If the reform of the NHS, with its clear identification of the objectives of purchasers and providers, is implemented intelligently it will increase substantially the demand for economic evaluation of competing health care treatments. Purchasers need the results of this work in order to prioritize treatments and decide which treatments will be funded and which will not. In a cash limited NHS it is inevitable that some beneficial treatments will not be funded. If limited NHS resources are not targeted efficiently, resources will be wasted and the opportunity cost of this inefficiency will be that some patients, who would benefit from care, will be deprived of treatment.

In health care systems where the focus of policy concern is cost containment rather than rationing, policy makers will also focus on the results of economic evaluation and mechanisms such as those used in Oregon. Decision makers in insurance-based health care systems, both public and private, typically control costs by manipulating reimbursement rules. A logical method of determining such rules is to use the results of economic evaluation which identify the relative costs and outcomes of competing treatments.

In the pharmaceutical sector there is likely to be rapid development in the use of economic evaluation techniques, including the use of quality of life measures. It is proposed both in Australia and Ontario to make the reimbursement of new drugs dependent on their being demonstrated to be superior, in terms of cost effectiveness, to rival treatments[5,20,9]. These policies are likely to be copied by other countries and extended to a broader range of innovative and existing technologies.

Central to the process of prioritizing health care treatments and containing costs is the measurement of the quality of life. An increasing number of treatments, especially from the pharmaceutical industry, will affect predominately the quality rather than the length of life. Without careful measurement of these effects the case for funding such treatments will be incomplete and purchasers in public and private health care systems will direct resources to other proven therapies.

# References

1. Acheson, E.D. *Medical Record Linkage*. Published by the Oxford University Press for the Nuffield Provincial Hospitals Trust, London, 1967.
2. Black, D. *An Anthology of False Antitheses*. Nuffield Provincial Hospitals Trust, London, 1984.
3. Clifton, F. *The State of Physick, Ancient and Modern Briefly Considered*. London, 1732.
4. Cochrane, A.L. *Effectiveness and Efficiency: Random Reflections on Health Services*. Nuffield Provincial Hospitals Trust, London, 1972.
5. Commonwealth of Australia *Guidelines for the Pharmaceutical Industry on Preparation of Submissions to the Pharmaceutic Benefits Advisory Committee*. Canberra, Department of Health, Housing and Community Services, 1990.

6.  Culyer, A.J., Maynard, A. and Posnett, J. (eds) *Competition in Health Care: Reforming the NHS*. London, Macmillan, 1990.

7.  Department of Health and Social Security. *Forrest Report. Breast Cancer Screening*, London, DH, 1986.

8.  Department of Health, Standing Medical Advisory Committee. *Blood Cholesterol Testing: the Cost-Effectiveness of Opportunistic Cholesterol Testing*, London, DHSS, 1990.

9.  Drummond, M.F. *Australian Guidelines for Cost-Effectiveness Studies of Pharmaceuticals: the Thin End of the Boomerang?* Discussion Paper 88. University of York, Centre for Health Economics, 1991.

10. Fallowfield, L. *The Quality of Life: the Missing Measurement in Health Care*. London, Souvenir Press (E & A) Ltd, 1990.

11. Fuchs, V. Rationing health care. *N. Engl. J. Med.*, 1985; 311, 24: 1572–1573.

12. Health Services Commission. *The 1991 Prioritization of Health Services*. Salem, Oregon, 1991.

13. Henderson, J., Goldacre, M.J., Griffith, M. and Simmons, H.M. Day case surgery: geographical variation, trends and remission rates. *J. Epidemiol. Commun. Health*, 1989; 43: 301–305.

14. Kind, P. *Hospital Deaths – the Missing Link: Measuring Outcome in Hospital Activity Data*. Discussion Paper no 44, University of York, Centre for Health Economics, 1988.

15. *Lancet* (editorial) 1841; 650–651.

16. Leese, B., Hutton, J. and Maynard, A. *The Costs and Benefits of the Use of Erythropoietin in the Treatment of Anaemia arising from Chronic Renal Failure*. Occasional Paper. University of York, Centre for Health Economics, 1990.

17. Maynard, A. Priorities: follow the Oregon trail? *Med. Audit News*, 1992; 2: 2.

18. McKeown, T. *The Role of Modern Medicine*, 2nd edn. London, Blackwell Scientific Publications, 1979.

19. Nightingale, F. *Some Notes on Hospitals*, London, Longman, 1863.

20. Ontario Ministry of Health, *Guidelines for Preparation of Economic Analysis to be Included in Submissions to Drug Programs Branch for Listing in the Ontario Drug Benefit Formulary/Comparative Drug Index*. Ontario, Drug Programs Branch, Ministry of Health, 1991.

21. Pickard, J.D., Bailey, S., Sanderson, H., Rees, M. and Garfield, J.S. Step towards cost–benefit analysis of regional neurosurgical care. *Br. Med. J.*, 1990; 301: 629–635.

22. Rosser, R., Kind, P. and Williams, A. Valuation of the quality of life: some psychometric evidence. In Jones-Lee, M.W. (ed.) *The Value of Life and Safety*. Amsterdam, North Holland, 1982.

23. Spilker, B. (ed.) *Quality of Life Assessment in Clinical Trials*. New York, Raven Press, 1990.

24. Spilker, B., Molinek, F.R., Johnston, K.A., Simpson, R.L. and Tilson, H.H. Quality of life bibliography and indexes, *Med. Care*, 28: 12 (December suppl.).

25. Steinbrook, R. and Lo, B. The Oregon Medicaid Demonstration Project: will it produce adequate health care? *N. Engl. J. Med.*, 1992: 326, 5: 340–344.

26. Tarlov, A.R., Ware, J.E., Greenfield, S., Nelson, E.C., Perrin, E. and Zubkof, M. The medical outcomes study, *J. Am. Med. Assoc.*, 1989; 262, 7: 925–930.

27. Teeling Smith, G. The economics of hypertension and stroke. *Am. Heart J.*, 1990; 119, 3, Part 2 (Suppl.): 725–728.
28. Williams, A. 'need' – an economic exegesis. In Culyer, A.J. and Wright, K.G. (eds) *Economic Aspects of Health Services*. Martin Robertson, 1978.
29. Williams, A. Economics of coronary artery bypass grafting. *Br. Med. J.*, 1985; 249: 326–329.
30. The EuroQol Group. EuroQol – a new facility for the measurement of health related quality of life. *Health Policy*, 1990; 16: 199–208.

# 27 The importance of quality of life in policy decisions

**Alan Williams**

The crucial policy decisions within the health care system are concerned with the setting of priorities. The need to set priorities arises from the fact that no country in the world, not even the richest, can afford to do all the things that it is now possible to do to improve the health of its citizens. In that situation, it is no longer sufficient, in the competition for resources, solely to show that a particular intervention is beneficial, though that still is (or should be) a necessary condition for funding. To be successful in that competition an intervention should be demonstrably more beneficial, per unit of resource used, than some minimum cut-off level. Rich countries can obviously afford to set that cut-off point further down the cost-effectiveness ratings than can poor countries, but what every country needs is a rank ordering of interventions by their cost-effectiveness, with those that yield the largest benefits per unit of resource to the forefront of the list, and those that are very costly in relation to their benefits placed at the rear of the queue. That is the rather stark nature of the policy problem we all face, though it presents itself in various guises, according to context.

This chapter will bypass the many problems which arise in the identification and measurement of the relevant costs of interventions, and concentrate on the measurement of their benefits (or effectiveness). In doing so the important issue of how to design and conduct trials so that the benefits of an intervention can reliably and accurately be attributed to it will be ignored. Similarly, additional life expectancy as a health benefit will be ignored initially, in order to concentrate on quality of life issues, though it will be considered later when the problem of establishing trade-offs between quality and quantity of life is discussed. As a final ground-clearing remark, the term 'intervention' includes any action which is intended to improve someone's health (or to reduce the rate at which it deteriorates), whether that action is a diagnostic technique, a medical or nursing therapy, counselling or social service support, educational or preventive measures, a change in administrative or budgetary responsibilities, the relief of the poverty, better housing, or whatever. In practice, however, this chapter will concentrate on ostensibly therapeutic medical interventions.

The general theme of this review is that the kind of quality of life measurements that need to be made will depend on the intended use of such measurements. However, it is also reasonable to be guided by the principle that there is no great merit in being more complicated and comprehensive than is necessary for the purpose in hand, unless the immediate task is being seen as a stepping stone towards a more ambitious longer term goal. Thus, there could be a variety of approaches to the task of measuring quality of life, none of which could be said to be right or wrong by any absolute standard, but each of which could be judged to be more or less appropriate to a particular task. Thus what is needed, as a mind-clearing device, is an array of 'diagnostic' questions which enable those engaged in quality of life measurement to see what kind of quality of life measure is needed for a particular purpose, and for what kind of purpose a particular kind of quality of life measure is appropriate. It should also help each of us to see how our work relates (if at all) to that of others. The following poses a first shot at such an array of questions.

In quality of life measurement for policy decisions seven key stages have to be considered:

1. select the salient descriptive characteristics relevant to health;

2. choose an operational definition and categorization of the selected characteristics;

3. choose an appropriate type of measurement (if necessary);

4.* choose an appropriate valuation method;

5.* choose appropriate respondents;

6. analyse and present the data in a manner relevant to the decision on which it is to bear;

7. make explicit any ethical or moral implications of the technique of measurement that has been adopted.

Stages 4 and 5 have been asterisked because they can be avoided in some circumscribed applications of quality of life measurement, but unfortunately they cannot be avoided if the objective is to tackle the policy decision outlined in the first paragraph. This is the essence of the difference between those who stop at quality of life profiles and those who are compelled to go on to generate a single index. If that statement is too cryptic to be readily accepted at present, it may be ignored until these seven stages have been discussed in more detail. To do this various sub-questions that arise within each broad heading, will be posed, and although space constraints mean these questions will be left rather bare and unadorned, their import should be all the clearer for that.

## QUESTIONS CONCERNING KEY STAGES IN QUALITY OF LIFE MEASUREMENT

### Select the salient descriptive characteristic

This process will be influenced by:

- The broad strategic purpose: Is it to be used over a wide range of conditions/treatments? or limited to a specific clinical setting?
- The investigatory strategy: The investigator may be working within a particular conceptual structure which dictates the organization of the material in a particular way (the theoretical approach) or may be content to try to impose order on the material once it has been collected (the empirical approach).
- Whose perceptions are important? If patients, then open-ended, un-prompted eliciting of ordinary people's personal constructs of health are initially required, though it may be advisable to prompt later. If those with the most experience or closest observations of a wide range of different health states, then the judgements of these people about what the impact is of ill health upon quality of life will be what is required. If the investigator is concerned only with certain specific elements, then that will determine what is included or excluded.
- How will information essentially be collected? Is the instrument for fairly routine use by busy people with no special training?; or for self-assessment by patients?; or for use by highly-trained and well-disciplined research staff for whom it is a significant part of their work?
- Data-handling constraints: There may be severe limits on the type and volume of material that can be handled once it is collected, which will set a limit on the number and type of characteristics that can be included.

### Choose an operation definition and categorization of the selected characteristics

- Items may be grouped by empirical methods (e.g. by cluster or factor analysis) or by prior theoretical considerations (e.g. using broader classificatory schemes which distinguish physical functioning, feelings, and social interaction).

- Alternative descriptions need testing for replicability, inter-observer bias, and validity.
- The complete scheme needs to be tested to ensure that is assigns all patients unambiguously to one (and only one) composite category.

### Choose an appropriate type of measurement (if necessary)

- Is it necessary? Is it possible that a descriptive categorization of patients (which would emerge from the stages outlined above) will be sufficient for the purpose in hand? (e.g. if the object was to try to explain why patients move from one composite category to another, with reference, perhaps, to age, sex, condition, treatment, and social class).
- If the purpose is to go beyond explanation to prediction, then measurement will be concerned with attaching weights to characteristics (or to composite categories) according to their contribution to diagnosis or forecasting the future course of a disease in terms of survival or quality of life.
- If the purpose is to evaluate whether (and by how much) a treatment benefits a patient, then the weights attached to the characteristics (or to the composite categories) should reflect the relevant person's valuations of each of those characteristics (or composite categories).

*In the following two sections it is assumed that the overall purpose is evaluation and that a single index number is required.*

### Choose an appropriate valuation method

- What is to be valued?
    - Is the 'unit' to be valued; some specified period of time spent experiencing a particular characteristic or composite category?; or some specific time profile made up of a succession of different characteristics or composite categories?
    - Is it to be presented as a certain or as an uncertain prospect?
    - Are quality of life and life expectancy to be valued together or separately?
- What kinds of valuation would be unacceptable? Would a valuation method be regarded as inappropriate if it were strongly influenced by the respondents' ability to pay?, socio-economic 'worth'?, risk aversion or gambling propensity?, current or recent experience of ill health?, any other factors?
- What mathematical properties must the measure have? Ordinal, interval, ratio?

- What degree of accuracy/robustness is required?
- Will any 'off-the-shelf' instrument do?
- If not:
    - What resources are available to develop a bespoke instrument?
    - How complex and/or demanding a technique can respondents cope with? Amongst the available techniques (each with different implications for the nature of the data generated) are: category rating, magnitude estimates, visual analogue scales, time trade-off, standard gamble, analysis of behavioural data (legal awards, willingness to pay).
    - How sensitive is the valuation method to the manner in which material is presented to respondents?

## Choose appropriate respondents

According to the purpose of the measurement these could be: patients with a particular condition (or their relatives); patients undergoing a particular treatment (or their relatives); patients generally; the population generally; some professional group associated with the provision of health care (specifically or generally); policy makers at local or national level.

## Analyse and present data in a manner relevant to the decision on which it is to bear

Individual valuations will vary, and the key issue here is how much of this variance to suppress, and how to condense what goes forward in a manner least likely to mislead the recipient (e.g. on what basis should aggregation proceed, should some summary measure of central tendency and/or variance be used, or whole distributions presented raw? How much interaction between variables should be explicitly noted?)

## Make explicit any ethical or moral implications of the technique of measurement that has been adopted

All measures concerned with policy decisions imply some interpersonal comparisons of welfare. Even routine measures such as mortality rates imply that one death is the same as another death. The choice between different clinical interventions according to, say, 2-year survival rates implies (a) to survive less than two years is worthless; (b) no matter how much longer than 2 years people survive, it carries no extra benefit; (c) quality of life is irrelevant; (d) it does not matter how much each intervention costs and (e) all individuals are equal. Each of these is a very strong ethical assertion, and none of them is typically made explicit when applying this criterion in clinical trials. In quality of life measurement, we must set a better example and tease out and state as clearly as we can the interpersonal welfare assumptions entailed in our measures.

## POSSIBLE SET OF ANSWERS

For policy-decision purposes, a quality of life measure than can be used over a wide range of conditions/treatments, as an adjustment factor on life expectancy, and which is cast in everyday terms that patients understand, is needed. It should be capable of being used routinely by observers who are busy people with no specific training and also suitable for self-assessment by patients. It should not contain many items of information about health state (perhaps not more than 20) and these should be selected according to their importance to people generally, and avoid things that are narrowly specific to a particular treatment or condition. Since the broad purpose is evaluative, the weights attached to each combination of characteristics should reflect people's relative valuations of those combinations of characteristics. Ideally, the relative values of a whole array of possible future time paths of health (ending in variable dates of death) should be established, but this is far too ambitious a task with the limited intellectual and material resources available at present. There is therefore a tendency to work with more limited building blocks, such as a specified time spent in a specified state (possibly with a specified probability) and then stringing these individual units together to build up a time path by aggregation (with or without discounting to reflect time preference). Life expectancy and quality of life must be systematically interrelated in the valuation process, since it is essential that trade-offs between quality of life and quantity of life can be encompassed in policy decisions. Generally, valuations influenced by wealth (ability to pay) and (less surely) socio-economic worth are not officially acceptable in the context of the National Health Service in the UK, though there are strong suggestions that certain social roles (e.g. being the parents of young children) do (and should) entitle a person to preferential treatment over otherwise identical cases[5]. Since the objective is to compare the relative value of the benefits of different treatments, an interval scale is required as a minimum, though the choice between category rating, magnitude estimation, visual analogue scale and time trade-off methods of achieving such a scale is not one that needs to be made on a *priori* grounds. The choice of respondents for the valuations themselves is problematical. On political grounds one might argue that it is the valuations of the politically legitimate authority (e.g. in Britain the members of the Health Authority or Health Board) that are relevant and need to be elicited but they may feel that it is not their personal values which should count, but their perceptions of the valuations of the people they represent. This would then bring them into accord with the present author's 'scientific' view, which is that researchers need to elicit the valuations of a very large number of people (2000 or more) with a variety of backgrounds and knowledge and experiences of the health care system, so that whether or not there is systematic bias between different subgroups (doctors, nurses, patients, healthy people, old/young, male/female, or by education, religious beliefs, etc.) can be determined.

Unfortunately, but unsurprisingly, there is no measure available at present which satisfies all these desiderata, and until something better is available I have adopted Rosser's Classification of Illness States, and its associated valuation matrix, as the closest approximation available. (See Ref. 2 for details).

## THE QUALITY ADJUSTED LIFE YEAR (QALY)

The basic idea behind this concept is deceptively simple. It is that if an extra year of healthy (i.e. good quality) life-expectancy is worth one, then an extra year of unhealthy (i.e. poor quality) life-expectancy must be worth less than one (for why otherwise do people seek to be healthy?). The problem is how to determine how much less than one an unhealthy year of life-expectancy is worth.

Suppose a second measurement convention is adopted, namely that being dead is worth zero, it produces two fixed points in the valuation scale. However, while one is an upper limit to the valuations that people may express, zero is not a lower limit, because some people may regard some living states as of such poor quality that they are worse than being dead. This seems to be a common finding in the work of those who construct health status indexes, and it is present in the responses of 70 people on which Rosser's valuation matrix (Table 27.1) is based (for more detail, see Ref. 2).

It will be seen that Rosser's classification works on eight disability and four distress categories, but since the worst disability category (unconscious) is not differentiated with respect to the degree of distress involved, this gives us 29 different combinations of disability and distress, each of which represents one quality of life (though Rosser does not use that term, and indeed disapproves of it as constituting too ambitious a claim for its import).

Using the Rosser valuation matrix, as a table of quality-adjustment factors on simple life-expectancy for use across individuals, has the following important implications:

(i)  three years in a state valued at 0.67 is as beneficial as two years of good health (each valued at one), if the effect of discounting is ignored;

(ii)  being dead is regarded as equally bad for everybody (in the absence of

**Table 27.1** Rosser's valuation matrix: responses of all 70 respondents (Fixed points: healthy = 1, dead = 0)

| Disability rating | | Distress rating | | | |
|---|---|---|---|---|---|
| | | A none | B mild | C moderate | D severe |
| I. | None | 1.000 | 0.995 | 0.990 | 0.967 |
| II. | Slight social | 0.990 | 0.986 | 0.973 | 0.932 |
| III. | Severe social, slight work | 0.980 | 0.972 | 0.956 | 0.912 |
| IV. | Severe work | 0.964 | 0.956 | 0.942 | 0.870 |
| V. | Unable to work | 0.946 | 0.935 | 0.900 | 0.700 |
| VI. | Chair-bound | 0.875 | 0.845 | 0.680 | 0.000 |
| VII. | Bed-bound | 0.677 | 0.564 | 0.000 | −1.486 |
| VIII. | Unconscious | −1.028 | | | |

good empirical evidence to the contrary, this seems a properly neutral assumption);

(iii) an extra year of healthy life-expectancy is regarded as equally valuable to everybody (irrespective of their personal characteristics or socio-economic roles).

It will be noted from (i) that the matrix contains within it all the information we need for the quality/quantity trade-offs, but what usually seems to exercise people more is (iii), so perhaps this warrants further clarification and consideration.

Note that in the context of policy decisions, implication (iii) does not say that an extra year of healthy life-expectancy is actually of equal value to everybody, but that it is to be regarded as such in policy making. This is thus a strong, specific, egalitarian ethic of distributive justice, and is to be accepted or rejected as such, and not regarded simply as the most convenient arithmetical procedure for adding things together. If some alternative principle of distributive justice were thought to be more appropriate, the information requirements would become more demanding, and the arithmetic more complicated, but that is all. The important thing is that the implied ethical principle be made explicit, and if it is acceptable, what follows from it should also be acceptable. If it is not acceptable, an alternative is to be formulated to replace it. In the absence of any such clearly formulated alternative at present, it is best to continue to use what might be termed the simple egalitarian rule, i.e. implication (iii).

## USE OF THE QALY FOR POLICY DECISIONS

There are a variety of policy decisions in which quality of life measures, incorporated in QALYs could be relevant. At a clinical level, the establishing of priorities between different kinds of patient for a given treatment (e.g. renal dialysis, coronary artery bypass grafts, or intensive care). At the level of a whole clinical practice or speciality, the ordering of priorities for the deployment of staff and other resources (e.g., in orthopaedics between hip replacement, upper limb replacement, scoliosis, and the treatment of low back pain). At a still higher level there is the priority problem facing health authorities when differentiating between specialities or conditions, such as how to strike the balance between heart disease, kidney failure, arthritis and cancer, where different specialties each claim to be able to offer beneficial treatment if given the resources to expand. At national level there is the balance between primary care and hospital care to be considered, between prevention and cure, between regions, and between proven therapy and research and training. As we move from the first to the last level the problems become more and more broad-ranging, but since all are concerned ultimately with the improvement of people's life expectancy and quality of life, and all are competing for the same pool of resources, then the cost-effectiveness criterion enunciated earlier is, in principle, the test by which priorities between them should be settled.

At present, such approaches are limited, but a few illustrative examples indicating the methods of approach are given below.

The problem of priority setting for patient selection within a particular treatment mode was addressed in a study[3] which estimated that the expected present value of the QALYs to be gained by coronary artery bypass grafting compared with drug management for the treatment of angina, for a male aged 55 with good left-ventricular function and no complicating concurrent conditions, varied markedly according to the severity of the angina and the implicated coronary anatomy (Table 27.2). This work has since been further

**Table 27.2** Expected present value of extra QALYs gained from coronary artery bypass grafting over medical management in the treatment of angina pectoris (Reproduced from Ref. 3, with permission)

| Coronary anatomy | Degree of angina | | |
|---|---|---|---|
| | Severe | Moderate | Mild |
| Left main (LMD) | 2¾ | 2¼ | 1¼ |
| 3 vessel (3VD) | 2¼ | 1¼ | ½ |
| 2 vessel (2VD) | 1¼ | ¾ | ¼ |
| 1 vessel (1VD) | ¼ | ¼ | 0 |

**Table 27.3** Cost per QALY for some selected cardiological procedures in 1985. (Reproduced from Ref. 3, with permission)

| Procedure | Cost per QALY (£'000) |
|---|---|
| Pacemaker implantation for atrioventricular heart block | 0.7 |
| Valve replacement for aortic stenosis | 0.9 |
| CABG for severe angina and LMD | 1.0 |
| CABG for moderate angina and 2VD | 4. |
| Heart transplantation | 5.0 |

refined, with respect to the site of lesion (proximal or distal), and these results have been published[6].

At the level of clinical practice, work in cardiology and cardiac surgery provides further examples, and comparisons have been made between costs per QALY for a variety of procedures within those specialties[3] (Table 27.3).

More recent data on the costs and benefits of heart transplantation suggest that the cost per QALY for that procedure are more like £8000 than the £5000 cited in the 1985 article[3].

When it comes to comparisons between specialties, some selective work has been reported (Williams[3], see Table 27.4). More recently the North West Regional Health Authority has been experimenting with the use of cost per QALY estimates as supplementary information in determining priorities for the allocation of funds for the development of Regional Specialties (for further details see Gudex)[1], and a good impression of these results can be gleaned from Table 27.5.

Prevention versus cure is rather more difficult territory, but some tentative work on strategies for the prevention of coronary heart disease[4] suggests

**Table 27.4** Cost per QALY for some selected non-cardiological procedures in 1985. (Reproduced from Ref. 3, with permission)

| Procedure | Cost per QALY (£'000) |
|---|---|
| Total hip replacement | 0.8 |
| Kidney transplantation (cadaver) | 3.0 |
| Haemodialysis at home | 11.0 |
| Haemodialysis in hospital | 14.0 |

**Table 27.5** Cost per QALY (£) for selected bids in a particular regional health authority for funds (reproduced from Ref. 1, with permission)

| | QALYs gained per patient (discounted at 5%) | Annual cost per patient | Total cost (discounted at 5%) | Cost per QALY |
|---|---|---|---|---|
| Continuous ambulatory peritoneal dialysis (4 years) | 3.4 | 12866 | 45676 | 13434[**] |
| Haemodialysis (8 years) | 6.1 | 8569 | 55354 | 9075[**] |
| Treatment of cystic fibrosis with ceftazidime (over 22 years) | 0.4 | 250 | 3290 | 8225[**] |
| Kidney transplant (lasting 10 years) | 7.4 | 10452 | 10452 | 1413[*] |
| Shoulder joint replacement (lasting 10 years) | 0.9 | 533 | 533 | 592[*] |
| Scoliosis surgery idiopathic adolescent | 1.2 | 3143 | 3143 | 2619[*] |
| neuromuscular illness | 16.2 | 3143 | 3143 | 194[*] |

[*] Represents one-off costs per case, and benefits discounted over life of case.
[**] Represents recurring annual costs and annual QALYs per case.

**Table 27.6** Cost per QALY for three strategies open to GPs for the prevention of coronary heart disease[*]

| Strategy | Approximate cost per QALY |
|---|---|
| Advice to stop smoking | Less than £180 |
| Action to control severe hypertension | £1700 (or perhaps somewhat lower) |
| Action to control total serum cholesterol levels | £1700 (or perhaps slightly higher) |

[*] Based on screening 1000 male patients over 40 years of age consulting their GPs for any reason whatever. (For details see Ref. 4)

costs per QALY for three such strategies as indicated in Table 27.6. General practitioners counselling patients to give up smoking, even without follow up, seem a very good buy!

Determining the proper balance between research, teaching and the practice of proven therapy is an ambitious exercise that this chapter has not yet dared tackle empirically, though some procedural suggestions can be made on the research aspect. It is commonly objected that the rigid application of the cost-per-QALY criterion will stifle progress in medicine, because many of the interventions which are now commonplace (and cost-effective) started off being very expensive in relation to the rather uncertain benefits they initially generated during the experimental stage. This is a valid objection, and it points to a two-stage competition. Any intervention which is too costly in relation to its benefits to be worth funding out of the therapeutic budget of the health service, could enter a different competition for research funding. In this competition, however, the rules are somewhat different. Activities yielding very-high-cost-QALYs should continue only if there is a reasonable prospect that their effectiveness will rise significantly and/or their costs will fall significantly: and if they are funded separately as research activities, pursued subject to proper research protocols, subject to independent evaluation, and with full disclosure of data.

## CONCLUSIONS

Quality of life measurement, when systematically related to life-expectancy, as a way of measuring the relative value of the benefits of different interventions, has a tremendous future at all levels from the monitoring of individual performance, through clinical trials, to the establishment of priorities at all levels in health care. In the last role it will also need to be systematically related to the costs of the respective interventions. However, there is so much ground to be covered that it is likely to be several decades before we can expect to see this kind of data used routinely for policy decisions. In the meantime we must concentrate on ensuring that it can be used for all major decisions, and be ready to respond to decision makers at all levels who are willing to join in the development of work or to offer a test-bed for the application of the techniques in their own day-to-day work. That way it should be possible to ensure that patients' quality of life is kept effectively to the forefront in policy decisions about health care.

### References

1. Gudex, C. QALYs and their use by the Health Service, University of York, Centre for Health Economics, Discussion Paper No. 20, October 1986.
2. Kind, P., Rosser, R. and Williams, A. Valuation of quality of life: some psychometric evidence. In Jones-Lee, M. W. (ed.) *The Value of Life and Safety*. Amsterdam, North-Holland, 1982, pp. 159—170.
3. Williams, A. Economics of coronary artery bypass grafting. *Br. Med. J.* 1985;291:325—329.
4. Williams, A. Screening for risk of CHD: is it a wise use of resources? In Oliver,

M., Ashley-Miller, M. and Wood, D. (eds) *Strategy for Screening for Risk of Coronary Heart Disease*. Chichester, John Wiley, 1987, pp. 97—105.

5.  Williams, A. Economics and the Rational Use of Medical Technology. In Rutten, F. and Reiser, S. (eds) *The Economics of Medical Technology*. Berlin, Springer-Verlag, 1988, pp. 109–120.

6.  Williams, A. The cost-effectiveness approach to the treatment of angina. In Patterson, D. (ed.) *The Management of Angina Pectoris*, Tunbridge Wells, Castle House Publications, 1987, pp. 131–141.

# Appendices

The following appendices are included to provide information on the nature of the questions included and how they may be asked of and answered by the patients. They are not always full versions of the instruments and do not include sufficient detail on definitions of individual items to enable them to be used to obtain an assessment of a patient's health status. Readers wishing to use one (or more) of the instruments are asked to contact the author(s) directly for their permission to use the instrument and to obtain full details.

## APPENDIX 1: QUALITY OF WELL-BEING SCALE

### A. Elements with calculated weights

| Label | Step no. | Step definitions | Weights |
|-------|----------|-----------------|---------|
| Mobility (MOB) | 5 | No limitation in driving or use of public transportation (bus, train, plane, subway) for health reasons | –0.000 |
| | 4,3 | Did not drive a car *or* did not use public transportation, for health reasons (< age 16, did not ride in a car, or had more help to use public transportation than usual for age) | –0.062 |
| | 2,1 | In hospital (nursing home, hospice, home for the retarded, mental hospital etc.) as a bed patient overnight | –0.090 |
| | 0 | Death | –0.090 |
| Physical activity (PAC) | 4 | No limitations for health reasons | –0.000 |
| | 3,2 | Found it difficult (or did not try) to lift, stoop, bend over, or use stairs or inclines, *and/or* limped, used a cane, crutches, or walker, *or* had any other physical limitation making it hard (or did not try) to walk as far or as fast as others of the same age, for health reasons, *or* in wheelchair, but controlled its movements without help | –0.060 |
| | 1 | In bed, chair, or couch for most or all of the day (health related?) *or* in wheelchair and did not control movement without help | –0.077 |
| | 0 | Death | –0.077 |
| Social activity (SAC) | 5 | Performed major role (work, home-making, school, retirement etc.) and other (personal, community, religious, social, recreational) activities, with no limitations for health reasons | –0.000 |
| | 4,3,2 | Limited in or did not perform major or other role activities for health reasons, but performed self-care (feeding, bathing, dressing, toilet) | –0.061 |
| | 1 | Did not perform self-care activities (or had more help than usual) for age for health reasons | –0.106 |
| | 0 | Death | –0.106 |

**B. Symptoms/problems complexes (CPX) with calculating weights**

| CPX no. | CPX description | Weights |
|---------|-----------------|---------|
| 1 | Death (not on respondent's card) | −0.727 |
| 2 | Loss of conciousness such as seizure (fits), fainting, or coma (out cold or knocked out) | −0.407 |
| 3 | Burn over large areas of face, body, arms or legs | −0.367 |
| 4 | Pain, bleeding, itching, or discharge (drainage) from sexual organs – does not include normal menstrual (monthly) bleeding | −0.349 |
| 5 | Trouble learning, remembering, or thinking clearly | −0.340 |
| 6 | Any combination of one or more hands, feet, arms, or legs either missing, deformed, crooked), paralysed (unable to move), or broken – including wearing artificial limbs or braces | −0.333 |
| 7 | Pain, stiffness, weakness, numbness, or other discomfort in chest, stomach (including hernia or rupture), side, neck, back, hips, or any joint of hands, feet, arms or legs | −0.299 |
| 8 | Pain, burning, bleeding, itching, or other difficulty with rectum, bowel movements, or urination (passing water) | −0.292 |
| 9 | Sick or upset stomach, vomiting or loose bowel movements, with or without fever, chills, or aching all over | −0.290 |
| 10 | General tiredness, weakness, or weight loss | −0.259 |
| 11 | Cough, wheezing, or shortness of breath with or without fever, chills or aching all over | −0.257 |
| 12 | Spells of feeling upset, being depressed, or crying | −0.257 |
| 13 | Headache, or dizziness, or ringing in ears, or spells of feeling hot, or nervous, or shaky | −0.244 |
| 14 | Burning or itching rash on large areas of face, body, arms or legs | −0.240 |
| 15 | Trouble talking, such as lisp, stuttering, hoarseness, or being unable to speak | −0.237 |
| 16 | Pain or discomfort in one or both eyes (such as burning or itching) or any trouble seeing after correction | −0.230 |
| 17 | Overweight for age or height or skin defect of face, body, arms or legs, such as scars, pimples, warts, bruises, or changes in colour | −0.186 |
| 18 | Pain in ear, tooth, jaw, throat, lips, tongue, several missing or crooked permanent teeth – including wearing bridges or false teeth; stuffy, runny nose; or any trouble hearing – including wearing a hearing aid | −0.170 |
| 19 | Taking medication or staying on a prescribed diet for health reasons | −0.144 |
| 20 | Wore eyeglasses or contact lenses | −0.101 |
| 21 | Breathing smog or unpleasant air | −0.101 |
| 22 | No symptoms or problems (not on respondent's card) | −0.000 |
| 23 | Standard symptom/problem (not on respondent's card) | −0.257 |

### C. Calculating formulas

*Formula 1: Point-in-time well-being score for an individual (W):*

$$W = 1 + (CPXwt) + (MOBwt) + (PACwt) + (SACwt)$$

where wt is the preference-weighted measure for each factor and CPX is symptom/problem complex. For example, the *W* score for a person with the following description profile may be calculated for one day as follows:

| Quality of well-being element | Description | Weight |
|---|---|---|
| CPX-11 | Cough, wheezing, or shortness of breath, with or without fever, chill, or aching all over | −0.257 |
| MOB-5 | No limitations | −0.000 |
| PAC-1 | In bed, chair, or couch for most or all of the day, health related | −0.077 |
| SAC-2 | Performed no major role activity, health related, but did perform self-care activities | −0.061 |

$$W = 1 + (-0.257) + (-0.077) + (-0.061) = 0.605$$

Formula 2: General health policy model formula for well-years (*WY*) as an output measure:

$$WY = [\text{No. of persons} \times (CPXwt + MOBwt + PACwt + SACwt)] \times \text{Time}$$

## APPENDIX 2: THE NOTTINGHAM HEALTH PROFILE

PATIENT NUMBER ☐ ☐ ☐
STUDY NUMBER ☐ ☐ ☐
CENTRE NUMBER ☐ ☐ ☐

HOW WOULD YOU DESCRIBE YOUR HEALTH AT PRESENT?

VERY GOOD ☐
GOOD ☐
FAIR ☐
POOR ☐
VERY POOR ☐

BEFORE YOU START PLEASE BE SURE TO READ THE INSTRUCTIONS.

DATE: . . . . . . . . . . . . . . .

**PART I**

For Office use only

Listed below are some problems people may have in their daily life. Look down the list and put a tick in the box under **yes** for any problem you have at the moment. Tick the box under **no** for any problem you do not have. **Please answer every question.** If you are not sure whether to answer yes or no, tick whichever answer you think is **more true** at the moment.

| | YES | NO |
|---|---|---|
| I'm tired all the time | ☐ | ☐ |
| I have pain at night | ☐ | ☐ |
| Things are getting me down | ☐ | ☐ |

| | YES | NO |
|---|---|---|
| I have unbearable pain | ☐ | ☐ |
| I take tablets to help me sleep | ☐ | ☐ |
| I've forgotten what it's like to enjoy myself | ☐ | ☐ |

| | YES | NO |
|---|---|---|
| I'm feeling on edge | ☐ | ☐ |
| I find it painful to change position | ☐ | ☐ |
| I feel lonely | ☐ | ☐ |

| | YES | NO |
|---|---|---|
| I can only walk about indoors | ☐ | ☐ |
| I find it hard to bend | ☐ | ☐ |
| Everything is an effort | ☐ | ☐ |

| | YES | NO |
|---|---|---|
| I'm waking up in the early hours of the morning | ☐ | ☐ |
| I'm unable to walk at all | ☐ | ☐ |
| I'm finding it hard to make contact with people | ☐ | ☐ |

| | YES | NO |
|---|---|---|
| The days seem to drag | ☐ | ☐ |
| I have trouble getting up and down stairs/steps | ☐ | ☐ |
| I find it hard to reach for things | ☐ | ☐ |

**PART I continued**

For Office use only

Remember, if you are not sure whether to answer yes or no to a problem, tick whichever answer you think is **more true** at the moment.

|                                               | YES | NO |
|-----------------------------------------------|-----|-----|
| I'm in pain when I walk                        | ☐   | ☐  |
| I lose my temper easily these days             | ☐   | ☐  |
| I feel there is nobody I am close to           | ☐   | ☐  |

|                                               | YES | NO |
|-----------------------------------------------|-----|-----|
| I lie awake for most of the night              | ☐   | ☐  |
| I feel as if I'm losing control                | ☐   | ☐  |
| I'm in pain when I'm standing                  | ☐   | ☐  |

|                                               | YES | NO |
|-----------------------------------------------|-----|-----|
| I find it hard to dress myself                 | ☐   | ☐  |
| I soon run out of energy                       | ☐   | ☐  |
| I find it hard to stand for long (e.g. at the kitchen sink, waiting for a bus) | ☐ | ☐ |

|                                               | YES | NO |
|-----------------------------------------------|-----|-----|
| I'm in constant pain                           | ☐   | ☐  |
| It takes me a long time to get to sleep        | ☐   | ☐  |
| I feel I am a burden to people                 | ☐   | ☐  |

|                                               | YES | NO |
|-----------------------------------------------|-----|-----|
| Worry is keeping me awake at night             | ☐   | ☐  |
| I feel that life is not worth living           | ☐   | ☐  |
| I sleep badly at night                         | ☐   | ☐  |

|                                               | YES | NO |
|-----------------------------------------------|-----|-----|
| I'm finding it hard to get on with people      | ☐   | ☐  |
| I need help to walk about outside (e.g. a walking aid or something to support me) | ☐ | ☐ |
| I'm in pain when going up and down stairs/steps | ☐   | ☐  |

|                                               | YES | NO |
|-----------------------------------------------|-----|-----|
| I wake up feeling depressed                    | ☐   | ☐  |
| I'm in pain when sitting                       | ☐   | ☐  |

Now please go back to the beginning and make sure you have answered **yes** or no to every question.

**Part II**

For Office use only

We would like you to think about the activities in your life which may be affected by health problems.
In the list below, tick **yes** for each activity in your life which is being affected by your state of health. Tick **no** for each activity which is not being affected, **or which does not apply to you.**

IS YOUR PRESENT STATE OF HEALTH CAUSING PROBLEMS WITH YOUR . . . .

|    |                                                                                              | YES | NO |
|----|----------------------------------------------------------------------------------------------|-----|----|
| 1. | JOB OF WORK<br>(that is, paid employment)                                                     | ☐   | ☐  |
| 2. | LOOKING AFTER THE HOME<br>(Examples: cleaning & cooking, repairs odd jobs around the home etc.) | ☐   | ☐  |
| 3. | SOCIAL LIFE<br>(Examples: going out, seeing friends, going to the pub etc.)                    | ☐   | ☐  |
| 4. | HOME LIFE<br>(That is: relationship with other people in your home)                            | ☐   | ☐  |
| 5. | SEX LIFE                                                                                       | ☐   | ☐  |
| 6. | INTERESTS AND HOBBIES<br>(Examples: sports, arts and crafts, do-it-yourself etc.)             | ☐   | ☐  |
| 7. | HOLIDAYS<br>(Examples: summer or winter holidays, weekends away etc.)                          | ☐   | ☐  |

## APPENDIX 3: THE McMASTER HEALTH INDEX QUESTIONNAIRE

### Section A: Physical function items

1.  Today are you physically able to run a short distance, say 300 feet, if you are in hurry? (This is about the length of a football field or soccer pitch.)

    1  NO
    2  YES

2.  Today, do you (or would you) have any physical difficulty at all with

    | | DIFFICULTY | NO DIFFICULTY |
    |---|---|---|
    | a.  walking as far as a mile? | 1 | 2 |
    | b.  climbing up 2 flights of stairs? | 1 | 2 |
    | c.  standing up from and/or sitting? down in a chair? | 1 | 2 |
    | d.  feeding yourself? | 1 | 2 |
    | e.  undressing? | 1 | 2 |
    | f.  washing (face and hands), shaving (men), and/or combing hair? | 1 | 2 |
    | g.  shopping? | 1 | 2 |
    | h.  cooking? | 1 | 2 |
    | i.  dusting and/or light housework? | 1 | 2 |
    | j.  cleaning floors? | 1 | 2 |

3.  Today, are you physically able to take part in any sports (hockey, swimming, bowling, golf, and so forth) or excercise regularly?

    1  NO
    2  YES

4.  At present, are you physically able to walk out-of-doors by yourself when the weather is good?

    1  NO
    2  YES

    a.  What is the farthest you can walk by yourself
       1  ONE MILE OR MORE
       2  LESS THAN 1 MILE BUT MORE THAN 30 FEET (ABOUT THE SIDE OF A HOUSE)
       3  LESS THAN 30 FEET

    b.  Are you able to walk by yourself?
       4  BETWEEN ROOMS
       5  ONLY WITHIN A ROOM
       6  CAN'T WALK AT ALL

5.  Today, do you (or would you) have any physical difficulty at all travelling by bus whenever necessary? (Circle your answer)

    1  NO
    2  YES

6.    Today, do you have any physical difficulty at all travelling by car whenever necessary?

    1  NO
    2  YES

7.    Do you have any physical difficulty at all driving a car by yourself?

    1  NO → GO TO Q.8
    2  YES

8.    Do you wear glasses?

    1  NO
    2  YES

a. Do you have any trouble seeing ordinary newsprint when you wear your glasses?

  1 NEVER
  2 SOMETIMES
  3 ALWAYS

c. Do you have any trouble seeing ordinary newsprint?

  1 NEVER
  2 SOMETIMES
  3 ALWAYS

b. Do you have a headache after watching television or reading when you wear your glasses?

  1 NEVER
  2 SOMETIMES } GO TO Q.9
  3 ALWAYS

d. Do you have a headache after watching television or reading?

  1 NEVER
  2 SOMETIMES } GO TO Q.9
  3 ALWAYS

9.    Do you wear a hearing aid?

    1  NO
    2  YES

a. Do you have trouble hearing in a normal conversation with several other persons when you wear your hearing aid?
  1 NEVER
  2 SOMETIMES
  3 ALWAYS

c. Do you have trouble hearing in a normal conversation with several other persons?
  1 NEVER
  2 SOMETIMES
  3 ALWAYS

b. Do you have trouble hearing the radio or television when you wear your hearing aid?
  1 NEVER
  2 SOMETIMES
  3 ALWAYS

d. Do you have trouble hearing the radio or television?
  1 NEVER
  2 SOMETIMES
  3 ALWAYS

## Section B: Emotional function items

Often people's health affects the way they feel about life. For these next questions, please circle the choice that is closest to the way you feel about each statement.

     If you STRONGLY AGREE, circle 1
     If you AGREE, circle 2
     If you are NEUTRAL, circle 3
     If you DISAGREE, circle 4
     If you STRONGLY DISAGREE, circle 5

|  | STRONGLY AGREE | | | STRONGLY DISAGREE | |
|---|---|---|---|---|---|
| 10. I sometimes feel that my life is not very useful. | 1 | 2 | 3 | 4 | 5 |
| 11. Everyone should have someone in his life whose happiness means as much to him as his own. | 1 | 2 | 3 | 4 | 5 |
| 12. I am a useful person to have around. | 1 | 2 | 3 | 4 | 5 |
| 13. I am inclined to feel that I'm a failure. | 1 | 2 | 3 | 4 | 5 |
| 14. Many people are unhappy because they do not know what they want out of life. | 1 | 2 | 3 | 4 | 5 |
| 15. In a society where almost everyone is out for himself, people soon come to distrust each other. | 1 | 2 | 3 | 4 | 5 |
| 16. I am a quick thinker. | 1 | 2 | 3 | 4 | 5 |
| 17. Some people feel that they run their lives pretty much the way they want to and this is the case with me. | 1 | 2 | 3 | 4 | 5 |
| 18. There are many people who don't know what to do with their lives. | 1 | 2 | 3 | 4 | 5 |
| 19. Most people don't realize how much their lives are controlled by plots hatched in secret by others. | 1 | 2 | 3 | 4 | 5 |
| 20. People feel affectionate towards me. | 1 | 2 | 3 | 4 | 5 |
| 21. I would say I nearly always finish things once I start them. | 1 | 2 | 3 | 4 | 5 |
| 22. When I make plans ahead, I usually get to carry out things the way I expected. | 1 | 2 | 3 | 4 | 5 |

| | | | | | |
|---|---|---|---|---|---|
| 23. I think most married people lead trapped (frustrated or miserable) lives | 1 | 2 | 3 | 4 | 5 |
| 24. It's hardly fair to bring children into the world the way things look for the future. | 1 | 2 | 3 | 4 | 5 |
| 25. Some people feel as if other people push them around a good bit, and I feel this way too. | 1 | 2 | 3 | 4 | 5 |
| 26. I am usually alert. | 1 | 2 | 3 | 4 | 5 |
| 27. Nowadays a person has to live pretty much for today and let tomorrow take care of itself. | 1 | 2 | 3 | 4 | 5 |

## Section C: Social function items

This section contains some questions on general health and on your social activities.

28. How would you say your health is today? Would you say your health is (Circle your answer)
    1 VERY GOOD
    2 PRETTY GOOD
    3 NOT TOO GOOD

29. Taking all things together, how would you say things are today? Would you say you are
    1 VERY HAPPY
    2 PRETTY HAPPY
    3. NOT VERY HAPPY

30. In general, how satisfying do you find the way you're spending your life today? Would you call it
    1 COMPLETELY SATISFYING
    2 PRETTY SATISFYING
    3 NOT VERY SATISFYING

31. How would you say your *physical* functioning is today? (By this we mean the ability to move around, see, hear, and talk.)
    1 GOOD
    2 GOOD TO FAIR
    3 FAIR
    4 FAIR TO POOR
    5 POOR

32. How would you say your *social* functioning is today? (By this we mean your ability to work, to have friends, and to get along with your family.)
    1 GOOD
    2 GOOD TO FAIR
    3 FAIR
    4 FAIR TO POOR
    5 POOR

33. How would you say your *emotional* functioning is today? (By this we mean your ability to remain in good spirits most of the time and to be usually happy and satisfied with your life.) (Circle your answer)
1 GOOD
2 GOOD TO FAIR
3 FAIR
4 FAIR TO POOR
5 POOR

34. Are you presently working on a job for wages, either full- or part-time?
1  YES → GO TO Q. 35
2  NO . . . a. Are you presently
                1 ON VACATION
                2 ON SICK LEAVE
                3 RETIRED
                4 A STUDENT
                5 A HOUSEWIFE
                6 OTHER (please specify)

_____

35. How much time, in a one-week period, do you usually spend watching television?
1 NONE
2 LESS THAN THREE HOURS A WEEK
3 LESS THAN ONE HOUR A DAY
4 MORE THAN TWO HOURS A DAY

36. Which of the following describe your usual social and recreational activities?
a.   going to church?
     1 NO
     2 YES

b.   going to a relative's home?
     1 NO
     2 YES
c.   any other activities? (please specify)

_____

37. Has anyone visited you in the last week? (Circle your answer)
a.   a relative?
     1 NO
     2 YES

b.   a friend?
     1 NO
     2 YES

c.   a regious group member?
     1 NO
     2 YES

d.   a social agency representative?
     1 NO
     2 YES

38. Do you have a telephone?
    1  NO → GO TO Q. 41
    2  YES

39. Have you used your telephone in the last week to call
    a.    a friend?
          1 NO
          2 YES

    b.    a religious group member?
          1 NO
          2 YES

    c.    a social agency representative?
          1 NO
          2 YES

40. Have you been called in the last week by a social agency representative?
          1 NO
          2 YES

41. How long has it been since you last had a holiday? (Write in number '0' if
    presently on holidays.)
    ___MONTHS *OR* ___YEARS

42. *During the last year*, have any of the following things happened to you?
    a.    separation from your spouse?
          1 NO
          2 YES

    b.    divorce?
          1 NO
          2 YES

    c.    going on welfare during the last year?
          1 NO
          2 YES

    d.    trouble getting along with friends/relatives during the last year?
          1 NO
          2 YES

    e.    retired from work during the last year?
          1 NO
          2 YES

    f.    some other problem or change in your life? (please specify)
          _____

## APPENDIX 4. THE INDEX OF HEALTH-RELATED QUALITY OF LIFE (IHQL)

**INSTRUCTIONS:** Read each question carefully and answer by putting a tick in the position which best describes how things have been for you. Please answer all questions.

**HEALTH-RELATED QUALITY OF LIFE:** Has your state of health caused any impairment in your quality of life in the past week?

|  | None | Mild | Moderate | Severe | Extreme |
|---|---|---|---|---|---|
| Impairment in quality of life |  |  |  |  |  |

**DISABILITY:** Which level of disability best describes the way things have been for you in the past week?

|  | |
|---|---|
| | No disability |
| | Slight disability which only interferes with social life |
| | Severe social disability and/or slight impairment of performance at work. Able to do all housework except heavy tasks |
| | Choice of work or performance at work severely limited. Housewives and old people able to do light housework only, but able to go out shopping |
| | Unable to undertake any paid employment. Unable to continue any education. Housewives only able to perform a few simple tasks. Old people confined to home except for escorted outings and short walks and unable to do shopping |
| | Confined to a chair or to a wheelchair or able to move around in the home only with support from an assistant |
| | Confined to bed |
| | Unconscious |

**DISCOMFORT:** Which level of discomfort best describes the way things have been for you in the past week?

| | |
|---|---|
| | No discomfort |
| | Slight discomfort |
| | Moderate discomfort |
| | Severe discomfort |
| | Extreme discomfort |

**DISTRESS:** Which level of distress best describes the way things have been for you in the past week?

| | |
|---|---|
| | No distress |
| | Slight distress |
| | Moderate distress |
| | Severe distress |
| | Extreme distressed and/or actively suicidal |

**DISABILITY:**  In this section we ask more detailed questions about any disability you may have had in the past week.

**SELF-CARE:**  In the past week; have you been able to care for yourself in the following ways?

| | Only with assistance | Not at all |
|---|---|---|
| Wash | | |
| Dress | | |
| Feed | | |

If YES
tick here . . . .

**MOBILITY:**  In the past week; has your mobility been restricted in any of the following ways?

| | By yourself but with some difficulty | Only if assisted e.g. by equipment or another person | Totally unable |
|---|---|---|---|
| Walk | | | |
| Travel | | | |

If NO
tick here . . . .

**PHYSICAL DISABILITY:**  Have you had any physical disability from any of the following in the past week?

| | Some | Severe |
|---|---|---|
| Paralysis | | |
| Amputation | | |
| Weakness | | |
| Involuntary movements | | |
| Tremor | | |
| Stiffness | | |

If NO
tick here . . . .

**STAYING AWAY FROM HOME FOR TREATMENT:**  In the past week; have you had to stay away from home for health treatment in any of the following places?

| | |
|---|---|
| General hospital | |
| Psychiatric unit in general hospital | |
| Mental hospital | |
| Intensive care unit | |
| Hospice | |
| Hostel or other (specify) | |

If NO
tick here . . . .

**CONSCIOUSNESS:** In the past week; has your level of consciousness been impaired in any of the following ways? Have you . . . . ?

| | Sometimes | All the time |
|---|---|---|
| Been unconscious? | | |
| Had any other impairment of consciousness? (please specify) | | |

If NO tick here . . . .

**THINKING:** In the past week; have you had any of the following problems with your ability to think?

| | Mild | Moderate | Severe | Extreme |
|---|---|---|---|---|
| Memory loss | | | | |
| Loss of concentration | | | | |

| | Some | Severe |
|---|---|---|
| Confusion (muddled thinking) | | |
| Disorientation      in time | | |
|      in place | | |
|      in person | | |

If NO tick here . . . .

**BODY FUNCTIONS:** In the past week; have you been . . . . ?

| | | Continuously | Intermittently |
|---|---|---|---|
| Incontinent | Bowel | | |
| | Bladder | | |
| Dependent on a machine for body functions (please state what kind of machine) | Inside body | | |
| | Outside body | | |
| Transplant dependent (please specify which part of the body) | | | |

If NO, tick here . . . .

**MEDICINES/DRUGS/SUBSTANCES:** In the past week; have you been reliant on any medicines/drugs/substances that are . . . . ?

| | Tick if YES |
|---|---|
| Prescribed | |
| Mind affecting | |
| Addictive | |

If NO, tick here . . . .

**SENSORY LOSS:**   Have any of your senses been impaired in the past week?

|  | Partial loss – corrected | Partial loss – uncorrected | Complete loss |
|---|---|---|---|
| Sight |  |  |  |
| Hearing |  |  |  |
| Taste |  |  |  |
| Smell |  |  |  |
| Touch |  |  |  |

If NO, tick here . . . .

**TRANSMISSIBILITY:**   Do you have a condition which could be either infectious to others or inherited by your children?   If YES, how much have you been concerned about this in the past week?

|  | Not at all | Slightly | Moderately | Extremely |
|---|---|---|---|---|
| Risk of infecting others |  |  |  |  |
| Risk of your children inheriting your condition |  |  |  |  |

If NO, tick here . . .

**OCCUPATIONAL, SOCIAL AND FAMILY ROLES:**   In the past week; has your state of health impaired your ability to perform any of the following roles?   If YES, please indicate . . . .

|  | No | Mildly | Moderately | Severely | Totally |
|---|---|---|---|---|---|
| MAIN OCCUPATION e.g. work, house-work, study |  |  |  |  |  |
| OTHER OCCUPATION(S) e.g. part-time job, house-work |  |  |  |  |  |
| FINANCIAL:   Providing income/ financial resources |  |  |  |  |  |
| SOCIAL:   Social activities, recreation, hobbies, holidays |  |  |  |  |  |
| FAMILY:   Family responsibilities and/or caring for dependents |  |  |  |  |  |

**DISCOMFORT:**  In this section we ask about any discomfort you may have had in the past week.

**PAIN/PHYSICAL DISCOMFORT:**  Have you had any pain/physical discomfort in the past week?

If YES, please indicate . . . .

|  | Occasionally | Frequently | Almost all the time |
|---|---|---|---|
| Slight |  |  |  |
| Moderate |  |  |  |
| Severe |  |  |  |
| Agonizing |  |  |  |

If NO,
please tick here . . . .

**SYMPTOMS:**  Have you had any of the following symptoms in the past week?

|  | Some | Severe |
|---|---|---|
| Breathlessness |  |  |
| Disfigurement |  |  |
| Fatigue, lack of energy |  |  |
| Poor appetite |  |  |

|  |  | Tick if YES |
|---|---|---|
| Eating disturbance | Overeating |  |
|  | Bingeing |  |
|  | Self-starving |  |
| Nausea and vomiting | Nausea |  |
|  | Vomiting (not self-induced) |  |
| Sleep disturbance | Too much sleep |  |
|  | Sleeping but not rested |  |
|  | Difficulty in onset |  |
|  | Interrupted sleep |  |
|  | Waking early – not sleeping again |  |

If NO,
tick here . . . .

**DISTRESS:** In this section we ask about distressing feelings and experiences, your relationships with other people and your personal sense of fulfilment.

**MOOD:** Have you had any problem with your mood in the past week? If YES, please indicate . . . .

|  | Mildly | Moderately | Severely | Extremely |
|---|---|---|---|---|
| DEPRESSED |  |  |  |  |
| ANXIOUS |  |  |  |  |
| Elated for no apparent reason (manic, high) |  |  |  |  |

If NO,
tick here . . . .

**DISTRESSING TREATMENT:** In the past week; has your state of health required you to have treatment which has been distressing to you?

If YES . . . .

|  | Mild | Moderate | Severe | Extreme |
|---|---|---|---|---|
| Amount of distress due to treatment |  |  |  |  |

If NO,
tick here . . . .

**SOCIAL NETWORK:** In the past week; have you had problems with the following types of contact with people?

|  | Tick if YES |
|---|---|
| Face to face |  |
| Telephone |  |
| Written letter |  |

If NO,
tick here . . . .

In the past week; how many of your contacts with people have been . . . .?

|  | A lot | A few | None |
|---|---|---|---|
| Supportive |  |  |  |
| Non-supportive |  |  |  |
| Hostile |  |  |  |
| Demanding |  |  |  |
| Of a type that makes you feel needed |  |  |  |

How many of your contacts with people this week were with . . . .?

|  | None | A few | Most |
|---|---|---|---|
| Health professionals or social service workers (as opposed to family or friends) |  |  |  |

**COMMUNICATION:**  In the past week; has your state of health impaired your ability to communicate with people in any of the following ways?

|  | Mild | Moderate | Severe | Extremely severe |
|---|---|---|---|---|
| Speech |  |  |  |  |
| Writing |  |  |  |  |
| Non-verbal expressions or gestures (absent or abnormal) |  |  |  |  |

If NO,
tick here . . . .

**INTIMACY:**
Do you have a close relationship?          YES . . . .          NO . . . .

If YES; would you describe this relationship as . . ?

|  | YES | NO |
|---|---|---|
| Warm |  |  |
| Confiding |  |  |
| Listening |  |  |
| One you can depend on |  |  |

**SEXUAL FUNCTION:**
Does sex feature in your life?          YES . . . .          NO . . . .

If Yes, has the condition of your health affected your sex-life in the past week? Have you had problems with . . . . ?

|  | Some | Severe |
|---|---|---|
| Loss of interest |  |  |
| Loss of enjoyment |  |  |
| Inability to perform |  |  |

Tick here,
if NO to all these . . . .

**FULFILMENT:** Here we explore aspects of life fulfilment which may be affected by the condition of your health

Do you feel . . . ?

|  | No | Partly | A lot |
|---|---|---|---|
| BLAMED:   Do you sense that others blame you for the state of your health? |  |  |  |
| STIGMATIZED:   Do you feel discriminated against because of the state of your health? |  |  |  |
| SOCIALLY UNACCEPTABLE:   Do you feel that your state of health is socially unacceptable? |  |  |  |
| LOSS OF MEANING:   Has your state of health led to a loss of meaning in your life? |  |  |  |
| DISSATISFIED WITH LIFE:   Has your health impaired your sense of satisfaction? |  |  |  |
| BORED:   Have you felt bored because of the state of your health? |  |  |  |
| FRUSTRATED:   Have you felt frustrated because of the state of your health? |  |  |  |
| A BURDEN TO OTHERS:   Has the state of your health made you feel a burden to others? |  |  |  |
| LOSS OF AMBITION:   Has the state of your health prevented you from meeting your goals? |  |  |  |

Do you feel . . . ?

|  | Yes | Partly | No |
|---|---|---|---|
| THAT YOU UNDERSTAND:   Do you feel that you understand the state of your health? |  |  |  |
| INFORMED:   Have you been told as much as you need to know about your state of health? |  |  |  |

**ATTITUDE**: What has your attitude towards the condition of your health been in the past week? Has it been . . . ?

|  | Tick if YES |
|---|---|
| Fighting |  |
| Resenting |  |
| Accepting with resignation |  |
| Positively accepting |  |
| Hopeless |  |
| Denying |  |
| Guilty |  |
| Justly punished |  |
| Disappointed |  |

**PERCEIVED PROGNOSIS**:   How do you view the way your condition will be in the future? Do you see it . . . . ?

| Cured | Improved | The same | Worse | Fatal |
|---|---|---|---|---|
|  |  |  |  |  |

THANK YOU FOR BEING SO HELPFUL

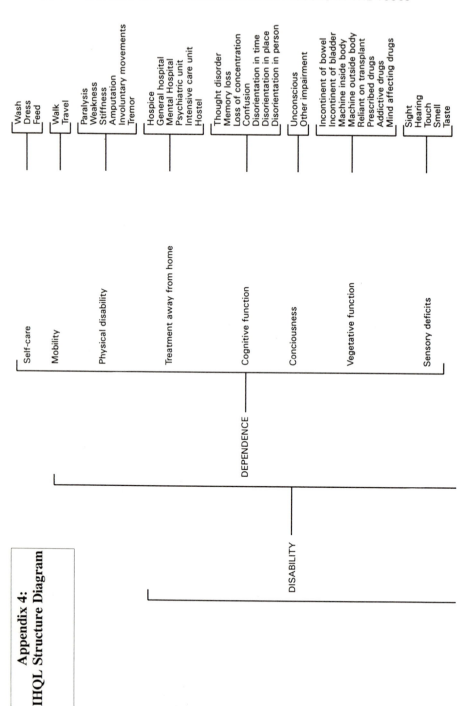

**Appendix 4:**
**IHQL Structure Diagram**

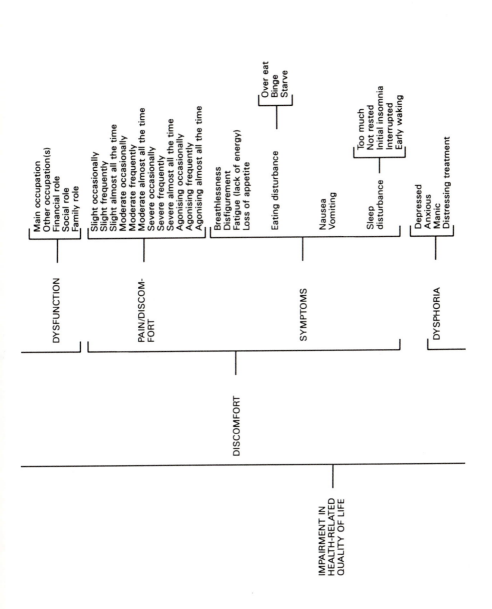

*Continued*

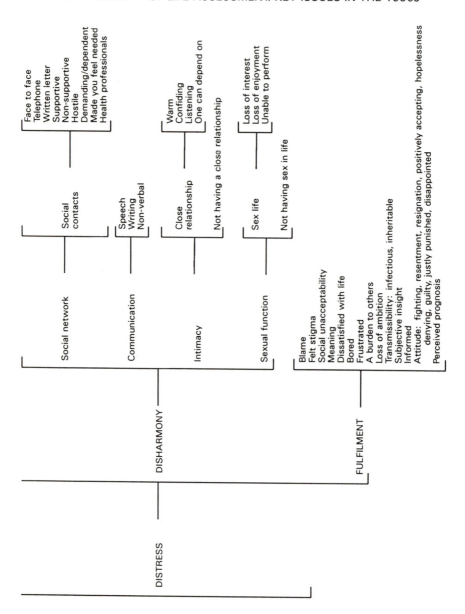

## APPENDIX 5: QUESTIONNAIRE ON HEALTH-RELATED QUALITY OF LIFE (15D©/HARRI SINTONEN)*

**Please read first through all the response alternatives of each question and then tick (x) from each question that alternative which best describes your present status.**

## QUESTION 1.

1 ( ) I am able to move (walk) normally, i.e. without difficulties indoors, outdoors and on stairs

2 ( ) I am able to move (walk) without difficulties indoors, but outdoors and/or on stairs with difficulties

3 ( ) I am able to move (walk) without help indoors (with or without appliances), but outdoors and/or on stairs only with help from others

4 ( ) I am able to move (walk) only with help from others indoors also

5 ( ) I am completely bed-ridden and unable to move about; if helped, I may sit on a chair

## QUESTION 2.

1 ( ) I see normally, i.e. I see to read a paper without difficulty either with or without glasses

2 ( ) I see to read a paper with difficulty either with or without glasses

3 ( ) I do not see to read a paper with or without glasses, but I see to move about without a guide (I would see to move about, if I were otherwise able to move about)

4 ( ) I do (I would) not see to move about without a guide, i.e. I am almost or completely blind

## QUESTION 3.

1 ( ) I hear normally (i.e. well) normal voice (with or without a hearing aid)

2 ( ) I hear normal voice with difficulty, in conversation louder than normal voice has to be used

3 ( ) I hear even loud voice poorly, I am almost deaf

4 ( ) I am completely deaf

---

* The questionnare may still experience some changes before being in the 'final' form.

## QUESTION 4.

1 ( ) I am able to breathe normally, i.e. no shortness of breath or other difficulty in breathing

2 ( ) I have shortness of breath when quickening my pace on even ground

3 ( ) I have shortness of breath on even ground at the walking pace of others of the same age

4 ( ) I must stop because of shortness of breath

5 ( ) I have shortness of breath when dressing, washing or at rest

## QUESTION 5.

1 ( ) I am able to sleep normally, i.e. no problems with sleeping

2 ( ) I have slight difficulty in sleeping, e.g. difficulty in falling asleep, I wake up too early, I wake up occasionally at night

3 ( ) I have considerable difficulty in sleeping, e.g. I must use often or regularly sleeping pills, I wake up regularly 1−2 times a night

4 ( ) I suffer from serious sleeplessness, e.g. difficulty in sleeping even with sleeping pills, I am awake most of the night

## QUESTION 6.

1 ( ) I am able to eat by myself without any difficulty or help

2 ( ) I am able to eat by myself without help, but with difficulty (e.g. slowly or with special appliances)

3 ( ) I need some help from others in eating

4 ( ) I am unable to eat by myself at all, I must be fed by others

5 ( ) I am unable to eat by myself at all, I must be fed through tubes or by intravenous fluids

## QUESTION 7.

1 ( ) I am able to speak normally, i.e. clearly and fluently

2 ( ) I am able to speak incoherently, but understandably, my voice trembles or changes pitch, my speech is stuttering

3 ( ) My speech is so slurred and confused that others have difficulties in understanding

4 ( ) I am dumb or my speech is not at all understandable, I communicate only by gestures

## QUESTION 8.

1 ( )  I am able to control the bladder normally, I have no 'accidents'

2 ( )  I have slight difficulty in controlling the bladder; possibly I have had one 'accident' in two weeks

3 ( )  I have occasional difficulty in controlling the bladder; possibly I have had a few 'accidents' in two weeks

4 ( )  I have regular difficulty in controlling the bladder; I have had quite often 'accidents' in two weeks

5 ( )  I am completely unable to control the bladder

## QUESTION 9.

1 ( )  I am able to do paid work or household work normally

2 ( )  I am able to do paid work or household work with a slightly reduced efficiency or with slight difficulty

3 ( )  I am able to do paid work or household work with considerably reduced efficiency or with considerable difficulty, I am able to accomplish only a part of usual tasks at work or at home

4 ( )  I am able to accomplish only a small part of usual tasks at work or at home, I am almost unable to work

5 ( )  I am not at all able to do paid work or household work, I am completely unable to work

## QUESTION 10.

1 ( )  I am able to participate normally (as usual) in social interaction and activities, e.g. clubs, meetings, visits, etc.

2 ( )  Because of my health I have had to restrict slightly my usual participation in social interaction and activities

3 ( )  Because of my health, I have had to restrict considerably my usual participation in social interaction and activities

4 ( )  Because of my health, I have had to give up almost entirely my usual participation in social interaction and activities

5 ( )  Because of my health, I have had to give up completely my participation in social interaction and activities

## QUESTION 11.

1 ( )  I am able to think clearly and logically, my memory functions quite perfectly

2 ( )  I have slight difficulties in thinking clearly and logically, my memory does not function quite perfectly

3 ( )  I have considerable difficulties in thinking clearly and logically, I have some loss of memory

4 ( )  I have great difficulties in thinking clearly and logically, I have considerable loss of memory

5 ( )  I am confused at all times and disoriented in place and time

## QUESTION 12.

1 ( )  I am not at all in pain and/or ache

2 ( )  I am in a slight pain and/or ache

3 ( )  I am in a sharp pain and/or ache

4 ( )  I am in an unbearable pain and/or ache

## QUESTION 13.

1 ( )  I do not feel at all sad, blue or depressed

2 ( )  I feel slightly sad, blue or depressed

3 ( )  I feel quite sad, blue or depressed

4 ( )  I feel very sad, blue or depressed

5 ( )  I feel extremely sad, blue or depressed

## QUESTION 14.

1 ( )  I do not feel at all distressed or fearful

2 ( )  I feel slightly distressed or fearful

3 ( )  I feel considerably distressed or fearful

4 ( )  I feel very distressed or fearful

5 ( )  I feel extremely distressed or fearful

## QUESTION 15.

1 ( )  I do not feel at all sick

2 ( )  I feel slightly sick

3 ( )  I feel quite sick

4 ( )  I feel very sick

5 ( )  I feel extremely sick

We are trying to find out what people think about health. We are going to describe a few health states that people can be in. We want you to indicate how good or bad each of these states would be for a person like you. There are no right or wrong answers. Here we are interested only in your personal view.

To help people say how good or bad a health state is, we have drawn a scale (rather like a thermometer) on which the best state you can imagine is marked by 100 and the worst state you can imagine is marked by 0.

We would like you to indicate on this scale how good or bad is your own health today, in your opinion. Please do this by drawing a line from the box below to whichever point on the scale indicates how good or bad your current health state is.

Your own health
state today

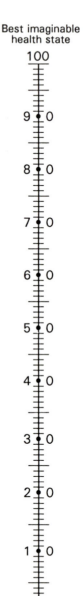

Best imaginable
health state

Worst
imaginable
health state

- We now want you to consider some other health states.

- Remember, we want you to indicate how good or bad each of these states would be for a person like you.

- They are described, on either side of the scale, on the page opposite.

- When thinking about each health state imagine that it will last for one year. What happens after that is not known and should not be taken into account.

- Please draw **one** line from each box to whichever point on the scale indicates how good or bad the state described in that box is.

- It does not matter if your lines cross each other.

Best imaginable
health state

| No problems in walking about | 100 | No problems in walking about |
| No problems with self-care | | No problems with self-care |
| Some problems with performing usual activities (e.g. work, study, housework, family or leisure activities) | 90 | No problems with performing usual activities (e.g. work, study, housework, family or leisure activities) |
| No pain or discomfort | 80 | Moderate pain or discomfort |
| Not anxious or depressed | | Not anxious or depressed |

| No problems in walking about | 70 | Some problems in walking about |
| No problems with self-care | | Some problems with washing or dressing self |
| No problems with performing usual activities (e.g. work, study, housework, family or leisure activities) | 60 | Some problems with performing usual activities (e.g. work, study, housework, family or leisure activities) |
| No pain or discomfort | | Extreme pain or discomfort |
| Not anxious or depressed | 50 | Extremely anxious or depressed |

| Some problems in walking about | 40 | Confined to bed |
| No problems with self-care | | Unable to wash or dress self |
| Some problems with performing usual activities (e.g. work, study, housework, family or leisure activities) | 30 | Unable to perform usual activities (e.g. work, study, housework, family or leisure activities) |
| Extreme pain or discomfort | | Extreme pain or discomfort |
| Moderately anxious or depressed | 20 | Extremely anxious or depressed |

| No problems in walking about | | Confined to bed |
| No problems with self-care | 10 | Unable to wash or dress self |
| No problems with performing usual activities (e.g. work, study, housework, family or leisure activities) | | Unable to perform usual activities (e.g. work, study, housework, family or leisure activities) |
| Moderate pain or discomfort | 0 | Moderate pain or discomfort |
| Moderately anxious or depressed | | Not anxious or depressed |

Worst
imaginable
health state

**PLEASE CHECK THAT YOU HAVE DRAWN ONE LINE FROM EACH BOX**
(that is, 8 lines in all)

In the same way as on the previous page, please indicate how good or bad these additional states are, by drawing a line from each box to a point on the scale. You will find that 2 of these states (marked *) are repeated from the previous page

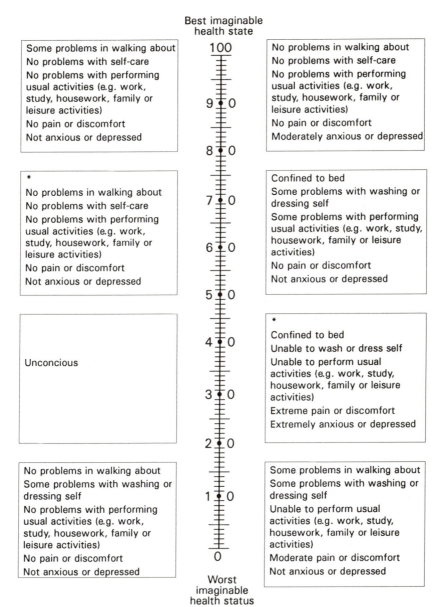

Best imaginable health state

| Some problems in walking about | No problems in walking about |
| No problems with self-care | No problems with self-care |
| No problems with performing usual activities (e.g. work, study, housework, family or leisure activities) | No problems with performing usual activities (e.g. work, study, housework, family or leisure activities) |
| No pain or discomfort | No pain or discomfort |
| Not anxious or depressed | Moderately anxious or depressed |

100

90

80

| *
No problems in walking about
No problems with self-care
No problems with performing usual activities (e.g. work, study, housework, family or leisure activities)
No pain or discomfort
Not anxious or depressed | Confined to bed
Some problems with washing or dressing self
Some problems with performing usual activities (e.g. work, study, housework, family or leisure activities)
No pain or discomfort
Not anxious or depressed |

70

60

50

| Unconcious | *
Confined to bed
Unable to wash or dress self
Unable to perform usual activities (e.g. work, study, housework, family or leisure activities)
Extreme pain or discomfort
Extremely anxious or depressed |

40

30

20

| No problems in walking about
Some problems with washing or dressing self
No problems with performing usual activities (e.g. work, study, housework, family or leisure activities)
No pain or discomfort
Not anxious or depressed | Some problems in walking about
Some problems with washing or dressing self
Unable to perform usual activities (e.g. work, study, housework, family or leisure activities)
Moderate pain or discomfort
Not anxious or depressed |

10

0

Worst imaginable health status

**PLEASE CHECK THAT YOU HAVE DRAWN ONE LINE FROM EACH BOX**
(that is, 8 lines in all)

- In the previous pages we asked you to say how good or bad various health states are in your view.

- We would now like you to tell us how good or bad you feel the state 'dead' is, compared with being in the other states for one year.

- Please turn back to pages 5 **and** 6 and draw a line across the thermometer at the point you would locate the state 'dead'

- Remember we would like you to do this on **both** pages 4 and 5.

# Index

## DATE DUE

| iLL(PIT) | | | |
|---|---|---|---|
| 789412 | | | |
| OCT 07 1996 | | | |
| 12/18/95 | | | |
| AG 1 5 '96 | | | |
| NO 3 0 '96 | | | |
| JAN 2 7 1998 | | | |
| FEB 2 8 1998 | | | |
| SEP 2 5 2008 | | | |
| | | | |
| | | | |
| | | | |
| | | | |
| | | | |
| | | | |
| | | | |